I-75 and the 401

A Traveler's Guide between TORONTO and MIAMI

Christine Marks
LL.B., B.A. (Hon. Psych.)

with

Emily Marks & Lizzy Marks

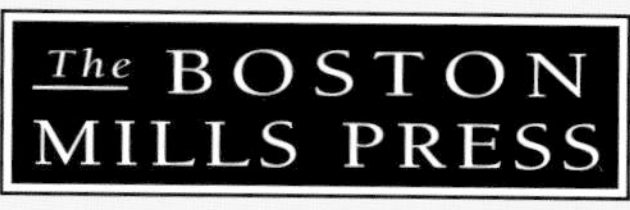

www.bostonmillspress.com

A BOSTON MILLS PRESS BOOK

Library and Archives Canada Cataloguing in Publication

Marks, Christine, 1965-
Interstate 75 and the 401 : a traveler's guide between Toronto and Miami / Christine Marks. -- Updated 4th ed.
Previous eds. have title I-75 and the 401.

ISBN-13: 978-1-55046-526-6 ISBN-10: 1-55046-526-0

1. Interstate 75--Guidebooks. 2. Macdonald-Cartier Freeway (Ont.)--Guidebooks.
3. Automobile travel--Ontario--Guidebooks. 4. Automobile travel--Southern States--
Guidebooks. 5. Automobile travel--Middle West--Guidebooks. 6. Ontario--Guidebooks.
7. Middle West--Guidebooks. 8. Southern States--Guidebooks.
I. Marks, Christine, 1965- . I-75 and the 401. II. Title.
GV1024.M37 2009 917.304'931 C2009-902140-4

First Printing

Publisher Cataloging-in-Publication Data (U.S.)

Marks, Christine.
Interstate 75 and the 401 : a traveler's guide between Toronto and Miami / Christine Marks.
Updated 4th ed.
Originally published as: I-75 and the 401.
[256] p. : photos. (some col.), col. maps ; cm.
Includes savings coupons for accommodations, restaurants, attractions, further information.
Summary: A comprehensive guide that covers Ontario Highway 401 to the Canada-U.S. border at Detroit
then south along I-75 to Florida. A quick reference section by exit shows details for gas stations,
restaurants and lodgings, with plenty of interesting side trips to sites nearby.

ISBN-13: 978-1-55046-526-6 ISBN-10: 1-55046-526-0

1. Interstate 75--Guidebooks. 2. Macdonald-Cartier Freeway (Ont.)--Guidebooks.
3. Automobile travel--Ontario--Guidebooks. 4. Automobile travel--Southern States--Guidebooks.
5. Automobile travel--Middle West--Guidebooks. 6. Ontario--Guidebooks.
7. Middle West--Guidebooks. 8. Southern States--Guidebooks.
I. Marks, Christine, 1965- . I-75 and the 401. II. Title.
917.304/931 dc22 GV1024.M377 2009

Published by Boston Mills Press
132 Main Street, Erin, Ontario, Canada N0B 1T0
Tel 519-833-2407 Fax 519-833-2195
e-mail: books@bostonmillspress.com www.bostonmillspress.com

In Canada: Distributed by Firefly Books Ltd.
66 Leek Crescent, Richmond Hill, Ontario, Canada L4B 1H1

In the United States: Distributed by Firefly Books (U.S.) Inc.
P.O. Box 1338, Ellicott Station, Buffalo, New York, USA 14205

The publisher acknowledges the financial support of the Government of Canada through the
Book Publishing Industry Development Program (BPIDP) for its publishing efforts.

Original cover design: Susan Darrach Design • Revised cover and book design: McCorkindale Advertising & Design

Back cover: from top right clockwise: Toledo Zoo, photo by Linda Milks, courtesy the Greater Toledo Convention & Visitors Bureau.
Historic nightly illumination tour courtesy Macon-Bibb County Convention & Visitors Bureau. Florida s beaches,
courtesy St. Petersburg/Clearwater Area Convention and Visitors Bureau. Niagara Falls, Ontario, courtesy Ontario Ministry
of Economic Development, Trade & Tourism. Parade of Breeds courtesy Kentucky Department of Travel Development.
The mountains of Tennessee, Courtesy Tennessee Department of Tourist Development. The Ambassador Bridge and
Detroit, Michigan skyline, photo by Vito Palmisano, courtesy Metro Detroit Convention & Visitors Bureau.
Page 1: Toronto skyline, courtesy Toronto Convention & Visitors Association.
Miami skyline, courtesy Greater Miami Visitors and Convention Bureau.

Printed in China

The first edition of this travel guide was published when my youngest daughter, Lizzy, was just one year old. Back then I was okay with "North" at the bottom of the page. The folks at Boston Mills Press cured me of that. A lot has changed since then, but always on this page in the first 3 editions I would say "this is for my girls." This time will be different. Emily and Lizzy both were such an integral part of this project it's not "for them" it's "from them"! We worked long and hard together to check existing entries, contact sources, and then to select and organize the new information for this edition. I am so especially proud of their emerging photography skills and have included many of the photos they captured from our excursions. They love to "get out there" and while they interviewed or took photos and notes, I beamed. This was exactly what I had hoped for 13 years ago: these experiences have been good for us and made our family stronger! Since the last edition our family has grown: I'm very thankful that my fiancé, Craig Russ, understands how important this book is to the three of us. Craig is my rock, and his pride and confidence in the three of us out on the road two thousand miles away encouraged me to truly enjoy traveling alone with my girls. My mother, Kathryn Poulton, on the other hand, just worried from the moment I put her two grandbabies into the car until I returned them back safely — but that's how she loves us and I wouldn't have it any other way.

For my girls, Emily and Elizabeth.
I love you both so much.

Way past deadline, we needed a lot of help and encouragement and the good people at Boston Mills Press were generous with both. My publisher, John Denison, rolled up his sleeves and really helped us with many, many tedious jobs. Johnny, you've been the best friend the three of us could ask for all these years — thank you for everything. Chris McCorkindale and Sue Breen at McCorkindale Advertising & Design in Waterloo, Ontario, managed to stay patient with me even though I added pressure by passing my delays onto their lap. This book looks fantastic, thank you so much, Chris and Sue! And of course, without the expertise and financial backing of Firefly Books, we wouldn't have any of this! Cheers to all of you!

As always, we've relied on the assistance of the Visitors and Convention Bureaus along the route. There are many people who have touched this edition and I hope I don't miss anyone. A big "thank you" to:,Angela Moore (Tifton CVB, GA), Belle Jackson (Berea Tourism, KY), Bev Rose (Dayton CVB, OH), Bill AuCoin (St. Petersburg-Clearwater CVB, FL), Candace Davis (Chattanooga CVB, TN),Carlynne Foster (Tennessee Department of Tourist Development), Carolina Bustamante and Stuart Newman of Stuart Newman Associates (Florida Keys Tourism), Cathy Bingham (Oxford County CVB, ON), Cathy Miller (Toledo CVB, OH), Charlie Haz and Jennifer Haz (Greater Miami Convention & Visitors Bureau. FL), Denise Spiegel (Orlando CVB, FL), Deann Bechtol (Miami County CVB, OH), Deanna Majchrzak (Detroit Metro CVB), Donna Grube (Auglaize & Mercer Counties CVB, OH), Erin Burns Freeman (Knoxville Tourism & Sports Corporation, TN), Nancy Hamilton, Lee County CVB, FL), Harvey Campbell (Columbia County, FL), Jennifer Huber (Charlotte Harbor CVB, FL), Jeff Raible (Sidney & Shelby Chambers of Commerce, OH), Joelle Cavitt (Cleveland/ Bradley Chamber of Commerce, OH), John Pricher (Alachua County Visitors and Convention Bureau, FL), Justine Palinska (Tourism Toronto, ONT), Karen Beavers (Tourism London ONT), Karen Cummings (County of Elgin, ONT), Kay Phillips (Dalton CVB,, GA), Laura Barrett (Henry County Chamber of Commerce, GA), Lee Rose (Lee County CVB, FL), Marcheta Keefer (Alachua County CVB, FL), Marge Bateman (Kentucky Department of Travel), Mary Haban (St. Petersburg/Clearwater CVB, FL), Mary A. Morris (Adel-Cook County Chamber of Commerce, GA), Megan Spears(Clayton County CVB, GA), Peggy Scott (London-Laurel County Tourist Commission, KY), Patty Halls (Convention & Visitors Bureau of Windsor, Essex County & Pelee Island, ONT),Regina Wheeler (Cartersville-Bartow County CVB, GA), Roland Loog, (Gainesville CVB, FL), Ross Czarnik (Cincinnati USA CVB, OH), Ruth Sykes (Macon CVB, GA), Sheila Averett Jones (Perry Area CVB, OH), Shelda Spencer Rees (Chattanooga Area CVB, TN), Shelly Bechard (Chatham-Kent CVB, ONT), Susan at the Suwannee Chamber of Commerce, Stefanie Paupeck (Georgia Department of Economic Development (GDEcD)), Teresa Mullis (Catoosa County Chamber of Commerce, GA), Lee Rose (Lee County VCB, FL), Wanda Kemp (High Springs CVB, FL)

The P.R. people with several properties in Florida were extremely helpful: Jack Guy and Michelle Boyd (Sheraton Sand Key Resort, Clearwater Beach), Jenny Kerr (Biscayne Lady Yacht Charters & Island Queen Cruises, Miami FL), Kelly Prieto (Tradewinds Island Grand Resort, St. Pete Beach), Angela Geml (Columbia Restaurant on Sand Key, Clearwater, FL) and Kathy White (Salvador Dali Museum), come to mind and so does Jeannie Bigos from the Outrigger Resort in Fort Myers Beach and Debra Illes from the diving museum in the Florida Keys, Mary Kay Ryan from the Longboat Key Club Resort (Florida), Mark Hubbard (Snorkeling at Hubbard's Marina, Tierra Verde, FL), Ralph Heath (Suncoast Seabird Sanctuary, Indian Shores, FL), and Jim Handy from the Handy family that have been welcoming guests to Kentucky for four generations, Barry Harris with Newport Beachside Hotel & Resort (Florida), Robin Schlaudecker and Shannon O'Berry at the Islander Resort (Florida Keys), Frank Holtslag (Circa39 hotel in Miami, FL), Laura Quinn (Florida Keys Wild Bird Rehabilitation Center), the Lazy Dog Kayak Guides (Key West, FL), Brian Geller (Ocean Pointe Suites, Key Largo, FL), and Amy or Sean Kelly, hosts of, and Tasha Dupree, PR contact for Island City House.

TORONTO to MIAMI & the Florida Keys via Highway 401 & Interstate I-75

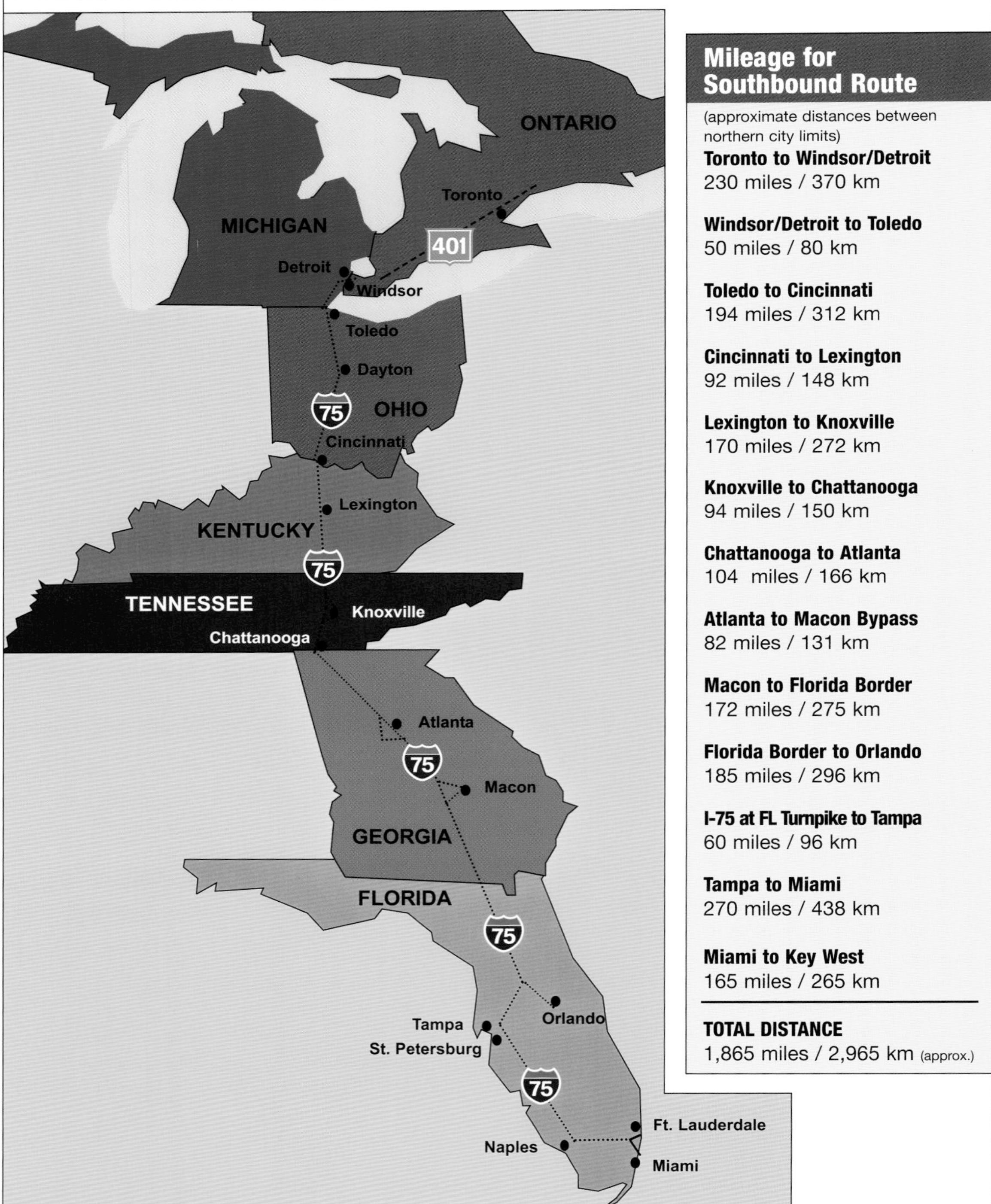

Mileage for Southbound Route

(approximate distances between northern city limits)

Toronto to Windsor/Detroit
230 miles / 370 km

Windsor/Detroit to Toledo
50 miles / 80 km

Toledo to Cincinnati
194 miles / 312 km

Cincinnati to Lexington
92 miles / 148 km

Lexington to Knoxville
170 miles / 272 km

Knoxville to Chattanooga
94 miles / 150 km

Chattanooga to Atlanta
104 miles / 166 km

Atlanta to Macon Bypass
82 miles / 131 km

Macon to Florida Border
172 miles / 275 km

Florida Border to Orlando
185 miles / 296 km

I-75 at FL Turnpike to Tampa
60 miles / 96 km

Tampa to Miami
270 miles / 438 km

Miami to Key West
165 miles / 265 km

TOTAL DISTANCE
1,865 miles / 2,965 km (approx.)

CONTENTS

HOW TO SAVE $$$ AND GET THE MOST FROM THIS BOOK

USING THE HIGHWAY EXIT GUIDE

LISTINGS

will indicate the services you should find close to the exit on the indicated side of the highway.

LOCATIONS MARKED BY LOGOS

Logos are like welcome mats set out by the managers of locations that are particularly interested in serving our readers. A logo shows exactly where you will find this service. Several offer special savings: look for coupons on the same page! Please contact us with any comments or complaints you may have about these locations.

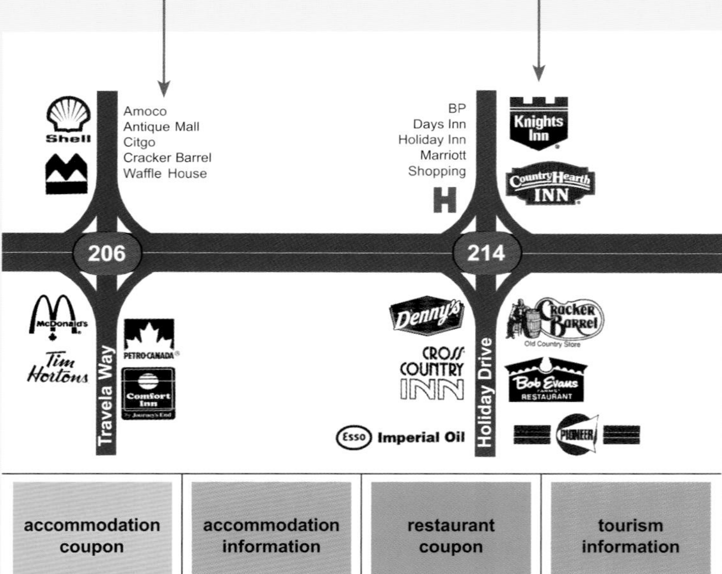

MONEY-SAVING COUPONS!

Money-saving and time-saving coupons are found on both the Canadian and American Exitguide pages.

Most of the savings are for accommodations but there are also coupons for food, drink, and merchandise. Free information packages from Tourism Associations can be obtained by calling the numbers listed in the bar at the top of the page or you can mail in the information coupons.

And please note, most of the participating proprietors suggest you simply present this book to the front desk cashier who will likely clip the coupons for you. If clipping is not required to obtain your discount, you'll be free to use the coupons over and over again or you can pass them along when you lend your book to friends and family members who travel.

TIPS FOR DRIVERS

1. READ THE BOOK BEFORE YOU GO

This book is a highway of information...so you'll know the highway like the back of your hand! You'll discover that many cities that aren't typical stop-overs are well worth a side-trip.

2. FLIP THE PAGES AS YOU DRIVE ALONG

Most of the U.S. map pages are 20 miles. Most of the Canadian map pages are 20 km. Just count the pages and multiply by 20 to figure out how far you have yet to go!

3. THIS IS NOT A COFFEE-TABLE BOOK

The pages are meant to be easy to tear out! Write notes, do the crossword puzzle (Tennessee).

4. TELL US ABOUT YOUR EXPERIENCES

Our database of services is being constantly updated because some businesses we show on the map may have unfortunately gone and others have been established since this edition of the book was printed. Please let us know what's new! And do not hesitate to write to us about your experiences on Highway 401 and the Interstate I-75.

E-mail me at
christine.marks@sympatico.ca

BEFORE YOU GO

Whether you are a commuter or a vacationer leaving for Cincinnati, Atlanta or the Gulf Coast (or just arm-chair traveling), we wish you a wonderful journey and hope that this book will add to your traveling pleasure.

NOTE: In the upper right hand corner of each map pages in this Exitguide, you'll find corresponding thumbnail diagrams of the province or state. Several of the larger city centers along the route are indicated for your quick reference.

Look for the "**X**." It will give you an indication of your relative progress along the highway.

Before you go, you may want to order the superlative tourism packages offered by each state (or province).

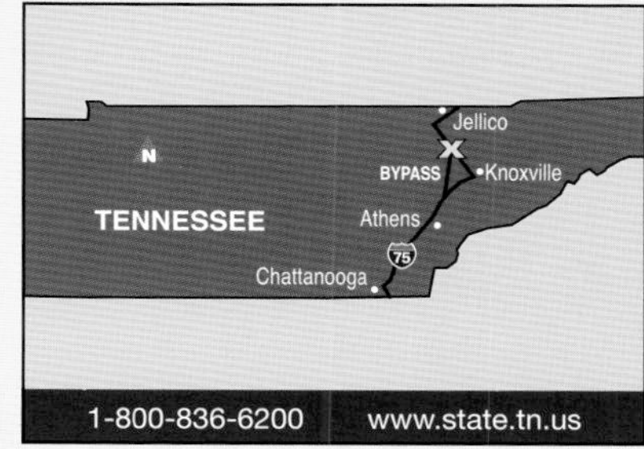

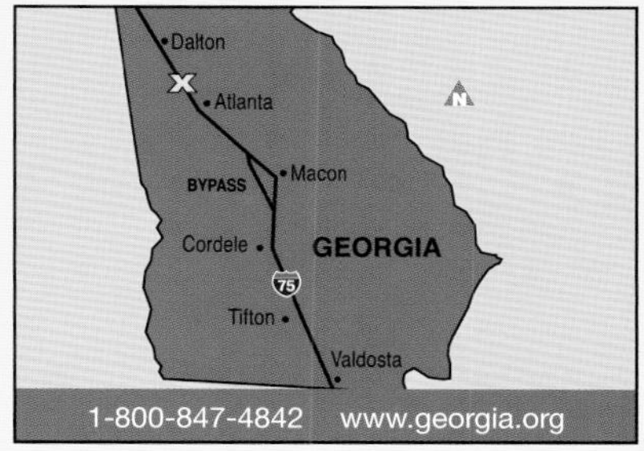

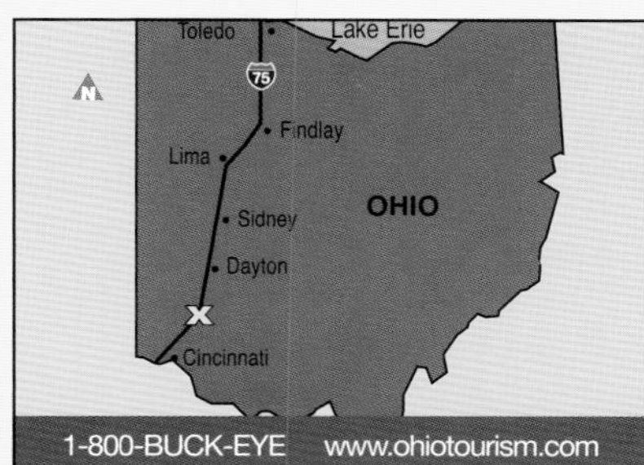

Welcome to Ontario

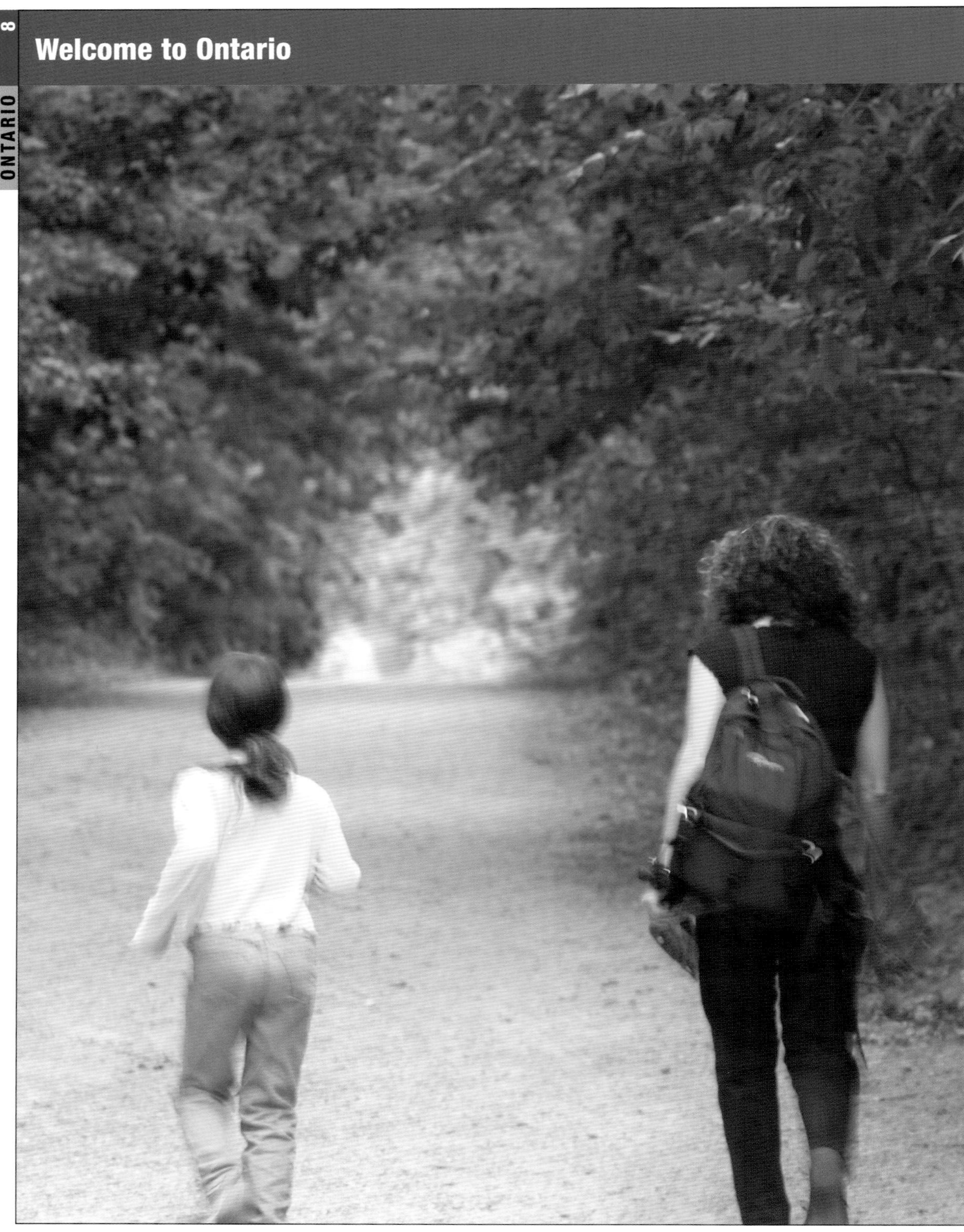

Hiking on Mount Nemo, near Milton, Ontario with my daughter Lizzy.
Photo by Stephen D'Agostino.

York Region
ONTARIO

York Region Tourism
17250 Yonge St., Newmarket, ON Canada L3Y 6Z1
905-883-3442 or 1-888-448-0000 **www.region.york.on.ca**

International travelers recognize two main attractions in York Region: Canada's premier theme park, **Canada's Wonderland,** and the **McMichael Canadian Art Collection.**

With more than 25 public and 25 private golf courses, York Region is a mecca for avid golfers.

Local visitors wish that they could keep secret the scenic trails, museums, and the myriad quaint shops and diverse restaurants you'll find in the visitors guide package for Ontario's Rising Star, York Region.

Attractions & Festivals

CEDAR BEACH PARK
Luxury trailer park for families less than a 1-hour drive from Toronto. Musselman's Lake, Stouffville. 905-642-1700

THE McMICHAEL CANADIAN ART COLLECTION
Canadian art treasures, including magnificent works by Group of Seven, First Nations, Inuit and contemporary artists. Woodland setting. Award-winning restaurant. Superb gift shop. Tours. Islington Ave., Kleinburg. 905-893-1121 www.McMichael.com 1-888-213-1121

CANADA'S WONDERLAND
Featuring 160 attractions, 50 thrill rides and Canada's largest outdoor wave pool. 9580 Jane St., Maple, ON L6A 1S6 www.canadaswonderland.com 905-832-7000

KANATA SUMMER FESTIVAL & MAIN STREET NEWMARKET EVENTS
A well-attended celebration of the birthday of Canada. Events include the Car Club Demolition Derby, a dance, fireworks and the Championship Cat Show. Late June to early July. 905-895-5193

Toronto
ONTARIO

Tourism Toronto (Toronto Convention & Visitors Association)
P.O. Box 126, 207 Queen's Quay West, Toronto, ON Canada M5J 1A7
416-203-2500 or 1-800-499-2514 **www.seetorontonow.com**

Historical Notes

The first known settlements of the Toronto area were those of the Seneca and Mississauga nations.

Early colonization in this area centered on the east bank of the Humber River and was near the crossing of several ancient native trails going west to the Mississippi and north to Lake Simcoe and into the wilderness.

Explorers, traders and missionaries exploited the land and water routes and eventually the name Toronto was applied to one of three forts built in the area by the French to protect their trade with First Nations against the English and other European competitors. By 1759 the forts were destroyed, but the area remained a trading center.

Toronto's magnificent skyline, *surrounded by Lake Ontario, captured from Toronto's Centre Island.* Courtesy Toronto Convention & Visitors Association

Canada came under British sovereignity at the end of the Seven Years' War with France (1763) and throughout and after the U.S. War of Independence the Toronto area became a haven for American colonists who preferred to remain under British rule. A great number of British immigrants settled in the area during the 19th century and Toronto was largely an Anglo-Saxon community. In the 1950s a large number of European immigrants joined the population. Today the vibrant, thriving, cosmopolitan, greater Toronto area is Canada's largest community and its commercial, financial and cultural heart.

Tourism, both international and local, is a Toronto specialty.

Toronto
ONTARIO

Tourism Toronto (Toronto Convention & Visitors Association)
P.O. Box 126, 207 Queen's Quay West, Toronto, ON Canada M5J 1A7
416-203-2500 or 1-800-499-2514 **www.seetorontonow.com**

Ontario Place. *Family entertainment complex situated on Toronto's waterfront featuring rides, attractions, IMAX® films and great live entertainment. Home to the Molson Amphitheatre and Atlantis Pavilions.* Courtesy Toronto Convention & Visitors Association

Live Entertainment in Toronto—Broadway North

FORD CENTRE for the PERFORMING ARTS, 5040 Yonge St., 416-733-9388
The PRINCESS of WALES THEATRE, 300 King St W., 1-800-461-3333
ELGIN & WINTERGARDEN THEATRE, 189 Yonge St., 416-314-2901
MASSEY HALL, 178 Victoria St., 416-872-4255 www.masseyhall.com
ROY THOMPSON HALL, 60 Simcoe St., 416-872-4255
SONY CENTRE for the PERFORMING ARTS, 1 Front St. E., 416-393-7469
The ROYAL ALEXANDRA THEATRE, 260 King St. W., 1-800-461-3333
ST. LAWRENCE CENTRE for the ARTS, 27 Front St. E., 416-366-7723 www.stlc.com
SOUL PEPPER THEATRE COMPANY, 55 Mill St., 416-866-8666
THE CANADIAN STAGE THEATRE, 26 Berkeley St., 416-368-3110
PANASONIC THEATRE, 651 Yonge St., 416-872-1111
TORONTO TRUCK THEATRE, 94 Belmont St., 416-922-0084
THE POOR ALEX, 296 Brunswick Ave., 416-324-9863
FACTORY THEATRE, 125 Bathurst St., 416-504-9971 www.factorytheatre.ca
TARRAGON THEATRE, 30 Bridgman Ave., 416-531-1827
THEATRE FRANCAISE, 26 Berkeley St., 416-534-6604
FAMOUS PEOPLE PLAYERS Dinner Theatre, 110 Sudbury St., 416-534-6604
LAUGH RESORT COMEDY CLUB, 370 King St. W., 416-364-5233
THEATRE PASSE MURAILLE, 16 Ryerson Ave., 416-504-PLAY
BUDDIES IN BAD TIMES THEATRE, 12 Alexander St., 416-975-9130
NATIVE EARTH PERFORMING ARTS, 55 Mill St., 416-531-1402
SECOND CITY, 51 Mercer St., 416-343-0011
YUK YUK'S COMEDY CABARET, 224 Richmond St. W., 416-967-6426
AL GREEN THEATRE, 750 Spadina Ave., 416-924-6211
CANADIAN OPERA COMPANY, 145 Queen St W., 416-924-6211
CANON THEATRE, 244 Victoria St., 416-872-1212
DIESEL PLAYHOUSE, 56 Blue Jays Way, 416-971-5656
FRINGE OF TORONTO Festival Theatre, 344 Bloor St. W., 416-966-1062
JUST FOR LAUGHS Toronto Festival, 416-355-2655 www.hahaha.com
KOFFLER CENTRE of the ARTS, 4566 Bathurst St., 416-636-1880

Entertainment Trivia

Toronto has more than 40 live theaters and is the 2nd-largest theater center in North America.

Toronto follows only Hollywood and New York as a location for filmmakers. Two popular spots for filming are Casa Loma and Kensington Market, which once doubled as a street market in Iran. Casa Loma is a 98-room castle, built in 1914 with solid gold fixtures, an electric elevator and an indoor pool.

Silent film star Mary Pickford, also once known as America's Sweetheart, lived on University Avenue at the site of what is now the Hospital for Sick Children.

Superman, the Man of Steel, fought the "battle for truth, justice and the American way." Joe Schuster, the creator of the character, was born in Toronto. He based the *Daily Planet* newspaper on the *Toronto Daily Star*.

Toronto
ONTARIO

Tourism Toronto (Toronto Convention & Visitors Association)
P.O. Box 126, 207 Queen's Quay West, Toronto, ON Canada M5J 1A7
416-203-2500 or 1-800-499-2514 **www.seetorontonow.com**

Toronto & Area Sports

Glen Abbey Golf Club
1333 Dorval Dr., Oakville. Designed by Jack Nicklaus, Canada's No. 1 public golf course opens late April to late October Reservations. In late July, Glen Abbey is home to the RBC Canadian Open on the PGA Tour. 905-844-1800 or 1-800-571-OPEN.

Toronto Blue Jays Baseball
Opens in April Rogers Centre stadium. Two-time World Series champs. 416-341-1234 www.bluejays.com

The Honda Indy Toronto
Exhibition Place. One of the city's largest, most celebrated sporting events. Stars and cars of the Indy Car series roar into Toronto mid-July. 416-588-7223

The Queen's Plate
Mid-July. Thoroughbred and harness horses at Woodbine Racetrack. 416-675-6110

Canadian Open
Canada's international men's tennis championships. Mid-August. York University International Tennis Centre. 416-203-2500

Canadian International Air Show. Canadian National Exhibition, waterfront. Late August. 416-303-6000

Toronto Argonauts
Rogers Centre. Our football heroes begin their season in October. 416-341-2714 www.argonauts.ca

Toronto Maple Leafs
Hockey heroes begin their season at the Air Canada Centre in October. www.mapleleafs.com

Toronto Raptors
The NBA franchise hits the Air Canada Centre courts in November. www.raptors.com

Air Canada Centre
40 Bay St., 416-815-5500 www.theaircanadacentre.com

Rogers Centre & CN Tower. *Toronto's Rogers Centre (with a fully retractable roof) seats 55,000 for baseball. Next door is the CN Tower.*
Courtesy Toronto Convention & Visitors Association

Inner Golf
99 Sudbury St., 416-538-4653 www.innergolf.ca

Ricoh Coliseum
100 Princess Blvd., 416-263-3900 www.ricohcoliseum.com

Rogers Centre
1 Blue Jays Way, 416-341-2770 www.rogerscentre.com

Tennis Canada
1 Shoreham Dr., 416-665-9777 www.tenniscanada.com

Toronto FC. Major League Soccer
Exhibition Place, 416-360-4625 www.torontofc.ca

Goodlife Fitness Toronto Marathon. Near the middle of October. Marathon starts at Mel Lastman Square in North York and ends at Queen's Park. As many as 4,000 runners as well as 30 wheelchair athletes will participate. 416-972-1062

TORONTO SPORTS TRIVIA

5-pin bowling was invented by Tommy Ryan from Toronto.

The world's most sought after race horse was Northern Dancer. This winner of the Kentucky Derby, the Belmont Stakes, and also Canada's Queen's Plate, commanded the highest stud fee for any thoroughbred in the world.

Tourism Toronto (Toronto Convention & Visitors Association)
P.O. Box 126, 207 Queen's Quay West, Toronto, ON Canada M5J 1A7
416-203-2500 or 1-800-499-2514 **www.seetorontonow.com**

TORONTO ANNUAL SHOWS & FESTIVALS

JANUARY

- **Toronto International Boat Show.** Mid-Jan. Exhibition Place. Canada's largest boat display.
- **National Home Show.** Mid-Jan. Metro Toronto Convention Centre.

FEBRUARY

- **Winter City Festival and Winterlicious.** Mid-Feb. Nathan Phillips Square Free
- **Canadian International Auto Show.** Mid-Feb. Metro Toronto Convention Centre.

MARCH

- **Canadian Music Festival.** Early Mar. Performances at 35 downtown clubs and halls.
- **Spring Fling.** Mid-Mar. Roger's Centre indoor carnival: midway, live entertainment and games.
- **Toronto Sportsmens' Show.** Mid-Mar. Exhibition Place. Canada's largest outdoors show.
- **One-of-a-Kind Springtime Craft Show & Sale.** March. Exhibition Place.
- **The Cottage Life Show.** Late March. International Centre. 400 exhibitors. www.cottagelife.com

APRIL

- **Metro Home Show.** Early Apr. Metro Toronto Convention Centre.
- **Clothing Show** Late Apr. Exhibition Place.
- **Creative Festival.** Mid-Apr. Exhibition Place. Supplies and demos.

MAY

- **Ontario Place** opens Mid-May. www.ontarioplace.com
- **Canada's Wonderland** season opens Mid-May.

JUNE

- **Toronto International Festival Caravan.** Mid-June. Explore different world cultures at 50 pavilions.
- **Gay & Lesbian Pride Week.** www.pridetoronto.com
- **Telus Toronto International Dragon Boat Race Festival.** Mid-June. Centre Island. Over 30 races and many multicultural events.
- **Festival of Fire.** June and July. Ontario Place. World's largest offshore international competition.
- **Fringe of Toronto Festival.** Late June. Annex neighborhood. Over 500 performances by more than 80 international theater companies.
- **Great Race North American.** Late June. The world's premier vintage auto event's finish line crosses the Bloor-Yorkville neighborhood.

JULY

- **Caribana.** Two weeks, late July. Famous Caribbean festival.

Photo © Tourism Toronto

JULY continued

- **Honda Indy.** Mid-July. Exhibition Place.
- **Toronto Outdoor Art Exhibition.** Mid-July. Nathan Phillips Square, near City Hall. North America's largest outdoor art festival. Juried www.torontooutdoorart.org
- **Beaches International Jazz Festival.** Late July. Free. 100 bands. www.beachesjazz.com

AUGUST

- **Canadian National Exhibition.** Mid-Aug. Canada's most highly attended annual event. www.theex.com
- **Canadian International Air Show.** Near Labour Day weekend. www.cias.org

SEPTEMBER

- **Toronto International Film Festival.** Early Sept. Ranked among top 4 film festivals in the world. www.tiffg.ca

OCTOBER

- **International Festival of Authors.** Mid-Oct. Harbourfront Centre. Largest literary fest of its type.

NOVEMBER

- **Royal Agricultural Winter Fair.** Early Nov. Largest indoor agricultural fair in the world. www.royalfair.org
- **One-of-A-Kind Fall Craft Show & Sale.** Late Nov. Exhibition Place. Works by many of Canadian artists.

DECEMBER

- **New Year's Eve at City Hall.** Nathan Phillips Square. Fun-filled party and countdown.

Toronto
ONTARIO

Tourism Toronto (Toronto Convention & Visitors Association)
P.O. Box 126, 207 Queen's Quay West, Toronto, ON Canada M5J 1A7
416-203-2500 or 1-800-499-2514 **www.seetorontonow.com**

Attractions

Art Gallery of Ontario
17 Dundas St. W. www.ago.net

Bata Shoe Museum
327 Bloor St. W. 416-979-7799

The Beaches Neighborhood
Iona Ave. www.beachestoronto.com

Black Creek Pioneer Village
Downsview 416-661-6600

CN Tower Ltd.
301 Front St. W. 416-868-6937

Casa Loma
1 Auston Terrace 416-923-1171

Centreville Amusement Park
Toronto Islands 416-203-0405

Eskimo Art Gallery Inc.
12 Queens Quay W. 416-366-3000

Fort York 100 Garrison Rd.
416-392-6907

The Grange
317 Dundas St. W. 416-979-6660

Greektown
Danforth Ave. 416-469-5634

Toronto Antique Centre
276 King Street W. 416-345-9941

Isaacs/Innuit Gallery
9 Prince Arthur Ave. 416-921-9985

Hockey Hall of Fame
BCE Place, 30 Yonge St. 416-360-7735
www.hhof.com

Holocaust Centre of Toronto
4600 Bathurst St. 416-635-2883

Mackenzie House
82 Bond St. 416-392-6915

Marine Museum of Toronto
Exhibition Pl. 888-675-7437

Market Gallery
95 Front St. E. 416-392-7604

Medieval Times Dinner
Exhibition Place 888-935-6878

Toronto Archives and Records
255 Spadina 416-397-5000

Toronto's distinctively beautiful Casa Loma.
Courtesy the Ontario Ministry of Economic Development, Trade & Tourism, c. 1996.

Toronto Zoo 361A Old Finch Ave.,
Scarborough 416-392-5929

Gardiner Museum of Ceramic Art
111 Queen's Park 416-586-8080

Museum for Textiles
55 Centre Ave. 416-599-5321

Ontario Parliament Buildings
College & University St. 416-325-7500

Ontario Place
955 Lake Shore Blvd. W. 416-314-9900

Ontario Science Centre 770 Don
Mills Rd., North York 888-696-1110

Power Plant Art Gallery
231 Queens Quay 416-973-4949

Queen's Quay Terminal
207 Queens Quay W. 416-203-0510

Redpath Sugar Museum
95 Queens Quay E. 416-586-5549

Royal Ontario Museum
100 Queen's Park 416-586-8000

Showcase Antique Mall
610 Queen St. W. 416-703-MALL

The Jane-Finch Sunday Market
77 Ellsworth Ave. 416-635-5286

Music

Roy Thompson Hall 60 Simcoe St.,
Toronto, 416-593-4828

Toronto Symphony Orchestra & Toronto Mendelssohn Choir
Roy Thompson Hall, 416-598-0422

Massey Hall 178 Victoria St.,
416-363-7624

Ford Centre for the Performing Arts 5040 Yonge St., North York, 416-733-9388

Opera & Ballet

The National Ballet of Canada and **The Canadian Opera Company**
The Four Seasons Centre for the Performing Arts, 145 Queen St. W.
www.nationalballet.ca

Fleck Dance Theatre
207 Queens Quay W., 416-973-4000

Opera Atelier
157 King St. E. 416-703-3767
www.operaatelier.com

The Toronto Operetta Theatre
947 Queen St. E. 416-922-2912
www.torontooperetta.com

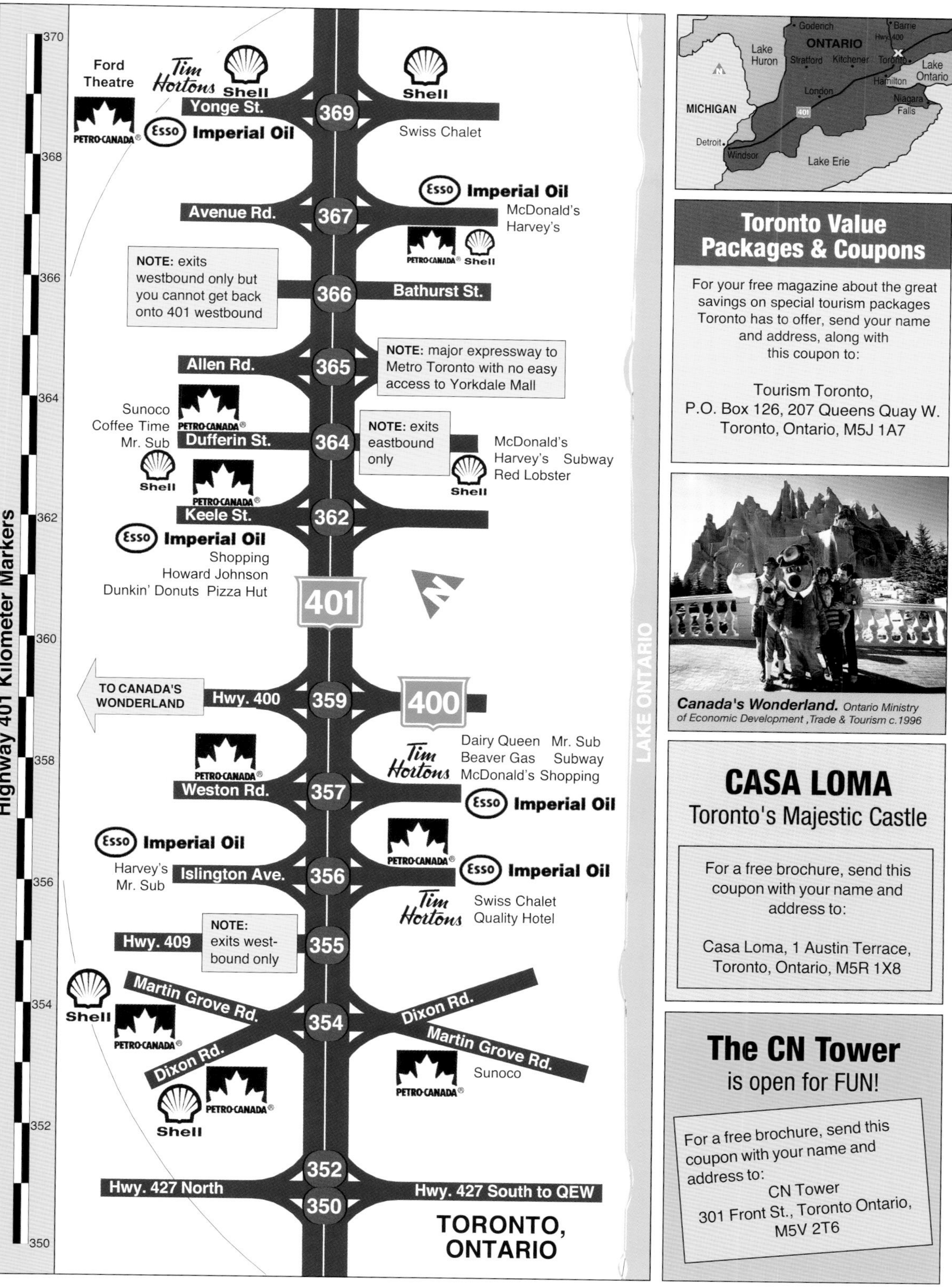
Highway 401 Kilometer Markers
370
368
366
364
362
360
358
356
354
352
350
Ford Theatre
Tim Hortons
Shell
Shell
Yonge St.
369
PETRO-CANADA
Esso Imperial Oil
Swiss Chalet
Esso Imperial Oil
Avenue Rd.
367
McDonald's
Harvey's
PETRO-CANADA
Shell
NOTE: exits westbound only but you cannot get back onto 401 westbound
366
Bathurst St.
Allen Rd.
365
NOTE: major expressway to Metro Toronto with no easy access to Yorkdale Mall
Sunoco
Coffee Time
Mr. Sub
PETRO-CANADA
Dufferin St.
364
NOTE: exits eastbound only
McDonald's
Harvey's Subway
Red Lobster
Shell
PETRO-CANADA
Shell
Keele St.
362
Esso Imperial Oil
Shopping
Howard Johnson
Dunkin' Donuts Pizza Hut
401
N
TO CANADA'S WONDERLAND
Hwy. 400
359
400
PETRO-CANADA
Tim Hortons
Dairy Queen Mr. Sub
Beaver Gas Subway
McDonald's Shopping
Weston Rd.
357
Esso Imperial Oil
Esso Imperial Oil
Harvey's
Mr. Sub
Islington Ave.
356
PETRO-CANADA
Esso Imperial Oil
Tim Hortons
Swiss Chalet
Quality Hotel
Hwy. 409
NOTE: exits westbound only
355
Shell
Martin Grove Rd.
PETRO-CANADA
354
Dixon Rd.
Martin Grove Rd.
Dixon Rd.
PETRO-CANADA
Sunoco
Shell
PETRO-CANADA
352
Hwy. 427 North
350
Hwy. 427 South to QEW
TORONTO, ONTARIO
LAKE ONTARIO
Goderich
Barrie
Hwy. 400
ONTARIO
Lake Huron
Stratford
Kitchener
Toronto
Lake Ontario
Hamilton
London
MICHIGAN
401
Niagara Falls
Detroit
Windsor
Lake Erie
Toronto Value Packages & Coupons
For your free magazine about the great savings on special tourism packages Toronto has to offer, send your name and address, along with this coupon to:
Tourism Toronto,
P.O. Box 126, 207 Queens Quay W.
Toronto, Ontario, M5J 1A7
CASA LOMA
Toronto's Majestic Castle
For a free brochure, send this coupon with your name and address to:
Casa Loma, 1 Austin Terrace,
Toronto, Ontario, M5R 1X8
The CN Tower
is open for FUN!
For a free brochure, send this coupon with your name and address to:
CN Tower
301 Front St., Toronto Ontario,
M5V 2T6

Canada's Wonderland. *Ontario Ministry of Economic Development, Trade & Tourism c.1996*

Toronto
ONTARIO

Tourism Toronto (Toronto Convention & Visitors Association)
P.O. Box 126, 207 Queen's Quay West, Toronto, ON Canada M5J 1A7
416-203-2500 or 1-800-499-2514 **www.seetorontonow.com**

Toronto Trivia

Inventions & Inventors

Two researchers at the University of Toronto, **Dr. Frederick Banting** and **Dr. Charles Best,** invented insulin, which now helps to keep millions of diabetics alive. The first injection of insulin was given in 1922 at Toronto General Hospital.

The paint roller was created by **Norman Breakey** of Toronto in 1940.

Hundreds of thousands of the world's infants spent much of their first year of life eating Pablum which was created at Toronto's internationally renowned **Hospital for Sick Children.** The hospital owned the patent on Pablum; sales helped defer research costs.

Sir Sandford Fleming invented a timely concept in Toronto in the 19th century called Standard Time.

Records & Famous Firsts

Toronto is Canada's largest city. Toronto has more than 4,000 restaurants and approximately 21,000 first-class hotel rooms with an additional 5,000 rooms in motels, guest houses and college residences.

The *Guinness Book of World Records* has certified that the the world's tallest free-standing structure is the 555.33-metre-tall **CN Tower** in Toronto. It is over 1,800 feet high! The CN Tower has the world's longest concrete staircase, with 2,570 steps that would take a physically fit person twenty minutes to descend.

Toronto's **Yonge Street** is the world's longest street (at 1,178 miles). It runs from Toronto's Queens Quay to Rainy River. Yonge Street was named after Sir George Yonge, British Secretary for War 1782-1794.

The **Canadian National Exhibition's** new flagpole was erected in 1977. It is a 184-foot Douglas Fir. It is believed to be the world's tallest wooden flagpole.

People

Author **Arthur Hailey** of Hotel and Airport fame once worked in Toronto as assistant editor of Maclean-Hunter's magazine Bus and Truck Transport.

Lady Iris Mountbatten, granddaughter of Queen Victoria's daughter Princess Beatrice, lives in Toronto.

One of Ernest Hemingway's first jobs was at the *Toronto Star* newspaper in the 1920s. He was paid $150 the first year. "Papa" Hemingway was not totally impressed by the city and he once remarked that he had to buy chocolate from a bootlegger because "stores can't sell candy on Sundays."

Bits & Pieces

William Lyon MacKenzie was elected the first mayor of the city of Toronto in 1834.

The population of York at the time of the War of 1812 was only about 700.

In the city of Toronto there are approximately 50,000 street lights.

The first postage stamp to be used in Canada was designed in Toronto in 1851 by **Sir Sanford Fleming.**

Toronto has about 42 foreign language newspapers.

2,500 ounces of gold were used as a coloring agent in the 14,000 windows of the **Royal Bank Plaza** building.

Toronto's subway system has the highest per capita ridership in North America. In 1881 Torontonians were able to buy 25 Toronto Street Railway tickets for one dollar.

The **Eaton Centre** is the 2nd-largest shopping center in Canada. More than 1,000,000 people visit it weekly.

Toronto's renowned **Canadian National Exhibition,** held from mid-August to early September, is the world's largest annual fair.

Some people say it couldn't be more appropriate. The seat of government for the province of Ontario Legislature in Toronto, built in 1896, but before the politicians called this property home, the land was used for a lunatic asylum!

Toronto's official motto is "Industry, Intelligence, Integrity."

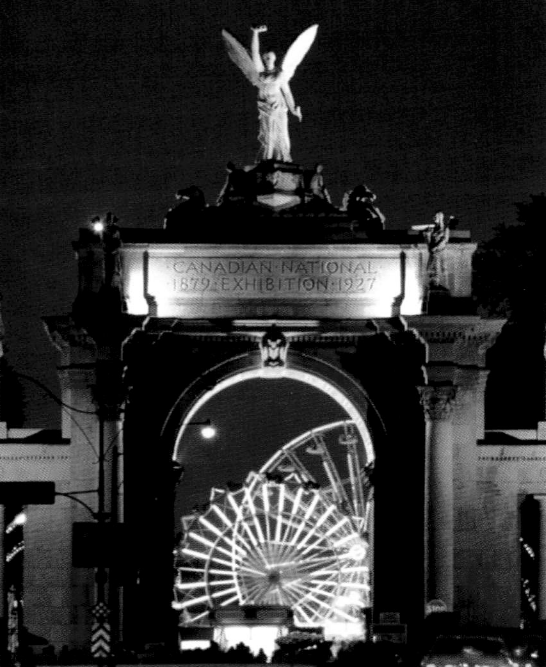

Canadian National Exhibition
Courtesy Tourism Toronto

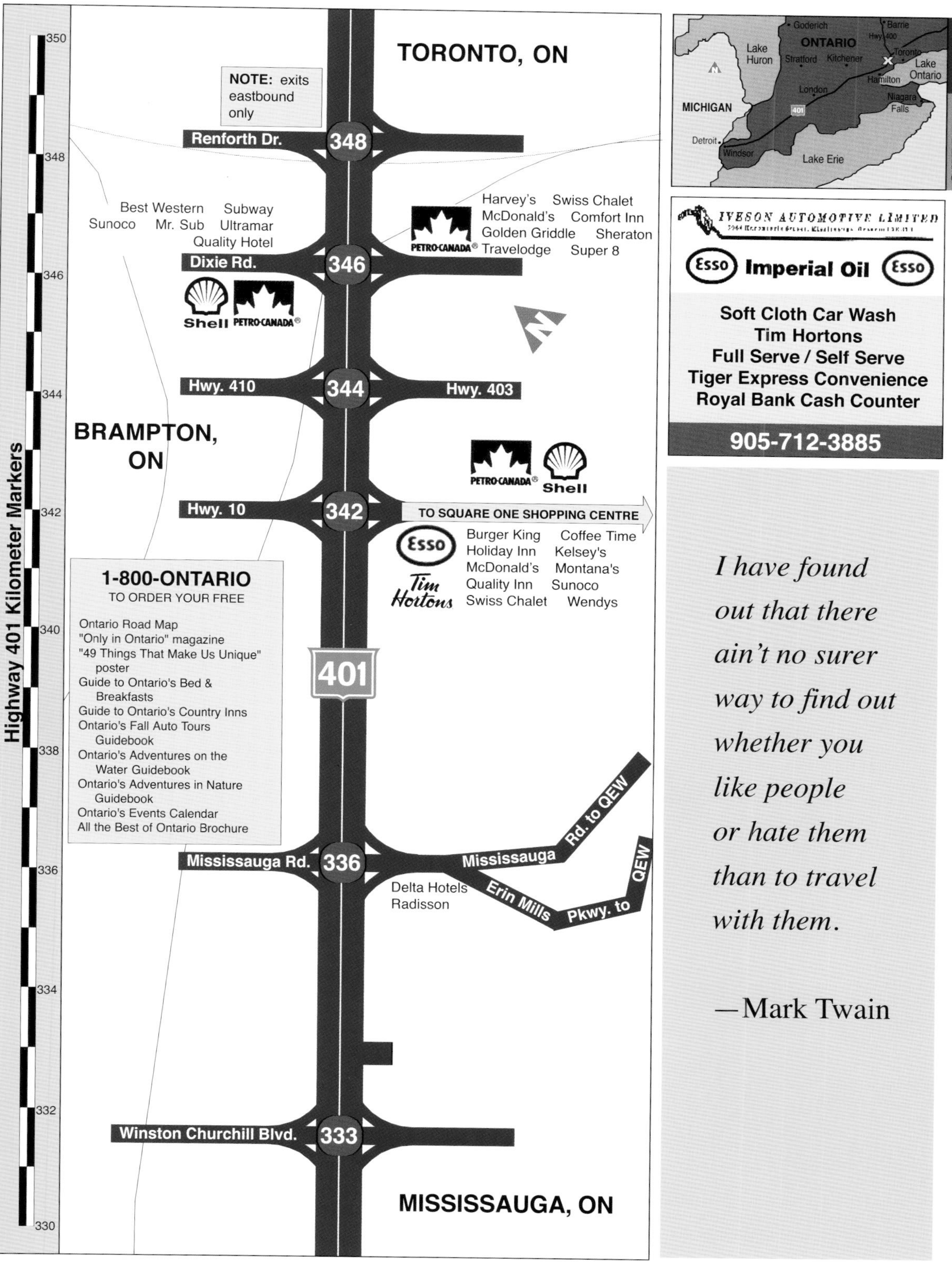

TORONTO, ON
NOTE: exits eastbound only
Renforth Dr.
348
Harvey's Swiss Chalet
McDonald's Comfort Inn
Golden Griddle Sheraton
Travelodge Super 8
PETRO-CANADA
Best Western Subway
Sunoco Mr. Sub Ultramar
Quality Hotel
Dixie Rd.
346
Shell
PETRO-CANADA
N
Hwy. 410
344
Hwy. 403
BRAMPTON, ON
PETRO-CANADA
Shell
Hwy. 10
342
TO SQUARE ONE SHOPPING CENTRE
Esso
Tim Hortons
Burger King Coffee Time
Holiday Inn Kelsey's
McDonald's Montana's
Quality Inn Sunoco
Swiss Chalet Wendys
1-800-ONTARIO
TO ORDER YOUR FREE
Ontario Road Map
"Only in Ontario" magazine
"49 Things That Make Us Unique" poster
Guide to Ontario's Bed & Breakfasts
Guide to Ontario's Country Inns
Ontario's Fall Auto Tours Guidebook
Ontario's Adventures on the Water Guidebook
Ontario's Adventures in Nature Guidebook
Ontario's Events Calendar
All the Best of Ontario Brochure
401
Mississauga Rd.
336
Mississauga Rd. to QEW
Erin Mills Pkwy. to QEW
Delta Hotels
Radisson
Winston Churchill Blvd.
333
MISSISSAUGA, ON
Highway 401 Kilometer Markers
350
348
346
344
342
340
338
336
334
332
330
Goderich
Barrie
Hwy 400
Lake Huron
ONTARIO
Stratford
Kitchener
Toronto
Lake Ontario
Hamilton
London
Niagara Falls
MICHIGAN
Detroit
Windsor
Lake Erie
17
ONTARIO
IVESON AUTOMOTIVE LIMITED
Esso Imperial Oil Esso
Soft Cloth Car Wash
Tim Hortons
Full Serve / Self Serve
Tiger Express Convenience
Royal Bank Cash Counter
905-712-3885
I have found out that there ain't no surer way to find out whether you like people or hate them than to travel with them.
—Mark Twain

Halton Region
ONTARIO

Halton Hills Chamber of Commerce
328 Guelph Street, Georgetown, ON Canada L7G 4B5
Tel: 905-877-7119 **www.haltonhillschamber.on.ca**

HISTORY OF THE TOWN OF CAMPBELLVILLE

The tiny town was named for its first settler, John Campbell. You can still see his 1832 log home at **37 Campbell Ave.** It is now stuccoed.

After damming the stream to provide waterpower for his sawmill, Campbell set about to attract other settlers by improving the roads and designing a plan for the town layout. Blacksmiths, storekeepers and cobblers were the first to set up shop, followed by a mill, churches and a schoolhouse. In 1880 the hamlet built a train depot for the Credit Valley Railway.

Today the town attracts shoppers and tourists. Reminders of the past fill the many antique boutiques that are frequented by both Canadian and American treasure-seekers.

***In nearby St. Jacobs,** Mennonites can be seen traveling to and from their homes in horse-drawn carriages. Courtesy Ontario Ministry of Economic Development, Trade & Tourism, c. 1996. Call 1-800-265-3353 for more information. www.stjacobs.com*

Hiking on the Escarpment

I can always make my sister Cath laugh when I bring out the "Hiking with Mom" memories. My energetic mother would haul my teenage sister and I to Campbellville on a weekend for a bite to eat, a browse through the shops, and a very large ice cream cone.

Too cool to admit to our feelings of dread, my sister and I would be especially talkative during the short drive to one of the conservation parks nearby. Soon we'd be trying not to lose sight of "Hiker-mama."

Sometimes we would take a more daring route along the panoramic cliffs of Mount Nemo. Other times we would walk the boardwalk around the mysteriously still Crawford Lake. Either way, mom would hush our complaints about our aches and pains with a smile and a "this is good for ya."

Those were good times. Today I appreciate the natural beauty of this area and I love to hike on the Escarpment. I've become a hiker-mama who never hesitates to drag her two girls along.

Attractions

Campbellville Area
This village is known for antique and specialty shops, inns, bed and breakfasts, art galleries, restaurants and tea rooms.

Chudleigh's
Milton. An apple farm with apples and apple baked goods as well as Ontario honey, cheddar and maple syrup. Farm animals, children's play area and pony rides (seasonal). 905-878-2725 or 905-826-1252

Conservation Areas
- **Kelso/Glen Eden Ski & Snowboard Centre,** Milton. 905-878-5011
- **Milton Falls,** Milton. 905-854-0262
- **Mount Nemo,** Burlington. 905-336-1158
- **Mounstberg Wildlife Centre,** Campbellville. 905-854-2276
- **Rattlesnake Point,** Milton. 905-878-1147

Crawford Lake Native Village
Milton. Reconstructed 15th century Iroquoian village. 905-854-0234

Country Heritage Park
144 Townline Rd, Milton, L9T 2Y3. Over 30 buildings and displays on scenic 80-acre site. Farm animals, free wagon rides, costumed interpreters, many special events including craft and trade demonstrations throughout the year. 905-878-8151

Halton Region Museum
Milton. Halton's history is presented in the museum and other buildings on the 19th century Alexander Homestead Site, with the Escarpment for a backdrop. Year-round, Mon. to Fri. 10 a.m.-4 p.m., Sun. and holidays noon-4 p.m. 905-875-2200 museum.region.halton.on.ca

Mohawk Raceway
Campbellville. Harness racing, trotters and pacers. Terrace Dining Room. Hwy. 401 at Guelph Rd. (exit 312). 416-675-3993 or 1-888-675-RACE.

Milton Farmers' Market
A main street market. Mid-May to Oct., Sat. only from 7 a.m.-noon. 905-878-0581

Streetcar Car Museum
(Ontario Electric R.R.)
Milton. Operational railway museum. Street-cars and radials travel 3 km of right-of-way through a scenic wooded area. Gift shop. Unlimited rides with daily admission. Ride vintage streetcars. Guelph Line 15 km north of 401. May 4 to Oct. 26. 519-856-9802 519-856-9802. www.hcry.org

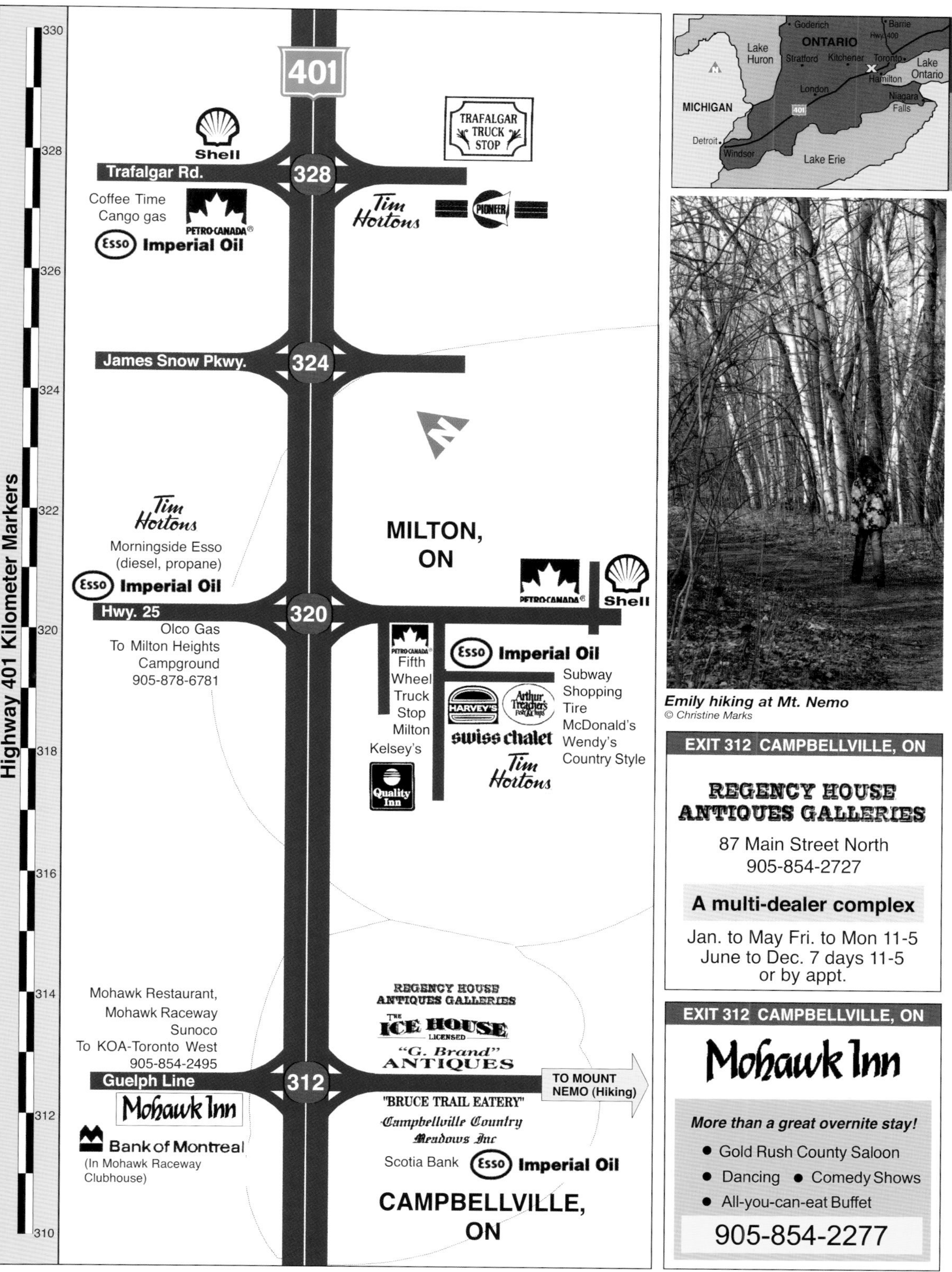
Highway 401 Kilometer Markers
330
328
326
324
322
320
318
316
314
312
310
401
Shell
TRAFALGAR TRUCK STOP
Trafalgar Rd.
328
Coffee Time
Cango gas
PETRO-CANADA
Esso Imperial Oil
Tim Hortons
PIONEER
James Snow Pkwy.
324
Tim Hortons
Morningside Esso
(diesel, propane)
Esso Imperial Oil
MILTON,
ON
PETRO-CANADA
Shell
Hwy. 25
320
Olco Gas
To Milton Heights
Campground
905-878-6781
PETRO-CANADA
Fifth
Wheel
Truck
Stop
Milton
Kelsey's
Quality Inn
Esso Imperial Oil
HARVEY'S
Arthur Treacher's
swiss chalet
Tim Hortons
Subway
Shopping
Tire
McDonald's
Wendy's
Country Style
Mohawk Restaurant,
Mohawk Raceway
Sunoco
To KOA-Toronto West
905-854-2495
Guelph Line
312
Mohawk Inn
Bank of Montreal
(In Mohawk Raceway
Clubhouse)
REGENCY HOUSE
ANTIQUES GALLERIES
THE ICE HOUSE
LICENSED
"G. Brand"
ANTIQUES
TO MOUNT
NEMO (Hiking)
"BRUCE TRAIL EATERY"
Campbellville Country
Meadows Inc
Scotia Bank
Esso Imperial Oil
CAMPBELLVILLE,
ON
Goderich
Barrie
Hwy. 400
Lake
Huron
ONTARIO
Stratford
Kitchener
Toronto
Lake
Ontario
Hamilton
MICHIGAN
London
401
Niagara
Falls
Detroit
Windsor
Lake Erie

Emily hiking at Mt. Nemo
© Christine Marks

Wellington County
ONTARIO

Guelph Visitor & Convention Services
55 Wyndham St. N., Guelph, ON Canada N1H 1A1
www.guelph.ca

Many of the small towns and villages of **Wellington County** were founded by English, Scottish and Irish settlers in the early 1800s. Today Wellington County is known for its flea markets, antique shops, and its list of popular celtic festivals and special events.

Guelph is the largest city in Wellington County. **John Galt,** a Scotsman and an organizer of the Canada Company, founded Guelph in 1827. Galt named the town in honor of the British Royal Family whose name was Guelph (from the House of Hanover).

Guelph has an impressive collection of some 60 heritage buildings. The Speed River has many beautiful and historical homes bordering its slopes. Among them is the birthplace of **John McCrae** (1872-1918), who was moved to write "In Flanders Fields" after the Battle of Ypres. The 1800s-style lattice-covered footbridge and Riverside Park also grace the river.

The two nearby villages of **Fergus** and **Elora** won't disappoint you. **Fergus** is the site of the extremely popular Fergus Highland Games and home to the Wellington County Museum and Archives.

The 70-foot gorge, overhanging rock ledges, small caves, waterfall and pine-needle-carpeted footpaths makes **Elora** an Ontario beauty mark! Elora's excellent restaurants always delight. One fine summer evening not long ago, I quite enjoyed a beautiful plate of salmon while being serenaded in the intimate but friendly atmosphere of the *La Cachette* riverbank patio.

Local Trivia

- **Ontario Veterinary College (OVC),** now part of the University of Guelph, was founded in 1862, making it the oldest operating veterinary school in North America.
- The first wire coat hangers were made in Guelph.
- The first two-way police-car radios were used in Guelph.
- The first jock-strap was made in Guelph by the Guelph Elastic Hosiery Company.
- Guelph is the site of Canada's first wet/dry re-cycling facility.

Fergus Scottish Festival and Highland Games. *A weekend celebration of Celtic music, dance and traditions.* *www.fergusscottishfestival.com*

Attractions & Festivals

The Arboretum
Guelph. Nature walks through plant collections, several gardens and 2,900 kinds of trees and shrubs. Year-round. At the Univ. of Guelph Campus off East Ring Rd. Free. 519-824-4120 ext. 54110 www.uoguelph.ca/arboretum

Wellington County Museum & Archives
Fergus. Restored 1877 stone building housing archives, exhibitions. Hiking/ski trails. Mon. to Fri. 9:30 a.m.-4:30 p.m., Sat. and Sun. 1 p.m.-5 p.m. On County Rd. 18. www.wcm.on.ca 519-846-0916

Elora Gorge
May to Oct. 10 to dusk, Jan. to Mar. 10 a.m.-5 p.m. 519-846-9742 www.grandriver.ca

The Ale Trail
Guelph. Meet brew masters and taste true craft beers at F&M Brewery, Sleeman Brewery and other nearby breweries. Mid-Apr. to mid-Oct., Sat. and Sun. 1 p.m.-4:30 p.m. Free. 1-800-334-4519 www.AleTrail.on.ca

Guelph Arts Council Historical Walking Tours
5 tours. May to Oct. Sun. 2 p.m.-4 p.m. Admission: $2. 519-836-3280

Elora Trout Festival
On the banks of the Grand River. June. Free. 519-846-0331

Guelph Spring Festival
Chamber, classical, jazz and world music celebration with free community concerts and admission events. Early June. 519-821-3210

MacDonald Stewart Art Centre and Donald Forster Sculpture Park
Seven galleries with art from local to international sources featuring renowned collection of Inuit art. Sculpture park with 19 Canadian works. 358 Gordon St. Free. 519-837-0010 msac@uoguelph.ca

The Elora Festival
Celebration of song. International talent, with choral focus. Early-July to early-Aug. 519-846-0331 www.elorafestival.com

Fergus Scottish Festival
An official ABA Top 100 Tourist Event. Mid-Aug. 519-787-0099 www.fergusscottishfestival.com

Guelph Jazz Festival
Local and international jazz artists. Indoor/outdoor concerts plus free events. Early Sept. 519-763-4952 www.guelphjazzfestival.com

Did you know that **the International Plowing Match 2000** was held in Guelph, Ontario.

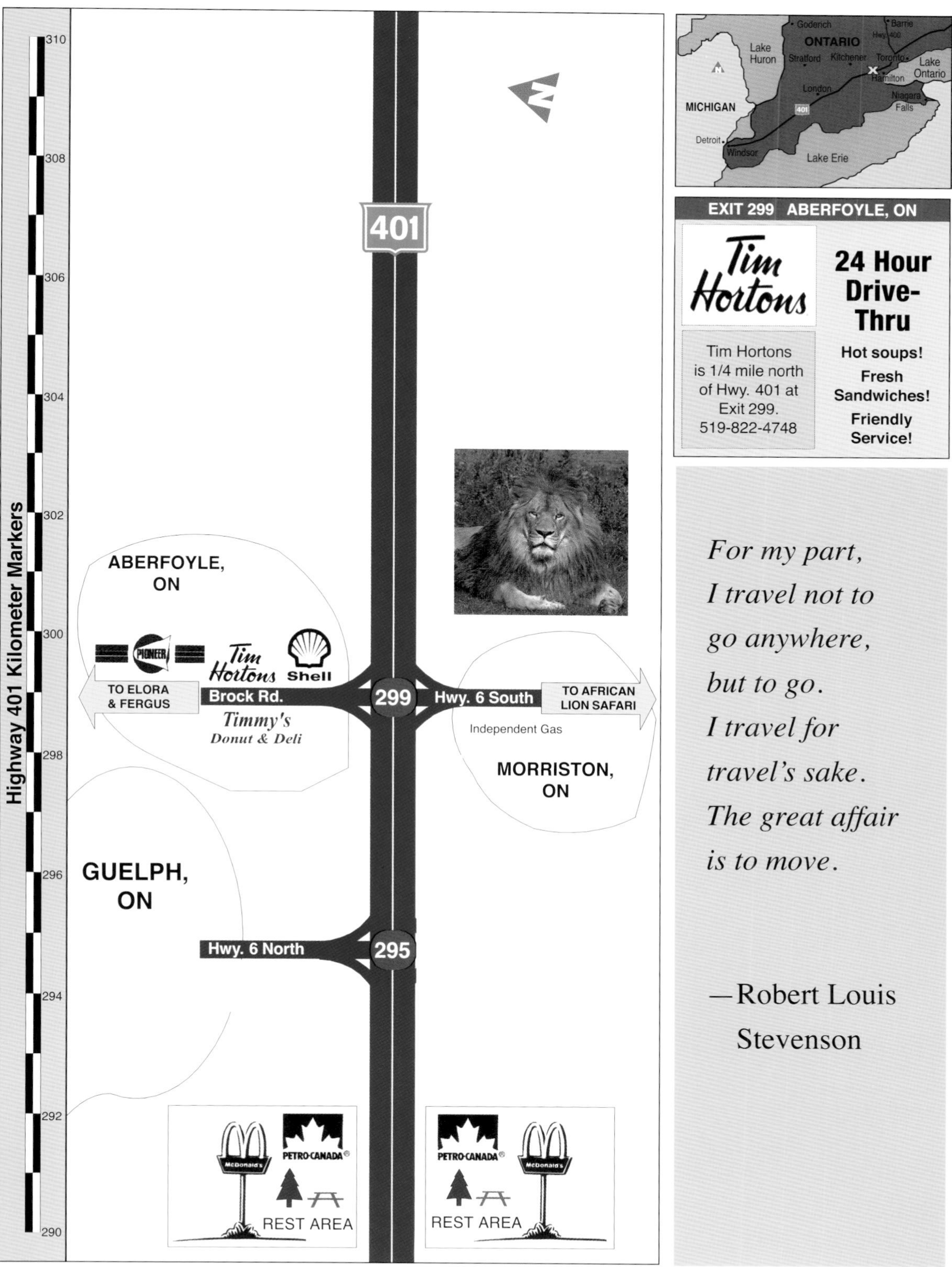

For my part,
I travel not to
go anywhere,
but to go.
I travel for
travel's sake.
The great affair
is to move.

—Robert Louis Stevenson

Waterloo Region
ONTARIO

Your Kitchener Store / KW Tourism
183-185 King Street W, Kitchener, ON, Canada N2G 1A7
519-745-3536 or 1-800-265-6959 **www.explorewaterlooregion.com**

Many of Waterloo Region's earliest settlements were Mennonite communities, a fact which makes this region culturally and architecturally unique. And every so often today you'll meet a horse-drawn Mennonite vehicle on the country roads.

KITCHENER-WATERLOO

K-W is known worldwide for its **Oktoberfest** celebration, and nationally for its museums and galleries. I especially recommend the **Canadian Clay & Glass Gallery** and the **Doon Heritage Crossroads Museum** (exit 275).

ST. JACOBS

Most of the nearly 100 unique shops, inns and restaurants of **St. Jacobs** are open year-round. You can watch craftspeople and artists at work, sample ethnic delicacies and buy unique gifts from the 400 different counters in the farm market. Shop till you drop at the 25-store Factory Outlet Mall! Peruse the aisles of the multi-dealer antique mall. I always look forward to a meal at St. Jacobs **Stone Crock Restaurant, Vidalia's Market Dining** or **Benjamin's Restaurant.**

CAMBRIDGE

Cambridge offers shopping bonanzas. **Southworks Outlet Mall** boasts savings of up to 70% on quality name products: Biltmore, Kodiak, Grower Direct, Stetson, Wolverine, Gore-Tex, Florsheim, & Muskoka Lakes. The Shirt Store, The **Tiger Brand Factory Outlet, Shamporium Factory Outlet** and a huge antique mall are also close by.

VILLAGE OF BLAIR

One minute from the 401 (exit 275) is the tiny **Village of Blair.** Here you'll enjoy browsing through the shelves at Blair House Gifts. While **The Lamb's Inn,** a brick and wood building erected in 1837, is now known as the **Garden Gate,** it remains the place to meet for area residents. Well worth a visit, Garden Gate Ltd. is one of Canada's finest manufacturers of quality ornamental concrete fountains, statuary and accessories. Stretch your legs or walk the dog along the scenic **river bank trail** that is just past the Village.

Attractions & Festivals

African Lion Safari
Canada's original safari adventure. Animal shows, cruise the "African Queen", scenic train rides, kids Jungle Playground, Pets' Corner, drive through Game Reserves (view and photograph 1,000 exotic animals and birds). Daily late Apr. to late Oct. Safari Rd. between Hwys. #6 and 8, Cambridge. 1-800-461-WILD www.lionsafari.com

Canadian Clay & Glass Gallery
Clay, glass, stained glass and enamel. Year-round, Waterloo. 519-746-1882

Doon Heritage Crossroads
Tour 20 historic buildings with costumed interpreters. Canadian archives, artifacts, children's educational programs, changing collections and German folk art. Spring and summer daily 10 a.m.-4:30 p.m.; Sept. to Dec. weekdays. Hwy. 401 exit 275, Kitchener. 519-748-1914 www.region.waterloo.on.ca/doon

Homer Watson House & Gallery
Art gallery in the Canadian landscape artist's original studio. Tues. to Sun., 12 noon-4:30 p.m. Kitchener. Free. 519-748-4377

Joseph Schneider Haus
Kitchener's oldest Pennsylvania German Mennonite home, restored to 1856. 466 Queen St. S., Kitchener, ON N2G 1W7 519-742-7752 www.region.waterloo.on.ca.jsh

Woodside National Historic Site
Boyhood home of Prime Minister William Lyon Mackenzie King restored to the Victorian style of the 1890's. Open Daily mid-May to Dec. 519-741-5684 ParksCanada.pch.gc.ca/parks/ontario/woodside

St. Jacobs Quilt and Fibre Art Festival
The last weekend in May. 1-800-265-3353 www.stjacobs.com

Grandriver Film Festival
October. Internation short film competition. 519-622-0043

Garden Gate Ltd
Canada's finest manufacturer of garden ornaments. 369 Pinebush Rd., Cambridge 519-624-0688 www.gardengateltd.com

Mill Race Festival of Traditional Folk Music
Art exhibit, music, dance. Late July. 12 noon-12 a.m. 519-653-1424

Waterloo Busker Carnival
Magic, comedy, acrobats, jugglers and more on King St. in Uptown Waterloo. Late Aug. 519-747-8769

Cambridge Fall Fair
Dickson Park. Mid-Sept. 519-621-9140 www.cambridgefallfair.com

Kitchener-Waterloo Oktoberfest
Mid-Oct. Nine days of old fashioned fun. World's second-largest, and North America's largest, Bavarian festival. 519-570-4267 www.oktoberfest.ca

St. Jacobs Harvest Festival
Early Oct. Farmers market/flea market. Agri-events, line dancing, sheep shearing and charity auction. 519-747-1830

Christkindl Market
A 400 year old German tradition. Crafts, food and music. Early Dec. Thurs. 4 p.m.-8 p.m.; Fri. 10 a.m.-8 p.m., Sat. 9 a.m.-8 p.m.; Sun. 12 noon-6 p.m. Kitchener City Hall. Free. 519-741-2388 www.christkindl.ca

Outlet Shopping

- **Kitchener Farmers Market** 519-741-2287
- **St. Jacobs Factory Outlet Mall** 1-800-265-3353
- **Southworks Outlet Mall**, Cambridge 519-740-0380
- **Biltmore Stetson Hat, Endlines, Florsheim Shoes, Shamporium, The Shirt Store, Antiques,** and **Tiger Brand Outlet,** Cambridge 519-621-5722

Camping

- **Grand River Conservation Authority** has 8 campgrounds in the area. May to Oct. 519-621-2761
- **Green Acre Park,** Waterloo. 345 sites, pull-throughs, close to St. Jacobs Farmers Market and Outlet Mall. 519-885-1758
- **Laurel Creek Conservation Area,** Waterloo. 725-acre lake. 519-884-6620

Highway 401 Kilometer Markers
290
288
286
284
282
280
278
276
274
272
270
401
CAMBRIDGE, ON
N
Townline Rd.
286
Imperial Oil
Esso
NOTE: 284 exits eastbound only. Re-access via exit 286
284
Franklin Blvd.
Shell
Tim Hortons
Jamieson Pkwy.
Holiday Inn
Comfort Inn
PETRO-CANADA
Burger King
Casey's
Harvey's Kelsey's
McDonald's Super 8
Taco Bell
Shell
To Green Acres RV Park 519-885-1758
Hwy. 24
282
Hespler Rd.
Esso
PETRO-CANADA
swiss chalet
KITCHENER-WATERLOO, ON
Tim Hortons
Hwy. 8 Overpass
Bank of Montreal
In Sports-world
To Kitchener, Waterloo & St. Jacobs
King St./Hwy. 8
To Pine Valley Park Campground
519-623-4998
pinevall@golden.net
Tim Hortons
PETRO-CANADA
Tim Hortons
McDonald's
Sunoco
HARVEY'S
278 A/B
"Old" Hwy. 8
RIVER BREEZE BED & BREAKFAST
see our ad on p. 31
Shell
PETRO-CANADA
To Bingemans Park Campground
519-744-1555
Fountain St.
Wink's Sunoco & convenience
To Doon Heritage Crossroads
BLAIR HOUSE GIFTS
Please see our ad above
Blair Rd.
Homer Watson Blvd.
275
Fountain St.
GARDEN GATE LTD.
Ornamental Concrete
1679 Blair Rd., Cambridge ON N3H 4R8 519-653-4545
Pioneer Dr.
Tim Hortons
New Dundee Rd.
Baker's Dozen Donuts open 24 hrs
RODEWAY SUITES
Village of BLAIR
Goderich
Barrie
Hwy. 400
ONTARIO
Lake Huron
Stratford
Kitchener
Toronto
Lake Ontario
Hamilton
London
Niagara Falls
MICHIGAN
401
Detroit
Windsor
Lake Erie
23
ONTARIO
EXIT 275 CAMBRIDGE, ON
BLAIR HOUSE GIFTS
519-650-2041
1660 Blair Rd. Cambridge, ON N3H 4R8
EXITS 284 & 282 CAMBRIDGE
Michelle & Mark Trombley
welcome you to their 401 service stations
Esso
Imperial Oil
Esso
TWENTY-FOUR CAR WASH
519-624-2093 684 Hespeler Rd.
•Esso •Bank Machine •Tim Hortons
•Touchless Car Wash
JAMIESON PKWY. CAR WASH
519-658-2910 100 Jamieson Pkwy.
•Esso •Car Wash •Tim Hortons
EXIT 278B KITCHENER, ON
BED & BREAKFAST
11 Sunbridge Cr., 519-743-4557
1-877-743-4557
• Jacuzzi, heated pool, whirlpool tubs
• Close to Markets, St. Jacobs & Universities
• Full breakfast
• Pets with res.
• Great trails
• Credit cards
* WHEN YOU PRESENT THIS INVITATION
EXIT 275 KITCHENER, ON
RODEWAY SUITES
55 New Dundee Rd.
519-895-2272
FEATURES
• Spacious guest rooms have kitchenette with microwave, fridge and sink
• In-room coffee maker/Cable TV
• Complimentary continental breakfast
• Pets allowed upon request
• Ample parking for large vehicles
Close to shopping, attractions, college & university, restaurants, market

Festival Country
ONTARIO

Festival Country is the second of the three tourism regions you pass through when you drive the stretch of Highway 401 that connects Toronto to Windsor. The other two tourism regions are Metropolitan Toronto and South-western Ontario.

Festival Country encompasses eight counties, three of which are linked by the 401: Waterloo Region, Wellington County, and Halton Region. **Niagara Falls, Oktoberfest,** and **African Lion Safari** are the big ticket attractions.

Festival Country is such a beautiful area that you'll be tempted to pick up a real estate paper before you leave. You don't want to miss the many fine vineyards and orchards, the spectacular **Niagara Falls,** or the **Royal Botanical Gardens** in Hamilton.

Festival Country is multi-faceted, from its Mennonite farms and markets to the bustling city centers of Hamilton, Guelph and Kitchener-Waterloo. **St. Jacobs**, known for Old Order Mennonites traveling by horse and buggy on main streets and country roads, operates the largest Farmers' market in Canada. The **Six Nations Reserve,** near Brantford, is the largest native settlement in Canada.

As the name suggests, there are festivals. The most notable ones are the **Shaw Festival** and **Oktoberfest** but the Highland Games, Pow Wows, farm fairs, flower festivals, wine festivals and winter carnivals should round out your list of possibilities. I do wish everyone could experience the breath-taking **Lilac Festival** at the **Royal Botanical Gardens** in Hamilton in Springtime. The fragrant breeze cresting the hill is truly therapeutic! 905-527-1158

Niagara is a popular year-round destination for our family. During autumn, we'll make day-trips to the Falls and avoid the seasonal pricing. The Niagara Parkway is a spectacular drive with plenty of beautiful picnic areas and hiking trails. In early spring, the dazzling display of naturalized daffodils and blossoming magnolia trees never fails. Most often we stop at the Gorge and Whirlpool Rapids so we can watch the braver tourists board the Spanish Aerocar.

Just south of the falls is a lesser known attraction, the Niagara Parks Greenhouse. It's free. Inside you'll find a grand assortment of identified tropical plants as well as native greenery. Look up! Hummingbirds are hiding in the hanging baskets and flitting from room to room.

My two girls thought the 2000 free-flying butterflies of 50 species at **Niagara Parks Butterfly Conservatory** was magical. Here, the delightful photography opportunities are as limitless as your exploring time. The conditions are warm and humid, so it's a good idea to dress lightly if you intend to visit the Conservatory for any length of time.

Niagara Area Attractions

Odrohekta, Gateway to the Six Nations Community, Brantford. 519-758-5444

Casino Niagara 1-888-946-3255

African Lion Safari 1-800-461-WILD

Butterfly Conservatory
Niagara Falls. The jewel of the Parkway! The exotic collection of tropical plants and free flowing water create a humid rainforest environment for the 2000 butterfly specimens. About 40 species of butterflies are on display at any time. 1-877-642-7275

Journey Behind the Falls
Since 1887, this unique attraction has been thrilling visitors with up close views of Niagara Falls. You will be provided with lightweight raincoats before you descend the 125 feet elevator and then you are left to explore on your own the 150 feet of tunnels burrowing behind the thunderous sheet of water. www.niagarapark.com

Niagara Parks Floral Clock
Fully operational and 40 feet in diameter, this clock features more than 15,000 plants. www.niagarapark.com

Niagara Glen
Hiking trails take you close to the Gorge. www.niagarapark.com

Whirlpool Public Golf Course
18-hole world-renowned course. 905-356-1140

Laura Secord Homestead
In Queenston, you'll enjoy the home of Laura Secord, heroine of the War of 1812. www.niagarapark.com

Mackenzie Heritage Printery
This restored home of William Lyon Mackenzie details the history of letter-presses and printing. Queenston. www.niagarapark.com

Great Gorge Adventure
The boardwalk stretches alongside the spectacular whitewater rapids. www.niagarapark.com

Niagara Parks Botanical Gardens
North of the Falls is a 100-acre property filled with vegetable and herb gardens, floral distractions and an arboretum. www.niagarapark.com

Historic Fort Erie
In this recreated 1812 British Garrison you are invited to step back into time with the help of military displays and the Discovery Room. www.niagarapark.com

Niagara Falls. *The grandeur of the world-famous attraction is just one facet of the scenic Niagara Parkway between Fort Erie and Niagara Falls, a drive that Winston Churchill claimed to be his favorite.*
Courtesy Southern Ontario Tourism Organization

Clifton Hill Attractions

Ripley's Moving Theater. 905-356-2261

Ripley's Believe It or Not. 905-356-2238

Movieland Museum of the Stars. 905-358-3061

Guinness World of Records Museum. 1-800-987-9852

Dinosaur Park Miniature Golf

Dazzleland Family Fun Center.

Cinema 180 Adventure Dome. 905-357-4330

House of Frankenstein. 905-357-9660

Fun House. 905-357-4330

Dracula's Haunted Castle. 905-357-1282

Circus World Gift Shop & Souvenirs. 905-356-5588

Mystery Maze. 905-357-4330

The Haunted House. 905-357-4330

Louis Tussaud's Waxworks. 905-374-6601

Hard Rock Cafe

Kelsey's Planet Hollywood

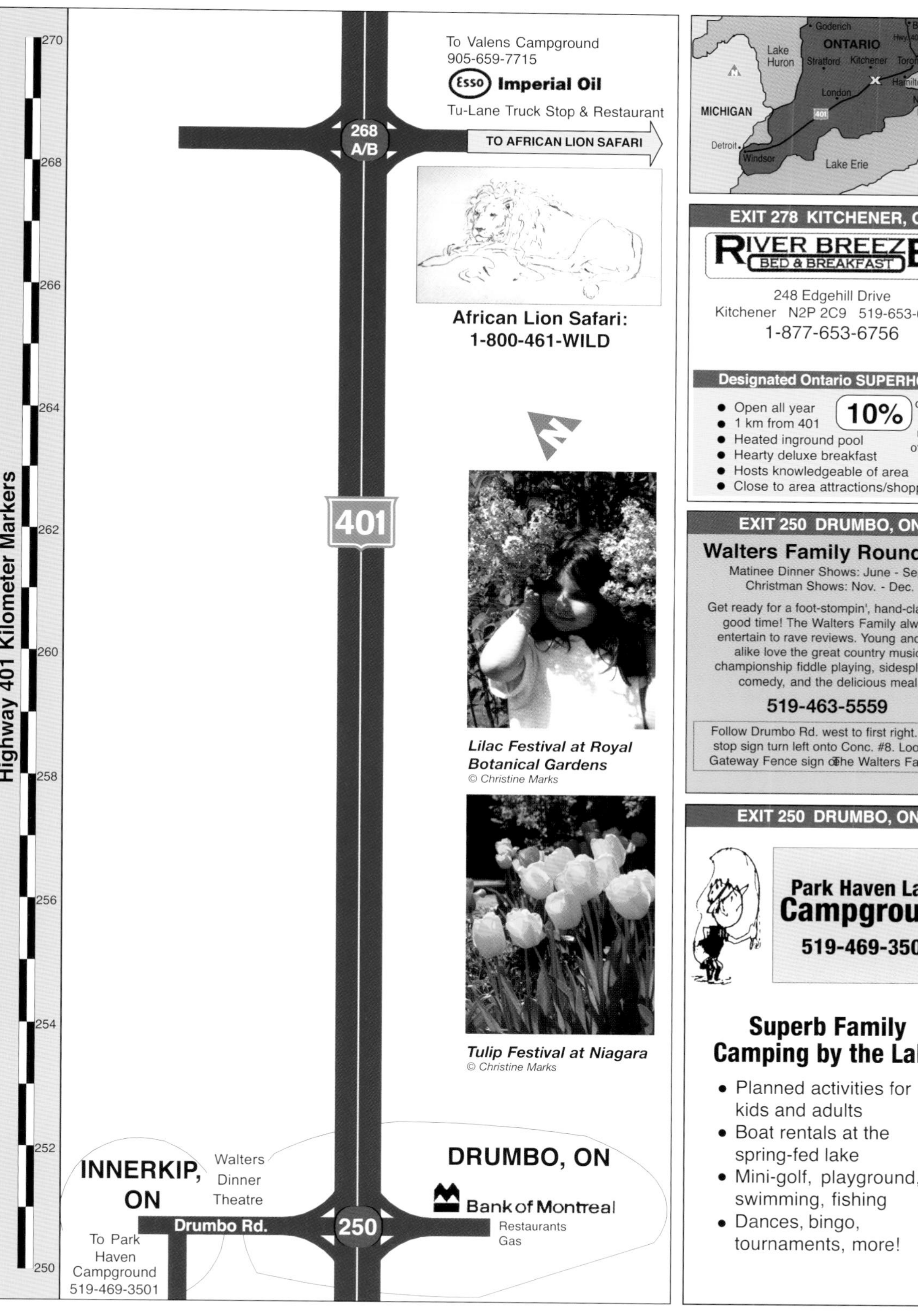

Lilac Festival at Royal Botanical Gardens
© Christine Marks

Tulip Festival at Niagara
© Christine Marks

EXIT 278 KITCHENER, ON

RIVER BREEZE BED & BREAKFAST

248 Edgehill Drive
Kitchener N2P 2C9 519-653-6756
1-877-653-6756

Designated Ontario SUPERHOST

- Open all year
- 1 km from 401
- Heated inground pool
- Hearty deluxe breakfast
- Hosts knowledgeable of area
- Close to area attractions/shopping

10% discount with mention of this ad

EXIT 250 DRUMBO, ON

Walters Family Round-Up

Matinee Dinner Shows: June - Sept.
Christman Shows: Nov. - Dec.

Get ready for a foot-stompin', hand-clappin', good time! The Walters Family always entertain to rave reviews. Young and old alike love the great country music, championship fiddle playing, sidesplitting comedy, and the delicious meal!

519-463-5559

Follow Drumbo Rd. west to first right. Next stop sign turn left onto Conc. #8. Look for Gateway Fence sign of "The Walters Family."

EXIT 250 DRUMBO, ON

Park Haven Lake Campground

519-469-3501

Superb Family Camping by the Lake

- Planned activities for kids and adults
- Boat rentals at the spring-fed lake
- Mini-golf, playground, swimming, fishing
- Dances, bingo, tournaments, more!

Oxford County
ONTARIO

Tourism Oxford
580 Bruin Blvd, Woodstock, ON Canada N4V 1E5
1-866-801-7368 **www.tourismoxford.ca**

Woodstock has a rich architectural heritage. Sites as new as the Woodstock Peace Lighthouse Gallery, or as old as our original public buildings (some with National Heritage Designations). Accommodations range from full-service hotels, motels and charming B & B's. Woodstock was the winner of the National Communities in Bloom title. Enjoy beautiful floral displays in public parks and beautifully landscaped residential sections, and woodland walking and biking trails. It's easy to see that we place a priority on the environment.

If live entertainment and art galleries are your thing, Woodstock has much to offer—award winning community theatre, world class choral music, the Woodstock Art Gallery and the Ross Butler Studio. Also consider live horse racing and slots or book a tee time at one of our 5 local golf courses.

Woodstock's convenient location is home to several international shows—Sally Creek Music Festival, The Dog Show, Dragon Races, Canada's Outdoor Farm Show, The Toy Show, and The Woodstock Wood Show.

If you're a photographer, you're only an F11 away from many breathtaking scenes. Nestled in the northern edge of town is Pittock Conservation Area, one of the longest manmade conservation bodies of water in Ontario. Great fishing, sailing, canoeing and camping too! And when you're out that way, visit Birtch Farms Estate Winery and Orchards. South of town is Jakeman's maple syrup farm, gift shop and walking trails with four seasons' personality. Drop by Tourism Oxford for literature to get your creative juices flowing.

TRIVIA

Oxford County's "Springbank Snow Countess" was the cow that set a world's record for lifetime butterfat production (9,062 pounds).

Local legend "Klondike" Joe Boyle has a 1,000-year-old Romanian cross and transplanted English ivy at his gravesite in the Presbyterian cemetery.

Woodstock Attractions

Woodstock Museum
The nationally designated Old Town Hall was originally built as Woodstock's first public market and concert hall in 1853, later serving as a fire hall, municipal offices, police lock-up, and county museum. Experience the reproduction wallpapered ceilings in the Grand Hall, featuring rotating exhibitions, year round. 519-537-8411 museum@city.woodstock.on.ca

Dairy Capital Cheese Shoppe
Specialty and imported products, cheeses, gourmet foods and gifts. Lunch served in diningroom or outdoor patio. Located in downtown Woodstock next to the Museum lawn. 519-537-7623

Birtch Farms Estate Winery and Orchards
Featuring winery tours and tastings, farm market, children's play area, farm animals, pick-your-own or ready picked apples and pumpkins and fall decorating crops, scarecrow making workshops, corn maze, wagon rides and groups tours by appointment. 519-469-3040 info@birtchfarms.com

Woodstock Raceway Slots
Live racing Saturdays May through September. Slots, bar and lunch room open 7 days a week. 519-537-4804

Woodstock Peace Lighthouse Gallery
This architectural gem and international place of pilgrimage is home to the largest 'icon' collection of its kind in the world. Also on display is a collection of ancient mapping and a lighthouse collection. Open daily. Guided tours by appointment. 519-539-0910 peacelighthouse@execulink.com

Ross Butler Studio
Operated by Ross' son David, this is the home to Canada's greatest agricultural artist's works. Open year round. 519-456-8155

Four seasons of beauty in Oxford County.
Photo by Ruth Anderson, courtesy Tourism Oxford

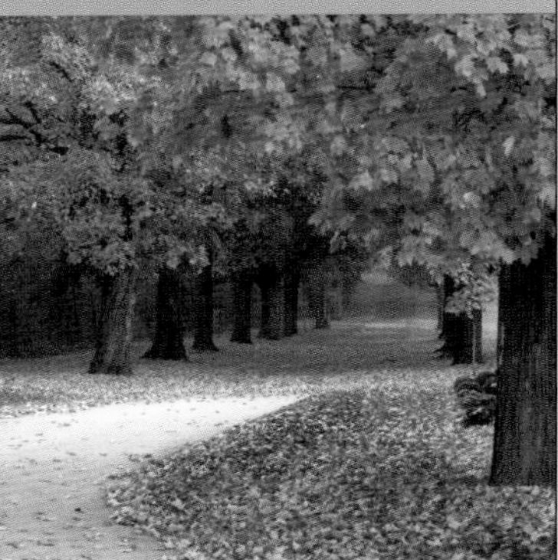

Hewitts Lane *Photo courtesy Tourism Oxford*

Downtown Woodstock boasts many boutiques and unique shops. Allow a few hours to explore. 519-537-5721 info@downtownwoodstock.ca

Pittock Conservation Area
250 treed modern campsite on the water, with store, pool, beach, boating, fishing, sailing. May to October. 519-539-5088

Canada's Outdoor Farm Show
For 10 years this show draws both international exhibitors (over 500) and audience to see the latest high tech demonstrations, on equipment, seed, and livestock. 1-800-563-5441 info@outdoorfarmshow.com

Sally Creek Music Festival Held in early July on the outskirts of Woodstock, this weekend of Bluegrass entertainment, jam sessions and musical fellowship is family oriented. 1-888-288-4423 74490 Oxford Rd. 17, Woodstock, ON. www.sallycreekmusicfestival.ca

Beautiful stately buildings.
Text/photo courtesy Tourism Oxford

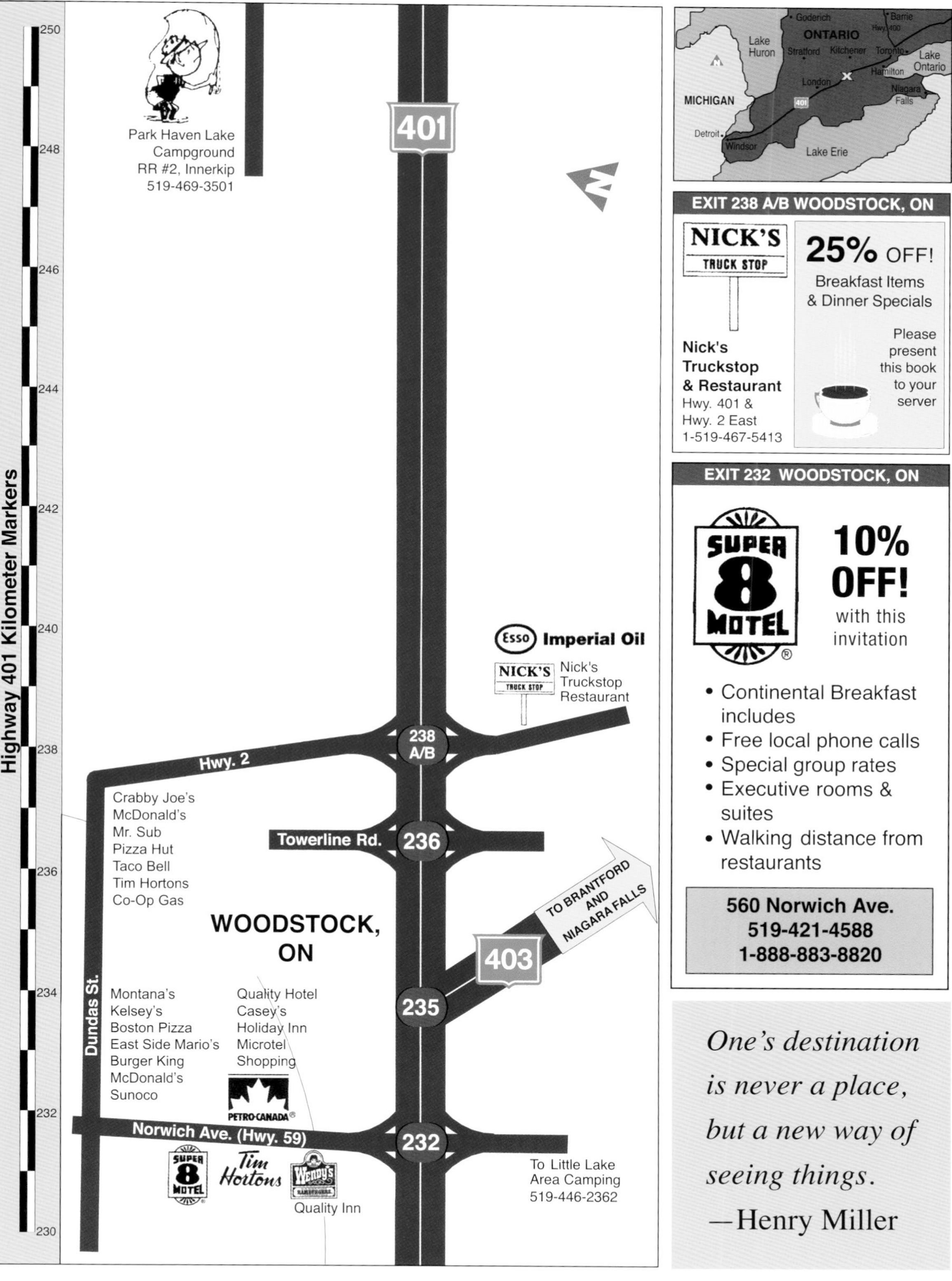

27
ONTARIO
Goderich
Barrie
Hwy. 400
ONTARIO
Lake Huron
Stratford
Kitchener
Toronto
Lake Ontario
Hamilton
London
Niagara Falls
MICHIGAN
401
Detroit
Windsor
Lake Erie
Highway 401 Kilometer Markers
250
248
246
244
242
240
238
236
234
232
230
Park Haven Lake Campground
RR #2, Innerkip
519-469-3501
401
Esso Imperial Oil
NICK'S TRUCK STOP
Nick's Truckstop Restaurant
Hwy. 2
238 A/B
Crabby Joe's
McDonald's
Mr. Sub
Pizza Hut
Taco Bell
Tim Hortons
Co-Op Gas
Towerline Rd.
236
TO BRANTFORD AND NIAGARA FALLS
WOODSTOCK, ON
403
235
Dundas St.
Montana's
Kelsey's
Boston Pizza
East Side Mario's
Burger King
McDonald's
Sunoco
Quality Hotel
Casey's
Holiday Inn
Microtel
Shopping
PETRO-CANADA
Norwich Ave. (Hwy. 59)
232
SUPER 8 MOTEL
Tim Hortons
Wendy's
Quality Inn
To Little Lake Area Camping
519-446-2362
EXIT 238 A/B WOODSTOCK, ON
NICK'S TRUCK STOP
25% OFF!
Breakfast Items & Dinner Specials
Please present this book to your server
Nick's Truckstop & Restaurant
Hwy. 401 & Hwy. 2 East
1-519-467-5413
EXIT 232 WOODSTOCK, ON
SUPER 8 MOTEL
10% OFF!
with this invitation
• Continental Breakfast includes
• Free local phone calls
• Special group rates
• Executive rooms & suites
• Walking distance from restaurants
560 Norwich Ave.
519-421-4588
1-888-883-8820
One's destination is never a place, but a new way of seeing things.
—Henry Miller

Oxford County
ONTARIO

Tourism Oxford
580 Bruin Blvd, Woodstock, ON Canada N4V 1E5
1-866-801-7368 **www.tourismoxford.ca**

CANADA'S DAIRY CAPITAL

TILLSONBURG
Several cultural attractions like Annandale National Historic Site—a Victorian treasure and museum, the Otter Valley Playhouse, the Station Arts Centre—a hub of artistic activity, and Lake Lisgar' popular splash park—a wonderful way to spend a day or two. Coyle's Country Store just north of town on Highway 19 is a shopping treasure, too.

TAVISTOCK
Find out why Quehl's Restaurant in Tavistock has been serving delicious meals since the 1930's. A great stop on your way to Stratford. Smalltown friendliness for shopping, too!

THAMESFORD
Mention Thamesford and Calithumpian Days come to mind. Friendly merchants, a modern library, and a picturesque picnic area along the river are also highlights.

EMBRO
Home of the famous Highland Games and the Thistle Theatre, as well as the popular Workshop supply for woodworking hobbyists. It's also the birthplace of Reverend George Leslie Mackay, who travelled to the other side of the world in the 1800's performing missionary deeds in Taiwan. The golf course just outside of Embro is always a popular spot.

LAKESIDE
Lake Sunova at Lakeside is the home of the annual MultiSport Canada Triathlon and Danceland, where 'big band' style dancing attracts crowds every Saturday night.

INNERKIP AND BRIGHT
This area is home to the Walter's Dinner Theatre where daily dinner theatre packs the restored barn with visitors from Canada and the USA. The premier 28-hole golf course at Innerkip is challenging and in demand.

INGERSOLL
The annual Canterbury Folk Festival is just one of the draws of this community. The Ingersoll Cheese Museum and local sports hall of fame, along with the Ingersoll Creative Arts Centre are conveniently located minutes from the 401 at the Elm Hurst Inn turnoff. And once again, their 18-hole golf course will please even the most discerning golfer. Downtown Ingersoll has a nice choice of restaurants and unique shops, too.

Norwich Area
Slow down for the Amish buggies in the Norwich area.

Embro Highland Games.
Text/photo courtesy Tourism Oxford

Woodstock's rich architectural heritage.
Text/photo courtesy Tourism Oxford

Festivals

Jakeman's MapleFest
April 519-539-1366

Calithumpian Days
Thamesford, May

Woodstock Community Challenge
May

Great Canadian Outdoor Expo
Woodstock 1-800-563-5441

MultiSport Canada Lakeside Triathlon
June 519-453-3255

World Crokinole Championships
Tavistock, June 519-655-2102

Tillsonburg Garden Tour
June 519-842-7843

Embro Highland Games
July 1 519-475-6061

SW Ontario Fiddle & Stepdance Champions
Tavistock, July 519-271-6115

Norwich Nostalgia Days
July 519-863-3328

Canterbury Folk Festival
Ingersoll, July 519-485-6337

Woodstock & Oxford Dog Show
July 519-462-1364 and 519-539-9078

Dragonboat Races
Pittock Lake, August 519-539-1291

Ingersoll Harvest Festival
September 519-485-0120

Cowapalooza and Wing Ding Festival
August 519-539-1291

Birtch's Apple Festival
September 519-469-3040

Canada's Outdoor Farm Show
Woodstock, Sept. 1-800-563-5441

Woodstock Wood Show
September 519-539-7772

Down Home Country Christmas
November 519-842-6151

Ingersoll Festival of Lights
Mid-November to mid-January. Hundreds of displays

Visit our Newest Travel Centre at Ingersoll

- 20,000 square feet of restaurants—Tim Horton's, Wendy's and Mr. Sub (including drive-thru service for Tim Horton's and Wendy's restaurants).
- A brand-name Nicholby's Express gift and convenience store.
- Desktop payphones with computer connections.
- The latest in video entertainment.
- The most up-to-date washroom amenities including separate family change rooms.

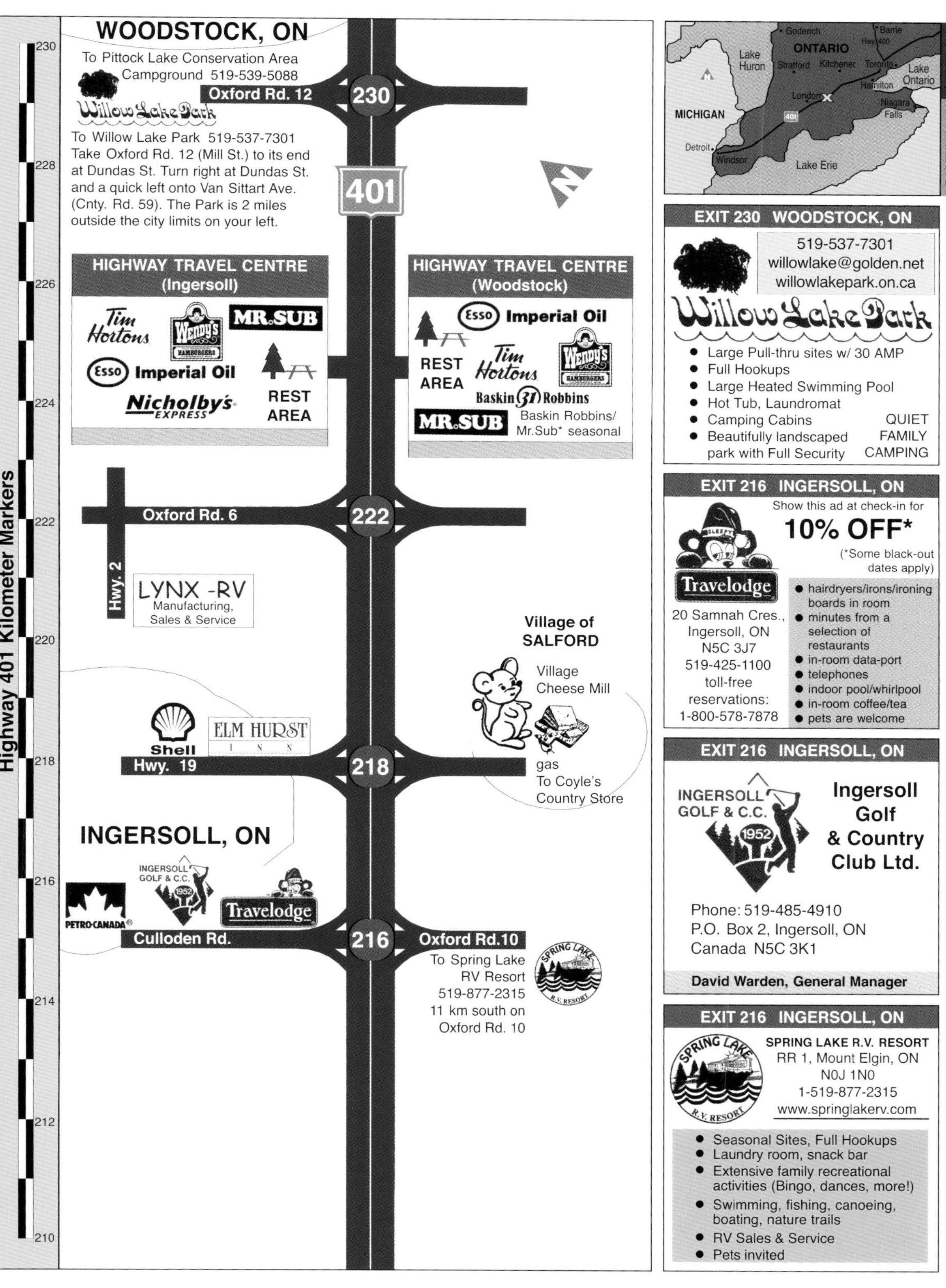

WOODSTOCK, ON
To Pittock Lake Conservation Area
Campground 519-539-5088
Willow Lake Park
To Willow Lake Park 519-537-7301
Take Oxford Rd. 12 (Mill St.) to its end at Dundas St. Turn right at Dundas St. and a quick left onto Van Sittart Ave. (Cnty. Rd. 59). The Park is 2 miles outside the city limits on your left.
Oxford Rd. 12
230
401
N
HIGHWAY TRAVEL CENTRE
(Ingersoll)
Tim Hortons
Wendy's Hamburgers
MR. SUB
Esso Imperial Oil
Nicholby's Express
REST AREA
HIGHWAY TRAVEL CENTRE
(Woodstock)
Esso Imperial Oil
REST AREA
Tim Hortons
Wendy's Hamburgers
Baskin 31 Robbins
MR. SUB
Baskin Robbins/
Mr.Sub* seasonal
Oxford Rd. 6
222
Hwy. 2
LYNX -RV
Manufacturing,
Sales & Service
Village of
SALFORD
Village
Cheese Mill
gas
To Coyle's
Country Store
Shell
ELM HURST INN
Hwy. 19
218
INGERSOLL, ON
INGERSOLL GOLF & C.C. 1952
PETRO-CANADA
Travelodge
Culloden Rd.
216
Oxford Rd.10
To Spring Lake
RV Resort
519-877-2315
11 km south on
Oxford Rd. 10
Spring Lake R.V. Resort
Highway 401 Kilometer Markers
230
228
226
224
222
220
218
216
214
212
210
Goderich
Barrie
Hwy 400
ONTARIO
Lake Huron
Stratford
Kitchener
Toronto
Lake Ontario
Hamilton
London
Niagara Falls
MICHIGAN
401
Detroit
Windsor
Lake Erie
29
ONTARIO
EXIT 230 WOODSTOCK, ON
519-537-7301
willowlake@golden.net
willowlakepark.on.ca
Willow Lake Park
• Large Pull-thru sites w/ 30 AMP
• Full Hookups
• Large Heated Swimming Pool
• Hot Tub, Laundromat
• Camping Cabins
• Beautifully landscaped park with Full Security
QUIET FAMILY CAMPING
EXIT 216 INGERSOLL, ON
Show this ad at check-in for
10% OFF*
(*Some black-out dates apply)
Sleepy
Travelodge
20 Samnah Cres.,
Ingersoll, ON
N5C 3J7
519-425-1100
toll-free
reservations:
1-800-578-7878
• hairdryers/irons/ironing boards in room
• minutes from a selection of restaurants
• in-room data-port
• telephones
• indoor pool/whirlpool
• in-room coffee/tea
• pets are welcome
EXIT 216 INGERSOLL, ON
INGERSOLL GOLF & C.C. 1952
Ingersoll Golf & Country Club Ltd.
Phone: 519-485-4910
P.O. Box 2, Ingersoll, ON
Canada N5C 3K1
David Warden, General Manager
EXIT 216 INGERSOLL, ON
Spring Lake R.V. Resort
SPRING LAKE R.V. RESORT
RR 1, Mount Elgin, ON
N0J 1N0
1-519-877-2315
www.springlakerv.com
• Seasonal Sites, Full Hookups
• Laundry room, snack bar
• Extensive family recreational activities (Bingo, dances, more!)
• Swimming, fishing, canoeing, boating, nature trails
• RV Sales & Service
• Pets invited

London
ONTARIO

Tourism London
267 Dundas Street, London, ON Canada N6A 1H2
519-661-6378 or 1-800-265-2602 **www.londontourism.ca**

THE FOREST CITY

The City of London was so admired when Governor Simcoe visited here in 1783, it became a candidate for the capital city. With a rich mix of traditional and contemporary, London is one of Ontario's showcase cities.

Like the city it was named for, London is anchored on the forks of the **River Thames,** and it too has beautifully preserved Victorian neighborhoods.

London earned the nickname "The Forest City" in recognition of the more than 1,500 acres of sculpted parks, many tree-lined avenues, and carefully groomed riverbanks. The city planner's preoccupation with natural beauty appears to have spilled over to the city's residents, whose fondness for gardening is evident.

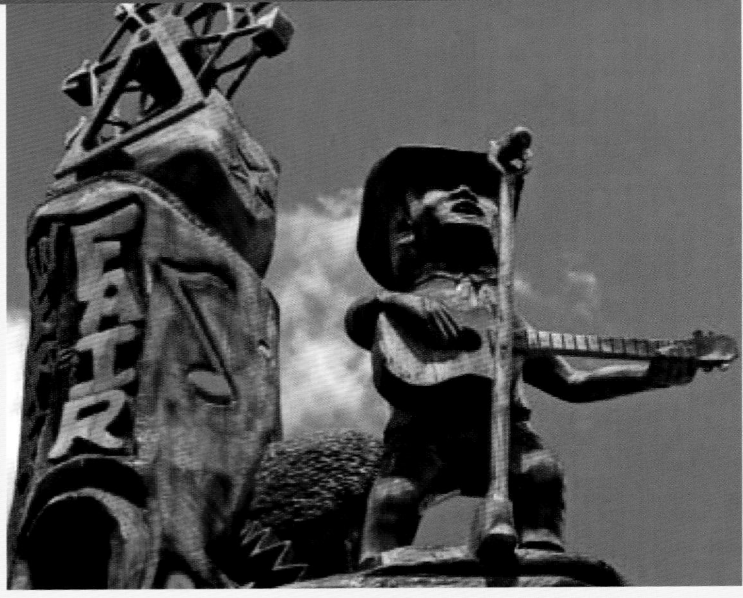

Tree Trunk Tom *Photo courtesy Tourism London*

Lizzy. Tree hugging in London, Ontario.

Outdoor Activities

The Tree Trunk Tour

One of London's newest attractions is surely a first! The Tree Trunk Tour enhances the city's reputation as the Forest City with this public art project. Call ahead for your walking tour map so you won't miss Squirreltopia, Mother Nature, or any of the other ten pieces by Robin Wenzoski or Neil Cox. With the support of STIHL Canada (a major manufacturer of chainsaws headquartered in London) Tourism London, The City of London and the Woodfield Community Association, these two artists spend about four weeks transforming each tree into a sculpture. 1-519-661-6378.

Feeding geese at one of London's Parks *Photo courtesy Tourism London*

Birding on Hawk Cliff

- **Early Spring.** View tundra swans en route to wintering grounds.
- **May.** See the brilliant colors of spring warblers.
- **Sept.** Find the American kestrel, the sharp-shinned hawk, hummingbirds and Monarch butterflies.
- **Fall.** Enjoy migrating broad-winged hawks soaring and sailing on thermals.
- **Late Fall.** Cooper's hawks, goshawks, red-shouldered hawks, red-tailed hawks and rough-legged hawks.

Once in a while you can catch a glimpse of a bald eagle, golden eagle or osprey.

Hawk Cliff, on the Lake Erie Shoreline east of Port Stanley. Call the Hawk Cliff Foundation, 519-782-4152

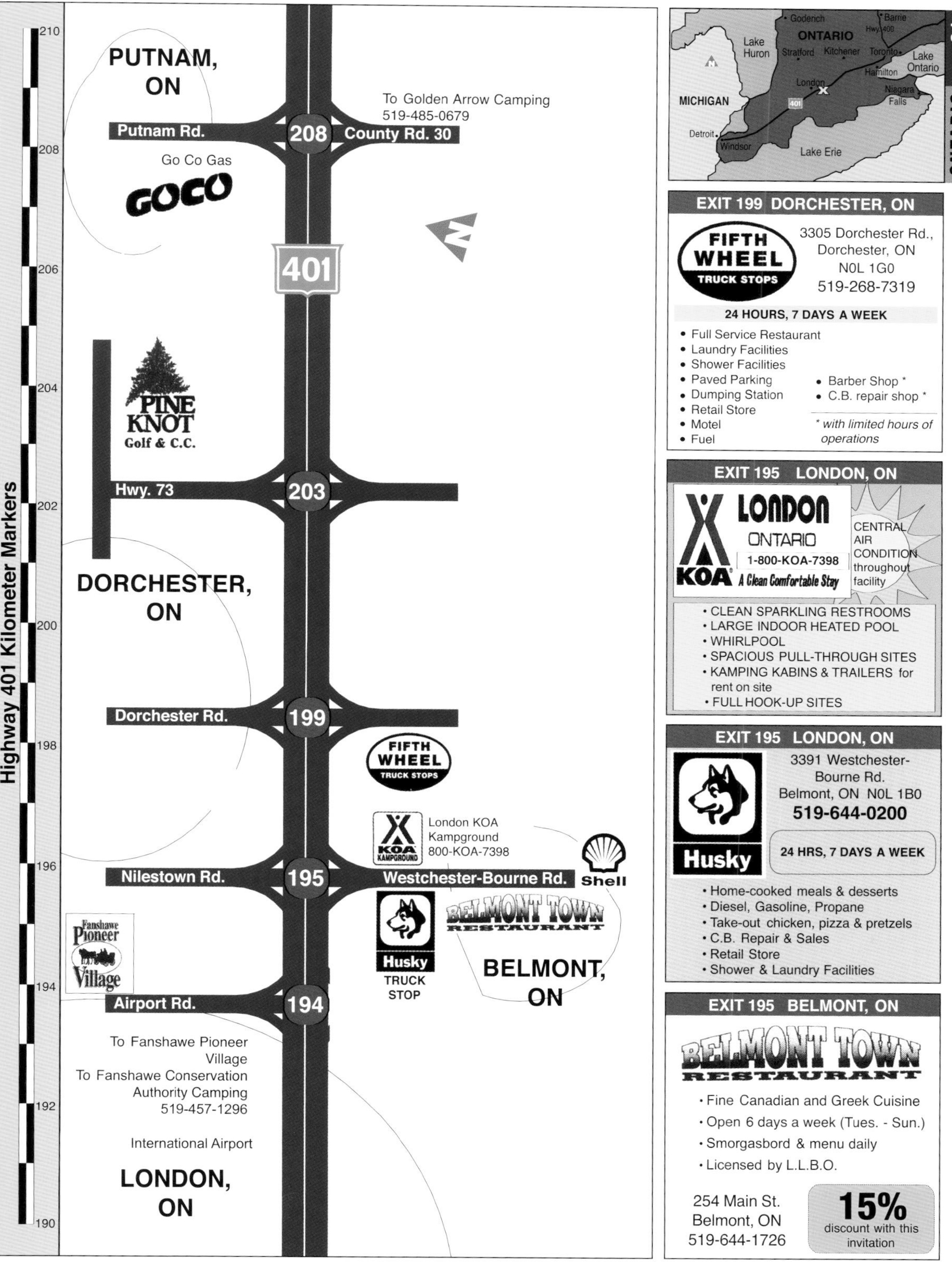

Highway 401 Kilometer Markers
210
208
206
204
202
200
198
196
194
192
190
PUTNAM, ON
Putnam Rd.
208
County Rd. 30
To Golden Arrow Camping
519-485-0679
Go Co Gas
GOCO
401
PINE KNOT
Golf & C.C.
Hwy. 73
203
DORCHESTER, ON
Dorchester Rd.
199
FIFTH WHEEL
TRUCK STOPS
London KOA
Kampground
800-KOA-7398
KOA KAMPGROUND
Shell
Nilestown Rd.
195
Westchester-Bourne Rd.
Husky
TRUCK STOP
BELMONT TOWN
RESTAURANT
BELMONT, ON
Fanshawe Pioneer Village
Airport Rd.
194
To Fanshawe Pioneer Village
To Fanshawe Conservation Authority Camping
519-457-1296
International Airport
LONDON, ON
Goderich
Barrie
Hwy. 400
ONTARIO
Lake Huron
Stratford
Kitchener
Toronto
Lake Ontario
Hamilton
London
Niagara Falls
MICHIGAN
401
Detroit
Windsor
Lake Erie

London
ONTARIO

Tourism London
267 Dundas Street, London, ON Canada N6A 1H2
519-661-6378 or 1-800-265-2602 **www.londontourism.ca**

Outdoor Activities

HORSEBACK RIDING
Cinch Stables Ltd. has been a year-round Western Riding center for over 20 years. Over 100 acres of trails and an indoor arena. Range of quality horses for all ages and skill levels. Lessons by certified teachers. Sleigh rides, ponies, wedding carriages and youth camp. 519-471-7071

DOWNHILL SKIING
London Ski Club (Boler Mountain). Downhill skiing, tubing, nature facilities, and ski school. Annual carnival in Feb. 519-657-8822

LONGWOODS ROAD CONSERVATION AREA Year-round, 9 to sunset. RR #1 Mount Brydges. 519-264-2420

LONDON MUSEUM of ARCHAEOLOGY
Indian village, museum, and gift shop open daily April to early Sept., and Tues. to Sun. from early Sept. to Dec. 1600 Attawandaron Rd. 519-473-1360

Ska-Nah-Doht IROQUOIAN VILLAGE
Open daily, mid-May to Sept., and Mon. to Fri. from Sept. to May. In Longwoods Road Conservation Area. 519-264-2420

TRIVIA

Cable TV was invented in London by Ed Jarmain in 1948 when he wired several of his neighbors' televisions to the large TV antenna at his residence.

London is known as **Test Town Canada** because it has been the number one product testing market location for decades.

The London Free Press was the first newspaper in Canada to microfilm back issues.

London is home to **Labatt Breweries.** John Labatt was kidnapped in 1934 and held for $150,000 ransom. He was held hostage for one day but was released without having to pay the ransom.

Canada's Block Parent program was founded here in 1968 by the local chapter of the National Council of Jewish Women.

In 1924, **Kellogg Canada Inc.** moved its operation from a small plant in Toronto to a large one in London, in part because the corn grown in this area is ideal for its famous Corn Flakes.

Storybook Gardens. *Courtesy Tourism London*

Attractions

Museum London
Tues. to Sun. Almost year-round. 519-661-0333

London Regional Children's Museum
Daily, almost year-round. 519-434-5726

Fanshawe Pioneer Village
May 1 to Dec. 18. 519-457-1296

Storybook Gardens in beautiful **Springbank Park**
May to early Oct. 519-661-5770

Royal Canadian Regiment Museum
Tues. to Sun., almost year-round. 519-660-5102

The Grand Theatre Oct. to May. 519-672-8800 or 1-800-265-1593

McIntosh Gallery, U.W.O. Tues. to Sun., almost year-round. 519-661-3181

Western Fair / Raceway
900 King St. 519-438-7203

Centennial Hall / Orchestra London
550 Wellington St. 519-672-1967

Eldon House Tues. to Sun. Almost year-round.519-661-0333

London Aquatic Centre
1045 Wonderland Rd. N. 519-641-7946

Banting National Historical Site
Tues. to Sat., almost year-round. 519-673-1752

Annual Events

London International Children's Festival Various locations, early June. 519-645-6739

Sunfest
Victoria Park, early-July. 519-432-4310

Home County Folk Festival
Victoria Park, mid-July. 519-432-4310

London Fringe Theatre Festival
Various locations, late July, early August. 519-434-0606

London Rib-Fest
Late July, early August. 519-963-0963

Festa Italiana
Covent Garden Market. mid-August 519-963-0963

Fiesta Del Sol,
Victoria Park, mid-August. 519-672-1522

Western Fair
Western Fairgrounds, early Sept. 519-438-7203 ext 222

Doors Open London
Various locations, mid-Sept. 519-645-2845

Double Decker Bus Tours
Late June until early Sept. 1-800-265-2902 or 519-661-5000

Tourism London
267 Dundas Street, London, ON Canada N6A 1H2
519-661-6378 or 1-800-265-2602 **www.londontourism.ca**

SPECIAL EVENTS

WESTERN FAIRGROUNDS ANNUAL EVENTS
900 King Street, 519-438-7203

- **Feb.** Cycle Show, Woodworking Show, Autorama Car Show, Southwestern Ontario Fishing & Outdoor Show, SW Ontario Golf & Vacation Show
- **March**. Western Fair Farm Show, London International Boat Show, and the London & St. Thomas Recreational Vehicle Show, Family Fun Fest
- **April.** Good Age Show, Craft Show, London Home and Garden Show, Poultry Industry Conference and Exhibition
- **May.** Rummage Sale
- **Sept.** Western Fair, Bridal Show
- **Oct.** International Travel Show, Fall Arts & Crafts Show.
- **Dec.** Christmas Craft Festival

FANSHAWE PIONEER VILLAGE SPECIAL EVENTS
519-457-1296

Special Events:

- **July.** Lantern Light and Mystery Tours
- **Aug.** Harvest Fest
- **Oct.** Fall on the Farm. Haunted Hay Ride.
- **Dec.** Victorian Village Christmas

Tree Trunk Tour
1-800-265-2602 or 519-661-5000
www.londontourism.ca

The Tree Trunk Tour demonstrates London's love of trees and is enhancing its reputation as the Forest City. The carvers have created sculptures that, instead of being confined to an art gallery, are right out on public streets.

ACCOMMODATIONS

AREA BED & BREAKFASTS

For a list of the bed & breakfast locations in the London area, contact: The London & Area Bed & Breakfasts www.londonbb.ca

AREA CAMPING

- Fanshawe Conservation Area 519-451-2800
- Golden Arrow Family Camping 519-485-0679
- London 401 / KOA 519-644-0222 Oriole Park 519-471-2720

DOWNTOWN ACCOMMODATIONS

- Delta London Armouries Hotel 1-800-668-9999 www.deltahotels.com
- Hilton London 1-800-445-8667 www.londonontario.hilton.com
- Holiday Inn Express Hotel & Suites 1-877-553-9992 www.hiexpress.com/londonon

DOWNTOWN continued

- London Executive Suites 1-800-265-5955 www.les-hotel.com
- Residence Inn by Marriott- London 1-877-4R-SUITES www.marriottresidenceinnlondon.com
- Station Park Inn 1-800-561-4574 www.stationparkinn.ca

SOUTH LONDON (near 401)

- Best Western Lamplighter Inn www.lamplighterinn.ca
- Comfort Inn *** 1-800-228-5150 www.choicehotels.ca/cn300
- Days Inn 1-800-DAYS-INN www.daysinnlondon.com
- Four Points Hotel - Sheraton London 1-800-325-3535 www.fourpoints.com/london
- Quality Suites www.choicehotels.ca/cn299
- Ramada Inn 1-800-303-3733 www.ramadainnlondon.com
- Travelodge London South *** 1-800-578-7878 www.travellodgelondon.com

London
ONTARIO

Tourism London
267 Dundas Street, London, ON Canada N6A 1H2
519-661-5000 or 1-800-265-2602 **www.londontourism.ca**

Wellington Road (Exit 186 A/B)
London, Ontario

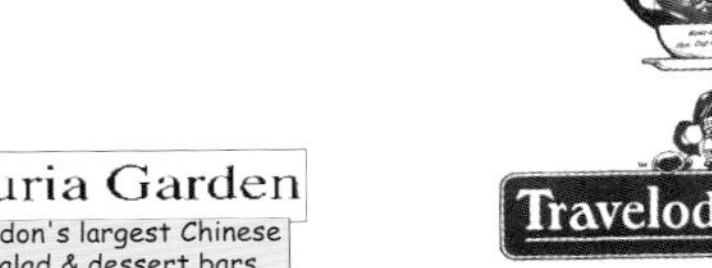

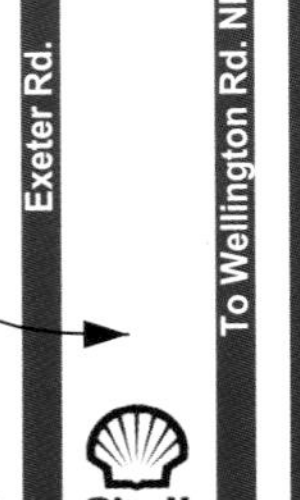

WHITE OAKS MALL
White Oaks Mall
1105 Wellington Rd.
London, ON
519-681-0434

Over 100 stores and services including *Wal-Mart * The Bay * SmithBooks * Wholesale Vision *Agnew * Halmark * Naturalizer * Black's Cameras * Tabi * Tim Hortons * KFC

Bank of Montreal
In White Oaks Mall

Archie's Seafood Restaurants
PETRO-CANADA
Esso Imperial Oil

Canadian Tire
Days Inn
Econolodge
Four Points
Sheraton
Howard Johnson
Sunoco
Wendys

London Home & Design Shopping Center -- over 30 stores including
*Antique Superstore
* Craft Superstore
* Super Pet * Winners
* Outback Steakhouse
* Sante Fe Store

Attractions Accessible from Exit 186 London, Ontario

6867 Wellington Rd.
London, ON
519-686-0027

Our family-owned, complete Garden-Center is open year-round.

* Mums * Roses * Poinsettias
* Perennials * Annuals
* Herbs * Giftware

Greens Galore
specializing in silk plants and trees
3014 Westminster Dr.
519-686-9692

Here's an invitation to come see our large selection of artificial :
*** Vines * Cacti * Ferns * Trees**
*** Palms * Bushes * Wreaths**

~~ Enjoy the beauty that greenery ~~
~~ brings to your home and office ~~
~~ without the work of real plants ~~

Visit Canada's oldest university art gallery!

Present this coupon for a free full-color reproduction of the watercolor painting "London 1847-52" by Sir Richard Airey (a view of early London) or other gift.

Tues-Thurs 12-7. Fri-Sun 12-4. 519-661-3181

COME JOIN IN THE FUN!

With this coupon receive
1 half-price child admission
with the purchase of a regular adult admission

❑ First Sat. in May to Labor Day open daily 10-8
❑ Labor Day to Thanksgiving Day open Mon. to Fri. 10-5, and Sat. & Sun. 10-6

For more info: **519-661-5770**

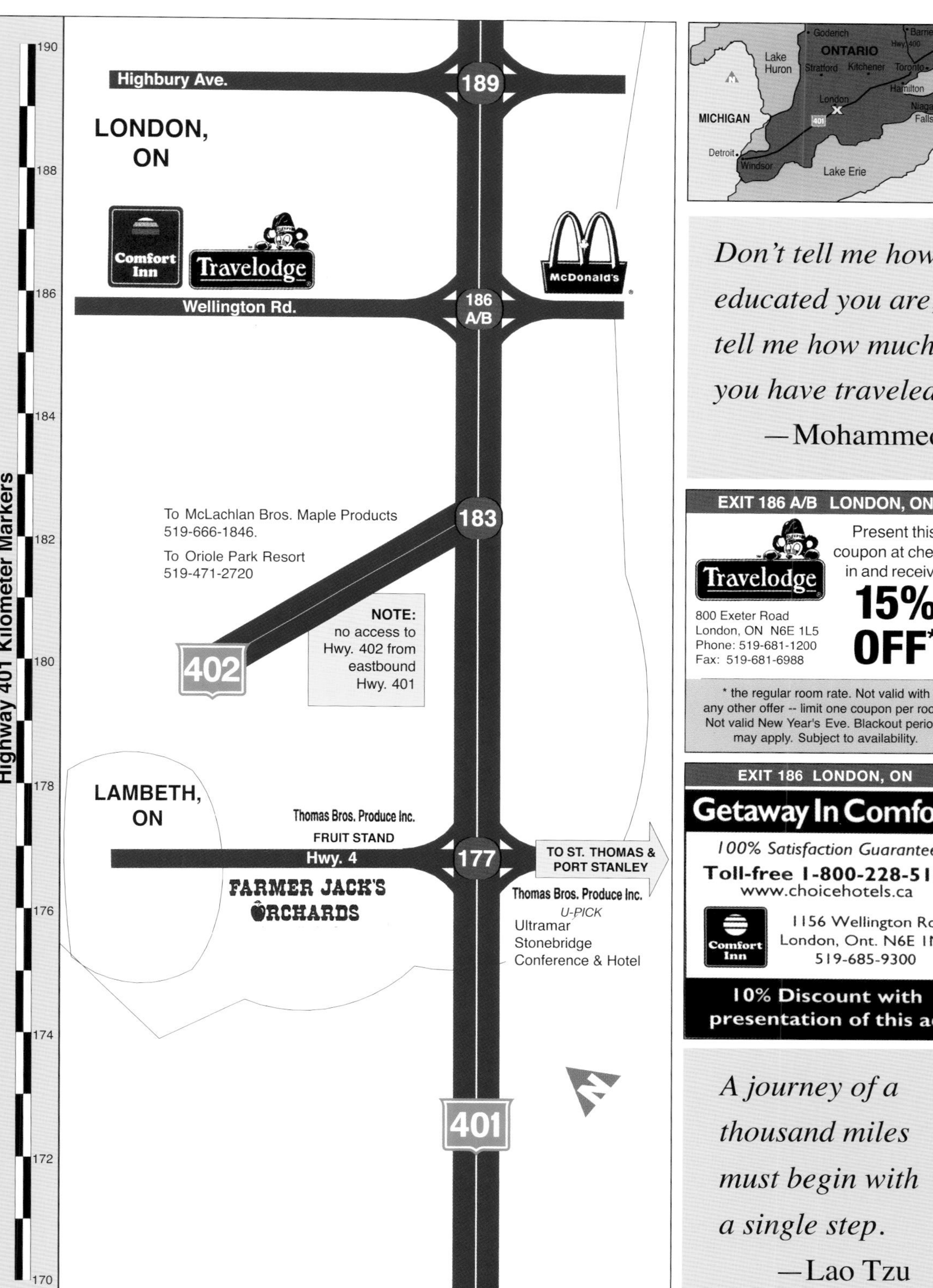

Don't tell me how educated you are, tell me how much you have traveled.

—Mohammed

A journey of a thousand miles must begin with a single step.

—Lao Tzu

St. Thomas
& Elgin County, ONTARIO

St. Thomas & Elgin Tourist Association
450 Sunset Dr., St. Thomas, ON Canada N5R 5V1
519-631-1480 ext. 137 or 1-877-GO ELGIN **www.elgintourist.com**

The tea rooms, antique shops, arts and crafts stores, country inns, summer theater, beaches, and hawks soaring over the cliffs will tempt you to visit **Elgin County.** Located halfway between Detroit and Toronto, it's a place to sit back and enjoy the hospitality.

Elgin offers visitors cruises on a **Mississippi Paddle Wheeler** and rides on the historical **Port Stanley Terminal Rail.**

Blessed with diverse soil types, Elgin offers a large selection of locally grown produce at the farms and fruit stands lining its country lanes. At many locations you are permitted to pick your own produce and take a tour. It's a great way to spend the day with your family!

Lake Erie's north shore is lined with beaches, river valleys, streams and wetlands. Here you can access conservation areas, provincial parks, lake bluffs and beaches and enjoy exceptional sights of many species of birds (especially raptors). The spring and fall migration routes are observed by many local and visiting bird enthusiasts.

Did you know that monarch butterflies also migrate in the fall? The bluffs and beaches of Elgin's north shore offer some of the best places to see these butterflies as they wait for favorable winds to carry them to Point Pelee and then on their way to Mexico.

To get to the north shore of Lake Erie, you can take any of the 401 exits numbered 129-177 or 195-208 and go south. If you go north, you'll find London (Middlesex County) and Woodstock (Oxford County).

TRIVIA

St. Thomas native **Joe Thornton** was Boston's first pick and first overall, in the 1997 NHL Entry Draft.

Thornton participates in the local summer hockey camp and hosts the 'Joe Thornton and Friends' game in the fall, which brings NHL and minor league players together to support the St. Thomas Stars hockey club.

Historic St. Thomas

St. Thomas (2-1/2 hours from Toronto; 2 hours from Detroit) is known for "the Hill" with its life-size statue of Jumbo.

Jumbo, the Barnum and Bailey Circus star, was billed as the largest elephant ever in captivity and he was probably the best-known animal that ever lived. He died in 1885 in a fatal collision with a Grand Trunk Railway locomotive.

Also located on the Hill is the **Old St. Thomas Church** (constructed in 1824); the **Elgin Military Museum,** which traces the County s military past; the **Elgin County Pioneer Museum;** and the **St. Thomas-Elgin Art Gallery.** Many fine old homes also grace the tree-lined streets of St. Thomas.

St. Thomas is proud of its beautiful parks. **Pinafore Park,** probably named after the popular Gilbert and Sullivan operetta, was developed by the St. Thomas Street Railway Company in the hopes that it would encourage passenger traffic. The park's flower displays, train, century-old pavilions and mature trees, playground, bandshell and stadium, as well as the trails by the pool, lake and Wildlife Sanctuary have been the city's pride since 1863.

Waterworks Park started out in the early 1900s as a small area around the PUC's pumping station. Now 25 acres have been set aside for quiet family recreation: 5,000 annuals surround ornamental shrubs, a footpath of narrow bridges spans tiny islands over a waterway of lilies, goldfish and other wildlife. Also enjoy the wading and swimming pool, nature trails and picnic areas throughout the park.

Calendar of Events

- **Canada Day Celebrations**
  Pinafore Park. July 1. 519-631-1680
- **Export "A" Ontario Open Golf Championship**
  St. Thomas Golf & Country Club. Early Aug. 519-631-4800
- **Canoe Races down the Big Otter**
  Mid- Aug. 519-631-8188
- **Elgin Historical Show**
  Mid-Aug. 519-631-6917
- **Ironhorse Festival & Railway Heritage Days** Railway Museum. Late Aug. 519-631-0936
- **Canada's Largest Fire Muster**
  Pinafore Park. Late Aug. 519-633-1563
- **Annual Auto Fest**
  Mid-June. Rare and classic vehicles are show-cased at the Saturday night cruise-in, where a section of Talbot Street is closed down from 5:30 to 9:30. Car show and shine in the park on Sunday. 519-765-3109
- **Festival of Lights**
  Pinafore Park. A delightful collection of seasonal displays by local merchants and associations. Proceeds to charity. Dec. 519-775-2303
- **Air Fair**
  St. Thomas Airport. London Flying Club. Early June. 519-473-9910

Historic St. Thomas

- **Art Gallery**
  St. Thomas-Elgin, Wed. to Sun. 301 Talbot St. 519-631-4040
- **Jumbo the Elephant, Elgin Military Museum** 519-633-7641, **Old St. Thomas Church, and Elgin County Pioneer Museum** 519-631-1680, all on the 'The Hill' on Talbot St.
- **Elgin County Railway Museum**
  In the historic 1913 Michigan Central Shops. 519-644-1874 or 519-631-0936 sjbecrm@elgin.net
- **Mary Rose Sanderson Gallery & Gifts**
  Across from Jumbo monument. 76 Talbot St. www.trilliumstudio.on.ca
- **Pinafore Park**
  Elm St. 519-631-1680
- **Talbot Trail Tea Room**
  Meals served. See the Ryckman Bros. Miniature Circus. 519-633-8040
- **Quai du Vin Winery**
  is more than a wine making business. Enjoy annual and weekend events like grape stomping. 45811 Fruit Ridge Lane, St. Thomas. 519-775-2216

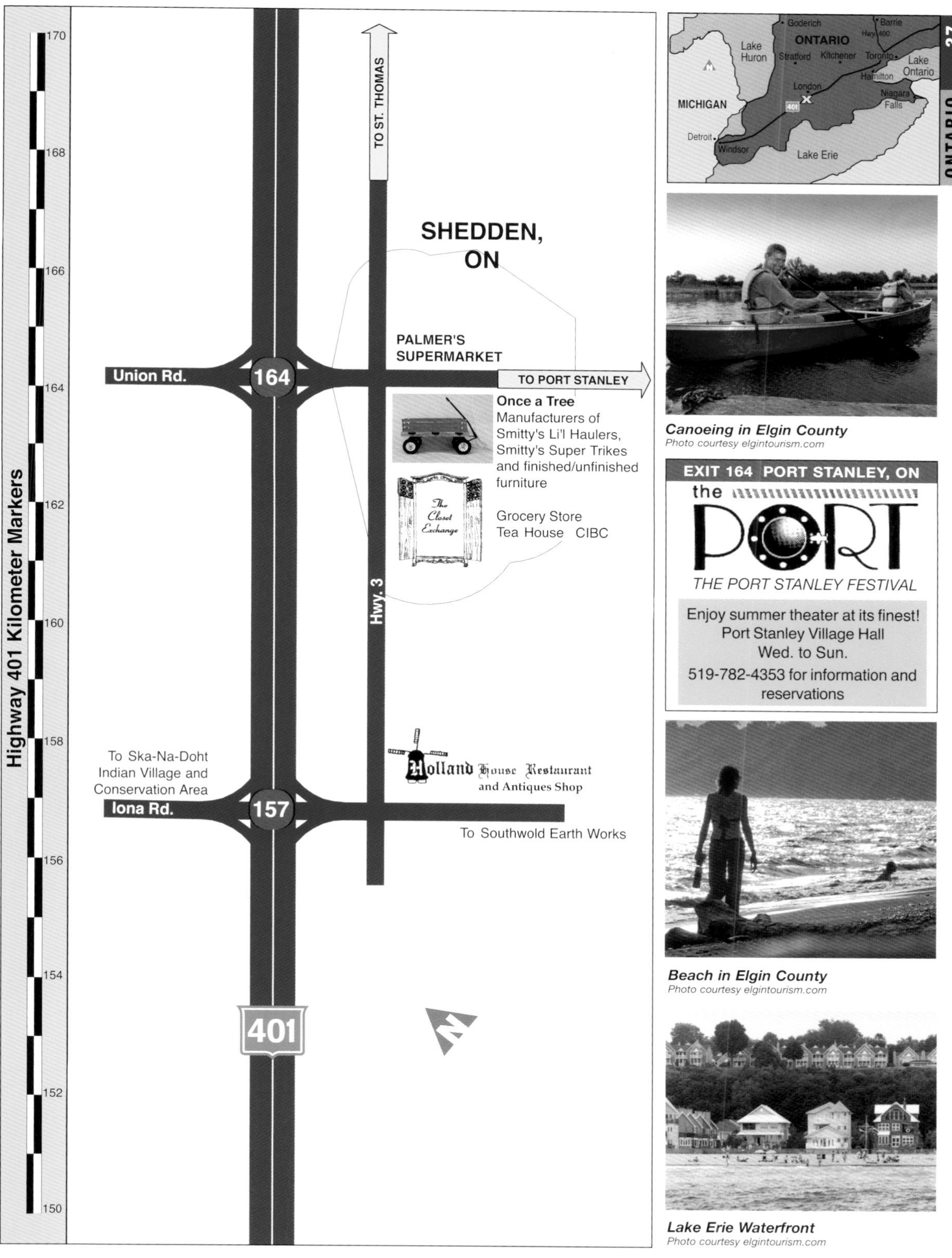

Canoeing in Elgin County
Photo courtesy elgintourism.com

Beach in Elgin County
Photo courtesy elgintourism.com

Lake Erie Waterfront
Photo courtesy elgintourism.com

Port Stanley
ONTARIO

St. Thomas & Elgin Tourist Association
450 Sunset Dr., St. Thomas, ON Canada N5R 5V1
519-631-1480 ext. 137 or 1-877-GO ELGIN **www.elgintourist.com**

This quaint fishing village has one of the few working harbors on the Lake Erie north shore and the historical King **George VI lift bridge** in the city center is a must-see. A fine stretch of clean, sandy beach lures day-trippers to Port Stanley and the unique boutiques, resident artists' galleries, shops, summer theater, scenic train ride, and relaxing paddle wheeler cruise brings them back.

Living 'in Port' has taught me a new appreciation for the seasons. We spent the whole year on the beach! The kids clambered over the ice that caked the winter shore, flew kites over the waves in spring and fall, and spent the entire summer in bathing suits making sand castles and throwing sticks for our new retriever puppy, "Suzie."

Shedden ONTARIO

If you love rhubarb, don't miss Shedden's **Rosy Rhubarb Days** in June. Enjoy the rhubarb baking contests, fairground exhibits, antique car show, border collie dog show, wagon rides, tractor displays and much more. 519-746-2600 www.rosyrhubarbfestival.com

While in Shedden chuckle at the Tearoom menu on the chalkboard in the restored old school, pick up a **"Smitty's Li'l Hauler"** wagon or other wooden marvel at **Once-A-Tree,** find an elusive Beanie Baby at **The Closet Exchange,** and enjoy healthy and delicious meals at **The Down Home Deli and Bakery.** Shedden Agricultural Fair in Aug. 519-764-2939. Great little shops!

Iona ONTARIO

The **Southwold Earthworks,** near Iona, offers self-directed tours of the Neutral Indian Village, dated 1500 A.D. Take 401 exit 157 to Hwy. 3.

Elgin Hiking Trail

From Port Stanley to the border of Elgin and Middlesex counties there is a 38-kilometer walking-only trail that is designated with white markers. It winds through valleys and ravines and along the wooded hillsides adjacent to Dodds Creek and Kettle Creek. The **Elgin Trail** has recently been connected to other trails, including the Thames Trail and the Bruce Trail. For a free brochure/map, call 519-633-3064.

Attractions

King George VI Lift Bridge

Port Stanley Festival Theatre
519-782-4353.

Port Stanley Train Ride 519-782-3730

Paul Schleusner Studio 519-782-4544
Mount Zion Pottery 519-782-4179
Murial Brown Studio 519-782-4493
P.B. Johnson Art Gallery & Studio
519-782-4577

Mackie's since 1911, 519-782-4390

Shaw's Ice Cream Since 1937

Harbour House Market
Antiques, Gifts & Collectable. 519-782-5108

Moore Water Gardens
Splendid! 1-800-728-6324

Elgin County Industry, Past and Present

In 1803, Colonel Talbot arrived on the north shores of Lake Erie to develop a settlement. After the construction of Hwy. 3 (Talbot Rd.) in 1809 the county began to prosper from agriculture and lumber. The fishing industry developed in the 1850s and the area became an important railway center.

St. Thomas, the largest city in the county, is the **"Railway Capital of Canada."** ON TRACK is a local group that encourages tourism by promoting the area's railway heritage.

NORTH AMERICAN RAILWAY HALL OF FAME has a CN5700 steam locomotive and baggage car, Wabash 51 diesel, L&PS electric L1 & NYC/Pulman sleeper car. 519-633-2535

STEAM ENGINE NO. 9 is being restored by the Southern Ontario Locomotion Restoration Society for operation as a tourist attraction in St. Thomas. For now it is on display for special occasions and almost year-round for public viewing at the Michigan Central Railway Shop in St. Thomas.

PORT STANLEY TERMINAL RAIL
Diesel engines pull both open and closed coaches through scenic Kettle Creek Valley. 519-782-3730
Of the several murals which beautify Elgin County, one is the largest train mural in Canada. You can watch the artists as they continue to paint new train murals on the downtown walls during the summertime.

IRON HORSE FESTIVAL. A community-based celebration of St. Thomas railway heritage at the end of Aug. Special events include a Rib Fest, Busker Contest, Car Show and Cruise Night, Midway, 1812 Battle Re-enactment, Mini Circus, Railway Heritage Days, and Craft Show. 519-633-2535 www.ironfestival.com

RAILWAY HERITAGE DAYS. Near the end of Aug. enjoy the railway vendors, entertainment, train rides and tours, food booths and rolling stock displays at the Michigan Central Railway Shops. 519-631-0936

PORT STANLEY. *Courtesy Ontario Ministry of Economic Development, Trade & Tourism, c. 1996*

Special Events

Port Stanley Summer Theatre
Wed. to Sat. 519-782-4353

St. Thomas Dragway April to October. Canada's Largest Drag Race held on Canada Day weekend. 519-775-2263 race@stthomasdragway.com

C.A.L.I.P.S.O. Days 519-782-3383

Hawk Cliff Migration
End of County Rd. 22. Early Sept., 519-782-4152

Great Chili Cook-Off
March. Mackie's on the Beach. 519-782-3360

Ontario Family Fishing Weekend early July. No fishing license necessary. Trout hatchery. 519-773-9037

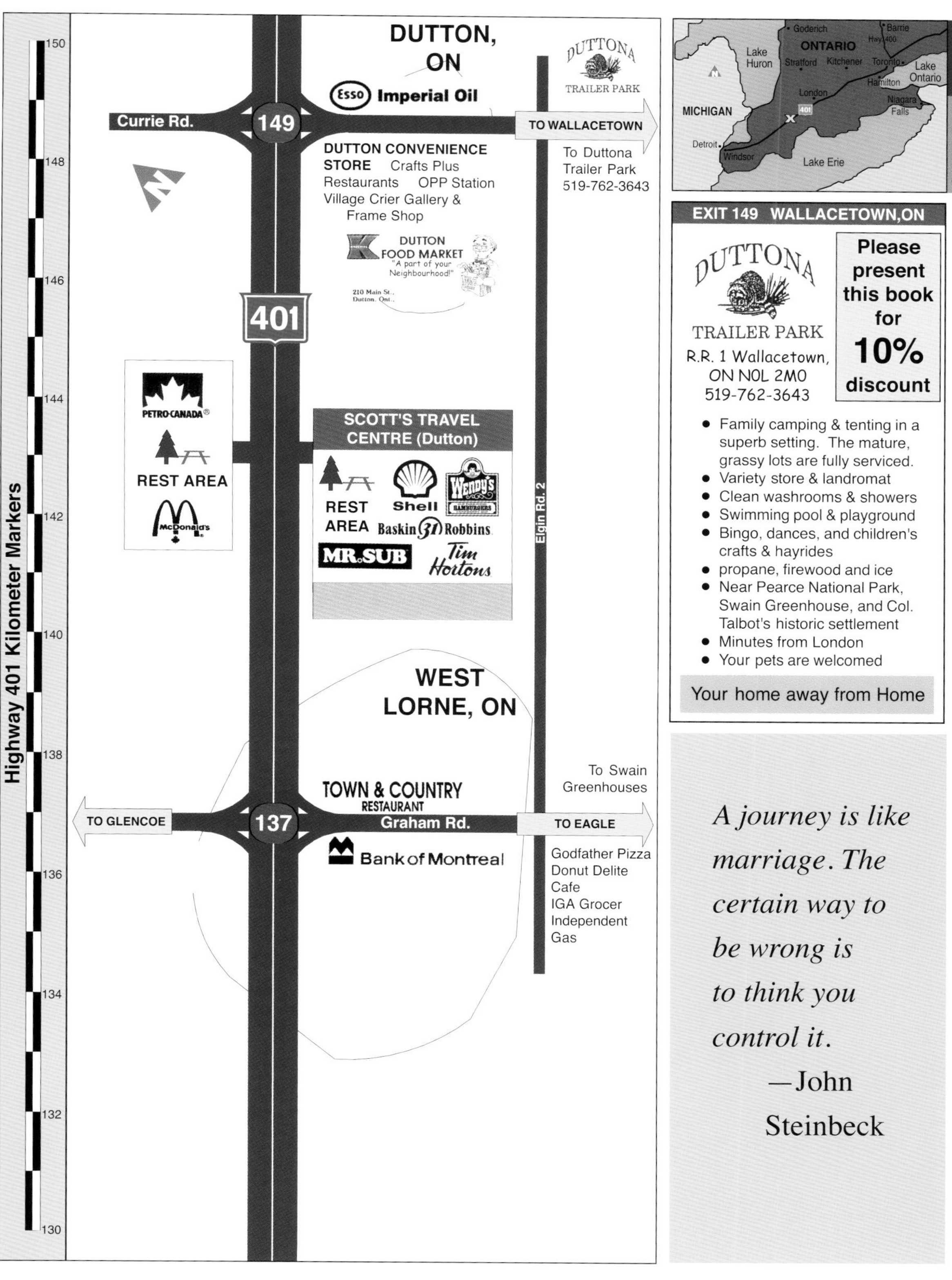
39
ONTARIO
Highway 401 Kilometer Markers
150
148
146
144
142
140
138
136
134
132
130
DUTTON, ON
Esso Imperial Oil
Currie Rd.
149
TO WALLACETOWN
DUTTONA TRAILER PARK
To Duttona Trailer Park 519-762-3643
DUTTON CONVENIENCE STORE Crafts Plus Restaurants OPP Station Village Crier Gallery & Frame Shop
DUTTON FOOD MARKET "A part of your Neighbourhood!"
210 Main St., Dutton, Ont.
401
PETRO-CANADA
REST AREA
McDonald's
SCOTT'S TRAVEL CENTRE (Dutton)
REST AREA
Shell
Wendy's HAMBURGERS
Baskin 31 Robbins
MR.SUB
Tim Hortons
Elgin Rd. 2
WEST LORNE, ON
To Swain Greenhouses
TOWN & COUNTRY RESTAURANT
TO GLENCOE
137
Graham Rd.
TO EAGLE
Bank of Montreal
Godfather Pizza
Donut Delite
Cafe
IGA Grocer
Independent
Gas
Goderich
Barrie
Hwy 400
ONTARIO
Lake Huron
Stratford
Kitchener
Toronto
Lake Ontario
Hamilton
London
Niagara Falls
MICHIGAN
401
Detroit
Windsor
Lake Erie
EXIT 149 WALLACETOWN,ON
DUTTONA TRAILER PARK
R.R. 1 Wallacetown, ON N0L 2M0
519-762-3643
Please present this book for 10% discount
• Family camping & tenting in a superb setting. The mature, grassy lots are fully serviced.
• Variety store & landromat
• Clean washrooms & showers
• Swimming pool & playground
• Bingo, dances, and children's crafts & hayrides
• propane, firewood and ice
• Near Pearce National Park, Swain Greenhouse, and Col. Talbot's historic settlement
• Minutes from London
• Your pets are welcomed
Your home away from Home
A journey is like marriage. The certain way to be wrong is to think you control it.
—John Steinbeck

St. Thomas & Elgin County, ONTARIO

St. Thomas & Elgin Tourist Association
450 Sunset Dr., St. Thomas, ON Canada N5R 5V1
519-631-1480 ext. 137 or 1-877-GO ELGIN **www.elgintourist.com**

DUTTON dates to 1891 and is still a mainstay of service for the agricultural community. Its Scottish heritage is celebrated on St. Andrew's Day and on Robbie Burns Night.

The historic sites include St. Peter's Church, one of the oldest churches in Southwestern Ontario. St. Peter's has been in continuous use since 1827 and the Cemetery is the resting place of Colonel Thomas Talbot.

Dutton Dunwich Street Dance & Sportfest. Mid-July. 519-762-3209 recreation@duttondunwich.on.ca

VILLAGE CRIER GALLERY & FRAME SHOP. Every Saturday from Easter to Thanksgiving, you can hear the village crier, dressed in full Scottish attire, cry forth his message outside the shop. The Ontario Guild of Town Criers' museum is Elgin's smallest, with only 24 square feet! The gallery displays for sale the works Dutton artist Jenny Phillips.

Port Stanley Marina. *Courtesy Ontario Ministry of Economic Development, Trade and Tourism, c. 1996*

Rodney ONTARIO

The Rodney Jail
135 Queen Str., Rodney, ON
519-785-0937
Obviously, there wasn't a lot of crime in Rodney in the late 1800s because the jail they chose to build is the smallest one in North America. Measuring 15' by 18', the building still boasts its original cell doors of riveted flat steel bars and offers two cells. Built in 1890, the jail now houses a book exchange. You can still see the inmates' carvings on the side of the cell walls.

Look forward to the antiques, crafts, shopping, and bed & breakfasts.

Visit farmgate markets for the very best in organic fruits and vegetables or pick-your-own produce. Blueberries are found at Blueberry Hill Farm at the intersection of Hwy. 3 and Hwy. 76. Apples abound at the Empire Valley Farm Market on Hwy. 3, west of Wallacetown. Tropicals fill the 4.5 acres of greenhouses at Swain Greenhouses near Eagle (exit 137). At Swain's you are invited to tour the garden and greenhouses, browse in the store and find refreshment in the cafeteria.

Rodney Agricultural Fair, mid-Sept. Horse-racing, tractor pull, cattle show and demolition derby. 519-762-2021

Gone Fishing in Elgin County

Known for yellow perch and walleye, Elgin County has many kilometers of lakeshore where you can tackle lake trout, salmon, whitefish, catfish, or small and largemouth bass.

FISHING CHARTERS

- **Lee-Jay Fishing Charters**
  Rodney, 519-785-2334
- **Boblane Marina**
  Port Bruce, 519-765-4312
- **North Erie Marina**
  Aylmer, 519-765-2010
- **Port Glasgow Yacht Club**
  Rodney, 519-785-0189
- **Portside Marina**
  Port Stanley, 519-782-3623
- **Stan's Marina**
  Port Stanley, 519-782-3553

Annual Events

Tagged Trout Derby
Catch any tagged trout in Springwater Conservation Area Reservoir near Aylmer, and win cash! 2 weeks in late April. 519-773-9037

Opening Day, Trout Season
Springwater Conservation Area, end of April. Reservoir stocked with rainbow trout. Wheelchair accessible. Children Free. 519-773-9037

Ontario Family Fishing Derby.
Enjoy fishing with your family at the Springwater reservoir during this fun weekend. Any size and type of fish can win a prize. Early June. 519-773-9037 No license necessary.

Fishing Derby Weekend
License free fishing at Lake Whittaker. Mid-July. 519-631-1270

Great Walleye Hunt & Rainbow Roundup
Port Stanley, Port Bruce, Port Burwell and Port Glasgow participate in this derby held the first 3 weeks in July. 519-782-4557

Port Glasgow Fish Fry & Waterfront Festival
Early Aug. 519-785-0560

Largemouth Bass Tournament
Springwater Conservation Area, home of Canada's live release record for largemouth bass! Win great prizes for largest bass. Competition for total length over 2 days with a 5-fish limit. Catch and release only. 519-773-9037

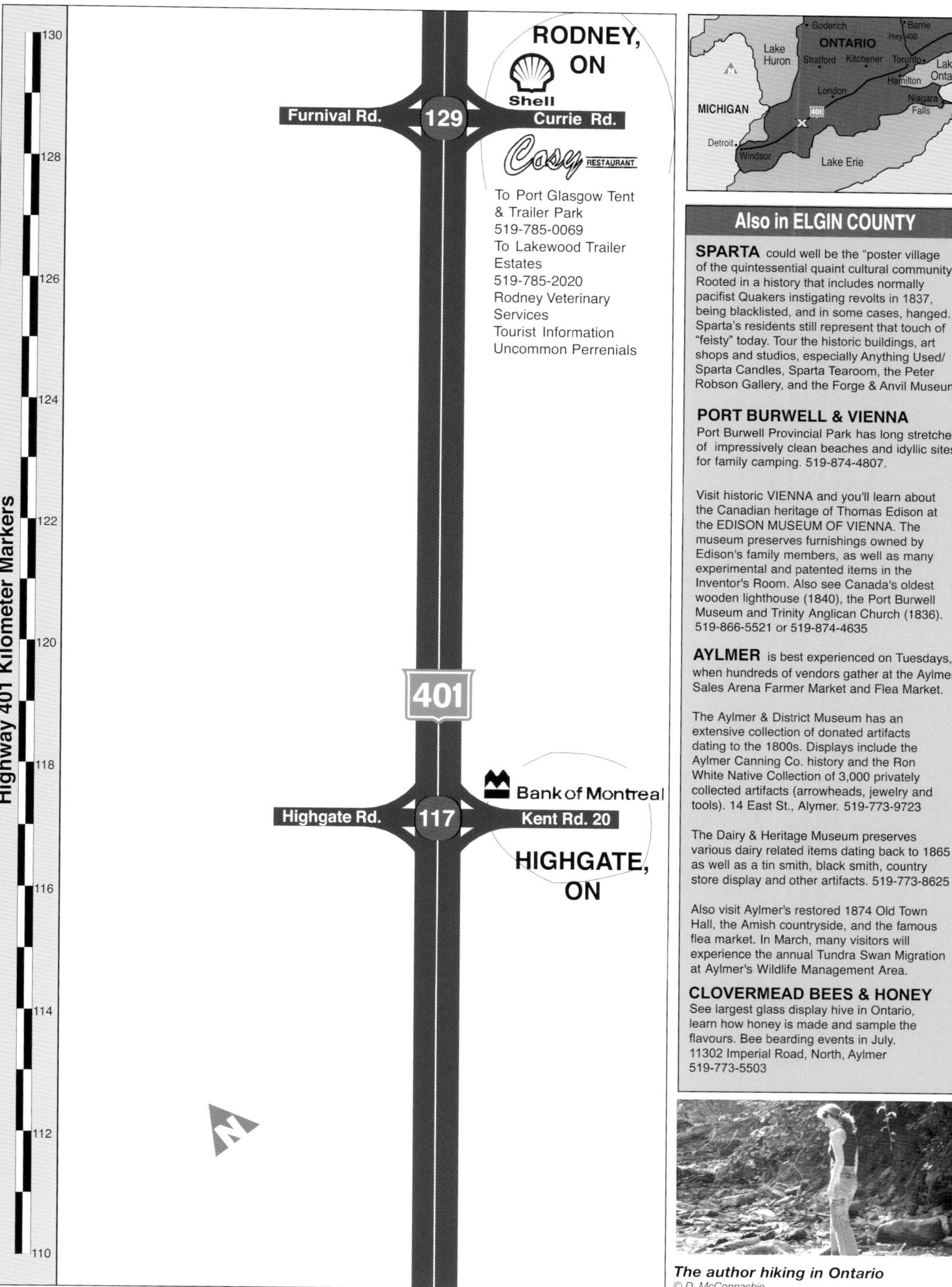

Also in ELGIN COUNTY

SPARTA could well be the "poster village of the quintessential quaint cultural community. Rooted in a history that includes normally pacifist Quakers instigating revolts in 1837, being blacklisted, and in some cases, hanged. Sparta's residents still represent that touch of "feisty" today. Tour the historic buildings, art shops and studios, especially Anything Used/ Sparta Candles, Sparta Tearoom, the Peter Robson Gallery, and the Forge & Anvil Museum.

PORT BURWELL & VIENNA
Port Burwell Provincial Park has long stretches of impressively clean beaches and idyllic sites for family camping. 519-874-4807.

Visit historic VIENNA and you'll learn about the Canadian heritage of Thomas Edison at the EDISON MUSEUM OF VIENNA. The museum preserves furnishings owned by Edison's family members, as well as many experimental and patented items in the Inventor's Room. Also see Canada's oldest wooden lighthouse (1840), the Port Burwell Museum and Trinity Anglican Church (1836). 519-866-5521 or 519-874-4635

AYLMER is best experienced on Tuesdays, when hundreds of vendors gather at the Aylmer Sales Arena Farmer Market and Flea Market.

The Aylmer & District Museum has an extensive collection of donated artifacts dating to the 1800s. Displays include the Aylmer Canning Co. history and the Ron White Native Collection of 3,000 privately collected artifacts (arrowheads, jewelry and tools). 14 East St., Alymer. 519-773-9723

The Dairy & Heritage Museum preserves various dairy related items dating back to 1865 as well as a tin smith, black smith, country store display and other artifacts. 519-773-8625

Also visit Aylmer's restored 1874 Old Town Hall, the Amish countryside, and the famous flea market. In March, many visitors will experience the annual Tundra Swan Migration at Aylmer's Wildlife Management Area.

CLOVERMEAD BEES & HONEY
See largest glass display hive in Ontario, learn how honey is made and sample the flavours. Bee bearding events in July.
11302 Imperial Road, North, Aylmer
519-773-5503

The author hiking in Ontario

© D. McConnachie

Chatham-Kent
ONTARIO

Municipality of Chatham-Kent — Department of Economic Development
435 Grand Ave. W., P.O. Box 944, Chatham, ON Canada N7L 3Z4
519-351-7700 or 1-800-561-6125 **www.cktourism.com**

CHATHAM-KENT has very clean beaches, first-rate hotels, great campgrounds and one-of-a-kind special events. There is also affordable city life.

Chatham-Kent offers panoramic driving tours. A popular one follows **Lake Erie's North Shore** and another follows the **St. Clair River.** Both have marked heritage sites that tell the stories of early settlers, the War of 1812, the Underground Railroad, and the bravery of the area's soldiers during the two world wars.

Former Hwys. 2, 40, and 21 provide quick access to the area's fruitstands and pick-your-own places.

Bordered by Lake St. Clair and Lake Erie, and with the Thames and the Sydenham Rivers flowing fast through the municipality, Chatham-Kent is popular with water-sports enthusiasts.

Explore Shipwrecks. Deep below the lake surface near Chatham-Kent divers can explore sunken ships lost in the 1800s. Many of the ships are virtually intact.

RONDEAU PROVINCIAL PARK is located on Chatham-Kent Road 15 (former Hwy. 51) near Morpeth on Lake Erie. The 11 kilometers of sandy beach, long nature trails, picnicking, fishing, sailing, interpretive programs, camping, canoeing, birding, swimming, the occasional bald eagle, the abundant white-tailed deer, and the southern hardwood forest, tulip trees and sassafras attract people to this beautiful park. 519-674-1770

TECUMSEH

THAMESVILLE is forever etched in Canadian history as the place where the famous Shawnee war chief **Tecumseh** disappeared in the War of 1812.

Take exit 109 and follow the attraction signs to the **Tecumseh Memorial.** Thamesville is also the birthplace of Canadian writer Robertson Davies and home to **Parks Blueberries.**

Ridgetown ONTARIO

Known as the "friendliest town in Ontario," Ridgetown charms visitors with Victorian architecture and tree-lined boulevards. You can tour the buffalo farm (519-674-0320) and the Ridgetown College of Agriculture by appointment (519-674-1588).

401 Wheels Inn
Courtesy Chatham-Kent Tourism

Attractions

THE RIDGE HOUSE MUSEUM
53 Erie St. This restored 1875 grand Victorian house has a permanent collection of authentic antique and locally made furniture. Revolving displays are changed by the curator each month. Perhaps, the most popular collection is the dazzling Christmas decoration show. Open Apr. 1 to Dec. 31. 519-674-2223

For Ridgetown events and attractions please call 519-674-5583

Events

- **Ridge House Museum,** 519-674-2223
- **Summerfest Agricultural College** Open House, mid-July, 519-674-1588
- **Ridgefest,** sidewalk sales, street dance, beer garden, buffalo ranch tours, mid-July, 519-674-2223
- **Ridgetown Antique Classic Car Show,** mid-July, 519-674-2223 (part of Ridgefest)
- **Highgate Agricultural Fair** September. 519-695-5915

Bothwell ONTARIO

During the American Civil War, Bothwell became a boomtown when its oil reserves were discovered. Many of the oil wells are still standing.

Attractions

The Fairfield Museum
The museum is situated on the old site of the town of Fairfield which was destroyed by invading American forces during the Battle of the Thames in 1813. Artifacts from both of the town's inhabiting cultures, the Delaware and the missionaries, are displayed. May to Oct., from Tues. to Sun. 519-692-4397

Moravian on the Thames
Moravian, the first Christian Indian town to be established in Canada (1792) is now a reserve where you can visit the New Fairfield Church, erected in 1848. 519-692-3936

Events

- **Bothwell Legion Archery** Fri. nights. 519-695-5874
- **Bothwell Figure Skating Carnival** March. 519-695-3004
- **Canada Day Pig Roast in the Park** 519-695-3700
- **Summer Festival** Dance, Fireman's breakfast, town-wide Yard Sale, Craft Show, Carnival, Kid's Fair and Parade first 2 weeks in Aug. 519-695-2942
- **Old Autos Vintage Car Show** Mid-Aug. Ontario's largest car show of its kind. 1-800-461-3457
- **Neighborhood Antique Tractor** Gathering, mid-Aug. 519-692-5375
- **Moraviantown Pow Wow** Mid-Aug. 519-692-3936
- **Scarecrow Contest** $600 prize. Oct. 519-692-5373

For more information about events and attractions in Bothwell please call 519-695-2844

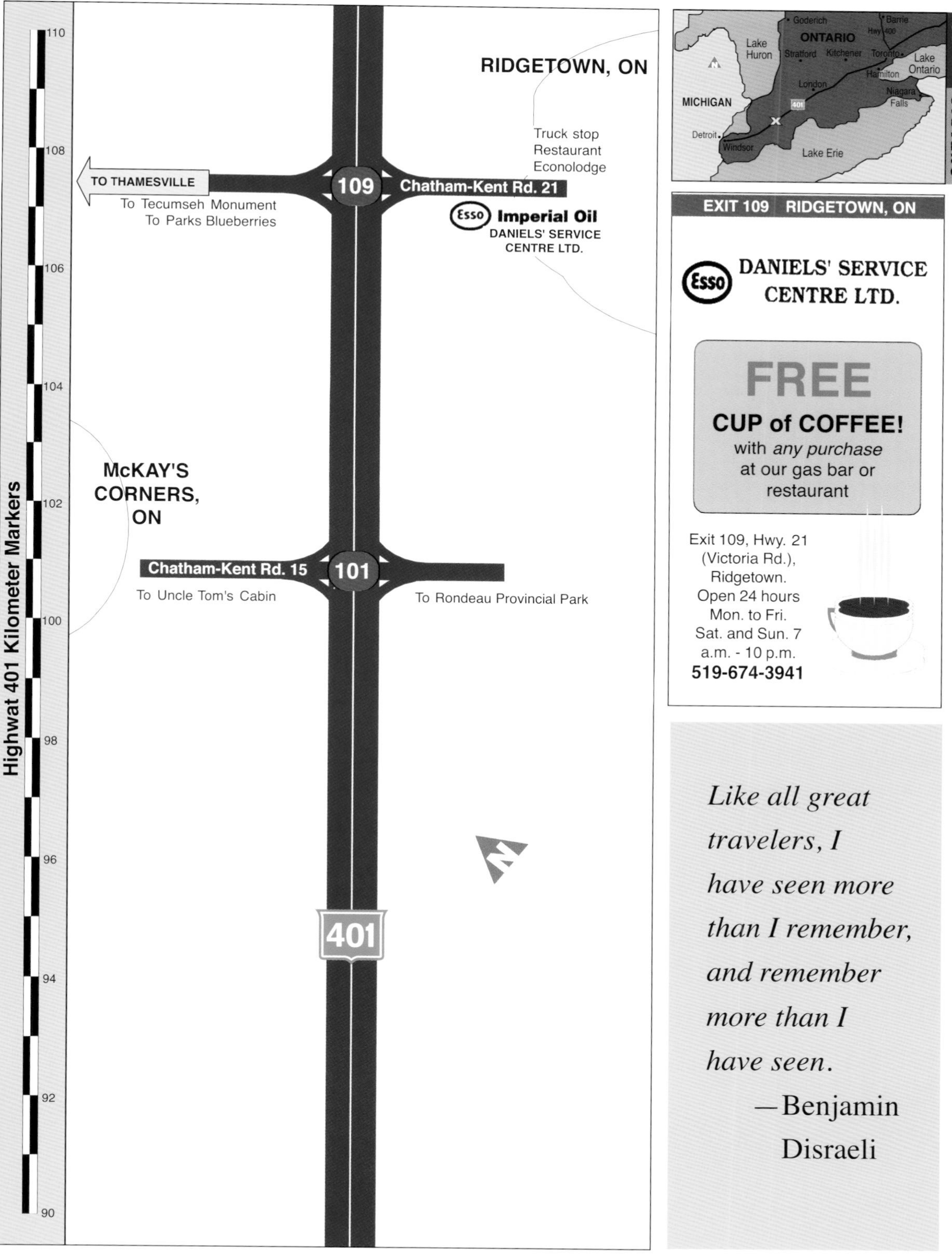

Highwat 401 Kilometer Markers
110
108
106
104
102
100
98
96
94
92
90
RIDGETOWN, ON
Truck stop
Restaurant
Econolodge
TO THAMESVILLE
109
Chatham-Kent Rd. 21
To Tecumseh Monument
To Parks Blueberries
Esso Imperial Oil
DANIELS' SERVICE CENTRE LTD.
McKAY'S CORNERS, ON
Chatham-Kent Rd. 15
101
To Uncle Tom's Cabin
To Rondeau Provincial Park
N
401
Goderich
Barrie
Hwy 400
ONTARIO
Lake Huron
Stratford
Kitchener
Toronto
Lake Ontario
Hamilton
London
MICHIGAN
401
Niagara Falls
Detroit
Windsor
Lake Erie
43
ONTARIO
EXIT 109 RIDGETOWN, ON
Esso DANIELS' SERVICE CENTRE LTD.
FREE
CUP of COFFEE!
with any purchase at our gas bar or restaurant
Exit 109, Hwy. 21 (Victoria Rd.), Ridgetown.
Open 24 hours Mon. to Fri.
Sat. and Sun. 7 a.m. - 10 p.m.
519-674-3941
Like all great travelers, I have seen more than I remember, and remember more than I have seen.
—Benjamin Disraeli

Chatham
ONTARIO

Municipality of Chatham-Kent — Department of Economic Development
435 Grand Ave. W., P.O. Box 944, Chatham, ON Canada N7L 3Z4
519-351-7700 or 1-800-561-6125 **www.cktourism.com**

Like the city it was named for, **Chatham** sits near the mouth of the Thames River. It originated as a naval dockyard in 1793.

The area's history is rich: it includes John Brown's plotting of a raid on **Harper's Ferry** (an event that helped to trigger the American Civil War) and the establishment of the northern terminus of the **Underground Railroad.** Chatham is home to the first Canadian inducted into the Baseball Hall of Fame, **Ferguson (Fergie) Jenkins.**

Be sure to visit the **Cultural Center,** the **Railroad Museum**, the **First Baptist Church (John Brown Meeting House),** and **Tecumseh Park.**

Tilbury ONTARIO

Tilbury attractions include the **175-year-old historic clock** located in the post office tower; the **Odette Memorial Library** and a **historical dashwheel** that is over 70 years old. Psst! Delicious roast chicken at the Blue Bonnet Restaurant!

Smugglers Marina
(Lighthouse Cove at the mouth of the Thames River), 100 serviced docks, 10' draft, gas, licenses, pub. RR #5, north of Tilbury. 519-682-2706

Wheatley ONTARIO

Wheatley welcomes you to explore Carolinian Canada, a unique forested habitat where birds, botanicals and butterflies found nowhere else thrive! The town has everything from herbs and antiques to fishing boats and shopping.

Campers Cove Family Camping boasts a sandy beach on Lake Erie and large shady lots with clean, modern facilities. Call ahead. 1-800-265-5833 or 519-825-4732 info@camperscove.ca

Wheatley Provincial Park. Over 100,000 visitors annually make this one of Ontario's most used and beloved parks. Canoeing, fishing, camping. 1 kilometer east of Wheatley on Hwy. 3. Reservations 519-825-4659

Two Creeks Conservation Area. Spring migration of songbirds. Nature trails along creek. Just north of Wheatley. Year-round. 519-354-7310

Chatham and Area Attractions

Chatham Cultural Centre
Theater productions, Art Gallery & Museum. Open daily 1 p.m.-5 p.m. 75 William St. N. Free admission to gallery/museum. 519-354-8338

First Baptist Church (John Brown Meeting House). Church founded in 1841 by refugee slaves. Call for information on worship services: 519-352-9552.

W.I.S.H. Centre
Cultural Room houses historical artifacts and slide presentations on the history of Chatham's Black community. 800-561-6125

Tecumseh Park
The park takes its name from Chief Tecumseh, who fought with the British during the War of 1812. Recreational activities, Concerts in the Park, and Festival of Nations are held in the summer. William St. 1-800-561-6125

Uncle Tom's Cabin Historic Site
See page 46. Rev. Josiah Henson's home and other restored historical buildings. Interpretive center and museum. Extensive selection of art and gifts from Africa. May 22 to Oct. 23, Tues. to Sun. 10 a.m.-4 p.m. July & Aug. open daily 10 a.m.-4 p.m., Sun. noon-4 p.m. RR #5, Park St., Dresden. 519-683-2978

Buxton National Historical Site & Museum Follow the Underground Railroad from slavery to freedom. The museum preserves material and artifacts of Raleigh, with special emphasis on its original settlers: the Black Settlement in North Buxton. May to Sept. Wed. to Sun. 1 p.m.-4:30 p.m. Or by appointment. On County Rd. 6 (the A.D. Shadd Road). 519-352-4799

Chatham and Area Special Events

- **Great Garage Sale**
  Chatham, early Mar and mid-Sept. 519-352-3888
- **Chatham Craft Show/Sales**
  Early Mar. and mid-Nov. 519-352-3888
- **Chesterfield Birding Tour**
  Wheatley Prov. Park, 6 a.m., May. 519-825-7131
- **Herb Faire**
  The Old Log House, Wheatley, mid-May. 519-825-7783
- **Dresden 50s & 60s Weekend, Pet and Hobby Parade, Classic Car Show** at conservation area, June. 519-683-4481
- **BMX Stadium Racing**
  Chatham, mid-June. 519-351-9300
- **Festival of Nations**
  Chatham, late June, early July. 519-360-1998
- **Chatham Concert Band**
  Tecumseh Park, summer, Wed. nights
- **Wheatley Fish Fest**
  Early Aug. 519-825-7131
- **Dresden Exhibition**
  Late July. 519-683-6194
- **Heritage Days**
  Thamesgrove conservation area, Chatham, late Sept. 519-351-2058
- **Chatham's Heritage House Tour**
  Late Sept. 519-351-2058
- **Wheatley Harvest Fest**
  Mid-Sept. 519-825-3929
- **Kent Kennel Klub Dog Show**
  Chatham, early Nov. 519-352-3888
- **Great Lakes Gun & Knife Show**
  Mid-Nov. 519-352-3888

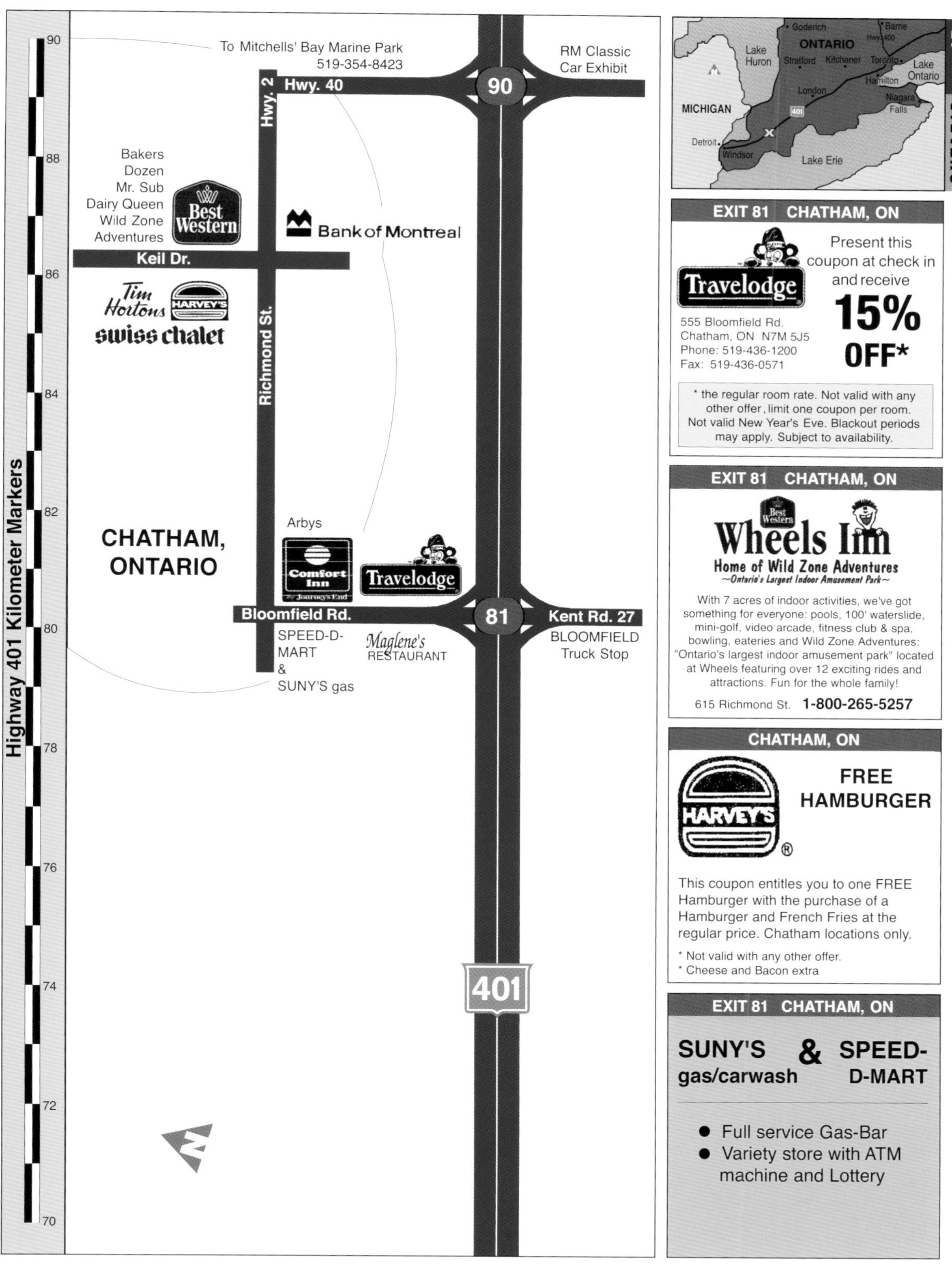

EXIT 81 CHATHAM, ON

Travelodge

555 Bloomfield Rd.
Chatham, ON N7M 5J5
Phone: 519-436-1200
Fax: 519-436-0571

Present this coupon at check in and receive

15% OFF*

* the regular room rate. Not valid with any other offer, limit one coupon per room. Not valid New Year's Eve. Blackout periods may apply. Subject to availability.

EXIT 81 CHATHAM, ON

Best Western

Wheels Inn

Home of Wild Zone Adventures

~Ontario's Largest Indoor Amusement Park~

With 7 acres of indoor activities, we've got something for everyone: pools, 100' waterslide, mini-golf, video arcade, fitness club & spa, bowling, eateries and Wild Zone Adventures: "Ontario's largest indoor amusement park" located at Wheels featuring over 12 exciting rides and attractions. Fun for the whole family!

615 Richmond St. **1-800-265-5257**

CHATHAM, ON

HARVEY'S®

FREE HAMBURGER

This coupon entitles you to one FREE Hamburger with the purchase of a Hamburger and French Fries at the regular price. Chatham locations only.

* Not valid with any other offer.
* Cheese and Bacon extra

EXIT 81 CHATHAM, ON

SUNY'S gas/carwash & SPEED-D-MART

- Full service Gas-Bar
- Variety store with ATM machine and Lottery

North Buxton
ONTARIO

Municipality of Chatham-Kent — Department of Economic Development
435 Grand Ave. W., P.O. Box 944, Chatham, ON Canada N7L 3Z4
519-351-7700 or 1-800-561-6125 **www.cktourism.com**

Once known as the Elgin Settlement, North Buxton served as a haven for fugitive slaves in the pre-Civil War years.

When the Reverend William King, a white Presbyterian minister and strict abolitionist, was willed his father-in-law's fourteen American slaves, he went south to meet the slaves in Ohio, then he set them free and offered them the opportunity to build a new life for themselves in a settlement he planned to build in Canada.

In return for clearing their own fields and building their own homes, the land was sold to the new settlers at a low price. Soon the settlement of 300 families flourished. Several descendants of the original settlers are residents of present-day North Buxton.

Dresden ONTARIO

A picturesque town on the bank of the Sydenham River, Dresden is steeped in history.

Reverend Josiah Henson established a colony for escaping slaves and became popular as the main character in Harriet Beecher Stowe's controversial 1852 novel, *Uncle Tom's Cabin*.

Take a guided tour of Henson's home and other unique 19th-century heritage buildings. Bring home one of the African art pieces or other gifts from the gallery. Enjoy the family picnic area.

Dresden also offers fine shopping on quiet streets and an exciting night of harness racing.

Rev. Josiah Henson (1789-1883)

Born in Maryland, Josiah Henson worked as a slave for 41 years. In 1830, he and his family escaped to Upper Canada via the Underground Railroad.

Through Josiah's leadership, the British American Institute, Canada's first Industrial School, was established. It was dedicated to the advancement of escaped slaves.

Josiah Henson's name became synonymous with the central character Uncle Tom, in Harriet Beecher Stowe's famous novel, Uncle Tom's Cabin. The novel sold 300,000 copies the first year. Uncle Tom's Cabin Historic Site provides a rare opportunity to learn, through Josiah's life, a multicultural story of inspirational courage and growth.

Uncle Tom's Cabin Historic Site. *Photo by Mark Wolfe, courtesy Chatham-Kent Tourism*

Uncle Tom's Cabin Historic Site

Current facilities, located on the original property purchased by Josiah, seek to portray the heritage of Josiah Henson's settlement.

The facilities include the newly restored Henson home, the James Harris House, where fugitive slaves may have resided, a church representative of the time, housing the pulpit used by Rev. Henson.

Also featured is a recently built interpretive center which contains a gift shop with souvenirs and books, and a museum housing many artifacts that relate to life in the Chatham area from the mid to late 19th century. Uncle Tom's Cabin Historic Site, on Park St., near Dresden. 519-683-2978 Open 10-4 Tuesday to Saturday, mid-May to end of October and some Mondays. Call ahead.

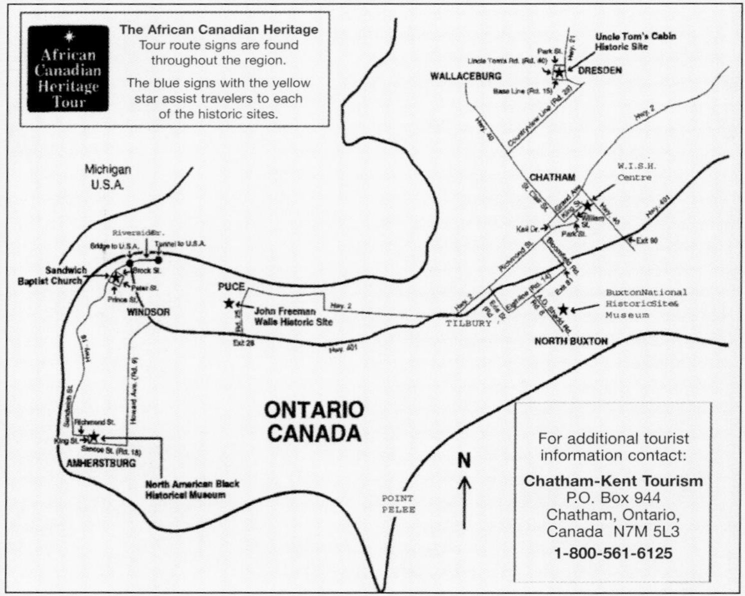

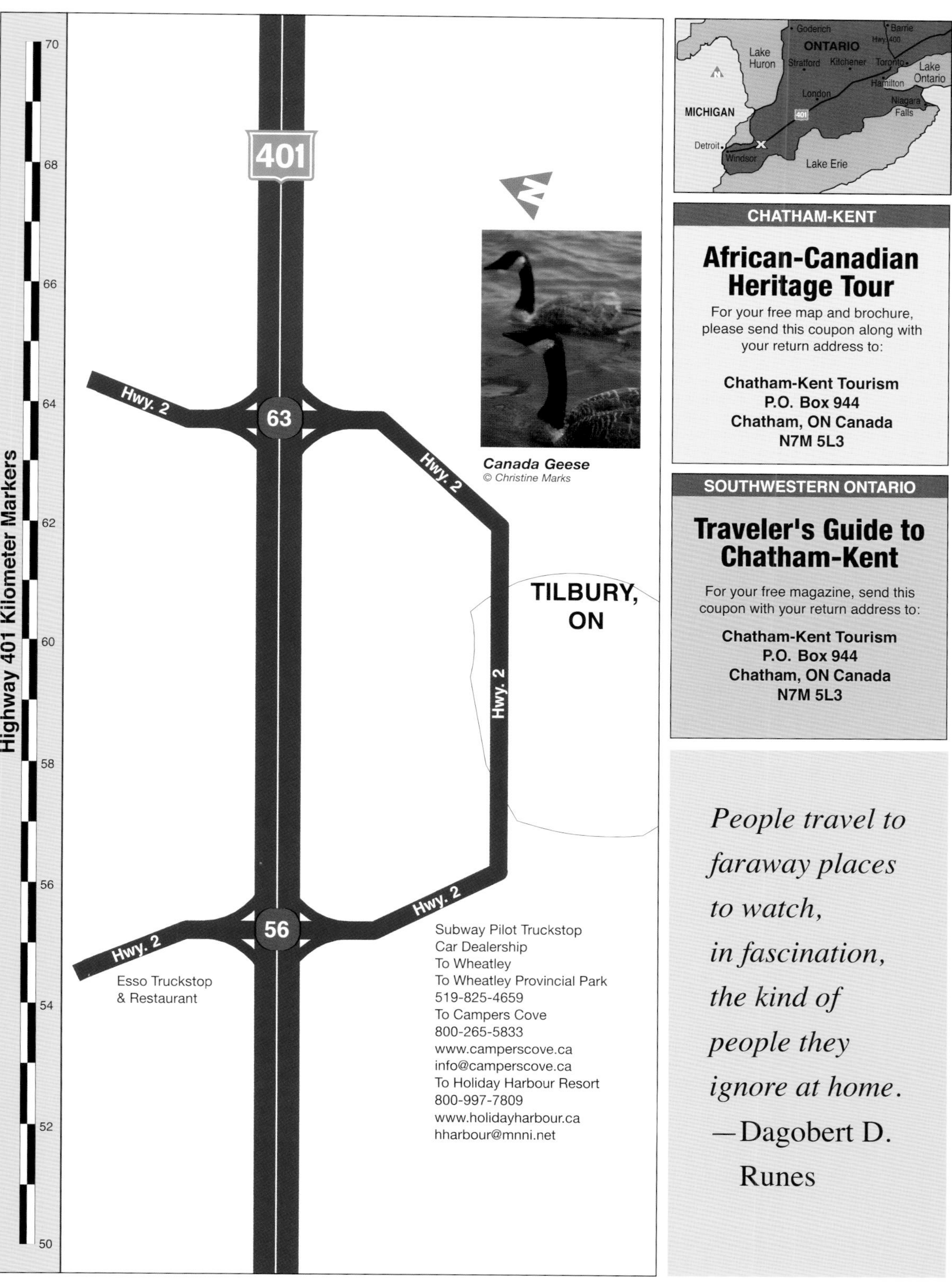

Canada Geese
© Christine Marks

CHATHAM-KENT

African-Canadian Heritage Tour

For your free map and brochure, please send this coupon along with your return address to:

Chatham-Kent Tourism
P.O. Box 944
Chatham, ON Canada
N7M 5L3

SOUTHWESTERN ONTARIO

Traveler's Guide to Chatham-Kent

For your free magazine, send this coupon with your return address to:

Chatham-Kent Tourism
P.O. Box 944
Chatham, ON Canada
N7M 5L3

People travel to faraway places to watch, in fascination, the kind of people they ignore at home.
—Dagobert D. Runes

Pelee Island
ONTARIO

Windsor, Essex County & Pelee Island Convention & Visitors Bureau
Suite 103, 333 Riverside Dr. W., Windsor, ON Canada N9A 5K4
519-255-6530 or 1-800-265-3633 **www.visitwindsor.com**

Where is Canada's most southerly inhabited point? **Point Pelee National Park** and **Pelee Island!**

Point Pelee National Park, a peninsula of green jutting out into the blue waters of Lake Erie, is one of the smallest national parks but it attracts nearly half a million visitors each year.

As a child I delighted in the migrations of birds (spring and fall) and monarch butterflies (late summer), the two special events which firmly anchor the park onto international maps.

My grandparents originated a tradition of taking the family to Point Pelee just about every Sunday, through rain, snow or shine!

In the spring we spent hours at the Marsh tip-toeing across the boardwalk or whispering across the water in grampa's home-made canoe. We would miss nothing.

Naturally, we spent lazy summer afternoons at one of the Park's several beaches, collecting shells and freckles.

In the fall, we explored nature trails and the shoreline, searching for wild grapes and flowers, and watching for deer, birds and butterflies.

My favorite season in the park was winter. I practiced skating for hours on the frozen marsh. I learned to snowshoe, eat dried fruit and walk "just as silent as a warrior" behind my grandfather so as not to disturb nature. We identified animal tracks in the snow.

My two best memories were of coming within a few feet of a majestic red fox on a trail near the Visitors Centre and of scoffing at the "deer crossing" road sign only to be left speechless as not one but two deer immediately bounded out in front of us!

Grampa's gone now and I appreciate his legacy. My little family continues to enjoy Point Pelee with regular visits.

The interpretive program and exhibits at the Visitors Centre are superlative. The resident nature interpreters fully answered our questions and spurred our minds in new directions with questions of their own. A transit service takes visitors on a memorable trip to the tip of the Point from April to October.

Pelee Island Winery Bottles
Photo courtesy visitwindsor.com

A Point of Interest: Pelee Island

Pelee Island is the largest island in the Lake Erie basin. It has a year-round population of just 275 residents.

Reserve your place on a ferry or fly in to tour this Island treat. www.ontarioferries.com

We spent a weekend on the Island a few summers ago but it wasn't enough! Watching the **M.V. JIIMAAN** ferry (1-800-661-2220) approach the Leamington dock was almost as much fun for us as the exciting hour-and-a-half long boat ride across the Pelee Basin to the Island.

We stayed at the **ANCHOR & WHEEL INN** (519-724-2195), an historic property owned by the Emrich family since 1971. The quiet hospitality and warm ambiance resonated with the Bed & Breakfast room's turn-of-the-century tin walls and ceilings. Camp sites and Guest Rooms were also available. It's best to confirm a reservation in order to sample the steaks and seafood served at their legendary "Island Restaurant." www.anchorwheelinn.com

We'd heard alot about the **SCUDDER BEACH BAR & GRILL** (519-724-2902).

The server, an "Islander," could have been a stand-up comedian. The local gossip she dished was almost as good as the meals. We were told that the outdoor bar and grill is *the* local nightspot.

We hiked out to see the oldest stone lighthouse on Lake Erie and we spent hours listening to the Island's most knowledgeable person, the curator of the Pelee Island Heritage Centre, Mr. Ron Tiessen.

You'll also find here a unique nature preserve, secluded beach, a celebrated Pheasant Farm, the Vin Villa Ruins, rare flora and fauna, prehistoric artifacts, and shipwrecks.

The very best part of the trip was our tour of the PELEE ISLAND WINE PAVILLION (1-800-597-3533). www.peleeisland.com

Out on the Pavillion, we barbecued our own lunch and watched the kids dance to the live music.

The highlight was the fascinating tour led by the Winery's publicity director. Our not knowing much about wine was no bar to her interest in educating us about the science and history of the wine industry.

We learned to identify the various types of grapes grown in the vineyards and the kinds of cork used to stop the bottles. And after viewing a short film on wine appreciation, we sampled a few of the many award-winning fine wines made at the Pelee Island Winery.

Whether for a daytrip, weekend or longer stay, Pelee Island is one place off the beaten path you're sure to enjoy. www. www.pelee.org

Explore Pelee, 519-325-TOUR. Local tour guides will show you all the secret magical spots of the Island and give historical accounts of life in Canada's most southern community. www.explorepelee.com

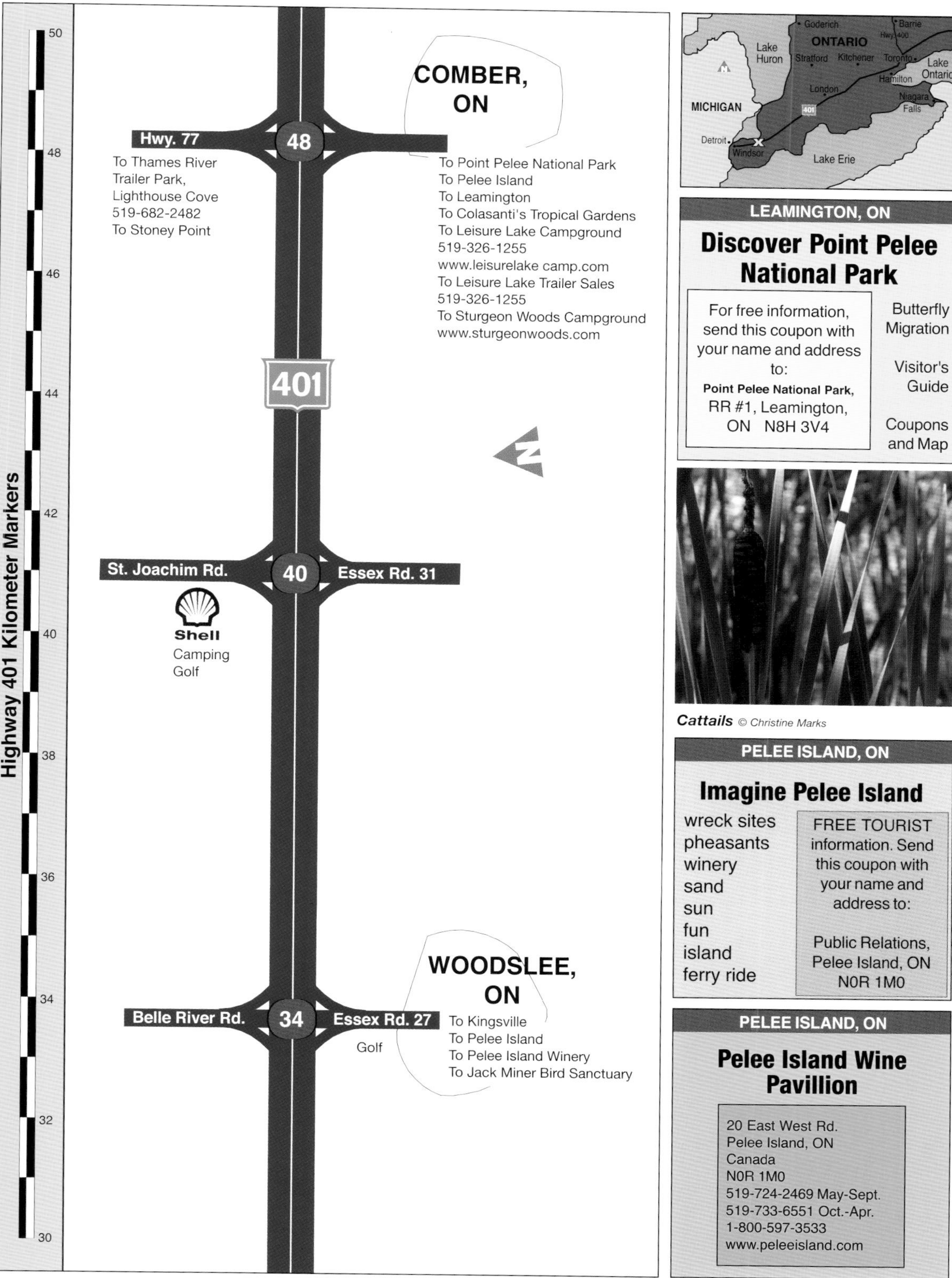
Highway 401 Kilometer Markers
50
48
46
44
42
40
38
36
34
32
30
COMBER, ON
Hwy. 77
48
To Thames River Trailer Park, Lighthouse Cove 519-682-2482
To Stoney Point
To Point Pelee National Park
To Pelee Island
To Leamington
To Colasanti's Tropical Gardens
To Leisure Lake Campground 519-326-1255 www.leisurelake camp.com
To Leisure Lake Trailer Sales 519-326-1255
To Sturgeon Woods Campground www.sturgeonwoods.com
401
N
St. Joachim Rd.
40
Essex Rd. 31
Shell
Camping
Golf
WOODSLEE, ON
Belle River Rd.
34
Essex Rd. 27
Golf
To Kingsville
To Pelee Island
To Pelee Island Winery
To Jack Miner Bird Sanctuary
Goderich
Barrie
ONTARIO
Hwy 400
Lake Huron
Stratford
Kitchener
Toronto
Lake Ontario
Hamilton
London
Niagara Falls
MICHIGAN
401
Detroit
Windsor
Lake Erie

Cattails *© Christine Marks*

Essex County
ONTARIO

Windsor, Essex County & Pelee Island Convention & Visitors Bureau
Suite 103, 333 Riverside Dr. W., Windsor, ON Canada N9A 5K4
519-255-6530 or 1-800-265-3633 **www.visitwindsor.com**

Essex County Being as south as California, as flat as the prairies, and having enriched black soil and a long growing season all contribute to Essex County's fabled growing conditions.

Its farm and related agricultural businesses reportedly earn $400 million dollar a year. There are some 2,200 farms, and about 300,000 acres of field crops. There are over 300 acres of greenhouses alone!

Windsor, Essex County and Pelee Island, as far as tourism regions of Ontario are concerned, is small; however, it submitted the thickest list of special events and attractions on file! Despite the fact that I was raised here, the area's diversity and growth surprised me.

Essex County embraces its long history. Numerous museums and historic sites can be found in Amherstburg, Essex, Harrow, Point Pelee and Windsor where the individuals, cultures and events that helped shape the area and Canada are presented for your consideration. The War of 1812, the Shawnee leader Tecumseh, the Upper Canada Rebellion and the Underground Railroad will come to life in the exhibits and costumed reenactments staged for your entertainment and education.

I'm particularly fond of the waterfront at Amherstburg and urge you to visit historic Fort Malden and the Navy Yard Park.

Wine tour at county winery.
Courtesy Windsor, Pelee Island & Essex County CVB

Did you know Essex County is a burgeoning wine region?
www.visitwindsor.com/wineries.asp

Attractions Near Windsor

Colasanti's Tropical Gardens
Over 20 greenhouses full of cactus, tropicals, exotic birds. Petting zoo, rides, mini putt, family entertainment center, orchards and buffet meals. Year-round. 1550 Road 3 East, Kingsville.
519-326-3287 www.colasanti.com

Colio Estate Wines
Tour and tasting. Year-round. Harrow.
519-738-2241 or 1-800-265-1322
www.coliowines.com

D'Angelo Estate Winery
Art in the Vineyard in Aug. Year-round free tours and seminars. Amherstburg.
519-736-7959 www.dangelowinery.com

Fort Malden National Historic Site
Built in 1796, this was a key British defensive post during the War of 1812 and the Rebellion of 1837. Call for dates of battle reenactments. Year-round. Amherstburg. Admission. 519-736-5416
www.parkscanada.gc.ca/malden

Holiday Beach Conservation Area
Camp, fish, swim, birding and picnicking. May to Nov. Near Amherstburg,
519-736-3772 or 888-487-4760
www.erca.org

Jack Miner Bird Sanctuary
World-celebrated sanctuary and migrational resting ground for Canada Geese. Won't disappoint you from mid-Oct. to end of Nov. Near Kingsville, Year-round, Mon. to Sat., 8:30 a.m.-5:30 p.m.
519-733-4034 or 1-877-289-8328
www.jackminer.com

John Freeman Walls Historic Site & Underground Railroad Museum
Tour where "the Underground Railroad has its end." Call for hours. On East Puce Rd., Puce. 519-258-6253
www.undergroundrailroadmuseum.com

Historic Amherstburg Visitor Centre (Apr-Nov) 519-736-8320. **Amherstburg Tourism Dept**. (Year-round) 800-413-9993
www.amherstburg.ca

John R. Park Homestead
Costumed guides at historic Lake Erie shore settlement. Picnic, nature trail and special events. Call for hours.
519-738-2029 www.erca.org
Blytheswood, near Leamington
915 County Rd. 50

Jones' Popcorn 519-326-7128

Leamington Info 1-800-250-3336
www.leamington.ca

Park House Museum
Candle-dipping, spinning, weaving and tinsmithing in the oldest house in Amherstburg. July to August daily. Rest of year Mon-Fri 519-736-2511
www.parkhousemuseum.com

Fort Malden Historic Park.
Courtesy Windsor, Pelee Island & Essex County CVB

Pelee Island Ferry Service Information Reservations: 1-800-661-2220 or 519-724-2115 for the 1-1/4 hour service from Leamington or Kingsville.

Navy Yard Park
This serene riverfront park was the scene of both 19th-century and War of 1812 battles. Sitting with chatty locals and identifying the flags on the lake freighters while you enjoy homemade ice cream from the nearby parlor makes quite a pleasing afternoon!

North American Black Historical Museum
Exhibits of African origins, slavery and emancipation. A celebration of achievement. Open July to August, Tues-Sun. Also open holiday weekends in August. Tours can be booked off-season. Amherstburg. 519-736-5434
www.blackhistoricalmuseum.com

Canadian Transportation Museum & Heritage Village
20,000 sq. ft. museum displays transportation exhibits from the mid-1800s up to the 1992 Dodge Viper. The Heritage Village features over a dozen buildings of local significance and displays artifacts from a bygone era. Kingsville, ON
519-776-6909 www.ctmhv.com

Crossing the Windsor-Detroit Border

N

401

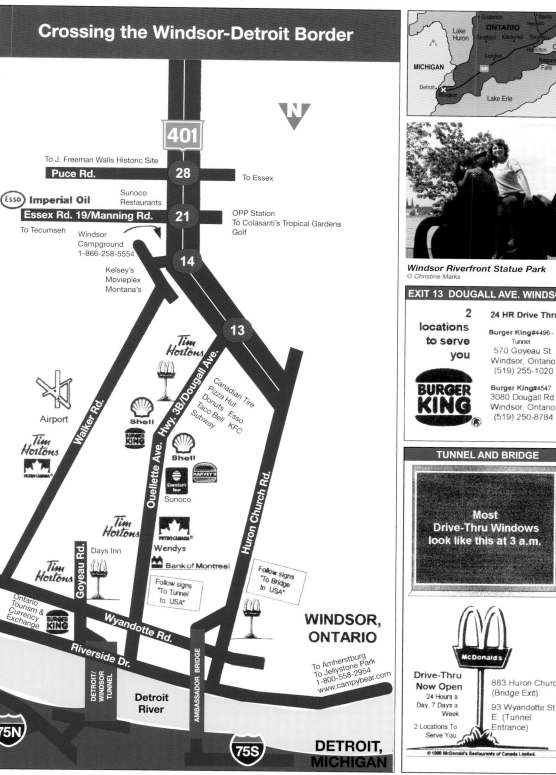

To J. Freeman Walls Historic Site

Puce Rd. 28 To Essex

Esso Imperial Oil

Sunoco Restaurants

Essex Rd. 19/Manning Rd. 21

OPP Station
To Colasanti's Tropical Gardens
Golf

To Tecumseh

Windsor Campground 1-866-258-5554

14

Kelsey's
Movieplex
Montana's

13

Airport

Walker Rd.

Tim Hortons

Petro Canada

Shell

Burger King

Hwy. 3B/Dougall Ave.

Canadian Tire
Pizza Hut
Donuts Esso
Taco Bell KFC
Subway

Shell

Harvey's

Comfort Inn

Sunoco

Ouellette Ave.

Huron Church Rd.

Tim Hortons

Petro Canada

Wendys

Days Inn

Bank of Montreal

Tim Hortons

Goyeau Rd.

Follow signs "To Tunnel to USA"

Follow signs "To Bridge to USA"

Ontario Tourism & Currency Exchange

Burger King

Wyandotte Rd.

Riverside Dr.

WINDSOR, ONTARIO

To Amherstburg
To Jellystone Park
1-800-558-2954
www.campybear.com

DETROIT/WINDSOR TUNNEL

Detroit River

AMBASSADOR BRIDGE

75N

75S

DETROIT, MICHIGAN

Windsor Riverfront Statue Park
© Christine Marks

EXIT 13 DOUGALL AVE. WINDSOR

Drive-Thru Windows
look like this at 3 a.m.
Drive-Thru Now Open
24 Hours a Day, 7 Days a Week
2 locations to serve you
883 Huron Church (Bridge Exit)
93 Wyandotte St. E. (Tunnel Entrance)
© 1998 McDonald's Restaurants of Canada Limited.

24 HR Drive Thru

Burger King#4496 - Tunnel
570 Goyeau St.
Windsor, Ontario
(519) 255-1020

Burger King#4547
3080 Dougall Rd.
Windsor, Ontario
(519) 250-8784

BURGER KING®

TUNNEL AND BRIDGE

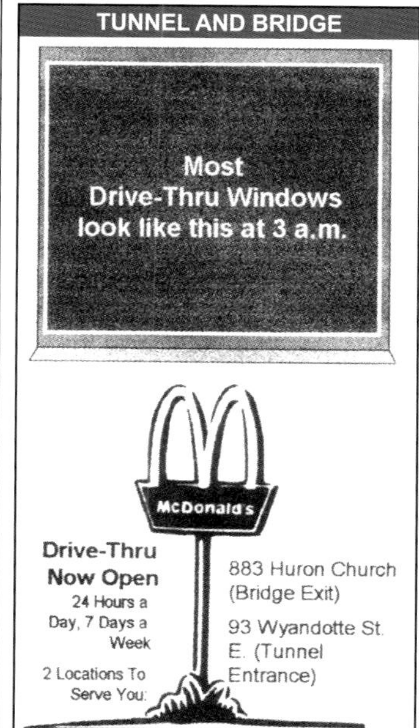

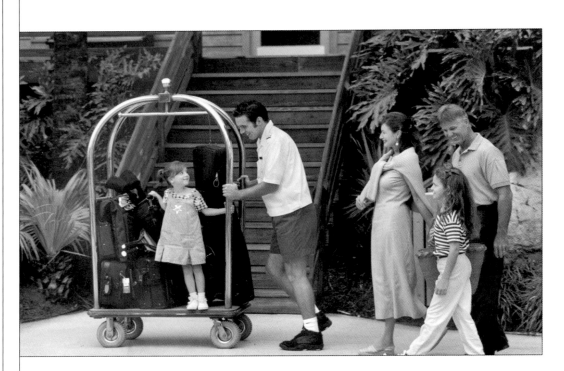

Essex County
ONTARIO

Windsor, Essex County & Pelee Island Convention & Visitors Bureau
Suite 103, 333 Riverside Dr. W., Windsor, ON Canada N9A 5K4
519-255-6530 or 1-800-265-3633 **www.visitwindsor.com**

Attractions in the City of Windsor

Casino Windsor at dusk.
Courtesy visitwindsor.com

Ambassador Bridge
4-lane bridge links the major highways of Detroit and Windsor. Also visit the Ambassador Duty Free Store, 1-800-GO-BRIDGE.
www.ambassadorbridge.com

The Art Gallery of Windsor
Changing exhibits and permanent collection, children's gallery, and sales. 401 Riverside Dr. W. Closed Mon. & Tues.
519-977-0013
www.agw.ca

Canadian Club Brand Heritage Centre,
Tours year-round. 2072 Riverside Dr. W., 519-973-9503
www.canadianclubwhisky.com

Caesars Windsor
377 Riverside Dr. E., 1-800-991-7777
www.caesarswindsor.com

Chrysler Theatre
519-252-8311 or 1-800-387-9181
www.chryslertheatre.com

PARKS & RECREATION
1-888-519-3333 www.citywindsor.ca

Jackson Park
65 acres of elegant gardens and a memorial to WWII veterans.
1-800-265-3633

Mackenzie Hall Cultural Community Centre Former courthouse built by Canadian Prime Minister Alexander Mackenzie in 1855. 3277 Sandwich St.
519-255-7600

Ojibway Park
315 acres of tallgrass prairie and savannah. Matchette Rd. and Broadway.
519-966-5852 www.ojibway.ca

The Riverfront
Much of the waterfront was reserved for public enjoyment and offers beautiful parks and gardens to watch ships from all over the world. The Peace Fountain is a floating water and colored light display in Coventry Gardens. Mid-May to mid-Oct. 11 a.m.-11:30 p.m. 1-888-519-3333

Royal Windsor Cruises
Sightseeing, lunch, dinner. May to Oct.
For reservations: 1-877-971-8843
www.senatorofwindsor.com

Vive Le Canada! Tours
Year-round by arrangement. 519-556-3511

Windsor's Community Museum
In the historic Francois Baby House, the museum presents Windsor's history.
254 Pitt St. W. Open Tues. to Sat. 10 a.m. -5 p.m., Sun. 2 a.m.-5 p.m. Free.
519-253-1812 www.citywindsor.ca

Willistead Manor
Tudor-Jacobean stately home built 1904-1906 by Hiram Walker's son. Silver sinks and marble fireplaces. Special events and tours. 1899 Niagara St.
519-253-2365 www.citywindsor.ca

The Windsor-Detroit Tunnel is the city-to-city connection preference. Tunnel Duty Free Shop, 519-258-7424. (Duty-Free Shops save 20 to 50%!) 465 Goyeau St.
1-800-669-2105 www.dwtunnel.com

Farmers Market at the Market Square
(Corner of Ottawa St. & Walker Rd.) Tues. to Fri. 8 a.m.-6 p.m., Sat. 7 a.m.-4 p.m.; Sun. 10 a.m.-3 p.m. 519-253-7374

Odette Sculpture Park
At Assumption and Centennial parks. Beautiful waterfront location includes over 20 sculptures on the waterfront. Year-round.

Windsor Wood Carving Museum
Only one in Ontario, showcasing tools, artifacts, historical and wildlife carvings. Year-round Tues. to Sat. 850 Ouellette St.
519-977-0823
www.windsorwoodcarvingmuseum.ca

Walkers Candies
Family-run facility. Homemade, hand-dipped treats the old fashioned way. Tours by request. www.walkerscandies.com
519-253-2019

OLG Slots at Windsor Raceway
519-969-8311 www.windsorraceway.com

Windsor Trivia

Windsor is Canada's southernmost city. Established in about 1749, it formed part of Ontario's oldest permanent settlement 240 years ago.

The first battle of the **War of 1812** was the **Battle of Windsor.**

Windsor was the first city in Canada to have an **electrified street railway** in 1886. Windsor had the first mile of concrete pavement in N. America, built in 1920.

Ford Motor Company of Canada was founded in Windsor, Aug. 17, 1904. The first fully Canadian-made auto was built in Windsor in 1913.

The Dodge brothers began their business careers in Windsor before going to Detroit in the early 1900s to form the **Dodge Motor Company.**

The Ambassador Bridge, at its opening in 1929, was the longest motor vehicle bridge in the world and still remains the longest international suspension bridge.

The Detroit/Windsor Tunnel, (completed 1930), is the world's only international underwater vehicle tunnel.

The **palm 'n turn,** a child-resistant lid for prescription drugs, was a Windsor first.

In 1962, Canterbury College of Windsor **(Univ. of Windsor)** became the first Anglican college in the world to affiliate with a Roman Catholic university.

Windsor Medical Services was the first doctor-sponsored, prepaid community health plan in Canada and was the forerunner to **OHIP**.

The first Community Chest in Canada originated in Windsor. Later it become the **United Way**. Windsor has ranked first in Canada in per capita giving for the past 16 years.

The **Windsor Lions Club** was the first Canadian Lions group. It founded White Cane Week and lobbied for the use of white canes into Ontario's legislation.

In 1962, Windsor was one of the first Canadian cities to establish a **senior citizens' center** and introduced the idea of a senior citizens' discount in 1970. Special discounts for seniors have since become widespread in North America.

Windsor
ONTARIO

Windsor, Essex County & Pelee Island Convention & Visitors Bureau
Suite 103, 333 Riverside Dr. W., Windsor, ON Canada N9A 5K4
519-255-6530 or 1-800-265-3633 **www.visitwindsor.com**

The **City of Windsor** has earned a few reputations over the years. Most of the nicknames were favorable: "The Rose City," "The Automotive Capital of Canada," "Canada's Most Generous City" and more recently "The Place To Be!'

By any name the city has earned an international reputation for its beautiful and abundant parkland. **Jackson Park's Queen Elizabeth II** sunken gardens feature a reflecting pool. The adjoining park and garden area is home to replicas of two WWII classic airplanes — a Hurricane Spitfire. These are accompanied by a monument to WWII veterans.

Dieppe Gardens, Ambassador Park, Assumption Park and **Coventry Gardens** with its famous **Peace Fountain** are all on the waterfront and offer spectacular views of the bridge and the Detroit skyline.

If you want to see the the largest fireworks display in North America, arrive early and win a spot at one of the riverfront parks for your lawn chair. You can shoot great photos of the multi-colored cascades reflecting on the mirrored surfaces of the skyscapers and river.

Known as the Automotive Capital of Canada, Windsor's corporate citizens include **Ford, General Motors** and **Chrysler.**

At one time Windsor earned a less favorable reputation as a result of its industrial economy. Today you'll find that Windsor is clean and green with an atmosphere of friendliness and generosity. Windsor initiated what was to become the United Way in Canada and has consistantly ranked first in Canada for per capita giving over the past 16 years! Windsor was also the first Canadian city to found a Goodfellows organization, a Lions Club and to open a senior citizens center.

Windsor's history goes back to the early 1640s. It spans the early pioneer days, the fur trade, settlement, a great fire, several wars, rebellions, and prohibition. Perhaps it is not surprising that one of Windsor's earliest, and today's most successful, companies is **Hiram Walker's Distillery!**

ANNUAL EVENTS: Windsor, Essex County& Pelee Island

Early FEBRUARY
Ice Wine Festival. D'Angelo Estate Winery, Amherstburg. 519-736-7959
www.dangelowinery.com

Festival of Ice. Colio Estate Wines, Harrow. 519-738-2241 or 1-800-265-1322
www.coliowines.com

Mid MARCH
Maple Syrup Festival Activities. John R. Park Homestead, Harrow. Contact for details/hours
519-738-2029 www.erca.org

First half of MAY
Point Pelee Festival of Birds. Point Pelee National Park, Leamington. 519-322-2365
www.pc.gc.ca/pointpelee

Mid-MAY
Shore & Songbird Celebration. Hillman Marsh Conservation Area, Leamington.
519-776-5209 ext. 308
www.erca.org

Early JUNE
Strawberry Festival. Gil Maure Park, LaSalle.
519-969-5699
www.lasallestrawberryfestival.com

Mid JUNE
Colchester Walleye Derby. Colchester Harbour, Colchester. 519-738-4025
www.derby.hcslions.com
Sponsored by Harrow Lions, features 6am and 7am launches, a food and beverage tent, and prizes totalling over $4500!

Early JUNE
Art in the Park. Willistead Park, Windsor.
519-253-6382
www.aipwindsor.com
One of Ontario's largest arts and crafts shows, featuring some 250 artists and artisans. The exhibitors display and retail their work at beautiful Willistead Park.

Weekends in JUNE
Carrousel of the Nations, Windsor
519-255-1127 or 1-877-237-9264
www.themcc.com
The Carrousel of the Nations is one of Ontario's longest-running annual June events. The festivities begin with Carrousel by the River, an outdoor family festival at the Riverfront Festival Plaza featuring international food, bazaar vendors, children's area and continuous live entertainment.

Mid-JUNE to early JULY
Windsor Summerfest. Civic Terrace, Festival Plaza, Windsor Riverfront 519-254-2880
www.summerfestwindsor.org
Live entertainment, World's Finest Shows midway, a Canada Day parade and celebrations, entertainment and a licensed venue in conjunction with the Target Fireworks over the Detroit River.

Late JUNE
Windsor Elvis Fest. Dieppe Park, Chrysler Theatre, Downtown Windsor. 519-254-1108
www.windsorelvisfest.com
Professional Elvis Tribute Artists and a classic car show are featured at this Graceland sanctioned preliminary competition for "The Ultimate Elvis Tribute Artist Contest™" held in Memphis, TN.

July 1 – CANADA DAY
July 1st is Canada's national holiday, marking the establishment of Canada as a new federation with its own constitution on July 1, 1867. Join in celebrations that take place throughout the region – Windsor's downtown waterfront (The Hbc Run for Canada, Canada Day Parade, giant cake, entertainment and more), Fort Malden National Historic Site in Amherstburg, and Pelee Island, to name a few.

Mid JULY
Festival Epicure: A Celebration of Food, Wine and Music. Riverfront Festival Plaza, Downtown Windsor.
519-971-5005
www.festivalepicure.com
A culinary array of the area's finest restaurants, wineries and eclectic mix of non-stop live music, all at a fabulous riverfront venue!

Bluesfest International. Riverfront Festival Plaza, Downtown Windsor. 519-977-9631
www.thebluesfest.com
Bluesfest International features four days of world-class blues and roots artists on the banks of the Detroit River.

The Windsor International Fringe Festival. Downtown Windsor. 519-258-9887
www.windsorfringe.com
Produced by Actors Theatre of Windsor (www.actorstheatreofwindsor.com), this 10-day festival will include the Windsor Fringe™ in five venues in Downtown Windsor, presenting 30 independent theatre companies as well as several free outdoor events: Buskin' to the Beat, The Visual Fringe (www.artcite.ca), Chalk & Chocolate Festival, and the Windsor International Buskers Festival (www.passthehat.com).

Dragon Boat Festival & Erie Street Festival of Food. Sandpoint Beach and Via Italia, Windsor.
519-250-0807
www.internationaldragonboats.com
Spectate or join in the fun yourself as paddlers from Canada and the United States raise funds for the fight against breast cancer. Festivities also take place with fine Italian food and entertainment in our "Little Italy."

Late JULY
Boblo Island International Jazz Festival, Boblo Island. 519-736-1111 or 1-877-222-2126
www.boblojazz.com
An eclectic mix of national and international sounds come together on one of Canada's premier resort islands. Food and beverages available.

ANNUAL EVENTS: Windsor, Essex County& Pelee Island continued...

Early AUGUST

Windsor Pride, Downtown Windsor.
519-973-4656 www.windsorpride.com
Five days of outstanding events to celebrate the LGBTT community in Windsor-Essex, culminating in the annual Pride Day and parade in downtown Windsor.

Pelee Fest, Pelee Island.
519-818-5511
www.pelee.org
Visit Pelee Island for a family festival featuring arts and crafts, children's games and activities and a festival tent with live entertainment... all with an Island flavour!

Essex County Steam & Gas Engine Show.
Co-An Park, McGregor.
519-839-4516
www.essexsteamandgasengine.com
Featuring tractors and machinery, steam and gas engines, parade (Sat.), flea market, crafts, bake sale, bean pot, souvenirs and various working displays.

Mid-AUGUST

Amherstburg Heritage Homecoming, Toddy Jones Park and Fort Malden National Historic Site, Amherstburg. 519-551-9840
www.uwindsor.ca/ahh
All are invited to join in this annual reunion and community event, celebrating the town's legacy as the final terminus on the Underground Railroad.

Leamington Tomato Festival. Seacliffe Park at Lake Erie, Leamington. 519-326-2878
www.leamingtontomatofestival.com
Free family event in Canada's Tomato Capitol featuring a parade, live entertainment, car show, children's village, "Tomato-Stomp" and "Hottest Tomato" contests, soapbox derby, pageant and much more!

Late AUGUST

Tecumseh Corn Festival. Lacasse Park, Tecumseh. 519-735-4756 www.tecumseh.ca
Fantastic entertainment for all — great tasting food (including delicious buttered corn-on-the-cob), parade, pageant, festival tents, carnival rides, live performances, food vendors, creative arts and crafts!

Art by the River. Fort Malden National Historic Site, Amherstburg. 519-736-2826
www.gibsonartgallery.com
Essex County's oldest arts and crafts show. Stroll the beautiful grounds. 150 artisans from across Ontario create an exceptional exhibition.

Early SEPTEMBER

Harrow Fair, Harrow Fairgrounds.
519-738-3262
www.harrowfair.com
This favourite "end of summer" event features competition in livestock, produce, horticulture and baking divisions. Arts and crafts, carnival rides, live entertainment, food and more!

Labour Day Weekend Windsor Karting Grand Prix. Downtown Windsor.
www.spkc.ca
A high profile street karting race at the Downtown Windsor waterfront.

Shores of Erie International Wine Festival, Grounds of Fort Malden National Historic Site, Amherstburg. 519-730-1001
www.soewinefestival.com
"A toast to the tastes!" The area's finest wineries, eateries and musicians come together on the shores of the scenic Detroit River.

Mid SEPTEMBER

Olde Sandwich Towne Festival, Mill and Russell Streets, Windsor. 519-728-1103
www.ostf.ca
Arts and heritage festival featuring a parade, activities and entertainment for young and old, antique boat/car exhibition, historic tours and reenactments, fireworks.

Festival of Hawks
Holiday Beach Conservation Area, Amherstburg.
519-776-5209 Ext. 308
www.erca.org

Late SEPTEMBER

Ruthven Apple Festival, Colasanti's Tropical Gardens, Ruthven. 519-776-6483
www.communitylivingessex.org
Musical entertainment, midway rides and games for children, the Apple Festival Car Show, craft and food vendors, parade, the Farmers' Market and more!

Essex-Kent Cage Bird Society Show, Exhibition & Fair, Fogolar Furlan Udine Bldg., Windsor. 519- 948-6398
www.essexkentcbs.com
North American breeders exhibiting canaries, finches, softbills, cockatiels, lovebirds, parrots and budgerigars, competing in various categories. Qualified, sanctioned judges, vendors on site. Spectators welcome!

OCTOBER

Migration Festival, Jack Miner Sanctuary, Lakeside Park and Kingsville High School, Kingsville. 519-733-2123
www.migrationfestival.ca
Weekend honouring Jack Miner, heritage and bird migration in Kingsville. Events include the outdoor show, market place, parade and children's events, plus a special anniversary celebration!

HOCKtoberfest Female Hockey Festival, South Windsor Arena, Forest Glade Arena, WFCU Centre (Windsor) and Vollmer Complex (Lasalle) 519- 816-8235
www.hocktoberfest.com
Over 80 teams from around the globe compete and participate in festivities, displays, clinics, manufacturers' exhibits, demos, contests and special events all celebrating women in hockey.

NOVEMBER

Windsor International Film Festival, Palace Cinemas, Lakeshore Cinemas, Art Gallery of Windsor. 519- 255-6530
www.windsorfilmfestival.ca
Bringing the best in Canadian and world cinema to southwestern Ontario, the Windsor International Film Festival presents a 10-day fall festival and year-round cinema series.

WINTER

Fantasy of Lights, Lakeside Park, Kingsville.
519-733-2123
www.fantasyoflights.ca
A spectacular viewing of holiday lights, displays and music throughout the winter season, featuring opening ceremonies, dinner with Santa, Santa Claus parade and New Year's Eve night!

DECEMBER

Windsor Santa Claus Parade, Riverside Dr. W. from Rankin to Brock Street. 519- 254-2880
www.santaparade.org
Enjoy this holiday tradition featuring floats, entertainers and bands from across Windsor, Michigan, Ohio, and Ontario as they march to the beat of Christmas tunes. Start time 6pm.

SIMILARITIES AND DIFFERENCES BETWEEN CANADA AND THE USA

"Facts are stubborn things; and whatever may be our wishes, our inclination, or the dictates of our passions, they cannot alter the state of facts and evidence." — John Adams

The following table consists of facts and statistics concerning Canada and the United States, as recent as January 1, 2007 (unless otherwise indicated). Source: www.unitednorthamerica.org

	CANADA	UNITED STATES	ANALYSIS
	Geography and Population Makeup		
Total Area[1]	9,984,670 sq km 3,855,103 sq mi	9,826,630 sq km 3,794,083 sq mi	Canada has 1.6% more area.
Land Area[1]	9,093,507 sq km 3,511,023 sq mi	9,161,923 sq km 3,537,438 sq mi	US has 0.7% more land.
Renewable Freshwater Supply[2]	2,901 cu km (1980)	2,478 cu km (1985)	Canada has 14.6% more renewable freshwater.
Energy Supply per capita (Equivalent Oil) (2004)[3]	8.06 tonnes	7.72 tonnes	Canada has 4.2% more energy per capita.
Major Protected Areas as % of Total Area (land) (2005)[3]	8.7%	25.1%	US has 2.9 times more naturally protected areas.
Population	33,390,141	301,139,947	US has 9.0 times more people.
Age Structure[1]	0-14 yrs: 17.3% 15-64 yrs: 69.2% 65 yrs +: 13.5%	0-14 yrs: 20.2% 15-64 yrs: 67.2% 65 yrs +: 12.6%	US has a slightly younger population.
Population Growth Rate[1]	0.87% growth	0.89% growth	US has a slightly higher growth rate.
Birth rate[1]	10.8 births/1,000 population	14.1 births/1,000 population	US has a 23.4% higher birth rate.
Death Rate[1]	7.9 deaths/1,000 population	8.3 deaths/1,000 population	US has a 4.8% higher death rate.
Net Migration Rate[1]	5.8 migrants/1,000 population	3.0 migrants/1,000 population	Canada has a 1.9 times higher migrant rate.
Sex Ratio[1]	0.98 male/female	0.97 male/female	Canada has a 1% greater male population.
Life Expectancy[1]	80.3 years	78.0 years	Canada has a 2.9% higher life expectancy.
Ethnic Groups	White: 85.6% Asian: 8.9% Native: 3.3% Black: 2.2% (2001)[4]	White: 81.7% Black: 13.4% Asian: 4.0% Native: 1.0% (2000)[5]	Canada has 3.9% more Whites, 2.2 times more Asians, and 3.3 times more Natives. US has 6.1 times more Blacks. All per capita. See below for further information.
Languages (spoken at home)	English: 70.7% French: 22.7% Spanish: 0.3% (2001)[4]	English: 82.1% Spanish: 10.7% French: 0.8% (2000)[5]	US has slightly more English speakers, and 35.7 times more Spanish speakers. Canada has 28.4 times more French speakers. All per capita.
Religions[1]	Roman Catholic: 42.6% Protestant: 23.3% Other: 18.1% None: 16% (2001)	Protestant: 52% Roman Catholic: 24% Other: 14% None: 10% (2002)	Canada has 18.6% more Roman Catholics, and 6% more non-religious people. US has 28.7 % more Protestants. All per capita.

	CANADA	UNITED STATES	ANALYSIS
		Economy	
GDP	$1.287 trillion USD[4]	$13.458 trillion USD[6]	US has 11.0 times greater GDP.
GDP per capita	$38,544 USD[4]	$44,690 USD[6]	US has 13.8% greater GDP per capita.
GDP growth rate (2005)[3]	1 year: 2.9% 10 year: 3.3%	1 year: 3.2% 10 year: 3.3%	US GDP is growing 0.3% more over a 1 year period. GDP rates are growing by the same rate over a 10 year period.
Personal Disposable Income per capita[7]	$22,491 USD	$31,794 USD	US has a 29.3% higher disposable income.
Unemployment Rate (2005)[3]	6.8%	5.1%	Canada has a 1.3 times higher unemployment rate.
Trading Partners — Exports / Imports	US: 79.2% / 65.5% UK: 2.5% / 2.4% Japan: 2.3% / 2.9%	Canada: 22.2% / 16.4% Mexico: 12.9% / 10.7%[5] China: 5.3% / 15.5%	US is Canada's largest trading partner. Canada is US's largest trading partner.
Government Surplus/Deficit as % of GDP (2004)[3]	0.68%	-4.72%	Canada's lending represents 0.68% of its GDP. US borrowing represents 4.72% of its GDP.
Government Debt as % of GDP (2004)[3]	72.2%	64%	Canada has 8.2 greater marketable debt as expressed in % of GDP.
Military Expenditure as % of GDP[1]	1.1% (2005)	4.1% (2005)	US spends 3.7 times more money on military as expressed in % of GDP.
Research & Development as % of GDP (2005)[3]	1.99%	2.68%	US spends 1.3 times more money on R&D as expressed in % of GDP.
ODA Development AID Expenditure as % of GNI (2005)[3]	0.34%	0.22%	Canada publicly spends 1.5 times more on development AID as expressed in % of GNI.
Educational Expenditure as % of GDP (2004)[3]	6.1%	7.3%	US spends 1.2% more money on education as expressed in % of GDP.
Health Care Expenditure as % of GDP (2004)[3]	9.9%	15.3	US spends 1.5 times more money on health care as expressed in % of GDP.
Total Government Expenditure as % of GDP (2004)[3]	40.5%	36.4%	Canada spends 4.1% more money in total as expressed in % of GDP.
Total Tax Receipts as % of GDP (2003)[3]	33.8%	25.6%	Canada collects 1.3 times more taxes as expressed in % of GDP.
Consumer Price Index annual change[3]	2.5%	4.3%	US has 1.7 times greater CPI.
Exchange Rate[8]	$0.882 USD	$1.134 CAD	US dollar is 11.8% greater in value.

Sources: 1. CIA World Factbook (http://www.cia.gov/cia/publications/factbook/) 2. Human Resources Development Canada (http://www.hrdc-drhc.gc.ca/) 3. IMD International (http://www.imd.ch/) 4. Nobel e-Museum (http://www.nobel.se/) 5. OECD (http://www.oecd.org/) 6. Statistics Canada (http://www.statcan.ca/) 7. United Nations Human Development Report (http://www.undp.org/hdro/) 8. United States Census Bureau (http://www.census.gov/) 9. United States Department of Labor (http://www.dol.gov/) 10. World Bank (http://www.worldbank.org/) 11. X-Rates (http://www.x-rates.com/)

CROSSING THE WINDSOR/DETROIT BORDER

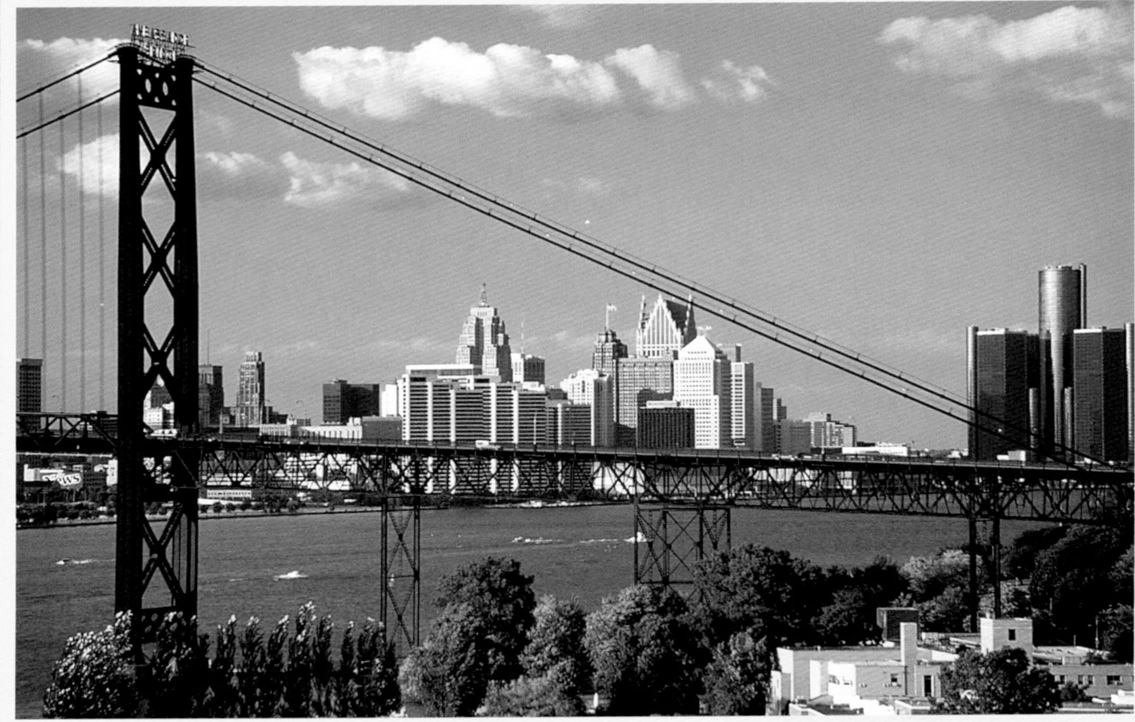

The Ambassador Bridge and Detroit skyline. *Vito Palmisano, courtesy Metro Detroit Convention & Visitors Bureau.*

I.D. When Crossing the Border

Resources to check:
- CrossingMadeEasy.com
- US Department of State www.travel.state.gov
- US Customs & Border Protection www.cbp.gov within USA 1-877-CBP-5511 outside USA 703-526-4200
- Canada Border Services Agency www.cbsa.gc.ca within Canada 1-800-461-9999 outside Canada 204-983-3500

- Visitors to Canada may be eligible for a a rebate of the Provincial sales Tax. 1-800-263-7965 (in Canada) 905-432-3431 (outside Canada) or www.rev.gov.on.ca

- Criminal record? Contact your nearest Canadian embassy, high commission or consulate or visit Citizenship and Immigration Canada's website: www.cic.gc.ca

- Allowance for Americans returning to USA: 313-442-0377 or visit: www.cbp.gov

- Criminal record? Call the Department of Homeland Security, Immigration & Customs Enforcement at 313-568-6042.

- Kids? Bring identification and, if applicable, a custody order.

- Take the prescription for your medication and glasses/contacts.

- Automobile insurance handy?

- Pets vaccinations up to date?

- Allowances for Canadians returning to Canada. Within Canada call 1-800-461-9999, outside Canada 506-636-5064 www.cbsa.gc.ca

"I Declare" is a free booklet for Canadians travelling outside Canada. 1-800-461-9999 www.cbsa.gc.ca

American Embassy in Ottawa, Canada
- 1-613-688-5335

U.S. Customs and Border Protection
- 1-800-973-2867 or 313-442-0368

Canadian Department of Foreign Affairs
- 1-800-267-8376 or 613-944-4000

Canadian Consulate in Detroit
- 313-567-2340

Canadian Consulate in Atlanta
- 404-532-2000

Canadian Consulate in Miami
- 305-579-1600

Michigan

Travel Michigan
300 N. Washington Square, Lansing, MI 48913
1-888-78-GREAT (1-888-784-7328) **www.michigan.org**

The State of Michigan

Motown, cars, sports, shopping, theater and museums! Michigan is also the most popular outdoor summer destination in the Midwest. Four Great Lakes surround the State of Michigan's borders.

It has more than 11,000 inland lakes and 36,000 miles of rivers and streams, 18 million acres of forest, hundreds of beaches, and 800 public golf courses! There are so many year-round activity choices, it's no wonder the Michigan Tourism line is very busy. Call anyway!

Michigan State Parks

With 99 State Parks to choose from in Michigan, you'll get what you are looking for, whether that may be lakeshore, sand-dunes, forest, or rocky crags! Enjoy camping, swimming, canoeing, hiking, horseback riding, hunting, fishing, skiing, and snowmobiling. It's a good idea to get camping reservations, especially in the summer. Some of the State Parks rent minicabins and rustic cabins. Again, it's best to make a reservation.

While camping in Michigan, I had the most memorable afternoon. We were dropped off upstream by the camp owner with a rental canoe ($5), and we half-floated, half-paddled (sometimes backwards!) our way for several hours down the Indian River back to our campsite. The willowy overhanging branches, and this slow, shallow, wispy river was as relaxing as a daydream.

Uniquely Michigan Terms

- "Upnorth" is used loosely for the great outdoors.
- "Trolls" is Upper Peninsula slang for lower peninsula resident. A troll is a creature that dwells below a bridge, and lower peninsula residents live south of the Mackinac Bridge, which links the two peninsulas!
- "Yoopers" or "U-Piners" is slang for Upper Peninsula residents.
- "Fudgies" refers to tourists, most especially the day-trippers.
- "Vernors" is used for ginger ale.

Michigan Trivia

Michigan's name is derived from the two Indian words michi-gama meaning "great lake."

Michigan's State motto is "Si quaeris peninsulam amoenam circumspice" - "if you seek a pleasant peninsula, look about you."

Detroit River and Ambassador Bridge at night.
Vito Palmisano, courtesy Metro Detroit Convention and Visitors Bureau

Michigan was admitted to the Union on January 26,1837, as the 26th state. State capital, Lansing, since 1847.

Michigan is in the heart of the largest body of surface freshwater in the world: the Great Lakes, which contain one-fifth of the world's supply.

The shore line of Michigan is 3,200 miles long and is the longest of any state except Alaska. It is longer than the entire Atlantic seaboard of the United States.

Approximately one-quarter of that Great Lakes shoreline is open to the public as beaches or other access sites.

Approximately 40,000 square miles of Great Lakes waters are within Michigan's borders.

Some 11,000 inland lakes dot Michigan's two peninsulas.

More than 36,000 miles of rivers and streams lace the state.

It is not surprising, then, that Michigan leads the nation in the number of pleasure boats registered: approximately 906,000.

Fifty-three percent of the state, or 19.3 million acres, is forested, constituting the fifth largest timberland in the nation (behind Georgia, Oregon, Alabama and North Carolina). If "Timberland" is defined as areas capable of supporting a viable timber industry, Michigan's timberland grew 6 percent from 1980 to 1993—the first increase since European settlement.

More than 100 species of trees have been identified in the forests of Michigan and that is more than in all of Europe! More than 90 percent of the Upper Peninsula's land is forested. Maples, aspen, oak, evergreen, and elms and other species are cut and shipped throughout the nation in all seasons.

Michigan proudly leads the nation in public golf courses with more than 800 currently open, and it also leads year after year in the number of courses opening and under construction with about 30 new ones per year.

With approximately 40 ski resorts, Michigan is one of the leading ski states.

Michigan is a leader for the nation in the number of registered snowmobiles (approximately 270,300).

More than 6,000 miles of snowmobile trails stitch most of the state together into a winter network and thousands of kilometers of cross-country ski trails add to the variety.

Despite the millions of acres of forests, resorts, golf courses, and major cities, Michigan remains one of America's leading agricultural states. It is second only to California in the variety of food and fiber crops grown within its borders with approximately 50 varieties.

Michigan leads the nation in the production of tart cherries, blueberries, and dry edible beans.

Michigan's State flower is the **Apple Blossom.** The State fish is the **Brook Trout. Petoskey** is the State stone and **Isle Royale Greenstone** is the State gem. The State tree is the **White Pine.** The **Robin** is the State bird. **Kalkaska** was adopted in 1990 as the official State soil type.

Detroit
MICHIGAN

Detroit Metro Convention & Visitors Bureau
211 W. Fort St., Suite 1000, Detroit, Michigan 48226
313-202-1999 or 1-800-DETROIT **www.visitdetroit.com**

Metro Detroit

In 1701, Antoine de la Mothe Cadillac traveled up the straits that would later be called the Detroit River. He liked the harbor and the fertile land and staked the French Flag on the shore. The name "Detroit" comes from the French "Detroit," meaning "of the straits."

By Detroit's 200th anniversary, there were almost one-quarter of a million residents, and the city was large enough to be granted a major league baseball franchise in 1901 when the American League was formed. Henry Ford's assembly line put the city on the road to prosperity. Just 30 years later, the population of Detroit had multiplied five times. Today, more than 4 million people live in Metropolitan Detroit.

Detroit's grand skyline is best viewed from the riverfront parks of its sister city across the border. Did you know that Detroit is actually *north* of Windsor? The bends in the straits have given elementary geography teachers headaches on both sides of the border!

The city was cleverly designed by Judge Woodward to resemble the spokes of a wheel. The main spokes shoot off from downtown at diagonal angles, which is great for moving traffic, but sometimes a little confusing. Before you visit, call the number above and order a free map of Detroit and all the attractions.

Downtown ethnic neighborhoods, Mexicantown, Dearborn (Arab-American), Hamtramck (Polish), Corktown and Greektown offer a great selection of authentic dishes.

The Fox Theatre, City Theater and Fillmore Detroit, the Gem Theater and Orchestra Hall grace the theater district.

I highly recommend the celebrated **Detroit Institute of Arts** with the huge bronze statue of *The Thinker* by Rodin out front. The Institute is found in **Detroit's University Cultural Centre** along with the **Detroit Public Library,** the **Detroit Historical Museum,** The **Charles H. Wright Museum of African American History** and the **Detroit Science Center.**

Area Attractions

Belle Isle
Year-round 1,000-acre park has the Belle Isle Nature Zoo, conservatory, Great Lakes Museum, picnic and recreational activities. Annual floral shows. Take bridge to East Grand Blvd. 313-852-4075. www.fobi.org/attractions.htm

Detroit Historical Museum
1840s, 1870s and 1900s "Streets of Detroit" scenes. 100 years of automotive history in the Motor City exhibit, costume, and desin gallery & library. 5401 Woodward Ave. 313-833-1805. www.detroithistorical.org

Detroit Institute of Arts
More than 100 galleries, one of the largest and most significant collections in the US. On display is Vincent van Gogh's self-portrait, the first van Gogh painting to enter a US museum collection. The museum underwent a renovation and expansion that was completed in 2007. Largest collection of Italian art outside of Italy. Ancient artifacts. Armor collection. Guided tour. 5200 Woodward Ave. 313-833-7900 www.dia.org

Detroit Science Center
Imax Dome Theater. Live science demonstrations and hands-on exhibit galleries. Focusing on space, life and physical science. One of the 10 largest science museums in the country. 5020 John R St. 313-577-8400 www.detroitsciencecenter.org

Motown Historical Museum
Original recording studio, artifacts and photographs. Guided tours available. 2648 W. Grand Blvd. 313-875-2264 www.motownmuseum.com

Charles H. Wright Museum of African American History
World's largest museum devoted to African American heritage and culture. 315 East Warren Ave. 313-494-5800 www.maah-detroit.org

Pewabic Pottery Gallery
National historic landmark recognizes the unique art form developed in Detroit in 1903. Pewabic tiles and vessels are in buildings throughout the nation. Archives, collections, education, giftshop. 10125 E. Jefferson Ave. 313-822-0954 www.pewabic.com

Holocaust Memorial Center
Research center documents the horror of the Holocaust and pre-Holocaust events. Free admission. 28123 Orchard Lake Rd., Farmington Hills. 248-553-2400 www.holocaustcenter.org

Cranbrook Institute of Science
One of the nation's greatest architectural treasures houses one of the world's leading centers for art, education and science. Natural history, mineral collection, planetarium, physics hall and art gallery. 39221 Woodward Ave., Bloomfield. www.cranbrook.edu

MotorCity Casino
Gaming, deluxe new hotel, dining and entertainment. 2901 Grand River Ave., Detroit. 866-782-9622 www.motorcitycasino.com

Edsel and Eleanor Ford House
87 acres on Lake St. Clair with a Cotswold-style house and original antiques and art collection. 1100 Lake Shore Rd., Grosse Pointe Shores. 313-884-4222 www.fordhouse.org

Meadow Brook Theater
The fourth largest historic house museum in the US, this 110-room, 88,000 sq ft Tudor-revival style mansion was the residence of Matilda Dodge (widow of auto pioneer John Dodge) and her second husband, lumber broker Alfred G. Wilson. A four million dollar home in 1929. Priceless art treasures. 7 plays annually. Tours at 1:30 p.m. 2200 N. Squirrel Rd., Rochester. 248-370-2100

Henry Ford Museum & Greenwich Village
America's most visited indoor/outdoor museum details America's evolution from rural to industrial superpower. Exhibits on transportation, communication, home arts, lighting, power & shop machinery and entertainment. Historic homes and workplaces of Edison, Ford, Wright Brothers and George Washington Carver on display in the village. Imax Theater. Year-round 9-5. 20900 Oakwood Blvd., Dearborn. 313-271-1620. www.thehenryford.org

Dine, shop, play and stay and tour the 73 story GM Renaissance Center. GM's global headquarters and location of GMnext showroom. 313-568-5600 www.gmrencen.com

Automotive Hall of Fame
Interactive exhibits recognize accomplishments of leaders in the automotive industry such as Dr. Porsche, Henry Ford and Soichiro Honda. Next to Henry Ford Museum. 313-240-4000. www.automotivehalloffame.org

Detroit Zoological Park
Animal lovers' paradise. Indoor/outdoor environments. 8450 W. 10 Mile Rd., Royal Oak. 248-541-5717 www.detroitzoo.org

Henry Ford Estate
National landmark called "Fair Lane" by the Ford family. Exhibits. Elaborate grounds. 4901 Evergreen Rd., U of Michigan, Dearborn. Tours. Memorial Day to Oct. 10 –7. 313-593-5590 www.henryfordestate.org

Greektown Casino
Slot machines, gaming and dining. 555 Lafayette Ave., Detroit. 888-771-4386 www.greektowncasino.com

MGM Grand Detroit Casino
Gaming, new hotel, celebrity chef restaurants and entertainment. 1777 Third St., Detroit. 1-877-888-2121 www.mgmgranddetroit.com

Morley Candy Makers
Morley Candy Makers. Free tour. www.morleycandy.com

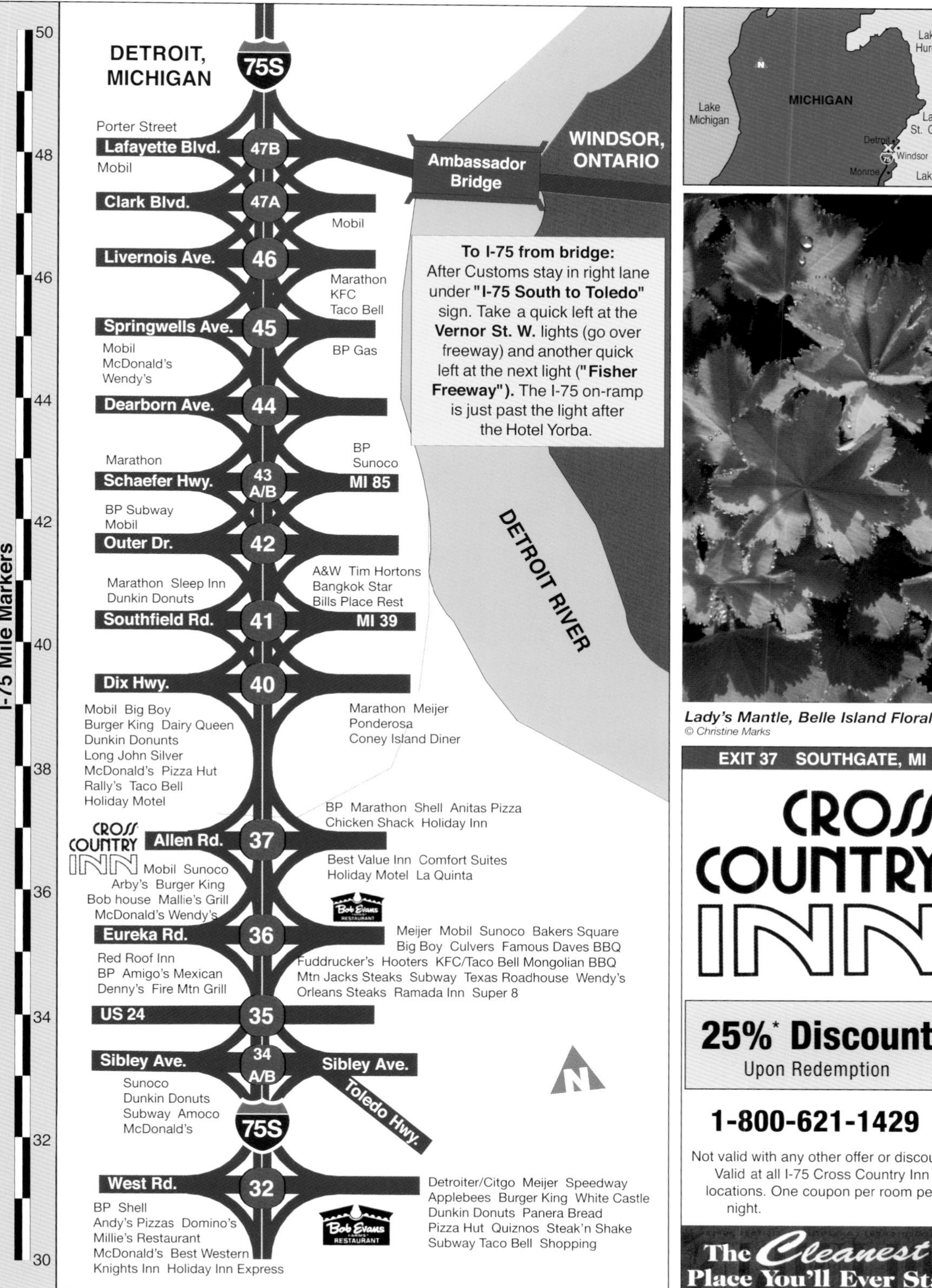

To I-75 from bridge:
After Customs stay in right lane under **"I-75 South to Toledo"** sign. Take a quick left at the **Vernor St. W.** lights (go over freeway) and another quick left at the next light (**"Fisher Freeway"**). The I-75 on-ramp is just past the light after the Hotel Yorba.

Lady's Mantle, Belle Island Floral
© Christine Marks

Detroit
MICHIGAN

Detroit Metro Convention & Visitors Bureau
211 W. Fort St., Suite 1000, Detroit, Michigan 48226
313-202-1999 or 1-800-DETROIT **www.visitdetroit.com**

Trivia

Detroit is known for its contributions to the automotive industry. So, it probably comes as no surprise to you that Detroit installed the first:

- traffic light (1915),
- the first mile of paved concrete road (1909), and
- the first urban freeway in the America (1942).

But I'll bet that you didn't know that Detroit also:

- has the oldest state fair in the U.S., the **Michigan State Fair** (since 1849). Held late Aug. to early Sept.
- is the potato chip capital of the world
- has the nation's oldest municipal aquarium on **Belle Isle** which is also the largest island park within any city
- has the only floating post office in the world, the **J.W. Westcott II**
- is the softball capital of the world
- is the only geographic location where Canada is south of the U.S.
- has the tallest hotel in N. America, **The Detroit Marriott Renaissance Center** which is also the largest privately-financed project in the world.
- has the largest annual fireworks display in the world
- is home of the typewriter, patented in 1829 by Detroiter William A. Burt
- developed the phrase "the real McCoy," based on Detroit inventor Elijah McCoy
- hosts North America's largest free jazz festival, the **Detroit International Jazz Festival** (Labor Day weekend)
- was the first city in the U.S. with individual telephone numbers (1879)
- is the site of the first electrical power plant, the Detroit Edison Company.
- has the largest NAACP membership of any U.S. city
- has the most registered bowlers in the U.S.

The Motor City

MAJOR INDUSTRY. Internationally known for automobile manufacturing and trade, the world headquarters for General Motors Corp., Ford Motor Co., Chrysler Corp., and Volkswagen of America are located in Metropolitan Detroit, Michigan.

The area also ranks as a leader in the production of: paints, non-electrical machinery and automation equipment for the pharmaceutical industry, rubber products, synthetic resins and garden seed.

National and international corporations headquartered here include: the Budd Company, Stroh Brewery Company, American National Resources and Federal Mogul. These companies help employ more than two million Detroiters. Detroit recently celebrated its American Automobile Centennial year. Tributes to modern transportation are everywhere: the **Henry Ford Museum, the Historical Museum, the Automotive Hall of Fame,** and Detroit's newest attraction, The **Spirit of Ford.**

Love fast cars? Try the *Detroit Grand Prix* on Belle Island.

For the classic beauties, attend the exclusive *Concours D'Elegance* car show at Meadowbrook Hall.

Want to see the new cars and concept cars? Don't miss the *International Auto Show* at Cobo Hall!

Henry Ford Museum & Greenfield Village

Established in 1929, **Henry Ford Museum and Greenfield Village®** is the most visited indoor/outdoor historical complex in America. With holdings of more than one million objects and 26 million documents, prints and photographs, it welcomes more than one million visitors annually.

The **Museum** celebrates resourcefulness and innovation with major collections in automobiles, home appliances, factory machinery, glassware, pewter and dishes.

Greenfield Village, adjacent to the Museum, is an 90-acre outdoor museum that features a collection of historic American homes, workplaces and community buildings that tell the story of both the famous and the not.

Henry Ford Museum, Detroit, MI.
Courtesy Metro Detroit Convention and Visitors Bureau.

Henry Ford Museum's permanent exhibitions include "The Automobile in American Life," a 60,000 square foot multi-media exhibition with 100 historically significant vehicles plus an original 1946 diner and 1950s drive-in movie. The village includes such national treasures as Thomas Edison's Menlo Park laboratory complex where more than 400 inventions were produced; the bicycle shop where the Wright brothers designed and built their first airplane; and the house where Noah Webster wrote his American dictionary.

The Henry Ford Museum and Greenfield Village® have long been one of my family's favorite destinations. With the new **IMAX®, Spirit of Ford,** and **Automobile Hall of Fame** buildings on the same attractions complex, I can't urge you strongly enough to visit the **Henry Ford Museum & Greenfield Village®.** 20900 Oakwood Blvd., Dearborn, MI 48121. 313-271-1620

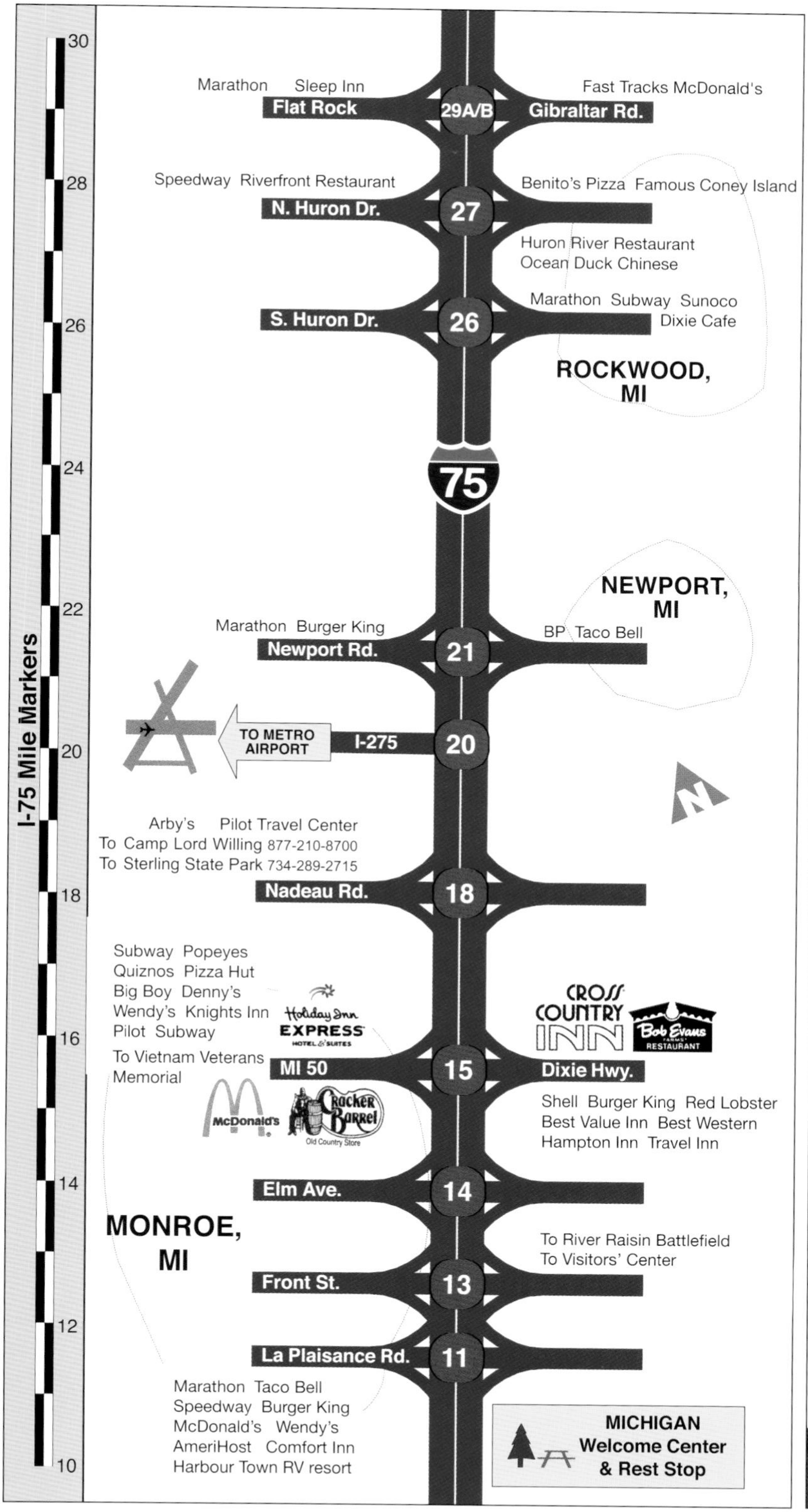

I-75 Mile Markers
30
28
26
24
22
20
18
16
14
12
10
Marathon Sleep Inn
Flat Rock
29A/B
Gibraltar Rd.
Fast Tracks McDonald's
Speedway Riverfront Restaurant
N. Huron Dr.
27
Benito's Pizza Famous Coney Island
Huron River Restaurant
Ocean Duck Chinese
Marathon Subway Sunoco
Dixie Cafe
S. Huron Dr.
26
ROCKWOOD, MI
75
NEWPORT, MI
Marathon Burger King
Newport Rd.
21
BP Taco Bell
TO METRO AIRPORT
I-275
20
N
Arby's Pilot Travel Center
To Camp Lord Willing 877-210-8700
To Sterling State Park 734-289-2715
Nadeau Rd.
18
Subway Popeyes
Quiznos Pizza Hut
Big Boy Denny's
Wendy's Knights Inn
Pilot Subway
To Vietnam Veterans Memorial
Holiday Inn EXPRESS HOTEL & SUITES
CROSS COUNTRY INN
Bob Evans RESTAURANT
MI 50
15
Dixie Hwy.
McDonald's
Cracker Barrel Old Country Store
Shell Burger King Red Lobster
Best Value Inn Best Western
Hampton Inn Travel Inn
Elm Ave.
14
MONROE, MI
To River Raisin Battlefield
To Visitors' Center
Front St.
13
La Plaisance Rd.
11
Marathon Taco Bell
Speedway Burger King
McDonald's Wendy's
AmeriHost Comfort Inn
Harbour Town RV resort
MICHIGAN Welcome Center & Rest Stop

Lake Huron
N
MICHIGAN
Lake Michigan
Lake St. Clair
Detroit
Windsor
Monroe
75
Lake Erie

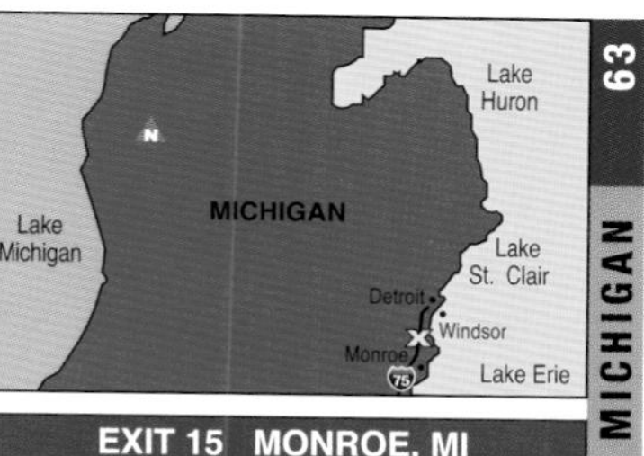

Detroit
MICHIGAN

DetroitMetro Convention & Visitors Bureau
211 W. Fort St., Suite 1000, Detroit, Michigan 48226
313-202-1999 or 1-800-DETROIT **www.visitdetroit.com**

DETROIT ZOO. While the Zoo is open year-round, we prefer to bring the girls to the zoo in the winter so we get a little exercise walking from one out-door habitat to another. Then we look forward to blankets of warm air as we enter indoor exhibits such as the free-flight aviary, primate house and reptile building.

DETROIT ART MUSEUM. Highlights of the collection include **Vincent van Gogh's** *Self Portrait*, *The Thinker* by **Auguste Rodin** and **Bruegel's** *The Wedding Dance.* I've been coming here for years! This past trip we focused on the excellent collection of armor, the European exhibit rooms, and the Egyptian fine art. We had a healthy lunch in the courtyard and enjoyed chatting with a cheerful custodian who not only knew the place like the back of his hand, but also delighted us with his gallery of stories.

DETROIT SCIENCE CENTRE. With more than 50 interactive exhibits in the Discovery Theatre, be prepared to learn about everything from space exploration to the microscopic world.

NEW! FORD FIELD**,** a $300 million domed stadium for the Detroit Lions is located next to brand new **COMERICA PARK,** the $300 million, Detroit Tigers open-air stadium. The two structures co-anchor an exciting new sports and entertainment district built in Detroit's existing theater district anchored on the Fox Theatre on Woodward Ave.

SOMETHING DIFFERENT. Most children get a kick out of camping. Imagine what a hero you'd be if you took them camping in a tepee! At least 6 Michigan State Parks rent the 20-foot-tall, canvas replicas of the traditional Native American structures. They sleep four. Don't worry about being on the ground: the tepees are equipped with soft cots and pads. 1-888-78-GREAT

OH SUGAR! Michigan is known for its many sugar bushes and maple syrup festivals. I'll never forget the delightfully surprised look on my oldest daughter's face when, for the first time, she licked the maple sap that she got on her finger "right from that tree, Mummy!"

Detroit Area Special Events

African World Festival
Detroit's largest ethnic festival presents cultures from around the world that are populated by people of African descent. 180 Artists' Marketplace, free concerts, international cuisine! 3rd weekend in Aug. at the Charles H. Wright Museum of African American History. 313-494-5853

America's Thanksgiving Parade®
2.2 mile stretch of Woodward Ave. from Mack Ave. to Jefferson Ave. 313-923-7400

Downtown Hoedown
World's largest free country music festival. Hart Plaza. Mid-May.

Chrysler Jeep Detroit APBA Gold Cup
Four-day "Indy 500" of boat-racing featuring world's fastest boats in five classes. Largest single-day attendance for a sporting event in the U.S. line the Detroit River to watch the hydroplanes often exceed 225 mph. Early July. Ticket sales: 800-359-7760

Comerica City Fest
Features food from 40 Detroit restaurants, demonstrations plus live entertainment. July 4th weekend. 313-927-2700 www.comericacityfest.com

Concours D'Elegance
The who's who of the automotive world are often seen viewing or judging in this "competition of elegance" on the beautiful grounds of Meadow Brook Hall. One week in August. 248-643-8645 www.mbhconcours.org

Detroit Belle Isle Grand Prix
30 champion cars take to one of the most challenging courses in the world, the streets of the Belle Isle Park. 3 days, mid-June. 313-222-7749 www.detroitgp.com

Detroit International Jazz Festival
The largest free jazz festival in North America, the event showcases local, regional, and international jazz artists at more than 100 free, open-air concerts. Labor Day weekend at Hart Plaza on the riverfront in downtown Detroit. 313-477-1248 www.detroitjazzfest.com

International Freedom Festival. More than 50 free events on both sides of the border over a two week period celebrate Canada Day (July 1) and Independence Day (July 4). A must-see is the breath-taking Hudson's Fireworks, the world's largest annual display of its kind. More on the festival is found on pages 59 and 60. 313-923-7400

Mexicantown Mercado
Detroit's Hispanic celebration of Mexican food, music and dance. The fiesta is held in the heart of Detroit's Mexicantown, on Bagley and 21st streets, two blocks north of the Ambassador Bridge every Sunday from mid-June to the end of summer. 313-967-9898

Michigan Renaissance Festival
In the 16th-century European village of Hollygrove, costumed townspeople, artisans, minstrels and magicians provide continuous entertainment and invite onlookers to participate in the fun. $15/adults. Seven weekend from mid-Aug. to late Sept., 10 a.m.-7 p.m. Exit 106 off I-75, one mile north of Mt. Holly between Pontiac and Flint. 1-800-601-4848 or 248-634-5552 www.michrenfest.com

Michigan State Fair
In Sept. 1849, the first State Fair was held in Detroit. The fair promotes family values with wholesome, traditional attractions such as livestock shows, and the display of award-winning produce, arts and crafts. Amuse-ment Park, food, games and a free concert. Late Aug./early Sept. 1120 W. State Fair Ave. (Eight Mile Rd. and Woodward Ave.) 313-369-8250 www,michigan.gov/mistatefair

North American International Auto Show.
Known as the "Motor City," Detroit hosts one of the world's largest auto shows. Visitors get first looks at new models, production cars, prototypes, and concept cars. Approx. 60 models make their worldwide debut at the show. Held in January, at the Cobo Arena, it attracts more than 6,000 media and 700,000 visitors (including my family!) every year. 313-438-2491 www.naias.com

Detroit Red Wings
Mark Hicks, courtesy Metro Detroit Convention and Visitors Bureau

Detroit's Professional Sports.

Named the "Best Sports City" by the *Sporting News,* Detroit is home to the:

- Detroit Lions Football (313-262-2003)
- Detroit Pistons Basketball (248-377-0100)
- Detroit Red Wings Hockey (313-396-7535)
- Detroit Rocker's Indoor Soccer (313-396-7070)
- Detroit Vipers IHL (248-377-0100)
- Detroit Tigers Baseball (313-962-4000), and
- Women's Professional Basketball, the Detroit Shock (248-377-0100).

MICHIGAN Residents

BERRY GORDY JR. With an $800 loan, this young factory worker created the Motown Sound and united a group of recording artists that would become loved by the world.

ROSA PARKS. Now a Detroiter, she became the "Mother of the Civil Rights Movement" when she refused to give up her bus seat to a white person.

JOE LOUIS. The Brown Bomber, the World Heavyweight Champ of 1937, symbolized American courage and honor during WWII.

RALPH BUNCHE. The winner of the 1950 Nobel Peace Prize was responsible for successfully mediating the Arab-Israeli War (1948).

ELIJAH McCOY. 19th-century inventor whose reputation for quality craftsmanship of 78 inventions spawned the phrase "The Real McCoy."

ARETHA FRANKLIN. The Queen of Soul still lives in her hometown, Metro Detroit, where she created her singing style at her father's church.

BEN CARSON. Dr. Carson made medical history as the first neurosurgeon to successfully perform brain separation on conjoined twins.

ANITA BAKER. The Grammy-winning pop artist and diva was born, raised and still makes her home in Detroit.

COLEMAN A. YOUNG. In 1973, the Tuskegee Airman became the first black mayor of Detroit. His term lasted for 20 years. Mr. Young was also a State Senator, civil and labor rights activist.

JUDY GARLAND
GILDA RADNER
TED NUGENT
THOMAS HEARNS
MARVELETTES
CASEY KASEM
STEVIE WONDER
ELLEN BURSTYN
DANNY THOMAS
GREEN HORNET RADIO SHOW
LONE RANGER RADIO SHOW
PIPER LAURIE
KIM HUNTER
ED MCMAHON
SMOKEY ROBINSON
DIANA ROSS
MARSHALL CRENSHAW
WALLY COX
ROBERT WAGNER
ROBIN WILLIAMS
FOUR TOPS
SUPREMES
ANITA BAKER
SELMA BLAIR
IGGY POP

TOM SKERRITT
SUZI QUATRO
BILL HALEY
MARTIN MILNER
DELLA REESE
DICK MARTIN
SONNY BONO
MARLO THOMAS
FRANCIS FORD COPPOLA
ALEX KARRAS
LEE MAJORS
GRAND FUNK
PAM DAWBER
TOM SELLECK
SHERILYN FENN
GERALD FORD
MAX GAIL
HENRY FORD
CHARLES LINDBERGH
KID ROCK
EMINEM (b. MARSHALL MATHERS)

KIRK GIBSON
DAVID ALLEN GRIER
HARRY MORGAN
ARTE JOHNSON
JAMES EARL JONES
TIM ALLEN
BLAIR UNDERWOOD
ALICE COOPER
TEMPTATIONS
CHARLES LINDBERG
MADONNA
JULIE HARRIS
GEORGE PEPPARD
JOHNNY DESMOND
GEORGE C. SCOTT
BOB SEGER
ALICE COLTRANE
LILY TOMLIN
DEL SHANNON
BOB EUBANKS

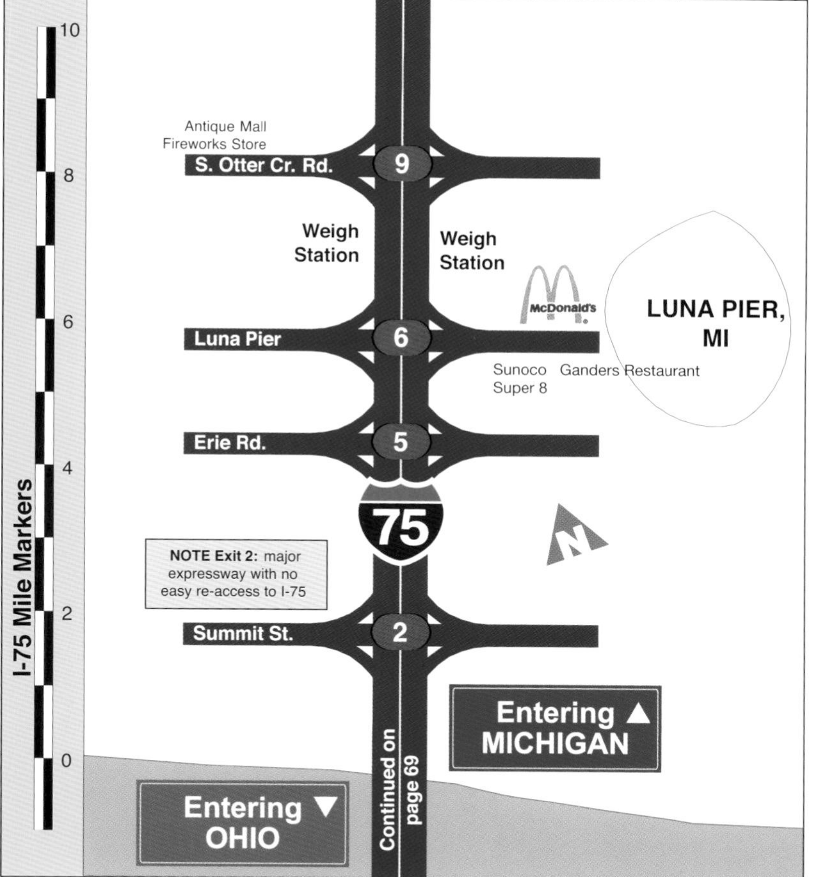

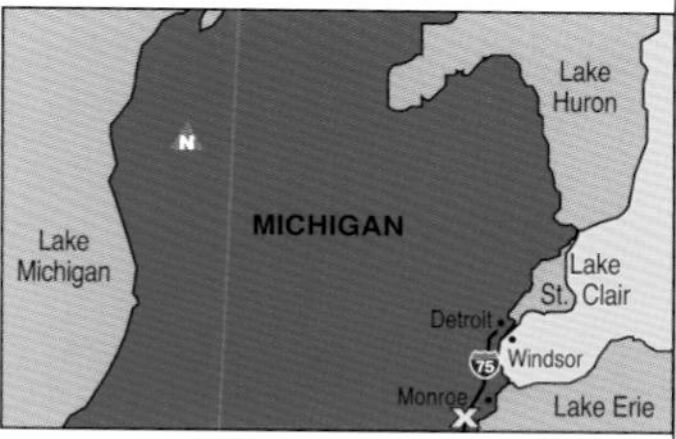

QUIZ: DATES IN DETROIT HISTORY

1. Detroit was founded in 1701 by a French explorer. What year was the city turned over to the British?
2. What year did George Washington force the British out of the city of Detroit and raise the American flag?
3. What year was all but one of Detroit's 200 buildings destroyed by fire?
4. What year was Michigan admitted to the Union as the 26th state?
5. When did Henry Ford build his first car in Detroit?
6. In what year was Detroit able to make this big boast: The Detroit Tigers won the World Series, the Detroit Lions were NFL champions AND the Detroit Red Wings won the Stanley Cup?
7. When was the first annual Detroit Grand Prix held on city streets?

ANSWERS

1. 1760 2. 1796 3. 1802
4. 1837 5. 1896 6. 1935
7. 1982

Ohio

Ohio Division of Travel and Tourism
P.O. Box 1001, Columbus OH 43216-1001
1-800-BUCKEYE **www.discoverohio.com**

History Notes

When the President of the United States signed the Ordinance of 1787, it created the "Northwest Territory," the land mass that is present-day Ohio, Indiana, Illinois, Michigan, Wisconsin and part of Minnesota.

All appointed by Congress, the territory was ruled by a governor, a secretary and three judges. In 1798, with a male adult population reaching 5,000, the settlers were allowed to elect house representatives. The first meeting was held in Cincinnati in 1799, and they elected Edward Tiffin as House Speaker and William Henry Harrison as representative to Congress.

In 1802, Congress passed an enabling bill that authorized Ohio to form a state government, and in 1803 Ohio was admitted to the union as the 17th state.

Chillicothe was chosen as the temporary capital for the new state of Ohio and so served until 1810 when the capital was moved to Zanesville. In 1812 the legislature sought a more central location and the capital was moved back to Chillicothe. Finally, the legislature decided to build a new capital on "the high banks of the Scioto River," and Columbus remains Ohio's permanent capital since 1816.

Ohio's Presidents

More U.S. presidents were born or reared in Ohio than in any other state in the union. Boasting a total of eight, Ohio has earned the nickname, "The Mother of Presidents."

State Symbols

Ohio has many symbols covering a wide variety of items found in the *Buckeye State.*

State Animal:	White-Tailed Deer
State Insect:	Ladybug
State Bird:	Cardinal
State Fossil:	Trilobite
State Motto:	"With God all things are possible"
State Flower:	Red Carnation
State Gemstone:	Flint
State Song:	"Beautiful Ohio"
State Tree:	American Horse Chestnut or the "Ohio Buckeye"
State Beverage:	Tomato Juice
State Rock Song:	"Hang On Sloopy"

OKTOBERFEST ZINZINNATI

Just one of the many festivals that take place in Ohio throughout the year.

Photo by Margaret Plowdrey Courtesy Greater Cincinnati Convention & Visitors Bureau

Trivia

Ohio is a state with many traditions and a rich history. Along with these traditions are numerous celebrated first achievements by Ohio and its famous citizenry. The collection of significant achievements would include:

- Ohio University in Athens was the first university in Ohio and the Northwest Territory (1804).
- The nation's first dental school was started in Bainbridge by Dr. John M. Harris (1824).
- The Ohio School for the Blind was the first state school for blind children.
- The Ohio State University is the largest single university campus in the country.
- The AFL (American Federation of Labor) was founded in Columbus in 1886.
- U.S. Senator James Kyle of Cedarville authored the bill that established Labor Day (1894).
- The world's first commercial chick hatchery was founded in Ohio (1897).
- The Procter & Gamble Co. in Cincinnati is the world's largest soap factory.
- The Wright Brothers of Dayton developed the first airplane.
- The National Football League was organized in Canton in 1920.
- U.S. Senator John Glenn from New Concord was the first American to orbit the earth in a spacecraft.
- Neil Armstrong of Wapakoneta was the first man on the moon.
- X-rays were first used in an operation by John Gilman in Marietta.
- The first successful blood transfusion was performed in Cleveland in 1905 by Dr. George Crile.
- W.F. Semple of Mount Vernon patented chewing gum in 1869.
- The Cincinnati *Red Stockings* became the world's first professional baseball team in 1868.
- Track star Jesse Owens, who won four gold medals during the 1936 Berlin Olympics, was born in Cleveland and graduated from The Ohio State University.

The Packard Museum, *Dayton, Ohio.*
Courtesy Ohio Department of Development, Division of Travel and Tourism

Toledo
OHIO

Greater Toledo Convention & Visitors Bureau
401 Jefferson Ave., Toledo, Ohio 43604-1067
419-321-6404 or 1-800-243-4667 (U.S./Can.) **www.dotoledo.com**

Toledo: More Than a Stopover

Your money goes a long way in Toledo. This friendly city offers more options than most: culture, sports, ethnic enclaves, shopping and festivals are accessible and affordable. So plan more than a weekend stay.

Complimenting the established Toledo destinations (**The Toledo Zoo, The Toledo Museum of Art** and the **Toledo Mud Hens Baseball Club)** is a number of attractions including the **Erie Street Market, the Center of Science and Industry** (or COSI Toledo), the **Libbey Glass Factory Outlet, Glass Pavilion, Metroparks of the Toledo area, Butterfly House, Sandpiper Boat,** tons of shopping, arts and entertainment, festivals and more.

Located in the Warehouse District at the **Erie St. Market** is the popular **Libbey Glass Factory Outlet** featuring 16,000 sq. ft. of glassware, dinnerware, flatware, glass giftware, candles and accessories. Established in 1832 and adjacent to the Erie St. Market is the Farmers Market selling fresh picked produce, baked goods, flowers, plants and poultry. Sat. & Wed. are your best bets. Libbey Glass Factory Outlet, 205 Erie St. 419-727-2374 **Libbey Glass Factory Outlet, 205 S. Erie St., 419-727-2374.**

Also downtown, overlooking the river you'll find Toledo's original brewpub, **The Maumee Bay Brewing Company.** In 1859, when **the Oliver House** opened its doors to the 10,000 citizens of Toledo, the city already had a telegraph line, a bridge across the Maumee River, and was a growing railroad center. **Oliver House** stands as the only remaining hotel designed by the architect, Isaiah Rogers, who was appointed Chief of the Bureau of Construction in the U.S. Treasury Department under President Abraham Lincoln. Today, the building is owned by the public and has been renovated to its original architectural splendor. Chief amongst its residents is the **Maumee Bay Brewing Company's Brew Pub,** which produces ales, lagers, and specialty brews in the German tradition using only four fine natural ingredients. From I-75 take US 280 South, to Summit St. and follow Summit St. to downtown Toledo. Left onto Oliver St. Left onto Broadway St. The address is 27 Broadway St., Toledo, Ohio. 419-241-1ALE

Visit The Docks for exceptional dining: Cousino`s Navy Bistro, The Real Seafood Company, Tango`s Mexican Cantina, Zia`s Italian, and Eileen`s Wine & Martini Bar.

The World Famous Toledo Mud Hens Baseball Club.
Fifth Third Field, 406 Washington St. Toledo. 419-893-9483. Courtesy Greater Toledo Convention and Visitors Bureau

Esquire magazine rates a 75-year-old Toledo restaurant among the top 40 steakhouses in the United States. Inside **Mancy's Steakhouse** door, an ancient wooden clown beckons you to come in and see the collection of treasures. Old things from all over the world will pique your curiosity and keep you sane as you take in the delicious aromas of the dishes just being served at the next table. You do need a reservation to try the famous steaks and seafood at Mancy's. At 953 Phillips St., Toledo, Ohio. 419-476-4154 www.mancys.com

Ever hear the former Toledo resident Jamie Farr's character on M*A*S*H talking about **"Tony Packo's?"** Those seven episodes gave this restaurant worldwide notoriety but there's no need for reservations! A family tradition of making Hungarian cuisine from scratch, great service, and a truly fun atmosphere has kept the locals and tourists coming in for more than 60 years. The restaurant has been restored to its original appearance in the 1930. The chili is guaranteed great! 1902 Front St., Toledo, Ohio. 419-691-6054 or 800-366-4218

Fifth Third Field *© www.dotoledo.com*

History Notes

French scout Etienne Brule visited the site of Toledo in 1615 and was met by the warring Erie Indians. This territory was claimed in 1689 by the French and later turned over to the British after the Indian War in 1763. Bet you didn't know that this area was once part of the Canadian Province of *Quebec,* from 1774 until the close of the American Revolution in 1783!

Fort Meigs, a 9-acre enclosure of massive timber and earthworks, was constructed in 1813 by William Henry Harrison. This fort successfully repelled the British invasion and earned for the Toledo area the reputation of "The Gibraltar of the Northwest."

The first white settlers into the area forbodingly known as "The Black Swamp" were Mennonites from Europe. It took ten years for them to dig the 100 miles of drainage ditches necessary to cultivate the land for farming. After the "Toledo War" in 1835, with both Michigan and Ohio claiming the territory. Congress gave it to Ohio in 1836.

In 1836, the State's first operational railroad line ran from Toledo to Adrian, Michigan, powered completely by horses.

Fort Meigs is the largest reconstructed wooden-walled fort in America. The fort along with a new museum and visitors center help bring history alive.

Toledo is known as the "Glass Capital of the World." It is also one of the largest petroleum refining locations in the nation, a busy Great Lakes port, and one of the largest rail centers in the U.S. And everyone knows that the Jeep is built in Toledo.

HOLY TOLEDO!
How did Toledo get its nickname?

- Maybe because Holy Rollers constantly criticized the city which had more saloons than churches?
- Possibly because its namesake is the "Holy City of Toledo," in Spain?
- Is it because nonviolent gangsters in the '20s and '30s were assured a refuge in the city by the Toledo police as long as they refrained from criminal activities while in the city?
- Was it the comments about poor attendance by vaudeville performers, who said every week was like Holy Week in Toledo?

Toledo
OHIO

Greater Toledo Convention & Visitors Bureau
401 Jefferson Ave., Toledo, Ohio 43604-1067
419-321-6404 or 1-800-243-4667 (U.S./Can.) **www.dotoledo.com**

Toledo is at the intersection of America's two most traveled highways, the I-75 and the I-80/90. Toledo prides itself in being affordable, accessible and accommodating. There's a world-class museum, a variety of dining adventures, nightlife options, a nationally ranked zoo, first-class performing arts venues, glass and ceramic outlets, and a long list of new attractions.

Edward Drummond Libbey started the glass industry in Toledo in 1888. When Libbey's superintendent of production, Michael Owens, devised the fully automatic glass bottle-making machine, Toledo immediately became the "Glass Capital of The World." **Owens-Illinois** (glass containers and glass tableware), **Libbey-Owens-Ford** (flat glass for automobiles and buildings), and **Owens-Corning and Manville** (fiberglass) are Toledo's main glass producers.

The **Toledo Museum of Art** is one of America's great museums. I've never been satisfied with anything less than a day, but whether you visit for an hour or longer, be prepared to lose yourself in this collection of treasures. The Great Masters are well-represented: works by El Greco, Rubens, Rembrandt, Gainsborough, Turner, van Gogh, Degas, Monet, Matisse, Picasso, Remington, Hopper and Nevelson grace the beautiful museum. There are endless collections from ancient Egypt, Greece and Rome. Marvel at the splendors of a room from a French chateau or a medieval cloister. Opened in 2006, the post-modern Glass Pavilion is the new home of the Toledo Museum of Art`s world-renowned glass collection, featuring more than 5,000 works of art from ancient to contemporary times. The Glass Pavilion received Travel & Leisures`s 2007 Design Award for Best Museum.

The Toledo Zoo is known as America's most complete zoo and it participates in the Species Survival Plan for 18 endangered species including lowland gorillas, cheetahs, orangutans, and snow leopards. The Hippoquarium is a popular attraction as is the new Kingdom of the Apes with its 17,000-square-foot outdoor Gorilla Meadow. The Toledo Zoo is one of the few places that exhibits koalas. Exotic and colorful birds sing and fly about as you make your way through the Aviary. The Formal and Rose Garden, Children's Zoo—Natures Neighborhood, hands-on exhibits, and railroad safari are delightful! Take I-75 exit 201A to 2 Hippo Way. Apr. to Sept. 10 a.m.- 5 p.m. Oct. to Mar. 10 a.m.-4 p.m. www.toledozoo.org 419-385-5721

Attractions

Old Road Dinner Train
90-minute excursions and dinner on board the 1956 GP 9 diesel electric trains in Blissfield, near Toledo. Open year-round. 517-486-5979

Arawanna II
Public departures from Rossford City Marina tours the Maumee River through Toledo, Maumee and Perrysburg. 1321 Chantilly Dr., Maumee. 419-255-6200

Cedar Point, Sandusky. 419-626-0830

Canal Experience
Learn what canal life was like aboard The Volunteer, a 60-foot replica of the time period. Providence Metropark, US 24 at SR 578, Grand Rapids, OH 419-407-9741

Culberton's Survival Center
Rescue and refuge for abused and abandoned exotic animals.
6340 Angola Rd., Holland, 419-865-3470

Farmers Market
In Warehouse District of Toledo. Apr. to Nov. Mon. to Fri. 8 a.m.-5 p.m., Sat. 6 a.m.-5 p.m. 525 Market St. 419-255-6765

Fort Meigs State Memorial
Largest walled fortification in U.S., built in 1813. Memorial Day to Labor Day, Wed. to Sat. 9:30 a.m.-5 p.m., Sun. noon-5 p.m. 2900 W. River Rd. Perrysburg. 419-874-4121.

Historic Old West End
Rich collection of late-Victorian architecture. For the 25-block neighborhood walking-tour brochure, call 419-259-5207

Isaac Ludwig Mill/Miami & Erie Canal
Working, restored saw and gristmill.
May to Oct. Wed. to Sun. and holidays 10 a.m.-5 p.m. 419-535-3050

Maumee Bay Brewing Company
Micro-brewery in the **1859 Oliver House,** in downtown Toledo. Home brew, famous homemade bread, gourmet coffee and other treats on the menu.
At 27 Broadway St. 419-243-1302

Queen of the Most Holy Rosary Cathedral
The only plateresque cathedral standing in the world today. Near the Toledo Museum of Art. 419-244-9575

SS Willis B. Boyer Museum Ship
This maritime museum in International Park, downtown Toledo, contains a restored 617-foot freighter. Call for guided tours.

Rutherford B. Hayes Presidential Center
The 19th President's Victorian mansion, presidential library and museum. Daily, year-round Mon. to Sat. 9 a.m.-5 p.m., Sun. noon-5 p.m. 1337 Hayes Ave., Fremont. 800-998-7737

Sandpiper Boat
Tours on the 100-passenger replica of an 1850s Miami & Erie Canal boat.
2144 Fordway, Toledo. 419-537-1212

Historic Sauder Farm & Craft Village
Rural Ohio in mid-1800s complete with blacksmith, potter and glassblower. Visit the quilt shop and general store.
Open daily, Apr. to Oct. On Ohio Rt. 2, Archbold. 800-590-9755

Schedel Arboretum & Gardens
Self-guided tour of 26 acres with two lakes, rose and iris garden and Japanese garden. 19255 Portage River Rd., Elmore. Open Apr. 15 to Oct. 31, Wed. to Sun. 10 a.m.-4 p.m. 419-862-3182

Toledo Botanical Garden
57 acres of roses, herbs, and wildflowers. Festival of Arts on the last weekend in June. 5403 Elmer Dr. 419-936-2986

Toledo Firefighters Museum
Vintage equipment. Summer open Sat. noon-4 p.m., winter open Sat. and Sun. noon-4 p.m. Admission is free.
918 Sylvania Ave. 419-478-3473

Toledo Museum of Art
See left for more information. Free. Tues. to Thurs. 10 a.m.-4 p.m., Fri. 10 a.m. -10 p.m., Sat 10 a.m.- 6 p.m., Sun. noon-6 p.m. 2445 Monroe St. 419-255-8000 or 800-644-6862. From I-75 exit 202A. Follow signs.

Wolcott House Museum
Stately home on the Maumee River and other buildings show life in the mid-1800s. Apr. to Dec. Wed. to Sun. 1 p.m.-4 p.m. 1031 River Rd, Maumee. 419-893-9602

The Toledo Museum of Art Peristyle
Home of Toledo Symphony Classics Series. 419-246-8000

Toledo Symphony Orchestra
Sept. to May. 419-246-8000

Toledo Opera
Valentine Theatre 419-255-7464
www.toledoopera.org

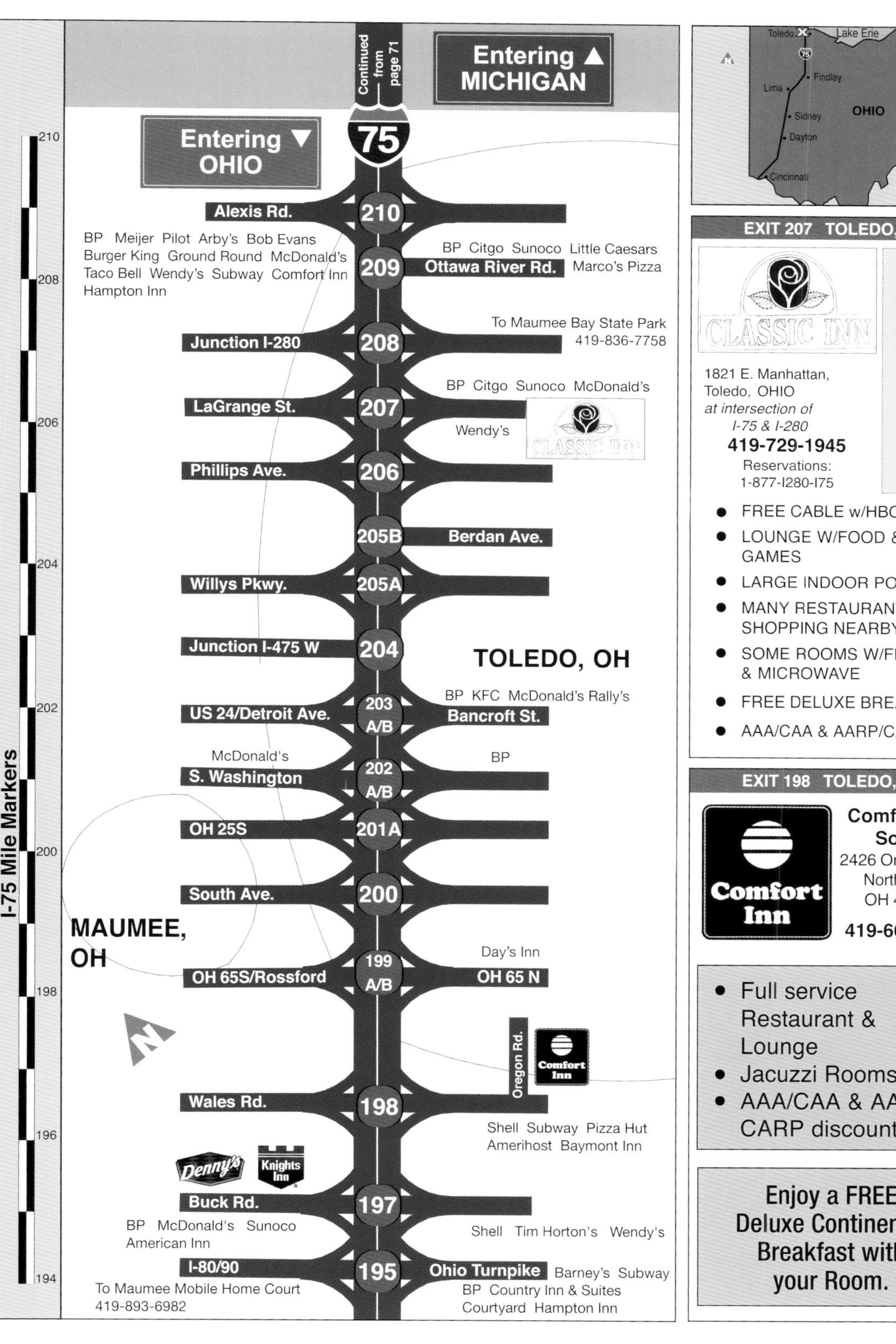
I-75 Mile Markers
210
208
206
204
202
200
198
196
194
Continued from page 71
Entering MICHIGAN
Entering OHIO
75
Alexis Rd.
210
BP Meijer Pilot Arby's Bob Evans Burger King Ground Round McDonald's Taco Bell Wendy's Subway Comfort Inn Hampton Inn
209
Ottawa River Rd.
BP Citgo Sunoco Little Caesars Marco's Pizza
Junction I-280
208
To Maumee Bay State Park 419-836-7758
LaGrange St.
207
BP Citgo Sunoco McDonald's
Wendy's
CLASSIC INN
Phillips Ave.
206
205B
Berdan Ave.
Willys Pkwy.
205A
Junction I-475 W
204
TOLEDO, OH
US 24/Detroit Ave.
203 A/B
BP KFC McDonald's Rally's
Bancroft St.
McDonald's
S. Washington
202 A/B
BP
OH 25S
201A
South Ave.
200
MAUMEE, OH
OH 65S/Rossford
199 A/B
Day's Inn
OH 65 N
N
Oregon Rd.
Comfort Inn
Wales Rd.
198
Shell Subway Pizza Hut Amerihost Baymont Inn
Denny's
Knights Inn
Buck Rd.
197
BP McDonald's Sunoco American Inn
Shell Tim Horton's Wendy's
I-80/90
195
Ohio Turnpike
Barney's Subway BP Country Inn & Suites Courtyard Hampton Inn
To Maumee Mobile Home Court 419-893-6982
Toledo
Lake Erie
75
Findlay
Lima
Sidney
OHIO
Dayton
Cincinnati

Toledo
OHIO

Greater Toledo Convention & Visitors Bureau
401 Jefferson Ave., Toledo, Ohio 43604-1067
419-321-6404 or 1-800-243-4667 (U.S./Can.) **www.dotoledo.com**

A Kid-Friendly Place

Looking for a great destination to take the kids for a summer weekend getaway? Take a peek at Toledo and Northwest Ohio. Recently ranked as the No. 1 kid-friendly city in the state, Toledo and Northwest Ohio has several new and expanded attractions that make it a popular family destination.

Whether it's visiting the new exhibits at The **Toledo Zoo** or a day at the beach at **Maumee Bay State Park,** Toledo and Northwest Ohio has something to do for the whole family at an affordable price!

The Centre of Science and Industry (or "COSI Toledo") has already set attendance records with more than 700,000 visitors exploring the hands-on science museum since it opened in 1977. COSI is a dynamic center of science, learning and interactive fun for kids of all ages featuring "Learning Worlds" including KIDSPACE, Life Force, Mind Zone, Whiz Bang Engineering, Water Works and more.

The Toledo Zoo With over 5,300 animals representing 760 species, the Toledo Zoo is one of the world's most complete zoos. It is also the region's top family destination. Visit the Arctic tundra, the wilds of Africa, a tropical rainforest, and the Sonoran Desert all in one day. More than one million visitors come each year to see polar bear cubs and baby giraffe.

Holy Toledo! More than half a million people come to Fifth Third Field to watch the Toledo Mud Hens play. Fifth Third Field, built in 2002, features a video scoreboard, sky boxes, and "The Roost" area near right field. 406 Washington St. www.mudhens.com

The Toledo Museum of Art's **Family Center** provides a hands-on play space for families every Tuesday, Thursday and Sunday. Kids ages three to 10 can explore costumes, games, books and puppets, design a gallery hunt with the advice of friendly Family Center volunteer, or enjoy storytelling, musical instruments and art activities. On Friday nights, the Museum stays open until 10:00 p.m. The Museum is free. Call for details about scheduled free tours, food, films, lectures and live music.

Toledo Museum of Art. *The new collection, "Hands-on Egypt," (not pictured) is an educational gallery specifically designed for touching! 419-255-8000 www.toledomuseum.org.* Photo: David Lehman, courtesy the Greater Toledo Convention and Visitors Bureau

Toledo Zoo. *"Arctic Encounter" is the zoo's largest exhibit. It features underwater viewing of polar bears and seals. Apr. to Sept. 10 a.m.-5 p.m., Oct. to March 10 a.m.-4 p.m. Closed for major holidays. 419-385-5721. I-75 exit 201A.*
Photo: Linda Milks, courtesy the Greater Toledo Convention & Visitors Bureau

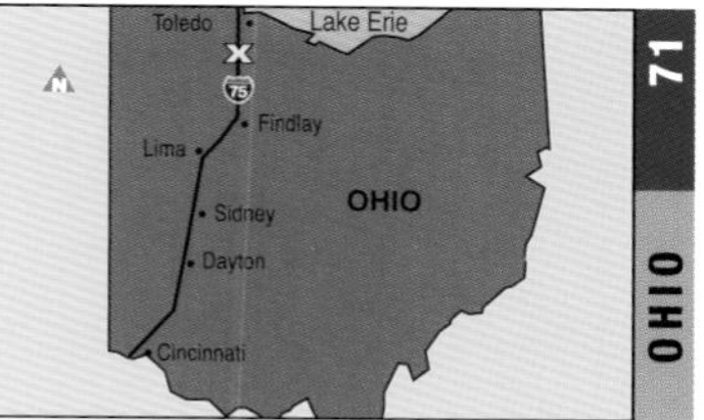

PERRYSBURG, OH

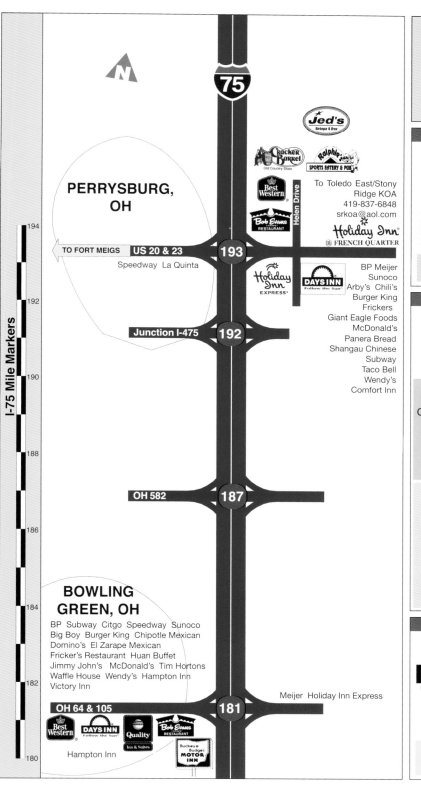

I-75 Mile Markers: 194, 192, 190, 188, 186, 184, 182, 180

75

Jed's Barbeque & Brew
Cracker Barrel Old Country Store
Ralphie's Sports Eatery & Pub
Best Western
Bob Evans Restaurant
Helen Drive

To Toledo East/Stony Ridge KOA
419-837-6848
srkoa@aol.com
Holiday Inn French Quarter

TO FORT MEIGS — US 20 & 23 — 193

Speedway La Quinta

Days Inn Follow the Sun

BP Meijer
Sunoco
Arby's Chili's
Burger King
Frickers
Giant Eagle Foods
McDonald's
Panera Bread
Shangau Chinese
Subway
Taco Bell
Wendy's
Comfort Inn

Junction I-475 — 192

OH 582 — 187

BOWLING GREEN, OH

BP Subway Citgo Speedway Sunoco
Big Boy Burger King Chipotle Mexican
Domino's El Zarape Mexican
Fricker's Restaurant Huan Buffet
Jimmy John's McDonald's Tim Hortons
Waffle House Wendy's Hampton Inn
Victory Inn

Meijer Holiday Inn Express

OH 64 & 105 — 181

Best Western Days Inn Quality Inn & Suites Bob Evans Restaurant
Buckeye Budget Motor Inn
Hampton Inn

Ohio

Ohio Division of Travel & Tourism
P.O. Box 1001, Columbus, Ohio 43216-1001
1-800-BUCKEYE **www.discoverohio.com**

Presidential Pathways

Ohio is nicknamed "The Mother of Presidents" for the eight presidents who called Ohio their home.

William Henry Harrison-9th President, 1841, North Bend, OH.

William Henry Harrison was born in Berkeley Plantation, Virginia, but he is considered an Ohio President because he resided here for many years prior to his presidency. After the War of 1812, Harrison settled in North Bend, in southwestern Ohio near the Ohio River. Harrison was the first President to die in office (just a month after being sworn in). **Harrison's Tomb,** a 60-foot monument, stands in North Bend.

Harrison fought in the Army as aide-de-camp to General Anthony Wayne and latter fought the Battle of Tippecanoe. He was later called "Old Tippecanoe." He won additional laurels in the battle of 1812, and is credited with defeating the combined British and Indian forces led, in part, by the famous Indian leader Tecumseh. Fort Meigs (Perrysburg), built under Harrison's guidance, was used in the War of 1812 and it was, at that time, the largest walled fortification in America.

Ulysses Simpson Grant-18th President, 1869-1877, Point Pleasant, OH.

Travelers to southwest Ohio can tour the **Grant Birthplace** in Point Pleasant, a restored one-story, three-room cottage built in 1817. In nearby Georgetown, a birthday party is held every April for the 18th President at the Grant Homestead where Grant's schoolhouse and boyhood home are located.

The son of an Ohio tanner, Grant attended West Point quite against his will. He graduated in the middle of his class but won military fame in various battles of the Civil War. After Lincoln appointed him General-in-Chief, he directed Sherman to drive through the South while he, along with the Army of the Potomac, pinned down Gen. Robert E. Lee's Army leading to Lee's surrender.

After retiring from the Presidency, Grant bought a partnership in a financial firm which went bankrupt just as Grant learned he had throat cancer. He won his race against death to produce a memoir that would pay off his debts and provide for his family. Soon after completing the last page in 1885, he died. The memoir ultimately earned nearly $450,000.

Rutherford Birchard Hayes-19th President, 1877-1881, Delaware, OH

Rutherford Hayes was born in Delaware (central Ohio) and attended Kenyon College and Harvard Law School. Hayes entered Congress in 1865, then served three terms as Governor of Ohio between 1867 and 1876. Hayes was elected to the Presidency over New York Governor Samuel J. Tilden by a margin of one electoral vote. Lucy Webb Hayes, carrying out her husband's orders to banish wine and liquor from the White House, delighted the Woman's Christian Temperance Union.

Hayes announced in advance of his election that he would serve only one term as President and so retired to **Spiegel Grove,** his home in Fremont (northwestern Ohio) at the conclusion of his term. The Victorian estate of Spiegel Grove is the highlight of the **Rutherford B. Hayes Presidential Center.** The landmark is the only presidential center that contains not only a U.S. president's residence, library, museum but also his tomb .

James Abram Garfield-20th President, 1881, Orange, OH.

James Garfield was the second president to be shot while in office. Doctors tried to find the bullet with a metal detector invented by Alexander Graham Bell but the device failed because Garfield was resting on a bed with metal springs—no one thought to move him!

Prior to his Presidency, Garfield rose to the rank of major general under President Lincoln, then served as a Congressman for 18 straight re-elections. Garfield was born near Orange outside of Cleveland in northeast Ohio. His home, nicknamed **Lawnfield** by reporters, is a National Historical Site in Mentor, about 20 miles east of Cleveland. **The James A Garfield National Historic Site** underwent an $11.8 million renovation completed in 1998. Two additional Garfield sites nearby include **The James A. Garfield Birthplace,** a humble log cabin along a woodland trail in Moreland Hills. Garfield was the last president born in a log cabin. **The James A. Garfield Monument** in Cleveland's historic Lake View Cemetery is an impressive 180-foot tower built of Ohio sandstone with a marble statue of Garfield ad the center piece.

Benjamin Harrison-23rd President, 1889-1893, North Bend, OH

The grandson of President William H. Harrison ("Old Tippecanoe"), Benjamin Harrison was born on a farm in the southwestern town of North Bend near the Ohio River. Of all the Chief Executives, only Benjamin Harrison was the grandson of a president. He attended Miami University in Ohio and studied law in Cincinnati. He later moved to Indianapolis, Indiana, where he practiced law and campaigned for the Republican Party.

Harrison is known for his "front-porch" campaigns, delivering short speeches to delegations that visited him in Indianapolis. Harrison is also remembered for signing the Sherman Anti-Trust Act and submitting the treaty to annex Hawaii that was later withdrawn by President Cleveland.

William McKinley-25th President, 1897-1901, Niles, OH

A two-term Governor of Ohio, President McKinley was born in the northeastern town of Niles, now the site of the National McKinley Birthplace Memorial. The memorial includes a library and museum. McKinley also served two terms as President, the second of which came to a tragic end in 1901 when he was shot while standing in a receiving line at the Buffalo Pan-American Exposition.

The **William McKinley National Monument** marks McKinley's tomb in Canton. In the same city, the **McKinley Museum of History, Science and Industry** features a planetarium, an entire street of old-fashioned shops and life-size "talking" animations of the President and his wife. The **Saxton McKinley House,** also located in Canton, houses the **National First Ladies' Library.**

William Howard Taft-27th President, 1909-1913, Cincinnati, OH

Born in the southwestern town of Cincinnati, Taft was the only man to become President and then chief justice. He graduated from Yale and studied law in Cincinnati, served as McKinley's chief civil administrator in the Philippines and was made Secretary of War by President Roosevelt.

When Taft was nominated to run on the Republic ticket for a second term, Roosevelt bolted the party to lead the progressives, thus guaranteeing the election of Woodrow Wilson. Taft then served as Professor of Law at Yale until President Harding made him Chief Justice of the United States.

In Cincinnati a widow's walk caps the **William Howard Taft National Historic Site,** the gracious Federal-style home where Taft was born. **The Taft Museum,** a National Historic Landmark, is located in the Baum-Longworth-Taft House. This Federal-period building was once home to William Taft's brother, Charles, and wife, Anna Sinton. The house became a museum in 1932 and is recognized as one of the finest small art museums in the country.

Warren Gamaliel Harding-29th President, 1921-1923, Blooming Grove, OH

Harding's background is a colorful one of a newspaper publisher, Ohio state senator, Lieutenant Governor and Governor. He delivered the noteworthy nominating address for President Taft at the 1912 Republican Convention. And Herbert Hoover served as his Secretary of Commerce.

Marion in central Ohio is the site of both **The Harding Home** and **The Harding Memorial.** Harding campaigned for the presidency on the front porch of his home and both Harding and his wife are buried at the memorial park.

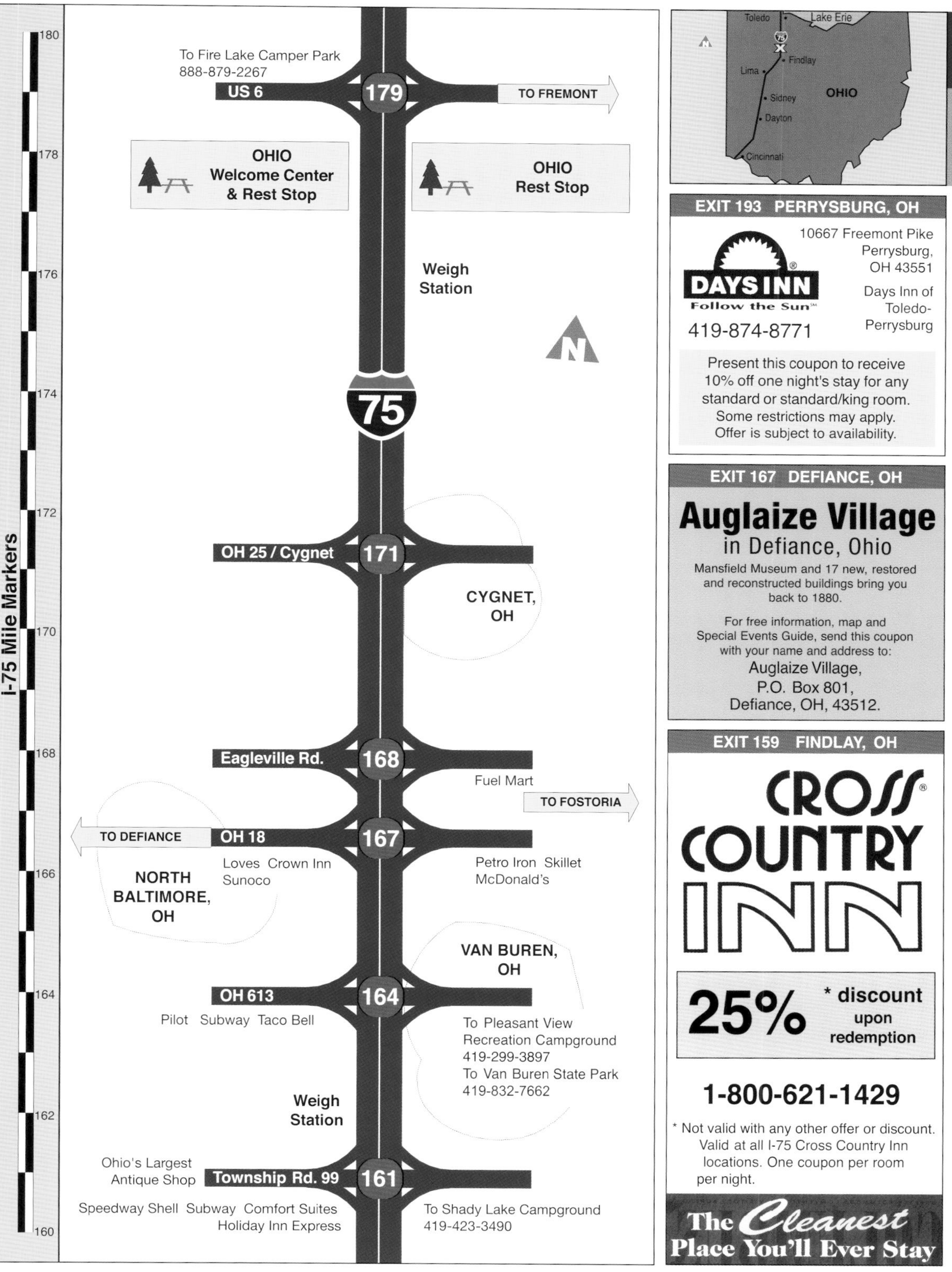
I-75 Mile Markers
180
178
176
174
172
170
168
166
164
162
160
To Fire Lake Camper Park
888-879-2267
US 6
179
TO FREMONT
OHIO
Welcome Center
& Rest Stop
OHIO
Rest Stop
Weigh
Station
N
75
OH 25 / Cygnet
171
CYGNET,
OH
Eagleville Rd.
168
Fuel Mart
TO FOSTORIA
TO DEFIANCE
OH 18
167
Loves Crown Inn
Sunoco
Petro Iron Skillet
McDonald's
NORTH
BALTIMORE,
OH
VAN BUREN,
OH
OH 613
164
Pilot Subway Taco Bell
To Pleasant View
Recreation Campground
419-299-3897
To Van Buren State Park
419-832-7662
Weigh
Station
Ohio's Largest
Antique Shop
Township Rd. 99
161
Speedway Shell Subway Comfort Suites
Holiday Inn Express
To Shady Lake Campground
419-423-3490
Toledo
Lake Erie
Findlay
Lima
OHIO
Sidney
Dayton
Cincinnati
EXIT 193 PERRYSBURG, OH
DAYS INN
Follow the Sun
419-874-8771
10667 Freemont Pike
Perrysburg,
OH 43551
Days Inn of
Toledo-
Perrysburg
Present this coupon to receive
10% off one night's stay for any
standard or standard/king room.
Some restrictions may apply.
Offer is subject to availability.
EXIT 167 DEFIANCE, OH
Auglaize Village
in Defiance, Ohio
Mansfield Museum and 17 new, restored
and reconstructed buildings bring you
back to 1880.
For free information, map and
Special Events Guide, send this coupon
with your name and address to:
Auglaize Village,
P.O. Box 801,
Defiance, OH, 43512.
EXIT 159 FINDLAY, OH
CROSS
COUNTRY
INN
25%
* discount
upon
redemption
1-800-621-1429
* Not valid with any other offer or discount.
Valid at all I-75 Cross Country Inn
locations. One coupon per room
per night.
The Cleanest
Place You'll Ever Stay

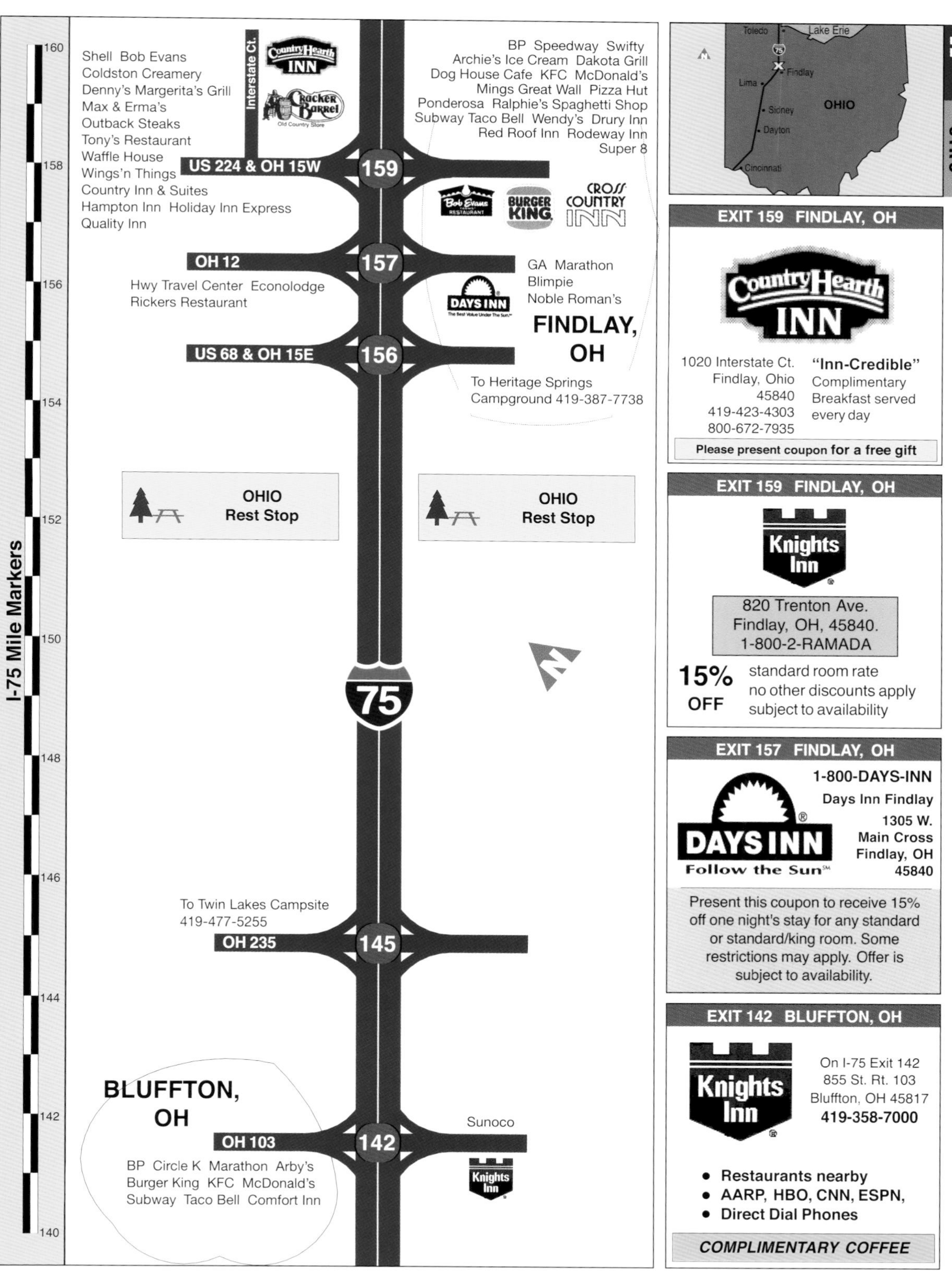

I-75 Mile Markers
160
158
156
154
152
150
148
146
144
142
140
Shell Bob Evans
Coldston Creamery
Denny's Margerita's Grill
Max & Erma's
Outback Steaks
Tony's Restaurant
Waffle House
Wings'n Things
Country Inn & Suites
Hampton Inn Holiday Inn Express
Quality Inn
Interstate Ct.
Country Hearth INN
Cracker Barrel
Old Country Store
BP Speedway Swifty
Archie's Ice Cream Dakota Grill
Dog House Cafe KFC McDonald's
Mings Great Wall Pizza Hut
Ponderosa Ralphie's Spaghetti Shop
Subway Taco Bell Wendy's Drury Inn
Red Roof Inn Rodeway Inn
Super 8
US 224 & OH 15W
159
Bob Evans
BURGER KING
CROSS COUNTRY INN
OH 12
157
Hwy Travel Center Econolodge
Rickers Restaurant
GA Marathon
Blimpie
Noble Roman's
DAYS INN
FINDLAY, OH
US 68 & OH 15E
156
To Heritage Springs
Campground 419-387-7738
OHIO
Rest Stop
OHIO
Rest Stop
75
N
To Twin Lakes Campsite
419-477-5255
OH 235
145
BLUFFTON, OH
OH 103
142
Sunoco
BP Circle K Marathon Arby's
Burger King KFC McDonald's
Subway Taco Bell Comfort Inn
Knights Inn
Toledo
Lake Erie
75
Findlay
Lima
OHIO
Sidney
Dayton
Cincinnati
75
OHIO
EXIT 159 FINDLAY, OH
Country Hearth INN
1020 Interstate Ct.
Findlay, Ohio
45840
419-423-4303
800-672-7935
"Inn-Credible"
Complimentary
Breakfast served
every day
Please present coupon for a free gift
EXIT 159 FINDLAY, OH
Knights Inn
820 Trenton Ave.
Findlay, OH, 45840.
1-800-2-RAMADA
15% OFF
standard room rate
no other discounts apply
subject to availability
EXIT 157 FINDLAY, OH
1-800-DAYS-INN
Days Inn Findlay
1305 W.
Main Cross
Findlay, OH
45840
DAYS INN
Follow the Sun
Present this coupon to receive 15% off one night's stay for any standard or standard/king room. Some restrictions may apply. Offer is subject to availability.
EXIT 142 BLUFFTON, OH
Knights Inn
On I-75 Exit 142
855 St. Rt. 103
Bluffton, OH 45817
419-358-7000
• Restaurants nearby
• AARP, HBO, CNN, ESPN,
• Direct Dial Phones
COMPLIMENTARY COFFEE

Lima/Allen County
OHIO

Lima/Allen County Convention & Visitors Bureau
147 North Main Street, Lima, Ohio 45801
419-222-6075 or 1-888-222-6075 **www.lima-allencvb.com**

Lima, pronounced "Ly-muh," in Allen County is the largest inland city in Northwest Ohio. It is a thriving business center and home to such products as the M1-A2 Abrams Tank.

Lima and Allen County's history is long and illustrious. French and English explorers made the area a major fur trading center in the 1700s. The area was known as the "Black Swamp" due to the heavily wooded swampland created by the last ice age's receding glaciers. The fertile soil enticed the first permanent settlement in 1831.

The City of Lima got its name from Lima, Peru, the place where the medicine to cure "swamp fever" came from. Allen County got its name from Col. John Allen who was a hero of the War of 1812.

RAILROAD HERITAGE. By the 1850s Lima was a major junction for five railroad freight and passenger lines. Lima Locomotive Works (founded in the 1870s) became the third-largest producer of locomotives in the nation. Lima is still known as the home of the Shay Locomotive. When oil was discovered in 1885 Lima became the "Oil Capital of the World" for at least the next two years. The oil barons of Lima built fabulous mansions on what would be known as the **Golden Block.**

THE ALLEN COUNTY MUSEUM has exhibits of Native American and early pioneer days, minerals and fossils. Local exhibits include the steam/electric rail era, firefighting and military displays.

Next to the Allen County Museum is the **MacDONELL HOUSE,** a historic home listed on the National Register of Historic Places. Located on the **GOLDEN BLOCK,** this 19-room Victorian mansion was built in 1885 during the oil boom and was recently donated to the Allen County Historical Society. Tour guides will point out the handcarved woodwork, combination chandeliers, the two-story stained-glass window on the grand staircase, a rare Viennese painting on a cobweb, and Mr. MacDonell's big game display in the Trophy Room. The contrast the living style provided by the old "Log House" that adjoins the MacDonell House is delightful.

Attractions

Allen County Museum
See left for more information. The recently expanded Allen County Museum has something for everyone. New to the facility is the Children's Discovery Center offering hands-on activities for kids of all ages. Check out exhibits of Native American and early pioneer days, Allen County's rich rail history, Public Enemy #1 John Dillinger/Sheriff Jess Sarber exhibit and more. This is the only AAM accredited county museum in the state of Ohio. Closed Mon. and holidays. Year-round open 1 p.m.-5 p.m., Tues. to Sun. 620 West Market St., Lima. 419-222-9426

The 1925 Shay Locomotive
620 West Market St., Lima. 419-222-9426

MacDonell House
See left for more information. Closed Mon. and holidays. Year-round, open 1 p.m.-5 p.m., Tues. to Sun. 632 West Market St., Lima. 419-224-1113

Lincoln Park Railway Exhibit
Outside display includes the last steam locomotive built in Lima, a 1882 Pullman luxurious private car, a Nickel Plate Caboose (1882). Year-round. Lincoln Park is on Elm Street behind the Lima Memorial Hospital. Contact Allen County Museum 419-222-9426.

John Dillinger and Sheriff Sarber Memorial Exhibit
In the Allen County Museum, you will get an accurate accounting of the John Dillinger story through videos, legal documents, and actual case photographs. 620 W. Market Street, Lima. 419-222-9426

The Plastic Outlet Store
World's largest assortment of plastic items from all over the world. Film. Exit 127 to Route 81, turn right onto Neubrecht Rd. 1390 Neubrecht Rd., Lima. 419-228-2242

Lima Symphony Orchestra
7 Town Sq., Lima. 419-222-5701

Artspace Art Gallery
65-67 Town Square, Lima. 419-222-1721

Tilton Farm
Travel around the 7-acre quarry; prepare yourself for a journey into the days of old, view collections including Civil War artifacts. By appointment only. 6555 Madden Rd. Lima. 419-648-6835

Artistic Creations Boutique
Renovated 1900s Victorian style home turned into giftshop. Open 10am – 5pm most days, later on Thursday. 6170 Harding Highway, Lima. 419-225-7463

DID YOU KNOW?

Phyllis Diller was born in Allen County in 1917.

Hugh Downs lived in Allen County from the age of two to nineteen.

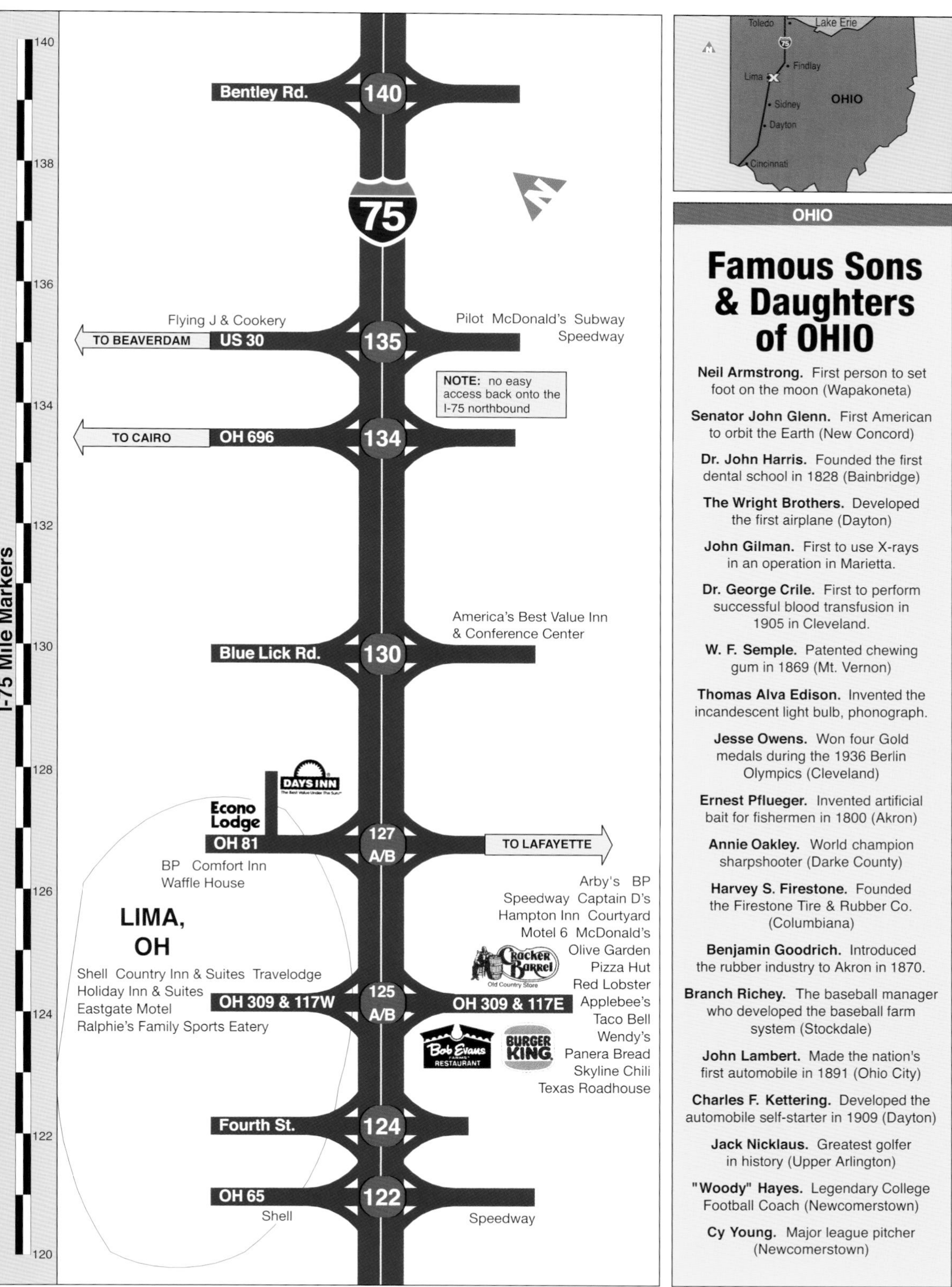

OHIO

Famous Sons & Daughters of OHIO

Neil Armstrong. First person to set foot on the moon (Wapakoneta)

Senator John Glenn. First American to orbit the Earth (New Concord)

Dr. John Harris. Founded the first dental school in 1828 (Bainbridge)

The Wright Brothers. Developed the first airplane (Dayton)

John Gilman. First to use X-rays in an operation in Marietta.

Dr. George Crile. First to perform successful blood transfusion in 1905 in Cleveland.

W. F. Semple. Patented chewing gum in 1869 (Mt. Vernon)

Thomas Alva Edison. Invented the incandescent light bulb, phonograph.

Jesse Owens. Won four Gold medals during the 1936 Berlin Olympics (Cleveland)

Ernest Pflueger. Invented artificial bait for fishermen in 1800 (Akron)

Annie Oakley. World champion sharpshooter (Darke County)

Harvey S. Firestone. Founded the Firestone Tire & Rubber Co. (Columbiana)

Benjamin Goodrich. Introduced the rubber industry to Akron in 1870.

Branch Richey. The baseball manager who developed the baseball farm system (Stockdale)

John Lambert. Made the nation's first automobile in 1891 (Ohio City)

Charles F. Kettering. Developed the automobile self-starter in 1909 (Dayton)

Jack Nicklaus. Greatest golfer in history (Upper Arlington)

"Woody" Hayes. Legendary College Football Coach (Newcomerstown)

Cy Young. Major league pitcher (Newcomerstown)

Auglaize & Mercer Counties OHIO

Auglaize & Mercer Counties Visitors Bureau
900 Edgewater Drive, St. Marys, Ohio 45885
419-394-1294 or 1-800-860-4762 **www.seemore.org**

History Notes

If you are interested in American history, the counties of Auglaize and Mercer boasts several notable events and places including the last Ohio capital of the Shawnee nation (Wapakoneta), the Greenville Treaty (signed at Fort Recovery), a War of 1812 fort (Fort Amanda), and St. Marys (once an important Indian trading center) that became headquarters for General William Henry Harrison.

The construction of the Miami & Erie Canal, with Grand Lake St. Marys as its primary feeder, encouraged the movement of people to this area more than 150 years ago.

Until the Hoover Dam was built, Grand Lake St. Marys was recognized as the largest man-made lake in the world. The lake is now a popular recreational area for picnics, swimming, boating, fishing and camping.

The tragic history of the Indian Wars of the 1790s is preserved in Fort Recovery. Two of the most dramatic Indian battles in U.S. history were fought here: the defeat of General Arthur St. Clair, and the defense of the Fort by General Anthony Wayne. The last fight (the Battle of Fallen Timbers) resulted in the Treaty of Greenville.

Fort Recovery State Memorial consists of blockhouses, a 101-foot replica of the obelisk Washington monument, and a museum. The museum exhibits detail the construction of the fort, the packhorse cannons, and period costumes. The largest collection of Indian artifacts in Ohio are identified and displayed here.

A pioneer cemetery, and the headwaters of the great Wabash River are also close by.

Bicycle Museum *© www.seemore.org*

Attractions

Auglaize County Courthouse
This remarkable Berea-style sandstone and tile-floored courthouse cost $259,481 to construct in 1894. Open Mon. to Fri. Wapakoneta. Call 419-738-3612 for more information.

Maria Stein Heritage Museum
This musum focuses on local history and includes displays on German settlement and the Sisters of the Precious Blood. Maria Stein is at the center of the thematic grouping of distinctive churches with towering spires topped with crosses: The Cross-Tipped Churches of Ohio. 2291 St. Johns Rd., Maria Stein. Museum open daily 1 p.m. - 4 p.m. from May to Oct. Closed Mon. and holidays. 419-925-4532

Auglaize County Historical Museum
223 S. Main St., St. Marys. 419-394-7069

State Fish Hatchery
25 large stock ponds raise walleye, saugeye and largemouth bass, as game fish. East Grand Lake St. Marys, Ohio Rt. 364. Year-round Mon. to Fri. 8 a.m.-4:30 p.m. 419-394-5170

Grand Lake St. Marys State Park
Enjoy camping, boating, fishing, hunting, hiking and swimming. 834 Edgewater Dr., in St. Marys. At 13,500 acres it is Ohio's largest inland lake. 419-394-3611

Fort Recovery State Museum
See left for more historical information. Fort Recovery is at the intersection of Ohio Rts. 49 and 119. May to Sept. open Tues. to Sun. 1 p.m.-5 p.m. 419-375-4649

Neil Armstrong Air & Space Museum
See description and photos on this page. Clearly visible from the I-75, take exit 111. The Space Museum is on Bellefontaine Rd., in Wapakoneta, Ohio. Open Mar. to Nov. daily, 9:30 a.m.-5 p.m. 419-738-8811.

Historic Canal Town St. Marys
The St. Marys River and waterways provide a natural north-south link between the Great Lakes and, via the Ohio River, the Gulf of Mexico. For more information call 419-394-1294.

Bicycle Museum of America
Oldest bicycle in America is housed in this historic building. 7 W. Monroe St., New Bremen. 419-629-9249

Neil Armstrong Air & Space Museum.

From the Wright Brothers pioneering designs to the first step on the moon, no one would argue that Ohio has led the nation in aviation. Neil Armstrong's first step on the moon (1969) and John Glenn's historic first orbit of the Earth and other achievements in flight are chronicled in the Neil Armstrong Air & Space Museum in Wapakoneta. John Glenn and Neil Armstrong are both from Ohio. Visitors can experience a simulated trip to the moon. Favorite displays include Neil Armstrong's collection, a moon rock, a F5D Skylancer plane, a Wright Model G Aero-boat, and the Gemini VIII spacecraft.

Two photos of museum courtesy Ohio Department of Development, Division of Travel and Tourism

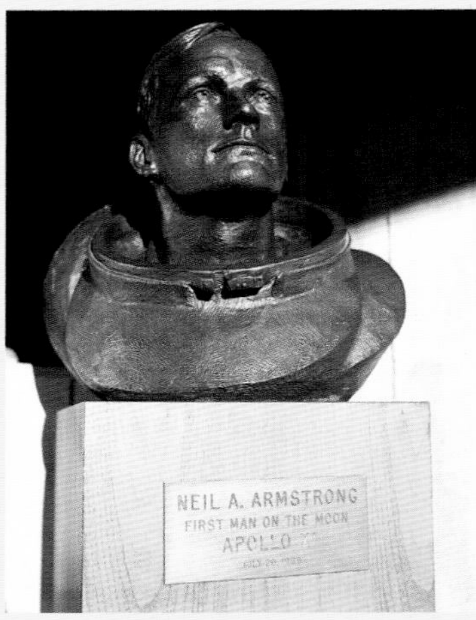

I-75 Mile Markers
120
118
116
114
112
110
108
106
104
102
100
Breese Rd.
120
Speedway
Cridersville Rd.
118
WAPAKONETA, OH
Neil Armstrong Air & Space Museum
113
OH 67
Dairy Queen
Burger King
Best Western
TA Marathon
Bellefontaine St.
111
Days Inn
BP Shell Arby's Bob Evans Capt D's
El Azteca Mexican Lucky Steer Restaurant
Pizza Hut Taco Bell Waffle House Wendy's
Holiday Inn Express Super 8 Comfort Inn & Suites
Shopping KOA (419-738-6016)
Note: Difficult reaccess to I-75 both directions
TO ST. MARYS, GRAND LAKE ST. MARYS, CELINA and FORT RECOVERY
US 33
110
TO BELLEFONTAINE
Difficult reaccess to I-75 both directions
To Glacier Lake Campgrounds
419-738-3005
To Indian Lake State Park
937-843-2717
75
N
Sunoco Budget Host Inn
OH 219
104
To Bicycle Museum of America
TO NEW BREMEN
OH 274
102
TO JACKSON CENTER
Bicycle Museum of America
© seemore.org
Toledo
Lake Erie
75
Findlay
Lima
Sidney
OHIO
Dayton
Cincinnati
79
OHIO
EXIT 111 WAPAKONETA, OH
Best Western
Bring in this ad and you'll
save 10%
off our rack rate w/coupon
Free Continental Breakfast
In-room Coffeemakers
USA Today delivered to your room Mon. to Fri.
1510 Saturn Dr., Wapakoneta, OH
419-738-8181
EXIT 111 WAPAKONETA, OH
SUPER 8 MOTEL
SAVE 10%
With this ad!
Some restrictions may apply
SUPER 8 MOTEL
* Wapakoneta *
1011 Lunar Dr.
419-738-8810
1-800-800-8000
Suites with whirlpools
Kitchenettes
Senior & Corporate Discounts
Large vehicle parking
Free HBO
Handicap room available
In-room Coffee-makers, hairdryers and microwave-refrigerator units
COMPLIMENTARY BREAKFAST
Life's great at Super 8
EXIT 92 SIDNEY, OH
20% OFF with coupon
DAYS INN
Follow the Sun
I-75 & St. Rt. 47
SIDNEY. OH
937-492-1104
1-800-DAYS INN
Color Cable TV
Free Continental Breakfast with Room
Free USA Today
EZ On/Off
12 Restaurants within 1 mile

Sidney/Shelby County
OHIO

Sidney Visitors Bureau
101 South Ohio Ave., 2nd Floor, Sidney, Ohio 45365
1-866-892-9122 **www.visitsidneyshelby.com**

This area was densely forested Indian hunting grounds until a French Canadian explorer, Peter Loramie, colonized it in 1769. Loramie and his large Indian entourage were forced out by General George Rogers Clark after the French and Indian Wars.

When General "Mad" Anthony Wayne established a fort here in 1794 settlers finally began to arrive. Roads were built and the county seat was chosen and named Sidney in honor of a well known poet and member of the British Parliament, Sir Phillip Sidney.

Early farmers produced enough food for the local need, that is until the construction of the Miami & Erie Canal reached Sidney in 1835 which connected the town to Cincinnati and Toledo. As Sidney's economy flourished an influx of settlers followed.

The dramatic effect of the canal can also be seen in the various architectural styles. Photo opportunities abound near **Sidney's Public Square** with its collection of beautifully restored historical and architecturally-significant buildings.

Bellefontaine/Logan County OHIO

The Greater Logan County Area Convention & Visitors Bureau
100 South Main Street, Bellefontaine, Ohio 43311
937-599-5121 or 1-888-LOGANCO **www.logancountyohio.com**

At 1550 feet above sea level, Bellefontaine is Ohio's highest point. The city also holds the world's record for the shortest street: McKinley Street.

Logan County was named for Colonel Benjamin Logan who, along with Daniel Boone and Simon Kenton, attacked the Native American villages along the Mad River under the commission of Gen. George Rogers Clark in 1786. Pioneering settlers were attracted to the diverse topography. The first railroad reached the city of Bellefontaine in 1837.

Famous residents of Logan county include Dr. Earl Sloan, founder of Sloan's Liniment; Wall Street Financial Broker Edward D. Jones, Christian author Norman Vincent Peale; and George W. Bartholomew, creator of Portland Cement.

Numerous natural attractions **(Indian Lake State Park, Ohio Caverns)** and recreational opportunities **(Marmon Valley Farm, Mad River Mountain)** attract millions of return visitors.

Miami County
OHIO

Miami County Visitors & Convention Bureau
405 S.W. Public Square - Suite 272, Troy, Ohio 45373
937-339-1044 or 1-800-348-8993 **www.visitmiamicounty.org**

Miami County embodies all of the very best aspects of America's Midwest. A cordial community always welcoming of visitors, we offer an uncommon blend of unique attractions including historic downtowns, antique shops, museums, festivals and events, and accommodations to suit your needs.

Blanketing the Miami County countryside is an exciting new trend for travelers. The Miami County Barn Quilt Tour! Decorating the landscape are true folk art renditions of traditional quit squares hand painted on numerous barns. Visitors will enjoy the beauty and simple elegance of the land as they make their way from town to town. Contact the Miami County Visitors & Convention Bureau for more information, 1-800-348-8993 or www.visitmiamicounty.org.

Traditional to most county fairs, the Miami County Fair has all the midway rides and delicious food one can handle, along with exhibits that demonstrate the unique qualities of the county. Each August at the fair ribbons are awarded in livestock competitions, arts & crafts, homemade foods, and photography among others. For more information 937-335-7492 or www.miamicountyohiofair.com

TROY

Held each year on the 1st full weekend in June, The Troy Strawberry Festival has it all from strawberry shortcake to strawberry burritos. With more than 250 arts & crafts booths, 70 food booths, live entertainment on four different stages, plenty of games, it's no wonder more than 200,000 people visit the festival each year! For more information, 937-339-7714 or www.troyohiochamber.com.

The WACO Military Experience Military show and swap meet comes to Troy in July. This event features Military aircraft and vehicles, historic re-enactors and collections, Veteran's organizations, the WACO Aircraft Museum, Plus American military time periods from the French and Indian War to the present including home front and adversaries. For more information, 937-339-9226 or www.wacoairmuseum.org.

On one day in August, downtown Troy transforms into a colorful world in celebration of the Troy Festival of Nations. Through the sharing of food, arts & crafts, music, story telling & dancing, our neighbors expand our horizons and our minds. Don't miss the parade! For more information call 937-339-1221.

Also in August come to downtown for an evening of music during the annual Troy Mayor's Concert. Dayton's Philharmonic Concert Band and Chorus will be there to treat you to magnificent music. For more information call 937-339-3114

In September celebrate Troy's role in aviation history by joining us at the WACO Celebration and Fly-In. WACO owners fly their aircraft back to Troy, the site of their manufacture. This event features aircraft displays, food vendors, kid's activities and a parade of WACOs.
For more information, 937-335-9226 or www.wacoairmuseum.org.

TIPP CITY

At one time Tipp City was known for growing a large variety of mums and the Tipp City Mum Festival celebrates this heritage each September. A parade strolls down historic Main Street and directly into the City Park, where arts, crafts, games, and entertainment are abundant.
For more information, 937-667-8631 or www.tippcitymumfestival.org.

On the second weekend in November you'll find the perfect start to the holiday season in Historic Downtown Tipp City at A Winter's Yuletide Gathering, where shopkeepers warmly invite you to their open house. Don't miss a visit by Santa, strolling carolers, musicians and carriage rides or the wonderful unique gifts and collectibles you will find! For more information, 937-667-9435.

PIQUA

Held in September, the Piqua Heritage Festival at Johnston Farm is a look at Ohio's early frontier and America's early ways. See pre-1800's encampments where traveling frontiersmen sell handmade items and participate in old fashioned games such as knife throwing and archery. Enjoy a large selection of homemade foods, old-time encampments, a Woodland Indian Museum, a working canal boat and an early 1800's farmstead. For more information, 937-773-5706 or www.piquaheritagefestival.com.

Piqua Historical Area State Memorial preserves the frontier of Ohio in the early 1800's. See the restored home of Federal Indian Agent Col. John Johnston, the oldest log barn in Ohio, learn about Woodland Indians and ride the "General Harrison" on a restored segment of the canal. For hours and more information, 1-800-752-2619 or www.ohiohistory.org.

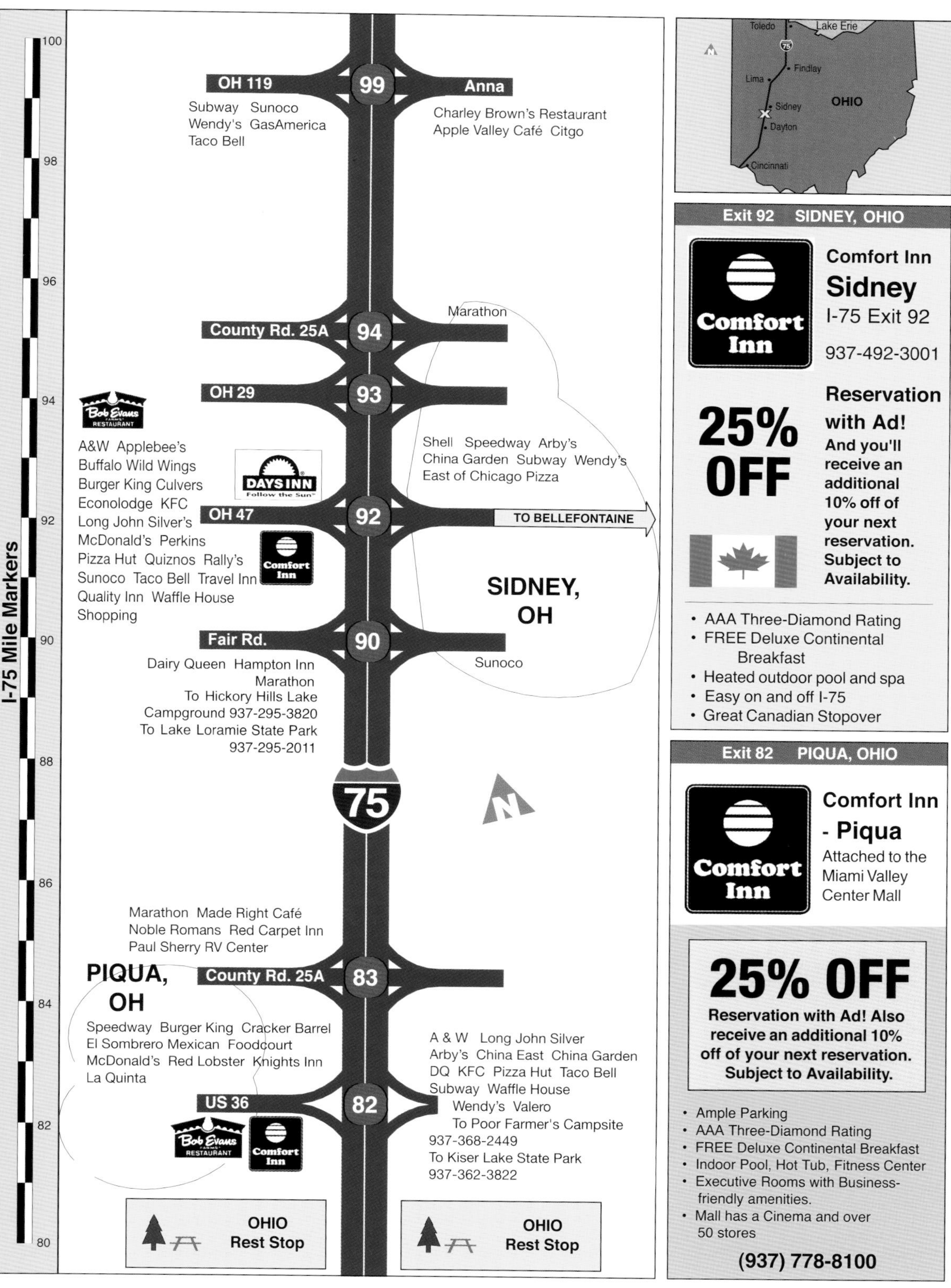
I-75 Mile Markers
100
98
96
94
92
90
88
86
84
82
80
OH 119
99
Anna
Subway Sunoco
Wendy's GasAmerica
Taco Bell
Charley Brown's Restaurant
Apple Valley Café Citgo
County Rd. 25A
94
Marathon
OH 29
93
A&W Applebee's
Buffalo Wild Wings
Burger King Culvers
Econolodge KFC
Long John Silver's
McDonald's Perkins
Pizza Hut Quiznos Rally's
Sunoco Taco Bell Travel Inn
Quality Inn Waffle House
Shopping
DAYS INN
Follow the Sun
Shell Speedway Arby's
China Garden Subway Wendy's
East of Chicago Pizza
OH 47
92
TO BELLEFONTAINE
Comfort Inn
SIDNEY, OH
Fair Rd.
90
Sunoco
Dairy Queen Hampton Inn
Marathon
To Hickory Hills Lake
Campground 937-295-3820
To Lake Loramie State Park
937-295-2011
75
N
Marathon Made Right Café
Noble Romans Red Carpet Inn
Paul Sherry RV Center
PIQUA, OH
County Rd. 25A
83
Speedway Burger King Cracker Barrel
El Sombrero Mexican Foodcourt
McDonald's Red Lobster Knights Inn
La Quinta
A & W Long John Silver
Arby's China East China Garden
DQ KFC Pizza Hut Taco Bell
Subway Waffle House
Wendy's Valero
To Poor Farmer's Campsite
937-368-2449
To Kiser Lake State Park
937-362-3822
US 36
82
Bob Evans
Comfort Inn
OHIO Rest Stop
OHIO Rest Stop
Toledo
Lake Erie
75
Findlay
Lima
Sidney
OHIO
Dayton
Cincinnati
N

Dayton/Montgomery County OHIO

Dayton/Montgomery County Convention & Visitors Bureau, Inc.
1 Chamber Plaza, Suite A, Dayton, Ohio 45402-2400
937-226-8211 or 800-221-8235 **www.daytoncvb.com**

The Woodland Arboretum Foundation

The admission to the **Historic Buildings and Grounds** is free, however, I suggest the guided tours, which are offered by appointment for a nominal fee. Or, if you prefer, borrow the audio-cassette for a self-guided tour.

The **Woodland Cemetery** is the final resting place of many prominent Americans including the Wright Brothers, Erma Bombeck, Paul Laurence Dunbar, not to mention the Gypsy King & Queen. The signed Tiffany stained glass window installed in the chapel is but one of the Woodland structures on the National Registry of Historic Places.

The 230-acre **Woodland Arboretum** has over 3,000 trees of 250 species gracing the grounds and is simply marvelous. The list of identified varieties includes eight of the largest trees of their kind in the State of Ohio.

Call ahead for details about the **special events** and **annual traditions** including flower sales, photo contests and the Stained Glass Annual Tour and Concert.

I-75 Southbound, use exit 52A.

I-75 Northbound, use exit 51. Cross Great Miami River via Stewart Street.

Go north on Alberta Street to your first right, which is the entrance to the Woodland Cemetery. Gates are open dawn to dusk, seven days a week.

118 Woodland Arboretum Ave.,
Dayton, Ohio 45409. 937-228-3221
www.woodlandcemetery.org

DAYTON: Birthplace of Aviation and Innovation

Orville and Wilbur Wright's fascination in flight began with an 1878 whirligig given to them by their father. That gift ultimately led the Dayton-born brothers to give the world the gift of flight, and the city continues to be home of innovators who have created everything from the stepladder to cellophane tape to space food.

Among Dayton's famous inventors and their inventions:

- **John Balsley:** Stepladder
- **Rufus Currier Bossard:** Photo-electric cell (the black light)
- **Carl Carlson:** Microfiche
- **Dr. William Hale Church:** Cellophane Tape
- **E.R. Churchwell:** Portable Crib
- **Leland Clark:** Human heart-lung machine
- **Luzern Custer:** Motorized wheelchairs
- **E.T. Fraze:** Pull tab and pop top beverage cans
- **Arthur Frei:** Ice cube tray with ejector mechanism
- **C. Francis Jenkins:** Movie projector, movie camera and film, movie theater
- **Charles Kettering:** Electric self-starter for automobiles
- **Maurice Krug:** Space food
- **Alfred Mellowes:** Self-contained refrigerator
- **Thomas Midgely:** Ethyl leaded gasoline
- **John Morton:** Parking meters
- **James Ritty:** Cash register
- **Daniel Webster Schaeffer:** Gas masks
- **Floyd Smith:** Parachute

Many other artists, athletes, actors and authors have called Dayton home, including poet laureate **Paul Laurence Dunbar,** actor **Martin Sheen,** cartoonist **Cathy Guisewite,** comedian **Jonathan Winters,** authors **John Jakes** and **Erma Bombeck,** talk show host **Phil Donahue**, Olympic track star **Edwin C. Moses,** and basketball star **Jim Paxson.**

The city honors its rich heritage in a variety of ways. **Edwin C. Moses Boulevard** and **Erma Bombeck Way** are major local thoroughfares.

The **Paul Laurence Dunbar home** is now a museum dedicated to his life and work.

America's Packard
A restored Packard showroom from the 1930s is the only museum dedicated to the classic **Packard automobile.**

Carillon Historical Park, *courtesy Ohio Dept. of Development, Division of Travel and Tourism*

A tribute to Dayton's more distant past is evident at the **SunWatch Indian Village,** which depicts daily life of the Fort Ancient Indians, who inhabited much of the Miami Valley roughly 800 years ago. See page 86.

In 2003, Dayton commemorated the **centennial anniversary** of Orville and Wilbur Wright's first flight into history with a yearlong celebration including an international arts festival, history and educational events, and the largest air show the world has ever seen.

Carillon Historic Park is a 65-acre historical and educational outdoor museum, much of which is devoted to the **Wright Brothers.**

Among the attractions is the original 1905 *Wright Flyer III,* restored under Orville Wright's direction and now a National Historic Landmark. Also here ia a replica of the Wright Cycle Company where, in 1903, the Wright Brothers built the world's first successful powered airplane.
www.carillonpark.org

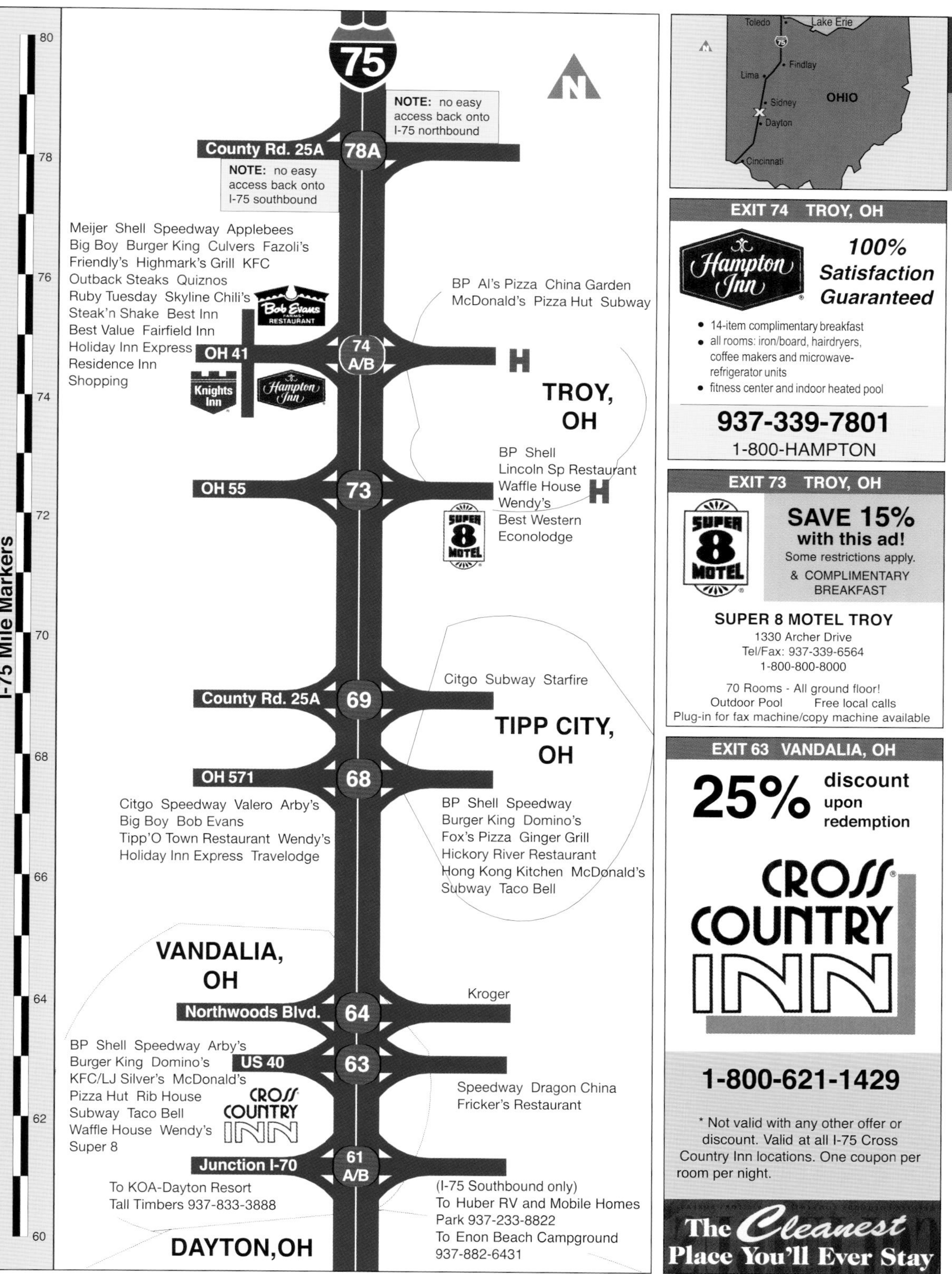
75
NOTE: no easy access back onto I-75 northbound
County Rd. 25A
78A
NOTE: no easy access back onto I-75 southbound
Meijer Shell Speedway Applebees
Big Boy Burger King Culvers Fazoli's
Friendly's Highmark's Grill KFC
Outback Steaks Quiznos
Ruby Tuesday Skyline Chili's
Steak'n Shake Best Inn
Best Value Fairfield Inn
Holiday Inn Express
Residence Inn
Shopping
Bob Evans
RESTAURANT
OH 41
74 A/B
Knights Inn
Hampton Inn
BP Al's Pizza China Garden
McDonald's Pizza Hut Subway
H
TROY, OH
BP Shell
Lincoln Sp Restaurant
Waffle House
Wendy's
Best Western
Econolodge
H
OH 55
73
SUPER 8 MOTEL
County Rd. 25A
69
Citgo Subway Starfire
TIPP CITY, OH
OH 571
68
Citgo Speedway Valero Arby's
Big Boy Bob Evans
Tipp'O Town Restaurant Wendy's
Holiday Inn Express Travelodge
BP Shell Speedway
Burger King Domino's
Fox's Pizza Ginger Grill
Hickory River Restaurant
Hong Kong Kitchen McDonald's
Subway Taco Bell
VANDALIA, OH
Northwoods Blvd.
64
Kroger
BP Shell Speedway Arby's
Burger King Domino's
KFC/LJ Silver's McDonald's
Pizza Hut Rib House
Subway Taco Bell
Waffle House Wendy's
Super 8
US 40
63
CROSS COUNTRY INN
Speedway Dragon China
Fricker's Restaurant
Junction I-70
61 A/B
To KOA-Dayton Resort
Tall Timbers 937-833-3888
(I-75 Southbound only)
To Huber RV and Mobile Homes Park 937-233-8822
To Enon Beach Campground 937-882-6431
DAYTON,OH
I-75 Mile Markers
80
78
76
74
72
70
68
66
64
62
60
Toledo
Lake Erie
Findlay
Lima
Sidney
Dayton
Cincinnati
OHIO
EXIT 74 TROY, OH
Hampton Inn
100% Satisfaction Guaranteed
• 14-item complimentary breakfast
• all rooms: iron/board, hairdryers, coffee makers and microwave-refrigerator units
• fitness center and indoor heated pool
937-339-7801
1-800-HAMPTON
EXIT 73 TROY, OH
SUPER 8 MOTEL
SAVE 15% with this ad!
Some restrictions apply.
& COMPLIMENTARY BREAKFAST
SUPER 8 MOTEL TROY
1330 Archer Drive
Tel/Fax: 937-339-6564
1-800-800-8000
70 Rooms - All ground floor!
Outdoor Pool Free local calls
Plug-in for fax machine/copy machine available
EXIT 63 VANDALIA, OH
25% discount upon redemption
CROSS COUNTRY INN
1-800-621-1429
* Not valid with any other offer or discount. Valid at all I-75 Cross Country Inn locations. One coupon per room per night.
The Cleanest Place You'll Ever Stay

Dayton/Montgomery County OHIO

Dayton/Montgomery County Convention & Visitors Bureau, Inc.
1 Chamber Plaza, Suite A, Dayton, Ohio 45402-2400
937-226-8211 or 800-221-8235 **www.daytoncvb.com**

Dayton, a city literally at the crossroads of America, offers unique recreational and educational opportunities around every corner. World-famous museums, dozens of unique attractions, professional arts organizations, miles of riverfront, acres of parkland, and a rich and colorful history draw hundreds of thousands of visitors to Dayton each year.

Dayton is one of the nation's top ten "90-minute land and air markets," which means that more than 5.6 million people can reach the city by land or air within just 90 minutes. Conveniently located at the "Crossroads of America" at the intersection of Interstate 70 and Interstate 75, Dayton is also accessible by nearly 30 daily non-stop jet service flights to Dayton International Airport.

Famous as the birthplace of Orville and Wilbur Wright, Dayton superlatives go far beyond aeronautics. World-class museums, historic sites, an impressive array of arts organizations and numerous settings—including everything from forests to prairies to wetland—have made Dayton one of America's most appealing cities.

United States Air Force Museum

If you are only going to make one detour along the I-75, you must visit the **U.S. Air Force Museum.** This free attraction is internationally recognized as the largest and oldest aviation museum in the world. With over 10 acres of indoor and outdoor exhibits, you'll see over 300 aircraft and missiles, plus thousands of personal artifacts, documents, photographs and mementos from the early 1900s to the present.

The Museum complex is operated by the U.S. Air Force and is located at the Wright-Patterson Air Force Base. Over one million visitors from across the nation and around the globe tour the Museum each year making it Ohio's number one non-commercial tourist attraction. The Museum is open daily, except Thanksgiving, Christmas and New Years Day, from 9 a.m. to 5 p.m. 1100 Spaatz St., Wright-Patterson Air Force Base, Ohio 45433-7102. 937-255-3286 www.wpafb.af.mil/museum

Attractions

Aviation Trail
Wright Dunbar Plaza, 22 S. William St. 937-225-7705 www.aviationtrailinc.org

Aullwood Audubon Center & Farm
100 Aullwood Rd. 937-890-7360 www.aullwood.center.audubon.org

Carillon Historical Park
65-acre historical park with local exhibits in 20 buildings including a replica of the Wright Cycle Company, the 1905 Wright Flyer III and a 1796 log house. Located on the banks of the Great Miami River in Dayton. 100 Carillon Blvd. Dayton. 937-293-3412 www.carillonpark.org America's Packard Museum

America's Packard Museum
See photo on page 66. 420 Ludlow St. 937-226-1917 www.americaspackard.org

The Dayton Art Institute
Free. 456 Belmonte Park N, Dayton. 937-223-5277 www.daytonartinstitute.org

Dayton International Airport
3600 Terminal Dr. 937-454-8200

Boonshoft Museum of Discovery
2600 DeWeese Pkwy. 937-275-7431 www.boonshoftmuseum.org

Five Rivers MetroParks 937-278-8231

International Women's Air & Space Museum
19 Summerhaven Rd., Dayton. 937-426-3519 www.iwasm.org

Miami Valley Dinner Theater
Route 73 at I-75 exit 38. 937-746-4554

National Afro-American Museum and Cultural Center
1350 Brush Row Rd., Wilberforce. 800-752-2603 www.ohiohistory.org

Kings Island
Open 7 days a week from Memorial Day through August 25, selected weekends in April, May Sept and Oct. 800-288-0808 www.visitkingsisland.com

SunWatch Indian Village
2301 W. River Rd., 937-268-8199 www.sunwatch.org

Paul Laurence Dunbar House State Memorial More information about Paul Laurence Dunbar and other Dayton's celebrated residents is found on page 82. Memorial is located at 219 Paul Laurence Dunbar St. 513-224-7061 www.ohiohistory.org

Woodland Cemetery and Arboretum
See page 82 for description and history of the cemetery and arboretum. 118 Woodland Ave. 937-228-3221 www.woodlandcemetery.org

The Wright Brothers Cycle Shop
Sat. 10 a.m.-4 p.m.; Sun. noon-4 p.m. Other hours are by appointment only. 22 S. Williams St.937-225-7705

The Wright Bros. Memorial
Huffman Prairie Flying Field in Dayton where Orville and Wilbur Wright first began testing their invention of powered flight. Call Five Rivers MetroParks for information. 937-275-PARK

U.S. Air Force Museum
Free. See photo and highlights on this page. Open daily, 9 a.m.-5 p.m. I-75 exit 58 or 54C, east 6 miles to Springfield St. at WPAFB. 937-255-3286

U.S. Air Force Museum, *courtesy Ohio Dept. of Development, Division of Travel and Tourism*

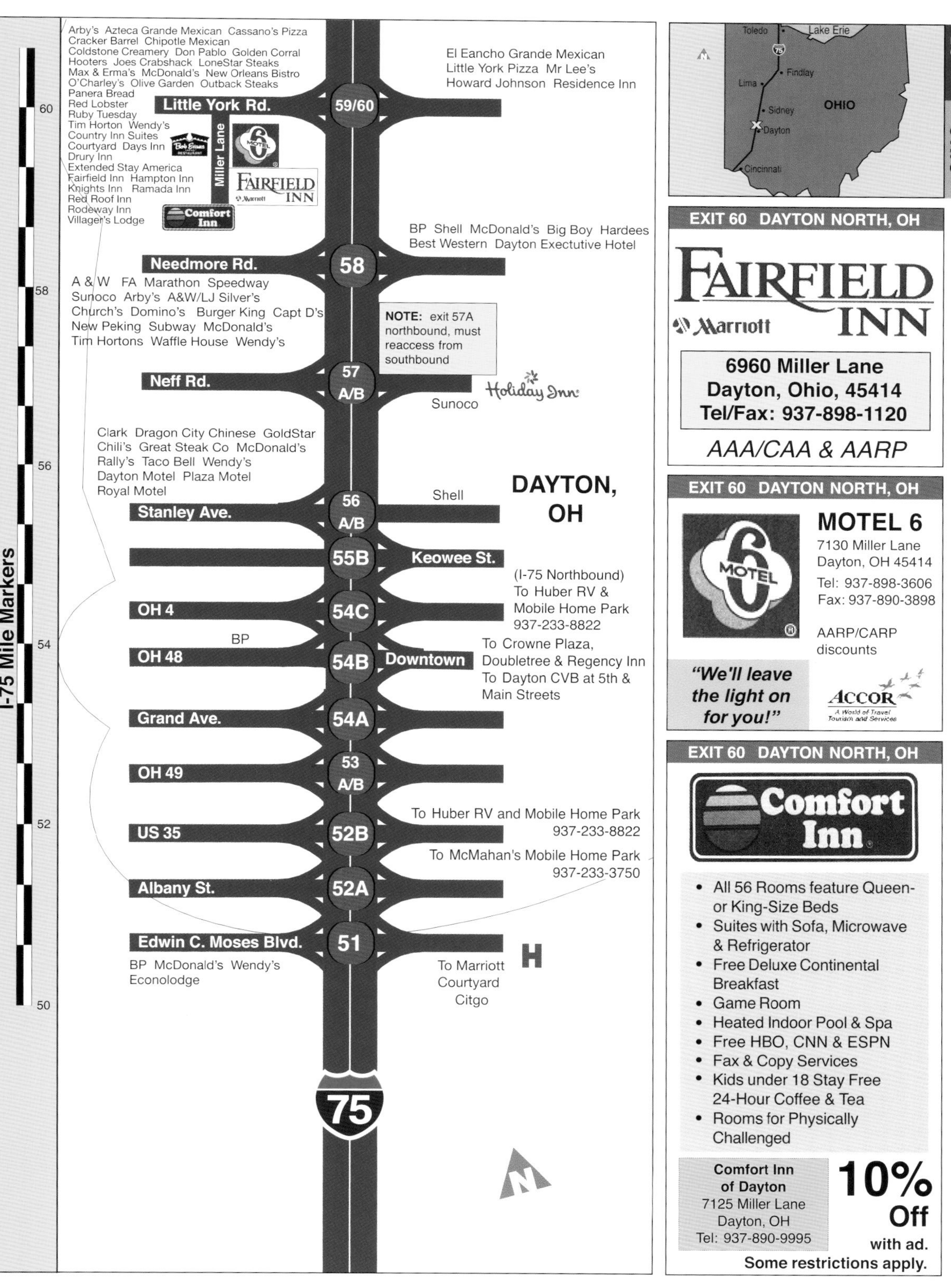
I-75 Mile Markers
60
58
56
54
52
50
Arby's Azteca Grande Mexican Cassano's Pizza
Cracker Barrel Chipotle Mexican
Coldstone Creamery Don Pablo Golden Corral
Hooters Joes Crabshack LoneStar Steaks
Max & Erma's McDonald's New Orleans Bistro
O'Charley's Olive Garden Outback Steaks
Panera Bread
Red Lobster
Ruby Tuesday
Tim Horton Wendy's
Country Inn Suites
Courtyard Days Inn
Drury Inn
Extended Stay America
Fairfield Inn Hampton Inn
Knights Inn Ramada Inn
Red Roof Inn
Rodeway Inn
Villager's Lodge
Little York Rd.
Miller Lane
59/60
El Eancho Grande Mexican
Little York Pizza Mr Lee's
Howard Johnson Residence Inn
FAIRFIELD INN
Comfort Inn
BP Shell McDonald's Big Boy Hardees
Best Western Dayton Exectutive Hotel
Needmore Rd.
58
A & W FA Marathon Speedway
Sunoco Arby's A&W/LJ Silver's
Church's Domino's Burger King Capt D's
New Peking Subway McDonald's
Tim Hortons Waffle House Wendy's
NOTE: exit 57A northbound, must reaccess from southbound
Neff Rd.
57 A/B
Holiday Inn
Sunoco
Clark Dragon City Chinese GoldStar
Chili's Great Steak Co McDonald's
Rally's Taco Bell Wendy's
Dayton Motel Plaza Motel
Royal Motel
Shell
DAYTON, OH
Stanley Ave.
56 A/B
55B
Keowee St.
(I-75 Northbound)
To Huber RV & Mobile Home Park
937-233-8822
OH 4
54C
BP
OH 48
54B
Downtown
To Crowne Plaza, Doubletree & Regency Inn
To Dayton CVB at 5th & Main Streets
Grand Ave.
54A
OH 49
53 A/B
To Huber RV and Mobile Home Park
937-233-8822
US 35
52B
To McMahan's Mobile Home Park
937-233-3750
Albany St.
52A
Edwin C. Moses Blvd.
51
BP McDonald's Wendy's
Econolodge
To Marriott
Courtyard
Citgo
H
75
N
Toledo
Lake Erie
75
Findlay
Lima
OHIO
Sidney
Dayton
Cincinnati

Dayton/Montgomery County OHIO

Dayton/Montgomery County Convention & Visitors Bureau, Inc.
1 Chamber Plaza, Suite A, Dayton, Ohio 45402-2400
937-226-8211 or 800-221-8235 **www.daytoncvb.com**

Outdoor Attractions

AVIATION TRAIL
The Dayton Aviation Trail is a self-guided tour highlighting various aviation landmarks located in the Dayton/Miami Valley area. Each site is marked by a blue and white Aviation Trail sign. A few of the highlights include: hearing a National Park Ranger recount the Wright Brothers early interest in flight at the Wright Cycle Company; seeing the original 1905 Wright Flyer III, the world's first practical airplane; watching a flyable look-alike of the Wrights' Model B, the world's first mass-produced airplane; and, walking the Huffman Prairie Flying Field where the Wrights tested their experimental machines. 937-443-0793

SunWatch INDIAN VILLAGE
The Fort Ancient Indians, some 800 years ago, settled along the banks of the Great Miami River. After 20 years of archaeological excavation, the SunWatch Indian Village offers a unique view of the lives of these early farmers. Call for information on the festival dates and special events. 2301 West River Rd., Dayton, Ohio. 937-268-8199

FIVE RIVERS METROPARKS
20 outstanding facilities comprise Dayton's famed Five Rivers MetroParks including the Carriage Hill MetroPark Farm Museum. At this living historical farm, the anvil still rings in the blacksmith shop, farm animals live in the barn, and crops grown some 100 years ago still thrive in the fields. Call for information about the special events including the Ice Harvest and Dulcimer Day. 937-275-PARK www.dayton.net/MetroParks

AULLWOOD AUDUBON CENTER AND FARM
The Aullwood Audubon Center and Farm, known as the Miami Valley's first educational farm, is a 350-acre sanctuary consisting of six miles of trails winding through prairie, woods, ponds and meadows. Here, visitors will discover a variety of native grasses and flowers, as well as 300 year old oak trees and threatened bird species, such as grasshopper sparrows, Henslow sparrows and bobolinks. Events include maple-syrup making in Feb. and March, a Wildlife Festival in May and an Apple Fest, Quilt Auction and Enchanted Forest in Sept. and Oct. 1000 Aullwood Rd., Dayton, Ohio. 937-890-7360

Special Events

Dayton Contemporary Dance Theater Winter Concert. Experience DCDC's worldwide reputation for energy-driven, modern and contemporary concert dance. Early Feb. Call for times and locations. 937-228-3232

Country Peddler Show. A magical weekend immersed in the beauty and tradition of the finest decorating and fashion designs in the country. Mid-Feb. Call for times. 937-228-3232

Dayton Auto Show. Dayton's largest downtown public show featuring the new cars, trucks, minivans and sport utility vehicles available in the Greater Dayton area. Dayton Convention Center. Early Mar. 937-443-4700

Art Quilt Exhibit. Aullwood Audubon Center and Farm. Early Mar. to early Apr., 1 p.m.-5 p.m. 937-890-7360

SunWatch Season Opening. Mid-Mar., open from noon-5 p.m. SunWatch Prehistoric Indian Village. 937-268-8199

Dayton Home and Garden Show. Home improvements, lawn and garden equipment, appliances, decorating services, landscaping and more. Open Mid-Mar. Dayton Convention Center. 800-274-6948

Bike Expo. Bicycle enthusiasts are invited to check out this free one-day event featuring "everything bikes." Events located at Stillwater Gardens MetroPark and Wegerzyn Gardens. 937-275-PARK

Israel Independence Day Celebration. Entertainment, food, games and crafts highlight this celebration of Israel's independence. Late Apr., 10 a.m.-4 p.m. Free at the U. of Dayton. 937-854-4150

Wildlife Festival. A family event with wild animals, good food, wagon rides, children's activities and exhibits. Early May, 10 a.m. - 5 p.m. Aullwood Audubon Center. 937-890-7360

Fiesta Latino Americana. Celebrate Hispanic culture with food, drink, arts, crafts and music. Mid-June. Free. Fraze Pavilion. 937-297-3720

Miamisburg Spring Fling Festival. Festival with arts and crafts booths, children's activities, food concessions, free entertainment, rides, games and more. Mid-May. Library Park, Downtown Miamisburg and Pipestone Golf Course. Free. 937-866-4532

Hamvention. Largest gathering of amateur Ham radio operators in the U.S. This three-day event features a trade show, flea market, seminars, speakers and awards banquet. Mid-May. Dayton Hara Complex. 937-276-6930

Dayton International Festival. Food, entertainment and cultural displays form 35 countries. Mid-May. Dayton Convention Center. 937-443-4700

Rail & Steam Festival. Full-scale static rail exhibits, scale train rides, garden railroads and other interesting trail-related activities. Late May. Carillon Historical Park. 937-293-2841

Hummel Expo. Three-day event in mid-June. At the Dayton Convention Center. 937-443-4700

Fiesta Latino Americana. Celebrate Hispanic culture with food, drink, arts, crafts and music. Mid-June. Free. Fraze Pavilion. 937-222-1505

National Advanced and Challenged Square Dance Competition. The highest level of square dancing. Mid-June. At the Dayton Convention Center. 937-443-4700

Ohio State Trapshooting Tournament. The best trapshooters in the state gather for this annual tournament at the end of June. Free admission for spectators. Amateur Trapshooting Grounds. 937-898-4638

Keeping the Tradition Pow Wow and Celebration. Late June. Many special events and opportunities. Caesar's Ford Park. 937-275-8599

Caribbean Night. Late June. Free. Fraze Pavilion. 937-297-3720

Trivia

Dayton's founding fathers included Benjamin Van Cleve, Daniel Cooper, Colonel George Newcom, and Jonathon Dayton. Jonathon Dayton, a New Jersey senator, was one of the original owners of the land and because his was the most pleasing sounding name, it was chosen for the name of the city.

In 1879, restauranteur James Ritty invented the cash register, but it took a tollkeeper on the Miami and Erie Canal to realize its advantage. John Patterson bought out Ritty's business and patent for $1,000 and his brother-in-law John Birch added the cash drawer and bell.

In 1903, Orville & Wilbur Wright, neither of whom graduated from their high school, invented the airplane.

In a barn near Dayton, Edward Deeds, Charles F. Kettering and William A. Chryst invented the first self-starting ignition system for the automobile. They sold the starter to the Cadillac Company. Wright-Patterson Air Force Base is the Dayton area's largest employer.

The Dayton Art Institute displays Claude Monet's masterpiece, *Waterlilies*. It was painted in 1903.

Mead, NCR and Reynolds & Reynolds are three Fortune 500 companies with headquarters in Dayton.

Renowned author Paul Laurence Dunbar, a Dayton native, worked as an elevator operator before he launched his writing career. Dunbar, the son of a former slave, attended school with Orville Wright.

Talk show host Phil Donahue was raised in Centerville and lived across the street from syndicated columnist and author Erma Bombeck early in their careers. Other Dayton residents: John Glenn, Edwin Moses, Thomas Watson (founded IBM), Virginia Hollinger (tennis), Jonathon Winters (entertainer), and Sam Hall (diving).

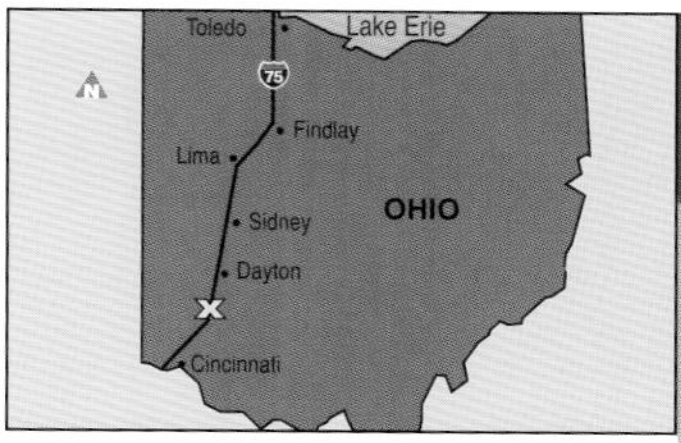

Toledo
Lake Erie
75
Findlay
Lima
Sidney
OHIO
Dayton
Cincinnati

Welcome to South Dayton

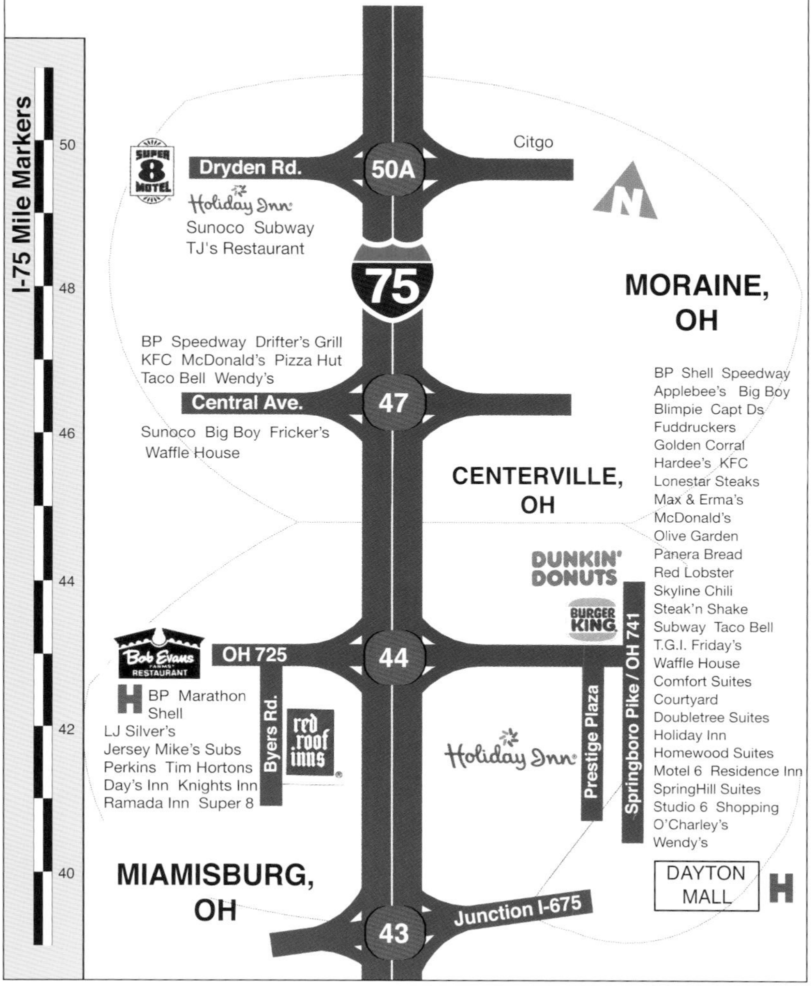

I-75 Mile Markers
50
48
46
44
42
40

Dryden Rd.
50A
Citgo
Holiday Inn
Sunoco Subway
TJ's Restaurant
75
MORAINE, OH

BP Speedway Drifter's Grill
KFC McDonald's Pizza Hut
Taco Bell Wendy's
Central Ave.
47
Sunoco Big Boy Fricker's
Waffle House
CENTERVILLE, OH

BP Shell Speedway
Applebee's Big Boy
Blimpie Capt Ds
Fuddruckers
Golden Corral
Hardee's KFC
Lonestar Steaks
Max & Erma's
McDonald's
Olive Garden
Panera Bread
Red Lobster
Skyline Chili
Steak'n Shake
Subway Taco Bell
T.G.I. Friday's
Waffle House
Comfort Suites
Courtyard
Doubletree Suites
Holiday Inn
Homewood Suites
Motel 6 Residence Inn
SpringHill Suites
Studio 6 Shopping
O'Charley's
Wendy's

DUNKIN' DONUTS
BURGER KING
Bob Evans Farms Restaurant
OH 725
44
H
BP Marathon
Shell
LJ Silver's
Jersey Mike's Subs
Perkins Tim Hortons
Day's Inn Knights Inn
Ramada Inn Super 8
Byers Rd.
red roof inns
Holiday Inn
Prestige Plaza
Springboro Pike / OH 741
DAYTON MALL
H
MIAMISBURG, OH
43
Junction I-675

Warren County
OHIO

Warren County Convention & Visitors Bureau
5412 Courseview Drive, Suite 200, Mason, Ohio 45040
800-791-4FUN **www.wccvb.org**

WARREN COUNTY
It would take four pages to detail the tourist opportunities in this impressive county. A quick sample includes the country's most popular seasonal amusement park, over 10 world-class golf courses, the highest concentration of antique shops in the U.S., the Underground Railroad, Quaker villages, Indian history (Fort Ancient, built by prehistoric moundbuilders), Ohio's oldest inn and restaurant (The Golden Lamb in Lebanon), first-class bed and breakfasts, and simply great camping.

SPRINGBORO
Founded in 1815 by Quaker pioneer Jonathon Wright (yes, he was kin to Orville and Wilbur) and named for the underground springs that once powered local grist and woolen mills, Springboro was a well-used stop on the Underground Railroad. The town is known for its golf and theater.

LEBANON
The Golden Lamb Inn, Ohio's oldest inn and restaurant, hosted 10 U.S. Presidents and served as a hub of stagecoach activity in the 1800s. Brick side-walks between the antique and specialty shops lead you to the Warren County Historical Society Museum, one of the nation's most outstanding county museums. The museum exhibits range from prehistoric to the Victorian age, with antique toys, archaeology collections, and Shaker artifacts. One of the finest examples of residential Greek Revival architecture in the Midwest is the Glendower State Memorial (1835). It is beautifully furnished with period pieces.

KINGS ISLAND AREA / MASON
Mason was named for Major William Mason, a Revolutionary War soldier and early owner of much of the land in the area. Near Mason, is one of the world's favorite seasonal theme parks. **Kings Island** has roller coasters, movie attractions, live entertainment and much more. Nearby, the Beach Waterpark is ranked in the nation's Top 10 by the *New York Times,* and is a splash for all ages. You will also enjoy the art galleries, antiques, shops and good food. Did you know that Mason is home to the ATP Tennis Championships and the Kroger Senior PGA Golf Classic?

WAYNESVILLE
Settled by English pioneers in 1797, Waynesville is the birthplace of not only chewing tobacco and branch banking but also the *Stetson* hat. Waynesville is well-known as the Antiques Capital of the Midwestern states.

Attractions

Kings Island
Open daily Memorial Day to Labor Day and some weekends in Apr., Sept. and Oct. From I-75 take exit 7 in Cincinnati to I-71 exit 25A. Kings Island Dr., Mason, OH. 800-288-0808 or 513-573-5700 www.visitkingsisland.com

The Beach Waterpark. Memorial Day to Labor Day. 2590 Waterpark Dr., Mason. (from I-75 take exit 7 to I-71 exit 25B). 800-886-SWIM or 513-398-SWIM

The Golf Center at Kings Island
Kroger PGA Senior Golf Classic in June. Mar. to Dec. 6042 Fairway Dr., in Mason, OH. 513-398-7700

Caesar Creek State Park Beach, boat ramps, skiing, trails, picnic areas. For camping see below. Year-round during daylight hours. 8570 E. Ohio Rt. 73, Waynesville, OH. 513-897-3055.

Caesar Creek *Camping* on Center Rd. off Ohio Rt. 380, call 513-488-4595

Yogi Bear's Kings Island Camp-Resort
Kings Island Dr., Mason. 800-344-9644

Cedarbrook Campground
760 Franklin Rd. (Ohio Rt. 123), near Lebanon. 513-932-7717

Spring Valley Frontier Campground
Camping, log cabins and cottages. Open year-round. 9580 Collett Rd., near Waynesville. 513-862-4510.

Fort Ancient Campground
On Ward-Koebel Rd. Use I-75 exit 7, then to I-71 exit 36. Lebanon. 513-289-2095

Caesar Creek Pioneer Village
Year-round self-guided tours. 3999 Pioneer Village Rd., Waynesville. 513-897-1120

Harveysburg Black School
First free black school in the Northwest Territory, operated by abolitionist Quakers. 1776 North St., P.O. Box 105, Harveysburg, OH (off Ohio Rt. 73). Tours only by appointment: 513-897-6195

Franklin's First Post Office
Restored 1805 log post office. Downtown Franklin, OH. 513-746-8295

Little Miami Scenic State Park & Bike Trail. 50-mile linear park on east bank of the river. 8570 E. Ohio Rt. 73, Waynesville, OH. 513-897-3055

Kings Island. *Courtesy Ohio Dept. of Development*

Turtle Creek Valley Railway
One-hour round-trip, Apr. to Dec. Ride-n-dine mystery tours. 198 S. Broadway, Lebanon, OH. 513-398-8584

Glendower State Memorial. Open Wed. to Sat. June to Labor Day. Weekends only Labor Day to Oct. 105 Cincinnati Ave., P.O. Box 223, Lebanon, OH. 513-932-1817

Golden Lamb Inn. 27 S. Broadway, Lebanon, OH. 513-932-5065

Fort Ancient State Memorial
National Historic Landmark, built by prehistoric moundbuilders. Chronicles Ohio's entire Indian heritage from prehistoric to modern times. Weekends, Apr. to May and Sept. to Oct., Wed. to Sun. from Memorial Day to Labor Day. 5123 Ohio Rt. 350, Oregonia, OH. 513-932-4421

Warren County Historical Society Museum. 105 S. Broadway, Lebanon, OH. Tues. to Sun. 513-932-1817

Heatherwoode Golf Course
On Ohio Rt. 741 south of Ohio Rt. 73. 88 Heatherwoode Blvd., Springboro, OH. 513-748-3222

Miami Valley Dinner Theatre
With 612 seats, the Miami Valley Dinner Theater is the fourth largest in the U.S., and southwest Ohio's only professional dinner theater. Open in 1975, the premises were designed specifically to house a dinner theater, so there are no poles obstructing the view. 765 W. Central Ave., P.O. Box 204, Springboro, OH. 513-746-4554

Harding Home & Museum
380 Mt. Vernon Avenue, Marion, OH, 43302. 740-387-9630 or 800-600-6894

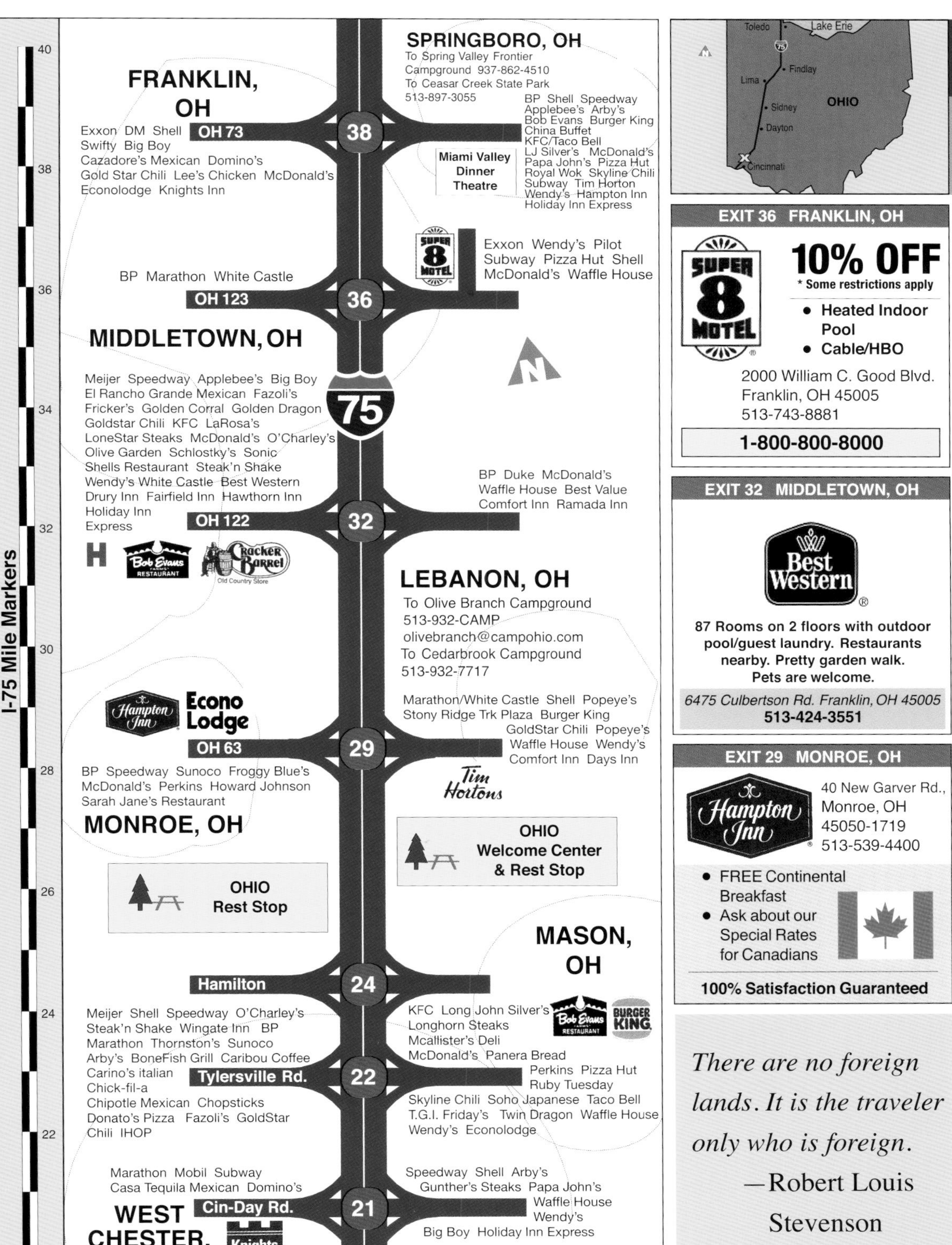
I-75 Mile Markers
40
38
36
34
32
30
28
26
24
22
20
SPRINGBORO, OH
To Spring Valley Frontier Campground 937-862-4510
To Ceasar Creek State Park 513-897-3055
BP Shell Speedway Applebee's Arby's Bob Evans Burger King China Buffet KFC/Taco Bell LJ Silver's McDonald's Papa John's Pizza Hut Royal Wok Skyline Chili Subway Tim Horton Wendy's Hampton Inn Holiday Inn Express
Miami Valley Dinner Theatre
FRANKLIN, OH
Exxon DM Shell Swifty Big Boy Cazadore's Mexican Domino's Gold Star Chili Lee's Chicken McDonald's Econolodge Knights Inn
OH 73
38
Super 8 Motel
Exxon Wendy's Pilot Subway Pizza Hut Shell McDonald's Waffle House
BP Marathon White Castle
OH 123
36
MIDDLETOWN, OH
N
75
Meijer Speedway Applebee's Big Boy El Rancho Grande Mexican Fazoli's Fricker's Golden Corral Golden Dragon Goldstar Chili KFC LaRosa's LoneStar Steaks McDonald's O'Charley's Olive Garden Schlostky's Sonic Shells Restaurant Steak'n Shake Wendy's White Castle Best Western Drury Inn Fairfield Inn Hawthorn Inn Holiday Inn Express
BP Duke McDonald's Waffle House Best Value Comfort Inn Ramada Inn
OH 122
32
H
Bob Evans Restaurant
Cracker Barrel Old Country Store
LEBANON, OH
To Olive Branch Campground 513-932-CAMP olivebranch@campohio.com
To Cedarbrook Campground 513-932-7717
Hampton Inn
Econo Lodge
Marathon/White Castle Shell Popeye's Stony Ridge Trk Plaza Burger King GoldStar Chili Popeye's Waffle House Wendy's Comfort Inn Days Inn
OH 63
29
BP Speedway Sunoco Froggy Blue's McDonald's Perkins Howard Johnson Sarah Jane's Restaurant
MONROE, OH
Tim Hortons
OHIO Welcome Center & Rest Stop
OHIO Rest Stop
MASON, OH
Hamilton
24
Meijer Shell Speedway O'Charley's Steak'n Shake Wingate Inn BP Marathon Thornston's Sunoco Arby's BoneFish Grill Caribou Coffee Carino's italian Chick-fil-a Chipotle Mexican Chopsticks Donato's Pizza Fazoli's GoldStar Chili IHOP
KFC Long John Silver's Longhorn Steaks Mcallister's Deli McDonald's Panera Bread Perkins Pizza Hut Ruby Tuesday Skyline Chili Soho Japanese Taco Bell T.G.I. Friday's Twin Dragon Waffle House Wendy's Econolodge
Bob Evans Restaurant
Burger King
Tylersville Rd.
22
Marathon Mobil Subway Casa Tequila Mexican Domino's
Speedway Shell Arby's Gunther's Steaks Papa John's Waffle House Wendy's Big Boy Holiday Inn Express
Cin-Day Rd.
21
WEST CHESTER, OH
Knights Inn
Toledo
Lake Erie
75
Findlay
Lima
Sidney
OHIO
Dayton
Cincinnati
EXIT 36 FRANKLIN, OH
Super 8 Motel
10% OFF
* Some restrictions apply
• Heated Indoor Pool
• Cable/HBO
2000 William C. Good Blvd. Franklin, OH 45005 513-743-8881
1-800-800-8000
EXIT 32 MIDDLETOWN, OH
Best Western
87 Rooms on 2 floors with outdoor pool/guest laundry. Restaurants nearby. Pretty garden walk. Pets are welcome.
6475 Culbertson Rd. Franklin, OH 45005
513-424-3551
EXIT 29 MONROE, OH
Hampton Inn
40 New Garver Rd., Monroe, OH 45050-1719 513-539-4400
• FREE Continental Breakfast
• Ask about our Special Rates for Canadians
100% Satisfaction Guaranteed

There are no foreign lands. It is the traveler only who is foreign.

—Robert Louis Stevenson

Cincinnati
OHIO

Greater Cincinnati Convention & Visitors Bureau
525 Vine St., Suite 1500, Cincinnati, Ohio 45202
513-621-2142 or 800--543-2613 **www.cincyusa.com**

There's a lot to love about Cincinnati. From the first glimpse of the impressive Cincinnati skyline to the last time you cross the river, you'll be blown away by the sweeping views and unique experiences. Take in a game with America's first professional baseball team. Stroll through one of the nationally recognized museums. Or taste a dish you won't forget – Cincinnati-style chilli. Whatever your taste you'll find it in Cincinnati USA.

The diverse architecture of this great city is best surveyed via a walking tour through the downtown area, which is graced with outdoor sculptures and parks.

Eden Park has **Krohn Conservatory**, **Playhouse in the Park** and the **Cincinnati Art Museum**.

Many choose a luncheon or dinner sightseeing cruise to see the city for the first time. Some of the excursion boat cruises offer to stop at the **Riverbend Music Center,** the famous outdoor amphitheater and summer home of the Cincinnati Pops. Many of the horse-drawn carriages begin their leisurely afternoon and evening city tours at the beautiful Fountain Square.

The **World's Sexiest Zoo** (according to Newsweek magazine) is well worth your time. The zoo features Komodo dragons, lowland gorillas, white tigers, and other rare animals. You and your children would be lucky to view the endangered species only found at the **Cincinnati Zoo & Botanical Garden.**

The **Cincinnati Museum Center** at Union Terminal is a magnificent example of Cincinnati's Art Deco style. Visitors can easily recognize Union Terminal for its massive 180-foot-diameter half-dome, an architectural wonder that's the largest in the Western Hemisphere. Once inside you can explore fantastic museums including the Cincinnati History Museum, Duke Energy Children's Museum, the Museum of Natural History & Science and the OMNIMAX Theater.

Great American Ballpark is home to baseball's first professional team, the Cincinnati Reds. Paul brown Stadium is home to the Cincinnati Bengals.

Cincinnati is consistently rated one of North America's most liveable cities and also one of the most "visitable." Whether you are visiting for an afternoon or a longer stay, it would be helpful to look over the Cincinnati USA Visitors Guide. Call the Cincinnati USA Convention & Visitors Bureau at 800-543-2613 or visit CincyUSA.com to order your visitors pack.

Cincinnati at night. *Chris Cone, courtesy Ohio Department of Development, Division of Travel and Tourism*

Attractions

BB Riverboats
Greater Cincinnati's oldest and largest riverboat company offers sailings year round. 101 Riverboat Row, Newport, Kentucky 41071 800-261-8586 www.bbriverboats.com

Cincinnati Art Museum
Spanning 6,000 years, the Museum treasures include painting, prints, drawings, photography, decorative arts, costumes and sculpture. 953 Eden Park, Cincinnati. 513-721-2787

Cincinnati Museum Center at Union Terminal
Explore 19,000 years of hands-on fun at the Museum of Natural History & Science, the Cincinnati History Museum and the Duke Energy Children's Museum. Experience the five story OMNIMAX Theatre. Minutes from I-75. 1301 Western Ave., Cincinnati. 800-733-2077 or 513-287-7000 www.cincymuseum.org

Cincinnati Opera
1243 Elm St., Cincinnati. 513-241-ARIA

The Cincinnati Playhouse in the Park
Eden Park, Cincinnati. 513-421-3888

The Cincinnati Reds Hall of Fame
100 Joe Nuxhall Way, Cincinnati. 513-765-7000

Cincinnati Symphony Orchestra
1241 Elm St. 513-381-3300

Cincinnati Zoo & Botanical Garden
Festival of Lights runs mid-Nov. to early Jan. 3400 Vine St. 513-281-4700 www.cincinnatizoo.org

Coney Island
6201 Kellogg Ave. Cincinnati. 513-232-8230

Harriet Beecher Stowe House
2950 Gilbert Ave. 513-751-0651

Jungle Jims' International Market
The food lover's paradise! Located at 5440 Dixie Way, Fairfield, OH. 513-674-6000 www.junglejims.com

Krohn Conservatory
Eden Park Dr. 513-421-4086

The Taft Museum
316 Pike St. 513-241-0343

National Underground Railroad Freedom Center
50 East Freedom Way, Cincinnati. 513-333-7500 www.freedomcenter.org

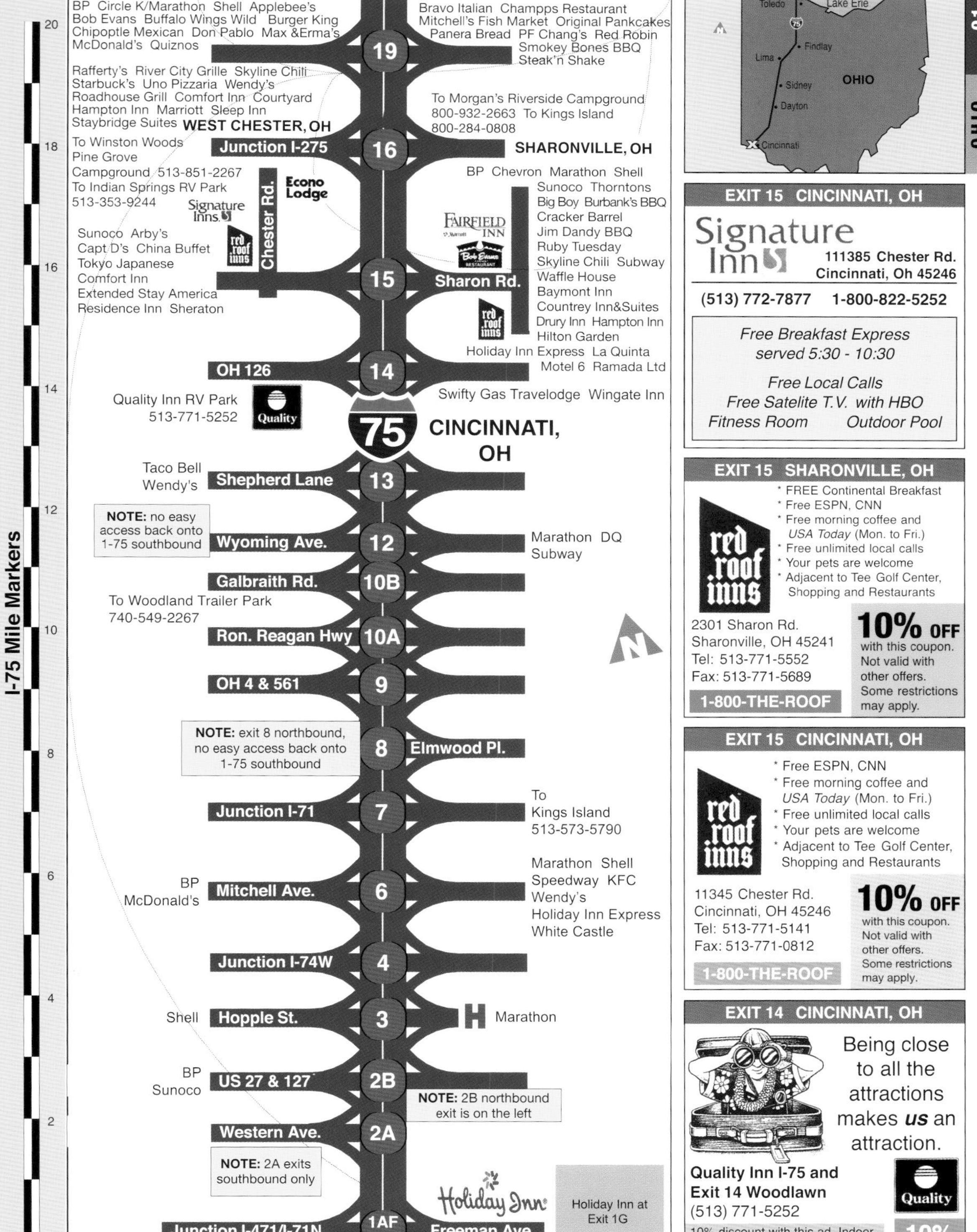
91
OHIO
Toledo
Lake Erie
75
Findlay
Lima
Sidney
OHIO
Dayton
Cincinnati
I-75 Mile Markers
20
18
16
14
12
10
8
6
4
2
0
BP Circle K/Marathon Shell Applebee's
Bob Evans Buffalo Wings Wild Burger King
Chipoptle Mexican Don Pablo Max &Erma's
McDonald's Quiznos
Bravo Italian Champps Restaurant
Mitchell's Fish Market Original Pankcakes
Panera Bread PF Chang's Red Robin
Smokey Bones BBQ
Steak'n Shake
19
Rafferty's River City Grille Skyline Chili
Starbuck's Uno Pizzaria Wendy's
Roadhouse Grill Comfort Inn Courtyard
Hampton Inn Marriott Sleep Inn
Staybridge Suites
WEST CHESTER, OH
To Morgan's Riverside Campground
800-932-2663 To Kings Island
800-284-0808
Junction I-275
16
SHARONVILLE, OH
To Winston Woods
Pine Grove
Campground 513-851-2267
To Indian Springs RV Park
513-353-9244
Signature Inns
Chester Rd.
Econo Lodge
BP Chevron Marathon Shell
Sunoco Thorntons
Big Boy Burbank's BBQ
Cracker Barrel
Jim Dandy BBQ
Ruby Tuesday
Skyline Chili Subway
Waffle House
Baymont Inn
Countrey Inn&Suites
Drury Inn Hampton Inn
Hilton Garden
Holiday Inn Express La Quinta
Motel 6 Ramada Ltd
Fairfield Inn
Bob Evans Restaurant
red roof inns
Sunoco Arby's
Capt D's China Buffet
Tokyo Japanese
Comfort Inn
Extended Stay America
Residence Inn Sheraton
15
Sharon Rd.
OH 126
14
Swifty Gas Travelodge Wingate Inn
Quality Inn RV Park
513-771-5252
Quality
75
CINCINNATI, OH
Taco Bell
Wendy's
Shepherd Lane
13
NOTE: no easy access back onto 1-75 southbound
Wyoming Ave.
12
Marathon DQ
Subway
Galbraith Rd.
10B
To Woodland Trailer Park
740-549-2267
Ron. Reagan Hwy
10A
N
OH 4 & 561
9
NOTE: exit 8 northbound, no easy access back onto 1-75 southbound
8
Elmwood Pl.
Junction I-71
7
To
Kings Island
513-573-5790
BP
McDonald's
Mitchell Ave.
6
Marathon Shell
Speedway KFC
Wendy's
Holiday Inn Express
White Castle
Junction I-74W
4
Shell
Hopple St.
3
H
Marathon
BP
Sunoco
US 27 & 127
2B
NOTE: 2B northbound exit is on the left
Western Ave.
2A
NOTE: 2A exits southbound only
Holiday Inn
Holiday Inn at Exit 1G
Junction I-471/I-71N
1AF GH
Freeman Ave.
EXIT 15 CINCINNATI, OH
Signature Inn
111385 Chester Rd.
Cincinnati, Oh 45246
(513) 772-7877 1-800-822-5252
Free Breakfast Express served 5:30 - 10:30
Free Local Calls
Free Satelite T.V. with HBO
Fitness Room Outdoor Pool
EXIT 15 SHARONVILLE, OH
red roof inns
* FREE Continental Breakfast
* Free ESPN, CNN
* Free morning coffee and USA Today (Mon. to Fri.)
* Free unlimited local calls
* Your pets are welcome
* Adjacent to Tee Golf Center, Shopping and Restaurants
2301 Sharon Rd.
Sharonville, OH 45241
Tel: 513-771-5552
Fax: 513-771-5689
1-800-THE-ROOF
10% OFF
with this coupon. Not valid with other offers. Some restrictions may apply.
EXIT 15 CINCINNATI, OH
red roof inns
* Free ESPN, CNN
* Free morning coffee and USA Today (Mon. to Fri.)
* Free unlimited local calls
* Your pets are welcome
* Adjacent to Tee Golf Center, Shopping and Restaurants
11345 Chester Rd.
Cincinnati, OH 45246
Tel: 513-771-5141
Fax: 513-771-0812
1-800-THE-ROOF
10% OFF
with this coupon. Not valid with other offers. Some restrictions may apply.
EXIT 14 CINCINNATI, OH
Being close to all the attractions makes us an attraction.
Quality Inn I-75 and Exit 14 Woodlawn
(513) 771-5252
Quality
10% discount with this ad. Indoor and outdoor pools. FREE in-room coffee and Continental breakfast.
10% OFF

Cincinnati
OHIO

Greater Cincinnati Convention & Visitors Bureau
525 Vine St., Suite 1500, Cincinnati, Ohio 45202
513-621-2142 or 800-543-2613 **www.cincyusa.com**

The River Rises:

All is new along Cincinnati's Historic Waterfront

The Ohio River has played a major role in the success of Cincinnati throughout its history. Today, more than 40 acres of lush parkland, state-of-the-art sports facilities, and entertainment venues are the draw among the busy banks of the Ohio River.

The Cincinnati Reds-the oldest professional baseball team in the country—just moved into a sparkling new old-style baseball stadium, **Great American Ball Park**. With just over 42,000 seats, closer views of the playing field, and different food and entertainment options the stadium—which anchors the east end of the riverfront developments—has proved to be a hit with fans and players alike.

Football fans can keep an eye on the downtown skyline and the riverfront while they watch the Cincinnati Bengals play at the new **Paul Brown Stadium**, a $400 million NFL showcase facility with an asymmetrical, open-ended design. Almost 70 percent of the seats are along the sidelines, providing close-to-the-action sight lines—even from upper-level luxury boxes and low-tiered end zones.

If you'd rather get out and play yourself, **Sawyer Point** is a vast public park, recreation and entertainment area stretching along the riverfront. There, you'll find **Yeatsman's Cove Park**, named for Griffin Yeatman who ran the "Square & Compass" tavern back in the 1970's, a popular spot for concerts, picnics, festivals and river watching. **The Public Landing**, which long ago was the hub of a thriving steamboat port, still serves Cincinnati's *Delta Queen* and the *Showboat Majestic*, acquired by the city in 1967 and added to the National Registry of Historic Places in 1980.

Also at Sawyer Point is **Bicentennial Commons**, a 22 acre park opened in June 1998 to celebrate the city's 200th birthday. It features the famous Flying Pig Sculptures, a bicentennial Brick Promenade, a working model of the Ohio river and its 20 canal locks and dams (from Pittsburgh, PA to Cairo, Il), A 12-foot statue of Cincinnatus (the Roman soldier

The new Lois & Richard Rosenthal Center for Contemporary Art, the vibrant Cincinnati Main Street and the Cincinnati Pops Orchestra in historic Music Hall.
Courtesy Greater Cincinnati Convention & Visitors Bureau

for which Cincinnati was named), as well as the P&G Pavilion which is used regularly for concerts and performances. Add to that a fitness area, playground, volleyball and tennis courts, an all-weather skating rink, fishing pier and the Schott Ampitheater, and it's easy to see what makes Cincinnati's riverfront such a popular place.

Just east of bicentennial commons, the **Theodore M. Berry International Friendship Park** opened in May, 2008 named after Cincinnati's first black mayor who died in October 2000. The 22 acre park is intended to celebrate international understanding and diversity. The $8.5 million project includes bike and walking paths connecting Bicentennial commons and the future Central Riverfront Park to the west. The park's design, which features intertwining walkways, continent-shaped gardens, a pavilion, a serpentine-shaped sitting wall and an earth mound sculpture in the shape of open hands, draws its inspiration from a child's friendship bracelet.

The riverfront plays host to major events throughout the year-everything from jazz festivals to **Riverfest**, a Labor Day fireworks display that has become one of the biggest fireworks events in the nation. Cincinnati celebrates its river heritage with the world's largest paddlewheel festival during the Tall Stacks Festival. This festival highlights the music and culture that traveled the river with a montage of entertainment including blues, jazz, heartland rock, gospel and Dixieland Jazz. You could also enjoy Party in the Park which rocks the river at Yeatman's Cove with Cincinnati's hottest bands and the coldest beer in town. All set against the Ohio river and the new Great American Ball Park, this party serves as your happy hour every Wednesday throughout the summer months.

And there's even more in the busy riverfront. Situated between both stadiums The National Underground Railroad Freedom Center pays tribute to all efforts to "abolish human enslavement and secure freedom for all people." Its location recognizes the significant role the people of Cincinnati played in supporting the Underground Railroad.

For more information about riverfront and other new developments in Concinnati, visit www.CincyUSA.com/

Cincinnati
OHIO

Greater Cincinnati Convention & Visitors Bureau
525 Vine St., Suite 1500, Cincinnati, Ohio 45202
513-621-2142 or 800-543-2613 **www.cincyusa.com**

Theater flourishes in Cincinnati.

Cincinnati's thriving arts scene offers something for everyone, including outstanding theater options. Boasting award-winning world-premieres, hot Broadway and off-Broadway shows, the largest number of community theaters per capita and several college theaters, including the School for Creative and Performing Arts, there is a never-ending selection of productions to choose from.

The **Fifth Third Bank Broadway in Cincinnati** ranks as one of the nation's largest presenters of professional touring Broadway productions with performances at the Aronoff Center for the Arts. (www.broadwayacrossamerica.com, 513-241-2345)

The **Cincinnati Arts Association** oversees programming and management of the Aronoff Center for the Arts and Music Hall. It presents high-quality, multi-disciplinary arts programs. The **Aronoff Center for the Arts**, which opened in 1995, is located in the heart of downtown Cincinnati. The facility consists of Procter & Gamble Hall, a 2,719-seat theater, the Jarson-Kaplan Theater, a 437-seat theater and the Fifth Third Bank Theater, a 150-seat studio theater. The spectacular red-brick **Music Hall**, a Victorian Gothic structure designed by Samuel Hannaford, built in 1878, contains a 3,397-seat hall, known for its extraordinary acoustics and its lavish old world decor. With plush seating for 3,397, it serves as home for the Cincinnati Opera, Cincinnati Symphony Orchestra, the fifth oldest orchestra in the United States, and the May Festival Chorus, the oldest continual choral festival in the Western Hemisphere. (www.cincinnatiarts.org, 513-721-3344)

The **Cincinnati Opera** is the second oldest company in the United States and offers four mainstage productions during the summer at Music Hall. (www.cincinnatiopera.com, 513-241-2742)

The **Cincinnati Playhouse in the Park**, nestled in Mt. Adams with a superb view of downtown Cincinnati, has been offering audiences the finest in professional theater for 45 years. The Playhouse attracts over 225,000 people annually to its two theaters, the 628-seat Robert S. Marx Theater and the intimate Thompson Shelterhouse, which seats 225. Under the direction of Producing Artistic Director Edward Stern, the Playhouse presents 11 productions September through June including comedies, dramas, classics and musicals. Each show runs at least four weeks, with eight performances per week scheduled for every day but Monday. One of America's first regional theaters, the Playhouse is a not-for-profit organization and is ranked as one of the 20 most popular attractions in the Tri-state. (www.cincyplay.com, 513-421-3888)

Mt. Adams (foreground), within walking distance of downtown Cincinnati (background), is a fashionable residential area with many sweeping views of the Ohio River. *Courtesy Greater Cincinnati Convention and Visitors Bureau*

The **Cincinnati Shakespeare Festival** features the best of Shakespeare and the classics. This professional classic theater performs nine productions, September through June. (www.cincyshakes.com, 513-381-BARD)

The **Ensemble Theatre of Cincinnati (ETC)**, is an exciting home to regional, world and off-Broadway premiere productions. ETC is a professional equity theatre dedicated to the production and development of new works and works new to the region. ETC has been home to premiere productions by such esteemed playwrights as Edward Albee, Lee Blessing, Jeffrey Hatcher, Warren Leight, and lanford Wilson. (www.cincyetc.com, 513-421-3555)

Shadowbox Cabaret South, located at newport on the Levee, just across the river from Cincinnati 1 Newport, Kentucky, offers high-energy, live entertainment, featuring sketch comedy, theatre and rock 'n' roll. Appetizer-style food and full bar service. Customized shows and corporate functions are available for groups. www.shadowboxcabaret.com 859-581-7625)

Showboat Majestic, a National Historic landmark located on Cincinnati's scenic riverfront, features the best in musicals, comedies and dramas. 937-376-4358

North of Cincinnati in Xenia, OH, **Blue Jacket**, cited as America's #1 historical, outdoor theatre, masterfully combines horses, cannons, stunning athleticism and flaming arrows. Blue Jacket offers backstage tours, frontier picnic dinners, gift shop, free parking and more. www.bluejacketdrama.com 937-376-4358

For a complete list of theaters (including community theaters) and performances in Cincinnati, visit www.CincinnatiArts.com. Visitor information is available at www.CincyUSA.com or 800-543-2613

Kentucky

Kentucky Department of Travel
500 Mero Street, 22 Floor, Frankfort, Kentucky 40601-1968
502-564-4930 or 1-800-225-8747 **www.kentuckytourism.com**

It would be a shame to just drive through Kentucky. Those of us who spend even a few days in Kentucky's majestic mountains, forests and sparkling lakes quickly find this state becomes a pleasant habit!

Watching those remarkable thoroughbreds canter up and down the rolling fields of manicured bluegrass bordered by long white stretches of perfect fencing, even for just a few moments, is like living in a painting or a poem.

You can best experience the state's equine history and culture throughout the year by visiting the **Kentucky Horse Park** in Lexington. To watch the powerful thoroughbreds in action, visit one of the state's many racetracks. Did you know that **Churchill Downs** in Louisville is home to the *Kentucky Derby,* and that **Keeneland** in Lexington is a National Historic Landmark?

Kentucky is known throughout the world for its horses but it is also known for its Kentucky Fried Chicken and world-class bourbon. Visit one of the eight distilleries that offer tours on the Bourbon Trail.

Adventure tourism is at its best in Kentucky with its 52 state parks, 21 major lakes, 14 river systems, 1,400 miles of trails and five national recreation areas: The **Big South Fork National River and Recreation Area;** the **Cumberland Gap National Historical Park;** the **Daniel Boone National Forest;** the **Land Between the Lakes;** and one of my favorite destinations, **Mammoth Cave,** which quietly boasts the world's longest cave system.

Kentucky's larger cities, Louisville, Lexington and Owensboro, offer great museums and performing arts companies.

Kentucky's heritage is preserved throughout the state and can be seen in museums, Civil War sites and historic homes. The state ranks fourth in the U.S. in the number of sites on the National Register. Some of the most popular sites include **Abraham Lincoln's Birthplace,** the **Blue Heron Mining Community** and **Fort Boonesborough,** which was founded by Daniel Boone.

Kentucky crafts are known throughout the world. **Berea,** the "folk arts and crafts capital of Kentucky," hosts notable craft fairs each spring and fall.

Northern Kentucky

The Northern Kentucky Convention & Visitors Bureau
50 E. River Center Blvd., Suite 200, Covington, Kentucky 41011
1-800-STAY-NKY **www.staynky.com**

Whether you call it the most northern part of the south or the most southern part of the north, you'll enjoy yourself along the riverfront across from Cincinnati. Dance, shop, dine or be entertained on shore. Take an cruise and see the bright blue **John Roebling Suspension Bridge** (opened in 1867, it was the prototype for the Brooklyn Bridge).

The world-class **Newport Aquarium** graces the Kentucky riverfront directly across the Ohio River from downtown Cincinnati. The $40-million Newport Aquarium features 11,000 animals representing 600 species in one million gallons of fresh and salt water, offering more that 60 exhibits in 100,000 square feet of display area.

The Newport Aquarium has 16 separate theme areas that take visitors through a world tour of underwater ecosystems. Among the featured exhibits is **Surrounded by Sharks.** The 380,000 gallons tank is bisected by a winding 84 foot underwater tunnel which gives visitors the true feeling of being underwater by utilizing seamless acrylic and clear flooring. This exhibit contains one of the country's largest open-air shark viewing areas with 25 sharks and some 2,200 other fish.

The Newport Aquarium is open daily, and ample parking is available on site.
The **Covington Riverside Drive area** or **"Riverwalk"** neighborhood is wonderful for a walking tour. Wrought-iron fencing enclose historic homes and sets the stage for beautiful river views. **MainStrasse Village** in Covington is an old German neighborhood full of shops, restaurants and festival activities. The 100-foot **Carroll Chimes Bell Tower** depicts the tale of the Pied Piper of Hamelin. The famous **Cathedral Basilica** of the Assumption is modeled after Notre Dame and has the largest stained-glass church window in the world.

While in Newport make sure to **Ride the Ducks.** This new town attraction carries you on an amphibious vehicle across the river into Ohio for a short tour then into the Ohio River for a river tour and then back onto dry land with a tour of the Newport area. Also in Newport is the World Peace Bell. The world's largest free-swinging bell was cast in France and journeyed up the Mississippi and Ohio Rivers for a Fourth of July dedication ceremony in 2000.

Another Northern Kentucky attraction, the **Belle of Cincinnati** is the signature boat of **BB Riverboats,** which operates a fleet of popular sightseeing and dining cruise boats on the Ohio River from its docks in Newport and Covington. The 201-foot long Belle of Cincinnati can carry 1,000 passengers on its four decks, making the sternwheeler twice as large as any other pleasure boat operating on local waters.

BB Riverboats operates cruises daily from both docks through Labor Day for sightseeing, lunch and dinner cruises, special events and private charters.

Newport on the Levee has become one of the major entertainment centers in Newport. With the Newport Aquarium as its anchor on one end, you will find a wide variety of restaurants and shops. Take a walk across the Ohio River on the Purple People Bridge and enjoy the sights of both shorelines from this fantastic viewpoint. Wander down to Riverboat Row and relax at James Taylor Park, the second most important military post in the country prior to the Civil War.

The $80 million **National Underground Railroad Freedom Center,** the first of its kind in the US, highlights Cincinnati and Northern Kentucky's key role in the Underground Railroad's heroic efforts to help slaves secure safe passage during the 19th century. The 158,000 sq. ft. center is the nation's largest museum commemorating the history of the Underground Railroad. Three interconnected buildings face the river and feature 38,000 sq. ft. of interactive exhibits, a 325-seat auditorium and an 8,000 sq. ft. welcome hall.

A little further south, on KY Rt. 338, is **Big Bone Lick State Park.** It is a preeminent archaeological site where great herds of prehistoric mammals came for salt at the end of the last ice age (12,000 to 20,000 years of age). Camping too! KY Rt. 338 near Richwood. 859-384-3522.

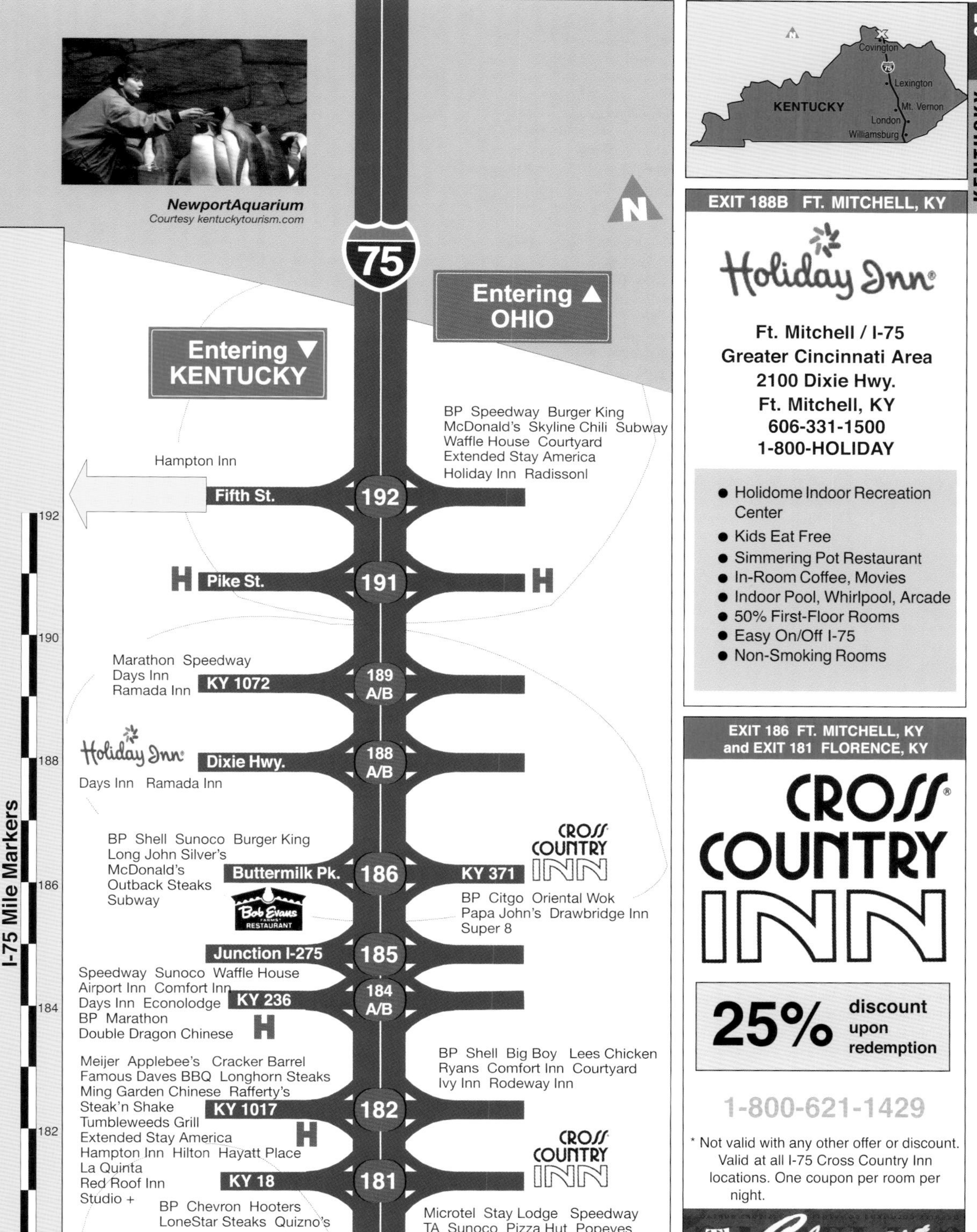
NewportAquarium
Courtesy kentuckytourism.com
75
N
Entering ▲ OHIO
Entering ▼ KENTUCKY
I-75 Mile Markers
192
190
188
186
184
182
180
BP Speedway Burger King
McDonald's Skyline Chili Subway
Waffle House Courtyard
Extended Stay America
Holiday Inn Radissonl
Hampton Inn
Fifth St.
192
H
Pike St.
191
H
Marathon Speedway
Days Inn
Ramada Inn
KY 1072
189 A/B
Holiday Inn
Dixie Hwy.
188 A/B
Days Inn Ramada Inn
BP Shell Sunoco Burger King
Long John Silver's
McDonald's
Outback Steaks
Subway
Buttermilk Pk.
186
KY 371
Cross Country Inn
Bob Evans Farms Restaurant
BP Citgo Oriental Wok
Papa John's Drawbridge Inn
Super 8
Junction I-275
185
Speedway Sunoco Waffle House
Airport Inn Comfort Inn
Days Inn Econolodge
BP Marathon
Double Dragon Chinese
KY 236
184 A/B
H
Meijer Applebee's Cracker Barrel
Famous Daves BBQ Longhorn Steaks
Ming Garden Chinese Rafferty's
Steak'n Shake
Tumbleweeds Grill
Extended Stay America
Hampton Inn Hilton Hayatt Place
La Quinta
Red Roof Inn
Studio +
KY 1017
182
H
BP Shell Big Boy Lees Chicken
Ryans Comfort Inn Courtyard
Ivy Inn Rodeway Inn
KY 18
181
Cross Country Inn
BP Chevron Hooters
LoneStar Steaks Quizno's
Microtel Stay Lodge Speedway
TA Sunoco Pizza Hut Popeyes
Best Value Inn Best Western
Covington
75
Lexington
KENTUCKY
Mt. Vernon
London
Williamsburg
EXIT 188B FT. MITCHELL, KY
Holiday Inn®
Ft. Mitchell / I-75
Greater Cincinnati Area
2100 Dixie Hwy.
Ft. Mitchell, KY
606-331-1500
1-800-HOLIDAY
● Holidome Indoor Recreation Center
● Kids Eat Free
● Simmering Pot Restaurant
● In-Room Coffee, Movies
● Indoor Pool, Whirlpool, Arcade
● 50% First-Floor Rooms
● Easy On/Off I-75
● Non-Smoking Rooms
EXIT 186 FT. MITCHELL, KY
and EXIT 181 FLORENCE, KY
CROSS COUNTRY INN®
25% discount upon redemption
1-800-621-1429
* Not valid with any other offer or discount. Valid at all I-75 Cross Country Inn locations. One coupon per room per night.
The Cleanest Place You'll Ever Stay

Kentucky

Kentucky Department of Travel
500 Mero Street, 22 Floor, Frankfort, Kentucky 40601-1968
502-564-4930 or 1-800-225-8747 **www.kentuckytourism.com**

DID YOU KNOW

that even though more than 30,000 Confederate soldiers left their Kentucky homes to fight for the South, according to official records, Kentucky never left the Union. In fact, more than 40,000 fought for the Union, including 20,000 African-Americans. You may recall that both the presidents of the United States, Abraham Lincoln, and the Confederate States, Jefferson Davis, were born in Kentucky. Kentucky's buffer zone between the urbanized, heavily industrialized North and the Deep South cotton plantations did not last long, and her refusal to enter a war that would divide its families dissolved.

Kentucky unwillingly became a battle ground and the base of operations for both the Union and the Confederacy. Kentucky's Civil War sites cover the entire state and many of the major ones are described on the diagram below.

KENTUCKY'S CIVIL WAR SITES TOUR

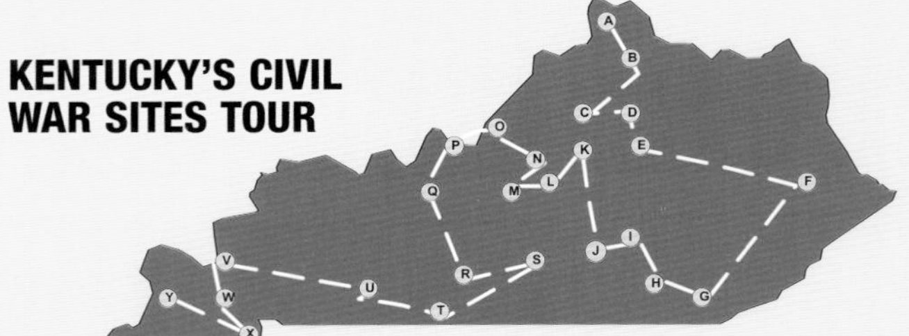

A. COVINGTON

Union military leaders first slowed the completion of the historic Roebling Suspension Bridge then encouraged its completion after deciding that it would be helpful in moving troops south. Still the bridge was not completed until 1866 and troops had to cross the Ohio on a military pontoon bridge just east of the present bridge. When the Confederates invaded Kentucky in the summer of 1862, federal troops fortified Covington with more than 20 forts and batteries in order to protect Cincinnati and the north.

B. LEXINGTON

Visit the Mary Todd Lincoln House and Gen. John Hunt Morgan's home. See the Fayette County Courthouse statues and the final resting place of many fine Kentuckians in the 19th-century cemetery.

C. FRANKFORT

The Commonwealth's capital has many research facilities including the Kentucky History Center, the State Capitol Rotunda with the statues of Jefferson Davis and Abraham Lincoln, the Frankfort Cemetery and the Military History Museum.

D. CAMP NELSON

The most important recruiting station for blacks in the state, Camp Nelson also served as a refuge for the families of the black troops. Following the war, Camp Nelson was one of the primary issuing centers for emancipation documents.

E. RICHMOND

A self-guided tour brochure with a taped narrative of tactically the most complete Confederate victory of the entire war can be obtained from the Richmond Tourism Commission 606-623-1000.

F. THE BATTLE OF MIDDLE CREEK

The largest battle in East Kentucky engaging the Union troops of the future President James A. Garfield and the Confederate troops of Kentucky politician Gen. Marshall on the high ridges near Prestonburg. After the Confederates retreated, Garfield was then promoted to brigadier general for his efforts.

G. CUMBERLAND GAP

Whoever controlled this mountain pass would be in a position to invade the other's territory. The gap changed hands four times throughout the war. Finally in 1863 the passage and its surrounding highlands were recaptured by the Union and remained in their hands until the end of the war. The Cumberland Gap National Historical Park's visitor centre has a good interpretation of the gaps' importance to the Civil War. The remains of numerous earthwork forts, many used by both armies, remain.

H. BARBOURVILLE

Site of the first Civil War battle fought in KY (Sept 1861). The Knox County Museum in the Barbourville Municipal Building has exhibits on this battle.

I. THE BATTLE OF WILDCAT MOUNTAIN

This site of the original Wilderness Road bed from the Civil War. Annual re-enactment each Spring. London, I-75 exit 49. 800-348-0095

J. THE BATTLE OF MILL SPRINGS

A decisive Union victory and one of the most important battles fought in the western theater, Jan. 19, 1862. 800-642-6287

K. PERRYVILLE

The battle of Perryville was the largest battle fought in Kentucky. The Southern troops won but were forced to retreat, abandoning Kentucky to the Union. The Perryville State Historic Site is on the actual battleground. Visit the museum and take a self-guided tour. Annual re-enactment early Oct.

L. THE BATTLE OF TEBBS BEND

Regarded as one of the bloodiest encounters of the war in the western theater, even though relatively small numbers were involved, and the fighting was of short duration.

M, N. HODGENVILLE/SPRINGFIELD

See the impressive monuments to Lincoln at the Abraham Lincoln Birthplace National Historic Site, the Abraham Lincoln Boyhood Home, the Lincoln Museum, and the Lincoln Homestead.

O. LOUISVILLE

None of the numerous forts this city constructed survive. Popular black history tour sites are the Eastern Cemetery and the Taylor Barracks. The new Lincoln memorial will be dedicated at Waterfront Park during the summer of 2009.

P. WEST POINT

Union supply depot near the mouth of the Salt River on the Ohio River. The Fort was oddly constructed in the shape of a horseshoe open on the north side.

Q. MUNFORDVILLE

Site of an important railroad saw two battles. Three of the forts are still standing. Walking tour brochure available at the Hart County Historical Society.

R. BOWLING GREEN

The heart of the Confederate defensive line, built to secure a southern foothold in the Commonwealth. Three forts are still standing.

S. GLASGOW

Home to the renovated Fort Williams, a Union earthworks built 1863.

T. FRANKLIN This most unique Civil War site still has the drawings and graffiti created by men who were incarcerated or inhabited the second floor of the old jail during the war. The jail is on the National Register of Historic Places.

U. HOPKINSVILLE/FAIRVIEW

The birthplace of Jefferson Davis is a monument to his life as the only president of the Confederacy. Breathtaking view of the countryside atop the 351-foot obelisk at the Jefferson Davis Monument State Historic Site on US-68.

V. PADUCAH

Gen. U.S. Grant moved his Union forces here and successfully repelled the larger rebel force in 1864. See Lang Park monument to Confederate Brigadier Gen. Lloyd Tilghman, the military museum, Oak Grove Cemetery and the collection of Lincoln memorabilia at the Alben Barkley Museum.

W. MAYFIELD Confederate Memorial Fountain.

X. WATER VALLEY

A monument to the Confederate soldiers who died nearby.

Y. COLUMBUS

One of Kentucky's most important Civil War sites, it was here in 1861 that Gen. Leonidas Polk occupied the town and facilitated the end of Kentucky's neutrality. Part of the Confederate defenses included stretching a chain across the river to keep the Union gunboats from moving south.

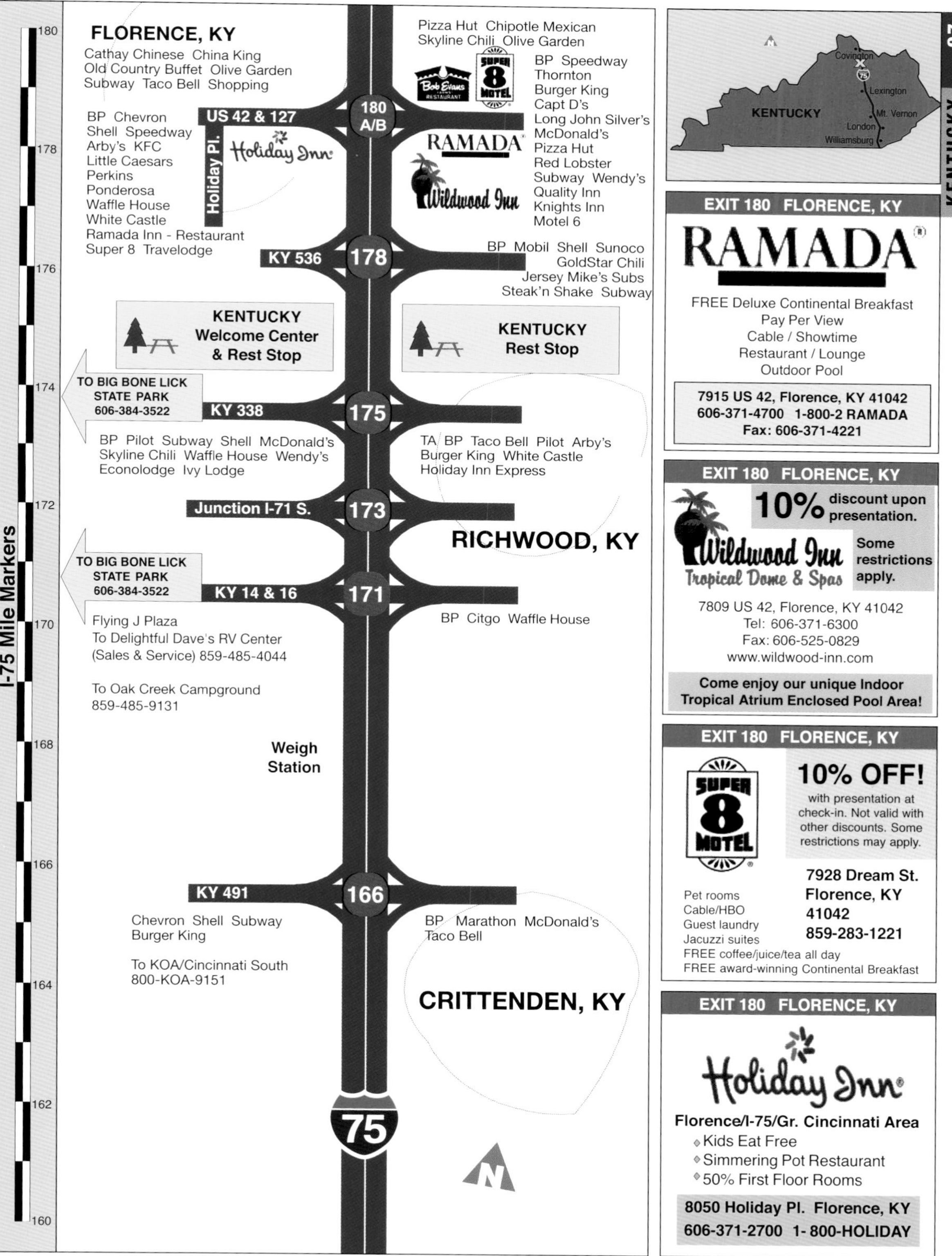
I-75 Mile Markers
180
178
176
174
172
170
168
166
164
162
160
FLORENCE, KY
Cathay Chinese China King
Old Country Buffet Olive Garden
Subway Taco Bell Shopping
BP Chevron
Shell Speedway
Arby's KFC
Little Caesars
Perkins
Ponderosa
Waffle House
White Castle
Ramada Inn - Restaurant
Super 8 Travelodge
US 42 & 127
180 A/B
Holiday Pl.
Holiday Inn
Pizza Hut Chipotle Mexican
Skyline Chili Olive Garden
Bob Evans Restaurant
Super 8 Motel
BP Speedway
Thornton
Burger King
Capt D's
Long John Silver's
McDonald's
Pizza Hut
Red Lobster
Subway Wendy's
Quality Inn
Knights Inn
Motel 6
RAMADA
Wildwood Inn
KY 536
178
BP Mobil Shell Sunoco
GoldStar Chili
Jersey Mike's Subs
Steak'n Shake Subway
KENTUCKY
Welcome Center
& Rest Stop
KENTUCKY
Rest Stop
TO BIG BONE LICK
STATE PARK
606-384-3522
KY 338
175
BP Pilot Subway Shell McDonald's
Skyline Chili Waffle House Wendy's
Econolodge Ivy Lodge
TA BP Taco Bell Pilot Arby's
Burger King White Castle
Holiday Inn Express
Junction I-71 S.
173
RICHWOOD, KY
TO BIG BONE LICK
STATE PARK
606-384-3522
KY 14 & 16
171
BP Citgo Waffle House
Flying J Plaza
To Delightful Dave's RV Center
(Sales & Service) 859-485-4044
To Oak Creek Campground
859-485-9131
Weigh
Station
KY 491
166
Chevron Shell Subway
Burger King
To KOA/Cincinnati South
800-KOA-9151
BP Marathon McDonald's
Taco Bell
CRITTENDEN, KY
75
N
KENTUCKY
Covington
Lexington
Mt. Vernon
London
Williamsburg
EXIT 180 FLORENCE, KY
RAMADA
FREE Deluxe Continental Breakfast
Pay Per View
Cable / Showtime
Restaurant / Lounge
Outdoor Pool
7915 US 42, Florence, KY 41042
606-371-4700 1-800-2 RAMADA
Fax: 606-371-4221
EXIT 180 FLORENCE, KY
10% discount upon presentation.
Wildwood Inn
Tropical Dome & Spas
Some restrictions apply.
7809 US 42, Florence, KY 41042
Tel: 606-371-6300
Fax: 606-525-0829
www.wildwood-inn.com
Come enjoy our unique Indoor
Tropical Atrium Enclosed Pool Area!
EXIT 180 FLORENCE, KY
Super 8 Motel
10% OFF!
with presentation at check-in. Not valid with other discounts. Some restrictions may apply.
7928 Dream St.
Florence, KY
41042
859-283-1221
Pet rooms
Cable/HBO
Guest laundry
Jacuzzi suites
FREE coffee/juice/tea all day
FREE award-winning Continental Breakfast
EXIT 180 FLORENCE, KY
Holiday Inn
Florence/I-75/Gr. Cincinnati Area
Kids Eat Free
Simmering Pot Restaurant
50% First Floor Rooms
8050 Holiday Pl. Florence, KY
606-371-2700 1-800-HOLIDAY

Williamstown
GRANT COUNTY

Williamstown/Grant County Tourist Commission
1116 Fashion Ridge Rd., Dry Ridge, KY 41035
859-824-3307 or 1-800-382-7117

The first building in what would become Grant County was known as Campbell's Block House. It is thought to have been built near Williamstown as early as 1784 by John Campbell, a trapper, hunter and trader who made regular trips here to trade with the Indians. The Block House later served to protect early settlers from Indian attacks. The first church, the Old Baptist Church on the Dry Ridge, was built nearby in 1799 for nine original members.

An early settler to the area, John Filson, surveyed a road through the wilderness (now the present route of the Norfolk Southern Railroad between Erlanger and Georgetown). It was called the Dry Ridge Trace and was heavily traveled. When the counties could no longer maintain it, the State converted it to a toll road and it became known as the Lexington Pike. It remained a toll road until the early 1900s when all Kentucky roads were made toll-free.

Grant County was named for one of 3 Grant brothers largely responsible for the pacification and settlement of Northern Kentucky. The Grants were nephews of Daniel Boone. William Arnold donated land for the county's public buildings and the county seat was named William's Town in his honor.

500 men fought for each side of the Civil War, but the County was largely pro-Southern, according to postwar election results.

Today, Grant County is largely rural. Its principal crops include tobacco, alfalfa and other hay, but is also a large producer of beef cattle. It is the 3rd-fastest growing county in Kentucky and is expected to become a bedroom community of Northern Kentucky and Cincinnati.

The four I-75 interchanges running through Grant County are all designated for expansion.

CRITTENDEN

Although not the residents' first choice for a name, it was incorporated in 1837 and named for John J. Crittenden. The area south and west of present-day Crittenden attracted settlers as early as 1790, and the first church, the Lebanon Presbyterian Church, was organized in 1796.

A **Kentucky Highway Historical Marker** on KY 491, west of Crittenden, states that Indians attacked the Andrew Brann family and cabin near the creek about 1805 and that the whole family was killed except the mother, who survived the scalping.

Barker's Blackberry Hill Winery offers winery tours by appointment. You can also pick your own blackberries in July and August (I-75 exit 166 east, from Crittenden follow KY-491 west, KY-1942 south, 16629 Mt. Zion-Verona Road, 606-428-0377).

DRY RIDGE

Many small communities on the crest of the dry ridge could have assumed this name, but the Dry Ridge Community was apparently so named in 1815 because of its proximity to the "Old Church on the Dry Ridge."

The **Dry Ridge Trace,** originally an Indian trail, followed the crest of the ridge and met up with the Big Bone-Blue Licks buffalo trail. Both served as passageways for early settlers and later became part of the Lexington Pike.

Dry Ridge was a trading center with general stores and taverns. In 1907 a fire destroyed several buildings including the newly constructed Southern Railroad depot. Another more disastrous fire in 1927 destroyed much of the business section.

Today the population of Dry Ridge is about 2,000 and there are about 30 stores in its outlet mall and about 120 businesses and professional offices. There is a variety of services at or near the I-75 interchange.

The **Dry Ridge Outlet Center,** at exit 159, has about 20 stores, 606-824-9516.
The Grant County visitor center is at 214 South Main in Williamstown, 1-800-382-7117.

And, yes, you *are* in a dry county, And, yes, you are in a dry county or maybe moist is a better description. In 2008, a bylaw was passed that allowed liquor to be sold in restaurants but you still won't find any liquor stores nearby.

WILLIAMSTOWN

The first name chosen for the town site was "Philadelphia," a name already chosen by another town in the state, so it was changed to honor the property owner who, in 1820, donated the land needed for public buildings.

The town began as a trading center, meeting place, and stopover point for livestock drovers who used the Lexington Pike. Once the Southern Railroad was constructed, the Lexington Pike's traffic, and Williamstown's economy, faltered. It was not until the turn of the century, with its cars and trucks, that the Lexington Pike would regain its importance and warrant the improvements and a new name: the US 25. You will cross US 25 several times as you drive the I-75 through Kentucky.

Williamstown also suffered several terrible fires, the last one in 1983. Lake Williamstown was created in part to combat the recurring fire problem and to serve the area residents with a dependable water source. By the 1980s, this lake produced 1.5 million gallons of water each day.

The 1,179-acre **Curtis Gates Lloyd Wildlife Management Area** is excellent for both bird watching and hiking. Four miles of dirt roads and trails wind through giant hardwoods, one of Kentucky's few virgin tree stands. Some of the white oak, black walnut, beech and hickory trees are 250 years old, with more than a three foot diameter. The area is home to deer, wild turkey, red and gray fox, red-tailed hawk, American kestrel, pileated woodpecker and the eastern bluebird. **Lake Leary,** a small fishing lake, is wheelchair accessible (from Crittenden follow US-25 south 1 mile, KY-491 east, 11300 Jonesville Road, 606-428-2262). Bullock Pen, Boltz, and Williamstown lakes are also in the area.

CORINTH

The history of Corinth dates back, according to the Corinth Christian Church records, to the late 1820s.

The effects of water shortages is evident in the number of fires this community suffered until the Corinth Water District was created in 1986. Water is now supplied by pipe from Williamstown.

Corinth is the smallest of Grant County's four incorporated areas.

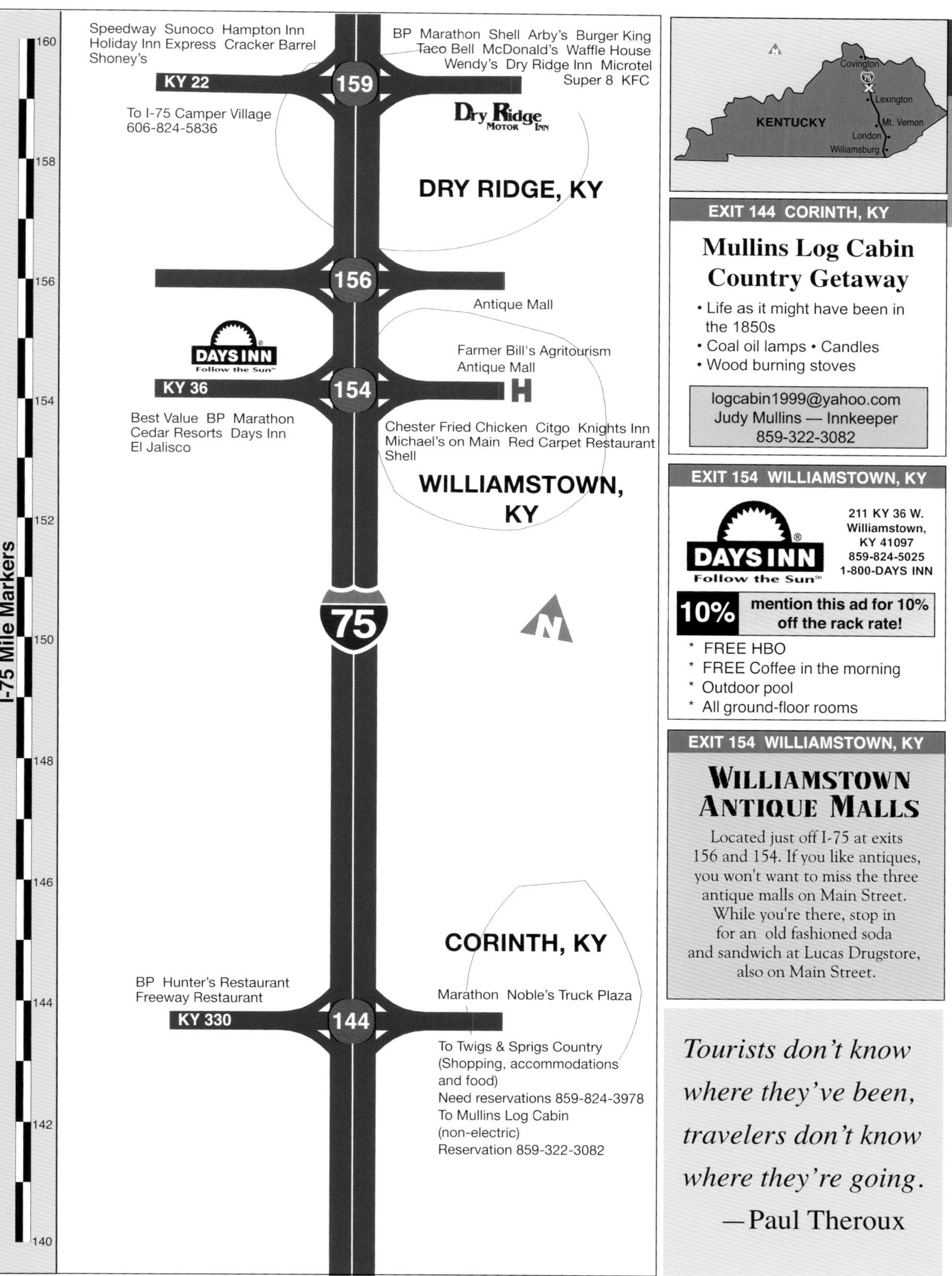
I-75 Mile Markers
160
158
156
154
152
150
148
146
144
142
140
Speedway Sunoco Hampton Inn
Holiday Inn Express Cracker Barrel
Shoney's
KY 22
159
BP Marathon Shell Arby's Burger King
Taco Bell McDonald's Waffle House
Wendy's Dry Ridge Inn Microtel
Super 8 KFC
To I-75 Camper Village
606-824-5836
Dry Ridge Motor Inn
DRY RIDGE, KY
156
Antique Mall
DAYS INN Follow the Sun
Farmer Bill's Agritourism
Antique Mall
KY 36
154
H
Best Value BP Marathon
Cedar Resorts Days Inn
El Jalisco
Chester Fried Chicken Citgo Knights Inn
Michael's on Main Red Carpet Restaurant
Shell
WILLIAMSTOWN, KY
75
N
CORINTH, KY
BP Hunter's Restaurant
Freeway Restaurant
KY 330
144
Marathon Noble's Truck Plaza
To Twigs & Sprigs Country
(Shopping, accommodations
and food)
Need reservations 859-824-3978
To Mullins Log Cabin
(non-electric)
Reservation 859-322-3082
Covington
Lexington
KENTUCKY
Mt. Vernon
London
Williamsburg
EXIT 144 CORINTH, KY
Mullins Log Cabin Country Getaway
• Life as it might have been in the 1850s
• Coal oil lamps • Candles
• Wood burning stoves
logcabin1999@yahoo.com
Judy Mullins — Innkeeper
859-322-3082
EXIT 154 WILLIAMSTOWN, KY
DAYS INN Follow the Sun
211 KY 36 W.
Williamstown, KY 41097
859-824-5025
1-800-DAYS INN
10% mention this ad for 10% off the rack rate!
* FREE HBO
* FREE Coffee in the morning
* Outdoor pool
* All ground-floor rooms
EXIT 154 WILLIAMSTOWN, KY
WILLIAMSTOWN ANTIQUE MALLS
Located just off I-75 at exits 156 and 154. If you like antiques, you won't want to miss the three antique malls on Main Street. While you're there, stop in for an old fashioned soda and sandwich at Lucas Drugstore, also on Main Street.
Tourists don't know where they've been, travelers don't know where they're going.
— Paul Theroux

Lexington
KENTUCKY

Lexington Convention & Visitors Bureau
301 East Vine Street, Lexington, Kentucky 40507-1513
859-233-7299 or 1-800-845-3959 **www.visitlex.com**

Antique Shopping

In Lexington and surrounding communities, antique shopping is an activity that never, so to speak, gets old.

In fact, to visit all the antique shops in the area, you'd have to plan to stay a while. There are more than 200 antique shops, ranging from large multi-dealer malls to small specialty stores, ready to tempt you with old Kentucky cabinetry, quilts, imported furniture, Shaker items, Depression glass, collectibles—you name it!

There's enough great antiquing within Lexington itself to keep you busy for days. In addition, virtually every surrounding community includes at least a few antique malls and shops, so it's easy to combine antique shopping with general sightseeing. As a writer for *The New York Times* put it, antiquing in the Bluegrass is "a chance to unearth some great buys in American antiques and, in the bargain, enjoy some of the most beautiful rural countryside anywhere."

Such a deal! And while all Bluegrass roads eventually lead to an antique shop or two, here are a few suggestions to get you started.

Spring through fall, the **Athens Schoolhouse Antique Show**, is held once a month at 6270 Athens – Walnut Hill in Lexington. From I-75 take exit 104 and travel one mile east on Athens – Boonesboro Rd. Admission $2.
859-225-7309
www.antiqueskentucky.com

You can bid for fine estate and other items at **Thompson & Riley** auctions, usually held on Tues. mornings at 710 East Main Street (859-252-6677).

Shopping at **Wakefield-Scearce Galleries** in Shelbyville, 47 miles west of Lexington via I-64 is a bit of the "British aisles" in the Bluegrass. Established in 1947, the shop specializes in imported English furniture, fine silver, paintings and objects of art. Sterling silver julep cups from Wakefield-Scearce are a great Kentucky gift or souvenir.

Text courtesy Teresa Day

Lexington, Kentucky: The Heart of the Bluegrass

Located at the heart of Central Kentucky's famed scenic **Bluegrass Region,** Lexington offers an appealing vacation alternative. The city is home to a downtown skyline overlooking acres of lush pastures. It's where bourbon was born and burley tobacco is raised. It's where champion horses are bred, foaled, trained, bought, sold, raced and retired.

Drive the back roads of Lexington and you will enjoy the views of grazing and galloping horses, lush meadows and extravagant barns (some have cupolas and chandeliers), contained by miles of pristine painted wood or historic stone fences.

Many of the city's most popular attractions celebrate the area's love of horses. Visitors can enjoy the excitement of horse racing at historic **Keeneland Race Course** or the **Red Mile Harness Track,** and take a behind-the-scenes look at the Thoroughbred industry at the **Thoroughbred Center,** a 2.5 acre park, contains seven lifesize and lifelike bronze racehorses streaking toward the finish line while brood mares, foals, and the great stallion Lexington "graze" in an overlooking field.

No stay in Lexington would be complete without spending a day at the **Kentucky Horse Park,** the world's first park devoted to the horse. The 1,200-acre working farm/educational theme park is a permanent home for many popular and rare horse breeds. Visitors meet retired equine champions, explore hands-on exhibits and attend Olympic-level equestrian events.

The city's combination of breathtaking countryside and big-city amenities make it an ideal vacation destination that offers something for everyone. Historic attractions, shopping, outdoor recreation, and great restaurants await year-round.

Settled in 1775, and known as the **"Athens of the West"** in the early 1800s, Lexington includes many fine historic homes and buildings.

Visitors can tour **Waveland,** a restored Southern plantation built by a relative of Daniel Boone; **Ashland,** the estate of the 18th-century stateman Henry Clay; the **Mary Todd Lincoln House,** the girlhood home of Abraham Lincoln's "First Lady"; and the **Hunt-Morgan House,** the restored Federal-style home of Confederate General John Hunt Morgan. **Park** historic district faces **Transylvania University,** the oldest university west of the Alleghenies.

Outdoor and family activities also abound in Lexington. Golfers can tackle challenging championship courses, such as Pete Dye-designed **Kearney Hill Links.**

The Explorium of Lexington, housed in a restored 19th-century commercial building, entertains youngsters with interactive exhibits and activities relating to scenic and, nature.

A variety of upscale restaurants, from European fare to regional cuisine, ensures every taste and budget will be catered to in Lexington. Local specialties include spoon bread, fried banana peppers, country ham, fried catfish and the Hot Brown sandwich.

Featuring some of the best shopping in Kentucky as well as family-owned Appalachian craft shops, Lexington offers shoppers an abundance of options for taking home unique gifts.

Lexington's lively arts scene includes the professional **Lexington Philharmonic** and other musical, theater and dance troops.

Lexington nightspots range from sing-along karaoke to live comedy. And, of course, there is **Bluegrass music** in the heart of the Bluegrass: the annual **Festival of the Bluegrass** in June draws top performers and international crowds.

Lexington's central location makes it an ideal base from which to explore the entire Bluegrass Region.

Within a short drive of Lexington are such attractions as **Shaker Village of Pleasant Hill,** the nation's largest restored Shaker community; the **Toyota Motor Manufacturing, U.S.A., Inc.** automaking facility; bourbon distilleries such as **Woodford Reserve Distillery, Maker's Mark** and **Buffalo Trace Distillery**; pioneer forts; historic railways; Kentucky's state capital; and **Berea,** "Kentucky's crafts capital."

Text courtesy Lexington Convention and Visitors Bureau. www.visitlex.com

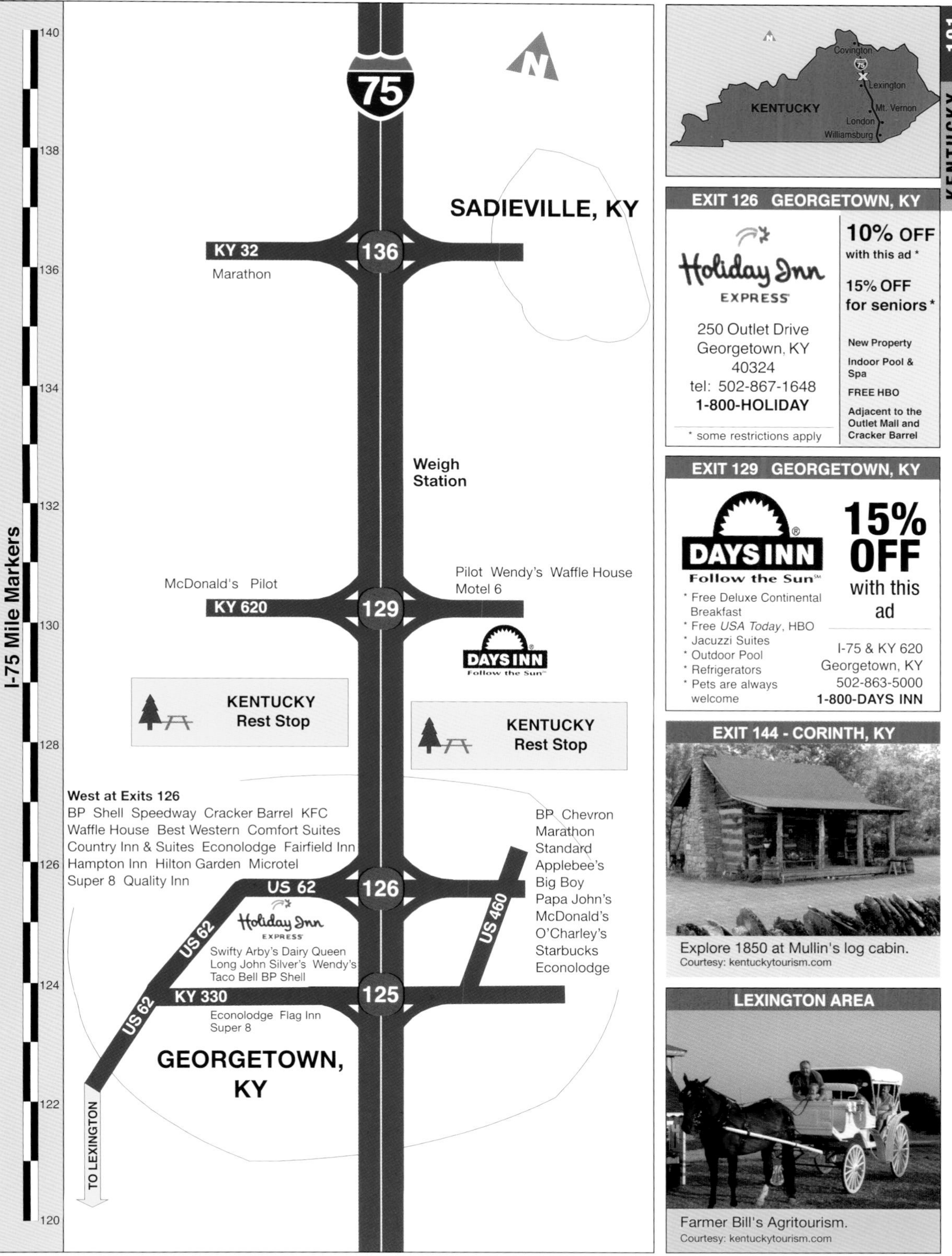

Explore 1850 at Mullin's log cabin.
Courtesy: kentuckytourism.com

Farmer Bill's Agritourism.
Courtesy: kentuckytourism.com

Lexington
KENTUCKY

Lexington Convention & Visitors Bureau
301 East Vine Street, Lexington, Kentucky 40507-1513
859-233-7299 or 1-800-845-3959 **www.visitlex.com**

TRIVIA

Lexington is located in the heart of the **Bluegrass region,** where the grass is dark green, not blue.

Finding a ticket to a **University of Kentucky Wildcat** basketball game is nearly impossible, season tickets are handed down from generation to generation and UK college students have access to the rest.

Transylvania University in downtown Lexington is the oldest university west of the Allegheny Mountains.

Lexington-area companies produce **Dixie cups** (James River-Dixie Northern Company), **Jif peanut butter** (T.J. Smuckers Co.), and **Speedo swimsuits** (Kentucky Textiles).

You can tour **Toyota Motor Manufacturing USA, Inc.** 10 minutes north of Lexington in Georgetown, KY, where they manufacture Camrys and Avalons.

Lexingtonians love to eat **hot browns** (open-faced sandwiches made with turkey and cheese), country ham (cured with salt or sugar and then boiled), beer cheese (spicy cheese spread that is delicious on crackers or vegetables), corn pudding (a rich corn casserole), and derby pie (a winning combination of sugar, eggs, butter, vanilla, chocolate chips and pecans.)

The largest **restored Shaker Village** in the United States is located in Harrodsburg, KY, 25 miles south of Lexington. The Shakers were a religious sect who lived peacefully and welcomed poor and hungry people into their community.

Lexington, Kentucky, is the largest of several Lexingtons in the United States. Others are Lexington, Massachusetts, a suburb of Boston; and similarly named cities in Nebraska, North Carolina, Oklahoma and Virginia.

Lexington has its very own **castle,** the real thing, complete with towers and turrets, located amongst horse farms just outside of downtown.

Area Festivals

Parade of Breeds
Courtesy Kentucky Department of Travel Development

Keeneland Thoroughbred racing in October and April. Stakes race every day, with the Bluegrass Stakes being the major prep race for the Kentucky Derby. 859-254-3412 or 800-456-3412

African-American Shaker History Weekend
Shaker Village of Pleasant Hill. Explores the contributions of African-Americans in Shaker communities. Feb. 859-734-5411

Rolex Kentucky Three-Day Event
U.S. Equestrian Team's Championship and International Trade Fair.Apr. 859-233-2362

High Hope Steeplechase at Kentucky Horse Park. Horse racing over brush and timber. May. 859-255-5727

Lexington Historic Preservation Week
Lectures and tours. May. 859-258-3265

MayFest
Gratz Park, Transylvania University. Variety of entertainment and art presentations. 859-231-7335

Annual Egyptian Event & Festival of the Bluegrass
Jamboree and trade fair. June. Kentucky Horse Park. 859-231-0771

Kentucky Hunter/Jumper Annual Show & Bluegrass Festival Hunter/Jumper Show. Kentucky Horse Park. $25,000 Grand Prix event. Aug. 859-266-6937

Bluegrass Trust Antique Show
Heritage Hall. Top dealers from around the country display furniture, silver and other collectors items. March 859-233-4567

Mt. Sterling Court Days
Mt. Sterling, KY. The "grand daddy" of all flea markets since 1796. Join the 100,000 visitors to a town whose population is around 5,000! Oct. 859-498-5343

Halloween Parade of Breeds
Kentucky Horse Park. Costumed riders. Great photo opportunities. 859-233-4303

Southern Lights Holiday Festival
Nov. to end of Dec., Kentucky Horse Park. 2.5-mile drive with an unforgettable 1 million lights and laser show. 859-255-5727

Christmas Chorus
Rupp Arena. 80 local choirs and Lexington Philharmonic celebrate the sounds of the season. 859-258-3026

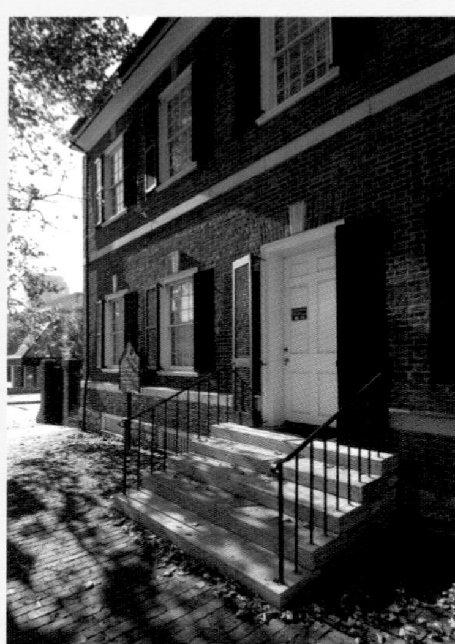

Mary Todd Lincoln House Lincoln. KY
www.kentuckytourism.com

Lexington
KENTUCKY

Lexington Convention & Visitors Bureau
301 East Vine Street, Lexington, Kentucky 40507-1513
859-233-7299 or 1-800-845-3959 **www.visitlex.com**

Horse Park

Mare and foal, *courtesy James Archambeault. Text courtesy Lexington Convention & Visitors Bureau*

An Extraordinary Park, with an Extraordinary Story

The horse is, of course, the theme of the **Kentucky Horse Park,** but what has made this scenic park the most popular attraction in Kentucky's Bluegrass region is its multi-faceted approach to this theme.

Here, a horse is not just a horse. It is history, art, competition, beauty and living legend.

Visitors to the Horse Park can see foals kicking up their heels in spring pastures, as well as bejeweled stallions prancing and snorting across the show ring. Inside the **International Museum of the Horse,** you can admire the world's finest collection of **miniature carriages,** then step outside and take a ride in a full-size one.

At the park's **fine art gallery,** you can admire a delicate terra cotta horse head from 8th-century Japan, while capturing your own masterpieces on film as you walk through the barn and paddock areas.

You'll see **racing trophies,** and meet champions who earn them, both in the flesh at the park's **Hall of Champions** and in bronze.

You may find yourself in the company of international royalty who have come to compete at top equestrian events, or meet inner-city youngsters who have forged positive partnerships with tamed wild horses in the park's **Mustang Troop drill team.**

The inspiration behind the Kentucky Horse Park is as old as Lexington itself; horses have always been an important part of the landscape and identity of the Bluegrass. The idea goes back nearly three decades. By the late 1960s, owners of Lexington's world-famous horse farms became increasingly concerned about insurance and safety issues relating to the traditional open-gate policy for visitors. They wanted to find a more structured way to show off the region's equine traditions.

In 1970, Lexington horse breeder John Gaines took a novel idea to state officials: a park in the heart of the Bluegrass that would celebrate the horse.

It took 8 years for his idea to become reality. In 1978, the $35-million Kentucky Horse Park opened with working horse farm exhibits, a museum, a race track, steeplechase course, polo field, display of breeds, a restaurant and a campground (Kentucky Horse Park State Park).

25 years later, these and additional facilities including an indoor arena, special event barns and a separate attraction, **The American Saddle Horse Museum,** plus a calendar of shows and special events attract nearly 1 million visitors to the Horse Park annually.

The park hosts regional, national and international competitions for horse breeds ranging from miniatures to Arabians.

The park has also become a popular setting for non-equine events, including the nation's **largest outdoor dog show** every Labor Day Weekend, a **Bluegrass music festival** every June, and **Southern Lights,** a drive-through Christmas season lights show combining equine and holiday exhibits.

The park's **National Horse Center** is now home to 30 prominent equine organizations, including the **U.S. Pony Club, USA Equestrian, the American Farriers Association** and **the Kentucky Thoroughbred Association.**

The park is also home base to central Kentucky **Riding for the Handicapped,** and the **Mustang Troop.**

The **"Hall of Champions"** has become the retirement home of many equine stars, including top Thoroughbred money earner John Henry who died October 8, 2007 and the champion stallion Cigar. Current residents include: Cigar, CH Gypsy Supreme, Kona Gold, DaHass, Western Dreamer, Staying Together, Alysheba (1987 Kentucky Derby Winner) and Funny Circle (2003 Kentucky Derby and Preakness Winner.)

Lexington
KENTUCKY

Lexington Convention & Visitors Bureau
301 East Vine Street, Lexington, Kentucky 40507-1513
859-233-7299 or 1-800-845-3959 **www.visitlex.com**

Who says you have to spend big bucks to have a good time? Not in Lexington and the Bluegrass Region. Here are great ways to have fun without paying admission.

1. Watch an early morning workout at **Keeneland Race Course** or the **Red Mile Harness Track**—or take a self-guided track tour. The Red Mile: 859-255-0752. Keeneland: 859-254-3412 or 800-456-3412.

2. Rev up your knowledge of a new kind of Kentucky horsepower at **Toyota Motor Manufacturing Kentucky, Inc.,** in Georgetown, where Toyota automobiles and engines are made for the world market. 800-866-4485

3. Explore the spirited Kentucky tradition of bourbon-making. Tour **Buffalo Trace,** maker of Ancient Age 502-696-5926 or 800-654-8471; **Austin Nichols Distilling Co.,** maker of Wild Turkey 502-839-4544; or **Woodford Reserve Distillery,** maker of Woodford Reserve 800-542-1812.

4. Snap a "photo finish" at the **Lexington's Thoroughbred Park,** Main and Midland streets where realistic, life-size bronze horse statues race and graze.

5. Thrill to the local version of "Palisades Park," the 470-acre **Raven Run Nature Sanctuary,** where hiking trails wind through meadows, woodlands and along streams in the scenic Palisades area. 859-272-6105

6. Admire Old Masters, American and Kentucky masterpieces and the nation's best traveling exhibits at the **University of Kentucky Art Museum.** 859-257-5716

7. Take a memorable (and memorial) stroll through **Lexington Cemetery,** nationally recognized for its arboretum and gardens, and final resting place of Henry Clay, Confederate General John Hunt Morgan, basketball coach Adolph Rupp and other famous Lexingtonians. 859-255-5522

8. Explore the area at your own pace, using the **Lexington Walk and Bluegrass Country Driving Tour**, available at the Convention and Visitors Bureau, 301 East Vine St. 859-233-7299 or 800-845-3959

9. Visit Kentucky Derby winners and other famous equine residents of the Bluegrass at area **horse farms;** the Lexington CVB can tell you which farms allow visitors. No admission charge; but tipping is recom mended. 859-233-7299 or 800-845-3959

10. Dig into Kentucky's "prehistory" and view arrowheads, tools, early pottery and other artifacts at the **Museum of Anthropology,** Lafferty Hall on the University of Kentucky campus. 859-257-8208.

11. Picnic where pioneer Daniel Boone once lived at **Boone Station State Historic Site,** Gentry Rd., Take I-75 exit 104 near Athens. Watch for signs.

Thoroughbred Park. *Photo: Jeff Rogers, text courtesy Teresa Day, Greater Lexington Convention & Visitors Bureau.*

12. Rub elbows with sheiks, movie stars and the horse set at **horse sales** at **Keeneland and Fasig-Tipton.** (But don't bid or you could spend millions!) 859-254-3412 and Fasig-Tipton horse sales: 859-255-1555

13. Sample the latest CDs on private head sets, try out computer games and software, or relax in the reading room at **Joseph-Beth Booksellers,** one the region's largest bookstores—and one of Lexingtonian's favorite places to meet and mingle. In the **Mall at Lexington Green,** Nicholasville Rd. 859-273-2911.

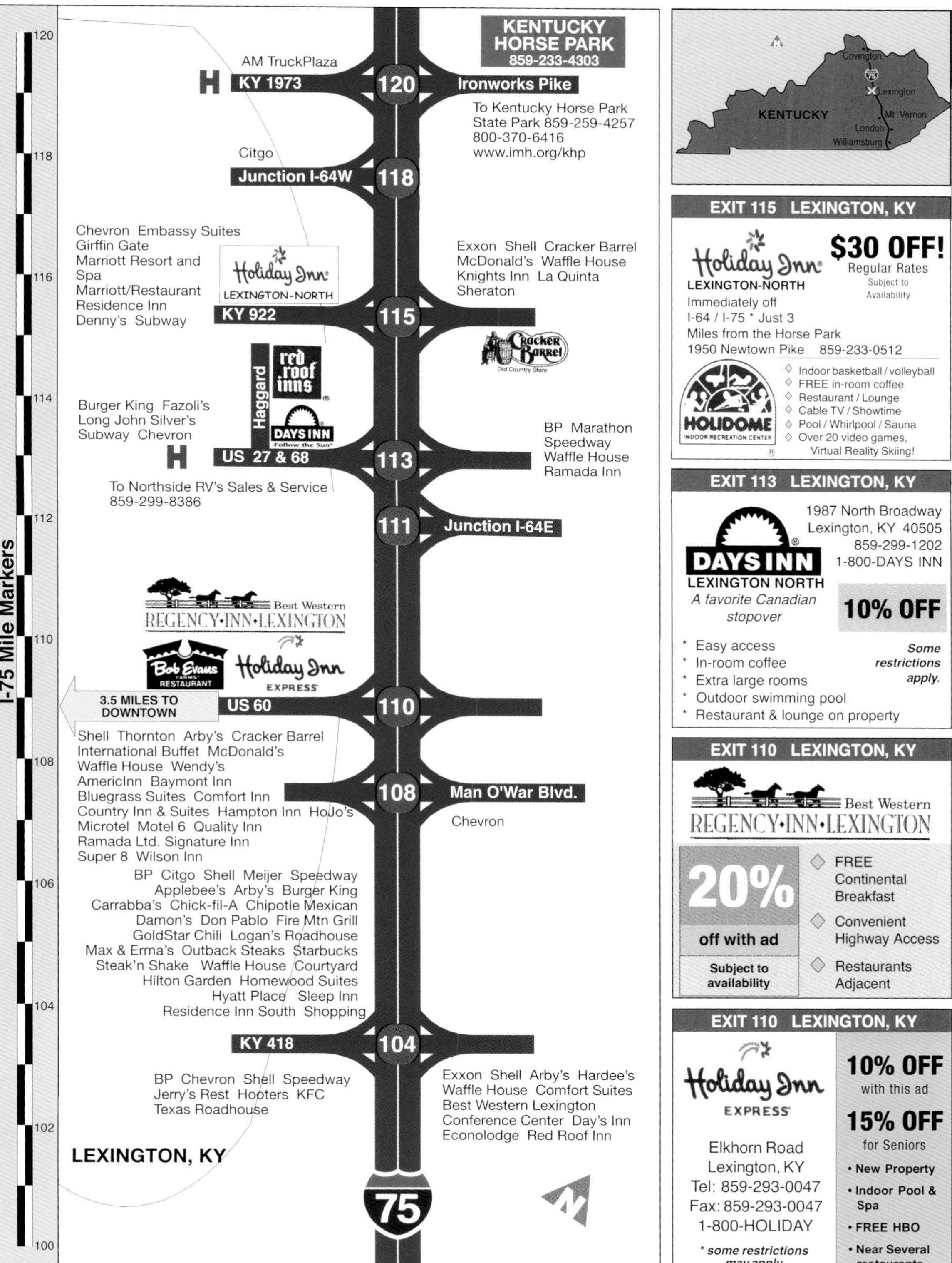

105
KENTUCKY
I-75 Mile Markers
120
118
116
114
112
110
108
106
104
102
100
KENTUCKY HORSE PARK
859-233-4303
AM TruckPlaza
H
KY 1973
120
Ironworks Pike
To Kentucky Horse Park
State Park 859-259-4257
800-370-6416
www.imh.org/khp
Citgo
Junction I-64W
118
Chevron Embassy Suites
Girffin Gate
Marriott Resort and Spa
Marriott/Restaurant
Residence Inn
Denny's Subway
Holiday Inn
LEXINGTON-NORTH
Exxon Shell Cracker Barrel
McDonald's Waffle House
Knights Inn La Quinta
Sheraton
KY 922
115
Cracker Barrel
Old Country Store
Haggard
red roof inns
DAYS INN
Follow the Sun
Burger King Fazoli's
Long John Silver's
Subway Chevron
H
BP Marathon
Speedway
Waffle House
Ramada Inn
US 27 & 68
113
To Northside RV's Sales & Service
859-299-8386
111
Junction I-64E
Best Western
REGENCY•INN•LEXINGTON
Bob Evans
RESTAURANT
Holiday Inn
EXPRESS
3.5 MILES TO DOWNTOWN
US 60
110
Shell Thornton Arby's Cracker Barrel
International Buffet McDonald's
Waffle House Wendy's
AmericInn Baymont Inn
Bluegrass Suites Comfort Inn
Country Inn & Suites Hampton Inn HoJo's
Microtel Motel 6 Quality Inn
Ramada Ltd. Signature Inn
Super 8 Wilson Inn
108
Man O'War Blvd.
Chevron
BP Citgo Shell Meijer Speedway
Applebee's Arby's Burger King
Carrabba's Chick-fil-A Chipotle Mexican
Damon's Don Pablo Fire Mtn Grill
GoldStar Chili Logan's Roadhouse
Max & Erma's Outback Steaks Starbucks
Steak'n Shake Waffle House Courtyard
Hilton Garden Homewood Suites
Hyatt Place Sleep Inn
Residence Inn South Shopping
KY 418
104
BP Chevron Shell Speedway
Jerry's Rest Hooters KFC
Texas Roadhouse
Exxon Shell Arby's Hardee's
Waffle House Comfort Suites
Best Western Lexington
Conference Center Day's Inn
Econolodge Red Roof Inn
LEXINGTON, KY
75
N
Covington
Lexington
KENTUCKY
Mt. Vernon
London
Williamsburg
EXIT 115 LEXINGTON, KY
Holiday Inn
LEXINGTON-NORTH
$30 OFF!
Regular Rates
Subject to Availability
Immediately off
I-64 / I-75 * Just 3
Miles from the Horse Park
1950 Newtown Pike 859-233-0512
HOLIDOME
INDOOR RECREATION CENTER
Indoor basketball / volleyball
FREE in-room coffee
Restaurant / Lounge
Cable TV / Showtime
Pool / Whirlpool / Sauna
Over 20 video games, Virtual Reality Skiing!
EXIT 113 LEXINGTON, KY
DAYS INN
LEXINGTON NORTH
A favorite Canadian stopover
1987 North Broadway
Lexington, KY 40505
859-299-1202
1-800-DAYS INN
10% OFF
* Easy access
* In-room coffee
* Extra large rooms
* Outdoor swimming pool
* Restaurant & lounge on property
Some restrictions apply.
EXIT 110 LEXINGTON, KY
Best Western
REGENCY•INN•LEXINGTON
20%
off with ad
Subject to availability
FREE Continental Breakfast
Convenient Highway Access
Restaurants Adjacent
EXIT 110 LEXINGTON, KY
Holiday Inn
EXPRESS
Elkhorn Road
Lexington, KY
Tel: 859-293-0047
Fax: 859-293-0047
1-800-HOLIDAY
* some restrictions may apply
10% OFF
with this ad
15% OFF
for Seniors
• New Property
• Indoor Pool & Spa
• FREE HBO
• Near Several restaurants

Richmond/Madison County, KENTUCKY

Richmond Tourism & Visitors Centre
345 Lancaster Avenue, Richmond, Kentucky 40475
859-626-8474 or 1-800-866-3705 **www.richmond.ky.us**

Colonel John Miller, a Revolutionary War soldier, founded Richmond in 1789. Despite the opposition of the Milford residents (the fight to retain the seat ended up in a brawl!), the Kentucky legislature permitted the county seat to be moved to the land owned by Colonel Miller. Court was held in his barn. On July 4, 1789, the site was officially named Richmond in honor of Miller's birthplace in Richmond, Virginia.

Richmond and Madison County will satisfy your love of American history. You can follow the Confederate troops on a self-guided tour of the Battle of Richmond. **Fort Boonesborough State Park** features a reconstructed Daniel Boone fort, Olympic-size pool, mini-golf, camping sites and sandy beach.

White Hall State Historic Site is the home of Cassius Marcellus Clay, the abolitionist, publisher and Minister to Russia. This 44-room Italianate mansion has shaded picnic areas, a gift shop and still has outside slave quarters. Richmond was also home to Kit Carson, the pioneer and explorer.

Richmond history is long. **Valley View Ferry** is the oldest continuous business on record in Kentucky (1780). Bybee Pottery is the oldest existing pottery west of the Alleghenies. Although records date to 1845, it is believed to have been established in 1809.

Richmond has the **Gibson Bay Golf Course,** a Par 72, 18-hole championship golf course designed by Michael Hurzdan. **Lake Reba Recreational Complex** has over 450 acres for fishing, boating and trails.

Hummel Planetarium and Space Theater, located on Eastern Kentucky University's campus, is the 11th-largest planetarium in the U.S.

Main Street Richmond is truly a shopper's dream and Richmond boasts one of the state's finest 19th-Century commercial districts.

Ft. Boonesborough, Richmond, KY
Courtesy: kentuckytourism.com

Attractions

Battle of Richmond Self-Guided Driving Tour
Follow the path of the Civil War *Battle of Richmond.* Audio cassettes available. Tour approximately 2 hours. Maps at Richmond Visitor Center, 345 Lancaster Ave. 1-800-866-3705

Bybee Pottery
World-famous family pottery business. Free tours offered daily. Open Mon. to Fri. 8 a.m.-4 p.m. US 52, Bybee, KY. See the photo above. 859-369-5350

Christopher "Kit" Carson's Birthplace
On Tates Creek Rd. off Hwy. 169, Richmond, KY. 1-800-866-3705

Daniel Boone Monument, on Eastern Kentucky University Campus, University Drive, Richmond, KY. 859-622-1000

Deer Run Riding Stables
Guided or unguided scenic trail rides. Pony rides, hayrides, fishing and kayaking. Closed Mon. 2001 River Circle Dr., Richmond, KY. 859-527-6339

Downtown Richmond
Has over 65 buildings on the National Register of Historic Places. Visit Main St., US 25, Richmond, KY. 1-800-866-3705.

Richmond Downtown Walking Tour of Homes
Richmond Visitor Center, 345 Lancaster Ave. 1-800-866-3705

Richmond Raceway
Stock-car racing each Sat. at 8 p.m. US 52 E, near Richmond. Call for complete directions. 859-623-9408

Fort Boonesborough State Park
Reconstructed fort with candle dipping, pottery turning, soap making. Sandy beach, picnics, camping and more. Take I-75 exit 95, to Richmond, KY. 859-527-3131

Gibson Bay Golf Course
2000 Gibson Bay Dr., on the Eastern By-Pass for Richmond. 859-623-0225

Hummel Planetarium & Space Center
Thurs., Fri. at 7:30 p.m.; Sat., Sun. at 3:30 p.m. and 7:30 p.m. Kit Carson Dr., Eastern By-Pass, Richmond, KY. 859-622-1547

Bybee Pottery, near Richmond, KY.
Courtesy: kentuckytourism.com

Lake Reba Recreational Complex
75 acres for fishing and boating. Other sports fields. Gibson Bay Dr., Eastern By-Pass, Richmond, KY. 859-623-8753

Madison County Courthouse
Main St., (or US 25S), Richmond, KY. Erected in 1849-50, the lobby showcases a boulder with an original 1770 inscription of Daniel Boone's signature. 1-800-866-3705

Meadowbrook Farm
Learn about the cattle, swine, sheep and fishery and other on site farming operations. On Meadowbrook Rd. (off KY 52), Richmond, 859-369-5426

Valley View Ferry
Kentucky's oldest continuous business, dating to 1785. Mon. to Sat. 6 a.m.-7 p.m., Sun. 9 a.m.-6 p.m. Tates Creek Rd., KY 169, Richmond, KY. 859-626-8143

White Hall State Historic Site
The historic home of Cassius Marcellus Clay. Gift shop, picnic area, guided tours. Off I-75 exit 95, White Hall Rd., Richmond, KY. 859-623-9178

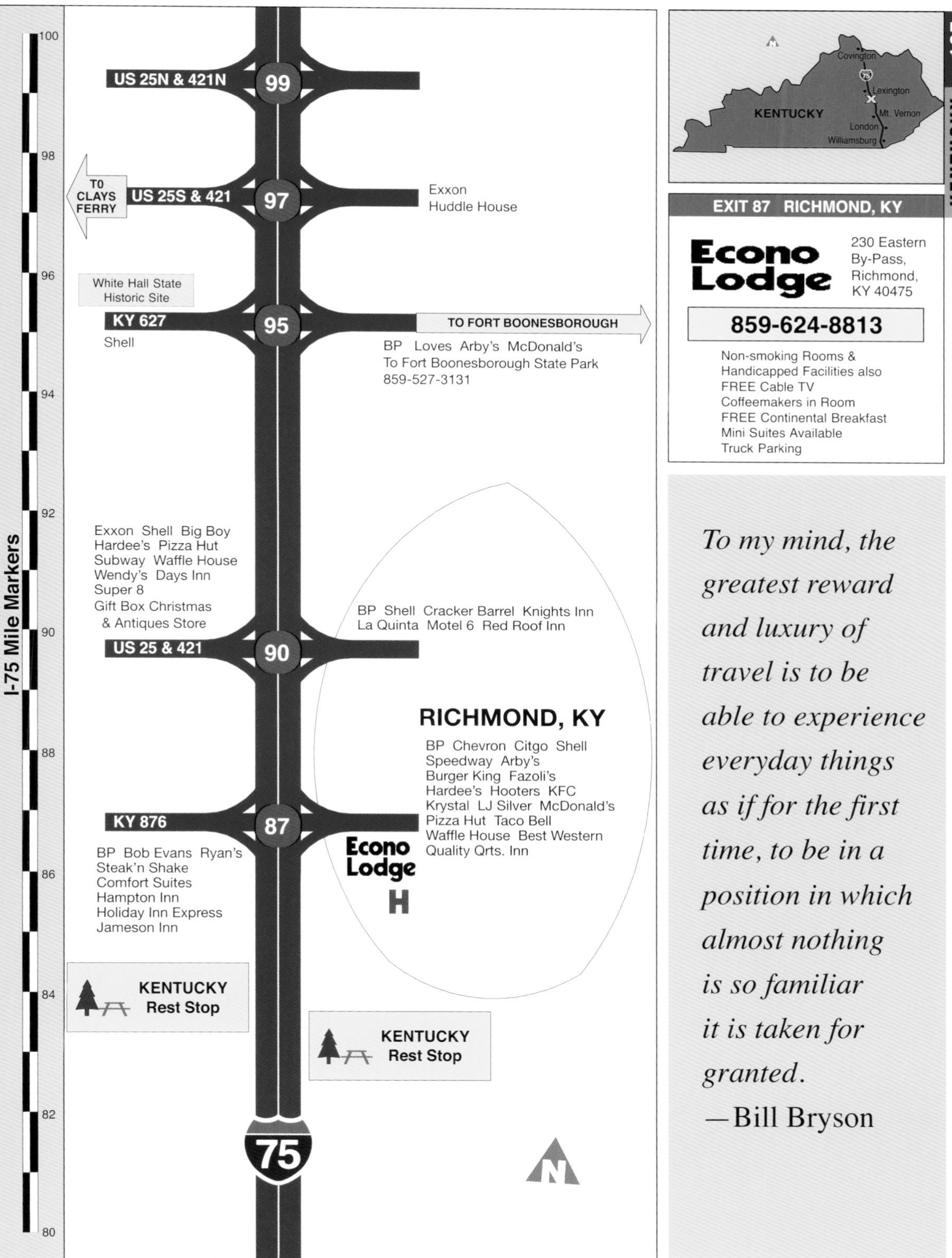

I-75 Mile Markers
100
98
96
94
92
90
88
86
84
82
80
US 25N & 421N
99
TO CLAYS FERRY
US 25S & 421
97
Exxon
Huddle House
White Hall State Historic Site
KY 627
95
TO FORT BOONESBOROUGH
Shell
BP Loves Arby's McDonald's
To Fort Boonesborough State Park
859-527-3131
Exxon Shell Big Boy
Hardee's Pizza Hut
Subway Waffle House
Wendy's Days Inn
Super 8
Gift Box Christmas & Antiques Store
BP Shell Cracker Barrel Knights Inn
La Quinta Motel 6 Red Roof Inn
US 25 & 421
90
RICHMOND, KY
BP Chevron Citgo Shell
Speedway Arby's
Burger King Fazoli's
Hardee's Hooters KFC
Krystal LJ Silver McDonald's
Pizza Hut Taco Bell
Waffle House Best Western
Quality Qrts. Inn
KY 876
87
Econo Lodge
H
BP Bob Evans Ryan's
Steak'n Shake
Comfort Suites
Hampton Inn
Holiday Inn Express
Jameson Inn
KENTUCKY Rest Stop
KENTUCKY Rest Stop
75
N
107
KENTUCKY
Covington
Lexington
KENTUCKY
Mt. Vernon
London
Williamsburg
EXIT 87 RICHMOND, KY
Econo Lodge
230 Eastern By-Pass, Richmond, KY 40475
859-624-8813
Non-smoking Rooms & Handicapped Facilities also
FREE Cable TV
Coffeemakers in Room
FREE Continental Breakfast
Mini Suites Available
Truck Parking
To my mind, the greatest reward and luxury of travel is to be able to experience everyday things as if for the first time, to be in a position in which almost nothing is so familiar it is taken for granted.
—Bill Bryson

Berea
KENTUCKY

Berea Welcome Center
201 N. Broadway, P.O. Box 556, Berea, Kentucky 40403
859-986-2540 or 1-800-598-5263 **www.berea.cc**

Renfro Valley and Kentucky's Bluegrass Music

What was once an obscure form of Southern country music popular with only a few 1000 people in Kentucky, Tennessee, and North Carolina has turned into a full-fledged musical discovery by millions of Americans and Europeans.

Bluegrass music got its name and musical form from Kentuckian **Bill Monroe & his Blue Grass Boys,** the most famous of the bluegrass bands. Monroe wrote Kentucky's official bluegrass song, "Blue Moon of Kentucky." While Monroe is considered the "father of bluegrass," Earl Scruggs, with his extraordinary banjo picking, is credited with popularizing it. The turning point in the popularization may have been the rendition by Scruggs and Lester Flatt of "The Ballad of Jed Clampett," the theme song of TV's "Beverly Hillbillies."

Several characteristics make bluegrass unmistakable to the informed listener. Most importantly, there is rarely either electrical amplification or percussion in a bluegrass band. A banjo is usually the lead instrument. The guitar, mandolin, string bass, and fiddle round out the ensemble, providing the driving rhythm and intricate harmonies that give bluegrass its contagious excitement.

Although modern bluegrass has evolved into a complex, standardized style, the threads of its development came from mountain ballads, folk songs, jazz, Dixieland, country and western, spirituals and gospel songs.

Kentucky has many spots that nurture unique musical sound. One is **Renfro Valley Country Music** off I-75 near Mt. Vernon. Founded in 1939 by John Lair, Renfro Valley is known for the traditional Barn Dance, the contemporary Renfro Valley Jamboree and the reverent **Sunday Morning Gatherin'.**

Renfro Valley is home to a village of craft studios and shops, the **John Lair Museum** (country music history), and other attractions. Many music-related events take place here throughout the year, including the Old Joe Clark Bluegrass Festival in July and the Fiddlers' Festival in November.

Folk Arts and Crafts of Kentucky

Each fall, the **Kentucky Guild of Artists and Craftsmen** holds craft fairs in Berea.

Daily craft demonstrations at the 2-day fair include pottery making, vegetable dyeing, silk screen printing, carving, and broom making. In addition to these two fairs is the Berea Craft Festival in July, which hosts more than 100 crafts people from across the country.

While in town, you'll want to visit the working studios of woodworkers, potters, quilters, jewelers, photographers, weavers and furniture makers and numerous shops and galleries offering the finest handcrafted work to be found anywhere.

Begin your tour at the Welcome Center in the historic train depot on N. Broadway. Ask for the map of the studios and antique shops locations.

Berea Craft Festival, Berea KY.
Courtesy: kentuckytourism.com

Berea College and Boone Tavern Hotel

Berea, located along the first trans-Appalachian route, retains many of the characteristics of the rugged pioneers who first settled Kentucky.

Spirited, individualistic, and self-sufficient, these men and women left a legacy that has been passed down in mountain ballads, folk dancing and crafts.

Berea College, the cornerstone of the community, was founded to provide education to mountain students with limited economic resources. Concern for the dignity of labor and the preservation of Appalachian crafts led to the establishment of college-operated student industries: weaving, wood turning, antique furniture reproduction, broom making, ceramics, needlecraft, and wrought iron working.

Since the school's founding in 1855, Berea College undergraduates have been required to work in the Student Labor Program to help meet the expenses of their education. Tours of the campus begin at **Boone Tavern Hotel.** 50 minutes. Free. Mon. to Fri. 9 a.m., 10 a.m. and 1 p.m.; Sat. 9 a.m. and 2 p.m. 859-986-9341 ext. 5018

Student-operated Boone Tavern,
with its fine dining and accommodations since the turn of the century, is on the college campus. It was built, in fact, in 1908 as lodging for house guests of the college. Today, the Georgian-Colonial tavern, just 1-1/2 miles from the I-75, is noted for fine regional Southern dishes such as Jefferson Davis Pie, spoon bread, corn sticks, Boone Tavern Chicken Pie and roast Kentucky lamb with caper gravy. Call 1-800-366-9358 for seating times and menu options. Courtesy: kentuckytourism.com

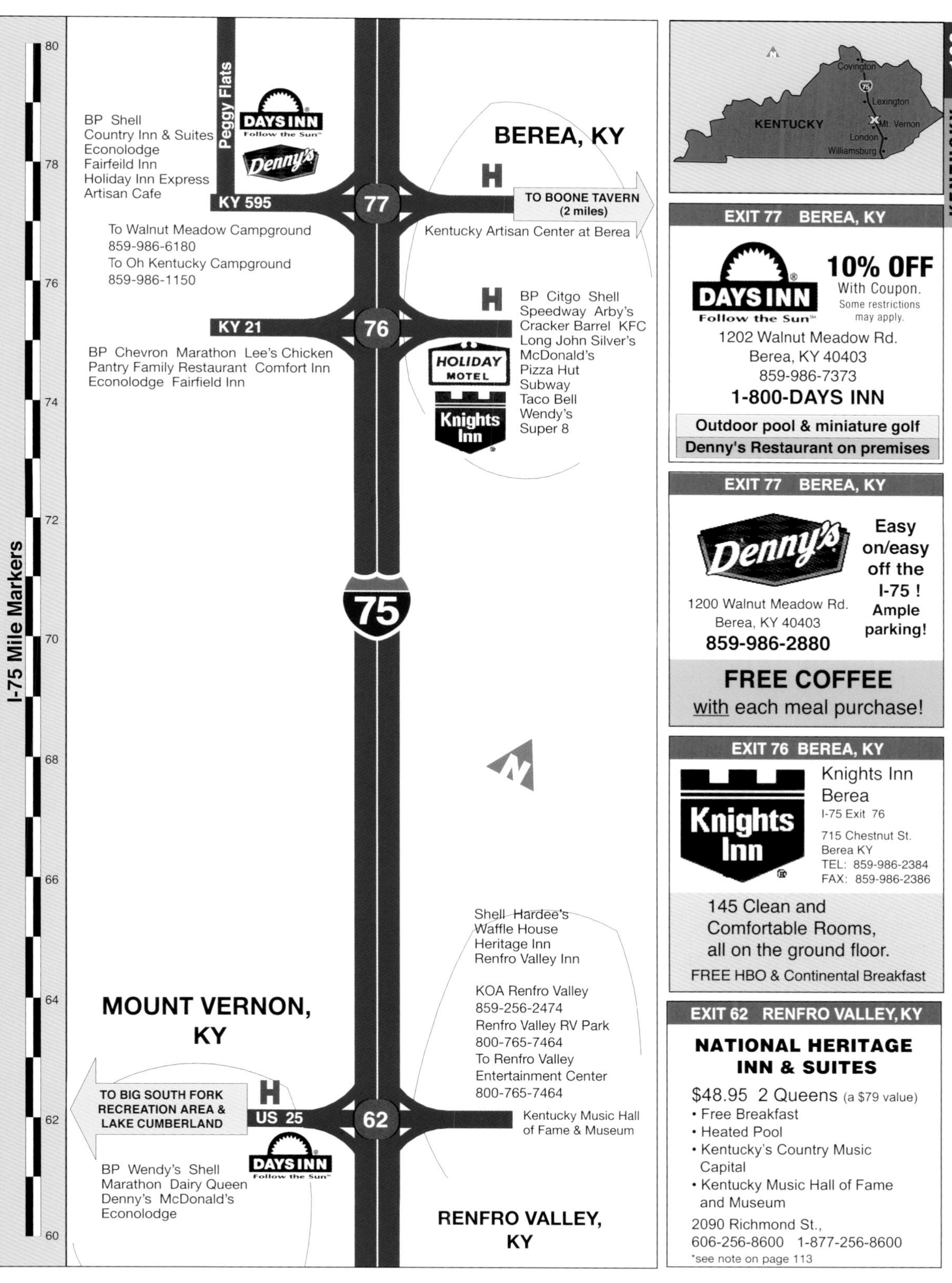
I-75 Mile Markers
80
78
76
74
72
70
68
66
64
62
60
Peggy Flats
BP Shell
Country Inn & Suites
Econolodge
Fairfeild Inn
Holiday Inn Express
Artisan Cafe
DAYS INN Follow the Sun
Denny's
BEREA, KY
KY 595
77
TO BOONE TAVERN (2 miles)
Kentucky Artisan Center at Berea
To Walnut Meadow Campground
859-986-6180
To Oh Kentucky Campground
859-986-1150
KY 21
76
BP Citgo Shell
Speedway Arby's
Cracker Barrel KFC
Long John Silver's
McDonald's
Pizza Hut
Subway
Taco Bell
Wendy's
Super 8
BP Chevron Marathon Lee's Chicken
Pantry Family Restaurant Comfort Inn
Econolodge Fairfield Inn
HOLIDAY MOTEL
Knights Inn
75
N
Shell Hardee's
Waffle House
Heritage Inn
Renfro Valley Inn
KOA Renfro Valley
859-256-2474
Renfro Valley RV Park
800-765-7464
To Renfro Valley
Entertainment Center
800-765-7464
MOUNT VERNON, KY
TO BIG SOUTH FORK RECREATION AREA & LAKE CUMBERLAND
US 25
62
Kentucky Music Hall of Fame & Museum
BP Wendy's Shell
Marathon Dairy Queen
Denny's McDonald's
Econolodge
DAYS INN Follow the Sun
RENFRO VALLEY, KY
Covington
Lexington
KENTUCKY
Mt. Vernon
London
Williamsburg
75
EXIT 77 BEREA, KY
DAYS INN Follow the Sun
10% OFF
With Coupon.
Some restrictions may apply.
1202 Walnut Meadow Rd.
Berea, KY 40403
859-986-7373
1-800-DAYS INN
Outdoor pool & miniature golf
Denny's Restaurant on premises
EXIT 77 BEREA, KY
Denny's
Easy on/easy off the I-75 !
Ample parking!
1200 Walnut Meadow Rd.
Berea, KY 40403
859-986-2880
FREE COFFEE
with each meal purchase!
EXIT 76 BEREA, KY
Knights Inn
Knights Inn
Berea
I-75 Exit 76
715 Chestnut St.
Berea KY
TEL: 859-986-2384
FAX: 859-986-2386
145 Clean and Comfortable Rooms, all on the ground floor.
FREE HBO & Continental Breakfast
EXIT 62 RENFRO VALLEY, KY
NATIONAL HERITAGE INN & SUITES
$48.95 2 Queens (a $79 value)
• Free Breakfast
• Heated Pool
• Kentucky's Country Music Capital
• Kentucky Music Hall of Fame and Museum
2090 Richmond St.,
606-256-8600 1-877-256-8600
*see note on page 113

Kentucky

Kentucky Department of Travel
500 Mero Street, 22nd Floor, Frankfort, Kentucky 40601-1968
502-564-4930 or 1-800-225-8747 **www.kentuckytourism.com**

Daniel Boone Country

Daniel Boone (1734-1820), hunted and explored Kentucky from 1767-74; cleared the Wilderness Road and founded **Fort Boonesborough** in 1775. Woods-man, explorer, settler, tavern-keeper and pioneer statesman, his life was a legend and he influenced Kentucky history like no other. Although the man was born in Pennsylvania in 1734, Kentucky is Daniel Boone country. Boone raised his family, buried two of his sons, and gave a daughter away in marriage in Kentucky.

Daniel Boone's wanderlust led him to explore "the West" and, in 1767, he first set foot in Kentucky. He laid claim to vast tracks of Kentucky soil, but by 1788 all were lost in legal battles. He lived in Kentucky with one of his sons for several years before moving further west. He died in Missouri in 1820. Thousands of settlers followed Boone's Kentucky trails which begin at **Cumberland Gap National Historical Park.** Cumberland Gap's location was documented in 1750 but the first white man known to use the Gap was Gabriel Arthur in 1764.

By 1769, Daniel Boone and a companion had scouted the area and spoke of the fabled Bluegrass Region. In 1775 just North of London, KY, Boone made the decision to blaze a new trail that would take him North to the Kentucky River. You can tour Boone's Trace by taking US Routes 25 and 388 through Kentucky's interior to Richmond and on to Fort Boonesborough, the Trace's terminus.

Kentucky-born Explorers & Frontiersmen

Judge Roy Bean (1825-1903)
Trader; bartender; infamous "hanging judge" of Langtry, Texas.

James Bowie (1796-1836)
Texas Ranger who died at the Alamo; designed the Bowie knife.

Kit Carson (1809-1868)
Indian agent; trapper; scout.

Floyd Collins (1887-1925)
Explorer whose entrapment and death in a cave became one of the most widely reported stories of the decade.

Kentucky's State Parks are the Finest

Seventeen resort parks have comfortable lodges complete with daily maid service. Unfortunately pets are not permitted. Sixteen of the parks have fully equipped housekeeping cottages. You can choose from a range of accommodations from efficiencies to 3-bedroom executive residences. Twenty-six have campsites with full hookups and dump stations. Many have historic sites, museums and give guided tours. Also noteworthy is the schedule of special events. The parks described on this page are handy to I-75.

BIG BONE LICK STATE PARK
Great herds of giant mastodons, mammoths and bison were attracted to the warm salt-water springs that bubbled to the earth at Big Bone Lick. The ground was marshy and entombed many of the great creatures, leaving their skeletons to be fossilized.

More than 500 acres with 62 camp sites with utilities. Gift shop, fishing and hiking trails.

Big Bone Lick State Park, 3380 Beaver Rd., Union, KY 41091-9627. I-75 exit 175, KY 338. 859-384-3522

LEVI JACKSON WILDERNESS ROAD STATE PARK in LONDON, KY.
This 900-acre park has 150 camp sites with utilities and is open year-round. There is a working pioneer grist mill, Mountain Life museum, gift shop, mini-golf, pool, special events, miles of hiking trails, groceries and playgrounds. Here you can hike two historic trails: Boone's Trace and the Wilderness Road which carried more than 200,000 settlers into Kentucky.

Levi Jackson State Park, 998 Levi Jackson Mill Rd., London, KY 40741-8944. I-75 exit 38. 859-878-8000

FORT BOONESBOROUGH STATE PARK
After fighting Indians and nature, Daniel Boone and his men finally reached the Kentucky River on Apr. 1, 1775, to settle the area now known as Fort Boonesborough. Today, Fort Boonesborough is a reconstructed working fort with period furnishings and pioneer craft demonstrations. The museum tells Daniel Boone's story through videos and displays.

153 acres with 167 camp sites with utilities. Open year-round. Swimming pool, dock with ramp, fishing, hiking.

Fort Boonesborough State Park, 4375 Boonesborough Rd., Richmond, KY 40475-9316. I-75 exit 95 (On I-64 exit at Winchester). 859-527-3131

GENERAL BURNSIDE STATE PARK
430 acres of camping, golf, boating, fishing and swimming at Kentucky's only island park. 94 camp sites with utilities, 18-hole golf course, pro shop, marina with rental boats and houseboats.

During the Civil War, Union General Ambrose Burnside patrolled this island for Confederate soldiers. Today it's a secluded lake with hidden coves and a thick forest cover.

General Burnside State Park, P.O. Box 488, Burnside, KY, 42519. 8 miles south of Somerset on US 27. 859-561-4104.

CUMBERLAND FALLS STATE RESORT PARK
Do you know what a moonbow is? This beautiful world-famous sight is only visible on this side of the world at Cumberland Falls State Resort Park when there is a clear night and a full moon. The mist of the waterfall fills the gorge and produces a night-time moonlit rainbow. The 125-foot wide waterfall is known as "Niagara of the South" and you can see it up close on a white-water rafting trip or scenic train excursion.

Nearly 1,700 acres. 52 lodge rooms, 20 Woodland rooms, 26 cottages and 50 camp sites with utilities year-round. Horseback riding, fishing, dining room, hiking trails and more.

CUMBERLAND FALLS STATE RESORT PARK
7351 KY 90, Corbin, KY, 40701-8814. Take Corbin Exit 29, to US 25W, then to KY 90. 859-528-4121

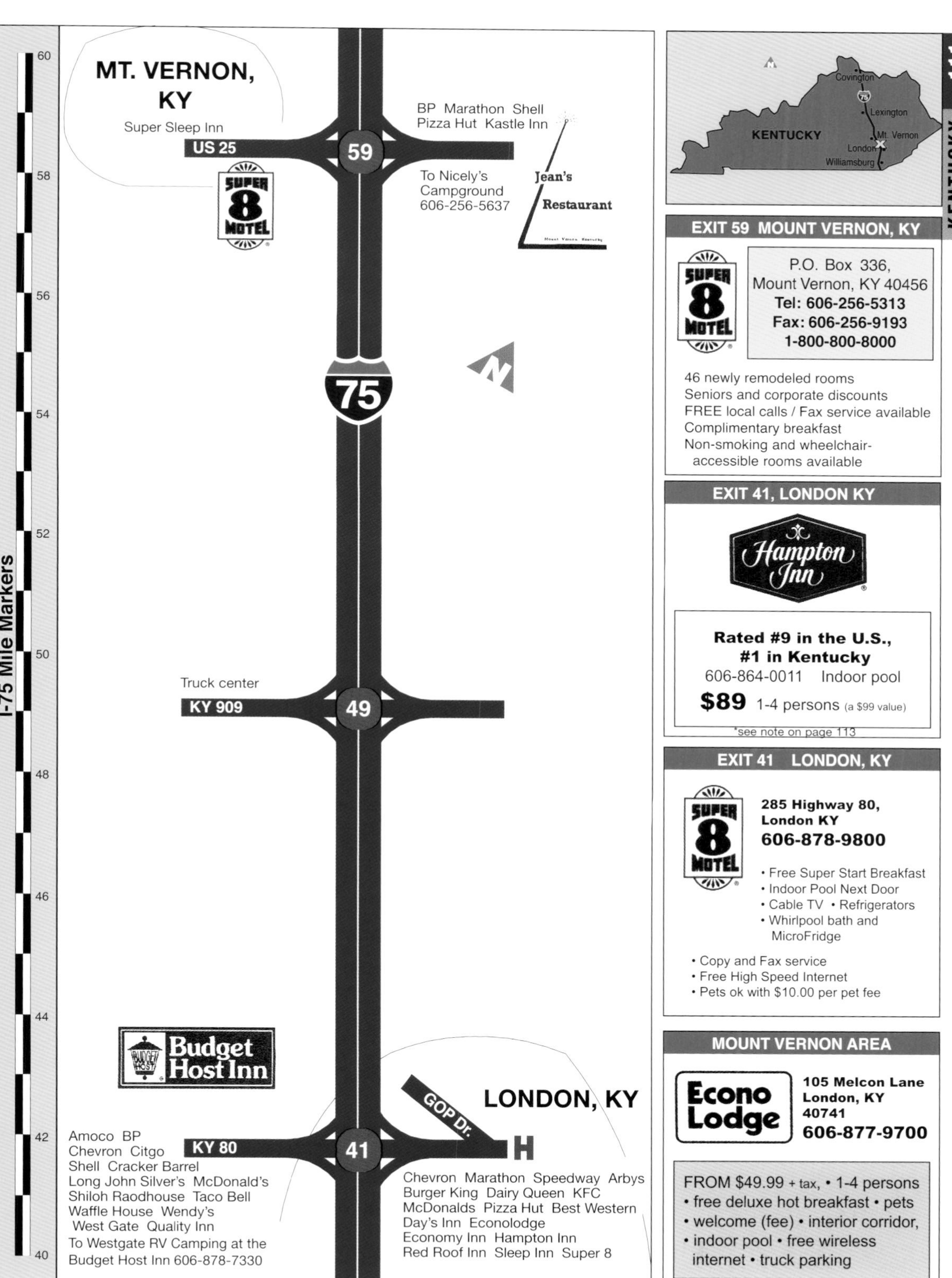
111
KENTUCKY
I-75 Mile Markers
60
58
56
54
52
50
48
46
44
42
40
MT. VERNON, KY
Super Sleep Inn
US 25
59
BP Marathon Shell
Pizza Hut Kastle Inn
To Nicely's Campground 606-256-5637
Jean's Restaurant
SUPER 8 MOTEL
75
N
Truck center
KY 909
49
Budget Host Inn
LONDON, KY
GOP Dr.
KY 80
41
H
Amoco BP
Chevron Citgo
Shell Cracker Barrel
Long John Silver's McDonald's
Shiloh Raodhouse Taco Bell
Waffle House Wendy's
West Gate Quality Inn
To Westgate RV Camping at the Budget Host Inn 606-878-7330
Chevron Marathon Speedway Arbys
Burger King Dairy Queen KFC
McDonalds Pizza Hut Best Western
Day's Inn Econolodge
Economy Inn Hampton Inn
Red Roof Inn Sleep Inn Super 8
Covington
Lexington
KENTUCKY
Mt. Vernon
London
Williamsburg
EXIT 59 MOUNT VERNON, KY
SUPER 8 MOTEL
P.O. Box 336,
Mount Vernon, KY 40456
Tel: 606-256-5313
Fax: 606-256-9193
1-800-800-8000
46 newly remodeled rooms
Seniors and corporate discounts
FREE local calls / Fax service available
Complimentary breakfast
Non-smoking and wheelchair-accessible rooms available
EXIT 41, LONDON KY
Hampton Inn
Rated #9 in the U.S.,
#1 in Kentucky
606-864-0011 Indoor pool
$89 1-4 persons (a $99 value)
*see note on page 113
EXIT 41 LONDON, KY
SUPER 8 MOTEL
285 Highway 80,
London KY
606-878-9800
• Free Super Start Breakfast
• Indoor Pool Next Door
• Cable TV • Refrigerators
• Whirlpool bath and MicroFridge
• Copy and Fax service
• Free High Speed Internet
• Pets ok with $10.00 per pet fee
MOUNT VERNON AREA
Econo Lodge
105 Melcon Lane
London, KY
40741
606-877-9700
FROM $49.99 + tax, • 1-4 persons
• free deluxe hot breakfast • pets
• welcome (fee) • interior corridor,
• indoor pool • free wireless
internet • truck parking

London
KENTUCKY

London-Laurel County Tourism Commission
140 West Daniel Boone Parkway, I-75 Exit 41, London, KY 40741
606-878-6900 or 1-800-348-0095 **www.corbinkytourism.com**

The London Visitor Center off I-75 exit 41 (Mon. to Sat. 9 a.m. - 5 p.m., 1-800-348-0095) has details on the outdoor recreation facilities as well as area shops such as **Fort Sequoyah, Dogpatch Trading Post, Country Crafts, Flea World** and **London Flea Market.** Be sure to ask about the annual **Civil War reenactment** of the *Battle of Camp Wildcat* and the **World Chicken Festival.** Also at this exit is the **Daniel Boone Motocross Park,** an AMA-sanctioned track with racing March to Nov. (On KY-80 W, 606-877-1364.

London is known to many as the home of **Levi Jackson Wilderness Road State Park.** The **Wilderness Road,** Kentucky's first true road built in 1796, and **Boone's Trace,** cut by Daniel Boone from Cumberland Gap to the Kentucky River, run through the park. You'll also see the only marked **burial grounds** along the Wilderness Road, the colorful **Mountain Life Museum,** and **McHargue's Mill** surrounded by the largest display of mill-stones in the country. Museum admission is $1.25, open 9 a.m. - 4:30 p.m. Camping and hiking from Apr. to Oct. The Mill is open May to Sept. I-75 exit 38 to US-25 South. 606-878-8000

Corbin
KENTUCKY

Corbin Tourist & Convention Commission
805 S. Main Street, Corbin, KY 40701
606-528-8860

If you take the Corbin exits 25 and 29, you will find one of Kentucky's finest recreational lakes: **Laurel River Lake.** This beautiful 5,600-acre lake is served by 1,500 motel rooms if that's any indication of its popularity!

Within an hour's drive from Corbin you will find several state and national parks and many major attractions including: **Big South Fork National Recreation Area, Cumberland Falls State Resort Park, Levi Jackson Wilderness Road State Park, Laurel Lake, Pine Mountain State Resort Park, Cumberland Gap National Historic Park, Daniel Boone National Forest, Renfro Valley Country Music Center, Corbin's Famous Annual Nibroc Festival & Kentucky Communities Crafts Village, Knox Historical Museum** and the **Dr. Thomas Walker State Historic Site.**

Great Tastes from the Bluegrass State

Traditional Kentucky favorites such as country ham, fried chicken, burgoo and hickory-smoked barbecue are as popular today as they were 150 years ago. The custom of curing ham, Kentucky style, began in frontier times and was born of the need to preserve meat for year-round use. Every family had its own smokehouse and secret curing methods.

Kentucky country ham differs from regular commercial ham in that it is cured by a dry-rub process rather than a soaking process. Sugar, salt, and other "secret" ingredients are rubbed into the aging ham at prescribed intervals. The curing ham grows stronger in flavor and aroma. A seasoned ham-lover seeks at least a year-old ham.

Hams are traditionally either baked, simmered or fried. Baked hams can be glazed with brown sugar, mustard, vinegar and cloves. All sorts of flavors can be simmered into country hams, from fruit juice to cola to sweet pickle juice. And who wouldn't enjoy a traditional Southern break-fast of fried ham, red-eye gravy, grits, scrambled eggs and homemade beaten biscuits?

***Colonel Sanders** restaurant & museum, Corbin, KY.*
Courtesy: kentuckytourism.com

Country ham is the basic ingredient of the **Hot Brown,** which originated at the Brown Hotel in Louisville. Morsels of turkey and ham on toast are covered with a cheese sauce, topped with bacon and a tomato slice and served piping hot.

An all-around favorite of Kentuckians is **fried chicken.** Forever clad in a white suit and string tie, the late Colonel Harland Sanders, has become the symbol of the Southern way of preparing chicken. His secret recipe for fried chicken, perfected at his small roadside restaurant, has created a worldwide corporation. Take exit 29 on US-25W to find the **Harland Sanders Cafe & Museum.** Dine in the restored restaurant, tour the Colonel's kitchen, and see artifacts and memorabilia. 7 a.m. - 11 p.m., handicapped accessible, 606-528-2163.

Barbecuing in Kentucky for a large group is an all-day job. Although beef and pork are used, the favorite meat is mutton. A hickory-smoked barbecue is made in a pit, an enclosed furnace-like structure that allows the meat to cook over low heat with hickory smoke. Occasionally the coals are dowsed with water to keep the meat from cooking too fast. Periodic basting with barbecue sauce gives the meat its flavor. It can take as long as 24 hours to barbecue a ham or pork side which is usually served with cole slaw, baked beans, potato salad, a slice of onion and barbecue sauce.

"Burgoo" is a thick stew popular at Derby time. Burgoo is usually cooked outdoors for 5 to 24 hours. Many think burgoo is made of everything available and edible. Not so! Real burgoo is made from specific recipes containing pork, veal, beef, lamb, chicken, and vegetables such as corn, cabbage, peppers, carrots, okra and potatoes.

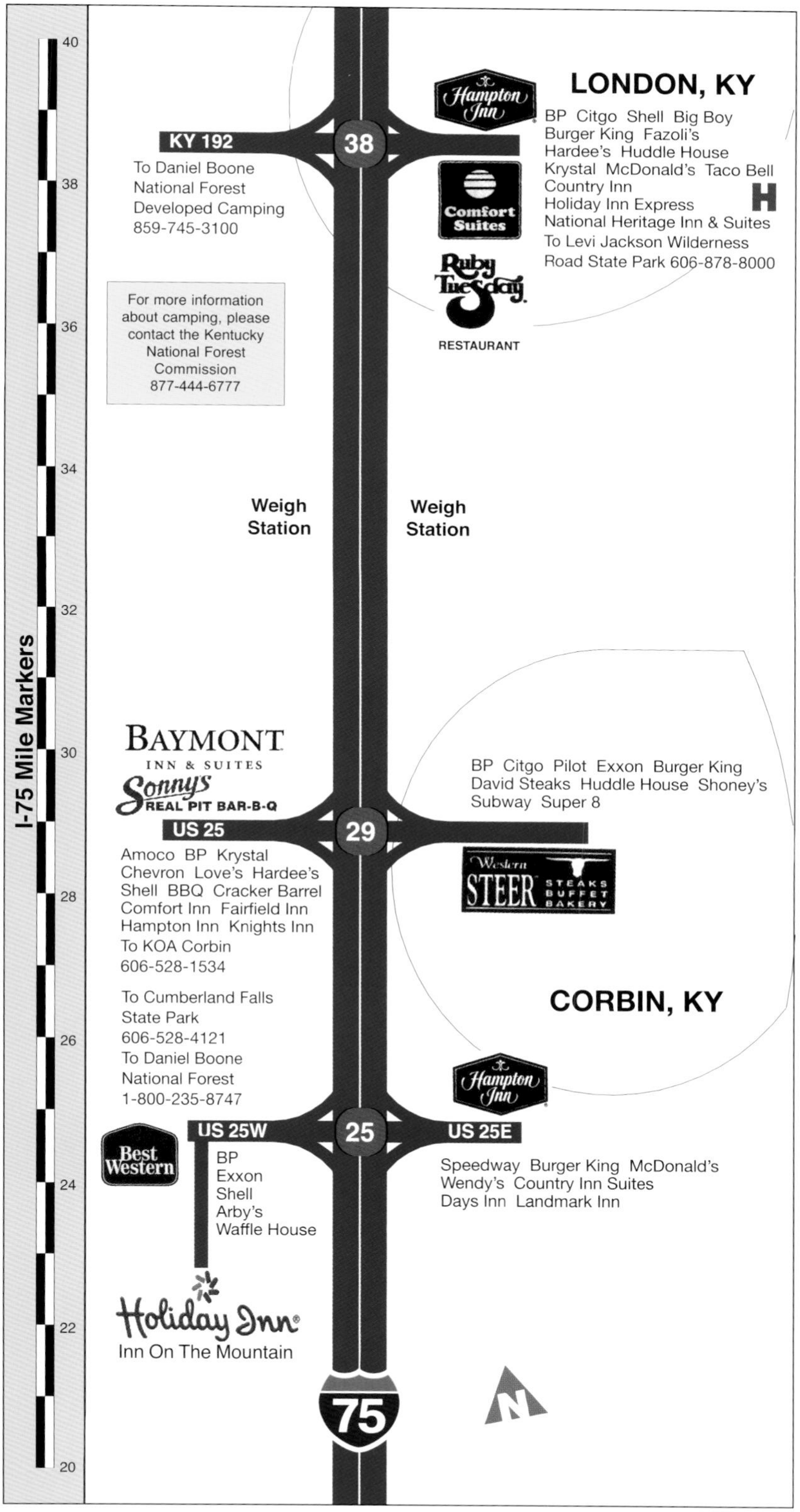

I-75 Mile Markers

40 38 36 34 32 30 28 26 24 22 20

LONDON, KY

BP Citgo Shell Big Boy
Burger King Fazoli's
Hardee's Huddle House
Krystal McDonald's Taco Bell
Country Inn
Holiday Inn Express
National Heritage Inn & Suites
To Levi Jackson Wilderness
Road State Park 606-878-8000

Comfort Suites

Ruby Tuesday RESTAURANT

KY 192 — 38

To Daniel Boone
National Forest
Developed Camping
859-745-3100

For more information about camping, please contact the Kentucky National Forest Commission 877-444-6777

Weigh Station

Weigh Station

BAYMONT INN & SUITES

Sonny's REAL PIT BAR-B-Q

US 25 — 29

Amoco BP Krystal
Chevron Love's Hardee's
Shell BBQ Cracker Barrel
Comfort Inn Fairfield Inn
Hampton Inn Knights Inn
To KOA Corbin
606-528-1534

To Cumberland Falls
State Park
606-528-4121
To Daniel Boone
National Forest
1-800-235-8747

BP Citgo Pilot Exxon Burger King
David Steaks Huddle House Shoney's
Subway Super 8

Western STEER STEAKS BUFFET BAKERY

CORBIN, KY

Hampton Inn

US 25W — 25 — US 25E

Best Western

BP
Exxon
Shell
Arby's
Waffle House

Holiday Inn
Inn On The Mountain

Speedway Burger King McDonald's
Wendy's Country Inn Suites
Days Inn Landmark Inn

75

EXIT 38 LONDON, KY

Hampton Inn

$69 1-4 GUESTS (An $89 Value)
606-877-1000

- Hilton Honors Points & Miles
- Interior and exterior entrance
- Next to Starbucks and Steak n Shake
- Hot & Cold breakfast bar

Voted London's Best for the last 5 years!

*see note below

EXIT 38 LONDON, KY

NATIONAL HERITAGE INN & SUITES

$39.95 ONE QUEEN (An $59.95 Value)
606-877-3400

- Free Breakfast bar
- Indoor pool
- Walk to Ruby Tuesday
- Golden Corral • Eldorado's
- Wal-Mart • Cinema & More

*see note below

EXIT 29 CORBIN, KY

$84 1-4 GUESTS (An $99 Value)
606-523-5696

- NEXT TO CRACKER BARREL
- HILTON HONORS POINTS & MILES
- RATED AS ONE OF THE BEST

*see note below

NOTE: THE BEST OF THE BEST

"We've known the Handy family for several years now; they have been welcoming guests to Kentucky for four generations. You can count on Jim Handy and his two sons to always give you a warm welcome and comforting stay. We highly recommend their three properties described above as well as their other I-75 locations including the National Heritage Inn and Suites (Exit 62) and the Hampton Inn (Exit 41).
"Rates quoted are 2009." Author's note.

Williamsburg
KENTUCKY

Williansburg Tourism Commission
650 S. Tenth St., Williamsburg, Kentucky 40769
606-549-0530 or 1-800-552-0530 **www.williamsburgky.com**

I never miss a chance to visit my favorite hotel, the beautiful **Cumberland Inn & Museum!**

The Cumberland Inn is truly one of South Central Kentucky's undiscovered treasures. Nestled within the lush Daniel Boone National Forest and resting at the foothills of the Appalachian Mountains, the Inn is located in one of the most picturesque portions of the country. The Cumberland Inn is surrounded by many famous area attractions like the Cumberland Falls, Big South Fork Scenic Railway and the Cumberland Museum featuring many different historic and cultural exhibits.

The Cumberland Inn is owned by Cumberland College, the majority of the associates are Cumberland College students, who are given the opportunity to work at the Inn to help pay for their college expenses.

The Inn is reminiscent of an old southern mansion. The lobby will captivate you—from the white marble floors to the hand-painted dome. The guest rooms are equally beautiful, spacious and impeccably clean. The Inn's **Athenaeum Restaurant** provides delicious food in a serene setting filled with leather-bound books, a player piano, a warm fire for the perfect atmosphere, and a beautiful view of the nearby Mountains.

For your idle time, relax and enjoy a swim in the indoor pool, complete with whirlpool, or visit the unique gift shop and museum. The superb service and luxurious rooms are offered at a very reasonable rate. The Inn is conveniently located off I-75 at exit 11. 649 South 10th St. Williamsburg, KY 40769. 1-800-315-0286 www.cumberlandinn.com

Williamsburg is just 11 miles north of the Kentucky-Tennessee border on the I-75 and is an excellent access point for the **Cumberland Falls** and **Big South Fork** areas. **The Kentucky Welcome Center**, also found at exit 11, is a full-service facility for travelers.

Kentucky's Eastern Highland: Tradition and Natural Beauty

Cloaked in the mist of tradition, quaint mountain folkways, and rugged scenic beauty, you'll find the unique heritage of **Kentucky's Eastern Highlands**.

Cumberland Gap, at the southeastern tip of Kentucky, was the portal to Western expansion. The **Cumberland Gap National Historic Park** is one of the most visited areas in the state. From its overlook you can see the sweep of mountains and forests that Daniel Boone saw more than 200 years ago.

The most prominent feature of the Highlands is the **Daniel Boone National Forest,** which stretches the length of the region. The 672,000-acre forest beckons to those who enjoy hiking, biking, camping and boating.

One of the most striking areas in the national forest is the **Red River Gorge Geological Area,** a virtual gallery of natural arches and bridges, palisades, and unique vegetation. Here you will find the striking **Natural Bridge** and **Natural Bridge State Resort Park.**

When conditions are right, you can see the only **moonbow** in the western hemisphere at majestic **Cumberland Falls** near Corbin. The largest waterfall east of the Rocky Mountains and south of Niagara Falls, it sends a 125-foot wide curtain of water over a drop of 70 feet.

In the far eastern tip of the state is the **Breaks of the Big Sandy River.** Often called the "Grand Canyon of the South," the Breaks is the largest canyon east of the Mississippi River. Enjoy the area's spectacular views at **Breaks Interstate Park** on the Kentucky-Virginia border.

Cave Run Lake and **Laurel River Lake,** two of the most popular lakes in the state, are at either end of the national forest. Other recreational lakes include **Grayson, Buckhorn, Paintsville, Dewey, Fishtrap** and **Greenbo.**

Seven of **Kentucky's State Parks** and day-use parks are located at these lakes and other scenic spots throughout the region, such as **Carter Caves** and **Pine Mountain.**

The Highlands have inspired musicians, artists, and writers the world over. One place to hear **mountain-inspired music** is at **Renfro Valley** near Mount Vernon, home of the Renfro Valley Barn Dance and the Sunday Morning Gatherin' radio broadcast since 1941.

The Highland's **craft heritage** is as rich as its crafts. Kentucky pottery, quilts, baskets, woodcrafts, and textiles are world-famous, and you can buy these treasures at craft cooperatives.

New to the area is the **Mountain Home Place,** located near the city of Paintsville, just off Country Music Hwy. 23 at Paintsville Lake. This Appalachian settlement and working farm recreates the workload of the 1850-1875 pioneers. When you first arrive, enjoy "The Land of Tomorrow" video narrated by actor Richard Thomas, who himself has family ties to the area. Then venture on to tour the HomePlace, where you'll see farm life as it was for a self-sufficient family of that period.

Text courtesy KY Department of Tourist Development

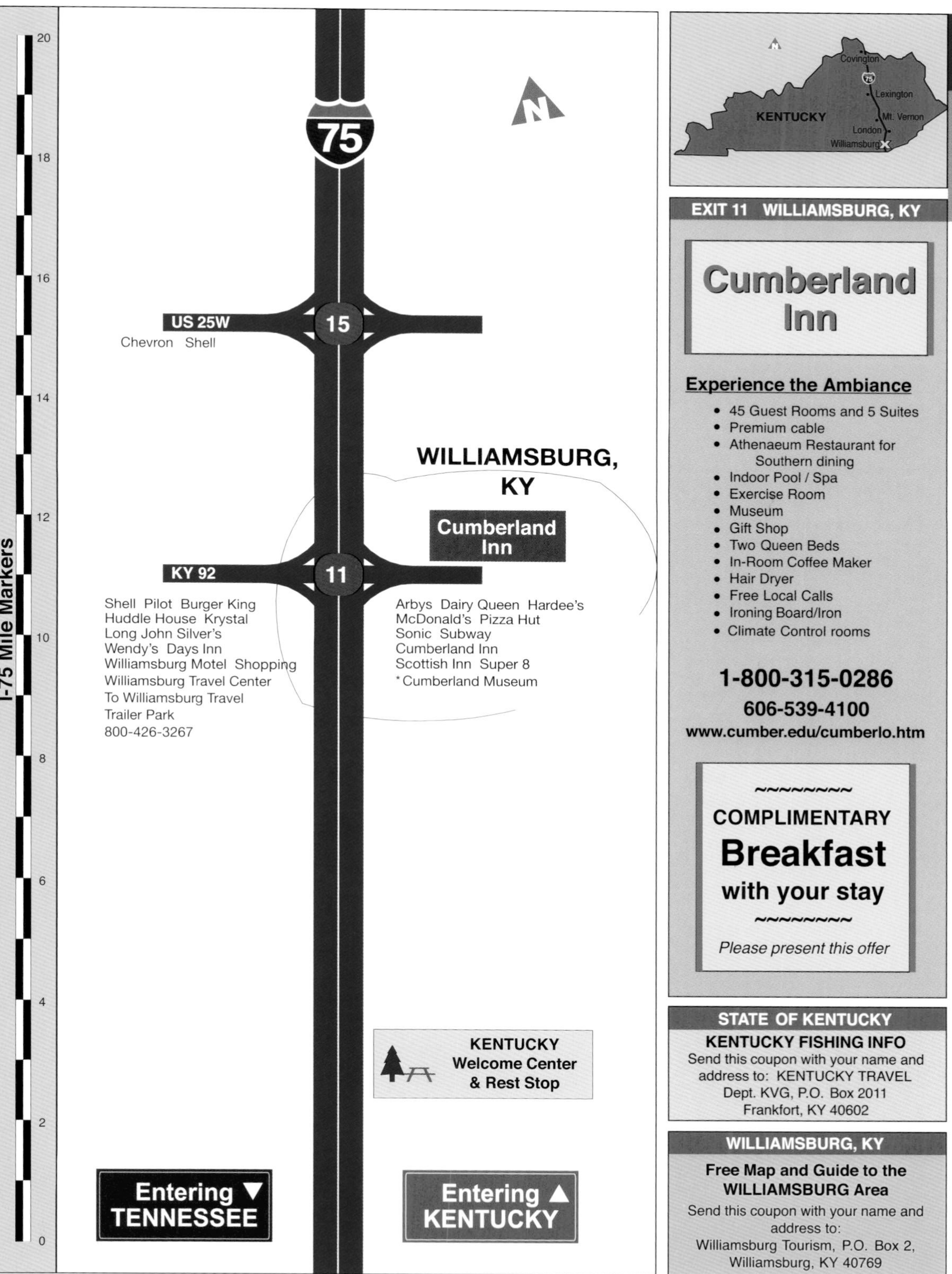
115
KENTUCKY
I-75 Mile Markers
20
18
16
14
12
10
8
6
4
2
0
75
N
US 25W
15
Chevron Shell
WILLIAMSBURG, KY
Cumberland Inn
KY 92
11
Shell Pilot Burger King
Huddle House Krystal
Long John Silver's
Wendy's Days Inn
Williamsburg Motel Shopping
Williamsburg Travel Center
To Williamsburg Travel
Trailer Park
800-426-3267
Arbys Dairy Queen Hardee's
McDonald's Pizza Hut
Sonic Subway
Cumberland Inn
Scottish Inn Super 8
*Cumberland Museum
KENTUCKY
Welcome Center
& Rest Stop
Entering ▼ TENNESSEE
Entering ▲ KENTUCKY
Covington
Lexington
KENTUCKY
Mt. Vernon
London
Williamsburg
EXIT 11 WILLIAMSBURG, KY
Cumberland Inn
Experience the Ambiance
• 45 Guest Rooms and 5 Suites
• Premium cable
• Athenaeum Restaurant for Southern dining
• Indoor Pool / Spa
• Exercise Room
• Museum
• Gift Shop
• Two Queen Beds
• In-Room Coffee Maker
• Hair Dryer
• Free Local Calls
• Ironing Board/Iron
• Climate Control rooms
1-800-315-0286
606-539-4100
www.cumber.edu/cumberlo.htm
COMPLIMENTARY
Breakfast
with your stay
Please present this offer
STATE OF KENTUCKY
KENTUCKY FISHING INFO
Send this coupon with your name and address to: KENTUCKY TRAVEL Dept. KVG, P.O. Box 2011 Frankfort, KY 40602
WILLIAMSBURG, KY
Free Map and Guide to the WILLIAMSBURG Area
Send this coupon with your name and address to:
Williamsburg Tourism, P.O. Box 2, Williamsburg, KY 40769

Tennessee

Tennessee Dept. of Tourist Development
312 Rosa Parks Ave. 25th Floor, Nashville, TN 37243
800-GO2-TENN **www.tnvacation.com**

The name "Tennessee" originated from the old Yuchi Indian word, "Tana-see," meaning "The Meeting Place." White men traveling in the area in the 1700s associated the word with the name of a Cherokee village and as the name of a river in Cherokee Territory.

"The Volunteer State." Tennessee earned its nickname by its remarkable record of furnishing volunteers in the War of 1812 and also in the Mexican War. Tennessee also ranks number one among other states in the total number of soldiers who fought in the War Between the States.

Two hundred years ago Tennessee was home to the Chickasaws, Cherokees and other native peoples. As settlers arrived aboard rafts, they kept many Indian names such as Sequatchie, Nolichucky, Hiwassee and Tennessee for the rivers.

The rivers are no longer transportation routes but they remain pristine enough to brew your coffee with, rich enough to fish for bass (Dale Hollow Lake holds the world record for smallmouth bass), and as fast or as slow as you like them. Make memories aboard a Mississippi Paddle Boat or race the rapids whitewater rafting! Did you know that the Ocoee River was the site for the 1996 Olympic Games Slalom Canoe/Kayak Competition?

1996 marked Tennessee's bicentennial.

The State is brimming with excitement. There's a full dance card awaiting you on a long list of new and traditional festivals. Tennessee is known for real country music, historic sights and attractions, theme parks and southern hospitality. It is also one of the world's greatest destinations for fishing.

Do you like to sing or just listen? Tennessee does both. The strains of Blues, Bluegrass, Country, and Rock and Roll are on the airwaves and the stage. Tennessee Ernie Ford, Elvis Presley, and Blues singer Bessie Smith were native Tennesseans.

With the zoo and nature parks, theme parks, military sites, art and science museums, shopping, antiques, markets and factory outlets, Tennessee's cities will keep you thrilled. The countryside also offers endless opportunities.

The Lost Sea is the world's largest underwater lake, Ober Gatlinburg Ski Resort is the world's largest artificial skiing surface. From Rock City on Chattanooga's Lookout Mountain you can see seven states.

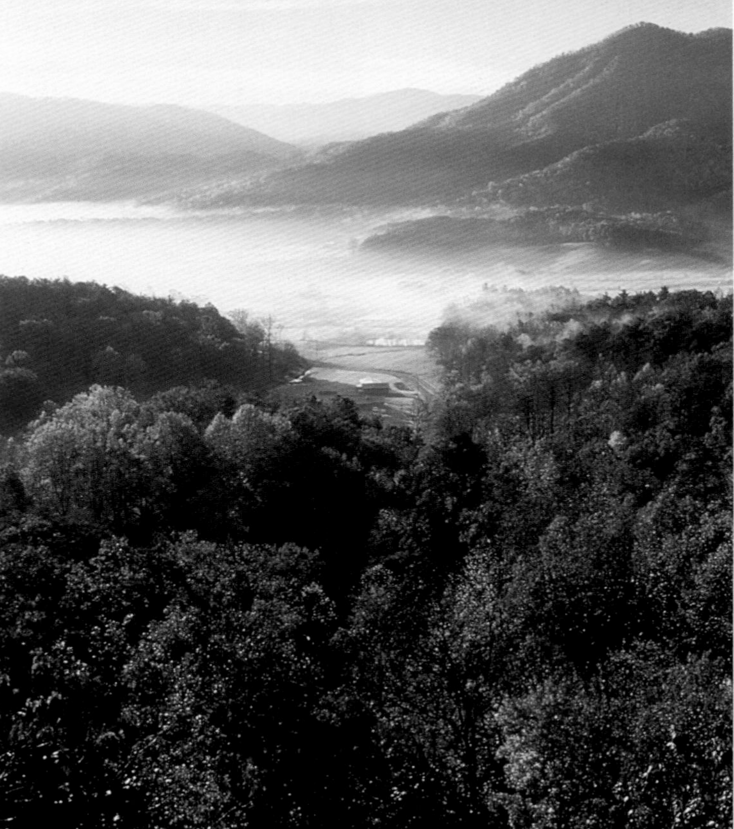

The Beautiful Mountains of Tennessee. *Courtesy Tennessee Department of Tourist Development*

Tennessee Trivia

Tennessee has produced three U.S. presidents: **Andrew Jackson,** 1829 to 1837; **James K. Polk,** 1845 to 1849; and **Andrew Johnson,** 1865 to 1869.

Other famous Tennesseans include frontiersman **Davy Crockett, Admiral David Farragut,** cavalry officer **Nathan Bedford Forrest,** U.S. Register of the Treasury **James Carroll Napier** (appointed 1911 by President William Howard Taft), World War I hero **Alvin York,** and **Cordell Hull** (secretary of state under Franklin D. Roosevelt).

Davy Crockett was not "born on a mountaintop in Tennessee," as the song says. He was born on the banks of Limestone Creek near Greeneville, where a replica of the Crocketts' log cabin stands today. More Civil War battles were fought in Tennessee than any other state except Virginia. The four national military parks in Tennessee are **Chickamauga-Chattanooga** in Chattanooga, **Stones River** in Murfreesboro, **Shiloh** near Savannah, and **Fort Donelson** near Dover.

Tennessee was the last state to secede from the Union during the War Between the States and the first state to be readmitted after the war. East Tennesseans were strongly pro-Union, while West and Middle Tennesseans were primarily on the side of the Confederacy.

Tennessee

Tennessee Dept. of Tourist Development
312 Rosa Parks Ave. 25th Floor, Nashville, TN 37243
800-GO2-TENN **www.tnvacation.com**

Founded by Ann Safley Houston, ***the Houston Museum of Decorative Art*** *is internationally known for its glassware, particularly its collection of more than 15,000 antique pitchers. Chattanooga, TN.* Courtesy Chattanooga Area Convention & Visitors Bureau

Considered one of the top-10 whitewater rivers in the U.S., the ***Ocoee River*** *has been the location of several major national and international competitions including the 1996 Olympic Games. A variety of rafting companies offer guided trips through the river's raging rapids. Ocoee, TN.* Courtesy Tennessee Tourist Development

Did You Know?

The Cherokee silversmith, **Sequoyah,** was the only known man in the history of the world to single-handedly develop an alphabet. His syllabus for the Cherokee Nation resulted in the first written language for a Native American people. The **Sequoyah Birthplace Museum** in Vonore, TN tells his story and is dedicated to the history and culture of Native Americans.

On August 21, 1920, Tennessee became the 36th state to ratify the 19th amendment to the U.S. Constitution, thus giving the nation's 17 million women the right to vote.

The worst earthquake in American history occurred in the winter of 1811-12 in northwestern Tennessee. The earthquake caused a vast land area to drop several feet and caused tidal waves on the Mississippi River. The river flowed backward into the depression, creating what is today known as Reelfoot Lake. During the winter months, Reelfoot Lake has the largest population of American bald eagles in the eastern United States.

The legendary railroad engineer **Casey Jones,** who was killed when his train crashed on April 30, 1900, lived in Jackson, Tennessee. Today there is a museum in his honor located in Jackson.

Oak Ridge, the secret city created in the 1940s, was instrumental in the development of the atomic bomb. Today, because of constant energy research, it is known as the Energy Capital of the World. It is the home of the American Museum of Science and Energy.

Tennessee has more than 3,800 documented caves. The *Guinness Book of World Records* lists the **"Lost Sea"** in Sweetwater, TN, as the largest underground lake in the U.S.

TENNESSEE'S STATE SYMBOLS

State Rocks:	Limestone and Agate
State Trees:	Tulip and poplar
State Wild Animal:	Raccoon
State Nickname:	The Volunteer State
State Birds:	Mockingbird & Bobwhite quail
State Insects:	Lady beetle (LadyBug), firefly & honeybee
State Gems:	freshwater pearl

Tennessee

Tennessee Dept. of Tourist Development
312 Rosa Parks Ave. 25th Floor, Nashville, TN 37243
800-GO2-TENN **www.tnvacation.com**

TENNESSEE TRAVELER

Tennessee Traveler Crossword

ACROSS

1. Water activity.
6. Desire or impulse.
10. Civil War cavalry group. (2 words)
15. Knoxville's big event. (2 words)
17. Strolling Jim and Midnight Sun.
19. Blount Mansion was Tennessee's first. (2 words)
20. Reelfoot's winter visitors.
21. Ornamental receptacle.
22. Negative answers.
23. Knoxville landmark: The ____ sphere.
24. Make a choice.
25. Cover.
26. Compass point.
27. Craft items.
31. Cry.
33. Civil War battlefield.
38. ____ and Behold!
39. Uncle Nabob's wife.
40. President Jackson or Johnson.
42. Alvin York was one.
44. Like a fox.
45. Engineering college (Abbr.)
46. Stat for 7 down.
47. Russian image.
48. Right angle building wing.
49. Columbia animal honoree.
50. Grand Ole Opry medium.
51. Soak up.
53. Travel necessity.
54. Wildflower part.
55. President Jackson's home.
60. Starting point for Nashville songwriter.
63. Check hers at Barbara Mandrell Country. (2 words)
64. Parthenon supports.
67. Japanese drink.
68. Loretta to Mooney.
70. Sailing vessel.
71. Reptile zoo residents.
74. Picnic coolant.
76. Stage exclamation.
78. First name initials for country music stars Rogers, Nelson and Murray.
79. Set aside legally, as a marriage.
81. Gatlinburg Christmas tradition.
85. Dayton "Monkey Trial" figure.
86. Tennessee, Cumberland and Mississippi. (2 words)
87. Common or horse.
88. Motel vacancy sign.
89. Disguise.

DOWN

1. Morning after feeling.
2. Museum of Appalachia location.
3. Country music's mecca. (3 words)
4. Master of Laws degree. (Abbr.)
5. Paradises.
6. Flying saucers.
7. Veteran Dodger pitcher: Herb ____.
8. American soldiers.
9. Before.
10. Vacation postcard deliverer. (3 words)
11. Famous for its rhododendron.
12. Organization. (Abbr.)
13. Norway's capital.
14. Sneak a look.
16. Twitty City attraction: Conway's ____.
18. Concorde.
23. World's largest underground lake: The Lost ______.
27. Record making material.
28. Music Row agent's product.
29. Hang glider's element.
30. Mississippi River showcase: ____ Island.
32. Davy Crockett event at Limestone.
34. Byrdstown native and FDR Secretary of State.
35. ___ bellum, as Belle Meade mansion.
36. America's most visited national park. (2 words)
37. Reelfoot eagle's home.
41. Summer temperature.
42. Dollywood's owner.
43. Tennessee's premier white water river.
45. Nashville has many. (2 words)
49. Memphis blues artist: ______ Rainey.
52. Printer's measure.
53. Microbe.
54. First king of Israel.
56. Goofs. (2 words)
57. Better ____ and make up than stay mad. (2 words)
58. Actor Guinness.
59. __ Big Orange!
61. __ your own thing.
62. 6,643 at Clingman's Dome; 6,593 at Mount LeCounte; 6,313 at Roan Mountain. (Abbr.)
65. The advantage of a vacation. (2 words)
66. Bridges.
69. Bristol Speedway activity.
71. Dale Hollow Lake's world record species.
72. Jonesborough opening: "__ upon a time."
73. Author unknown. (Abbr.)
75. The Tennessee Plowboy.
77. Chart for a Nashville recording session. (Abbr.)
80. Confederate Army's top commander.
82. Wide shoe size.
83. Civil War Rifleman's chief asset.
84. Creator of "The Great Lakes of the South."

For more information contact the Director of Information, Tennessee Department of Tourist Development, Room T, Box 23170, Nashville, Tennessee 37202 or telephone (615) 741-2159.

I-75 Mile Markers: 160, 158, 156, 154, 152, 150, 148, 146, 144, 142, 140

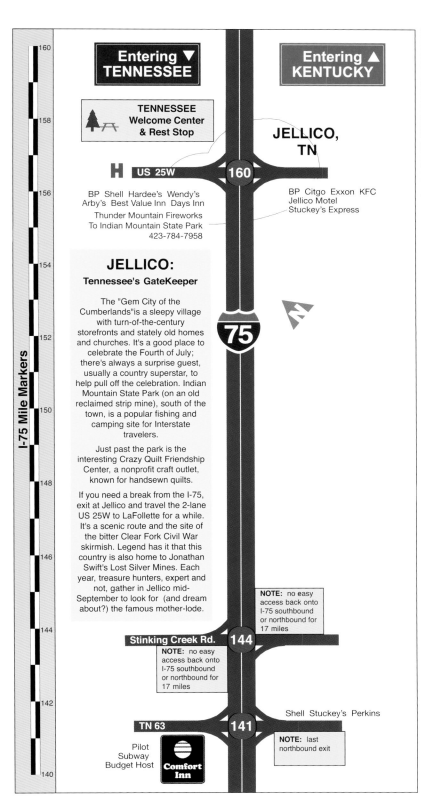

Entering ▼ TENNESSEE

Entering ▲ KENTUCKY

TENNESSEE Welcome Center & Rest Stop

JELLICO, TN

US 25W — Exit 160

BP Shell Hardee's Wendy's
Arby's Best Value Inn Days Inn
Thunder Mountain Fireworks
To Indian Mountain State Park
423-784-7958

BP Citgo Exxon KFC
Jellico Motel
Stuckey's Express

JELLICO:

Tennessee's GateKeeper

The "Gem City of the Cumberlands"is a sleepy village with turn-of-the-century storefronts and stately old homes and churches. It's a good place to celebrate the Fourth of July; there's always a surprise guest, usually a country superstar, to help pull off the celebration. Indian Mountain State Park (on an old reclaimed strip mine), south of the town, is a popular fishing and camping site for Interstate travelers.

Just past the park is the interesting Crazy Quilt Friendship Center, a nonprofit craft outlet, known for handsewn quilts.

If you need a break from the I-75, exit at Jellico and travel the 2-lane US 25W to LaFollette for a while. It's a scenic route and the site of the bitter Clear Fork Civil War skirmish. Legend has it that this country is also home to Jonathan Swift's Lost Silver Mines. Each year, treasure hunters, expert and not, gather in Jellico mid-September to look for (and dream about?) the famous mother-lode.

75

NOTE: no easy access back onto I-75 southbound or northbound for 17 miles

Stinking Creek Rd. — Exit 144

NOTE: no easy access back onto I-75 southbound or northbound for 17 miles

TN 63 — Exit 141

Shell Stuckey's Perkins

Pilot
Subway
Budget Host
Comfort Inn

NOTE: last northbound exit

Anderson County
TENNESSEE

Anderson County Tourism Council
115 Welcom Lane, Clinton, TN 37716
865-457-4547 or 1-800-524-3602 **www.yallcome.org**

LAKE CITY
Notable attractions: **Savage Gardens** has the greatest collection of wildflowers outside the Great Smoky Mountains. Enjoy the 1/2-mile tourpath through the gardens which were first planted in the 1930s. Free. Weekends in the spring, 423-426-6495. **Norris Dam State Park** has an 18th-century gristmilll, a pioneer museum, camping and cabins. US 441, I-75 exits 128 and 122. 423-632-1825

NORRIS DAM
On US 441, the first and northernmost dam built by TVA for flood control (opened 1935), has some of the state's best fishing. You can tour the power-house from 8 a.m.-3 p.m. daily, picnic and take a great photograph or two of fishermen in the shallow tailwaters of the dam. Use I-75 exits 128 or 122. 423-632-1825

NORRIS
On Hwy. 61, 1 mile east of I-75 exit 122, is the famous 65-acre museum/farm/village complex called the Museum of Appalachia. This museum contains over 30 authentic log buildings, many farm animals, the Appalachian Hall of Fame and 250,000 artifacts in a huge display barn on the lifestyle of rural Appalachia. The gift shop contains shaker baskets, toys, jewelry, white oak baskets, cookbooks, quilts, and other crafts.

At the same exit you'll find the brand new Anderson County Visitors Center complete with interactive displays relating to local tourism and a gift shop where you can buy quality pottery, baskets, quilts, books, maps and more at reasonable prices.

CLINTON
800-524-3602 The **Green McAdoo Cultural Center** is a new attraction devoted to the 12 young people who were the first students to desegregate a state-supported high school. (Aug 27, 1956) Clinton High School holds the honor of having the first African American to graduate from a public high school in the South. Learn the fascinating history of the twelve and how they changed the nation. Open Tues-Sat., 10am – 5pm.

The **Appalachian Arts Craft Center** is a highly recognized educational facility with over 200 members. Buy pottery, weavings, quilts, baskets, wood carvings, Appalachian Folk Art, dolls and toys. Mon-Sat 10am-6pm, Sunday 1-5pm, year-round but closed Sundays and Mondays in January and February.

Museum of Appalachia's Annual Tennessee Fall Homecoming Welcomes Visitors from Around the World

It was fall, about 20 years ago, when a few folk gathered at John Rice Irwin's **Museum of Appalachia** pioneer farm/village in Norris, for molasses making. Some old-timers brought their whittling sticks, and some told stories and several engaged in other almost forgotten activities; and a goodly number brought fiddles, guitars and banjos. This casual get-together became one of the largest, old-time craft, music and early American cultural festivals.

The American Bus Association has chosen it as one of the "Top 100 Events in North America" and the Southeast Tourism Society voted it as one of the "Top 20 October Events."

Homecoming is a celebration of the culture and heritage of Appalachian pioneer, mountain and rural life. The 250 musicians who perform include some of the most well-known purveyors of old-time music. The non-professional mountain musicians are just as popular!

Early pioneer activities include cane grinding with a mule-powered mill, molasses boiling, lye soap making, yarn spinning, rail splitting, saw milling, and sheep herding.

Hundreds of craftspeople will be making and selling their wares in the village.

Members of the Smoky Mountain Antique Engine and Tractor Association will have dozens of century-old one-cylinder engines; and they will demonstrate how the engines are used to power corn mills, a well digger, a butter churn, an ice-cream maker, and other early contrivances.

Numerous country cooks will prepare and serve regional food from wood burning stoves, including such favorites as pinto beans, corn bread, fried pies, country ham and biscuits, pit barbecue, chicken and dumplings, homemade desserts and much more.

Museum of Appalachia's Tennessee Fall Homecoming. *Sherman Wooten, chairmaker, is one of several hundred old-time mountain craftspeople and musicians who regularly participate in the Homecoming. One of the nation's largest and most popular mountain, folk, music and craft festivals, Tennessee's annual Homecoming is hosted by the acclaimed Museum farm and village in Norris, TN. Photo and text courtesy Tennessee Tourist Development*

Annual Events

Wildflower Walks at Norris Dam State Park. Late March and all of April.

Clinch River Antique Spring Fair, Clinto. Early May. 865-457-2559

Lavender Festival, mid-June.

Fall Color Cruises around Norris Lake. 865-426-7461

Christmas in Old Appalachia at Museum of Appalachia. Early December until Dec. 24, 8am-5pm. Homemade decorations & gifts, musicians playing and singing Christmas Carols near the open fires and traditionally decorated Christmas trees all add to the experience. 865-494-7680 www.museumofappalachia.com

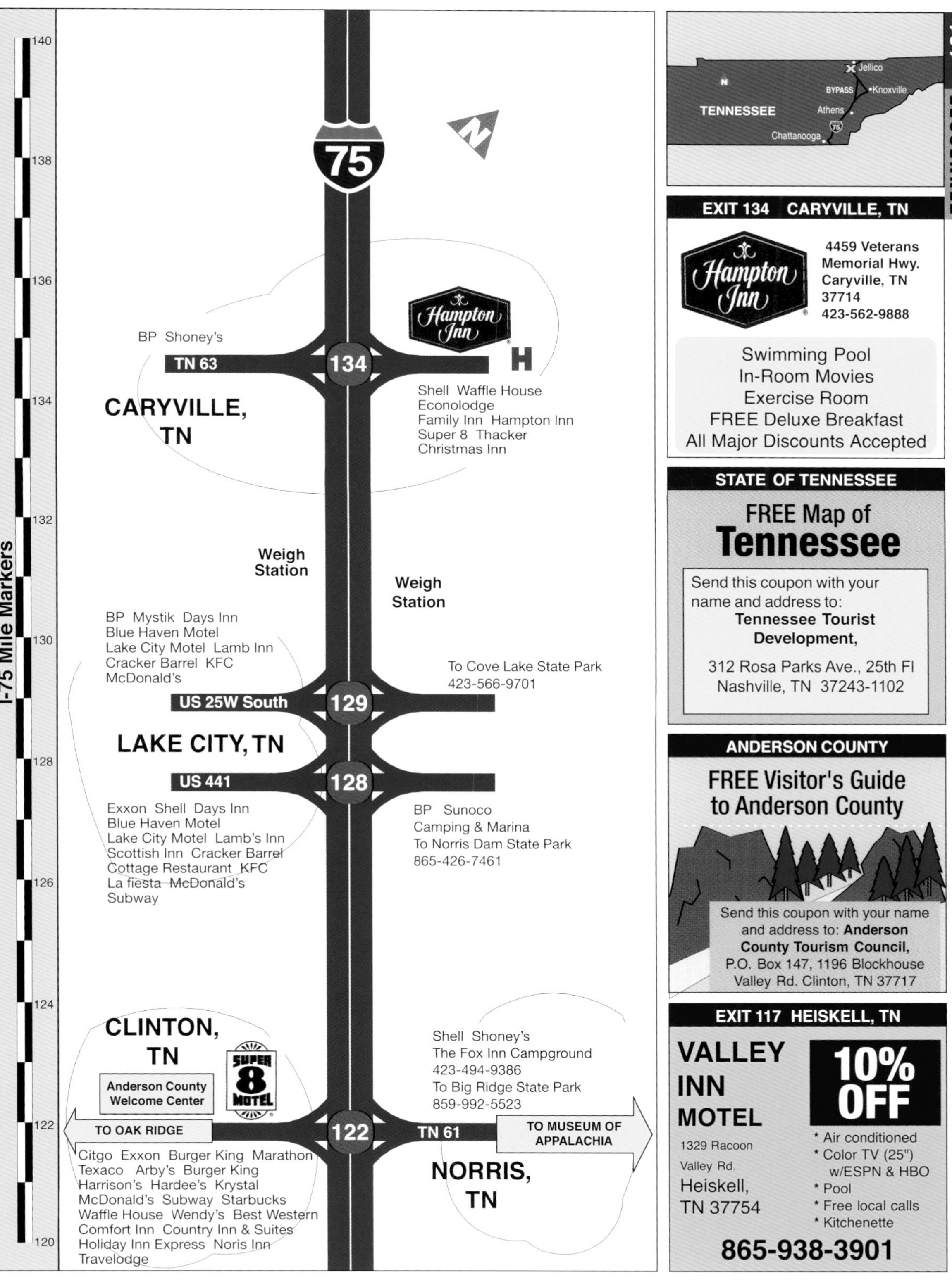
I-75 Mile Markers
140
138
136
134
132
130
128
126
124
122
120
75
BP Shoney's
TN 63
134
CARYVILLE, TN
Shell Waffle House
Econolodge
Family Inn Hampton Inn
Super 8 Thacker
Christmas Inn
Weigh Station
Weigh Station
BP Mystik Days Inn
Blue Haven Motel
Lake City Motel Lamb Inn
Cracker Barrel KFC
McDonald's
To Cove Lake State Park
423-566-9701
US 25W South
129
LAKE CITY, TN
US 441
128
Exxon Shell Days Inn
Blue Haven Motel
Lake City Motel Lamb's Inn
Scottish Inn Cracker Barrel
Cottage Restaurant KFC
La fiesta McDonald's
Subway
BP Sunoco
Camping & Marina
To Norris Dam State Park
865-426-7461
CLINTON, TN
Anderson County Welcome Center
SUPER 8 MOTEL
Shell Shoney's
The Fox Inn Campground
423-494-9386
To Big Ridge State Park
859-992-5523
TO OAK RIDGE
122
TN 61
TO MUSEUM OF APPALACHIA
Citgo Exxon Burger King Marathon
Texaco Arby's Burger King
Harrison's Hardee's Krystal
McDonald's Subway Starbucks
Waffle House Wendy's Best Western
Comfort Inn Country Inn & Suites
Holiday Inn Express Noris Inn
Travelodge
NORRIS, TN
TENNESSEE
Jellico
BYPASS
Knoxville
Athens
Chattanooga
EXIT 134 CARYVILLE, TN
Hampton Inn
4459 Veterans Memorial Hwy.
Caryville, TN 37714
423-562-9888
Swimming Pool
In-Room Movies
Exercise Room
FREE Deluxe Breakfast
All Major Discounts Accepted
STATE OF TENNESSEE
FREE Map of Tennessee
Send this coupon with your name and address to:
Tennessee Tourist Development,
312 Rosa Parks Ave., 25th Fl
Nashville, TN 37243-1102
ANDERSON COUNTY
FREE Visitor's Guide to Anderson County
Send this coupon with your name and address to: Anderson County Tourism Council,
P.O. Box 147, 1196 Blockhouse Valley Rd. Clinton, TN 37717
EXIT 117 HEISKELL, TN
VALLEY INN MOTEL
1329 Racoon Valley Rd.
Heiskell, TN 37754
10% OFF
* Air conditioned
* Color TV (25") w/ESPN & HBO
* Pool
* Free local calls
* Kitchenette
865-938-3901

Knoxville
TENNESSEE

Knoxville Tourism & Sports Corporation, Knoxville Visitor Center
301 South Gay St., , Knoxville, TN, 37902
865-532-7263 or 1-800-727-8045 **www.knoxville.org**

KNOXVILLE: Where Good Times and Good Friends Await You

Steeped with southern hospitality and tradition, Knoxville provides incredible cultural, historical, outdoor and family-friendly experiences. Knoxville has it all: culinary delights, museums, nightlife and championship sports.

A charming adventure awaits you in Knoxville's downtown area. The Market Square District is a pedestrian-only area full of unique shops, restaurants and nightlife. Gay Street holds several signature Knoxville restaurants and shops such as Mast General store and Downtown Grill & Brewery.

Knoxville is also the perfect city for exploration and adventure. The Knoxville Zoo offers exhibits of exotic animals such as the African Lion, Red Panda and the Snow Leopard. For those interested in history Knoxville offers several world-class museums.

Knoxville is naturally blessed with the beauty of the Tennessee River and the Great Smoky Mountains.

Also to discover in the KNOXVILLE area:

- luxuriate in a cruise down the Tennessee River aboard the **Star of Knoxville,** an authentic paddlewheeler
- fill your days and nights with entertainment, history and culture in the **Market Square.**
- visit the **World's Fair Park,** home to the **Knoxville Museum of Art;** and the Sunsphere which offers a 360 degree view high above the Knoxville skyline.
- experience one of Knoxville's many festivals including the **Dogwood Arts Festival** in April, Sundown in the City (Spring) or Christmas in the City (December).

The urban gateway to the Great Smoky Mountains, Knoxville *is the home of the University of Tennessee and headquarters for the Tennessee Valley Authority. In the foreground stands the Sunsphere, theme structure of the 1982 World's Fair. Courtesy of Tennessee Tourist Development*

Knoxville's Sunsphere Reopens

The Knoxville skyline has one distinctive structure, a large golden globe. This structure is the Sunsphere, a 266-foot-tall steel truss structure topped with a 74-foot bronze sphere.

The Sunsphere was created as a theme structure for the 1982 World's Fair. Because the theme of the 1982 fair was Energy Turns the World, the theme structure for the fair was to be a monument to the sun, the source of all energy. During the fair, the Sunsphere was used as a reception hall for formal events and spaces for a local office. The Sunsphere was reopened to the public on July 5, 2007, in time for the 25th anniversary of the 1982 World's Fair.

Once inside the structure (free admission by the way, courtesy of Mayor Haslam), visitors have a 360-degree view of the city from more than 200 feet above the

World's Fair Park. Located at a dozen viewing points are domes with info about the buildings and history of the point's lookout. These panel points include sites such as the Tennessee Theater and Gay Street. The future of the city is also featured on the observation deck as a computerized image shows new plans such as a rendition of riverfront, a new pedestrian bridge, and a renovated Neyland Stadium.

123
TENNESSEE
I-75 Mile Markers
120
118
116
114
112
110
108
HEISKELL, TN
SEE OUR AD ON PREVIOUS PAGE
VALLEY INN MOTEL
NOTE: Map of highway is exaggerated to indicate how turns will appear.
BP Pilot
ROUTE 170
117
Raccoon Valley
To Knoxville North KOA
865-933-6393
To Escapees Raccoon Valley RV Park
865-947-9776
75
Comfort Inn
SHONEY'S
BP Buddy's BBQ
Chevron
McDonald's
Krystal Subway
Wendy's
Country Inn Suites
Holiday Inn Express
Exxon Shell
Hardee's
Waffle House
TN 131
112
BP Scottish Inn
Burger King Chili's
McDonald's
To Camper's Corner Sales & Service
865-688-4733 rbrodt2088@aol.com
Callahan Drive
110
RODEWAY INN
Quality Inn
Weigel's Knight's Inn
Citgo Pilot Conoco Arby's
Burger King Great American Steaks
IHOP McDonald's Outback Steaks
Red Lobster Subway Waffle House
Best Value Clarion Inn Econolodge
Motel 6 Super 8
To Bob Cox Camper Country
Sales & Service
865-688-0823
DAYS INN Follow the Sun
Ryan's
Merchant Dr.
108
MANDARIN HOUSE
CHINESE RESTAURANT
BP Citgo
Pilot
Applebee's
Cracker Barrel
Hooters
Logan's Roadhouse
O'Charley's Pizza Hut
Starbucks Waffle House
Best Western
Comfort Inn
Econolodge
Hampton Inn
Sleep Inn
Original Book Exchange
Papermill Dr.
I-40 Exit 383
NOTE: to continue **southbound,** follow signs to Junction I-640/ I-40. The exit is on your right.
NOTE: for **southbound** Knoxville Bypass, follow signs to Junction I-75/I-640. The exit is on your right.
75S
40W
75S
640 W
I-40 Exit 385
I-640 Exit 1
I-640 Exit 3
640 W
NOTE: to continue **northbound** take I-40 exit 385 and follow signs "I-640, Keep Right to Lexington." The exit is on
75N
640E
TN 62
40W
NOTE: to continue **northbound,** follow signs "North to Lexington" and take I-640 exit 3. The exit is on your right.
275
for downtown KNOXVILLE
for downtown KNOXVILLE
N
NOTE: Map is exaggerated
KNOXVILLE, TN
Jellico
BYPASS
Knoxville
TENNESSEE
Athens
Chattanooga
75
EXIT 112 KNOXVILLE, TN
Comfort Inn
323 E. Emory Rd
Powell, TN 37849
(behind Shoney's)
865-938-5500
◆ 72 Beautifully Appointed Rooms
◆ Suites available with: VCR, microwave, refrigerator, hot tub, sofa sleeper
◆ Free Cable TV, HBO and ESPN
◆ Free Deluxe Continental Breakfast
◆ Children 18 and under stay free
EXIT 110 KNOXVILLE, TN
RODEWAY INN
(865) 687-3500
6730 Central Ave. Pk. Knoxville, TN 37912
◆ 90 Newly Renovated Rooms
◆ King Rooms Available
◆ Indoor Heated Pool (adjacent)
◆ Full service Restaurant (adjacent)
◆ Free Local Calls
◆ Free Cable TV, HBO and Disney
◆ Children 18 and under stay free
EXIT 110 KNOXVILLE, TN
Quality Inn
6712 Central Ave. Pk.
Knoxville, TN 37912
(865) 689-6600
◆ 130 Tastefully Decorated Rooms
◆ Jacuzzi, Executive, King Suites
◆ Heated Indoor Pool
◆ Full Service Restaurant
◆ Free Local Calls
◆ Free HBO and Disney
◆ Children 18 and under stay free
EXIT 108 KNOXVILLE, TN
DAYS INN Follow the Sun
6325 Central Ave.
Knoxville, TN
37912
(865) 687-5800
◆ 109 Guest Rooms and 2 Lounges
◆ Suites and King Rooms
◆ Heated Indoor Pool, Whirlpool
◆ Restaurant
◆ Cable TV, SHO, and Disney
◆ Children 12 and under stay free
Free Continental Breakfast

Knoxville
TENNESSEE

Knoxville Tourism & Sports Corporation, Knoxville Visitor Center
301 South Gay St., Knoxville, TN, 37902
865-532-7263 or 1-800-727-8045 **www.knoxville.org**

Enjoy the WDXV Blue Plate Special Daily in the Knoxville Visitor Center

The WDVX Blue Plate Special began in 1997, the same year the radio station began broadcasting from a 14-ft camper studio in Norris, TN. The Blue Plate Special features a free, daily concert series from noon until 1pm with live performances by local and national artists who represent the WDVX programming tapestry of traditional and eclectic forms of American roots music. There's also a live webcast at www.WDVX.com

More than 16,000 people attended the free concerts in 2006, the WDVX Blue Plate Special received Museum/Attraction of the Year Award from the Knoxville Tourism Alliance.

Drop by the Knoxville Visitor Center on any day during the week from noon to 1pm and enjoy a good Southern lunch served from the Visitor's Center Café Gourmet. Who knows who might be entertaining that day? Past performers include Ricky Skaggs and Kentucky Thunder and Bela Fleck and the Fleckstones.

Area Attractions

Beck Cultural Exchange Center
History of African-Americans in Knoxville. Extensive archives. Free. Tues. to Sat., 10 a.m.-6 p.m. 1927 Dandridge Ave. 865-524-8461

Blount Mansion
Birthplace of Tennessee statehood. National landmark, built between 1792 and 1830. Mar. to Dec., Tues. to Sat. 9:30 a.m.-5 p.m., Sun. 12:30 p.m.-5 p.m.; Jan. to Feb., Tues. to Fri. 9:30 a.m.-5 p.m. 200 W. Hill Ave. 865-525-2375

Confederate Memorial Hall (Bleak House). Victorian mansion built in 1858 and occupied by Gen. James Longstreet during seige of Knoxville. Tour the Southern memorabilia. Library open to the public. Tues. to Fri. 1 p.m.-4 p.m. 3148 Kingston Pk. 865-522-2371

East Tennessee Discovery Center
Hands-on science, world culture, art, Planetarium, Mon. to Sat. 9 a.m.-5 p.m. 516 N. Beaman St. at Chilhowee Park. 865-637-1121

East Tennessee History Center
National Register of Historic Places building houses historical collection, library and archives. Mon. to Fri. Corner of Market and Clinch Aves. 865-544-5744

Ewing Gallery of Arts & Architecture
Contemporary works of art. Mon. to Thurs. 8:30 a.m.-8:00 p.m.; Fri. 8:30 a.m. -4:30 p.m., Sun. 1 p.m.-4 p.m. Free. 1715 Volunteer Blvd. on UT campus. 865-974-3200

Frank H. McClung Museum
Anthropology, archaeology, art, medicine, and ancient Egypt collections. Mon. to Fri. 9 a.m.-5 p.m., Sat. 10 a.m.-5 p.m., Sun. 1 p.m.-5 p.m. Free. 1327 Circle Park Dr. on UT campus. 865-974-2144

James White's Fort
Built in 1786 by Knoxville s founder, Gen. James White. De.c. to Feb. Mon. to Fri. 10 a.m.-4 p.m. Mar. to Dec. 15, Mon. to Sat. 9:30 a.m.-4:30 p.m. 205 E. Hill Ave. 865-525-6514

Knoxville Museum of Art
U.S. and world collections of art, museum shop, exploratory gallery, interactive center and education garden. Tues. to Thurs. and Sat. 10 a.m.-5 p.m., Fri. 10 a.m.-9 p.m., Sun. 11:30 a.m.-5 p.m.. 1050 World s Fair Park Dr. 865-525-6101

Knoxville Zoological Park
White tiger, red panda, cheetah, Gorilla Valley, Tortoise Territory, otters in the park and gardens. Daily. Near exit 392 off I-40. 865-637-5331

Mabry-Hazen House
Antebellum home served as HQ for both Confederate and Union forces during the Civil War. On the National Register of Historic Places. Apr. to Dec. Tues. to Fri. 10 a.m.-5 p.m, Sat. 10 a.m.-2 p.m. 1711 Dandridge Ave. 865-522-8661

Marble Springs (John Sevier Historic Site)
Plantation and log home of frontier military leader and Tennessee's first governor, John Sevier. Apr. to Oct. Tues. to Sat. 10 a.m.-5 p.m., Sun. 2 p.m.-5 p.m. Nov. to Mar. Tues to Sat. 1 p.m.-5 p.m. 1220 W. Gov. John Sevier Hwy. 865-573-5508

Ramsey House
100 acres of original plantation and the first stone house of Knox County, completed in 1797 by Col. Francis A. Ramsey. Mar. to Dec. Tues. to Sat. 10 a.m.-4 p.m., Sun. 1 p.m.-4 p.m. At 2614 Thorngrove Pike, 865-546-0745

Star of Knoxville Riverboat
Sightseeing cruises, lunch and dinner, Sun. brunch, starlight dancing. Apr. to Dec. daily. 300 Neyland Dr. 865-525-STAR

Joseph B. Wolffe Gallery of Sport Sculpture
Features the athlete sculptor R. Tait McKenzie. Mon. to Fri. 1 p.m.-5 p.m. 1914 Andy Holt Ave. at UT campus. 865-974-0967

Bijou Theatre
In addition to being housed in Knoxville's fourth oldest building, the Bijou has an atmosphere that's perfect for live music and performing arts. 803 Gay St. 865-522-0832

Alex Haley Statue at Haley Heritage Square
Magnificent statue honouring Alex Haley, author of Roots, who made Knoxville his home. Largest statue of an African-American in the nation. 1600 Danridge Ave. 800-727-8045.

Ijams Nature Center
A 150- acre nature sanctuary on the banks of the Tennessee River with mulched and paved trails, a waterfront boardwalk and wildlife viewing areas. 2915 Island Home Ave. 865-577-4717.

Volunteer Princess Cruises
Brings the concept of elegant entertaining afloat. Enjoy daily cruises. 956 Volunteer Landing Lane. 865-541-4556

Knoxville
TENNESSEE

Knoxville Tourism & Sports Corporation, Knoxville Visitor Center
301 South Gay St., Knoxville, TN, 37902
865-532-7263 or 1-800-727-8045 **www.knoxville.org**

The Pallisaded James White's Fort *was built in 1786 and was the beginning of the modern city of Knoxville. In 1791, Territorial Governor William Blount signed the Treaty of the Holston with the Cherokee Indians at this fort.*

Special Events

Dogwood Arts Festival
Walk along more than 60 miles of trails featuring some of the most spectacular trees of all kinds and colors. This popular event offers a chance to visit and admire beautiful gardens and take part in arts and craft fairs, while enjoying outdoor concerts from local musicians. April. Various locations throughout Knoxville. 865-637-4561

Rossini Festival
An annual celebration of the fun and excitement opera provides, this downtown festival features food, beverages, entertainment and a wide range of art vendors. Enjoy world-class opera performances, wine tasting and the vibrancy of this Italian street fair. Gay St and Market Square District. 865-524-0795 www.rossinifestival.org

Sundown in the City is a free outdoor concert series in Market Square District that has drawn thousands of people to downtown Knoxville on Thursday nights every spring and summer. The bands that perform at Sundown play a variety of music, from Reggae to rock and beyond. April-June, Thur night at 7pm. www.sundowninthecity.com

Kuumba Festival
Largest African American Cultural Arts festival in East Tennessee. Kuumba was established in 1989 by local Knoxville artists and community activists who were looking to showcase African American artists, therefore sharing, educating and exposing rich cultural art to the Knoxville community. June. Various locations. 865-546-9705

Festival on the Fourth
Festival on the Fourth is a night of entertainment to celebrate the birth of America. Featuring vendors, food and a variety of musical entertainment leading up to a fabulous fireworks display. July 4, World's Fair Park. 865-215-4248 wwwcityofknoxville.org

Chrysler Jeep Boomsday Festival
Largest Labor Day weekend fireworks show in the nation. Amusement games, children's activities, food, tons of vendors and live music are all part of the fun. Sunday before Labor Day, Neyland Drive and Volunteer Landing. www.boomsday.org

Hola Festival
Pick up your passport and travel to Spain and the Americas – right in the heart of Knoxville. A fun, hands-on experience, the Hola Festival is a daylong Hispanic-themed event featuring music, dance, homemade food, arts & crafts and cultural heritage displays. Market Square District, September. www.holafestival.org

Christmas in the City
The jolliest 8 weeks in the South! Highlights include the WDVX Holiday Ho-Ho-Hoedown, the WIVK/Fowler Christmas Parade and the Regal Festival of Lights. Nov. & Dec. Various locations. 865-215-4248

In 1786, General James White brought his family across the mountains from North Carolina to claim land given to him for his service in the American Revolution. White built his cabin where the Holston and French Broad Rivers join to form the Tennessee River. He later erected three other cabins to house visitors and built a stockade as a defense against possible attacks.

James White was a kindly man, so he housed many settlers as they began to pour over the mountains. Through land grants from the State of North Carolina, James White owned all land on which the city of Knoxville would later be built. In 1790, William Blount of North Carolina was appointed governor of the Territory Southwest of the River Ohio and selected White's fort as the site of the capitol. On Oct. 1, 1791, the new town was christened Knoxville, in honor of Major General Henry Knox, who, as Secretary of War, was William Blount's superior in Indian affairs.

In 1796, the Southwest Territory became the state of Tennessee, the 16th state in the Union. Knoxville became the first Capitol of Tennessee and remained so until 1812. Since that time, community interest has kept James White's log house from deterioration. The home of James White has been restored and furnished with furniture, tools and artifacts of the period. In addition to the main house, other buildings include a guest house, blacksmith shop, loom house, smokehouse and museum.

Robert McGinnis, the on-site director at James White Fort, happens to be an eighth generation descendent of James White. Daily tours provide a glimpse into the living conditions and life struggles of the period.

Special events "Beary Merry Christmas," a celebration for children and their teddy bears, and the "Candlelight Tour," a formal decorated tour through the fort. In April, during the Dogwood Arts Festival, "Spring Fling at the Fort" includes arts and crafts and demonstrations. In August, relive a day in the life of the Cherokee Indians during "Cherokee Heritage Days." The Cherokee will demonstrate tomahawk throwing and blow gun weaponry.

205 E. Hill Avenue in downtown Knoxville. Dec. 16 to Feb. 28 from 10 a.m. until 4 p.m., Mon. through Fri.; March 1 to Dec. 15 from 9:30 a.m. until 4:30 p.m., Mon. through Sat. Last tour at 3:30 p.m. Closed Sundays and all major holidays. Admission charge.

Knoxville
TENNESSEE

Knoxville Tourism & Sports Corporation, Knoxville Visitor Center
301 South Gay St., Knoxville, TN, 37902
865-532-7263 or 1-800-727-8045 **www.knoxville.org**

WOMEN'S BASKETBALL HALL OF FAME

The Women's Basketball Hall of Fame (WBHOF) is an international museum dedicated to preserving the history of women's basketball. Opened in June 1999, the Hall of Fame just celebrated its 10th anniversary and now proudly boasts 103 inductees.

The outside of the striking 32,000 sq. ft. building is graced with two remarkable basketballs. The world's largest basketball is located on the north end of the hall, weighing ten tons and sitting on top of a glass staircase that resembles a basketball net. A brick courtyard, shaped like a basketball is located on the southern side of the facility with many of the bricks engraved to honor inductees, guests and others who have chosen to leave their legacy at the Hall of Fame.

Once inside the facility you'll be greeted by a 17 ft bronze sculpture by California artist Elizabeth McQueen that represents the Hall's mission to "honor the past, celebrate the present and promote the future" of women's basketball. The Hall offers many multi-media presentations as well as artefacts, photographs, scrapbooks, medals, trophies and uniforms that bring the history of women's basketball to life. 700 Hall of Fame Dr. 865-633-9000 www.wbhof.com

Trivia

1. Which four cities haved served as Tennessee's state capitol?
2. During the Civil War battle of Mobile Bay, which Knoxville native uttered the famous "Damn the torpedoes! Full speed ahead!"?
3. Which Knoxville native directed *The Yearling, National Velvet* and more than 40 other Hollywood motion pictures?
4. Which James Agee's Pulitzer prize winning story takes place in Knoxville? See answers on next page.

Camping

The Crosseyed Cricket Campground
Year-round, 47 sites with full hookups, pool, fishing, boating, restaurant, showers. 751 Country Lane, Lenoir City. 865-986-5435

Jellystone Park
Mar. to mid-Dec. 85 sites with hookups, restaurant, pool. 9514 Diggs Gap Rd., Heiskell. 865-933-6600

House Mountain State Natural Area
5-acre House Mountain reaches 2,100 feet above sea level. 3930 Idumea Rd., Corryton. 865-933-6851

Lazy Acres on Tellico Lake
60 sites. Hook-ups, showers, boating & fishing. Year-round. Rt. 3, Jackson Bend Rd. 865-986-3316

Melton Hill Campground (year-round)
Over 90 sites, no hookups. Showers, boating. 400 W. Summit Hill, Knoxville. 865-988-9794

Bed & Breakfasts

Brookhaven Farm
12 rooms with private bath. Panoramic view. Also a spring-fed catch and release pond with paddleboats. 604 Brookhaven Ln., Seymour. 865-579-7979

The Country Inn. 11 rooms with private bath. On 18-hole golf course in foothills of the Great Smoky Mountains. 15 min. from Knoxville. 701 Chris-Haven Dr., Seymour. 865-577-8172

Middleton House Bed & Breakfast
15 rooms with private bath. 18th-century antiques with fireplace room, jacuzzi. 800 W. Hill Ave. in Knoxville. 865-524-8100

Mitchell's Bed & Breakfast
1 room with private bath. Neighborhood is tree-lined. Private entrance, efficiency. 1031 West Park Dr., Knoxville. 865-690-1488

Wayside Manor Bed & Breakfast
11 rooms, 10 w/ private bath. Pool, tennis, fireplace. good food. 4009 Old Knoxville Hwy. 33, Rockford. 865-970-4823

*Most famous as the first American zoo to successfully breed African elephants in captivity, the **Knoxville Zoological Gardens** is home to more than 1,000 animals.*
Courtesy of Tennessee Tourism Development.

KNOXVILLE ZOOLOGICAL GARDENS

The newest addition to the Knoxville Zoo is "Toadally Frogs," an exhibit where kids can hop around with the amphibians and learn to bellow like a bullfrog. "Bloomin' Butterflies" features hundreds of beautiful insects. Other popular exhibits include "Kids Cove," and "Stokely African Elephant Preserve."

Knoxville Zoo is located off exit 392A from I-40 West and is open every day except Christmas Day, from 9:30am to 6pm. 865-637-5331 (ext 300) www.knoxville-zoo.org

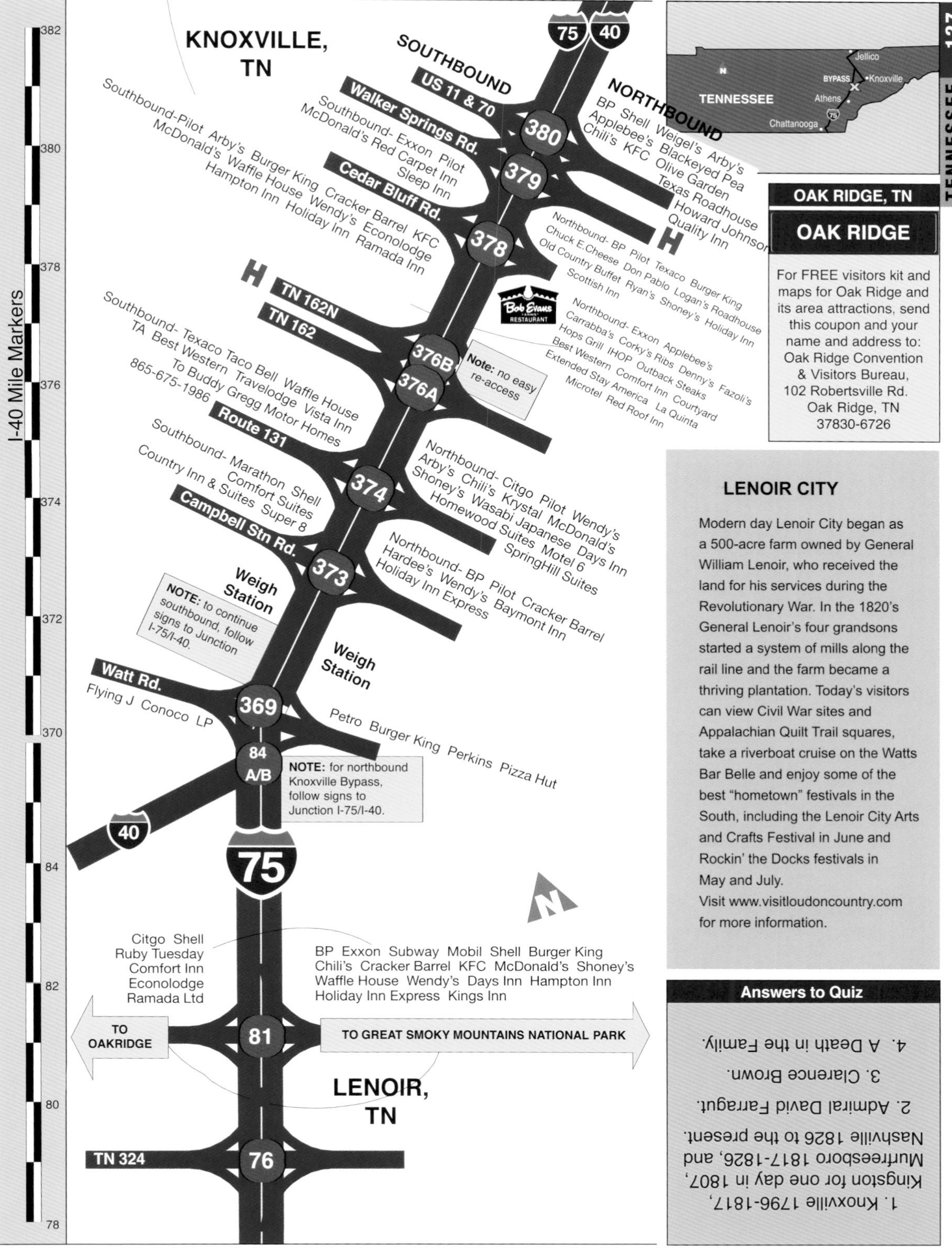

OAK RIDGE, TN

OAK RIDGE

For FREE visitors kit and maps for Oak Ridge and its area attractions, send this coupon and your name and address to:
Oak Ridge Convention & Visitors Bureau,
102 Robertsville Rd.
Oak Ridge, TN
37830-6726

LENOIR CITY

Modern day Lenoir City began as a 500-acre farm owned by General William Lenoir, who received the land for his services during the Revolutionary War. In the 1820's General Lenoir's four grandsons started a system of mills along the rail line and the farm became a thriving plantation. Today's visitors can view Civil War sites and Appalachian Quilt Trail squares, take a riverboat cruise on the Watts Bar Belle and enjoy some of the best "hometown" festivals in the South, including the Lenoir City Arts and Crafts Festival in June and Rockin' the Docks festivals in May and July.
Visit www.visitloudoncountry.com for more information.

Answers to Quiz

1. Knoxville 1796-1817, Kingston for one day in 1807, Murfreesboro 1817-1826, and Nashville 1826 to the present.
2. Admiral David Farragut.
3. Clarence Brown.
4. A Death in the Family.

Oak Ridge
TENNESSEE

Oak Ridge Convention & Visitors Bureau
102 Robertsville Rd. Suite C., Oak Ridge, Tennessee 37830-6726
865-482-7821 or 1-800-887-3429 **http://oakridgevisitor.com/home.html**

About 15 miles west of the I-75, the city of Oak Ridge may be a bit out of the way, but it's well worth a detour. With a population of only 28,000, this remarkable city offers the tourist more options than many much larger centers.

Secret City Unveiled

Oak Ridge is a city born of war, living for peace and growing through science. It celebrates more than 50 years of historic existence. In 1942, America was in the midst of a World War. Japan had just bombed Pearl Harbor and the United States was pulled into war with Germany, Italy and Japan.

President Franklin Delano Roosevelt had to act quickly, as Germany had overrun eastern Europe and was rumored to be attempting to develop a bomb of great magnitude and power. Albert Einstein wrote to Roosevelt about the power he theorized could be released from a particle many scientists said did not even exist, the atom. From these letters and conversations, a city was born. Nestled between the hills of East Tennessee, Oak Ridge was established in secret as part of the now historical *Manhattan Project.*

This area was chosen for its abundance of water, labor, transportation accessibility and electricity from the newly established Tennessee Valley Authority project, including the Norris Dam. It was also chosen because the project could be isolated from the outside world.

The city was built at a blazing pace as houses were being constructed every half-hour at the height of wartime construction. The city grew to a population of 75,000 people and Tennessee's fifth-largest city, yet the city remained unheard of to most people outside the gates.

Citizens were required to wear identification badges at all times and were sworn to secrecy. Soldiers guarding the security gates would not allow those without badges to leave or enter.

The U.S. government moved its top scientific minds into the area to research the possibilities of fission (splitting of the atom) at X-10, one of the facilities built during the Manhattan Project. Only a select few knew why Oak Ridge was established and what was being researched. In fact, it is rumored that when Roosevelt died in 1945, Vice-President Harry S. Truman did not know until he was inaugurated what research had been conducted or why. As the Manhattan Project progressed, more people filtered into the city to assist in the production of something they only knew was "important to the war effort."

By 1945, not only the state but the whole world knew what Oak Ridge had been researching, as *Fat Man* and *Little Boy,* the world's first atomic bombs, were dropped on Japan putting a quick, definite end to World War II.

Today, Oak Ridge has a population of nearly 30,000 and is situated in 92 square miles of East Tennessee beauty. The Oak Ridge public school system is consistently ranked the first in the state for academics. The city is located 15 minutes from West Knoxville and is surrounded by the natural beauty of lakes and mountains.

Oak Ridge is still a city of science, but instead of war, it is working for peace. Various types of research are conducted in Oak Ridge. Scientific contributions are made to energy, nuclear materials, medical and environmental research.

The three main plants, **Oak Ridge National Laboratory** (formerly **X-10**), **K-25** and **Y-12** are still functioning, but with this new purpose in mind. Other areas established during the war are now historical attractions which are viewed by visitors from all over the world.

These attractions include the **Graphite Reactor,** a number of displays at the American Museum of Science and Energy and overlooks allowing a panoramic look at K-25 while enjoying audio-visual presentations.

The **Graphite Reactor** was the world's first operating nuclear reactor and it is open Mon-Fri, June thru Sept to US citizens aged 10 and over.

The **American Museum of Science and Energy** displays the history of Oak Ridge in an exhibit area called the World War II Secret City Room, while the remainder of the museum is dedicated primarily to scientific displays of energy.

Visitors may also tour **Jackson Square Historical Park** and the **Emma Spray Garden.** The park is located on the original town site. The Emma Spray Garden features a centerpiece fountain and the "signature" sidewalk, which contains the names of past and present residents of the city. This area along with other *Manhattan Project* areas have been honored with Tennessee's largest single inclusion in the National Register of Historic Places. There is also some of the original "cemestos" (houses) located near Jackson's Square. Visitors can also see some of the original dormitories, shopping centers and guard gates which are located throughout the city.

Oak Ridge can suit everyone's recreational needs. The immediate area offers three lakes for summer fun: **Watts Bar, Melton Hill** and **Norris.**

Houseboats may be rented on nearby Watts Bar and Norris lakes, but the lakes are also excellent for water-skiing, swimming, sailing and fishing. For the back to basics visitor, Norris and Watts Bar lakes have campsites and cabins.

The world's record striped bass was caught in **Melton Hill Lake** (also stocked with muskies)**,** part of which is located within the Oak Ridge city limits.

Top competitive rowers in the country gather annually for a number of rowing events on the 2,000-metre course.

The **Bull Run Steam Plant,** also located on Melton Hill Lake, is one of the world's largest coal-fired steam plants.

Oak Ridge offers numerous golf courses and tennis courts. Hikers find the trails located in and around Oak Ridge to be relaxing and beautiful.

The **Children's Museum** is a cultural museum containing displays of the region's Appalachian heritage, arts and handicrafts. The museum has changing exhibits from the Smithsonian and other collections and programs which focus on art, history, science and world culture.

The **University of Tennessee Arboretum** has 250 acres of trails through forest and botanical gardens. Three trails are less than 1.5 miles long and visitors can identify the labeled plants.

Oak Ridge
TENNESSEE

Oak Ridge Convention & Visitors Bureau
102 Robertsville Rd. Suite C., Oak Ridge, Tennessee 37830-6726
865-482-7821 or 1-800-887-3429 **http://oakridgevisitor.com/home.html**

The Graphite Reactor *was the first nuclear reactor to operate continuously and is now a National Historic Landmark, open to the public. Photo/text on this and facing page courtesy Oak Ridge Convention & Visitors Bureau.*

The American Museum of Science & Energy.
Photo courtesy Oak Ridge Convention & Visitors Bureau.

DID YOU KNOW?
During the Manhattan Project, Oak Ridge was a heavily guarded city surrounded by security gates and fences. The city was built in secrecy during the 1940s and grew from a quiet rural area to a bustling city of 75,000 at the peak of the Manhattan Project.

DID YOU KNOW?
Bull Run Steam Plant, the final site on the city's 38-mile self-guided tour, is one of the world's largest, most fuel efficient coal-fired generating plants.

DID YOU KNOW?
The Costs of the Manhattan Project according to the Oak Ridge web sight link www.brook.edu/FP/PROJECTS/NUCWCOST/MANHATTN.HTM was $20 billion. The average cost per atomic device/bomb was $5 billion.

For more information, please try the following web sites:

http://www.bergen.org/AAST/manhattan_proj/a_manprj.html

http://www.em.doe.gov/circle/manhattn.html

http://www.brook.edu/FP/PROJECTS/NUCWCOST/WEAPONS.HTM

Attractions

Visitors Welcome Center
Open year round, Mon. to Fri. 9am – 5pm. 102 Robertsville Rd. Suite C, 800-887-3429

Oak Ridge Art Center
Year-round, Tues. to Fri. 9 a.m.-5 p.m. Free. 201 Badger Ave. 865-482-1441

Jackson Square Historic Park
Walking tour. Daily 7 a.m.-9:30 p.m. Free. Tennessee Ave. 865-482-8450

Oak Ridge K-25 Site Overlook
Former uranium enrichment plant. Daily 9 a.m.-7 p.m. Free. Hwy 58.

American Museum of Science & Energy (AMSE)
Open daily from 9 a.m.-5 p.m. and from June to Aug. open till 6 p.m. Free. 300 South Tuland Ave. 865-576-3200

University of Tennessee Arboretum
Open 8-sunset. Visitor s Center open Mon. to Fri. 8:30 a.m.-4:30 p.m. Free. On TN Rte. 62. 865-483-3571

Children's Museum of Oak Ridge
Sept. to May, Mon. to Fri. 9 a.m.-5 p.m., Sat. and Sun. 1:30 p.m.-4:30 p.m. 461 W Outer Dr. 865-482-1074

New Hope Visitors Center.
Mon-Thur 8am to 4:30pm., 602 Scarboro Rd.

DOE Facilities Public Bus Tour.
Register at AMSE. Free with admission Mon-Fri, June to Sept. US citizens 10 or older only.

Secret City Commemorative Walk.
1403 Oak Ridge Turnpike. Free. 800-887-3429

Secret City Festival.
Mid-June at Oak Ridge Community Center. Citywide celebration of the largest multi-battle WWII re-enactment in the South. Manhattan Project site tours will be offered throughout the weekend. www.secretcityfestival.com

Loudon County
TENNESSEE

Loudon County Visitors Bureau
1075 Hwy 321 North, Lenoir City, TN, 37771
865-986-6822 or 888-568-3662 **www.visitboudoncounty.com**

SEQUOYAH BIRTHPLACE MUSEUM

Citico Rd., Vonore
865-884-6246

Open year-round except major holidays.
Mon. to Sat. 9 a.m.-5 p.m.
Sun. 12 noon-5 p.m.

Sequoyah (1776-1843), a Cherokee Indian, was a soldier, statesman, silversmith and the creator of the innovative Cherokee writing system. Sequoyah single-handedly developed an alphabet for the Cherokees and it took him 12 years! The Cherokees were the only group of American Indians to develop a written language and they also published books and a newspaper.

The **Sequoyah Birthplace Museum** is Tennessee's only native-owned historic attraction. Here you can enjoy the beauty of the Great Smoky Mountains on the shores of the Tellico Lake and study the Cherokee myths and legends. Beautiful crafts and artwork by Cherokee Indians is for sale in the giftshop.

DID YOU KNOW?

Loudon County was created in 1870 from Roane, Monroe, Blount and McMinn counties. It was named for Fort Loudon, erected 1756 by the British and named in honor of the Earl of Loudon, commander-in-chief of British and American forces in the French and Indian War.

There are 20 major lakes and reservoirs in the state of Tennessee, and over 19,000 miles of warm and cold water streams, providing unlimited opportunities for fishing, sailing, houseboating, canoeing and white water rafting.

Loudon

Settled in 1790, this ferryboat port on the Tennessee River has become a small town destination for its shopping, dining, historic sites and award winning winery. The Carmichael Inn is a restored 1810 log cabin serving fabulous meals. 865-408-9712. The adjoining Orme Wilson building was built by R.T. Wilson who is said to be the inspiration for the character Rhett Butler in Gone With the Wind.

Camping, Exit 72. Knights Inn, 16 sites/RV pads, 15100 TN 72N, 423-458-5855 Lotterdale Cove Campground, on East Coast Tellico Pkwy has 90 sites, electricity. Apr. to Oct. 423-856-3832

Niota

Niota Depot is 3 miles east of I-75. Built in 1853, this is the oldest standing railroad depot in Tennessee. Now used as offices for the Town of Niota, the depot is open for tours during business hours. In the past, the town of Niota was featured in several magazine and television pieces due to its former all-woman government.

Coincidentally, Niota was home to Harry T. Burn, the Tennessee legislator who cast the deciding vote to ratify the historical amendment to the U.S. Constitution that gave women the right to vote.

Sweetwater & The Lost Sea

The Lost Sea
Cavern tour and glass-bottom boat rides on the 4.5-square-mile underground lake. Also enjoy the gift shop, restaurant, ice-cream parlor, picnic and nature trails. A nice afternoon excursion. Year-round. See photo below. 140 Lost Sea Rd., 6 miles off I-75 on TN 68. 423-337-6616

Tennessee Meiji Gakuin Japanese Culture Center
Bridges Japanese and American cultures with exhibits and events. 1314 Peachtree St. 4 miles east of Sweetwater, North on Hwy. 11. Mon. to Fri. 9 a.m.-4 p.m. 423-337-4245

Hillside Heaven Bed & Breakfast
Several rooms, 2 with private bath. Dine in a historic log cabin, enjoy the fireplace, wraparound porches. Across the highway from Lost Sea. Sweeping view of the Smokies and surrounding woodland. 2920 TN 68, Madisonville. 423-337-2714 or 1-800-394-7049

Sweetwater Valley KOA
More than 50 sites with hookups, plus groceries, pool. Open year-round. Located at 269 Murray s Chapel Rd. 423-213-3900 or 1-800-KOA-9224

*The Guiness Book of World Records lists **the Lost Sea** as the world's largest underground lake. The cavern has been designated a Registered Natural Landmark because of its abundance of rare anthodite or "cave flower" formations. Here, in Sweetwater, TN, is an opportunity for you to have a truly unique travel experience.*
Courtesy the Lost Sea, Tennessee.

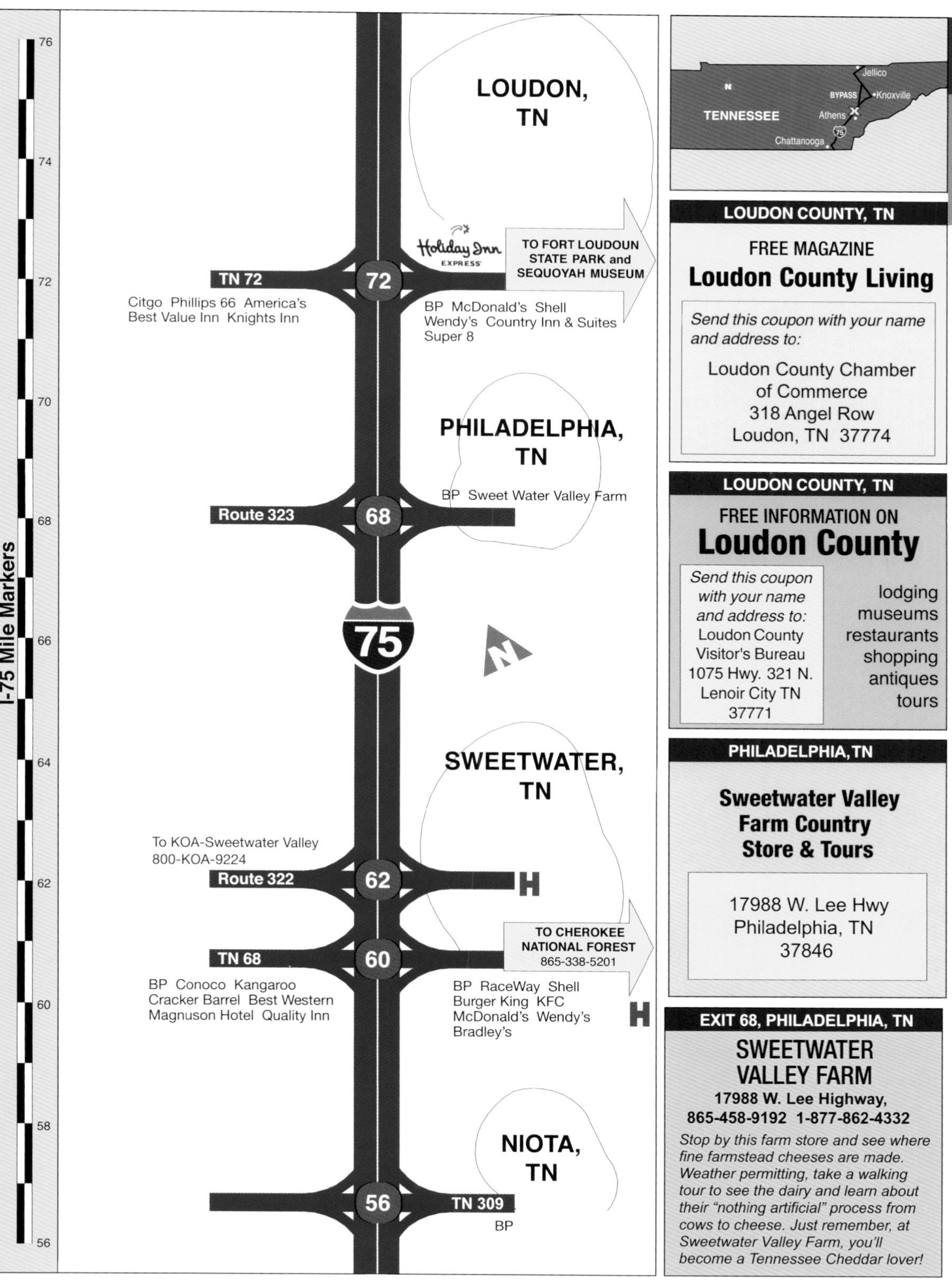
131
TENNESSEE
Jellico
BYPASS
Knoxville
TENNESSEE
Athens
75
Chattanooga
N
I-75 Mile Markers
76
74
72
70
68
66
64
62
60
58
56
LOUDON, TN
Holiday Inn EXPRESS
TO FORT LOUDOUN STATE PARK and SEQUOYAH MUSEUM
TN 72
72
Citgo Phillips 66 America's Best Value Inn Knights Inn
BP McDonald's Shell Wendy's Country Inn & Suites Super 8
PHILADELPHIA, TN
BP Sweet Water Valley Farm
Route 323
68
75
N
SWEETWATER, TN
To KOA-Sweetwater Valley 800-KOA-9224
Route 322
62
H
TO CHEROKEE NATIONAL FOREST 865-338-5201
TN 68
60
BP Conoco Kangaroo Cracker Barrel Best Western Magnuson Hotel Quality Inn
BP RaceWay Shell Burger King KFC McDonald's Wendy's Bradley's
H
NIOTA, TN
56
TN 309
BP
LOUDON COUNTY, TN
FREE MAGAZINE
Loudon County Living
Send this coupon with your name and address to:
Loudon County Chamber of Commerce
318 Angel Row
Loudon, TN 37774
LOUDON COUNTY, TN
FREE INFORMATION ON
Loudon County
Send this coupon with your name and address to:
Loudon County Visitor's Bureau
1075 Hwy. 321 N.
Lenoir City TN 37771
lodging
museums
restaurants
shopping
antiques
tours
PHILADELPHIA, TN
Sweetwater Valley Farm Country Store & Tours
17988 W. Lee Hwy
Philadelphia, TN
37846
EXIT 68, PHILADELPHIA, TN
SWEETWATER VALLEY FARM
17988 W. Lee Highway,
865-458-9192 1-877-862-4332
Stop by this farm store and see where fine farmstead cheeses are made. Weather permitting, take a walking tour to see the dairy and learn about their "nothing artificial" process from cows to cheese. Just remember, at Sweetwater Valley Farm, you'll become a Tennessee Cheddar lover!

McMinn County
TENNESSEE

Athens Area Chamber of Commerce
13 N. Jackson St., Athens, Tennessee 37303
423-745-0334 **www.athenschamber.org**

Less than 200 years ago the land now comprising McMinn and the surrounding counties was covered by dense forest. This area was then known as the "Cherokee Nation" and Chota was the capitol. This territory was part of the "Hiwassee District" ceded by the Cherokee Indians to the United States on February 26, 1819. The treaty was signed by John B. Calhoun, the Secretary of War and several Indian Chiefs. By the terms of the treaty a reservation of 640 acres was offered to anyone who chose to become a citizen of the United States. Very few accepted.

An act for the organization of McMinn County was passed by the State Legislature and the county was named in honor of Joseph McMinn, who was governor of Tennessee at the time.

The 435-square-miles of McMinn County consists of a series of low parallel ridges separated by swift flowing streams and valleys. The main creeks are Conasauga, Chestua, Mouse, Cane, Eastanallee, Spring and Rogers, all of which traverse the county from northeast to southwest, and empty into the Hiwassee River, which borders the county on the southwest.

The first town in the county was on the bank of the Hiwassee River and was named in honor of John C. Calhoun. In 1821-22, the town of Athens was laid out and in 1823 the courts of the county were moved there.

Ten miles to the southeast of Athens, and 125 miles north of Atlanta, lies the town of Etowah, in the shadow of the beautiful Unaka Mountains. The name in the Indian tongue means "Golden Water."

Riceville had its beginnings in 1855. C.N. Rice bought from the Indians the land on which the town now stands and established his home there. The first school was started on the Rice property in 1857.

Three brothers, James Bryant, Mortimer Bryant and Jacob Bryant established an industrial community located approximately 2 miles south of the present town of Englewood on the banks of the Chestua Creek. A dam was constructed in the creek to furnish water power for the mills.

The people are friendly and eager to talk about history with visitors. Stop by and steal a glimpse of the past.

Text courtesy Athens Area Chamber of Commerce.

Athens and McMinn County

The city takes its name from Athens in Greece. McMinn County is the leading Grade A milk producing county in the state. One of the nation's leading paper manufacturers is also located here, utilizing the vast expanse of timber.

Artist's Alcove
Area's best kept secret: pottery, jewelry, weaving, woodworking, glass, candles in a working potter's studio. Exit 49 or 52. 6 South St. 423-745-7312

McMinn County Living Heritage Museum
Small town life at the turn of the century. The **Annual Quilt Competition & Show,** mid-Feb. to late April, is one of the South's largest. Mon. to Fri. 10 a.m.-5 p.m. Sat. and Sun. 2 p.m.-6 p.m. 522 West Madison Ave., Athens. 423-745-0329

Mayfield Dairy Farms Visitor Center
Ice cream made fresh daily for over 75 years! Free tours, a short film presentation and, best of all, free tastings! 4.3 miles east from exit 52 on I-75. Mon. to Fri. 9 a.m.-5 p.m., Sat. 9 a.m.-2 p.m. 4 Mayfield Lane. 1-800-MAYFIELD www.mayfielddairy.com

Historic Downtown Athens
Revitalized downtown offers Southern Charm as you dine or shop. 5 antique shops plus book stores, fine gifts, 3 jewelers, notable pawn shop, and several architectural interests (restored facades, wide brick sidewalks). 423-745-0334

Woodlawn Bed & Breakfast
National Historic Register. On five acres in downtown Athens, this 1858 historic Greek revival home is one of the oldest masonry structures in the county. During the Civil War it served as a hospital for Union soldiers. Original smokehouse, 13.5 foot ceilings, 4 rooms with private baths. 110 Keith Lane. 423-745-8211 or 1-800-745-8213 www.woodlawn.com

Globe Swift Air Museum
Authentic restored versions of the original Globe and Temco Swift airplanes on display. Free. **National Swift Fly-In Airshow** on Memorial Day weekend. 7 miles from I-75, east on TN 30. McMinn County Airport, on County Rd. 552. Daily 9 a.m.-4 p.m., except Nov. to Mar., Mon. to Fri. 9 a.m.-4 p.m. 423-745-9547

Riceville

Mouse Creek Nursery
2-acre nursery grows 600 varieties of perennials. June to Feb. Tues. to Fri. 9 a.m. -5 p.m., Sat. 9 a.m.-12 noon. 2 miles east of I-75 on County Rd 67. 423-462-2666

Sunshine Hollow Bakery and Daylily Exhibition Gardens
1000 varieties of daylilies and hosta on display May to June. Year-round. Homemade pecan fruitcake at the Bakery Outlet open Nov. to Dec. Mon. to Sat. 9 a.m.-5 p.m., Sun 1 p.m.-5 p.m. 8 miles west of I-75. Exit 42. 1-800-669-2005 www.sunshinehollow.com

Riceville Wallpaper Outlet
Large selection of name-brand wallpaper. Tues. to Sat. 10 a.m.-4:30 p.m. 3 miles east of I-75. 423-462-2675

Calhoun

Calhoun, the first white settlement in the county, had a stockade where Cherokee Indians were held prior to their relocation on the Trail of Tears. Today it is noted for its **Meadowland Arts & Crafts Festival,** the resting place of Tennessee's 6th Governor, Joseph McMinn, and of course, great fishing on the Hiwassee River.

Windswept Farm (B&B)
Panoramic mountain views, tastefully decorated cottages & cabins. Children welcome. 2889 Hwy. 163, Delano, TN 37325 1-800-874-5684. I-75 exit 36 and go east. South 5 miles on Hwy 11, then east on Rte 163 (11 miles).

POP QUIZ!!
What famous Tennessean held every elective office at the local, state and federal level, including President of the United States?

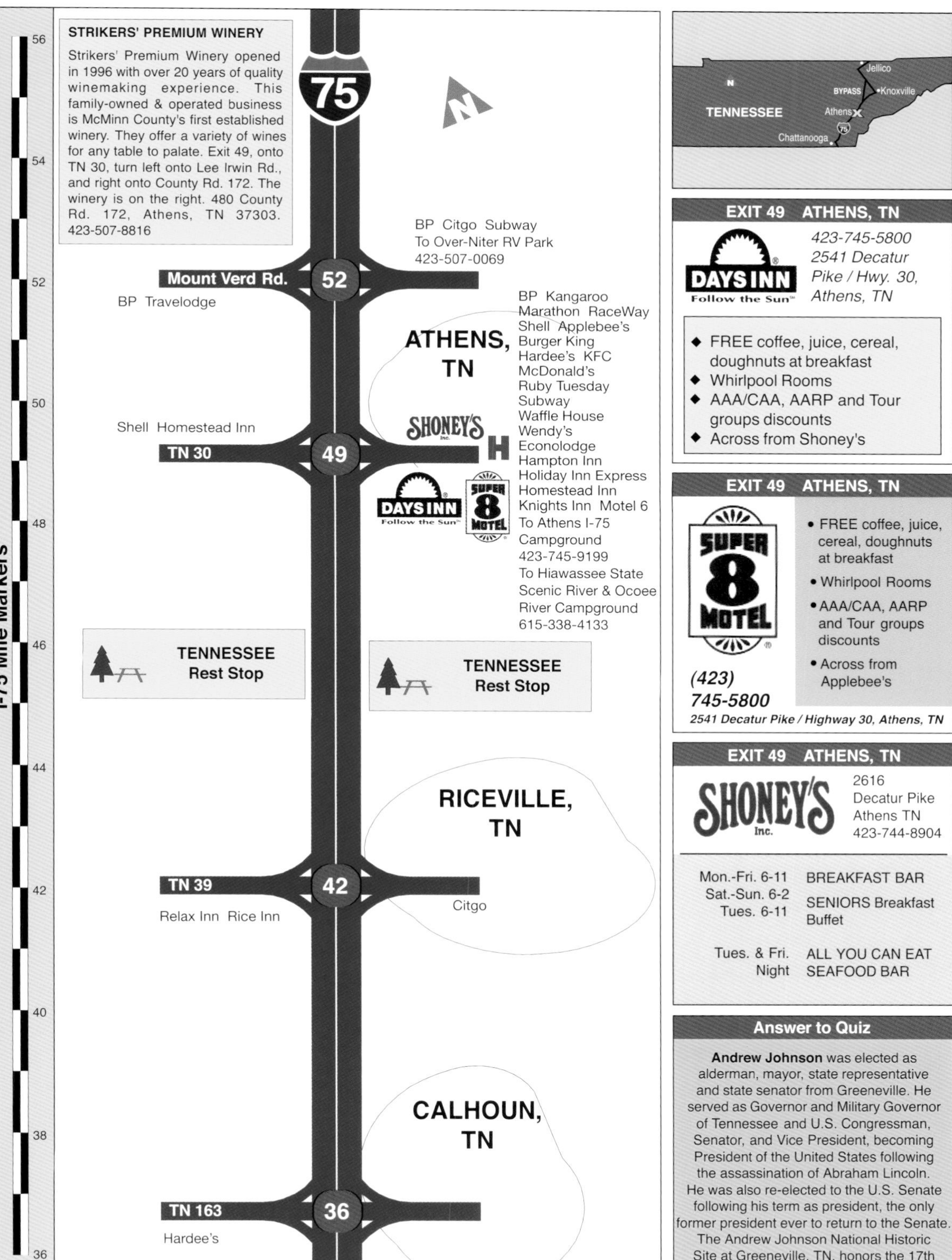

Answer to Quiz

Andrew Johnson was elected as alderman, mayor, state representative and state senator from Greeneville. He served as Governor and Military Governor of Tennessee and U.S. Congressman, Senator, and Vice President, becoming President of the United States following the assassination of Abraham Lincoln. He was also re-elected to the U.S. Senate following his term as president, the only former president ever to return to the Senate. The Andrew Johnson National Historic Site at Greeneville, TN, honors the 17th President of the United States.

Cleveland/Bradley County TENNESSEE

Cleveland/Bradley County Convention & Visitors Bureau
225 Keith Street, SW.,P.O. Box 2275, Cleveland, Tennessee 37320-2275
423-472-6587 or 1-800-472-6588 **www.visitclevelandtn.com**

Bradley County was created 1836 from Cherokee lands and named in honor of Edward Bradley a fellow officer and friend of Andrew Jackson in the War of 1812. The City of Cleveland, incorporated in 1842, was named for Col. Benjamin Cleveland, a revolutionary War veteran and one of the heroes at King's Mountain.

The world watched as the community of Cleveland played host to the 1996 Olympic Canoe/Kayak Competition on the famous **Ocoee River.** The Ocoee is the premier whitewater river of the southeast and the site of the first modern Olympic event on a natural river. For a picture of the Ocoee see the "Welcome to Tennessee" pages.

Cleveland is also the gateway to the **Cherokee National Forest,** Tennessee's only national forest and 625,000 acres of unspoiled natural beauty for your camping and hiking adventures. **Red Clay State Historical Area** marks the last capital of the Cherokee nation before the *Trail of Tears.* This and other important Cherokee landmarks can be found in and around Cleveland.

Explore the area's unique antique experience by picking up an Antiques and Collectibles Trail brochure from the Cleveland/Bradley Chamber of Commerce. If you feel the need to stretch your legs, enjoy the city's wonderful scenery on the Greenway of Cleveland/Bradley County, which provides a beautiful pathway for walkers, joggers, bicyclists and skaters. The Greenway connects with the city's sidewalk system to take in beautiful Historic Downtown Cleveland.

How about a fresh, delicious treat? Apple Valley Orchard, a featured favorite in Southern Living magazine, has incredible apples (including their own variety) and some of the best apple pies you've ever tasted. Visit Morris Vineyard and Winery to sample a vast selection of fine wines for all tastes, all produced and bottled on location. Morris Vineyard is one of the few vineyards that still offer pick-your-own-fruit – all with incredible views of the Appalachian Mountains. For more info see the list on the right.

Some interesting and well-attended festivals include the Evening Shade Concert Series, the Cherokee Days of Recognition, the Nillie Bipper Arts & Crafts Festival, the Downtown Halloween Block Party and Carols in the City. This area is also a sports haven with national softball and soccer tournaments, as well as golf, horseback riding, bowling, fishing and watersports.

Attractions

Apple Valley Orchards
Open Jan – mid-April & mid-June to end of July, Tues-Sat, 9-5, Sunday noon-6pm. Open Aug to Dec, Mon-Sat, 9-6, Sunday noon-6pm. Farm market, bakery and delicious fresh apples. 351 Weese Rd, SE. 423-472-3044

The Cherokee Chieftain sculpture is the focal point of downtown's **Johnston Park.** Carved from a tree by sculptor Peter "Wolf" Toth in 1973.

Cherokee National Forest
Camping, hiking, fishing, hunting and boating. The **Forest's Scenic Byway,** the first scenic byway designated in the nation, winds along **Parksville Lake,** the **Ocoee River** and mountaintops. 423-476-9700

Historic Charleston/Calhoun Driving Tour
Go back in time with this informative driving tour of the historic sites contained in the charming towns of Charleston and its northern sister city, Calhoun. From Cherokee beginnings and Civil War skirmishes, to tremendous social and cultural developments, these two small southern river towns may be small, but their place in history is significant and largely untold… until now. 423-472-6587

Cleveland Downtown Historic Greenway. Walking tour of local folklore. 2145 Keith St. 423-472-6587

Cleveland Speedway
The Speedway is a 1/3 mile clay-banked dirt track oval car racing facility that has been around more than 30 years. The track is equipped with state-of-the-art computers and is one of the south's premier dirt racks. Five divisions compete. Gates open at 5pm, races at 7pm. 423-479-8574

Ocoee River.
In Cherokee National Forest
Whitewater rafting, kayaking and canoeing at various skill levels. The Ocoee River's Class III and IV rapids make it the most popular whitewater river in the nation and the site for the 1996 Olympic Whitewater events. 423-472-6587

Primitive Settlement
Restored and furnished log cabins and relics from early America. 6 miles east of Cleveland on Kinser Rd. Apr. to Oct. 9 a.m.-4 p.m. 423-476-5096

Ducktown Basin Museum
The first state-owned historical industrial site is the large copper deposit first mined by the Cherokee and "discovered" by European settlers in 1843. Nature at its best as you approach the site. Nonprofit museum in the **Burra Burra Mine Historic District.** 423-496-5778

Hiwassee State Scenic River
was the first designated Scenic River in TN and is a popular nature photography site. Also primitive camping, fishing and canoeing. 423-338-5201

Morris Winery & Vineyard
Largest pick-your-own grapes farm. Widest variety in Aug. Other fruits in season. Mon. to Sat. 8 a.m.-8 p.m. and 1 p.m.-6 p.m. on Sun. 423-479-7311 or 423-472-1612

Red Clay State Historic Area. *This model farm illustrates the Cherokee Indian lifestyle. Red Clay was the last council ground of the Cherokee Nation before their forced removal to Western territories in 1838 on the "Trail of Tears." Pure running water still flows from the "Council Spring," a natural feature that attracted the Cherokee to the site (produces over 400,000 gallons of sapphire-blue water per day). Reconstructed Cherokee farm and council house, interpretive center, theater, exhibits and artifacts. Open March to November from 8 a.m.-sunset and from December to February open 8 a.m.-4:30 p.m. Take Blue Springs Rd. or Dalton Pike off Hwy. 64 Bypass and follow signs. 423-478-0339. Courtesy Tennessee Tourism Development*

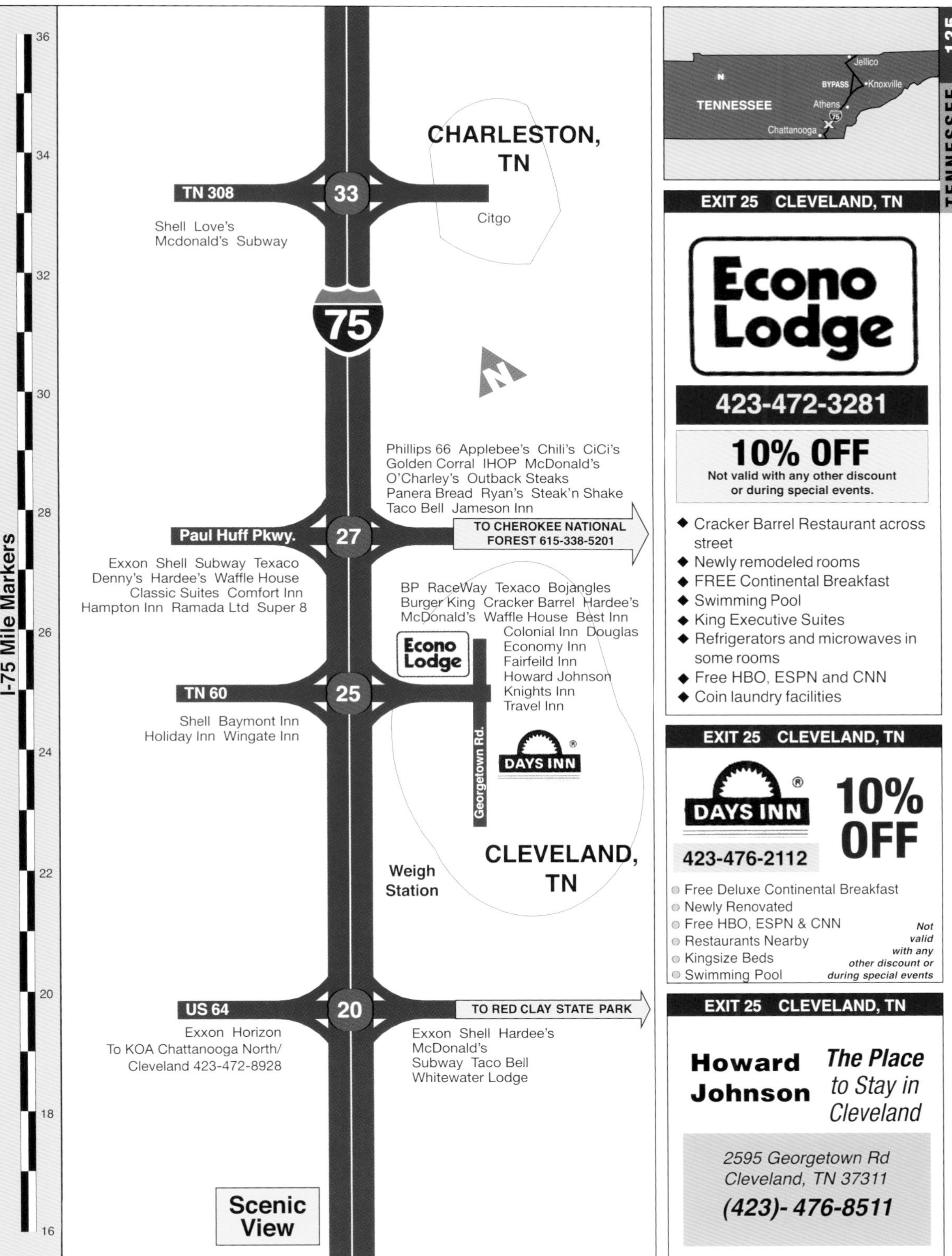
I-75 Mile Markers
36
34
32
30
28
26
24
22
20
18
16
CHARLESTON, TN
TN 308
33
Shell Love's
Mcdonald's Subway
Citgo
75
N
Phillips 66 Applebee's Chili's CiCi's
Golden Corral IHOP McDonald's
O'Charley's Outback Steaks
Panera Bread Ryan's Steak'n Shake
Taco Bell Jameson Inn
Paul Huff Pkwy.
27
TO CHEROKEE NATIONAL FOREST 615-338-5201
Exxon Shell Subway Texaco
Denny's Hardee's Waffle House
Classic Suites Comfort Inn
Hampton Inn Ramada Ltd Super 8
BP RaceWay Texaco Bojangles
Burger King Cracker Barrel Hardee's
McDonald's Waffle House Best Inn
Colonial Inn Douglas
Economy Inn
Fairfeild Inn
Howard Johnson
Knights Inn
Travel Inn
Econo Lodge
TN 60
25
Shell Baymont Inn
Holiday Inn Wingate Inn
Georgetown Rd.
DAYS INN
CLEVELAND, TN
Weigh Station
US 64
20
TO RED CLAY STATE PARK
Exxon Horizon
To KOA Chattanooga North/
Cleveland 423-472-8928
Exxon Shell Hardee's
McDonald's
Subway Taco Bell
Whitewater Lodge
Scenic View
Jellico
BYPASS
Knoxville
TENNESSEE
Athens
Chattanooga

Chattanooga
TENNESSEE

Chattanooga Area Convention & Visitors Bureau
2 Broad St., Chattanooga, Tennessee 37402
423-424-4430 or 1-800-322-3344 **www.chattanoogafun.com**

Hamilton County was created in 1819 from Rhea County and Indian lands and named in honor of Alexander Hamilton (1757-1804), American statesman, Revolutionary War soldier, member of the Continental Congress and secretary of the U.S. treasury under President Washington. The history of the area centered upon present-day Chattanooga is long. Prior to the visit of the Spanish expedition led by Hernando De Soto in 1540, the Chattanooga area was the capital of one of the greatest Indian cultures in history, the highly-civilized Cherokee Nation.

The British established the colony of Carolina which included all of the Tennessee country in 1663. About the same time, the French from the Mississippi Valley also claimed this area. With the construction of "The Old French Store" in 1761, Chattanooga became a trading center. The store was the first structure built by European men and the site is now marked by a historical plaque.

In 1763 England gained title to the territory at the close of the French and Indian War. Chief Dragging Canoe's Chickamauga Indians, a splinter group of Cherokees, moved to South Chickamauga Creek in 1777 and resisted European settlement and cooperated with the British in the American Revolution. Ignoring federal policy, militiamen destroyed the primary Chickamauga Indian towns in 1794, ending the struggle between the Indians and the settlers.

In 1796 Tennessee became the 16th state. At that time Indian lands comprised about three-quarters of the Chattanooga area.

One of Chattanooga's oldest cemeteries, at the site of the old Brainerd Mission, was built by the Congregational and Presbyterian Churches, and named for missionary David Brainerd. It served as a school for Cherokees and was the first in America where domestic arts and agriculture were taught to Indians. The small cemetery contains the graves of Indians and missionaries. Its leaders encouraged Sequoyah who presented his syllabary to the Cherokee Nation 1821.

The infamous "Trail of Tears" started by boat from Chattanooga in 1838. John Ross, the Principal Chief of the Cherokees for 38 years and the founder of Chattanooga, who had successfully resisted for ten years the removal of his people to the Oklahoma territory, went by riverboat. His wife was one of the thousands who died.

Lookout Mountain, *Sprawled in the famous Moccasin Bend of the Tennessee River, Chattanooga's skyline is dominated by the imposing **Lookout Mountain**, site of several major attractions including **Rock City, Ruby Falls, Point Park and the Incline Railway**. Courtesy Tennessee Tourism Development*

Lookout Mountain Flight Park & Training Center

With beautiful mountains and the temperate climate of the sunny South, the area near Chattanooga has become the hang gliding capital of the East as well as the home of America's largest hang gliding school, **Lookout Mountain Flight Park & Training Center (LMFP).**

Founded in 1978, the school graduates more than 125 hang glider pilots each year. In fact, 1 of every 5 novice-rated pilots in the U.S. learns to hang glide at this training center. The training program has been so successful that the United States Hang Gliding Assoc. (USHGA) has adopted LMFP's training manual as the official flight training manual for the sport.

Tandem flights, meaning 2 people on a larger glider, have become very popular at **Lookout Mountain.** A certified tandem instructor launches, flies and lands the glider, with a passenger at his or her side. Both pilot and passenger are in their own harnesses and hooked securely to the glider. No hang gliding experience is necessary. The pilot gives all the necessary instruction been towed up by an ultra-light aircraft.

Lookout Mountain
begins just inside Chattanooga's city limits and continues southwest more than 50 miles, crossing into Georgia and then Alabama. The flight park's mountain launch site is 1,350 feet above Lookout Valley, with training hills 15 minutes away near the town of Trenton, Georgia.

The long straight ridges and wind conditions in the Chattanooga area are often ideal for modern hang gliding. Hang gliders can fly in any direction, and the pilot circles when he or she encounters "bubbles" of rising air called "thermals," allowing pilots to rise thousands of feet into the sky and fly for hours at a time.

Flight distances exceeding 100 miles have been achieved from LMFP with the local distance record set on a flight beginning at **Lookout Mountain Flight Park** and ending 154 miles later in Swords, Georgia, about 70 miles east of Atlanta. Flights of 100 miles or more take four to 8 hours to complete and typically carry the hang glider to altitudes of 4,000 to 8,000 feet above the ground.

Modern hang gliders are well-designed and tested, and certified by an industry group. The sport is self-regulated by the USHGA, under basic regulations established by the Federal Aviation Administration. Hang glider pilots are trained by USHGA-certified instructors.

Contact:
Lookout Mountain Attractions

3518 S. Broad St.,
Chattanooga, TN, 37409
423-820-4030 800-825-8366
www.lookoutmountain.com

Chattanooga Area Convention & Visitors Bureau
2 Broad St., Chattanooga, Tennessee 37402
423-424-4430 or 1-800-322-3344 **www.chattanoogafun.com**

The Southern Belle Riverboat lights up the evening sky along the Tennessee River. *Photo courtesy Greater Chattanooga Convention and Visitors Bureau.*

Reflection Riding Arboretum & Botanical Garden

Centuries before the first European explorer gazed on the beauty of the **Tennessee Valley** and the mountains that surround it, Indians roamed the land. On the side of **Lookout Mountain,** a 35-foot high stone face stoically stares over one of the most beautiful places in Tennessee. Indian legend tells that the face once belonged to a great chief who was the last of his tribe. The chief prayed to his gods that his nation would not be forgotten and as he prayed, a great storm swept up the valley and etched his face into the mountain.

Lookout Mountain's Great Stone Face is just one of the many landmarks that can be found in the 300-acre nature park known as **Reflection Riding,** created by John A. Chambliss and his wife. It has been said that the most beautiful place during spring is **Reflection Riding,** when thousands of wildflowers are in full bloom and grace the trails around the park (over 300 wildflower species have been identified in the park).

Reflection Riding has also preserved the historical aspects of the park. The **Great Indian Warpath,** which once stretched from Alabama to New York, remains in its original condition. It is believed that DeSoto's Expedition in 1540 once traveled on the Warpath. A portion of the **St. Augustine Cisca Trail,** which ran between St. Augustine, FL, and Man-chester, TN, is also preserved.

In 1807, the **Old Federal Road,** which stretched from Augusta, GA, to Nashville was the first road through the Cherokee Nation. The portion of it than ran through the park has been maintained.

Lookout Mountain has been the site of several battles. Cherokee Chief Dragging Canoe was defeated by John Sevier's militia here one year after the Revolutionary War ended. During the Civil War's campaign for Chattanooga, several skirmishes were fought on the land in this garden.

Throughout the preserve, markers have been placed to remind visitors of the rich history surrounding **Lookout Mountain**. Millstones, brought by the first European settlers in 1803, still lie beside Lookout Creek. Among the buildings in the garden is Cherokee Chief Walking Stick's log cabin, one of the oldest structures in Tennessee.

Chattanooga Nature Center and Reflection Riding Arboretum and Botanical Garden
400 Garden Rd., Chattanooga, TN 37419
423-821-1160 www.ridetheincline.com

Lookout Mountain Incline

Experience the thrill of riding "America's most amazing mile" as the **Incline** climbs Lookout Mountain. Chattanooga and its surrounding mountains and valleys come alive as the trolley-style rail cars travel into the clouds. The breathtaking grade of the track, 72.7% near the top, gives the **Incline** the unique distinction of being the world's steepest passenger railway.

From the mountain top, the **Incline's Lookout Mountain** Upper Station observation deck offers visitors a panoramic view from the highest overlook on the mountain.

On Nov. 16, 1895, the historic **Incline** began transporting residents and visitors between Chattanooga and the top of **Lookout Mountain.** On a clear day visitors can see 200 miles to the Great Smoky Mountains. While visiting the mountain, observe the Incline's two 100-horsepower electric motors that power the large drums which operate the cable from the Lookout Mountain station's machine rooms.

Built in 1895 as a fast, inexpensive means of transport, the **Incline Railway** provided easy access to the cool temperatures of the picturesque mountain. Lookout Mountain quickly developed into a popular summer vacation resort area during the late 19th and early 20th centuries, and is still popular today. Just a short, three-block walk from the Incline's Lookout Mountain Station is Point Park, a unit of the **Chickamauga/Chattanooga National Military Park** and the site of one of the most dramatic Civil War battles. Visitors can stand on the same bluff that General U.S. Grant did in 1863 and be thrilled by the view.

At the **Point Park Visitors Center** view the magnificent Walker painting "Battle Above the Clouds." Relax in the visitors center auditorium and listen to a brief taped narration explaining the battle and painting's history.

Lookout Mountain Incline Railway is at the foot and top of Lookout Mountain. From I-75 take I-24 to exit 178, take Lookout Mountain exit and follow the Incline signs. Year-round, makes 3 or 4 trips per hour. 827 East Brow Rd., Lookout Mountain, TN 37350. 423-821-4224

Chattanooga
TENNESSEE

Chattanooga Area Convention & Visitors Bureau
2 Broad St., Chattanooga, Tennessee 37402
423-424-4430 or 1-800-322-3344 **www.chattanoogafun.com**

DOWNTOWN CHATTANOOGA ATTRACTIONS

Tennessee Aquarium IMAX® 3D Theater This six-story, state-of-the-art 3D theater showcases the ultimate in film and sound technology. Open daily except Thanksgiving Day & Christmas Day. Next to TN Aquarium at 201 Chestnut St., Chatt. 1-800-265-0695 or 423-266-IMAX www.tnaqua.org. See page 146.

Creative Discovery Museum Search for lost dinosaur bones in the field science lab. Create art with many different media in an artist's studio. Compose your own tunes in a musician's studio and explore an inventor's workshop just for kids! **Brand NEW River Play Exhibit**, gives children a chance to splash around in an interactive water course. Children can plot a kid-size riverboat, scale a crow's nest high atop a 2 1/2 story climbing structure, build sailboats and make water wheels spin and buckets spill. Just two blocks from TN Aquarium at 321 Chestnut St., Chatt. 423-756-2738 www.cdmfun.org

Tennessee Aquarium Allow yourself two hours when you take the self-guided tour of the Tennessee Aquarium. You'll want to immerse yourself in the striking new surroundings where 9,000 animals make their homes. See an anaconda, a bonnethead shark, a giant alligator snapping turtle, piranhas, monstrous arapaimas and gliding stingrays. Open daily except Thanksgiving and Christmas Day. Tickets sold from 10 a.m.- 6 p.m. 1 Broad St., Chatt. 1-800-262-0695 www.tnaqua.org

Houston Museum of Decorative Arts A fabulous collection of antiques and decorative art objects, including collections of antique glass and porcelain considered to be among the finest in the world. Guided tours. Gift shop. 201 High St., Chatt. 423-267-7176

Hunter Museum of American Art The most complete collection of American art in the Southeast. Tues. to Sat. 9:30 a.m.- 5 p.m., Sun. 12- 5 p.m. 10 Bluff View, Chatt. 423-267-0968 www.huntermuseum.org

Lookout Mountain Incline Railway World's steepest passenger railway. 827 East Brow Rd., Lookout Mountain. 423-821-4224 www.ridetheincline.com

Jack Daniels Whiskey Distillery. Lynchburg is the seat of Moore County and even though it is home to the distillery, it's a dry county and has been ever since Prohibition. Take a guided tour and learn the complete history of the whiskey and some interesting stories about Mr. Jack too! Tours last about 75 minutes, starting every 15 minutes, 9am-4:30pm. Jack Daniel's great-grandniece, Lynne Tolley, is the proprietor of the local Boarding House Restaurant (noonday meals) and is also the official taster at the Distillery. About a two-hour drive from Chattanooga. Take I-24 west towards Nashville. Take exit 111 (Manchester) and go left on Hwy 55 all the way to Lynchburg. 931-759-6180 www.jackdaniels.com

Photo/text of the **Tennessee Valley Railway Museum** courtesy Tennessee Dept. of Tourist Development

Chattanooga Choo Choo & the Tennessee Valley Railroad

Americans have always had a fascination with railroads. For a time in America, the only way to travel was by rail. Towns across the country were proud to have their own depots.

Wanting to preserve the railroad's proud heritage, a group of Chattanooga residents formed the **Tennessee Valley Railroad Museum** in 1961. Today, an impressive collection of classic pieces from railroading history have been assembled to make the largest operating historic railroad in the South.

The collection is any train lover's dream. **Steam locomotive 4501,** built in 1911, is the pride of the museum. **The Eden Isle,** a 1917 office car with 3 bedrooms and 4 bathrooms, and the **Clover Colony,** a stainless steel Pullman sleeping car, are other treasures you can tour that was once used by Marilyn Monroe.

The Tennessee Valley Railroad owns 40 acres, including 4 railroad bridges and a historic tunnel through Missionary Ridge that played an important role during the Civil War's *Battle for Chattanooga.* It was the railroad that made Chattanooga such a strategic location during the Civil War. The route the museum follows shows the first rail lines. During the season (June to Aug.), the **Downtown Arrow Train** makes runs between the museum and the **Chattanooga Choo Choo.**

In 1941, the "King of Swing," Glenn Miller, released a song composed for the film *Sun Valley Serenade.* The song reached number 1 on the Hit Parade and sold more than 1 million copies as a single. Did you know that Miller was awarded the record industry's first gold record for "*The Chattanooga Choo Choo*"?

Chattanoogans have been in love with railroads since the departure of their first train in 1909. At the height of Chattanooga's train days, 14 tracks were in use and 68 trains arrived and departed each day. The last train left in 1970 and the depot was boarded up.

In 1971 a group of investors restored the depot and the **Chattanooga Choo Choo** opened as an historical hotel. Coaches were bought and each car was converted into 2 hotel rooms. The **Chattanooga Choo Choo** offers 365 comfortable rooms and suites, including 48 rooms aboard the traincars. Guests are able to play tennis and swim in either the outdoor or indoor pool. Visitors may roam the formal gardens, tour the 30-acre complex in a 1924 New Orleans trolley, eat in one of 5 restaurants, and shop in the specialty stores. The H.O. gauge model railroad on display is complete with more than 3,000 feet of track, and 1,000 model freight cars, and is one of the largest in the U.S.

Tennessee Valley Railroad
Apr. to Nov. 4119 Cromwell Rd.
423-894-8028. www.tvrail.com

Chattanooga Choo Choo Holiday Inn
1400 Market St. Chattanooga, TN 37402.
Telephone: 423-266-5000 or
1-800-TRACK-29 www.choochoo.com

Chattanooga
TENNESSEE

Chattanooga Area Convention & Visitors Bureau
2 Broad St., Chattanooga, Tennessee 37402
423-424-4430 or 1-800-322-3344 **www.chattanoogafun.com**

*Some remaining **Rock City Barns** such as this one near Chattanooga are designated Historic Landmarks. Photo/text courtesy Tennessee Department of Tourist Development.*

Rock City Gardens

Over 70 years ago, Frieda Carter developed a 10-acre garden on a mountaintop near Chattanooga, TN. Her husband found inspiration in his wife's work and he improved her pine-needle path among the huge boulders and natural rock formations in the "city of rocks." **Rock City Gardens** opened in 1932.When the visitor numbers subsided after a brief flurry of business, Garnet Carter hired Clark Byers to paint barn roofs with messages. For 32 years, Byers painted the famous **"See Rock City"** slogan on over 900 barns in 19 states from Michigan to Texas to Florida.

In the 1950's **Rock City** developed a bird-house campaign to compliment their barn advertising, but the Beautification Act of 1965 brought an end to both companies. Barn slogans and birdhouses were painted over. Only 85 barns remain today.

The "See Rock City" slogan can still be seen around the world in British subways, French countrysides and Japanese gardens. During Desert Storm, soldiers erected a Rock City birdhouse in the desert sands of Kuwait.

Rock City has been a natural attraction that provides entertainment for the whole family: see the towering rock formations, beautiful gardens, the wonderful view from **Lover's Leap** and the award-winning gardens with their year-round dazzling colors.

Take I-24 (I-75 exit 2 from downtown Chattanooga) and follow Rock City/ Lookout Mountain signs. Only 6 miles from downtown Chattanooga on TN 58 and GA 157. Open year-round except Christmas Day from 8:30 a.m.-5 p.m. Summer hours 8:30 a.m.-8 p.m. 1400 Patten Rd. Lookout Mountain, Georgia. 706-820-2531 www.seerockcity.com **Enchanted Garden of Lights** in Nov. to Dec., opens 6 p.m.-9 p.m.

The Charm of Ruby Falls

Visitors come from all over the world to see the 145-foot natural under-ground waterfall with no known beginning, where 300 gallons of water funnel each minute into a crystal-clear, 4-foot deep pool. Here you will find glistening stalagmites made from white onyx, rock formations that resemble steak and potatoes, an angel's wing, an elephant's foot and a thermometer locked on 58 degrees year-round.

Remaining a vital part of the allure for Chattanooga, **Ruby Falls** is one of its oldest, most popular attractions. **Lookout Mountain Caverns**, which welcomes hundreds of thousands of visitors each year, was once used during the Civil War as a retreat and camp ground for both Confederate and Union Troops. For over 6 decades, **Ruby Falls** has been one of the most popular attractions in southeast Tennessee. Another feature that enhances **Ruby Falls**' charm is the addition of the **Fun Forest**, a playground for children of all ages. Parents can relax under the covered deck area and enjoy a snack from the Fun Forest Grill or take in the spectacular view of Chattanooga from the **Ruby Falls Tower**.

Open every day except Christmas Day. 8 a.m.- 8 p.m. with tours continuously. **Ruby Falls**, Lookout Mountain, 1720 South Scenic Hwy., Chatt., TN. 423-821-2544 www.rubyfalls.com 800-755-7105

I-75 exit 2, then eastbound onto I-24, take exit 174 and follow signs to Lookout Mountain. Westbound I-24, take exit 178 and follow signs to Lookout Mountain. Or from Tennessee Aquarium, take South Broad Street.

Chattanooga
TENNESSEE

Chattanooga Area Convention & Visitors Bureau
2 Broad St., Chattanooga, Tennessee 37402
423-424-4430 or 1-800-322-3344 **www.chattanoogafun.com**

Attractions

River Gallery Sculpture Garden
Art and nature combined on two acres of beautifully landscaped grounds. Free. Bluff View Art District, Chatt. 423-267-7353

Chattanooga Riverboat Co. "Southern Belle"
Cruises departing from Ross's Landing. 201 Riverfront Pkwy., Chatt. 423-266-4488 or 800-766-2784 www.ChattanoogaRiverboat.com

Chatt. Regional History Museum $4/adults. Daily Mon. to Fri. 10 a.m.-4:30 p.m., Sat. & Sun. 11 a.m.-4:30 p.m. 400 Chestnut St., Chatt. 423-265-3247

International Towing & Recovery Museum
Exhibits of antique vehicles with wrecker and towing equipment dating back to 1916. Hall of fame. and gift shop. 3315 Broad St., Chatt. 423-267-3132

Chattanooga African-American Museum
200 E. Martin Luther King Blvd., Chatt. Unique collection of African art. 423-266-8658 www.caamhistory.org

Battles for Chattanooga Electric Map & Museum
At Point Park, the actual site of the famous "Battle above the Clouds." 1110 East Brow Rd., Lookout Mountain. 423-821-2812 www.battlesforchattanooga.com

Chattanooga Nature Center
Explore wetlands along a boardwalk, tour native plant gardens, observe native animals in southeastern forest and field habitats. Walk, drive or bike along the trails. Mon. to Sat. 9 a.m.-5 p.m. Sun. 1 p.m.-5 p.m. At the foot of Lookout Mountain, 400 Garden Rd., Chatt. 423-821-1160 www.chattanooganaturecenter.org

Raccoon Mountain Crystal Caverns
45-minute easy walking tour of spectacular underground scenery. Also wild cave tours. 319 West Hills Dr., Chatt. 423-821-9403

Jack Daniel's Distillery
Hwy 55, Lynchburg, TN 37352
931-759-6180 www.jackdaniels.com

Tennessee Aquarium Cove Forest Exhibit, *courtesy Chattanooga Area Convention and Visitors Bureau.*
Text courtesy Tennessee Department of Tourist Development

Tennessee Aquarium

The world's first and largest freshwater aquarium of its kind opened on May 1, 1992. The $45-million **Tennessee Aquarium** was created to celebrate the life-giving force of the river. It was founded to provide enjoyment, understanding and conservation of the earth's rivers. Visitors are guided on a journey beginning at the Tennessee River's source in the Appalachian Cove Forest, where a lush mountain forest has been recreated. River otters play under cascading waterfalls, as birds sing nearby. Visitors stand eye-to-eye with 80-pound catfish that prowl the depths of the detailed Tennessee River Gallery.

Discovery Falls magnifies the life of the animals too small to be seen in a normal environment. Observe salamanders, darters, and other creatures. Experience the misty climate when they enter the Mississippi Delta exhibit. Alligators slip into the black waters of the Mississippi, while water moccasins drape their lethal bodies over low hanging branches.

Sting rays, sharks, and colorful ocean fish can be seen in the Gulf of Mexico as visitors continue on their journey. The Rivers of the World exhibit allows visitors the chance to stand on the banks of the world's great rivers: North America's Tennessee and Mississippi, South America's Amazon, Africa's Zaire, Japan's Chimanto, and Siberia's Yenisey. Visitors can see deadly piranha, tigerfish and even a boa constrictor.

The aquarium has a spectacular 60-foot canyon, two living forests and more than 22 tanks. Through the more than 40 realistic exhibits, visitors are able to look at the life that surrounds the river. Funded entirely by the private sector, the **Tennessee Aquarium** has educational facilities that provide hands-on exhibits, a 200-seat auditorium, 2 fully-equipped classrooms and a wet lab. The on-site **IMAX® 3D Theater** opened in 1996. The expansion is set to open May, 2005.

Next to the **Chattanooga Visitor Center,** the **Aquarium** is located in the center of **Ross's Landing Plaza,** a part of the **Tennessee Riverpark and Riverwalk.** Tickets are sold from 10 a.m.-6 p.m. 1-800-262-0695 www.tnaqua.org Check-out the **NEW Seahorse Exhibit & Discovery Hall**.

CAMPING

Shipp's RV Center & Campground
Award-winning. On Chickamauga Creek. I-75 exit 1 if southbound and exit 1A if northbound. 6728 Ringgold Rd., Chatt. 800-222-4551 or 423-892-8275 www.shippsrv.com

Lookout Valley RV Park & Campground
At foot of Lookout Mountain. 3714 Cummings Hwy.423-821-3100

Best Holiday Trav-L-Park Four-star. Take I-72 "East Ridge" exit 1 if southbound or 1B if northbound, go right at top of ramp, and left at Amoco. 1709 Mack Smith Rd., Chatt. 706-891-9766 1-800-693-2877 www.chattacamp.com

Raccoon Campground
At foot of rustic Raccoon Mntn. 1 mile off I-24 at Lookout Valley Exit 174. 319 West Hills Dr., Chatt. 423-821-9403 800-823-2267

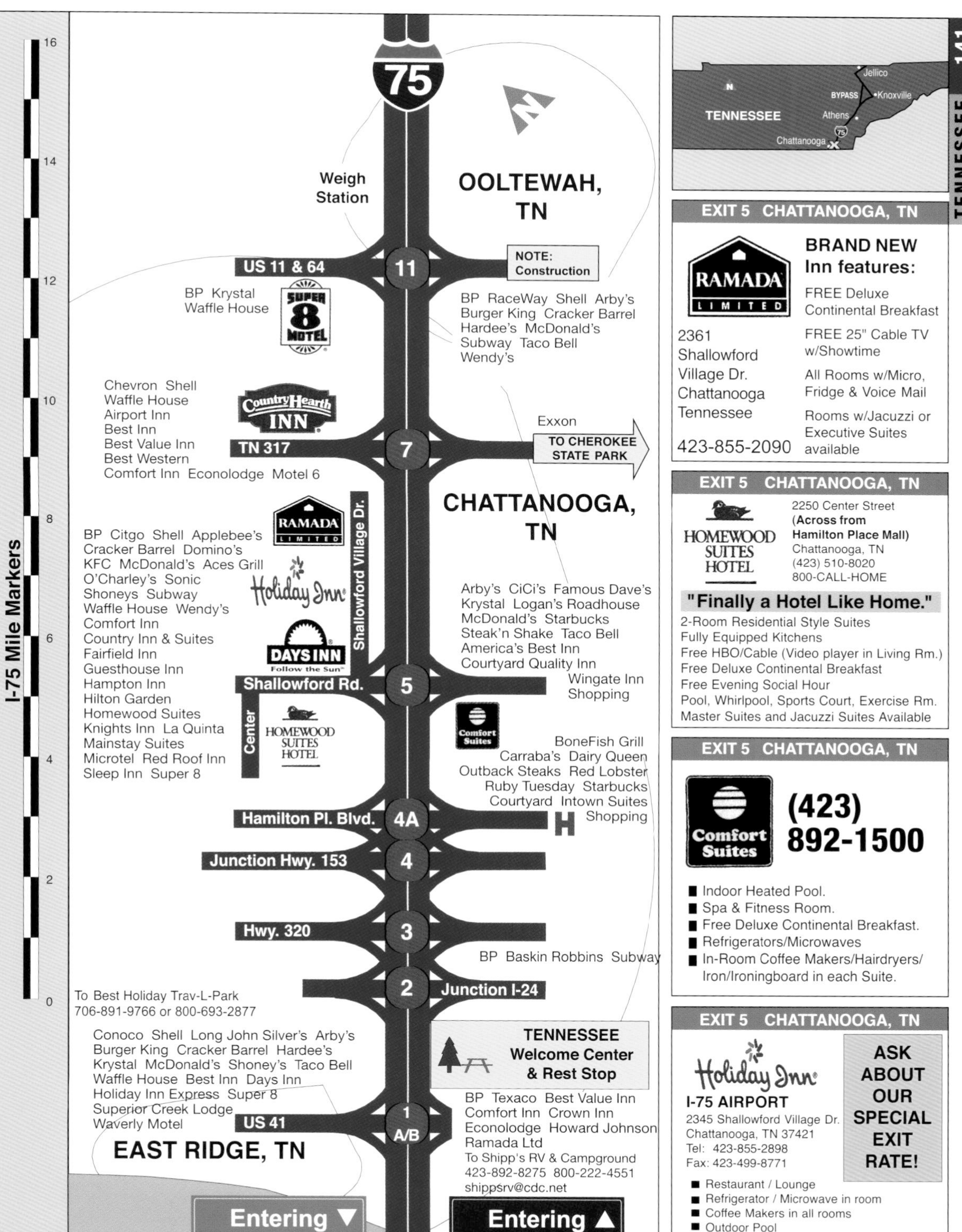

141
TENNESSEE
Jellico
BYPASS
Knoxville
TENNESSEE
Athens
75
Chattanooga
I-75 Mile Markers
16
14
12
10
8
6
4
2
0
75
N
Weigh Station
OOLTEWAH, TN
US 11 & 64
11
NOTE: Construction
BP Krystal
Waffle House
SUPER 8 MOTEL
BP RaceWay Shell Arby's
Burger King Cracker Barrel
Hardee's McDonald's
Subway Taco Bell
Wendy's
Chevron Shell
Waffle House
Airport Inn
Best Inn
Best Value Inn
Best Western
Comfort Inn Econolodge Motel 6
Country Hearth INN
Exxon
TN 317
7
TO CHEROKEE STATE PARK
CHATTANOOGA, TN
RAMADA LIMITED
Shallowford Village Dr.
BP Citgo Shell Applebee's
Cracker Barrel Domino's
KFC McDonald's Aces Grill
O'Charley's Sonic
Shoneys Subway
Waffle House Wendy's
Comfort Inn
Country Inn & Suites
Fairfield Inn
Guesthouse Inn
Hampton Inn
Hilton Garden
Homewood Suites
Knights Inn La Quinta
Mainstay Suites
Microtel Red Roof Inn
Sleep Inn Super 8
Holiday Inn
DAYS INN Follow the Sun
Arby's CiCi's Famous Dave's
Krystal Logan's Roadhouse
McDonald's Starbucks
Steak'n Shake Taco Bell
America's Best Inn
Courtyard Quality Inn
Shallowford Rd.
5
Wingate Inn
Shopping
Center
HOMEWOOD SUITES HOTEL
Comfort Suites
BoneFish Grill
Carraba's Dairy Queen
Outback Steaks Red Lobster
Ruby Tuesday Starbucks
Courtyard Intown Suites
Hamilton Pl. Blvd.
4A
H
Shopping
Junction Hwy. 153
4
Hwy. 320
3
BP Baskin Robbins Subway
2
Junction I-24
To Best Holiday Trav-L-Park
706-891-9766 or 800-693-2877
Conoco Shell Long John Silver's Arby's
Burger King Cracker Barrel Hardee's
Krystal McDonald's Shoney's Taco Bell
Waffle House Best Inn Days Inn
Holiday Inn Express Super 8
Superior Creek Lodge
Waverly Motel
TENNESSEE Welcome Center & Rest Stop
US 41
1 A/B
BP Texaco Best Value Inn
Comfort Inn Crown Inn
Econolodge Howard Johnson
Ramada Ltd
To Shipp's RV & Campground
423-892-8275 800-222-4551
shippsrv@cdc.net
EAST RIDGE, TN
Entering GEORGIA
Entering TENNESSEE
EXIT 5 CHATTANOOGA, TN
RAMADA LIMITED
BRAND NEW Inn features:
FREE Deluxe Continental Breakfast
FREE 25" Cable TV w/Showtime
All Rooms w/Micro, Fridge & Voice Mail
Rooms w/Jacuzzi or Executive Suites available
2361 Shallowford Village Dr. Chattanooga Tennessee
423-855-2090
EXIT 5 CHATTANOOGA, TN
HOMEWOOD SUITES HOTEL
2250 Center Street
(Across from Hamilton Place Mall)
Chattanooga, TN
(423) 510-8020
800-CALL-HOME
"Finally a Hotel Like Home."
2-Room Residential Style Suites
Fully Equipped Kitchens
Free HBO/Cable (Video player in Living Rm.)
Free Deluxe Continental Breakfast
Free Evening Social Hour
Pool, Whirlpool, Sports Court, Exercise Rm.
Master Suites and Jacuzzi Suites Available
EXIT 5 CHATTANOOGA, TN
Comfort Suites
(423) 892-1500
Indoor Heated Pool.
Spa & Fitness Room.
Free Deluxe Continental Breakfast.
Refrigerators/Microwaves
In-Room Coffee Makers/Hairdryers/ Iron/Ironingboard in each Suite.
EXIT 5 CHATTANOOGA, TN
Holiday Inn
I-75 AIRPORT
2345 Shallowford Village Dr.
Chattanooga, TN 37421
Tel: 423-855-2898
Fax: 423-499-8771
ASK ABOUT OUR SPECIAL EXIT RATE!
Restaurant / Lounge
Refrigerator / Microwave in room
Coffee Makers in all rooms
Outdoor Pool
Indoor Pool privileges next door
Free Local Calls

Georgia

Georgia Department of Economic Development
75 Fifth St., NW, Suite 1200, Atlanta, GA 30308
404-962-4000 or 1-800-VISIT-GA **www.exploregeorgia.org**

Georgia's History

Georgia was one of the original 13 colonies and was established by the English in 1733 at Savannah. The region's history, however, dates back many centuries earlier to a period when the Creek and Cherokee inhabited the area. The Native American settlements, although widespread and highly developed throughout the region, were gradually reduced with the European settlement of the New World.

It wasn't until 1730, however, that a group of English settlers made plans to establish a separate colony and name it after King George II. Just a few decades later, in 1776, Georgia joined the fight against the British for independence. The Revolutionary War ended in 1783, and Georgia became the fourth state in the Union to ratify the United States Constitution.

Soon after the Revolutionary War, settlers and land companies began developing the new state resulting, in 1838, in the forced removal of the remaining Native Americans to Oklahoma on the tragic "Trail of Tears."

Atlanta, developed as a transportation crossroads and became a city in 1845. But with the start of the Civil War in 1861, Georgia's progress came to a halt. In 1863, General William Sherman's Union forces marched across Georgia, burning and destroying nearly everything in their path. This devastation was later immortalized in Atlanta author Margaret Mitchell's classic novel, *Gone With The Wind.*

Following the Civil War, Georgia's cities prospered and her economy gradually recovered. The manufacturing and trade industries began expanding. Railway construction resumed, banking activities increased and towns grew and prospered. Through the turn of the century and on through two World Wars, the state continued to experience industrial and business growth.

The largest cities in Georgia are Atlanta, the capital city, and Columbus, Savannah, Macon, and Albany.

Welcome to Georgia

The Georgia State Capitol *in Atlanta, GA, is one of two U.S. capitols whose dome is sheeted in gold. The gold was brought from Georgia's own Dahlonega in the Northeast Georgia mountains.*
Photo courtesy Georgia Department of Industry, Trade & Tourism

Blue Ridge Mountains — Brasstown Valley Resort, Hiawassee

Georgia Department of Economic Development
75 Fifth St., NW, Suite 1200, Atlanta, GA 30308
404-962-4000 or 1-800-VISIT-GA **www.exploregeorgia.org**

The Stone Mountain Memorial Carving, near Atlanta, *is the world's largest single piece of sculptural art. The carving depicts (from left to right) Confederate President Jefferson Davis, Generals Robert E. Lee and Thomas "Stonewall" Jackson. Stone Mountain, GA. Photo courtesy Georgia Department of Industry, Trade & Tourism*

Georgia Aquarium in Atlanta *© Georgia Department of Economic Development*

Georgia ranks 10th among the 50 states of the United States in population, according to the most recent reports from the U.S. Census Bureau.

Georgia is the largest state east of the Mississippi and is larger than any other state in the southeastern region of the United States. The state is 315 miles long from north to south.

Georgia is the home of two former U.S. presidents: **Jimmy Carter** and the late **Franklin Delano Roosevelt.**

OTHER GEORGIANS OF NOTE

Martin Luther King Jr.
Civil rights leader and winner of the Nobel Peace Prize, 1964.

Ted Turner
Creator of the Cable News Network, CNN and the owner of Georgia's professional sports teams: the Atlanta Braves and the Atlanta Hawks.

Juliette Gordon Low
Founder of he Girl Scouts in Savannah, Georgia, in 1912.

Newt Gingrich
Former Speaker of the U.S. House of Representatives.

Andrew Young
First black U.S. ambassador to the United Nations, first black Georgian elected to Congress since the Civil War and Mayor of Atlanta, 1981-1989.

Margaret Mitchell
Author of the book *Gone With the Wind.*

Sidney Lanier
Famous poet born in Macon, Georgia.

Lewis Grizzard
Famous humorist, columnist and author.

Alice Walker
Pulitzer Prize-winning author of *The Color Purple.*

Carson McCullers
Noted columnist and author of *Member of the Wedding* and *The Heart is a Lonely Hunter.*

Georgia

Georgia Department of Economic Development
75 Fifth St., NW, Suite 1200, Atlanta, GA 30308
404-962-4000 or 1-800-VISIT-GA **www.exploregeorgia.org**

Georgia's Original Peoples

Georgia's history begins with its prehistoric people, the **Mound Builders,** who roamed the land and built the great mounds you can see at the **Kolomoki Mounds State Historic Park** in southwest Georgia, at the **Ocmulgee National Indian Mounds** near Macon, and near Cartersville at the **Etowah Mounds.** The I-75 takes you near the last two of these three sites.

En route to the Mississippi River in 1540, Hernando De Soto probably met the Creek Indians of southwest Georgia. The Cherokee tribe settled the northeast and northwest of present-day Georgia. You can tour what was once the the Cherokee capital, **New Echota,** near Calhoun. In 1928, the first newspaper to use an Indian language (the bilingual Cherokee Phoenix) was published in New Echota. The Cherokee tribe was removed from Georgia in 1838.

DID YOU KNOW?

Georgia's major industry is textiles.

Georgia has over 48,000 farms with an estimated total income of over $17.5 billion.

It is one of the largest chicken and egg producers in the U.S. Peanuts are Georgia's largest crop followed by pecans, tobacco, soybeans and corn. The state is known for its peaches and is a national leader in the production of watermelon.

The fourth-largest class of manufactured goods is paper, paperboard and pulpwood.

Georgia Red Clay is the most valuable mined product in Georgia and Georgia leads the nation in both clay and granite production.

Tourism is Georgia's second-largest industry.

The Hay House, *the gem of Macon, GA, is a striking example of one of Georgia's beautiful homes, many of which are open for tours. The interior of Hay House is simply beautiful. Macon is particularly proud of its architectural collection and it has done something very special to encourage visitors to "come see how beautiful our city is." Each evening the many significant treasures on their architectural tour are illuminated by various methods to provide visitors with a very different, very dramatic, experience. Something you will write home about! Much more to be found on this tour and the city of Macon in the pages that follow.*
Photo courtesy Georgia Department of Industry, Trade & Tourism

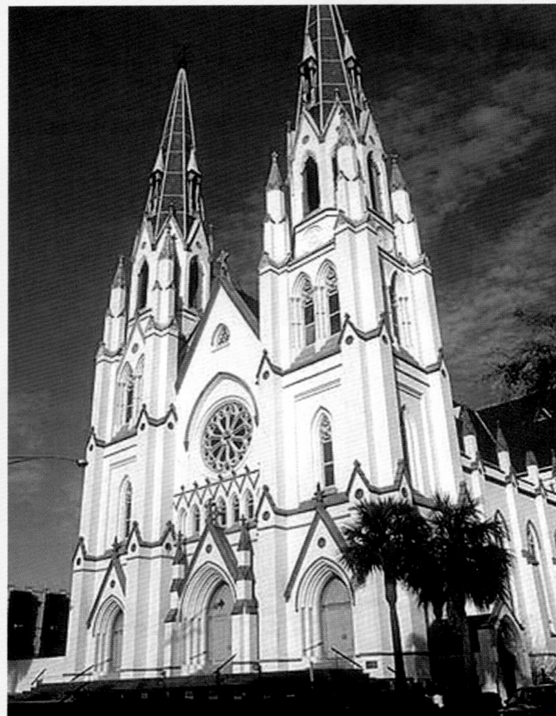

Take a side-trip to Savannah to see the striking ***Cathedral of St. John the Baptist,*** *the oldest Roman Catholic congregation in Georgia. Dedicated in 1876, this cathedral is one of the many examples of Savannah's charming past.*

Photo courtesy Georgia Department of Industry, Trade & Tourism

Georgia Department of Economic Development
75 Fifth St., NW, Suite 1200, Atlanta, GA 30308
404-962-4000 or 1-800-VISIT-GA **www.exploregeorgia.org**

***Chehaw Wild Animal Park**, designed by Jim Fowler, the host of Wild Kingdom. It is nestled among the pines in Albany, GA. Photo courtesy Georgia Department of Industry, Trade & Tourism*

***Bass fishing at George Bagby State Park.** Photo courtesy Georgia Department of Industry, Trade & Tourism*

EARLY GEORGIA HISTORY

- **1540** Hernando DeSoto was probably the first white man to visit Georgia.
- **1562** Jean Ribault, a French sailor surveyed the coast of Georgia in order to establish a colony of French Huguenots.
- **1565** Pedro Menendez de Aviles of Spain drives out the French and sets up posts on the coast.
- **1721** The British Empire's southern outpost maintained for over 10 years near present day Darien, Georgia.
- **1733** James Edwards and 120 English settlers colonize what would become Savannah. They call the colony "Georgia."
- **1735** Founders of the Methodist Church, John & Charles Wesley arrive in Georgia.
- **1736** General Oglethorp and his Highlanders establish a settlement near Fort King George and call it "Darien."
- **1775** Revolutionary War begins.
- **1776** 3 Georgians sign the Declaration of Independence: Button Gwinnett, Lyman Hall & George Walton.
- **1778** Georgia becomes one of the first states of the United States.
- **1779** British troops capture almost all of Georgia.
- **1782** America and its allies drive out the English.
- **1783** The Revolutionary War ends.
- **1788** Georgia becomes the 4th state in the Union to ratify the U.S. Constitution.
- **1783** Eli Whitney's invention, the cotton gin, causes an industrial revolution in Georgia's cotton industry.
- **1785** The first university in the U.S., The U. of Georgia, receives it charter.
- **1795** "The Yazoo Fraud." Large land companies defraud state legislators into selling Georgia land at $0.015/acre.
- **1828** Dahlonega started the first U.S. gold rush.
- **1838** Natives removed from Georgia. Known as "The Trail of Tears."
- **1860** Abraham Lincoln elected President of the United States.
- **1861** Georgia becomes 5th Southern state to secede from the Union.
- **1863** Confederate troops win bloody battle of Chickamauga.
- **1864** William T. Sherman's Union forces burn Atlanta to the ground.
- **1864** Sherman's march to the sea; capture of Savannah.
- **1865** Gen. Robert E. Lee surrenders to Ulysses S. Grant, the Civil War is over.

Catoosa County
GEORGIA

Catoosa County Area Chamber of Commerce
264 Catoosa Circle, Ringgold, GA 30736
706-965-5201 **www.catoosachamberofcommerce.com**

Chickamauga–Chattanooga National Military Park

In the fall of 1863, two armies clashed in an effort to gain control of a vital transportation hub that led straight into the heart of Dixie. Over a period of nine weeks, the Confederate and Union armies fought two major battles, each side claiming one victory. In the end, the champion would hold the key to the Deep South: Chattanooga.

For three days in September, one of the bloodiest battles of the Civil War was fought between General Bragg's Confederates and General Rosecrans' Army of the Cumberland at the cost of 34,000 casualties.

CHICKAMAUGA-CHATTANOOGA NATIONAL MILITARY PARK
is the nation's oldest, largest, and most visited national military park. The park's 8 separate areas total more than 8,000 acres, including the battlefield at Chickamauga where Union and Confederate armies lost 34,000 men on September 19th and 20th, 1863. Courtesy: Georgia Department of Economic Dev.

POINT PARK *(below) on Lookout Mountain marks the site of the famous Civil War "Battle Above the Clouds," fought in Nov., 1863. Photo/text Courtesy Tennessee Tourist Development and Chattanooga Area Convention & Visitors Bureau.*

Bragg was determined not to repeat a previous defeat and shortly after dawn on Sept. 19, the Battle of Chickamauga began. The battle was fought over a 4-mile area that was covered with dense woods and thick underbrush, unlike most battles which were fought on open fields. The fighting was desperate, often resulting in hand-to-hand combat. For 2 days, Bragg unsuccessfully tried to drive a wedge in the Union lines.

Bragg's victory came when Rosecrans was forced to aid Thomas' Corps, who struggled against repeated Confederate assaults. A gap was opened, enabling Gen. James Longstreet's troops to smash through the Federal line.

Rosecrans' defeat pushed the Union troops back into Chattanooga. The Confederates chased after the fleeing army and occupied Missionary Ridge, Lookout Mountain and Chattanooga Valley, effectively putting the city under siege. By placing artillery at key spots around Chattanooga, the Confederates prevented supplies from reaching the Union army. Unless there was a break in the Confederate noose, Rosecrans would have to surrender or starve.

Aware of Rosecrans plight, Washington sent 36,000 reinforcements, and General Ulysses S. Grant assumed overall command. When Grant arrived in October, the situation changed. Federal troops were able to open a short supply route in late October thus breaking some of the Confederate hold. On Nov. 23, Thomas' men attacked the Confederates at Orchard Knob. The Battle of Chattanooga had begun.

The following day, Lookout Mountain was encompassed by a thick fog. Taking advantage of the fog, Hooker's soldiers pushed the Confederates away from Cravens House, who were at the time using it as a headquarters. Bragg retreated from Lookout Mountain to his stronghold along Missionary Ridge. By Nov. 25, Bragg had concentrated most of his forces along the ridge. Sensing a victory, Grant sent forces to attack the Confederate flanks.

With the Union offensive, the Confederate line collapsed. With the siege lifted and the battle won, the Union army was in control of Tennessee. The following spring, Sherman used Chattanooga as his base on his infamous "March to the Sea."

Twenty-five years after the Civil War, Congress authorized the first four national military parks: **Chickamauga and Chattanooga, Shiloh, Gettysburg** and **Vicksburg.**

The first and the largest of the four was Chickamauga and Chattanooga. President Benjamin Harrison established the park when he signed the declaration on Aug. 19, 1890. The park was officially dedicated on Sept. 18-20, 1895, 32 years after the Battle of Chickamauga. Veterans placed 1,400 monuments and markers along the battlelines.

The **Point Park Visitor Center** is the home of James Walker's 13' x 33' painting, *The Battle Above the Clouds*. Inside Point Park are three gun batteries that mark a segment of the siege lines. In the center of the park is the **New York Peace Memorial** that depicts a Union and Confederate soldier shaking hands under a flag that symbolizes peace and brotherly love.

The **Ochs Museum** and Overlook was dedicated Nov. 12, 1940. named in honor of Adolph S. Ochs, owner-publisher of the *New York Times* and the *Chattanooga Times,* the exhibits tell the story of the Battle of Chattanooga and its role in determining the outcome of the Civil War.

The **Chickamauga Battlefield Visitor Center** features a state-of-the-art audio-visual program that explains the battle and its place in the Civil War. Also in the visitor center is the **Claude E. and Zemada O. Fuller Collection of American Military Arms.** The Fuller Guns are considered to be the best collection of Springfield longrifles in the world. The Collection includes other rare items and weapons. The Park features self-guided tours, monuments and historical tablets, plus several hiking and horse trails.

There is also The Old Stone Church Museum which served as a hospital for wounded soldiers from both sides. www.6thcavalrymuseum.com

DID YOU KNOW?

Ringgold Depot is one of the few remaining antebellum railroad depots in the state. Built in 1849, the depot was significant during the Civil War as a supply depot for Confederate troops.

Dalton
Atlanta
BYPASS
Macon
Cordele
GEORGIA
75
Tifton
Valdosta

Opry at the Ringgold Depot

Talented performers from throughout the Tri-state area come to the Ringgold Opry to share in the legacy of traditional acoustic music. All the "pickin" takes place every Saturday night at 7:30 p.m., rain or shine, on stage at the Ringgold Depot. Award winning fiddler, singer and actor Randall Franks, known to millions as "Officer Randy Goode" on TV's "In the Heat of the Night," often appears on stage at the Ringgold Opry. Two-time Old Time Banjo Player of the Year and SPBGMA Entertainer of the Year nominee Gary Waldrep also performs here. This historic depot was built in 1850 as a rail link between Atlanta and Chattanooga, TN.

For more information call 706-965-3933.

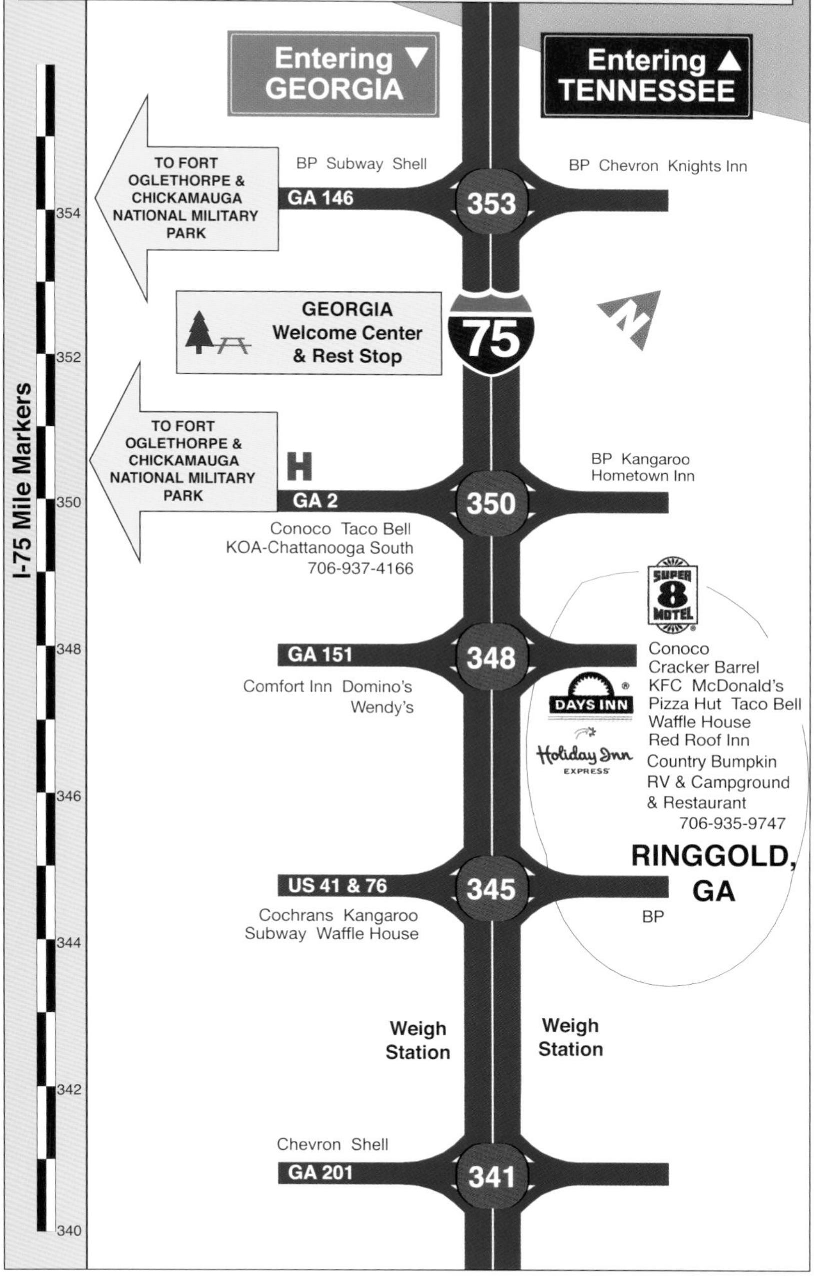

Entering GEORGIA
Entering TENNESSEE
I-75 Mile Markers
354
352
350
348
346
344
342
340
TO FORT OGLETHORPE & CHICKAMAUGA NATIONAL MILITARY PARK
BP Subway Shell
GA 146
353
BP Chevron Knights Inn
GEORGIA Welcome Center & Rest Stop
75
N
TO FORT OGLETHORPE & CHICKAMAUGA NATIONAL MILITARY PARK
H
GA 2
350
BP Kangaroo
Hometown Inn
Conoco Taco Bell
KOA-Chattanooga South
706-937-4166
GA 151
348
Comfort Inn Domino's
Wendy's
SUPER 8 MOTEL
Conoco
Cracker Barrel
KFC McDonald's
Pizza Hut Taco Bell
Waffle House
Red Roof Inn
Country Bumpkin
RV & Campground
& Restaurant
706-935-9747
DAYS INN
Holiday Inn EXPRESS
RINGGOLD, GA
US 41 & 76
345
Cochrans Kangaroo
Subway Waffle House
BP
Weigh Station
Weigh Station
Chevron Shell
GA 201
341

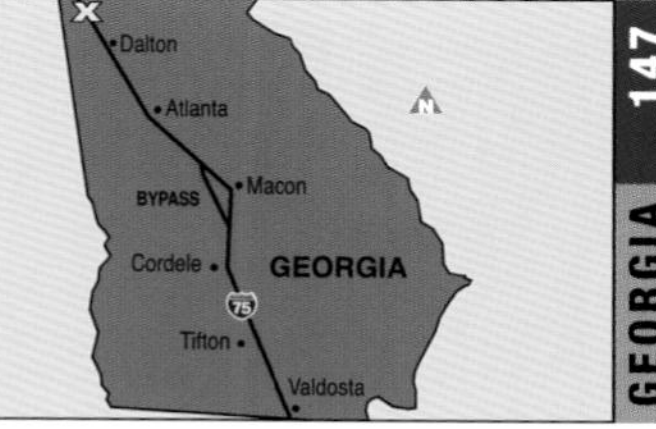

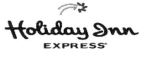

Dalton
GEORGIA

Dalton Area Convention & Visitors Bureau
PO Box 6177, Dalton, GA 30722
706-876-1620 or 800-331-3258 **www.visitdaltonga.com**

Dalton History

The Dalton settlement, carved from Cherokee lands in the mid 1800's, was strategically located on the W&A railroad which connected Atlanta and Chattanooga. It is a noted manufacturing town that once housed a Confederate hospital in the Civil War. Thousands of soldiers camped here in 1863-64 and in May of 1864, when the Atlanta campaign began, Sherman's troops met Johnston's Confederates along Rocky Face Ridge. You can study 32 Civil War markers that commemorate important history in the area at places like **Dug Gap Battle Park,** and the **Civil War Cemetery.**

DALTON: THE WORLD'S CARPET CAPITAL

In 1895 Catherine Evans Whitener turned her skill at creating legendary tufted bedspreads into a multi-million dollar business and led Dalton to become the Carpet and Textile Capital of the World. The industry grew very rapidly into machine manufactured spreads and rugs, and then into carpet.

The carpet industry based in Dalton produces over 40% of the world's carpet or 70% of the U.S. total. In fact, the manufacturer in Georgia with the largest number of employees is a carpet manufacturer. Over 1.5 billion square yards of carpet is produced yearly in the U.S. with a dollar value at mill level of $9.9 billion and $15 billion at retail.

Did you know that, of all carpet produced, 75% is residential and 25% is commercial. 40% of the total is replacement carpet.

Presently there are over 3.1 billion pounds of face fibers consumed per year, with nylon accounting for 63.6% of the total, polypropylene (olefin) 28.5%, polyester 7.5%, and wool 0.47%. The creation of nylon bulk continuous filament yarn precipitated Dalton's carpet industry. 75% of the yarn used by the carpet industry is produced and processed in Georgia.

Over 100 carpet outlets are located in the Dalton area. You will see the signs for them along your way. They are worth the visit if for nothing else than to see other visitors from all over pull up in trucks to take dozens of the carpets and other purchases home!

Attractions

Crown Gardens and Archives
Museum in the Crown Cotton Mill offices building, 1885, in a National Register Historic District. Exhibits from Dalton's textile industry with emphasis on the chenille bedspread industry which precipitated the carpet industry, Cherokee Indian history, artifacts of the Civil War, and Georgia poet Robert Loveman. Tues. to Sat. from 10 a.m.-5 p.m. At 715 Chattanooga Ave. 706-278-0217

Blunt House Built in 1848 as the home of the first mayor, postmaster and religious leader. On the National Register of Historic Places. Open by appointment. 506 S. Thornton Ave. 706-278-0217

Dalton Depot A Train Depot built in 1852 and in use until 1978, a National Historic Register site, now in use as an upscale restaurant/lounge. In the lobby is the original beginning point for surveying the city of Dalton. Groups welcome. 110 Depot Street in downtown Dalton. 706-226-3160

Dug Gap Battle Park Breastworks built by Civil War soldiers during the Atlanta campaign, 1864, open to the public during daylight hours. Free. W. Dug Gap Battle Mountain Road, 1/2 mile from I-75. 706-278-0217

Backroads and Battlefields For those who like to take the paths less traveled, drive the backroads and battlefields of northwest Georgia. Make Dalton your home base and explore the mountains, history, and unique treasures of the region. Pick up a guide at the Dalton Visitors Center. 800-331-3258 www.nwgabackroads.org

Prater's Mill An historic grist mill, built in 1855 with slave labor, on the National Register of Historic Places. Grounds open to the public during daylight hours. On Ga. Hwy. 2 about 1 mile east of Ga. 71 and 10 miles north of Dalton.

Special Events

Eastman Southeastern Gun & Knife Show. Jan. and Aug. 706-272-7676

Civil War Trade Show
Feb. 706-272-7676

Prater's Mill Country Fair Columbus Day weekend. Craftsfolk, food, entertainment, sales and demonstrations. 706-694-6455

Railroad Viewing Downtown Dalton is the only place outside of Atlanta where railfans can gather to observe the convergence of two different rail lines: CSX and Norfolk-Southern. The area by the 1914 Norfolk-Southern depot just off E. Morris St. is a great place to set up your camera and capture images of these modern machines. I-75, Exit 333, Walnut Avenue east, left on Thornton Ave., right on E. Morris St. 800-331-3258

Chickamauga National Military Park, Concert in the Park Saturday just before July 4th.

Vann House Days of Indian Heritage
July. Tour the only mansion built by a native American. 706-695-6060

Red Clay Park hosts the weekend **Cherokee Days of Recognition.** August. 800-331-3258

Historic Wink Theatre This 1941 "small-town version of the Fox Theatre in Atlanta" in downtown dalton offers a variety of entertainment just about every weekend of the year from concerts and theatrical productions to symphonies and classic old movies. I-75, Exit 333, Walnut Avenue east, left on Thornton Ave., right on Crawford St. 706-226-WINK

Creative Arts Guild hosts a Fall Festival of Arts and Crafts. Sept. 706-278-0168.

Annual Battle of Tunnel Hill, GA Reenactment. Civil War soldier demonstration. Sept. 706-673-5152

Hamilton House Museum (GCWHT)
The Hamilton House Museum is Dalton's oldest brick home and features exhibits devoted to Dalton's textile industry; Civil War materials and artifacts; Cherokee Indian history; and Georgia poet Robert Loveman, plus collections of local heritage groups. The Hamilton House is located at 701 Chattanooga Ave. and is open by appointment. Admission charged. Call the Whitfield Murray Historical Society at 706-278-0217.

County Fair Each October. Rides, livestock and exhibits. 706-278-1712

Chief Vann House sponsors a Moravian Christmas with traditional decorations and entertainment. December. 706-695-6060

Tunnel Hill Cannon Dalton, GA
Photo courtesy Dalton Area CVB

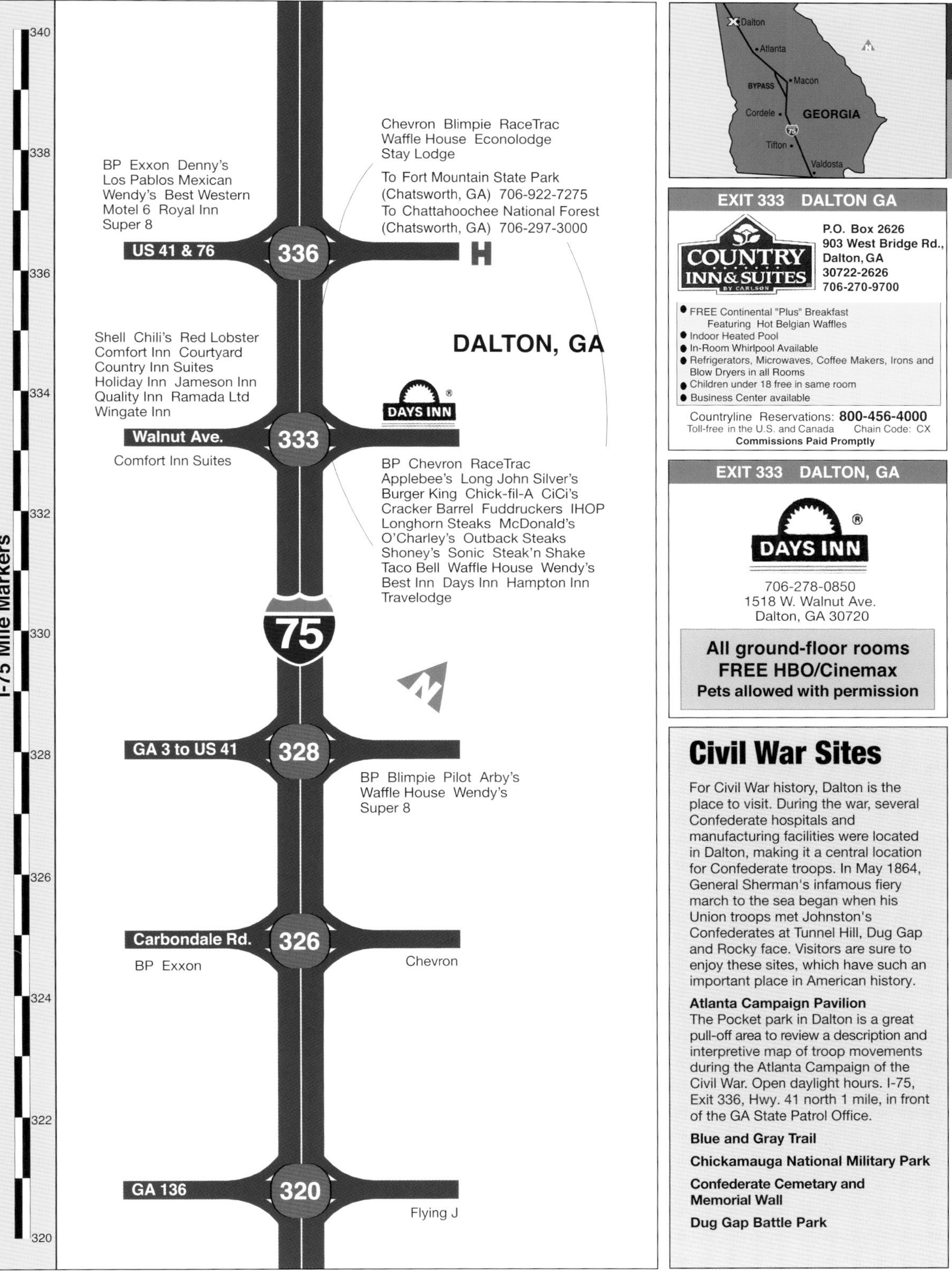
149
GEORGIA
Dalton
Atlanta
Macon
BYPASS
Cordele
GEORGIA
75
Tifton
Valdosta
I-75 Mile Markers
340
338
336
334
332
330
328
326
324
322
320
BP Exxon Denny's
Los Pablos Mexican
Wendy's Best Western
Motel 6 Royal Inn
Super 8
Chevron Blimpie RaceTrac
Waffle House Econolodge
Stay Lodge
To Fort Mountain State Park
(Chatsworth, GA) 706-922-7275
To Chattahoochee National Forest
(Chatsworth, GA) 706-297-3000
US 41 & 76
336
H
DALTON, GA
Shell Chili's Red Lobster
Comfort Inn Courtyard
Country Inn Suites
Holiday Inn Jameson Inn
Quality Inn Ramada Ltd
Wingate Inn
DAYS INN
Walnut Ave.
333
Comfort Inn Suites
BP Chevron RaceTrac
Applebee's Long John Silver's
Burger King Chick-fil-A CiCi's
Cracker Barrel Fuddruckers IHOP
Longhorn Steaks McDonald's
O'Charley's Outback Steaks
Shoney's Sonic Steak'n Shake
Taco Bell Waffle House Wendy's
Best Inn Days Inn Hampton Inn
Travelodge
75
N
GA 3 to US 41
328
BP Blimpie Pilot Arby's
Waffle House Wendy's
Super 8
Carbondale Rd.
326
BP Exxon
Chevron
GA 136
320
Flying J
EXIT 333 DALTON GA
COUNTRY INN & SUITES BY CARLSON
P.O. Box 2626
903 West Bridge Rd.,
Dalton, GA
30722-2626
706-270-9700
FREE Continental "Plus" Breakfast Featuring Hot Belgian Waffles
Indoor Heated Pool
In-Room Whirlpool Available
Refrigerators, Microwaves, Coffee Makers, Irons and Blow Dryers in all Rooms
Children under 18 free in same room
Business Center available
Countryline Reservations: 800-456-4000
Toll-free in the U.S. and Canada Chain Code: CX
Commissions Paid Promptly
EXIT 333 DALTON, GA
DAYS INN
706-278-0850
1518 W. Walnut Ave.
Dalton, GA 30720
All ground-floor rooms
FREE HBO/Cinemax
Pets allowed with permission
Civil War Sites
For Civil War history, Dalton is the place to visit. During the war, several Confederate hospitals and manufacturing facilities were located in Dalton, making it a central location for Confederate troops. In May 1864, General Sherman's infamous fiery march to the sea began when his Union troops met Johnston's Confederates at Tunnel Hill, Dug Gap and Rocky face. Visitors are sure to enjoy these sites, which have such an important place in American history.
Atlanta Campaign Pavilion
The Pocket park in Dalton is a great pull-off area to review a description and interpretive map of troop movements during the Atlanta Campaign of the Civil War. Open daylight hours. I-75, Exit 336, Hwy. 41 north 1 mile, in front of the GA State Patrol Office.
Blue and Gray Trail
Chickamauga National Military Park
Confederate Cemetery and Memorial Wall
Dug Gap Battle Park

Gordon County
Georgia

Gordon County Chamber of Commerce
300 South Wall Street, Calhoun, Georgia 30701
706-625-3200 or 1-800-887-3811 **www.gordonchamber.org**

American historians know **Gordon County.** The scene of the Native American people's most significant political act is located at New Echota, now a 198-acre restored Cherokee village open to the public. In 1819, New Echota (near Calhoun) was chosen as the Cherokee capital, and by 1828 the busy town had its own newspaper, *The Cherokee Phoenix,* written in their native language using the alphabet designed by the Cherokee **Sequoyah.** The town and farms prospered until the Cherokees were moved on the "Trail of Tears."

Gordon County was named for Gen. William Washington Gordon, a prominent State Senator and the first president of the Georgia Central Railroad. Calhoun, the county seat, once named Oothcaloga, was re-named for U.S. Vice-President J.C. Calhoun.

A little over a decade after the county's founding, Union and Confederate troops clashed in the 1864 Civil War *Battle of Resaca.* **The Confederate Cemetery** at Resaca is the resting place of hundreds who died during the 2-day battle. Each year, the Battle of Resaca is recreated on the site.

Oakleigh, the home of the **Gordon County Historical Society,** is another Civil War site. Here, in this lovely antebellum home, General Sherman made headquarters as he advanced through Georgia on his famous "March to the Sea." Several historical displays, including a collection of more than 1,500 dolls are housed here.

With the arrival of the cotton mills and the tufted textile industry, Gordon County became known for its roadside displays of tufted chenille bedspreads, robes, and mats. This cottage industry quickly developed into several highly profitable international textile and carpet companies. The **Calhoun Outlet Center** is at I-75 exit 312.

Salacoa Creek Park near Calhoun is a camping and fishing haven with 343 acres of scenic woodland and a lake. The **John's Mountain Wildlife Management Area** in the scenic **Chattahoochee National Forest** has sparkling trout streams, wooded hiking trails, many deer, a picnic area, and a scenic vista called "John's Mountain Overlook." There is tent camping in the **Pocket Recreation Area** in **Chattahoochee National Forest.**

Attractions

Overlook." There is tent camping in the **Pocket Recreation Area** in **Chattahoochee National Forest.**

1864 Battle of Resaca Re-enactment
Annual observance on the actual battlesite the 3rd weekend in May. On Saturday, re-enactors camp in the style of the day. Visitors are always encouraged to talk with the soldiers and tour the encampment. Enjoy various other activities and then on Sunday, the actual battle gets under way at 2:00 p.m. and ends with a memorial service. Exit 320 from I-75 and follow the signs to Battlefield.
706-625-3200 or 1-800-887-3811

Salacoa Creek Park
Swimming, boating, picnicking, well-equipped camping and fishing. Early Mar. to late Sept., 7 days a week. I-75 exit 315, east on GA Hwy. 156.
706-629-3490

Calhoun Outlet Center
Nearly 90 stores. Jan. to Feb. Mon. to Sat. 10 a.m.-7 p.m., Sun. 12 noon-6 p.m.; Mar. to Dec. Mon. to Sat. 10 a.m. -9 p.m., and Sun. 12 noon-6 p.m. I-75 exit 312. 455 Belwood Rd. Calhoun. 706-602-1300 or 1-800-866-5900.

Fields Ferry Golf Club, Calhoun
Championship 18-hole daily fee course designed by Arthur L. Davis. Year-round. I-75 exit 315, east on GA Hwy. 156. Turn left onto Hunts Gin Rd. and take the first fork to the right. Pro shop: 706-625-5666.

Pocket Recreation Area in the **Chattahoochee National Forest.**
Apr. to mid-Nov. I-75 exit 320, to GA Hwy 136 east from LaFayette for 13.5 miles. Turn right (south) at Villanow on Pocket Road for approximately 7 miles to the Recreation Area. 706-638-1085

New Echota State Historic Site
Film and museum exhibits, reconstructed print shop and other buildings. History of the Cherokee alphabet and newspaper. Year-round, Tues. to Sat. 9 a.m.-5 p.m., Sun. 2 p.m.-5:30 p.m. 1211 Chatsworth Hwy. N.E. Calhoun. 706-629-8151

Adairsville, GA Exit 306

Barnsley Gardens, Adairsville, GA
Courtesy Cartersville CVB

Barnsley Gardens Resort
(Bartow County)
A charming English-style village resort offers sumptuously appointed cottages, several fine dining venues, a full-service spa and intimate meeting spaces. Recreational highlights include a Jim Fazio-designed championship golf course, tennis courts, trout fishing pond, Orvis Shooting Grounds, Orvis Fly-Fishing school, Springbank Quail Preserve and hiking trails. Thirty acres of heirloom gardens are open to the public Mon-Sat 8am – 6pm, Sunday 8am-5pm. Gardens admission is $10 Adults, $8 Seniors (55 plus) and $5 children and students.

GEORGIA'S OFFICIAL SYMBOLS

Bird:	Brown Thrasher
Butterfly:	Tiger Swallowtail
Crop:	Peanuts
Fish:	Largemouth Bass
Flower:	Cherokee Rose
Fossil:	Shark's Tooth
Fruit:	Peach
Game Bird:	Bobwhite Quail
Gem:	Quartz
Insect:	Honeybee
Marine Mammal:	Right Whale
Reptile:	Gopher Tortoise
Tree:	Live Oak
Vegetable:	Vidalia Onion
Wildflower:	Azalea

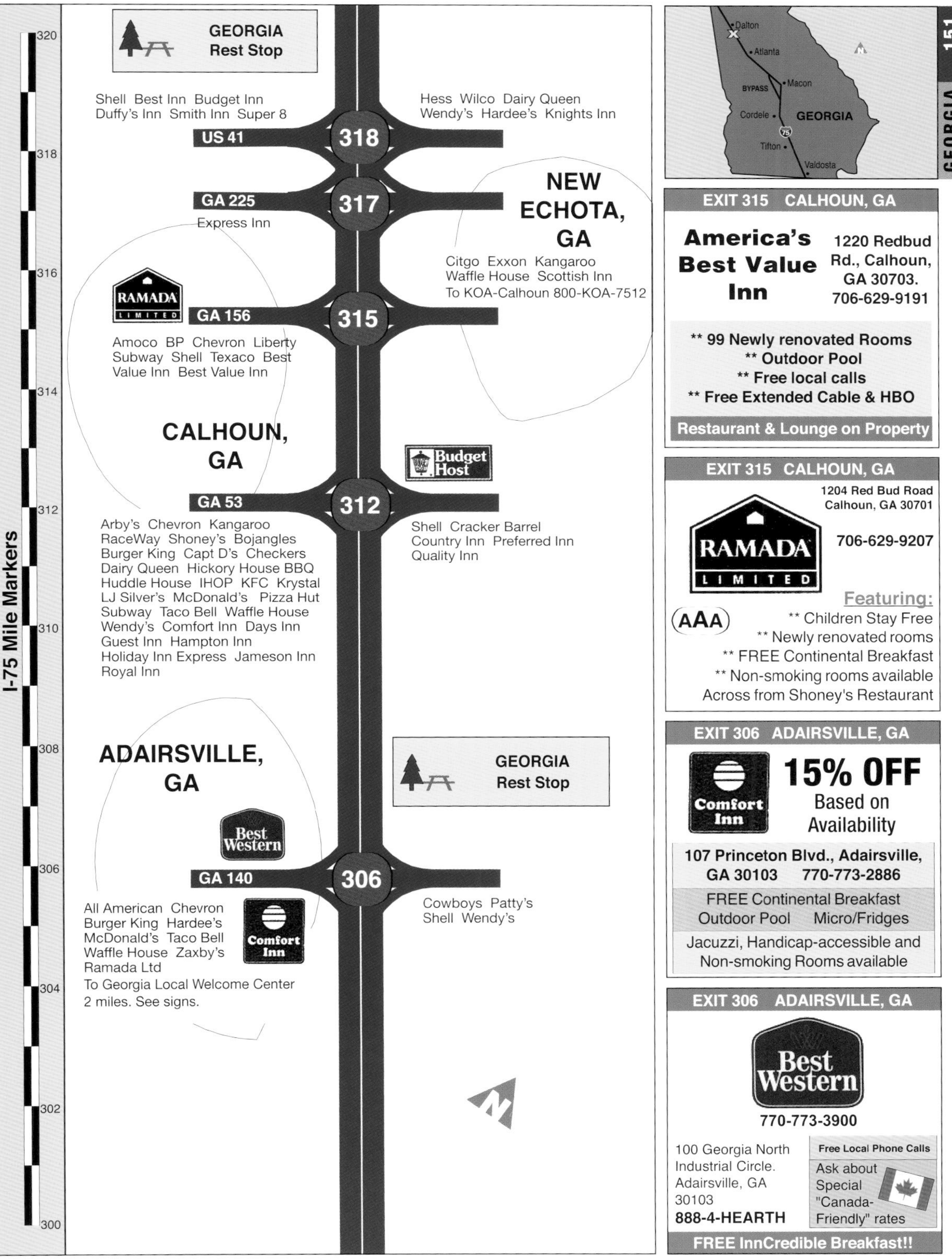
I-75 Mile Markers
320
318
316
314
312
310
308
306
304
302
300
GEORGIA
Rest Stop
Shell Best Inn Budget Inn
Duffy's Inn Smith Inn Super 8
Hess Wilco Dairy Queen
Wendy's Hardee's Knights Inn
US 41
318
GA 225
317
Express Inn
NEW
ECHOTA,
GA
Citgo Exxon Kangaroo
Waffle House Scottish Inn
To KOA-Calhoun 800-KOA-7512
RAMADA LIMITED
GA 156
315
Amoco BP Chevron Liberty
Subway Shell Texaco Best
Value Inn Best Value Inn
CALHOUN,
GA
Budget Host
GA 53
312
Arby's Chevron Kangaroo
RaceWay Shoney's Bojangles
Burger King Capt D's Checkers
Dairy Queen Hickory House BBQ
Huddle House IHOP KFC Krystal
LJ Silver's McDonald's Pizza Hut
Subway Taco Bell Waffle House
Wendy's Comfort Inn Days Inn
Guest Inn Hampton Inn
Holiday Inn Express Jameson Inn
Royal Inn
Shell Cracker Barrel
Country Inn Preferred Inn
Quality Inn
ADAIRSVILLE,
GA
GEORGIA
Rest Stop
Best Western
GA 140
306
All American Chevron
Burger King Hardee's
McDonald's Taco Bell
Waffle House Zaxby's
Ramada Ltd
To Georgia Local Welcome Center
2 miles. See signs.
Comfort Inn
Cowboys Patty's
Shell Wendy's
N
Dalton
Atlanta
Macon
BYPASS
Cordele
GEORGIA
75
Tifton
Valdosta

Cartersville
GEORGIA

Cartersville, Bartow Co. Convention & Visitors Bureau
P.O. Box 200397, Cartersville, Georgia 30120
770-387-1357 or 1-800-733-2280 **www.notatlanta.org**

ETOWAH INDIANS, *Cartersville, GA Photo/ text courtesy Georgia Dept. of Industry, Trade & Tourism*

History of the Cartersville Area

More than 450 years ago Cartersville was visited the Etowah Indian settlement along the Etowah River. Here, as in other Native American villages, the Spaniards engaged in violent confrontations with the villagers.

The Etowah Mounds site was inhabited by a tribe of the Mississippian culture between A.D. 700 and 1600. Re-creations of the site reveal that the chief priests governed their fortified villages from atop earthen mounds overlooking the central ceremonial plaza. We know that when a chief priest died, his home was destroyed and he was buried atop the mound. Then a large layer of dirt was added as a foundation for the new Chief's home.

The Natives' class structure was relative to the height of the Mounds on which they lived and to the placement of common huts nearby. In addition to operating within a class system, the Etowah enjoyed an intricate system of trading, were accomplished craftsmen, and practiced sophisticated religions.

A series of events led to the demise of the Etowah. De Soto's visit seemed to be an important factor. Aside from the skirmishes which killed many village inhabitants, the Natives had little immunity to the European diseases introduced to them.

In the years following the De Soto expedition, the Mississippian culture slowly began to fade from the Etowah River Valley. In addition to the European invasion, there is evidence of a tragic occurrence during a burial ceremony. Perhaps the Etowah people believed this would bring about great misfortune to their tribe, or perhaps misfortune actually occurred. Regardless, the accident may have led to the abandonment of the Etowah Burial Mounds. While no one knows for sure what happened to the Etowah tribe, the Creek Indians are believed to be their descendants.

The Creek Nation occupied the Etowah Valley territory in Cartersville until the late 1700s. The Creeks lived in large permanent towns or plazas which were very similar to the arrangements of the Etowah people. By 1650, the Cherokee Nation had migrated southward, occupying more than 40,000 square miles in the southern Appalachian. Cherokee and Creek lived peacefully as neighbors until the late 1700s when a great war occurred. This war resulted in the retreat of the Creek Nation to land south of the Chattahoochee River.

Around the 1800s, the Cherokee were at home in the Etowah Valley. They adopted a government patterned after the United States, dressed in European-style dress, and used European agriculture and home-building methods.

In 1828 the rumor that De Soto's gold was discovered in the North Georgia mountains induced a law, passed by the State of Georgia, which nullified the Cherokee Nation government. Thus began the removal of the Cherokee Nation to the area of Red Clay, Tennessee. In 1832, the U.S. Supreme Court ruled in favor of the Cherokee, but the ruling was never enforced by President Andrew Jackson. Following a controversial "Treaty of New Echota," the "Trail of Tears" was executed.

After the removal of the Cherokee, North Georgia was opened to settlers from the Georgia Land Lottery. Many wealthy landholders from coastal Georgia ventured north to stake their claim. Two Savannah residents, Sir Godfrey Barnsley and William Henry Stiles, brought fame, fortune and legends along with them. Their passage, made famous by Eugenia Price's Savannah Quartet, is one of great Southern intrigue.

Stiles came to Cassville in the early 1830s. After surveying the area, Stiles settled southwest of Cassville along the Etowah River. His letters home to Savannah encouraged family and friends to join him. One friend who did just that was Godfrey Barnsley. Barnsley and his wife, Julia Scarborough, created a beautiful estate.

The manor house, an Italianate-style mansion, was the centerpiece of the English-style gardens which boasted every known variety of rose.

Barnsley's estate evolved into a magnificent showplace with tapestries, paintings, Venetian glass, Italian marble and Persian silks. Notable Barnsley family heirlooms included a clock that belonged to Marie Antionette and a table which had belonged to an emperor of Brazil. See photo on page 168. Despite the death of Barnsley's wife, the estate flourished until the the Civil War. Barnsley's primary business was shipping and he turned his ships over to the Confederacy.

The Barnsley empire slowly declined. The tornado in 1906 removed the roof and the grounds were left unattended and the manor house endured in ruins. In 1988, the remaining acreage of the Barnsley estate was purchased by Prince Hubertus Fugger of Germany. The Prince and his family instantly fell in love with their property and hired renowned horticulturalists to restore the lifeless gardens. No longer owned by Prince Fugger's family, the estate has become the Barnsley Gardens Resort. This luxury resort offers 87 guestrooms in 33 English-style cottages, a Jim Fazio-designed championship golf course, a full service spa and fine dining.

The Civil War and General Sherman's wrath changed the south and especially Bartow County, however, numerous Civil War sites within Bartow remain as they were in 1864.

Today, over 450 years after De Soto embarked in search of gold, great treasures can be found at the Tellus: Northwest Georgia Science Museum. This museum (a favorite of mine) is an innovative show place of minerals, fossils and gemstones found locally and across the world. Visitors can buy locally produced quality jewelery, fossils and other gifts from the earth at the Jewelry Gift Shop. I-75 exit 293. See page 160 for more info about the Tellus: Northwest Georgia Science Museum.

Dalton
Atlanta
Macon
BYPASS
Cordele
GEORGIA
75
Tifton
Valdosta

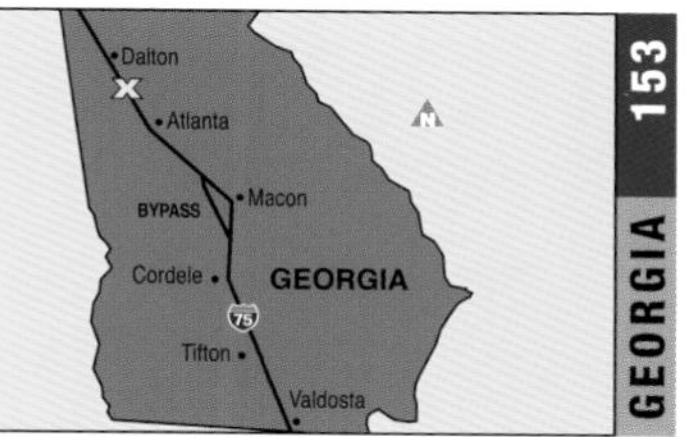

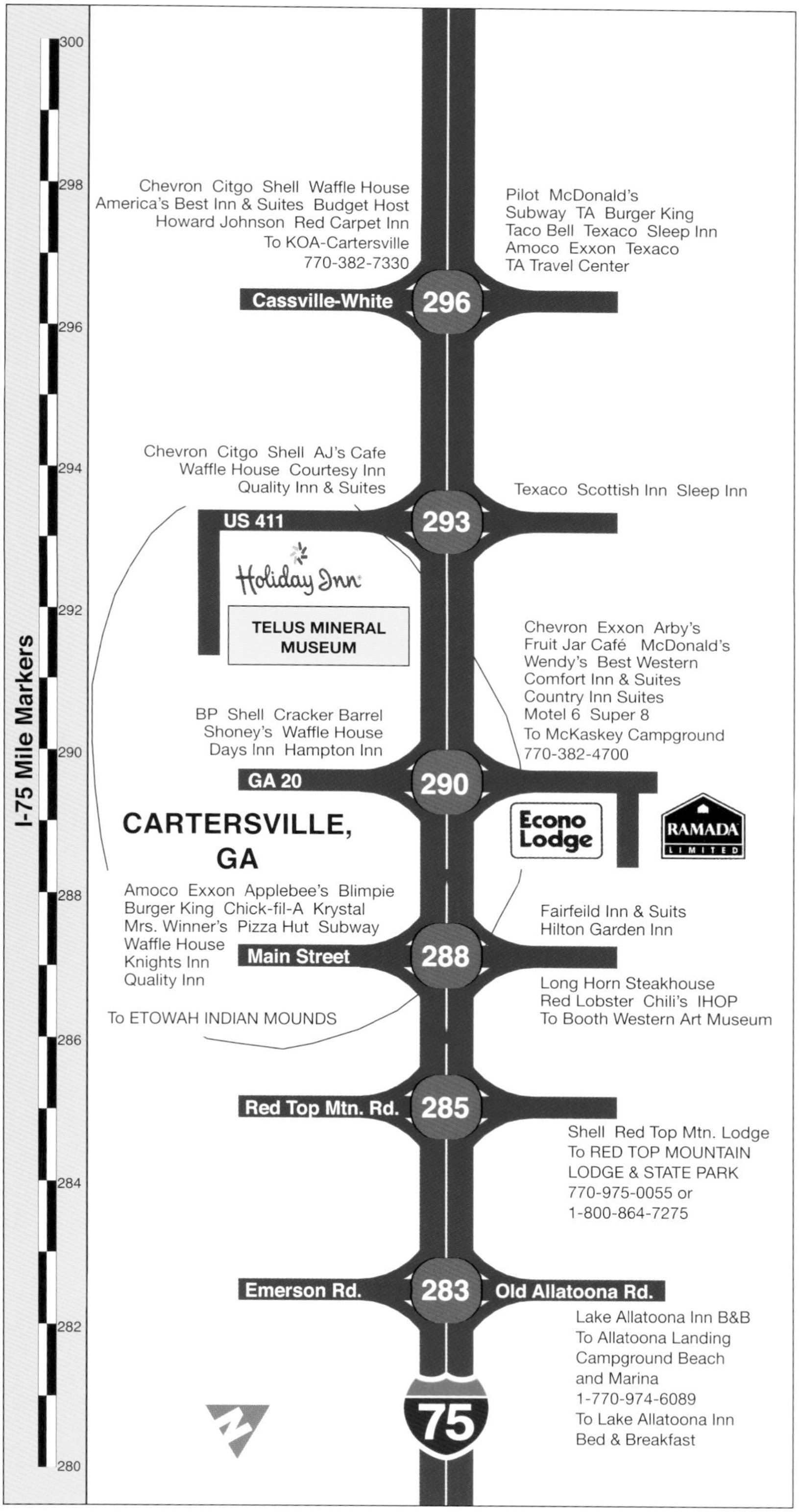

I-75 Mile Markers
300
298
296
294
292
290
288
286
284
282
280
Chevron Citgo Shell Waffle House
America's Best Inn & Suites Budget Host
Howard Johnson Red Carpet Inn
To KOA-Cartersville
770-382-7330
Pilot McDonald's
Subway TA Burger King
Taco Bell Texaco Sleep Inn
Amoco Exxon Texaco
TA Travel Center
Cassville-White
296
Chevron Citgo Shell AJ's Cafe
Waffle House Courtesy Inn
Quality Inn & Suites
Texaco Scottish Inn Sleep Inn
US 411
293
Holiday Inn
TELUS MINERAL MUSEUM
Chevron Exxon Arby's
Fruit Jar Café McDonald's
Wendy's Best Western
Comfort Inn & Suites
Country Inn Suites
Motel 6 Super 8
To McKaskey Campground
770-382-4700
BP Shell Cracker Barrel
Shoney's Waffle House
Days Inn Hampton Inn
GA 20
290
CARTERSVILLE, GA
Econo Lodge
RAMADA LIMITED
Amoco Exxon Applebee's Blimpie
Burger King Chick-fil-A Krystal
Mrs. Winner's Pizza Hut Subway
Waffle House
Knights Inn
Quality Inn
Fairfeild Inn & Suits
Hilton Garden Inn
Main Street
288
Long Horn Steakhouse
Red Lobster Chili's IHOP
To Booth Western Art Museum
To ETOWAH INDIAN MOUNDS
Red Top Mtn. Rd.
285
Shell Red Top Mtn. Lodge
To RED TOP MOUNTAIN
LODGE & STATE PARK
770-975-0055 or
1-800-864-7275
Emerson Rd.
283
Old Allatoona Rd.
Lake Allatoona Inn B&B
To Allatoona Landing
Campground Beach
and Marina
1-770-974-6089
To Lake Allatoona Inn
Bed & Breakfast
75

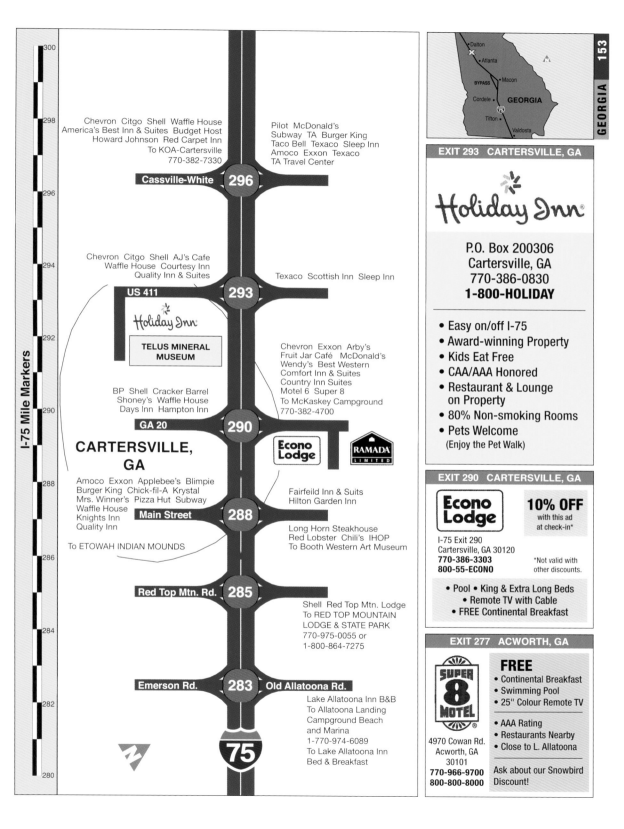

Cartersville
GEORGIA

Cartersville, Bartow Co. Convention & Visitors Bureau
P.O. Box 200397, Cartersville, Georgia 30120
770-387-1357 or 1-800-733-2280 **www.notatlanta.org**

TRIVIA

The site of Georgia's first Supreme Court decision was Cassville, in 1846.

Bartow County was the home of Rebecca Latimer Felton, the first woman to serve as U.S. Senator (1922).

Bartow County was the birthplace of the Confederate Memorial Day.

Bartow County is famous as the origin of the Lottie Moon Christmas Offering for Baptist Foreign Missions.

Bartow County is also home to these notables: Gangster Pretty Boy Floyd, Baseball great Rudy York, authors Bill Arp and Corra Harris and former Governor Joe Frank Harris.

Tellus: Northwest Georgia Science Museum

On July 31, 2007 the finest mineral museum in the southeastern US – the Weinman Mineral Museum – closed its doors to make way for a magnificent new museum that occupies more than 125,000 sq. ft. and features galleries devoted to minerals, fossils, transportation technology and hands-on science experiments. The 120-seat digital Planetarium hosts stargazing events and other family events staged throughout the day. The Weinman Mineral Gallery has one of the most comprehensive collections in the Southeast. The Fossil Gallery features a 40 ft. Tyrannosaurus rex. Collins Family "My Big Back Yard" has hand-on science exhibits. Science in motion relives major developments in science and technology. Open daily 10am – 5pm. Adults $12, Seniors $10, Children $8. Add planetarium show $3. Take exit 293, left on Tellus Drive beside the Holiday Inn. 100 Tellus Dr., Cartersville, GA 30120 770-606-5700 www.tellusmuseum.org

Attractions

ETOWAH INDIAN MOUNDS STATE HISTORIC SITE
Blue skies shine over the Etowah River Valley which was home to thousands of Native Americans from 900 to 1500 A.D. Today, the historic site consists of ceremonial mounds, an impressive interpretive museum and an archaeological site. Visit the Etowah Indian Mounds State Historic Site near Cartersville. 813 Indian Mounds Rd. 770-387-3747

WILDLIFE VIEWING AREAS at RED TOP MOUNTAIN STATE PARK
One of Georgia s most popular state parks, Red Top Mountain is located on Lake Allatoona on the I-75. Aside from an abundance of native deer and other wildlife, the park offers camping, swimming, boating, hiking and tennis. Lodging and dining is available in the 33-room lodge. Enjoy a meal in the relaxing **Mountain Cove Restaurant.** Reserve one of 18 guest cabins. 781 Red Top Mountain Rd. Cartersville. 770-975-0055

SUNSET ON LAKE ALLATOONA
This 12,000-acre lake has swimming, fishing, boating, hiking and beautiful sunsets. Public facilities and services on **Lake Allatoona** include marinas, boat rentals, lodging, restaurants, camping and picnic sites. The **Visitors Center** located at the **Lake Allatoona Dam and Overlook** has regional history, indigenous wildlife and details the production of electricity. The lake is maintained by the U.S. Army Corps of Engineers. 678-721-6700

WORLD'S FIRST COCA-COLA OUTDOOR WALL ADVERTISEMENT
The Coca-Cola sign on the east wall of Young Brothers Pharmacy in downtown Cartersville was painted in 1894 and is a welcome symbol to visitors from across the globe. It is authenticated by the Coca-Cola Company as the first outdoor painted wall sign for the world-renowned soft drink. You can get quite an interesting photo!
Young Brother's Coca-Cola Sign.
2 West Main St., Cartersville.
770-382-4010

Etowah Indian Mounds State Historic Site,
Cartersville, GA Courtesy Cartersville-Bartow County CVB

Cowboys and Indians in Georgia

is a travel package centered in Cartersville, Georgia, the home of the magnificent Booth Western Art Museum and gateway to Georgia's Chieftains Trail. Travel the trail and discover Southeastern Native American Heritage from the pre-historic Etowah Mounds at cartersville through to the beginning of the Trail of Tears.
1-800-733-2280
www.cowboysandindiansingeorgia.com

NOBLE HILL-WHEELER MEMORIAL FOUNDATION
African-American history museum and cultural center housed in the 1923 school that was the first constructed in northwest Georgia specifically for the education of black children.
Near Cassville, GA. 770-382-3392

BOOTH WESTERN ART MUSEUM
This museum displays a permanent collection of contemporary Western American Art. More than 200 paintings and sculptures, by more than 100 of the finest 20th contury Western artists, depict the history and legends of the Old West, as well as the modern day cowboy and Native Peoples. Additional galleries include: Civil War, Presidential, Western Illustration and Western Movie posters. Opened August 23, 2003. 501 Museum Drive, Cartersville 770-387-1300 www.boothmuseum.org.

BARTOW HISTORY CENTER
A site on Northwest Georgia's Blue & Gray Trail, this museum aims to preserve the cultural, industrial & agricultural heritage of Bartow County and NW Georgia. Workshops, farmsteads and mercantile archives from pioneer settlements to early 20th century will delight visitors. Mon-Sat. 10am-5pm. Thur till 8pm. $3 adults, $2.50 Seniors, $2 students. Exit 288, south 2 miles, right on Wall St. 13 N. Wall St., Cartersville, GA 30120. 777-382-3818 www.bartowhistorycenter.org

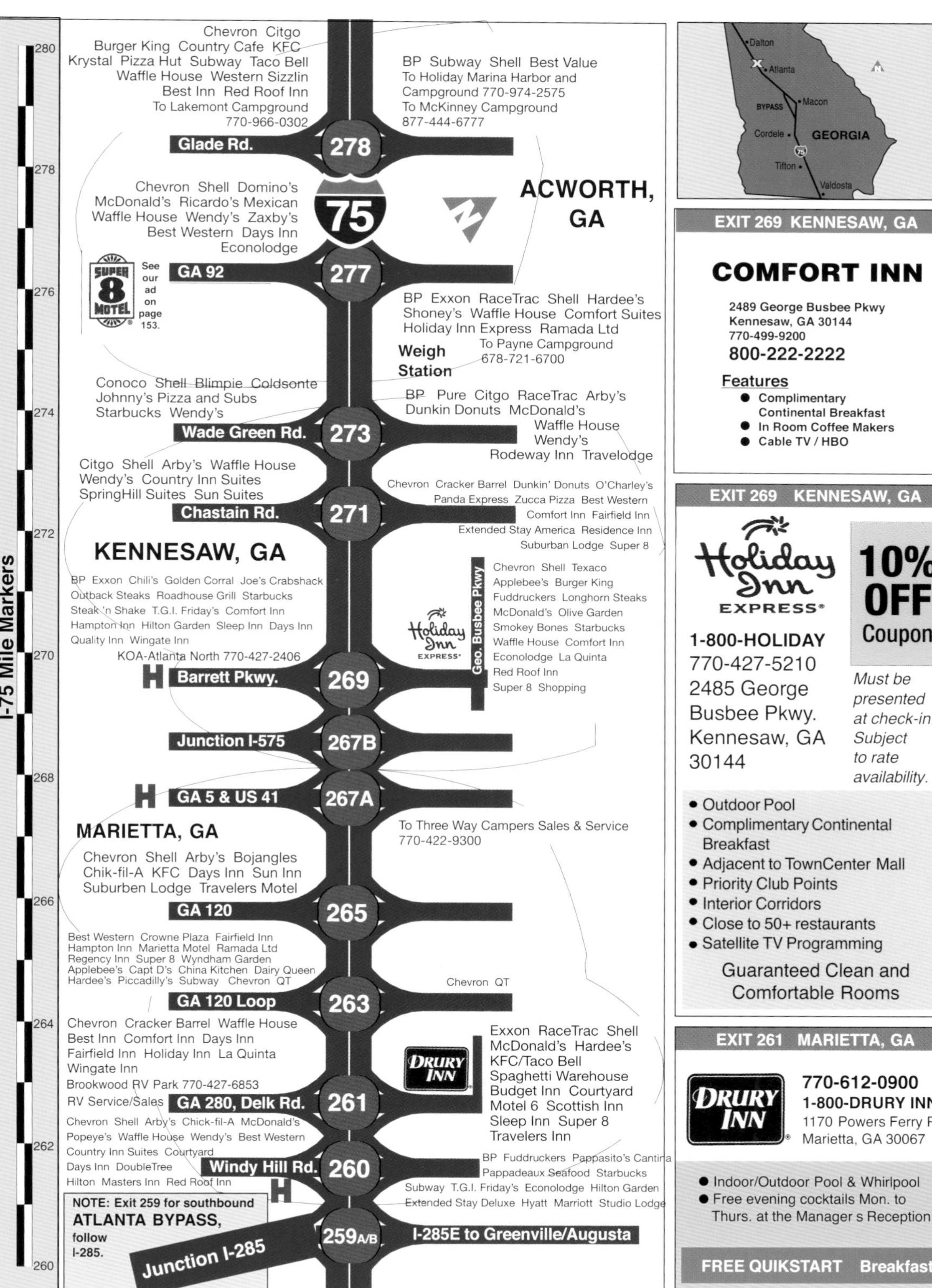
I-75 Mile Markers
280
278
276
274
272
270
268
266
264
262
260
Chevron Citgo
Burger King Country Cafe KFC
Krystal Pizza Hut Subway Taco Bell
Waffle House Western Sizzlin
Best Inn Red Roof Inn
To Lakemont Campground
770-966-0302
BP Subway Shell Best Value
To Holiday Marina Harbor and
Campground 770-974-2575
To McKinney Campground
877-444-6777
Glade Rd.
278
75
ACWORTH, GA
Chevron Shell Domino's
McDonald's Ricardo's Mexican
Waffle House Wendy's Zaxby's
Best Western Days Inn
Econolodge
SUPER 8 MOTEL
See our ad on page 153.
GA 92
277
BP Exxon RaceTrac Shell Hardee's
Shoney's Waffle House Comfort Suites
Holiday Inn Express Ramada Ltd
To Payne Campground
678-721-6700
Weigh Station
Conoco Shell Blimpie Coldsonte
Johnny's Pizza and Subs
Starbucks Wendy's
BP Pure Citgo RaceTrac Arby's
Dunkin Donuts McDonald's
Waffle House
Wendy's
Rodeway Inn Travelodge
Wade Green Rd.
273
Citgo Shell Arby's Waffle House
Wendy's Country Inn Suites
SpringHill Suites Sun Suites
Chevron Cracker Barrel Dunkin' Donuts O'Charley's
Panda Express Zucca Pizza Best Western
Comfort Inn Fairfield Inn
Extended Stay America Residence Inn
Suburban Lodge Super 8
Chastain Rd.
271
KENNESAW, GA
BP Exxon Chili's Golden Corral Joe's Crabshack
Outback Steaks Roadhouse Grill Starbucks
Steak 'n Shake T.G.I. Friday's Comfort Inn
Hampton Inn Hilton Garden Sleep Inn Days Inn
Quality Inn Wingate Inn
KOA-Atlanta North 770-427-2406
Geo. Busbee Pkwy
Chevron Shell Texaco
Applebee's Burger King
Fuddruckers Longhorn Steaks
McDonald's Olive Garden
Smokey Bones Starbucks
Waffle House Comfort Inn
Econolodge La Quinta
Red Roof Inn
Super 8 Shopping
Holiday Inn EXPRESS
H
Barrett Pkwy.
269
Junction I-575
267B
H
GA 5 & US 41
267A
To Three Way Campers Sales & Service
770-422-9300
MARIETTA, GA
Chevron Shell Arby's Bojangles
Chik-fil-A KFC Days Inn Sun Inn
Suburben Lodge Travelers Motel
GA 120
265
Best Western Crowne Plaza Fairfield Inn
Hampton Inn Marietta Motel Ramada Ltd
Regency Inn Super 8 Wyndham Garden
Applebee's Capt D's China Kitchen Dairy Queen
Hardee's Piccadilly's Subway Chevron QT
Chevron QT
GA 120 Loop
263
Chevron Cracker Barrel Waffle House
Best Inn Comfort Inn Days Inn
Fairfield Inn Holiday Inn La Quinta
Wingate Inn
Brookwood RV Park 770-427-6853
RV Service/Sales
Exxon RaceTrac Shell
McDonald's Hardee's
KFC/Taco Bell
Spaghetti Warehouse
Budget Inn Courtyard
Motel 6 Scottish Inn
Sleep Inn Super 8
Travelers Inn
DRURY INN
GA 280, Delk Rd.
261
Chevron Shell Arby's Chick-fil-A McDonald's
Popeye's Waffle House Wendy's Best Western
Country Inn Suites Courtyard
Days Inn DoubleTree
Hilton Masters Inn Red Roof Inn
Windy Hill Rd.
260
BP Fuddruckers Pappasito's Cantina
Pappadeaux Seafood Starbucks
Subway T.G.I. Friday's Econolodge Hilton Garden
Extended Stay Deluxe Hyatt Marriott Studio Lodge
H
NOTE: Exit 259 for southbound
ATLANTA BYPASS,
follow
I-285.
Junction I-285
259A/B
I-285E to Greenville/Augusta
Dalton
Atlanta
BYPASS
Macon
Cordele
GEORGIA
75
Tifton
Valdosta
EXIT 269 KENNESAW, GA
COMFORT INN
2489 George Busbee Pkwy
Kennesaw, GA 30144
770-499-9200
800-222-2222
Features
Complimentary Continental Breakfast
In Room Coffee Makers
Cable TV / HBO
EXIT 269 KENNESAW, GA
Holiday Inn EXPRESS
10% OFF Coupon
1-800-HOLIDAY
770-427-5210
2485 George Busbee Pkwy.
Kennesaw, GA 30144
Must be presented at check-in. Subject to rate availability.
Outdoor Pool
Complimentary Continental Breakfast
Adjacent to TownCenter Mall
Priority Club Points
Interior Corridors
Close to 50+ restaurants
Satellite TV Programming
Guaranteed Clean and Comfortable Rooms
EXIT 261 MARIETTA, GA
DRURY INN
770-612-0900
1-800-DRURY INN
1170 Powers Ferry Pl.
Marietta, GA 30067
Indoor/Outdoor Pool & Whirlpool
Free evening cocktails Mon. to Thurs. at the Manager s Reception
FREE QUIKSTART Breakfast

Atlanta
GEORGIA

Atlanta Convention & Visitors Bureau
Suite 100 - 233 Peachtree Street NE., Atlanta, Georgia 30303
404-521-6600 or 1-800-ATLANTA **www.atlanta.net**

Atlanta: From Railroad Hub To International City

Like its symbol, the phoenix of Egyptian mythology, Atlanta rose from the ashes of the Civil War to become the mecca of the new South, and is today an emerging international city. The first people to live in Georgia were prehistoric Indians called "Mound Builders." They were followed by the **Cherokee Indians**, who settled in the north, and the Creek, who populated the south.

The state was named after Great Britain's King George II. It was the last of the 13 original U.S. colonies. Atlanta began taking shape in the mid-1830s, when the Western & Atlanta Railroad selected the site as the southern end of its tracks. The town was called Terminus until 1843, when it was renamed Marthasville, after the daughter of Gov. Wilson Lumpkin. Two years later it was renamed **Atlanta**, a name suggested by the Atlanta-Pacific Railroad's founder.

By the outbreak of the Civil War, Atlanta was a major railroad hub, supply depot and manufacturing center. In 1864, Union General Sherman burned every business and more than two-thirds of the city's homes during his infamous "**March to the Sea**." Atlanta's resurgence began soon after. Within four years, the Georgia capital was moved to the city from Milledgeville and the drive to attract new business was under way. One man, newspaper editor H. W. Grady, earned much of the credit for coaxing the city toward a new economic agenda.

In the meantime, colleges and universities opened, telephones were introduced to the area and trolleys began to roll. In 1895, the well-attended Cotton States and International Exposition in Peidmont Park showed visitors and residents alike that Atlanta was headed in a new direction and was braced for the 20th century.

By the late 1920s, a downtown business sector, ringed by residential districts, had taken shape. At the same time, Atlanta Alderman William B. Hartsfield campaigned to turn a vacant racetrack into an airport. Today, **Hartsfield Atlanta International Airport** is among the world's busiest runways and feeds the city's vital service business. While the city continued its economic surge, it became known as the cradle of the Civil Rights Movement. Atlanta pre-empted much of the strife associated with the 1950s and 1960s by taking a lead in strengthening minority rights. The city s strongest identification with the movement was through native son, Dr. Martin Luther King Jr., but many others played important roles. In 1963, Atlanta Mayor Ivan Allen Jr. was the only Southern mayor to testify before Congress supporting the pending Civil Rights Bill. When Dr. King was slain in 1968, it was Mayor Allen who pleaded for calm. His request was met with anguished, but peaceful, mourning by the city.

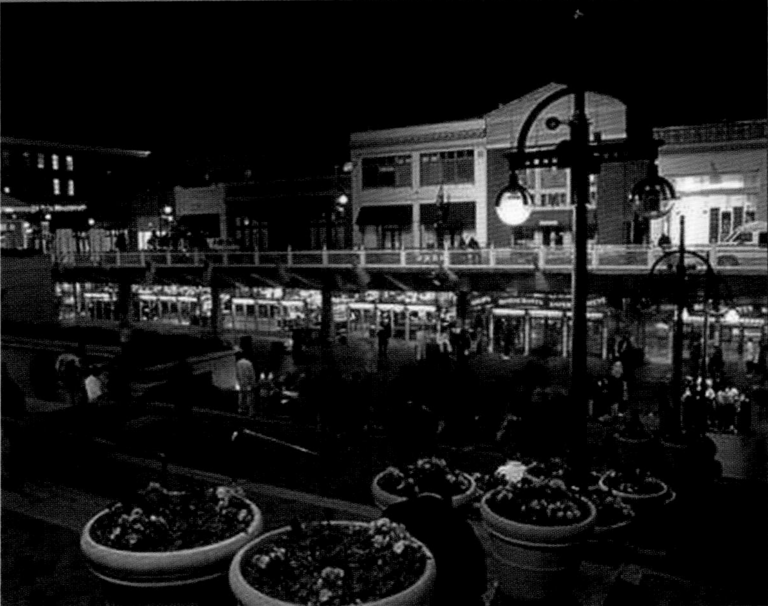

Underground Atlanta *is the 4-block area where the city of Atlanta originated in 1837 as a railroad terminus. By the late 1800s, the tracks presented a traffic hazard, so viaducts were built above the railyard and, gradually, the area bridged over was "lost." In the late 1960s, its gas-lit, cobblestoned streets were rediscovered, restored, and opened as a recreation of the Gay 90s with shops, restaurants, lounges and live entertainment. Photo/text courtesy Atlanta Convention & Visitors Bureau*

In 1965, the city built **Atlanta-Fulton Stadium,** despite the fact that it had not yet signed any teams to play there. In short order, however, baseball's **Braves** moved here from Milwaukee and the National Football League awarded Atlanta the **Falcons** expansion team. Did you know that Hank Aaron's historic home run number 715 occurred at Atlanta-Fulton stadium in April of 1974?

Much has been accomplished in the past 25 years to elevate Atlanta to world-class status. An efficient public transportation system, **MARTA**, was put in place, Underground Atlanta was added to the entertainment map, the Georgia World Congress Center made the city a convention hub and the Georgia Dome was built in 1992. Atlanta hosted the 1988 Democratic National Convention and the 1994 Super Bowl XXVIII and was awarded the 1996 Centennial Olympic Games and the 2002 NCAA Basketball Final Four.

Georgia's State Capitals:

Savannah (1733-1786)
Augusta (1786-1795)
Louisville (1796-1806)
Milledgeville (1807-1868)
Atlanta (1868-present)

Atlanta Convention & Visitors Bureau
Suite 100 - 233 Peachtree Street NE., Atlanta, Georgia 30303
404-521-6600 or 1-800-ATLANTA **www.atlanta.net**

ATLANTA TIMELINE

Atlanta has grown from a small railroad town in the 1800s to a thriving metropolis that hosted the world during the Centennial Olympic Games of 1996. The following timeline will take you from 1836, when Atlanta was formed as a railroad terminus through to the present.

Martin Luther King Memorial. *Dr. Martin Luther King was born in Atlanta on January 15, 1929. Thousands visit the gravesite each year to pay their respects. The Martin Luther King Memorial is just one of the interesting attractions of the Martin Luther King Historic District of Atlanta. Photo/text: Atlanta Convention & Visitor's Bureau*

1837. Area chosen for a new railroad terminus connecting Georgia and the Tennessee River.

1843. "Terminus" was renamed "Marthasville" in honor of Martha Lumpkin, the daughter of Georgia Governor Wilson Lumpkin.

1845. Marthasville was renamed Atlanta, a feminine form of "Atlantic," suggested by the founder of the Atlantic-Pacific Railroad.

1864. During the Civil War, Union General William T. Sherman burned Atlanta to the ground on his infamous "March to the Sea."

1868. Atlanta becomes the GA capital.

1877. Telephones were introduced in Atlanta.

1883. The Atlanta Journal was founded.

1886. Atlanta chosen for site of the Georgia Institute of Technology. Henry Grady made his "New South" speech in New York City, calling for the North's reconciliation with the South and economic diversification and industrialization of the region. A local drug store, Joseph Jacob's Pharmacy, began selling a new headache/hangover tonic called Coca-Cola invented by John S. Pemberton.

1889. Joel Hurt established **Inman Park** (the city's first planned suburb) and Atlanta's 1st electric trolley line, which ran to Inman Park.

1891. Asa Candler paid $2,300 to own Coca-Cola.

1892. Joel Hurt opened the Equitable Building, the city's first skyscraper.

1895. The **Cotton States and International Exposition** was held in Piedmont Park.

1898. The *Cyclorama* Civil War painting was acquired and displayed in Grant Park.

1917. Fire leaves 10,000 Atlantans homeless.

1919. E. Woodruff paid $25 M for Coca-Cola.

1922. Atlanta's first local radio stations, WSB and WGST, began broadcasting to Atlantans.

1926. William B. Hartsfield selected the site of Candler Field for the Atlanta airport. The Atlanta Historical Society was founded by W. McElreath. The High Museum of Art opened.

1930. Atlantan Bobby Jones won first "Grand Slam" in golf, the British Open, the British Amateur, the U.S. Open and the U.S. Amateur.

1935. Techwood Homes, dedicated by President Franklin D. Roosevelt, became Atlanta's pioneer housing project.

1936. Mitchell's *Gone with the Wind* is published.

1939. The movie *Gone With the Wind* made its world premiere in Atlanta.

1941. Delta moved its headquarters to Atlanta.

1948. Atlanta launched the city's first television station, WSB-TV.

1952. Through its "Plan of Improvement," the city of Atlanta incorporated surrounding areas, increasing population from 330,000 to 430,000.

1958. The **Temple of the Hebrew Benevolent Congregation** was bombed by what was believed to be racial extremists.

1959. Atlanta Constitution Editor Ralph McGill won a Pulitzer Prize for editorials on the Temple bombing.

1960. Elbert Tuttle was appointed Chief Judge of the 5th Circuit Court of Appeals. Under his leadership, the court sped up the desegregation process in Atlanta and the region by rapidly overturning court orders used as delay tactics.

1961. Ivan Allen Jr. defeated segregationist Lester Maddox in the mayoral election, and Atlanta s public schools were desegregated.

1961. A modern terminal was completed at Hartsfield Airport, and William B. Hartsfield described Atlanta as the "city too busy to hate."

1962. 106 Atlanta Art Association members and relatives died in a plane crash. Richard Rich led a $14 million fundraising drive to build the **Atlanta Memorial Arts Center,** now the Woodruff Arts Center, in their memory.

1964. Martin Luther King Jr. won the Nobel Peace Prize.

1965. The $18-million Atlanta-Fulton County Stadium was built in 364 days "on land we didn't own, with money we didn't have, and for teams we had not signed," said Ivan Allen. That same year the **Braves** moved from Milwaukee and the **Atlanta Falcons** became a new NFL expansion team.

1968. Dr. Martin Luther King Jr. was assassinated in Memphis, Tennessee.

1969. The opening of **Underground Atlanta** put Atlanta on the entertainment and social map.

1970. MARTA (Metropolitan Atlanta Rapid Transit Authority) purchased the Atlanta Transit System and began extending its routes, and engineering a rapid rail system.

1974. Atlanta Brave Hank Aaron hit his 715th home run, breaking Babe Ruth's major league homerun record.

1976. Georgia built the **Georgia World Congress Center,** the second-largest convention center in the world.

1988. Atlanta hosted the Democratic National Convention.

1989. Following a $142-million renovation, Underground Atlanta reopened.

1990. The National Football League announced Atlanta as host city for the Super Bowl XXVIII in 1994. In Tokyo, the International Olympic Committee named Atlanta as host for the 1996 Centennial Olympic Games.

1992. Atlanta opened the **Georgia Dome,** the largest cable-supported stadium in the world. The **Atlanta Braves** repeated the 1991 baseball season by winning the National League pennant and competing in the World Series against the **Toronto Blue Jays.**

Atlanta
GEORGIA

Atlanta Convention & Visitors Bureau
Suite 100 - 233 Peachtree Street NE., Atlanta, Georgia 30303
404-521-6600 or 1-800-ATLANTA **www.atlanta.net**

Auburn Avenue Research Library

The $10 million **Auburn Avenue Research Library on African-American Culture and History** opened in 1994. It is the nation's only other public library devoted to black culture.

The mission of the library is to collect, preserve and disseminate information on the African-American experience, with a special regional focus centered on Atlanta, the cradle of the civil rights movement.

The four-story, red-brick facility, located at Auburn Avenue and Courtland Street, holds 20,000 reference books, 50,000 pieces of microfilm and microfiche, 1,000 audio and video cassettes and 2,000 periodical volumes as well as photographs, manuscripts, letters and even a baseball autographed by Negro league stars. Along with its next-door neighbor, the **APEX Museum,** the library is seen as the western gateway into the **Sweet Auburn District** from downtown.

DID YOU KNOW?

THE GEORGIA WORLD CONGRESS CENTER

Recognized as the most heavily booked convention facility in the nation for major conventions, trade shows, consumer shows and corporate meetings.

The **Georgia World Congress Center** is booked at 82% of its practical maximum capacity years in advance.

It has events scheduled into 2019.

Since opening in 1976, the **Center** has hosted more than 14.8 million visitors. About half of these visitors came from other states.

By hosting many large trade shows as well as being the site of a growing number of international trade shows, the **Center** is considered one of the premier convention facilities in the world.

The Northside Drive entrance is large enough to hold the Titanic!

ATLANTA BYPASS (I-285)

Thanks goes to **Mary Ellen Barry** of Peterborough, Ontario, for making the excellent suggestion that we include the Atlanta Bypass in this edition of the Exitguide. A best bet during rush hour, the less hectic Atlanta Bypass route I-285 can also experience traffic problems. Tune into 750 AM for the latest traffic reports for Atlanta.

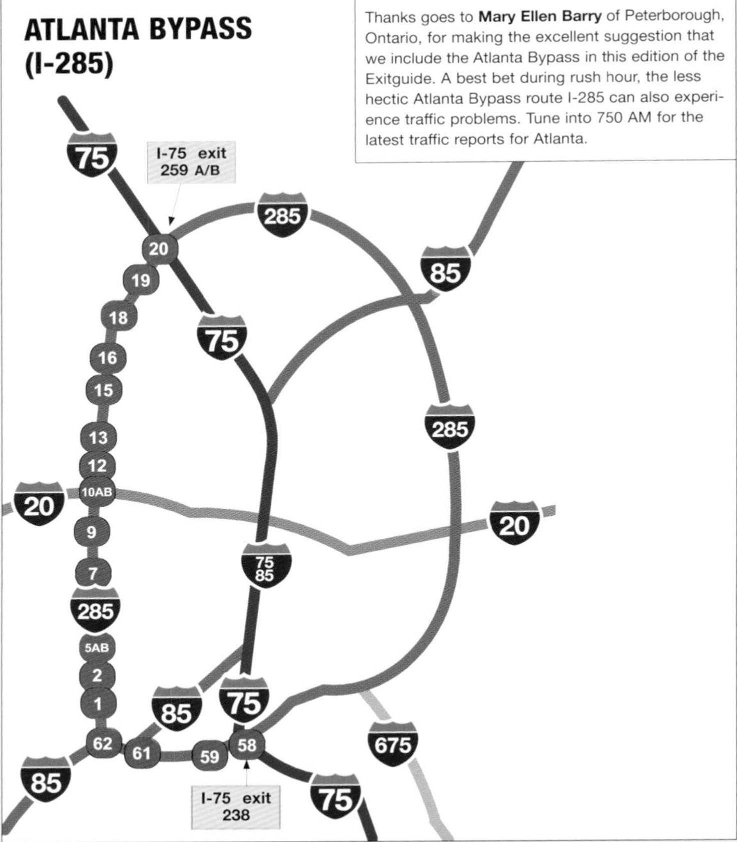

Atlanta Skyline. *Downtown Atlanta has more than 10,000 hotel rooms and more than one million square feet of exhibit space. Some of downtown Atlanta's tallest buildings include the cylindrical Westin Peachtree Plaza Hotel, the stair-shaped Georgia Pacific building, the twin tower One-ninety-one Peachtree building and the gold-domed Georgia State Capitol. Kevin C. Rose, courtesy of the Atlanta Convention & Visitors Bureau*

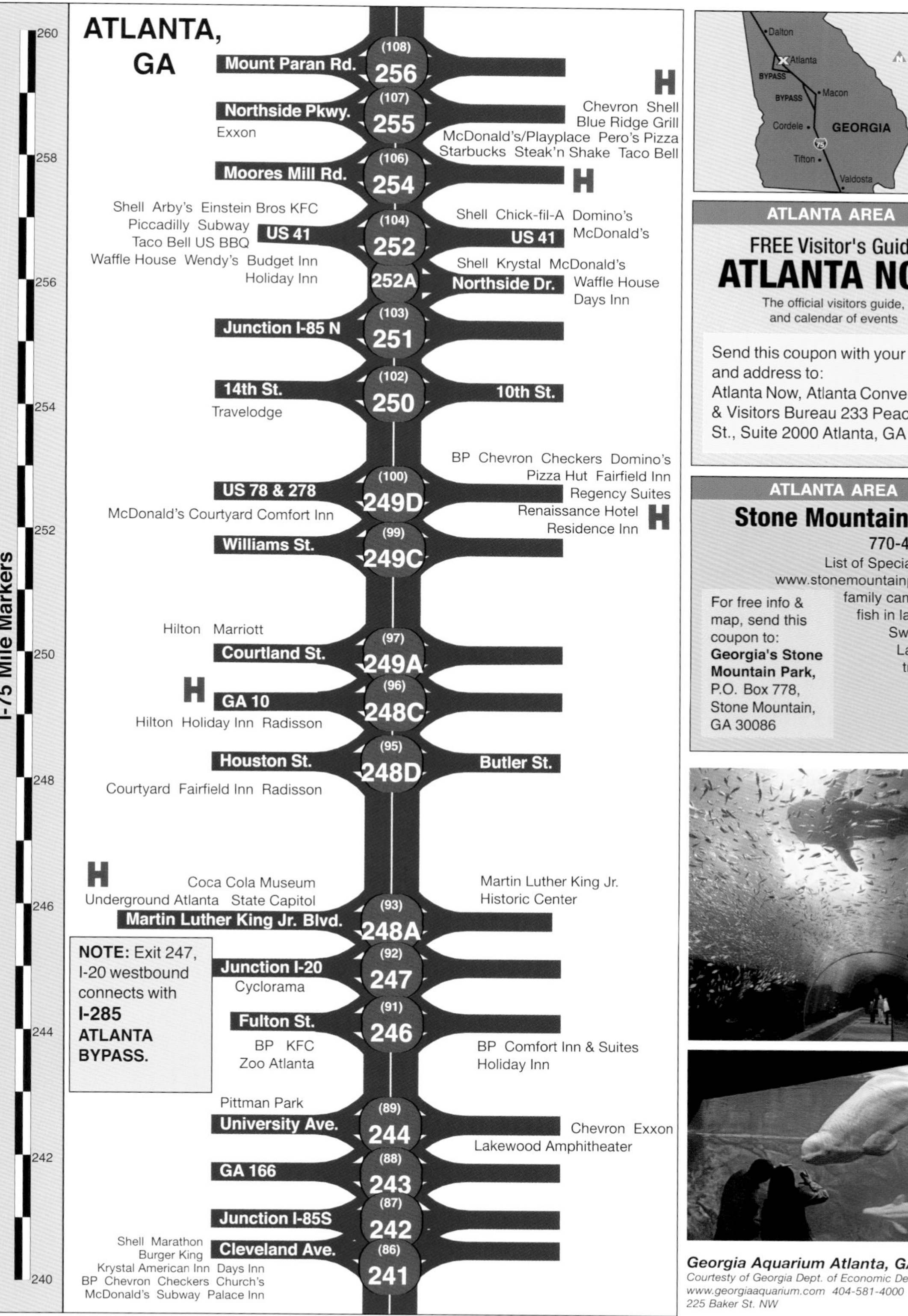
ATLANTA, GA
I-75 Mile Markers
260
258
256
254
252
250
248
246
244
242
240
Mount Paran Rd.
(108)
256
Northside Pkwy.
(107)
255
Exxon
Chevron Shell
Blue Ridge Grill
McDonald's/Playplace Pero's Pizza
Starbucks Steak'n Shake Taco Bell
Moores Mill Rd.
(106)
254
Shell Arby's Einstein Bros KFC
Piccadilly Subway
Taco Bell US BBQ
Waffle House Wendy's Budget Inn
Holiday Inn
US 41
(104)
252
US 41
Shell Chick-fil-A Domino's
McDonald's
252A
Northside Dr.
Shell Krystal McDonald's
Waffle House
Days Inn
Junction I-85 N
(103)
251
14th St.
(102)
250
10th St.
Travelodge
BP Chevron Checkers Domino's
Pizza Hut Fairfield Inn
Regency Suites
Renaissance Hotel
Residence Inn
US 78 & 278
(100)
249D
McDonald's Courtyard Comfort Inn
Williams St.
(99)
249C
Hilton Marriott
Courtland St.
(97)
249A
GA 10
(96)
248C
Hilton Holiday Inn Radisson
Houston St.
(95)
248D
Butler St.
Courtyard Fairfield Inn Radisson
Coca Cola Museum
Underground Atlanta State Capitol
Martin Luther King Jr.
Historic Center
Martin Luther King Jr. Blvd.
(93)
248A
NOTE: Exit 247, I-20 westbound connects with I-285 ATLANTA BYPASS.
Junction I-20
Cyclorama
(92)
247
Fulton St.
(91)
246
BP KFC
Zoo Atlanta
BP Comfort Inn & Suites
Holiday Inn
Pittman Park
University Ave.
(89)
244
Chevron Exxon
Lakewood Amphitheater
GA 166
(88)
243
Junction I-85S
(87)
242
Shell Marathon
Burger King
Krystal American Inn Days Inn
BP Chevron Checkers Church's
McDonald's Subway Palace Inn
Cleveland Ave.
(86)
241
Dalton
Atlanta
BYPASS
BYPASS
Macon
Cordele
GEORGIA
Tifton
Valdosta

Georgia Aquarium Atlanta, GA
Courtesty of Georgia Dept. of Economic Development
www.georgiaaquarium.com 404-581-4000
225 Baker St. NW

Atlanta
GEORGIA

Atlanta Convention & Visitors Bureau
Suite 100 - 233 Peachtree Street NE., Atlanta, Georgia 30303
404-521-6600 or 1-800-ATLANTA **www.atlanta.net**

The Inn at Eagles Landing
South of the airport off I-75. Small luxury hotel in a country club setting offering fine dining, golf, tennis, swimming, meeting and function room facility. Secluded and behind security gates. Very exclusive. 425 Country Club Drive, Stockbridge, GA 30281. 770-389-3118
jpc@eagleslanding.com

Arrowhead Campground
Closest campground (10 miles) to Downtown Atlanta adjacent to Six Flags off I-20. Offers all the amenities to make your stay memorable. Swimming pool, laundry, store, propane, hot showers, game room, basketball court, full hook-ups, 30-50 Amp, tent and group areas. Stream on site. MARTA bus pick-up 150 yard walk from camp. 7400 Six Flags Drive, S.W., Austell, GA 30168
1-800-631-8956

KOA Atlanta North
Year round camping. Full service pool, 30-50 amp service game room, meeting rooms, 230 sites-Monthly sites available. 2000 Old U.S. 41 Highway, Kennesaw, GA 30152
770-427-2406

WHO HAS WORLDWIDE HEADQUARTERS IN ATLANTA?

The American Cancer Society
Boys' and Girls' Club
C.A.R.E.
Coca-Cola
Coca-Cola Enterprises
Delta Air Lines, Inc.
Equifax, Inc.
Georgia-Pacific
Hayes Microcomputer Products, Inc.
Holiday Inn Worldwide
Home Depot, Inc.
National Center for Disease Control
Ritz-Carlton Hotel Company
Turner Broadcasting
United Parcel Services

Attractions In The Atlantic Area

American Adventures Amusement Park
Georgia's only amusement park designed specifically for families with kids, features rides appropriate for toddlers and more thrilling rides for older children. Enjoy the mini-golf and go-cart racing. **Foam Factory** is open daily all year, and the rides, golf and go-cart racing is open weekends and holidays in off-season (Oct. to Apr.) and daily late Spring to Sept. Kids $14.99 for all attractions; Foam Factory only $7.99; parents $2.99; toddlers $4.99. Exit 265 off I-75, 20 minutes from downtown Atlanta. 250 Cobb Pkwy., N. Marietta, GA 30062. 770-428-5217

Atlanta Brewing Company
Tour Atlanta's oldest and most beloved microbrewery. Observe how beer is produced and sample all of the brewery's craft beers. Taste tours are offered every Friday at 5:30 p.m. At 1219 Williams St., NW Atlanta, GA 30309. www.atlantabrewing.com

CNN Center
Newly renovated CNN Center is the global headquarters of Turner Broadcasting System and home to CNN's international news networks. Visitors are invited to take the daily **CNN Studio Tours,** 9 a.m.-6 p.m., (adults $8, senior citizens $6, children $5, children under 6 not permitted). Open daily, the **CNN Center complex** houses various restaurants and specialty stores including the **Braves Clubhouse Store** and **The Turner Store,** the **Omni Hotel at CNN Center,** a multi-screen movie theatre, and a **U.S. Postal Store.** The CNN Center is located across from Centennial Olympic Park. One CNN Center, Atlanta, GA 30303. 404-827-2300 www.cnn.com
turnerproperties@turner.com

Georgia's Stone Mountain Park
See photo on page 149. P.O. Box 778, Stone Mountain, GA 30086. 770-498-5690 or 800-401-2407
proberts@stonemountainpark.com

Thunder Road USA/Georgia Racing Hall of Fame
Immersive theaters and state-of-the-art interactives commemorate the people who define motorsports. Open in the fall of 2000. 415 Highway 53, East Dawsonville, GA 30534.
706-216-RACE trusa@alltel.net

World of Coca-Cola
The story of Coca-Cola told through exhibits, memorabilia, classic radio and television advertisements, a fanciful representation of the bottling process and a futuristic soda fountain. Shop from the largest selection of Coca-Cola merchandise in the "Everything Coca-Cola" store. Allow at least an hour for a self guided tour. Located adjacent to **Underground Atlanta.** Open Mon. to Sat., 9 a.m.-5 p.m., Sun. noon-6 p.m. (June, July, Aug. open Mon. to Sat. 9 a.m.-6 p.m.; Sun. 11 a.m.-6 p.m.) Closed Easter, Thanksgiving, Dec. 25, and 5 p.m. on Dec. 31. Adults $6, Seniors $4, Children $3 and children under 5 free with an adult admission. 55 Martin Luther King, Jr. Drive, Atlanta, GA 30303. 404-676-5151
abutler@na.ko.com

Zoo Atlanta
See the Giant Pandas of Chengdu, gorillas, orangutans, tigers, lions, giraffes, elephants, birds and more in natural habitats. Open Mon. to Sun. 9:30 a.m.-4:30 p.m. (5:30 p.m. on weekends). Closed on Thanksgiving, Dec. 25 and 31. Admissions: Adults $12, seniors $10, children ages 3-11 $8, children under 3 free. Free parking. 800 Cherokee Ave., Atlanta, GA 30315. 404-624-5600
phyllis.hooks@mindspring.com

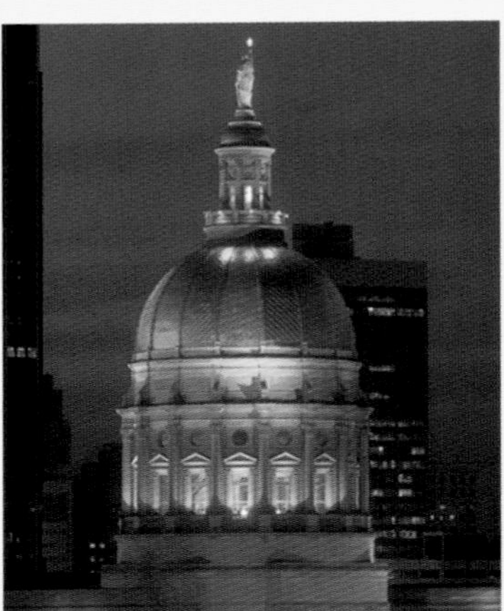

Georgia State Capitol Building.
Built in 1889, the Georgia State Capitol is topped with gold mined from Dahlonega, GA, the site of the nation's first gold rush. It houses the Georgia House of Representatives and the Senate, a Hall of Flags, a Hall of Fame, and the Georgia State Museum of Science and Industry. Tours of the building daily.

Kevin C. Rose, courtesy Atlanta Visitors and Convention Bureau

Atlanta
GEORGIA

Atlanta Convention & Visitors Bureau
Suite 100 - 233 Peachtree Street NE., Atlanta, Georgia 30303
404-521-6600 or 1-800-ATLANTA **www.atlanta.net**

Special Events In The Atlanta Area

Southeastern Flower Show
Late Feb. Atlanta Expo Center, 3650 Jonesboro Rd., SE Atlanta, GA 30354 (I-285 exit 40) 404-361-2000

Atlanta Journal-Constitution Auto Show Sponsored by Atlanta Journal and Constitution and Reed Expo. At the Georgia World Congress Ctr., 285 International Blvd., Atlanta, GA 30313. Mid-Mar. 404-223-4000 or www.ajcautoshow.com

Atlanta Dogwood Festival
Over fifty local and national performances on three stages, Rock Climbing, Kite Flying, National Disc-Dog Championship, Hot Air Balloons and much more. Early Apr. Piedmont Park, Atlanta, Ga 30309. 404-817-6851

Lasershow Spectacular
Enjoy colorful light shows on the mountain as images create dramatic stories, historic tales and comical characters, complemented with music that echoes throughout the park. Sat. nights, early Apr. to late Oct. $7/vehicle. Georgia's Stone Mountain Park, Hwy. 78, Stone Mountain, GA 30086. 770-498-5600 www.stonemountainpark.com

Music Midtown
An Atlanta festival music extravaganza, early May. Dozens of concerts on several stages with big name performers. 404-249-6400 www.musicmidtown.com

Civil War Encampment, Spring Campaign Features over 100 living history interpreters, authentic clothing, offerings of what life was like, musket and artillery firing; a guided tour to the award-winning exhibition "Turning Point: The American Civil War." Mid-July. Atlanta History Center, 130 West Paces Ferry Rd. NW, Atlanta, GA 30305. 404-814-4000 Late April Civil war full-scale encampment of both Union and Confederate soldiers staged near Antebellum Plantation, Stone Mountain Park. 770-498-5690 www.stonemountainpark.com

Folk Fest: Meet the Artists Party
The World's Greatest Folk Art Show & Sale, hosting 85 galleries with dealers from around the nation specializing in self-taught art, Folk Art, Outsider Art, and Southern Folk Pot. 15/adult. Mid-Aug. North Atlanta Trade Center, 1700 Jeurgens Ct., Norcross, GA 30093. 770-279-9853

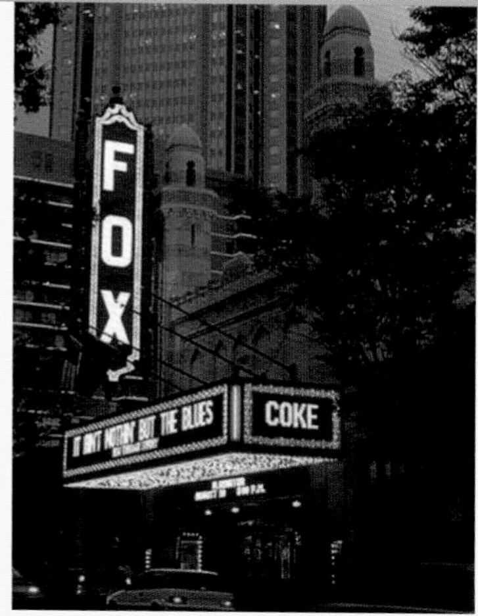

The Fox Theatre, *Atlanta, GA.*
On the National Register of Historic Places, the 1929 Moorish/Egyptian/Art Deco theater hosts broadway musicals, concerts, a summer movie series and other live shows. The Fox Theatre seats 4,518 and houses the nation's second-largest organ. Kevin C. Rose, courtesy Atlanta Visitors and Convention Bureau

Atlanta Jazz Festival
A week of jazz around Memorial Day. Different venues, huge stars. Many free events. Artists' booths and food. 404-0817-6851 www.atlantafestivals.com

National Black Arts Festival
Late July to Early Aug. Piedmont Park, Atlanta, Ga 30309. 404-817-6851 or 404-730-0177 www.nbaf.org info@piedmontpark.org

World Bodybuilding Championships
Mid-Sept. Atlanta Expo Center, 3650 Jonesboro Rd., SE Atlanta, GA 30354. (I-285 exit 40) 404-361-2000

Atlanta Motor Speedway
info@atlantamotorspeedway.com

NOPI Nationals
Motorsports Supershow. Mid-Sept. Atlanta Motor Speedway, 1500 Highway 19-41, P.O. Box 500, Hampton, GA 30228. 770-946-4211

A Tour of Southern Ghosts
Storytellers in authentic costumes tell stories by candlelight, romancing the past with folk tales of Civil War and Revolutionary ghosts. Evenings, late Oct. to Oct. 31. $7/vehicle. Georgia's Stone Mountain Park, Hwy. 78, Stone Mountain, GA 30086. 770-498-5600

In ATLANTA, You'll Find...

- 130 retail centers
- 57 public golf courses
- 54 public parks
- 100 streets with the name "Peachtree"
- The largest toll-free telephone dialing area in the world
- The largest suburban office park in the U.S.: **Perimeter Center** (3.5 million square feet of office/retail space, 400 acres)
- The 14th largest mall in the nation: **Mall of Georgia**
- The world s largest bas-relief sculpture and the world s largest exposed mass of granite: **Georgia's Stone Mountain Park**
- The largest federal regional concentration outside of Washington, D.C.
- The largest 10K race in the world: the **Peachtree Road Race** with 55,000 runners
- The second-largest theater organ in the nation: the **Fox Theatre**
- The oldest ballet company in the nation: the **Atlanta Ballet** (1929)
- The tallest hotel in the Western hemisphere: the **Westin Peachtree Plaza** (73 stories, 723 feet tall)
- The tallest building in the Southeast: **NationsBank Plaza** (55 stories and 1,023 feet)

Annual Scottish Festival & Scottish Games
Gathering of the clans at Stone Mountain. 2 days in mid-Oct. 770-498-5690

Clayton County
GEORGIA

Clayton County Convention & Visitors Bureau
104 N. Main St., Jonesboro, Georgia 30236
770-478-4800 or 1-800-662-7829 **www.visitscarlett.com**

History

Clayton calls itself "Atlanta's True South." They invite you to take their self-guided driving tour where you will learn the history of the strategic **Civil War Battle of Jonesboro:** "Four railway lines came together in Atlanta, linking the city to the entire Confederacy. In the July heat, Union troops had captured or damaged three of the railways. The fourth and final Confederate supply line ran right down the middle of a town called Jonesboro"

You can also step back in time at **Stately Oaks Plantation** and relive the legacy of *Gone With The Wind.* Of course, the real *Tara* is only a Hollywood studio set, but Clayton County was used by Margaret Mitchell as a historical foundation for her novel as she drew from the stories handed down to her by her Clayton County relatives, the Fitzgeralds. Did you know that *Gone With the Wind* has sold over 30 million copies?

Jonesboro Historic District is a nearly 300-acre area listed on the National Register of Historic Places. It contains almost all of the significant structures still surviving in and around the town of Jonesboro, including the **1867 Depot,** the **pre-Civil War downtown,** a **1922 Baptist Church,** an early 1800's **Methodist Superannuate Home,** the **1898 Courthouse/Masonic Lodge,** the **1869 Jail,** the **Confederate Cemetery** and more than a dozen beautiful southern mansions and plantations. Historical markers commemorate the significant places.

Spivey Hall

At Clayton State College, in nearby Morrow, you will find Spivey Hall, Atlanta's premier music recital facility. It is said to be built to acoustical perfection. The Albert Schweitzer Memorial Organ has thrilled audiences without fail. This 400-seat hall plays host to the world's finest musicians and vocalists, classical and jazz, during the Sept. to May season.

During the summer, jazz and pop performances are scheduled. More information below under Cultural Attractions.

"Spivey Hall is to music what light is to painting." ~ Robert Shaw

Clayton County Attractions

1867 Jonesboro Depot Welcome Center
Pick up a copy of the Historic Jonesboro Driving Tour map at the Jonesboro Depot Welcome Center. The Welcome Center also has Georgia tourism information, gifts and souvenirs. Open Monday-Friday 8:30 a.m.-5:30 p.m. and Saturday 10 a.m.-4 p.m. 104 North Main Street, Jonesboro. 770-478-4800 or 800-662-7829

Patrick R. Cleburne Confederate Memorial Cemetery
Here is the final resting place of 600 to 1000 Confederate soldiers who fell during the Battle of Jonesboro. The cemetery was laid out in the shape of the Confederate battle flag cemetery and is maintained by local members of the United Daughters of the Confederacy. It was the defeat of the Confederate forces at Jonesboro that resulted in the capture of Atlanta by General W.T. Sherman. Open daily. McDonough and Johnson Sts. Jonesboro.

Stately Oaks Historical Home and **Plantation Community** Built in 1839, this Greek Revival plantation home has its authentic outbuildings. Costumed guides will show you through **Stately Oaks,** the **Bethel One-Room Schoolhouse, Juddy's Country Store** and the original **Log Kitchen.** Entirely authentic, this plantation complex hosts several special events. Mon. to Sat. 10 a.m. -4 p.m. 100 Carriage Dr. at Jodeco Rd., Jonesboro. 770-473-0197

Atlanta Motor Speedway The biggest motorsports event in GA. 160,000 people attend NASCAR Winston Cup racing in May and Sept. Speedway gift shop. Behind-the-scenes Speedway tour: Mon. to Sat. 9 a.m.-5 p.m., Sun. 1 p.m.-5 p.m. Tara Blvd., Hampton. 770-946-4211 or for tours: 770-707-7970

Clayton County International Park
Sports and recreation water park! Site of the 1996 Olympic Beach Volleyball. A white sand beach rings a sparkling spring-fed lake, with a kiddie pool, Daily, seasonal, 10 a.m.-8 p.m. GA Highway 138, Jonesboro. 770-473-5425

Blalock Reservoir and Lake Shamrock
Unspoiled setting, 260-acre Blalock Reservoir is fully stocked with at least 6 generations of bream, channel cat and bass. Swimming. Apr. to Sept. 1, Wed. to Sun. Daily or season permits available at the gate. Lake Shamrock is a kids' fishin' hole (an adult must accompany child). No permit required for children under 12.

Newman Wetlands
With trails and an interpretive center, the **Newman Wetlands Center** was created to demonstrate the importance of wetlands in our environment. A wetlands video prepares guests to experience a 0.6-mile boardwalk trail through a created wetlands environment with over 200 species of birds, tree frogs, turtles, snakes, deer, mink, beaver and other such inhabitants. 2755 Freeman Rd. Hampton. 770-603-5606

Reynolds Nature Preserve
130 acres of unspoiled woodlands and wetlands. Interpretive center, piers, pavilions and bridges along 4 miles of foot-paths laid among ponds, streams and hardwood forest. Trails run in half-mile loops and bring hikers back to their starting point. **The Georgia Native Plants Trail** is wheelchair accessible and has braille trail markers. Daily, 8:30 a.m.-dusk. The interpretive center is open Mon. to Fri. 8:30 a.m.-5:30 p.m. Free. 5665 Reynolds Rd., Morrow. 770-961-9257

Atlanta State Farmers' Market
The largest open-air produce farmer's market in the U.S. and the 2nd-largest in the world. Daily. Exit 237. Forest Park. 404-675-1782

Jonesboro Antiques & Collectibles Shops
The Jonesboro Antique Shoppe, Simple Pleasures, Sweet Memories, and Trifles & Treasures stores have gift ideas and great finds. North and South Main Streets.

Southlake Mall I-75 exit 233, Morrow.

Road to Tara Museum
Experience an extraordinary collection of Gone With the Wind movie and book memorabilia. The museum is located in Jonesboro's historic train depot and displays various GWTW costumes, rare books and manuscripts, authentic theatre posters and much more. Mon-Fri, 8:30am – 5:30pm and Sat. 10am-4pm. 770-478-4800 800-662-7829

Southern Belles and Whistles Tour
Learn about the citizens of Jonesboro, its brave men and Southern Belles and the important role that Jonesboro and the railroad played in the Civil war. This air-conditioned mini-bus tour departs at 11am and 1pm from The Road to Tara Museum. Admission includes 70-minute tour, Road to Tara Museum and Old Jail/History Center. 770-478-4800 or 800-662-7829.

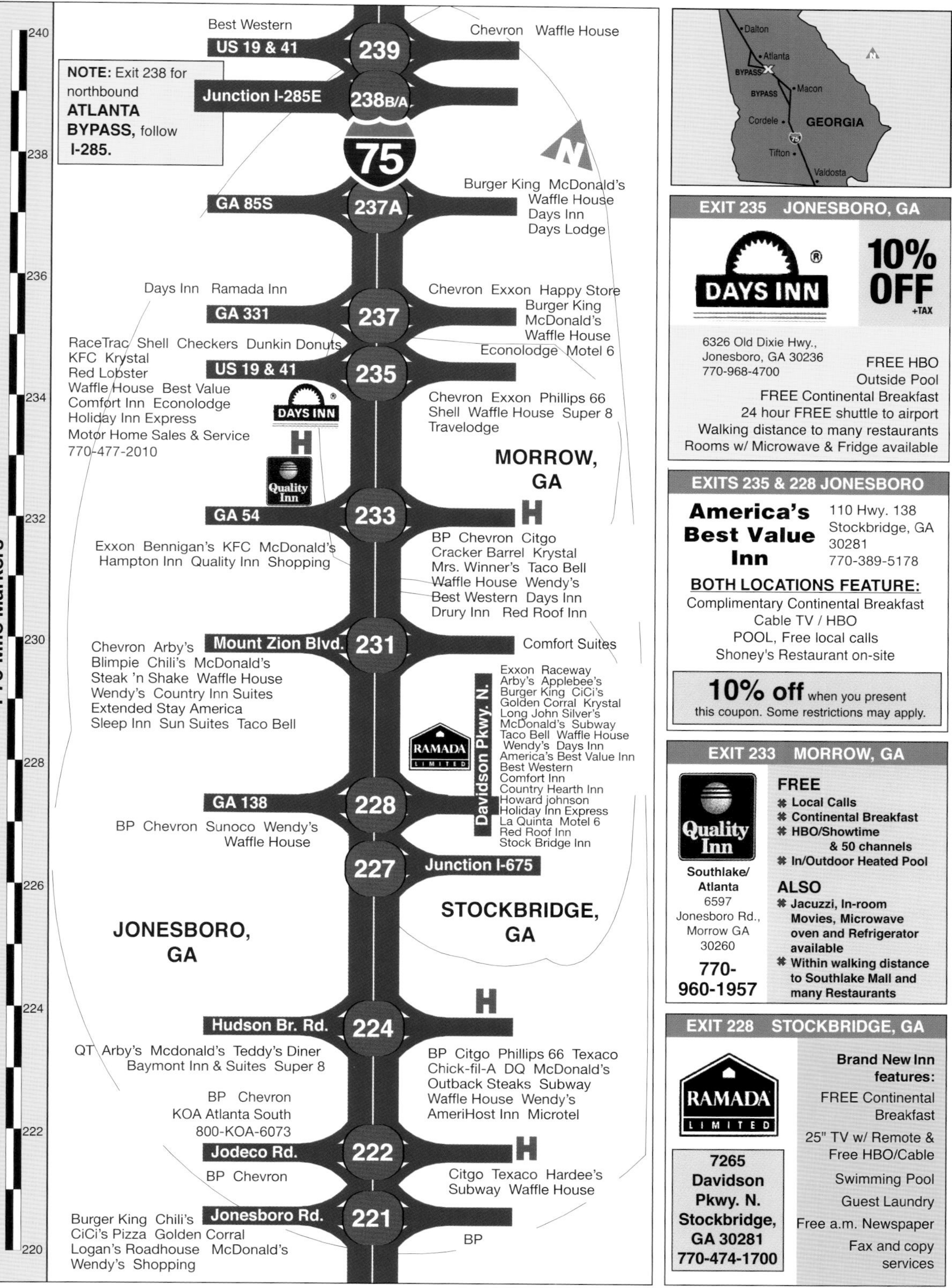
I-75 Mile Markers
240
238
236
234
232
230
228
226
224
222
220
NOTE: Exit 238 for northbound ATLANTA BYPASS, follow I-285.
Best Western
US 19 & 41
239
Chevron Waffle House
Junction I-285E
238B/A
75
N
GA 85S
237A
Burger King McDonald's Waffle House Days Inn Days Lodge
Days Inn Ramada Inn
GA 331
237
Chevron Exxon Happy Store Burger King McDonald's Waffle House
RaceTrac Shell Checkers Dunkin Donuts KFC Krystal Red Lobster Waffle House Best Value Comfort Inn Econolodge Holiday Inn Express
Motor Home Sales & Service 770-477-2010
US 19 & 41
235
Econolodge Motel 6
DAYS INN
Chevron Exxon Phillips 66 Shell Waffle House Super 8 Travelodge
H
Quality Inn
MORROW, GA
GA 54
233
H
Exxon Bennigan's KFC McDonald's Hampton Inn Quality Inn Shopping
BP Chevron Citgo Cracker Barrel Krystal Mrs. Winner's Taco Bell Waffle House Wendy's Best Western Days Inn Drury Inn Red Roof Inn
Mount Zion Blvd.
231
Comfort Suites
Chevron Arby's Blimpie Chili's McDonald's Steak 'n Shake Waffle House Wendy's Country Inn Suites Extended Stay America Sleep Inn Sun Suites Taco Bell
Davidson Pkwy. N.
Exxon Raceway Arby's Applebee's Burger King CiCi's Golden Corral Krystal Long John Silver's McDonald's Subway Taco Bell Waffle House Wendy's Days Inn America's Best Value Inn Best Western Comfort Inn Country Hearth Inn Howard Johnson Holiday Inn Express La Quinta Motel 6 Red Roof Inn Stock Bridge Inn
RAMADA LIMITED
GA 138
228
BP Chevron Sunoco Wendy's Waffle House
227
Junction I-675
STOCKBRIDGE, GA
JONESBORO, GA
H
Hudson Br. Rd.
224
QT Arby's Mcdonald's Teddy's Diner Baymont Inn & Suites Super 8
BP Citgo Phillips 66 Texaco Chick-fil-A DQ McDonald's Outback Steaks Subway Waffle House Wendy's AmeriHost Inn Microtel
BP Chevron KOA Atlanta South 800-KOA-6073
Jodeco Rd.
222
H
BP Chevron
Citgo Texaco Hardee's Subway Waffle House
Jonesboro Rd.
221
Burger King Chili's CiCi's Pizza Golden Corral Logan's Roadhouse McDonald's Wendy's Shopping
BP
Dalton
Atlanta
BYPASS
BYPASS
Macon
Cordele
GEORGIA
75
Tifton
Valdosta
N
EXIT 235 JONESBORO, GA
DAYS INN ®
10% OFF +TAX
6326 Old Dixie Hwy., Jonesboro, GA 30236 770-968-4700
FREE HBO
Outside Pool
FREE Continental Breakfast
24 hour FREE shuttle to airport
Walking distance to many restaurants
Rooms w/ Microwave & Fridge available
EXITS 235 & 228 JONESBORO
America's Best Value Inn
110 Hwy. 138 Stockbridge, GA 30281 770-389-5178
BOTH LOCATIONS FEATURE:
Complimentary Continental Breakfast
Cable TV / HBO
POOL, Free local calls
Shoney's Restaurant on-site
10% off when you present this coupon. Some restrictions may apply.
EXIT 233 MORROW, GA
Quality Inn
Southlake/ Atlanta 6597 Jonesboro Rd., Morrow GA 30260
770-960-1957
FREE
Local Calls
Continental Breakfast
HBO/Showtime & 50 channels
In/Outdoor Heated Pool
ALSO
Jacuzzi, In-room Movies, Microwave oven and Refrigerator available
Within walking distance to Southlake Mall and many Restaurants
EXIT 228 STOCKBRIDGE, GA
RAMADA LIMITED
7265 Davidson Pkwy. N. Stockbridge, GA 30281 770-474-1700
Brand New Inn features:
FREE Continental Breakfast
25" TV w/ Remote & Free HBO/Cable
Swimming Pool
Guest Laundry
Free a.m. Newspaper
Fax and copy services

Henry County
GEORGIA

Henry County Chamber of Commerce
1709 Highway 20W, McDonough, Georgia 30253
770-957-5786 **www.henrycvb.com**

Henry County

Henry County was founded in 1821 and named for the Revolutionary War patriot, Patrick Henry. McDonough and surrounding Henry County considers itself to be the benchmark for measuring Southern Hospitality. While **Henry County** is known for its quiet countryside graced with towering oaks and pines and the beautiful antebellum homes and gardens filled with Azalea and Dogwood, **Henry County** also has a reputation for great celebrations.

Locust Grove has a notable Old-Fashion Christmas (parade, stage entertainment, food, train rides and more.) Hampton celebrates transportation history during Planes, Trains and Automobiles and Stockbridge has the one-of-a-kind Ole Stockbridge Days (arts & crafts, food and children's activities.) Perhaps the best known celebration in Henry County is hosted in McDonough; you don't want to miss **McDonough's Geranium Festival and Craft show** in May.

McDonough boasts one of the loveliest old courthouse squares in Georgia, an area of the downtown lined with intriguing shops and restaurants.

Golf In The Atlanta Area

30 minutes from Atlanta, you can access 7 challenging courses offering 135 holes that won't put your bank card in the rough.

1. Georgia National Golf Club
1715 Lake Dow Rd. McDonough, GA. I-75 exit 218 (Hampton/GA 81). Turn east to McDonough. At the square, continue on GA 81 east and go 2 miles to Lake Dow Rd. Turn left and go 3.5 miles to the entrance on the left. 770-914-9994

2. Rum Creek Golf
107 St. Ives Court, Stockbridge, GA. This course is a new executive par three course which opened less than a year ago. Exit 224 (Hudson Bridge) go right approx. one mile to Flippen Road, turn right (north) onto Flippen and the course is approx. one mile on the right. 770-507-3538 www.rumcreekgolf.com

3. Crystal Lake Golf & Country Club.
100 Crystal Lake Blvd., Hampton, GA 30228. Located in a gated community surrounding a spectacular semi-private golf course with a unique but challenging design. Opened in 2006 but already noted as one of Atlanta's premier golf courses. 770-471-3233. www.crystallakecc.com

4. Green Valley Golf Club
434 Hwy. 155, McDonough, GA. I-75 to exit 216 (GA 155). Turn east. 1 mile to the course entrance on the left. 770-957-2800

5. Cotton Fields Golf Club
400 Industrial Blvd. McDonough, GA. I-75 to exit 218 (GA 20/81). Turn east. 1 block to the McDonalds Restaurant at Industrial Blvd. Turn right (south) and go 1 mile. Entrance on the left. 770-914-1442

6. Lake Spivey Golf Course
8255 Clubhouse Way, Jonesboro, GA. I-75 exit 228 (GA 38/ Jonesboro/ Stockbridge). Turn west and go 0.5 miles to Spivey Rd. Turn left and go 0.5 mile to Lake Spivey Country Club entrance. 770-471-GOLF

7. The Oakes Course
11240 Brown Bridge Rd. Covington, GA. I-20 to exit 44, Almond Rd./Porterdale. Turn south. Go 2 miles. Entrance is on left. 770-783-3801

8. Highland Golf Club
2271 Flat Shoals Rd. Conyers, GA. I-20 to exit 43, Salem Rd. Turn south, to the 1st light, Flat Shoals Rd. Turn left. 0.2 mile to the entrance on the right. 770-483-4235

Spalding County

Thomas Spalding's nickname was "Georgia's Benjamin Franklin." From a long line of hardy Scottish warriors, this father of 16 children worked tirelessly to promote and improve Georgia's agriculture. Spalding is best known for his service to his state and country. Spalding served as a member of the Constitutional Convention in 1798 and, in 1850, as chairman of the Great Convention at Milledgeville which produced the instrumental "Georgia Platform."

This area was first claimed by the Spaniards as part of Florida in the 1540s. In 1629 England declared the area to be part of South Carolina and finally, in 1764, it became an official part of the colony called Georgia. McIntosh Road follows the old Creek Indian trail which led to their meeting place at Indian Springs. The Spring was heavily sulfured and rumored to have healing powers.

Spalding County was formed in 1851. The land near Griffin (named for Gen. L. Griffin) was given away in a lottery. Most of the winners grew cotton on their 202-acre lots.

WHO AM I?

John Henry Holliday was born in Griffin GA on Aug. 14, 1851. He was baptized on Mar. 21st at the First Presbyterian Church of Griffin. John's father was Henry B. Holliday, first Clerk of the Court for Spalding County. Major Henry B. Holliday resigned from the Confederate Army in 1862 and moved his family to Valdosta, GA. The Hollidays were prominent citizens and Henry B. Holliday served several terms as Mayor of Valdosta.

In the early 1870s, John Henry Holliday completed his schooling at the Valdosta Institute. He entered the Pennsylvania College of Dental Surgery where he graduated. He moved to Atlanta, GA, where he set up his dental practice. Within a short time he moved his practice to Griffin GA. Doctor Holliday's Office was located in the One Hundred Block of West Solomon St. on the second floor (which is now Cain's Furniture). Doc Holliday practiced dentistry in his home town until 1873, when he was diagnosed as having tuberculosis and advised to move out West to the dryer climate. With his future shattered he started his journey west and unknowing to him, a place in Western history.

Doc Holliday was considered to be a man of class and distinction by those who knew him. However, with his pain increasing, he turned to whiskey. This sometimes altered his personality and took his temper beyond control. He soon became well known for both his temper and his skills with a gun.

No one knew Doc Holliday better than his best friend Marshall Wyatt Earp. As a Deputy Marshall, Doc stood at his friend's side when a fast gun was needed. He is best known for the day he stood with Wyatt and the Earp Brothers as they faced the Clanton gang on October 14, 1881. This was known as "The Gunfight at the OK Corral." Several movies were made about the Gunfight at the OK Corral. The movies plus the Wyatt Earp TV series that ran for several years has helped to make Doc Holliday one of America's favorite Western heroes.

Doc fought many battles, but none tougher than the one with tuberculosis. After 15 years of suffering, his life ended peacefully on Nov. 8th, 1887, in Glenwood Springs, Colorado.

Text courtesy Griffin—Spalding Chamber of Commerce

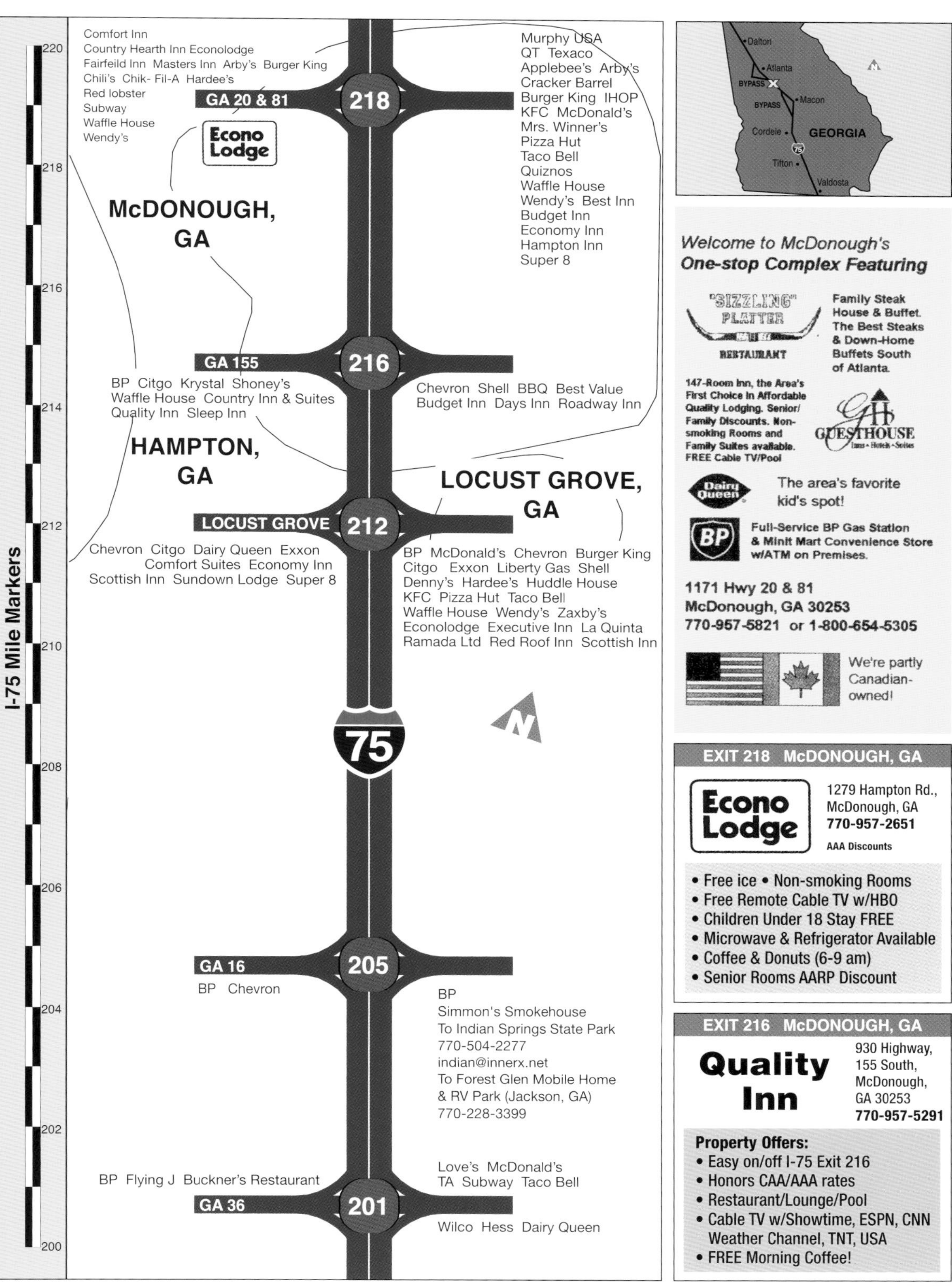

165
GEORGIA
Dalton
Atlanta
BYPASS
BYPASS
Macon
Cordele
GEORGIA
75
Tifton
Valdosta
I-75 Mile Markers
220
218
216
214
212
210
208
206
204
202
200
Comfort Inn
Country Hearth Inn Econolodge
Fairfeild Inn Masters Inn Arby's Burger King
Chili's Chik- Fil-A Hardee's
Red lobster
Subway
Waffle House
Wendy's
Econo Lodge
GA 20 & 81
218
Murphy USA
QT Texaco
Applebee's Arby's
Cracker Barrel
Burger King IHOP
KFC McDonald's
Mrs. Winner's
Pizza Hut
Taco Bell
Quiznos
Waffle House
Wendy's Best Inn
Budget Inn
Economy Inn
Hampton Inn
Super 8
McDONOUGH, GA
GA 155
216
BP Citgo Krystal Shoney's
Waffle House Country Inn & Suites
Quality Inn Sleep Inn
Chevron Shell BBQ Best Value
Budget Inn Days Inn Roadway Inn
HAMPTON, GA
LOCUST GROVE, GA
LOCUST GROVE
212
Chevron Citgo Dairy Queen Exxon
Comfort Suites Economy Inn
Scottish Inn Sundown Lodge Super 8
BP McDonald's Chevron Burger King
Citgo Exxon Liberty Gas Shell
Denny's Hardee's Huddle House
KFC Pizza Hut Taco Bell
Waffle House Wendy's Zaxby's
Econolodge Executive Inn La Quinta
Ramada Ltd Red Roof Inn Scottish Inn
75
N
GA 16
205
BP Chevron
BP
Simmon's Smokehouse
To Indian Springs State Park
770-504-2277
indian@innerx.net
To Forest Glen Mobile Home
& RV Park (Jackson, GA)
770-228-3399
BP Flying J Buckner's Restaurant
Love's McDonald's
TA Subway Taco Bell
GA 36
201
Wilco Hess Dairy Queen
Welcome to McDonough's
One-stop Complex Featuring
"SIZZLING" PLATTER RESTAURANT
Family Steak House & Buffet. The Best Steaks & Down-Home Buffets South of Atlanta.
147-Room Inn, the Area's First Choice in Affordable Quality Lodging. Senior/ Family Discounts. Non-smoking Rooms and Family Suites available. FREE Cable TV/Pool
GUESTHOUSE
Inns • Hotels • Suites
Dairy Queen
The area's favorite kid's spot!
BP
Full-Service BP Gas Station & Minit Mart Convenience Store w/ATM on Premises.
1171 Hwy 20 & 81
McDonough, GA 30253
770-957-5821 or 1-800-654-5305
We're partly Canadian-owned!
EXIT 218 McDONOUGH, GA
Econo Lodge
1279 Hampton Rd.,
McDonough, GA
770-957-2651
AAA Discounts
• Free ice • Non-smoking Rooms
• Free Remote Cable TV w/HBO
• Children Under 18 Stay FREE
• Microwave & Refrigerator Available
• Coffee & Donuts (6-9 am)
• Senior Rooms AARP Discount
EXIT 216 McDONOUGH, GA
Quality Inn
930 Highway,
155 South,
McDonough,
GA 30253
770-957-5291
Property Offers:
• Easy on/off I-75 Exit 216
• Honors CAA/AAA rates
• Restaurant/Lounge/Pool
• Cable TV w/Showtime, ESPN, CNN
Weather Channel, TNT, USA
• FREE Morning Coffee!

Forsyth-Monroe County
GEORGIA

Forsyth-Monroe County Chamber of Commerce
68 North Lee Street, Forsyth, GA 30129
478-994-9239 or 1-888-642-4628 **www.themiddleofeverywhere.com**

MONROE COUNTY
Nestled in the rolling hills of the Piedmont, Monroe County is rich with game, timber, lakes, minerals, fertile soils and warm hearts.

FORSYTHIA FESTIVAL
The Forsyth-Monroe County Chamber of Commerce holds their **Forsythia Festival** the second weekend in March. Enjoy the art shows, used book sale, 5K run, fishing tournament, and theatrical performances. The **2-day Arts & Crafts Show** plays on the forsythia theme and features the best of the area's artisans.

FORSYTH WALKING TOUR
28 buildings, many of which are on the National Register of Historic Places, are the focus of an afternoon's walk through Historic Forsyth. Begins at the monumental 1896 Courthouse in the Courthouse Square Historic District. I-75 exit 186. "Forsyth's old courthouse square looks like a picture postcard arriving a century late. People have liked it the way it is. So do we." Macon News, Apr. 5, 1983.

FRIED GREEN TOMATOES
Juliette, GA

At the turn of the century, Juliette was a railway depot community that boasted the "world's largest water powered grist mill." Then the train stopped coming and the town lay almost dormant until 1991.

In 1991 the producers of the movie *Fried Green Tomatoes at the Whistle Stop Cafe* discovered the river, railroad and quaint old stores that would serve as the perfect backdrop for the movie. The movie created tourism and today Juliette serves its visitors a variety of experiences: antique shops, souvenir shops and, of course, a meal of fried green tomatoes at the cafe. The fried catfish and lima beans (honest!) were delicious.

Whistle Stop Cafe is open Mon. to Sat. 8 a.m. - 2 p.m., and Sun. noon - 7 p.m. I-75 exit 186, go east 8 miles.

Attractions In The Forsyth Area

MONROE COUNTY MUSEUM
Monroe County owns and operates the museum situated in a quaint old train depot on Tift College Drive in Forsyth (I-75 exit 186). This building, constructed in 1899, has a restored caboose that is loved by the local children. The first railroad in Georgia was the Monroe Railroad and Banking Company, built in 1838 to run from Macon to Forsyth. When the train reached Forsyth, a unique turntable was used to reverse direction and return it to Macon. Tues. to Fri. 10 a.m.-5 p.m., Sat. 10 a.m.-5 p.m., Sun. 1 p.m.-5 p.m. 478-994-5070

PIEDMONT NATIONAL WILDLIFE REFUGE
The Piedmont is a conservation success story. Franklin D. Roosevelt signed an executive order in 1939 establishing the Piedmont National Wildlife Refuge in an effort to save this once vast and fertile forest that had been destroyed by the clearing of the European settlers in the early 1800s. With the soil-robbing cotton farms and the loss of the root system of the old trees, the Civil War ravages, a boll weevil infestation and the Great Depression, the land was largely abandoned and fell further victim during the Dust Bowl Era. Today the land is forested with clear streams, beaver dams, migrating waterfowl, red-cockaded woodpeckers, whitetail deer, bats, foxes, coyotes and bobcats. The park offers a visitor center, two different hiking trails along Allison Lake, and hunting and fishing. I-75 exit 186 in Forsyth and go east along the Juliette Road for 18 miles till you reach the refuge office and visitor centre. For information call or write: Piedmont National Wildlife Refuge, Route 1, Box 670, Round Oak, GA. 478-986-5441.

INDIAN SPRINGS STATE PARK
One of the oldest State Parks, Indian Springs has tent/trailer sites (full hookup), pedal/fishing boat rentals, cottages, swimming and fishing on the 105-acre lake. The Creek Indians believed this spring had magical healing and energizing powers. I-75 exit 205 to Jackson. Southeast on US 23. South on GA Hwy. 42 to the park. 7 a.m.-10 p.m. 678 Lake Clark Rd. Flovilla, GA. 770-504-2277

DAUSET TRAILS NATURE CENTER
Since its opening in 1978, Dauset Trails has provided enjoyment for visitors, young and old, as well as an educated appreciation for the environment of the 1,000 forested acres. Trained staff give you the opportunity to get the most from your outdoor experiences in birdwatching, hiking and photography. Indoor programs allow you to hold a live snake, learn about marsupials, and visit the injured and orphaned animals cared for on site. Camping is available by reservation for organized groups only. Group camping areas are located around a beautiful 6-acre lake. I-75 exit 198, east on High Falls Rd. for 4.5 miles, then 3.3 miles east on Mt. Vernon Rd. to entrance on the left. Mon. to Sat. 9 a.m.-5 p.m., Sun. 12 noon-5 p.m. 360 Mt. Vernon Church Rd. Jackson, GA. 770-775-6798

LAKE JULIETTE
Lake Juliette was built to provide a water source for Plant Scherer, an "electrical generating facility." The land surrounding the plant and the 3600-acre lake is available for fishing, hunting, and primitive camping. I-75 exit 186 to Juliette Road in Forsyth and go east to US 23. Take US 23 south to the Lake entrance. Lake Resources Manager, Georgia Power Company, 180 Dam Rd., Jackson, GA, 30233. 404-526-2741 or 404-994-7945

HIGH FALLS STATE PARK
995 acres, 140 tent and trailer sites, 650-acre lake. Great camping, excellent fishing and swimming is offered at this park which, in the early 1800s, was the site of a prosperous industrial town that turned into a ghost town when a major railroad bypassed it in 1880. See the historic waterfall, hike the two scenic trails and canoe. I-75 exit 198 at High Falls Rd. and go east 1.8 miles. High Falls State Park, Route 5, Box 202-A, Jackson, GA. 7 a.m.-10 p.m. 478-994-5080 OR 800-864-7275

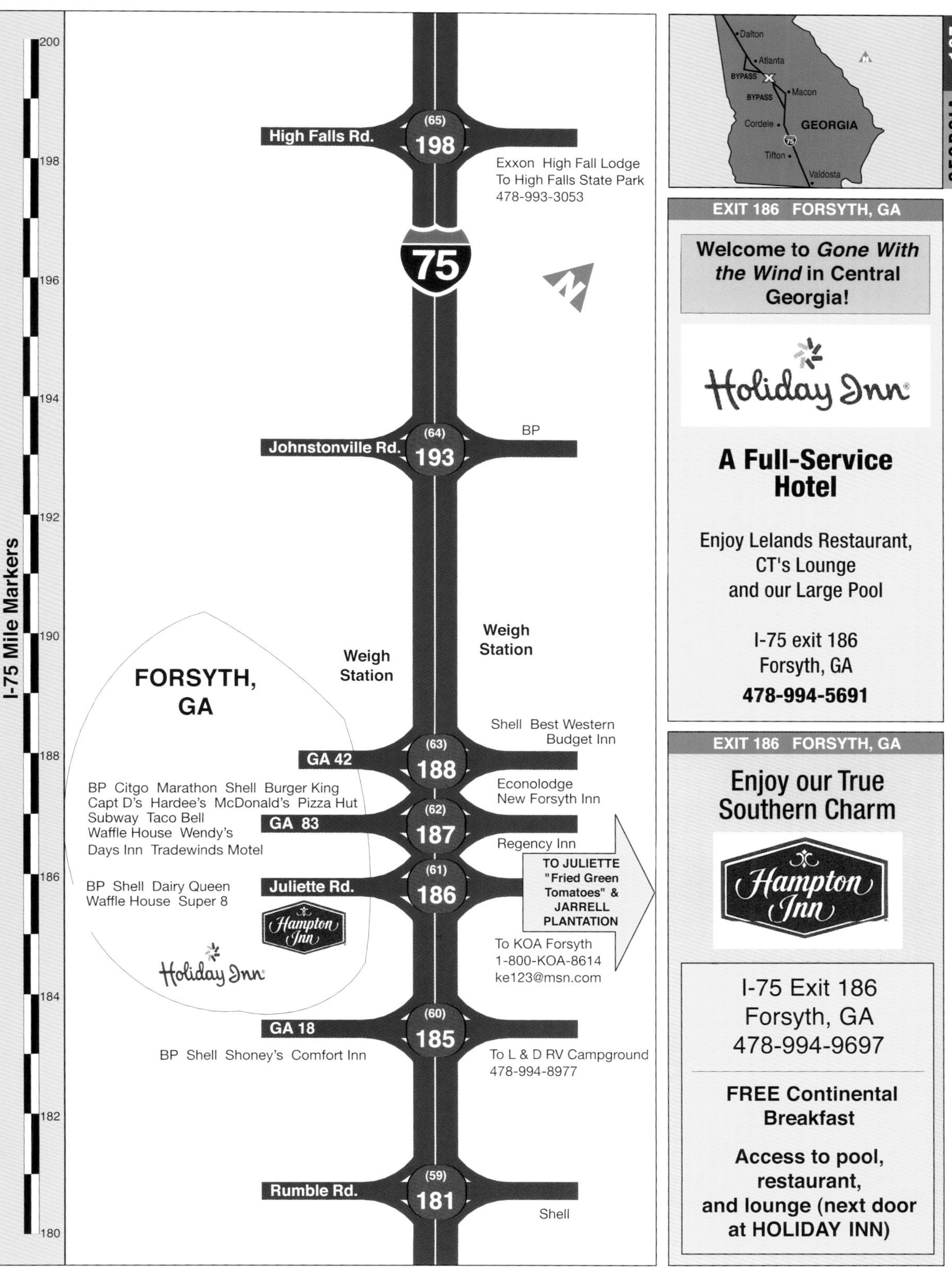
I-75 Mile Markers
200
198
196
194
192
190
188
186
184
182
180
75
High Falls Rd.
(65)
198
Exxon High Fall Lodge
To High Falls State Park
478-993-3053
Johnstonville Rd.
(64)
193
BP
Weigh Station
Weigh Station
FORSYTH, GA
GA 42
(63)
188
Shell Best Western
Budget Inn
BP Citgo Marathon Shell Burger King
Capt D's Hardee's McDonald's Pizza Hut
Subway Taco Bell
Waffle House Wendy's
Days Inn Tradewinds Motel
Econolodge
New Forsyth Inn
GA 83
(62)
187
Regency Inn
TO JULIETTE "Fried Green Tomatoes" & JARRELL PLANTATION
Juliette Rd.
(61)
186
BP Shell Dairy Queen
Waffle House Super 8
Hampton Inn
Holiday Inn
To KOA Forsyth
1-800-KOA-8614
ke123@msn.com
GA 18
(60)
185
BP Shell Shoney's Comfort Inn
To L & D RV Campground
478-994-8977
Rumble Rd.
(59)
181
Shell
Dalton
Atlanta
BYPASS
BYPASS
Macon
Cordele
GEORGIA
Tifton
Valdosta
75

Macon
GEORGIA

Macon GA CVB/Downtown Visitor Center
450 Martin Luther King Jr. Blvd., Macon, GA 31201-3300
478-743-3401 or 1-800-768-3401 **www.maconga.org**

THE SONG & SOUL OF THE SOUTH, MACON, GA, OFFERS THE BEST OF YESTERDAY AND TODAY

Did you know that Macon has more cherry blossoms than any other city in the world, including Washington, D.C., and the cities of Japan. It was proclaimed the **Cherry Blossom Capital of the World** by the Japanese Consulate General.

Macon's only casualty during the Civil War was the **Old Cannonball House,** into which a Union cannonball crashed.

Ocmulgee National Monument features one of the earliest public buildings in North America. The earth lodge, which visitors are welcome to explore, dates back 1,000 years.

Did you know that Macon is one of the only cities in Georgia that grew from a real frontier fort? **(Fort Benjamin Hawkins).** See a replica of the fort's 1806 blockhouse on Emery Highway.

Did you know that Macon has been the home of **Little Richard, Otis Redding, James Brown, Lena Horne, Razzy Bailey,** the **Allman Brothers Band** and **Capricorn Records?** Macon was also the home of the noted 19th-century poet and musician **Sidney Lanier.**

Macon has a rich baseball tradition. **Pete Rose** played for the Macon Peaches. **Vince Coleman** set the single-season minor league stolen-base record for the **Macon Red Birds.**

Macon is a rich source of African-American art, history and culture. It is home to the largest African-American museum in Georgia, **the Tubman Museum,** and the **Douglas Theatre** where **Lena Horne, Otis Redding** and **Count Basie** got their start.

Cannonball House, Macon GA
Photo courtesy of Georgia Dept of Economic Development

Beautiful downtown Macon. *Modern hotels and amenities, a beautifully restored historic district and even the site of an ancient Indian community at Ocmulgee National Monument offer Macon visitors the best of yesterday and today in the heart of the historic South. Courtesy Macon-Bibb County Convention and Visitors Bureau, Inc.*

Macon In A Nutshell

Macon, GA, has hosted ancient Indian tribes, explorers, river traders, cotton kings and presidents. In the early 1800s, the city fathers designed Macon after the ancient Gardens of Babylon. Today, wide avenues, lined with white-columned mansions and more than 200,000 flowering cherry trees lead the visitor through America's Dreamtown.

Modern hotels and amenities, a beautifully restored historic district and even the site of an ancient Indian community at **Ocmulgee National Monument** offer Macon visitors the best of yesterday and today in the heart of the historic South.

Tour Macon via carriage or van or explore independently, (tour brochures in several languages or tapes in English are available at the Convention and Visitors Bureau). In addition to the magnificent National Historic Landmark **Italian Renaissance Revival "Hay House," c. 1855-59,** built with luxuries far ahead of its time, visitors can tour antebellum Greek Revival mansions and Victorian cottages year-round. They can also experience a variety of modern-day museums, including the **Tubman African American Museum.**

America's Dreamtown also offers year-round festivals with events and special tours for all ages. Each Spring, Macon celebrates the **Cherry Blossom Festival,** a Top 20 Event in the Southeast, and one of the Top 100 Events in North America, offering more than 300 activities in the Cherry Blossom Capital of the World. Each summer, Macon hosts a variety of arts and cultural events, including **Macon's International Cherry Blossom Festival** (March), **Tubman Pan African Festival** (April), **Macon Gardens, Mansions & Moonlight Tours** (May), **Bragg Jam** (summer), **Ocmulgee Indian Celebration** (Sept.), **GA State Fair** (Sept.), **Christmas in Olde Macon** (Dec.), and the Macon, **GA Film Festival** (Feb.)

Visitors can shop in the leisurely atmosphere of Macon's centers and malls. Enjoy the many recreational opportunities, from golf to water sports. Dining — from exquisite, to soul food, to one of the nation's oldest hot dog stands — is sure to please. Everyone will enjoy this vibrant, beautiful Southern city.

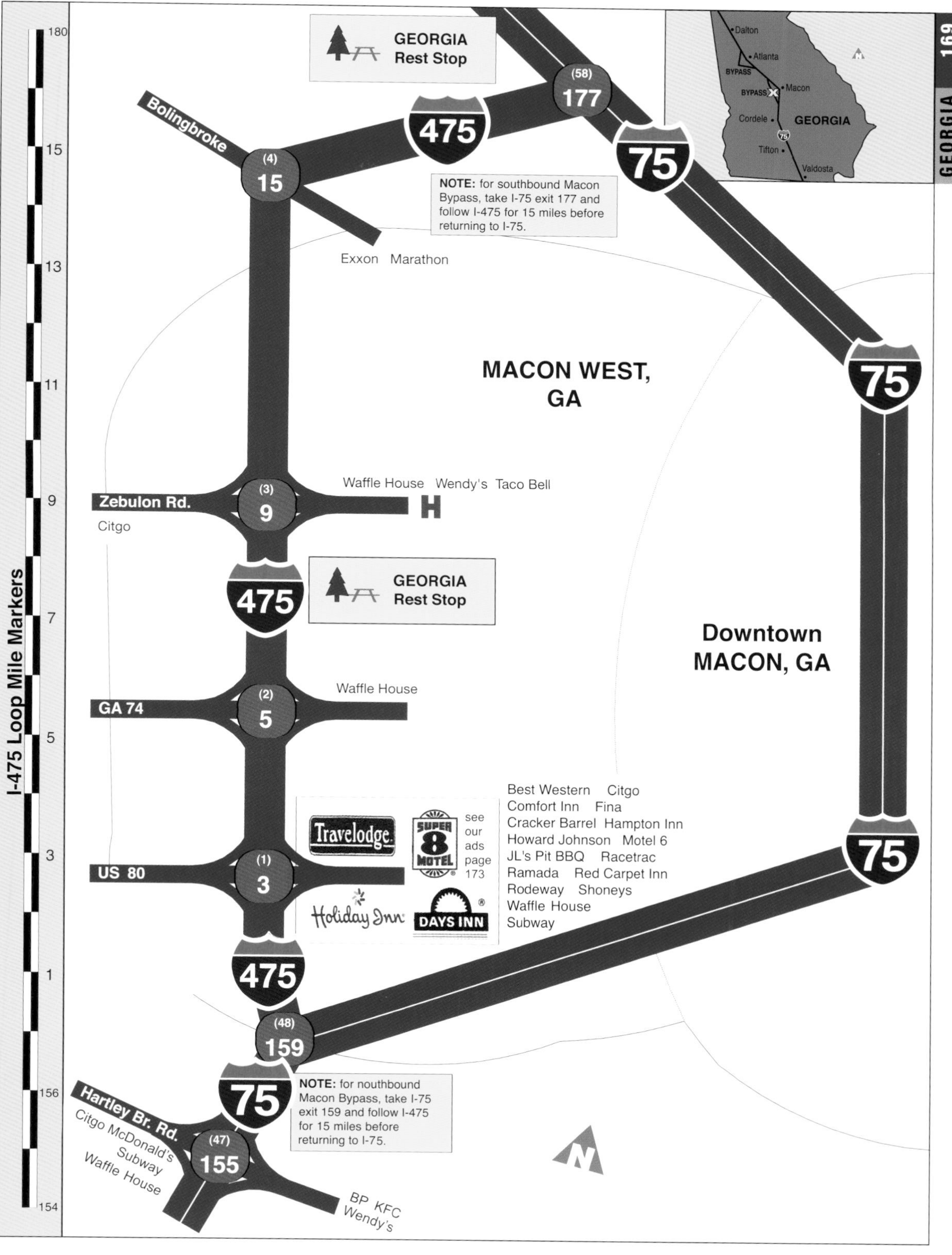
GEORGIA
Rest Stop
Bolingbroke
(4)
15
475
(58)
177
75
Dalton
Atlanta
BYPASS
BYPASS
Macon
Cordele
GEORGIA
Tifton
Valdosta
NOTE: for southbound Macon Bypass, take I-75 exit 177 and follow I-475 for 15 miles before returning to I-75.
Exxon Marathon
MACON WEST, GA
Zebulon Rd.
(3)
9
Waffle House Wendy's Taco Bell
Citgo
H
475
GEORGIA
Rest Stop
Downtown MACON, GA
GA 74
(2)
5
Waffle House
Travelodge
SUPER 8 MOTEL
see our ads page 173
Best Western Citgo
Comfort Inn Fina
Cracker Barrel Hampton Inn
Howard Johnson Motel 6
JL's Pit BBQ Racetrac
Ramada Red Carpet Inn
Rodeway Shoneys
Waffle House
Subway
US 80
(1)
3
Holiday Inn
DAYS INN
475
(48)
159
75
NOTE: for nouthbound Macon Bypass, take I-75 exit 159 and follow I-475 for 15 miles before returning to I-75.
Hartley Br. Rd.
Citgo McDonald's
Subway
Waffle House
(47)
155
BP KFC
Wendy's
N
I-475 Loop Mile Markers
180
15
13
11
9
7
5
3
1
156
154

Macon
GEORGIA

Macon GA CVB/Downtown Visitor Center
450 Martin Luther King Jr. Blvd., Macon, GA 31201-3300
478-743-3401 or 1-800-768-3401 **www.maconga.org**

GEORGIA MUSIC HALL OF FAME INDUCTEES (Partial List)

GOSPEL: Wendy Bagwell, Dr. Thomas Dorsey, The Lewis Family, Lee Roy Abernathy, Eva Mae LeFevre, and Hovie Lister

RHYTHM & BLUES: James Brown, Ray Charles, Isaac Hayes Graham Jackson, Gladys Knight & the Pipps, Curtis Mayfield, "Blind Willie" McTell, "Ma" Rainey, Otis Redding, "Piano Red" Perriman, and Chuck Willis

COUNTRY/FOLK: Bill Anderson, Chet Atkins, Beaudleax Bryant, Cotton Carrier, Fiddlin' John Carson, Ronnie Milsap, George Riley Puckett, Jerry Reed, Ray Stevens, and Gid Tanner & the Skillet Lickers

ROCK N' ROLL: Duane Allman, Buddy Buie / J.R. Cobb, Brenda Lee, Little Richard, Tommy Roe, Billy Joe Royal, Joe South, The Tams, and Dennis Yost & the Classic IV R.E.M.

JAZZ/SWING: Ray Eberle, Connie Haines, Fletcher Henderson, Lena Horne, Harry James, Johnny Mercer, and Joe Williams

PRODUCERS / MUSIC EXECUTIVES: Alex Cooley, Elmo Ellis, Emory Gordy Jr., Felton Jarvis, Joel Katz, Gwen Kessler, Bill Lowery, Zell Miller, Chips Moman, Ray Whitley, Phil Walden, Bob Richardson, Zenas "Daddy" Sears, Harold Shedd, and Sam Wallace

CLASSICAL: Albert Coleman, Roland Hayes, James Melton, and Robert Shaw

Georgia Music Hall of Fame

The Deep South, with its rich culture, has been an incubator for music since the pre-colonial days. Nowhere has that heritage been richer than in Georgia, which can probably boast more accomplished musicians per capital than most countries. Georgia has an amazing legacy, a rich musical heritage which ranges from the blues to the classics, and includes rock and roll, country and gospel. Macon and middle Georgia especially have produced musicians. Macon was selected as the site of the **Georgia Music Hall of Fame** because the city is home to the **Allman Brothers, Little Richard, Otis Redding** and others and because it is the geographic heart of Georgia.

Imagine yourself entering a small town in Georgia, strolling down the Main Street and sauntering into the Record Store, where you'll hear the music of **R.E.M., B-52's, Black Crowes, TLC, Kris Kross,** the **Allman Brothers Band** and more. Further along, slip into the absolutely authentic 1950's Soda Fountain, hear **"Little" Richard** and other Rock'n Roll greats on the jukebox, and, of course, enjoy a Coca-Cola poured by a real soda jerk.

The Jazz Club is where you'll hear the sophisticated music of **Lena Horne, Harry James, Johnny Mercer** and other golden legends. The Skillet Lickers' Cafe will resound with the country sounds of **Ronnie Milsap, Brenda Lee, Travis Tritt** and **Tricia Yearwood;** next stop is the Gospel Chapel, an exhibit that will move your heart and soul with the music of **Dr. Thomas Dorsey, Hovie Lister,** the **Statesman Quartet** and more. But wait, there's more. Just step into the Back Stage Alley which will sing the praises of those unsung heroes who make other artists (and sometimes themselves) sound and look so good. See the equipment used for intricate recordings and hear the work of many talented songwriters and producers such as **Bill Lowery, Buddy Buie, Jermaine Dupri** and **Dallas Austin.**

The Rhythm & Blues Revue is designed like a genuine blues nightclub with audio landscape. Enjoy **James Brown, Otis Redding, Gladys Knight and the Pips, Ray Charles, "Ma" Rainey, Clarence Carter** and many others perform in individual listening stations.

An inviting park, complete with benches is a place to rest and think of all you've seen and heard. A likeness of the late, great, **Otis Redding,** one of Georgia's musical giants graces this space, and welcomes you to the Hall of Fame exhibits. In the Gretsch Theater, you'll be able to select and view videos of many Georgia musicians, and see costumes and memorabilia celebrating the careers of Georgia's classical artists including **Mattiwilda Dodds, Robert Shaw, Jessye Norman, Bobby McDuffie** and more.

Before you leave, take Georgia Music History home: CDs, cassettes, videos and so much more can be purchased in the Gift Shop.

200 Martin Luther King Blvd.
Near the junction of I-75 and I-16 in Macon, GA. Mon. to Sat. 9 a.m.-4:30 p.m.,
Sun. 1 p.m.-4:30 p.m.
478-750-8555 or 1-800-GA-ROCKS

GEORGIA MUSIC HALL OF FAME *200 Martin Luther King Blvd., Macon, GA. 478-750-8555*
Photo/text courtesy Macon-Bibb County Convention & Visitors Bureau

Macon GA CVB/Downtown Visitor Center
450 Martin Luther King Jr. Blvd., Macon, GA 31201-3300
478-743-3401 or 1-800-768-3401 **www.maconga.org**

Lights On Macon

Historic Nightly Illumination Tour Creates Spectacular Georgia Attraction

Fireflies are not the only thing lighting up Historic Macon for nighttime visitors to this beautiful southern city. Already famous for its romantic, white-columned mansions and Victorian period architectural gems, Macon's Intown Historic District's existing beauty and tourism value have been expanded to include the illumination of more than 30 historic homes and buildings.

Inspired by light and sound presentations shown on historic chateaus and buildings in France and throughout Europe, the nightly tour offers visitors an opportunity to experience the ambience of what has been called one of the great historic cities in the American South.

Individually designed lighting highlights the most spectacular aspects of each home or building with dramatic illumination. A unique door might be softly lit, giving a warm, inviting feeling. A commanding turret may cast powerful shadows and represent the strength of a bygone era. And the delicate filegree of a Victorian period porch might be back lit, bringing to mind images of families who have spent comfortable southern nights basking in the glow of the beautiful city. Cupolas, stairways, stained glass, patterned brick work and graceful columns are some of the other architectural details that will captivate nighttime visitors.

The late Kenneth B. Dresser, a creative consultant for illumination projects at Walt Disney's Magic Kingdom and EPCOT, developed the Macon illumination plan.

The tour area begins with the National Historic Landmark Hay House, following Georgia Avenue up to College Street. At College Street a right turn leads to Bond Street, where another right turn takes the visitor to Coleman Hill to end back at Georgia Avenue. The tour area was chosen because of the great diversity of architectural style within a relatively contained area.

This night time program complements other cultural activities in downtown Macon, such as the **Georgia Music Hall of Fame,** restored **Historic Douglass Theater, Tubman African American Museum,** connecting **Pedestrian Plaza** and the **Georgia Sports Hall of Fame.** A variety of downtown restaurants, theatre and existing entertainment venues add to Macon's tourism experience.

Call 800-768-3401 for more information.
text/photo courtesy Macon-Bibb County C&VB

The Hay House. *Elegant, sophisticated in design, suitably furnished, Hay House was built 1855-60. Far ahead of its time in convenience and design, it had bathrooms, an elevator, an in-house ventilating system, intricate waterworks and even a secret room. Its 24 rooms and more than 18,000 square feet reflect the design trends of Second-Empire France and southern Europe in the 1850s. Almost unchanged since 1860, Hay House provides visitors the opportunity to experience the lifestyle of more than 120 years of gracious living. The property, including its handsomely landscaped grounds, is a National Historic Landmark. See the photo of the Hay House exterior in the Welcome to Georgia pages.*
934 Georgia Ave. Mon. to Sat. 10 a.m. - 5 p.m., Sun. 1 p.m. - 5 p.m. 478-742-8155

Macon
GEORGIA

Macon GA CVB/Downtown Visitor Center
450 Martin Luther King Jr. Blvd., Macon, GA 31201-3300
478-743-3401 or 1-800-768-3401 **www.maconga.org**

Museum of Arts and Sciences

$5/adults. $4/seniors. $2/children. **
Mon. to Thur. and Sat. 9 a.m.-5 p.m.,
Fri. 9 a.m.-9 p.m., Sun. 1 p.m.-5 p.m.
4182 Forsyth Rd. Macon, GA.
478-477-3232

At the Museum's **Discovery House,** visitors are invited to explore the various disciplines of the Museum: art, science and the humanities.

In **Uncle Charlie's Parlor,** curious visitors will find drawers full of rocks, butterflies, shells, dolls, swords and arrowheads embedded in tables and shelves and even a polar bear, all assembled to illustrate the value of keeping collections.

The **Mark Smith Planetarium** uses exciting visual and audio effects to take virtual journeys across the Earth and through space, bringing astronomy to life. The Indoor Zoo is an amazing habitat where tamarinds, snakes, alligators and other creatures are displayed.

Upstairs in the **Artist's Garret,** visitors follow their muse, expressing their own perspective on the world by building an architectural edifice in the brick bin, weaving on the rag loom, creating a sculpture on the nyloop wall or painting with a high tech toy by Invideo.

Shhh! As visitors enter the **Dream Room,** a sound sculpture by award-winning artist/composer Christopher Janney.
The lights go down and a programmed sequence of sounds come from above, below and behind, stimulating guests to use their ears, then draw their "vision" and post it for all to see.

Aspiring scientists can venture down to the **Scientist's Workshop** in the basement, where they learn to classify, measure, predict and infer. Also, guests can take a look at Zyghoriza, the Museum's 40-million-year old whale fossil and hunt for fossils at the Ziggy Dig.

Note: Admission is free each Mon. and Fri. evening 5 p.m.-9 p.m.!

A backdrop of more than 200,000 blushing Yoshino cherry trees makes Macon the Cherry Blossom Capital of the World! In March, the Macon Cherry Blossom Festival fills 10 days with events, performances, art, exhibits and Southern hospitality.
Courtesy Macon-Bibb County C&VB.

Special Events

SPRING

Macon's International Cherry Blossom Festival (March). This city-wide festival fills ten days with events, concerts, exhibits, arts & crafts, hot air balloons and more against a backdrop of more than 300,000 Yoshino cherry trees, the most in the world! www.cherryblossom.com 478-751-7429

Tubman Pan African Festival (April). This annual occasion centers on the theme of love, peace, unity and hope, with masquerades, Caribbean steel bands, Reggae, African music, dancers, films, children's entertainment and cultural demonstrations. www.tubmanmuseum.com 478-743-8544

Macon Gardens, Mansions & Moonlight Tours (May). Self-guided tours explore enchanting secret gardens and historic homes in Macon's loveliest neighborhoods. Garden market included. Proceeds benefit the National Historic Landmark Hay House. www.hayhouse.org 478-742-8155

SUMMER

Bragg Jam. This memorial to Macon brothers Braxx and Tate Bragg includes two days of cool concerts featuring local, regional and national acts, arts, children's events, the Ocmulgee Adventure Race and more. Proceeds benefit the Ocmulgee Heritage Trail. www.braggjam.org 478-722-9909

FALL

Ocmulgee Indian Celebration (Sept.). Native Americans gather at Ocmulgee National Monument to share their heritage at the 12,000-year-old site. www.nps.gov/ocmu 478-752-8257

Georgia State Fair (Sept.). From amusement rides to agricultural exhibits, this annual state fair has entertained visitors for more than 150 years, making it the longest running fair in the Southeast. www.georgiastatefair.com 478-746-7184

WINTER
Christmas in Olde Macon (dec.). Macon's historic house museums feature elegant holiday decorations with special evening tours, refreshment and music. 1-800-768-3401

Macon, GA, Film Festival (MAGA). Established in 2005, MAGA is rapidly becoming the South's newest hot topic of the film industry with a full week of film and associated activities each February. www.maconfilmfestival.com

Macon
GEORGIA

Macon GA CVB/Downtown Visitors Centre
450 Martin Luther King Jr. Blvd., Macon, GA 31201-3300
478-743-3401 or 1-800-768-3401 **www.maconga.org**

Macon Highlights

Woodruff House. *958 Bond St. Macon, GA 478-744-2715*
Built in 1836 for Jerry Cowles, a banker, by Macon master architect and builder Elam Alexander. Excellent Greek Revival architecture. Sold in 1847 to Col. Joseph Bond, one of the South's wealthiest cotton planters. In 1857 Col. Bond made the world's largest record-setting cotton sale, selling 2,200 bales of cotton for $100,000. Restored, owned and operated by Mercer University, the house is used for a variety of college and community activities. Courtesy Macon-Bibb County C&VB

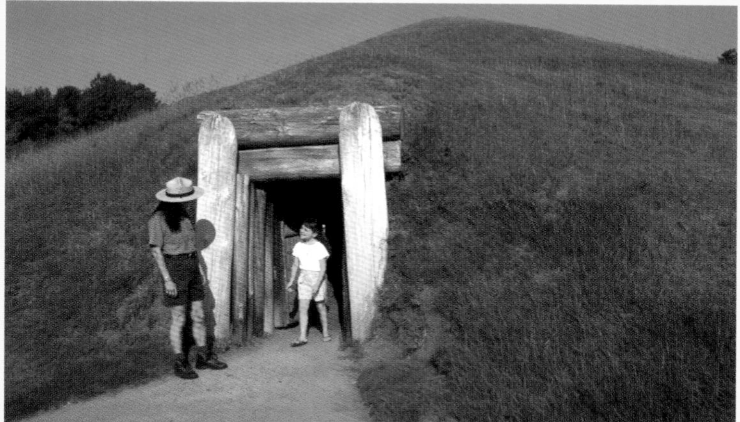

Ocmulgee National Monument. *Located on U.S. 80 East in Macon, GA. 1207 Emery Hwy. Pictured is the Ancient community's Earth Lodge, circa AD 1000. It was a ceremonial building, probably a meeting place for the town's political and religious leaders. It has been reconstructed to allow visitors to see it as it was at that time. A National Park, Ocmulgee features many mounds, each with its own purpose. Walking and driving trails provide a relaxing and interesting visit. Courtesy Macon-Bibb County C&VB*

Perry/Warner Robins, GEORGIA

Perry Area Convention & Visitors Bureau
101 General Courtney Hodges Blvd, Perry, GA 31069
912-988-8000 **www.perryga.com**

The Crossroads of Georgia

Known as the "Crossroads of Georgia" due to its ideal location in the geographic center of the state, Perry has long been a favorite travel stop. Here, dogwoods and azaleas bloom profusely during spring, and winter visitors are welcomed by day-brightening camellias.

The **Perry Area Welcome Center** is at I-75 exit 135 on General Courtney Hodges Blvd. The helpful staff can provide you with detailed local information and a fairly complete package for statewide attractions. There is plenty of parking for your RV, and a free dump station, off-leash dog park and wireless internet.

Many north and southbound tourists opt for a 90-mile alternative to I-75: **the Peach Blossom Trail** runs from Jonesboro (just south of Atlanta) along the U.S. 41 to the U.S. 341 (just north of Perry) down to Warner Robins and to the Museum of Aviation. In mid-March the trail is lined with a profusion of pink and white blossoms. From mid-May to mid-August this is where you get the juicy huge peaches Georgia is known for. There are plenty of roadside stands along the Peach Blossom Trail. To guide you along the historical trail with its variety of festivals and sights along the way, you might want to pick up the brochure at the Perry Welcome Center.

Just West of Perry is **Massee Lane Gardens** with its brick paths through acres of camellias (blooming Nov. to Mar.), Japanese gardens, and roses. This is the start of another trail, **Georgia's Andersonville Trail,** which is rich in Civil War history. It will take you to the **Andersonville Civil War National Historic Site,** the **Confederate Civil War prison** (where 13,669 Union prisoners died), a restored village, the **National Cemetery,** and the museum which chronicles all American wars from the Revolution to Gulf War. The trail ends in Plains, GA, home of former President Jimmy Carter.

In addition to the semi-annual **Mossy Creek Festival**, Perry hosts a wide array of spectacular annual events:
February: Georgia National Rodeo (www.gnfa.com)
March: Peaches to the Beaches Yard Sale
April: Perry Dogwood Festival (www.perrygachamber.com)
Oct: Georgia National Fair (georgianationalfair.com)
Dec: Christmas at the Crossroads.

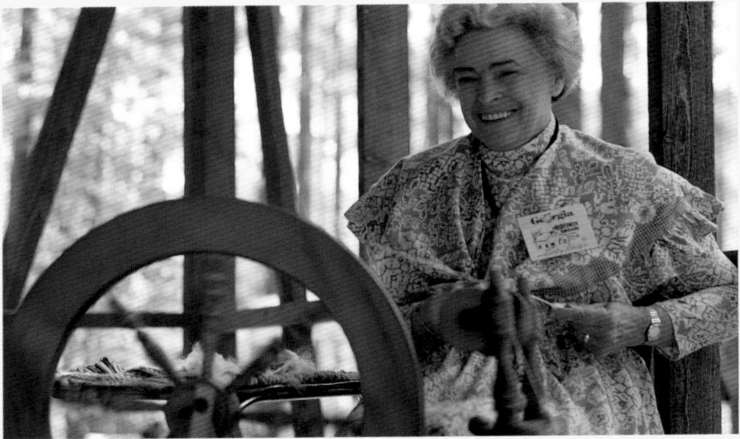

Mossy Creek Barnyard Arts & Crafts Festival. *I-75 exit 43A, go 3 miles east, or I-75 exit 142 (GA 96) and go 6 miles east to Lake Joy Rd. Sat. and Sun. 10 a.m.-6 p.m. 478-922-8265. Courtesy of the Georgia Dept. of Industry, Trade & Tourism*

Mossy Creek Barnyard Arts & Crafts Festival

Three miles from Perry is a beautiful pine thicket where the semi-annual award winning festival, **the Mossy Creek Barnyard Arts & Crafts Festival,** is held. Voted year after year as a Top 20 Event in the Southeast and one of the 75 best in the nation, exhibitors and visitors come to Perry from across the U.S. and Canada the third weekends of April and October to see "The Way it Used to Be."

Artists and craftspeople congregate here to display and demonstrate their unique skills. www.mossycreekfestival.com

People like Ernie Mills will demonstrate how he carves his working decoys. You might be lucky enough to watch Corky Gauger spin angora from live rabbits right before your eyes. You don't want to miss the handmade horse-drawn buggies, the cornshuck dolls, or the delicious home-made food and "secret" family recipe books!

Children look forward to the mule and wagon rides, the animal petting park, and especially the magical **Fantasy Forest,** where Larry the Leprechaun thrills them with his stories, magic and ventriloquism.

Robins Air Force Base/Museum of Aviation

The city of Warner Robins was named for Air Force Gen. A. Warner Robins. The city's major industry is **Robins Air Force Base** and main attraction is the **Museum of Aviation** which features more than 85 historic aircraft.

This museum is the fastest growing aviation attraction in the Southeast and is situated on a beautiful 43-acre site.

The collection of aviation memorabilia begins with WW I. Favorite displays include an original Norden bombsite, the "secret weapon" of WW II (Rosie the riveter), the WW I and WW II ace Gen. Frank "Monk" Hunter collection, Georgia's Black Eagles, German Luftwaffe items and the General Robert L. Scott (author of *God is My Copilot*) collection.

You can also see the SR-71 "spy plane" and buy souvenirs from the gift shop.

The Warner Robins Welcome Center is located at 142 Watson Blvd.

Warner Robins, GA 31093 478-922-5100

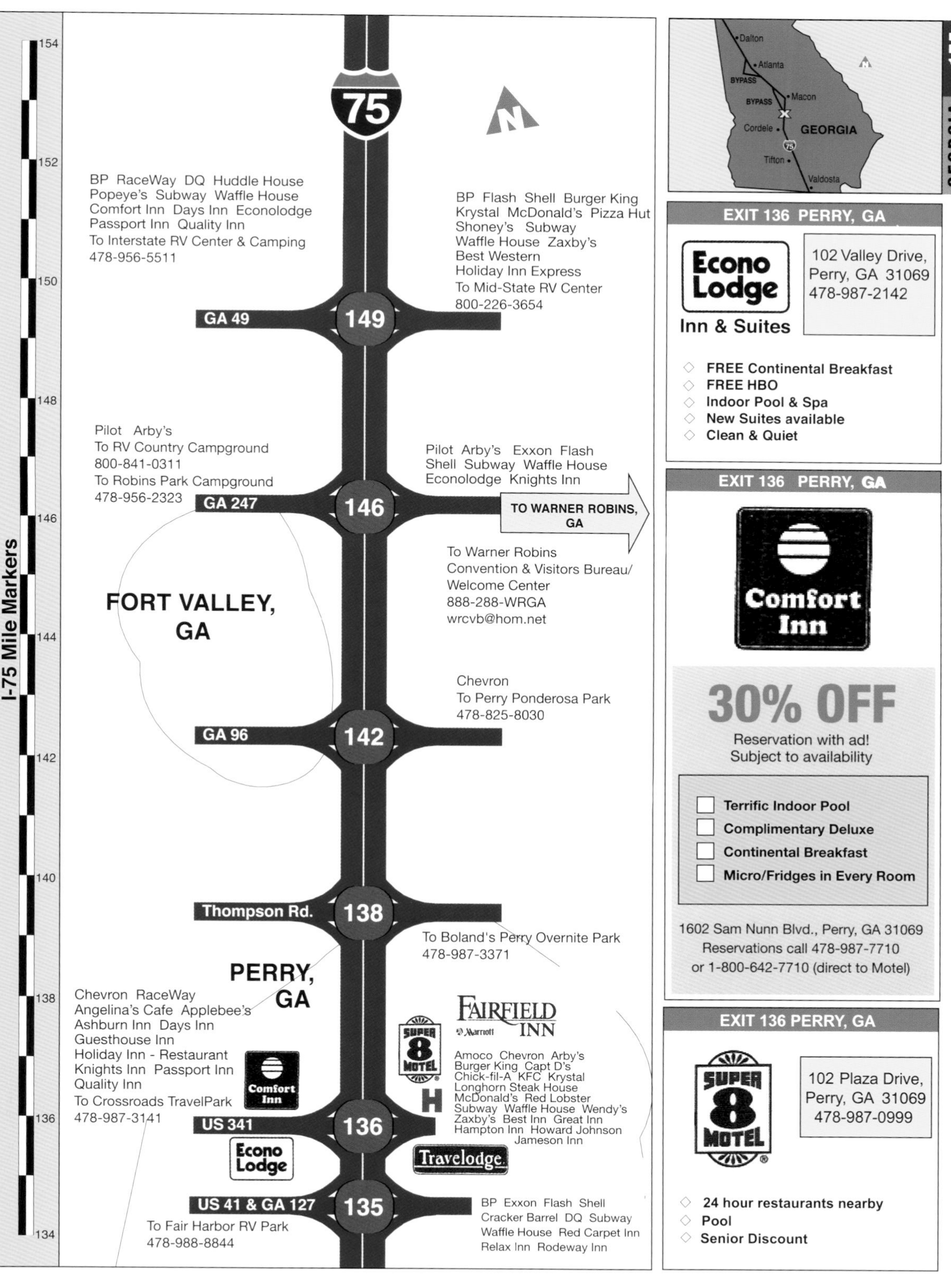

175
GEORGIA
Dalton
Atlanta
BYPASS
BYPASS
Macon
Cordele
GEORGIA
Tifton
Valdosta
I-75 Mile Markers
154
152
150
148
146
144
142
140
138
136
134
75
N
BP RaceWay DQ Huddle House
Popeye's Subway Waffle House
Comfort Inn Days Inn Econolodge
Passport Inn Quality Inn
To Interstate RV Center & Camping
478-956-5511
BP Flash Shell Burger King
Krystal McDonald's Pizza Hut
Shoney's Subway
Waffle House Zaxby's
Best Western
Holiday Inn Express
To Mid-State RV Center
800-226-3654
GA 49
149
Pilot Arby's
To RV Country Campground
800-841-0311
To Robins Park Campground
478-956-2323
Pilot Arby's Exxon Flash
Shell Subway Waffle House
Econolodge Knights Inn
GA 247
146
TO WARNER ROBINS, GA
To Warner Robins
Convention & Visitors Bureau/
Welcome Center
888-288-WRGA
wrcvb@hom.net
FORT VALLEY, GA
Chevron
To Perry Ponderosa Park
478-825-8030
GA 96
142
Thompson Rd.
138
To Boland's Perry Overnite Park
478-987-3371
PERRY, GA
Chevron RaceWay
Angelina's Cafe Applebee's
Ashburn Inn Days Inn
Guesthouse Inn
Holiday Inn - Restaurant
Knights Inn Passport Inn
Quality Inn
To Crossroads TravelPark
478-987-3141
Comfort Inn
FAIRFIELD INN
Marriott
SUPER 8 MOTEL
H
Amoco Chevron Arby's
Burger King Capt D's
Chick-fil-A KFC Krystal
Longhorn Steak House
McDonald's Red Lobster
Subway Waffle House Wendy's
Zaxby's Best Inn Great Inn
Hampton Inn Howard Johnson
Jameson Inn
US 341
136
Econo Lodge
Travelodge
US 41 & GA 127
135
To Fair Harbor RV Park
478-988-8844
BP Exxon Flash Shell
Cracker Barrel DQ Subway
Waffle House Red Carpet Inn
Relax Inn Rodeway Inn
EXIT 136 PERRY, GA
Econo Lodge
Inn & Suites
102 Valley Drive,
Perry, GA 31069
478-987-2142
FREE Continental Breakfast
FREE HBO
Indoor Pool & Spa
New Suites available
Clean & Quiet
EXIT 136 PERRY, GA
Comfort Inn
30% OFF
Reservation with ad!
Subject to availability
Terrific Indoor Pool
Complimentary Deluxe
Continental Breakfast
Micro/Fridges in Every Room
1602 Sam Nunn Blvd., Perry, GA 31069
Reservations call 478-987-7710
or 1-800-642-7710 (direct to Motel)
EXIT 136 PERRY, GA
SUPER 8 MOTEL
102 Plaza Drive,
Perry, GA 31069
478-987-0999
24 hour restaurants nearby
Pool
Senior Discount

Dooly County
GEORGIA

Dooly County Chamber of Commerce
P.O. Box 308, 117 E. Union St., Vienna, Georgia 31092
229-268-8275 **www.doolychamber.com**

DOOLY COUNTY is GEORGIA'S SECRET SPICE

This county, one of the earliest in Georgia, was named for Col. John Dooly, a resident who was murdered in his home. Dooly County's location near the I-75 and US 41 makes it an attractive place to stop. Busloads of people visit the local pecan processing and confectionary plant or they come to see the fields of cotton and peanuts, the cotton gin, and extensive hog operations.

The county seat, Vienna, was incorporated in 1841 and is notable for its carefully laid city plan: a large square for the courthouse flanked by perfectly parallel and straight streets crossing each other at perfect right angles.

The **Dooly County Courthouse,** in the heart of downtown Vienna, was recently restored and is listed on the National Register of Historic Places. It was built in 1891 of Georgia granite, slate, and brick.

Dooly Campground is another historical structure featuring an open-air tabernacle built with 110-year-old hand-hewn timbers.

Dooly County was, in part, shaped by the cotton industry, a fact that is well-documented in the **Georgia Cotton Museum** just minutes from the I-75 at exit 109.

Hunting is popular here. Some form of wild game is in season practically year-round, including trophy deer. Other recreational activities offered are fishing, horseback riding, water sports and golf.

A fantastic collection of **Wizard of Oz** memorabilia, the largest in the nation, is owned by Dooly Resident, Fred Causey. His collection contains more than 2,000 items, many of which were on display at the CNN Center in Atlanta.

Food means the world to Dooly County and the whole world knows! The annual **Big Pig Jig is** no longer a local secret, it's Georgia's Official Barbecue Cooking Championship! Held in November in Vienna. Hundreds of judges turn out for this event.

Big Pig Jig

Dooly County is conveniently located at the intersection of the I-75 and U.S. Highway 41, and it has long been a favorite place to make a detour to either the Andersonville Trail or the Presidential Pathways trail.

Also a favorite destination for traveling BBQ critics, the Georgia Barbecue Championship has lured not a few south-bound tourists to Dooly County for the weekend! This event, also know as the **Big Pig Jig,** is the state's oldest, largest and now, its official, barbecue championship. Twice it has been named as a Top 20 Event in the Southeast and a Top 100 Event in America.

Located in historic Vienna, GA, **the Big Pig Jig,** is a festival for the entire family centered around a barbecue pork cooking contest which includes approximately 120 teams competing for over $12,000 in cash and trophies. Barbecuers may enter any one or all three pork categories: **Whole Hog, Shoulder,** or **Ribs.** Teams may also compete in **Brunswick Stew, Barbecue Sauce, People's Choice,** and **Hog Calling** competitions.

Each team who enters the contest is an automatic entry in the Best Booth contest. The music concert begins by dark. Meat judging starts on Saturday at 10 a.m. and prizes are awarded by 6 p.m.Big Pig Jig is sanctioned by the **"Memphis in May" World Barbecue Cooking Championship.** The Georgia Grand Champion will represent **Big Pig Jig** and the State of Georgia at the Memphis Cookoff.

A scholarship pageant, parade, and storefront decorating contest will kick off the event in Vienna the Saturday before the cookoff weekend. Along with the cooking contest there is also a 5K Hog Jog run, local entertainers, a bounty of food and beverages and an enticing Arts and Crafts area.

The public is invited to compete for the Georgia Hog Calling Championship and trophy.

The Big Pig Jig facility is located at I-75, exit 109 in Vienna. Admission to the park is about $8 per day.

For more information write to:
Rhonda Lamb-Heath,
Big Pig Jig, PO Box 308,
Vienna, GA, 31092
229-268-8275 www.bigpigjig.com
Exit 109, Vienna, GA

PEOPLE & PLACES OF INTEREST

GUEST HOUSE. 217 5th Street. This is where Governor George Busbee was raised. Busbee served as the Governor of Georgia from 1974 to 1982.

WALTER F. GEORGE HOME. 305 E. Union St. U.S. Senator George (served from 1922 to 1957) was for 35 years a powerful member of what was known as the Southern Coalition and a champion of vocational education. He was chairman of the Foreign Relations and Finance Committees and architect of the North Atlantic Treaty Organization (NATO).

DOOLY CAMPGROUND. Built in 1875, this beautiful open air tabernacle is constructed of handcarved virgin timber. It is the site of many community activities including the annual Methodist Camp meeting.

ROGER KINGDOM. The two-time Olympic Gold Medal winner was born and raised in Dooly County.

EUGENE METHVIN, the editor of Readers Digest magazine was born and raised here. His parents once owned and operated the Vienna-News Observer.

JODY POWELL HOUSE. This is the home where President Jimmy Carter's popular press secretary was raised.

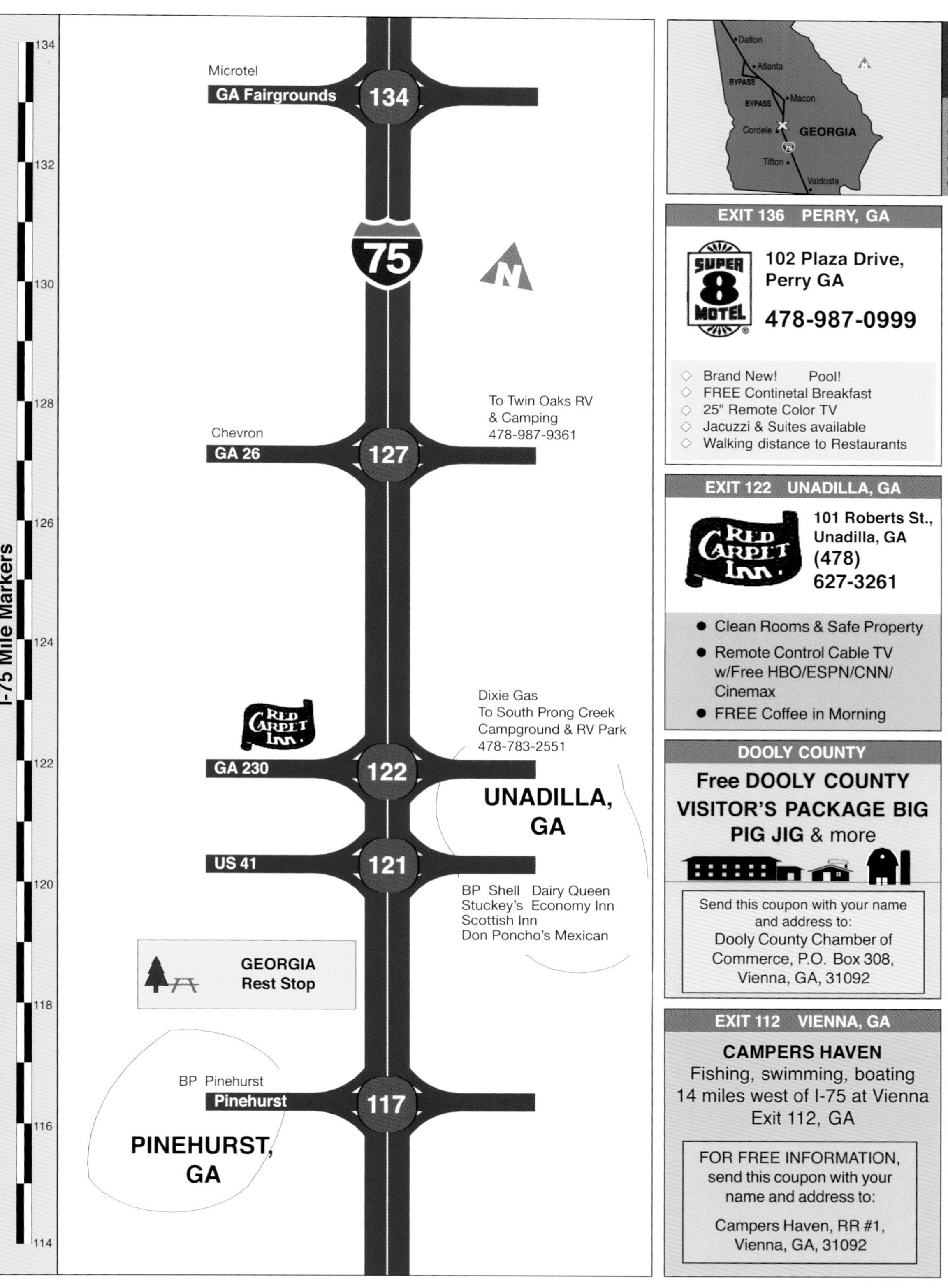

I-75 Mile Markers
134
132
130
128
126
124
122
120
118
116
114
Microtel
GA Fairgrounds
134
75
N
Chevron
GA 26
127
To Twin Oaks RV
& Camping
478-987-9361
Dixie Gas
To South Prong Creek
Campground & RV Park
478-783-2551
GA 230
122
UNADILLA,
GA
US 41
121
BP Shell Dairy Queen
Stuckey's Economy Inn
Scottish Inn
Don Poncho's Mexican
GEORGIA
Rest Stop
BP Pinehurst
Pinehurst
117
PINEHURST,
GA
177
GEORGIA
Dalton
Atlanta
BYPASS
BYPASS
Macon
Cordele
GEORGIA
Tifton
Valdosta
EXIT 136 PERRY, GA
SUPER 8 MOTEL
102 Plaza Drive,
Perry GA
478-987-0999
◇ Brand New! Pool!
◇ FREE Continetal Breakfast
◇ 25" Remote Color TV
◇ Jacuzzi & Suites available
◇ Walking distance to Restaurants
EXIT 122 UNADILLA, GA
Red Carpet Inn.
101 Roberts St.,
Unadilla, GA
(478)
627-3261
● Clean Rooms & Safe Property
● Remote Control Cable TV
w/Free HBO/ESPN/CNN/
Cinemax
● FREE Coffee in Morning
DOOLY COUNTY
Free DOOLY COUNTY
VISITOR'S PACKAGE BIG
PIG JIG & more
Send this coupon with your name
and address to:
Dooly County Chamber of
Commerce, P.O. Box 308,
Vienna, GA, 31092
EXIT 112 VIENNA, GA
CAMPERS HAVEN
Fishing, swimming, boating
14 miles west of I-75 at Vienna
Exit 112, GA
FOR FREE INFORMATION,
send this coupon with your
name and address to:
Campers Haven, RR #1,
Vienna, GA, 31092

Cordele/Crisp County, GEORGIA

Cordele-Crisp Chamber of Commerce
P.O. Box 158, 302 East 16th Avenue, Georgia 31015
229-273-1668 **www.cordele-crisp-chamber.com**

"THE WATERMELON CAPITAL OF THE WORLD"

Hernando de Soto's secretary, Rodrigo Ranjel, and his reporter, the Gentleman of Elva, chronicled in their diary what is thought to be the first Christian religious service in the Southeastern United States. The event occurred in the village of the peace-loving Ichisi Indian tribe, near present day Cordele, GA. This Mass was believed to have been celebrated on Apr. 1, 1540, while rested his men at this friendly Indian village.

One mile south of Cordele, on US 41, at the supposed site, you can visit the marker commemorating the event's Quadri-Centennial anniversary.

The area that is now Cordele was briefly Georgia's state capital. During the last days of the Confederacy, Georgia's war governor, Joseph E. Brown, used his farm property to escape from General Sherman's wrath, and "hide" the state's most important documents. At that time Gov. Brown's farm was known as "Dooly County Place." Dooly County Place was later sold and replaced with the today's Suwanee Hotel.

With the advancement of the railroad and the construction of the hydroelectric plant (the first county-owned electric system in the U.S.), Cordele was on the map.

Cordele was founded in 1888 and named for the oldest daughter of Colonel Samuel H. Hawkins, Miss Cordelia. Hawkins was president of the Savannah, Americus and Montgomery Railroad.

Crisp County was formed in 1905 from Dooly County. The new county was called Crisp in honor of Charles F. Crisp, a Georgia lawyer, judge and congressman. Judge Crisp served as Speaker of the House of Representatives from 1891 to 1893.

CORDELE is the Watermelon Capital of the World because they say they grow them bigger and more luscious than any place on earth! Cordele invites you to put their watermelon to the test at the **Watermelon Days Festival** celebrated annually along with the Fourth of July. Call 229-273-1668 for more information about this event and others held in the area.

Georgia Veterans Memorial State Park

All U.S. veterans who served, fought and died for freedom were honored when this State park, located on the 7,000-acre Lake Blackshear, was established. Visitors can access a fishing paradise. Lake Blackshear is the site of the national bass fishing tournament where nationwide entrants compete in several events and crowds line the shore to watch.

Georgia Veterans Memorial State Park offers over 1,300 acres for your recreation. The indoor museum interprets wars and battles from the 18th-century French and Indian War through Viet Nam. The outdoor museum displays some of the most famous war materials ever on display. Come see these planes, cannons, and tanks!

This park with a paved flying area is beloved by model airplane flying enthusiasts. Pull up your lawn chair or join in! This park is also well-known for its 18-hole championship public golf course!

The park offers tent and RV camping sites, a swimming pool and beach, 10 cottages for rent, a winterized group shelter, boating and waterskiing, as well as pioneer camping.

Park hours: 7 a.m.-10 p.m.
Georgia Veterans Memorial State Park, 2459-A US 280W, Cordele, GA. Located 9 miles west of I-75 (exit 101) near Cordele on US 280.
229-276-2371 or, for the golf course, 229-276-2377.

Historic Downtown

The construction of I-75 adversely affected the movement of traffic through downtown Cordele and the deterioration of the commercial architecture followed. In 1987, the city opted to join the Georgia Main Street Network and began revitalizing its downtown. In 1989, Cordele's downtown was added to the National Register of Historic Places list. Here are some brief descriptions of just a few of the many notable buildings:

1. Suwanee Hotel
Built on the former site of Civil War Gov. Brown's house, this English Vernacular Revival building was constructed of locally made bricks.

2. Carnegie Library
Designed in the Beaux Arts style and built in 1903, this was the second Carnegie Library built in Georgia.

3. Gainey's Drugstore
Downtown Cordele's first brick structure, built in 1889.

4. GS & F Depot
In 1895 this depot began serving freight and passengers until Union Station was constructed in 1903.

5. Thompson Building
Most date this English Vernacular Revival style building to 1903. Notable architectural details: a castelated cornice, an oriel window, stone cartouches marked with "T," and a stone window and door surrounded by beautifully ornate floral and egg and dart carvings.

The Andersonville Trail

Cordele is the 11th stop on this 75 mile sightseeing tour of the antique shops, museums, historic homes and local Southern fare of 12 quaint Georgia towns. The Confederate prison at the Andersonville National Historic Site, described on page 180, sounds quite interesting. Call 912-928-2303 to request a tour brochure.

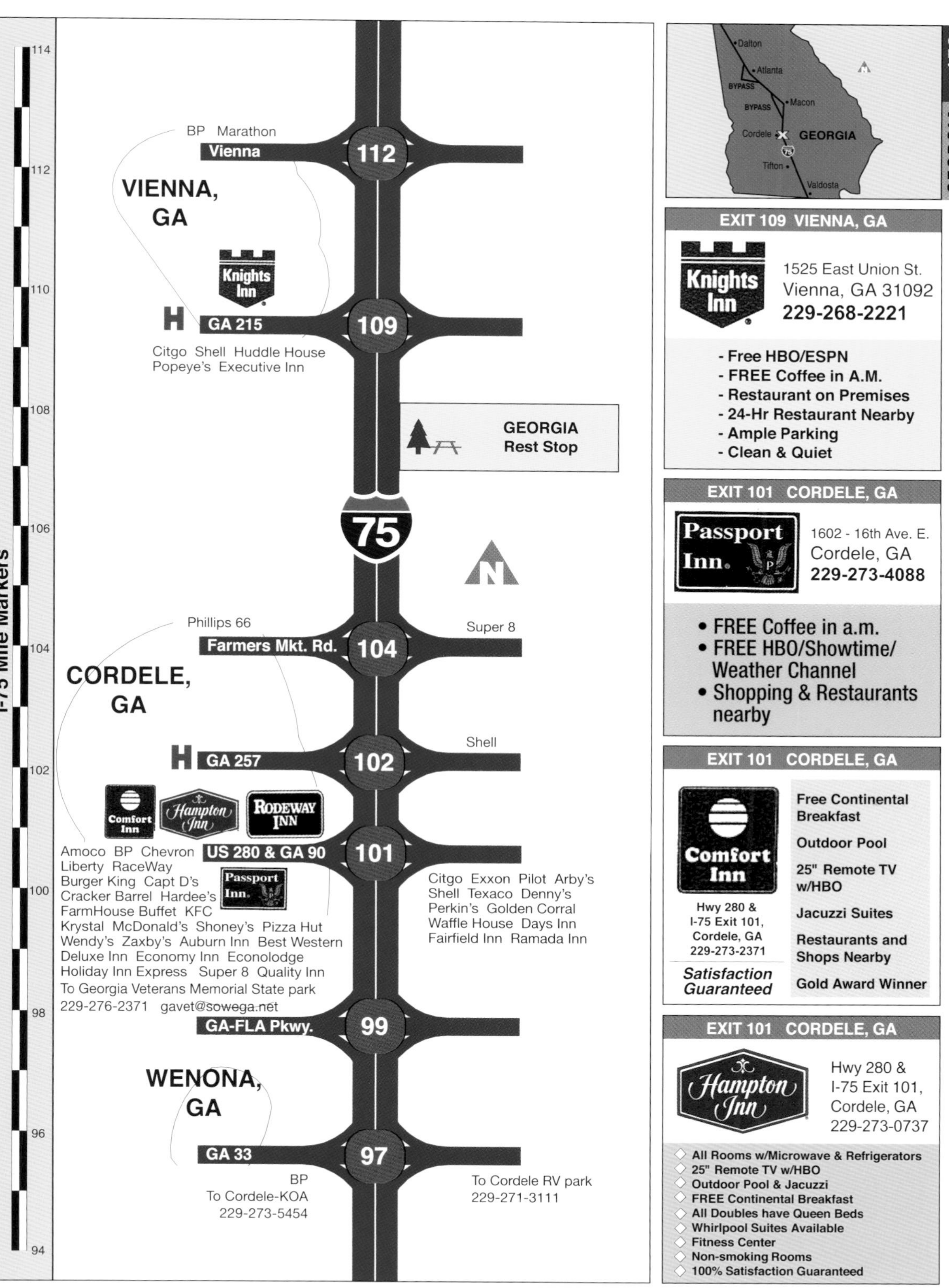

179
GEORGIA
I-75 Mile Markers
114
112
110
108
106
104
102
100
98
96
94
BP Marathon
Vienna
112
VIENNA, GA
Knights Inn
GA 215
109
Citgo Shell Huddle House
Popeye's Executive Inn
GEORGIA
Rest Stop
75
N
Phillips 66
Farmers Mkt. Rd.
104
Super 8
CORDELE, GA
GA 257
102
Shell
Comfort Inn
Hampton Inn
Rodeway Inn
US 280 & GA 90
101
Amoco BP Chevron
Liberty RaceWay
Burger King Capt D's
Cracker Barrel Hardee's
FarmHouse Buffet KFC
Krystal McDonald's Shoney's Pizza Hut
Wendy's Zaxby's Auburn Inn Best Western
Deluxe Inn Economy Inn Econolodge
Holiday Inn Express Super 8 Quality Inn
To Georgia Veterans Memorial State park
229-276-2371 gavet@sowega.net
Passport Inn
Citgo Exxon Pilot Arby's
Shell Texaco Denny's
Perkin's Golden Corral
Waffle House Days Inn
Fairfield Inn Ramada Inn
GA-FLA Pkwy.
99
WENONA, GA
GA 33
97
BP
To Cordele-KOA
229-273-5454
To Cordele RV park
229-271-3111
Dalton
Atlanta
BYPASS
BYPASS
Macon
Cordele
GEORGIA
75
Tifton
Valdosta
EXIT 109 VIENNA, GA
Knights Inn
1525 East Union St.
Vienna, GA 31092
229-268-2221
- Free HBO/ESPN
- FREE Coffee in A.M.
- Restaurant on Premises
- 24-Hr Restaurant Nearby
- Ample Parking
- Clean & Quiet
EXIT 101 CORDELE, GA
Passport Inn.
1602 - 16th Ave. E.
Cordele, GA
229-273-4088
• FREE Coffee in a.m.
• FREE HBO/Showtime/ Weather Channel
• Shopping & Restaurants nearby
EXIT 101 CORDELE, GA
Comfort Inn
Hwy 280 &
I-75 Exit 101,
Cordele, GA
229-273-2371
Satisfaction Guaranteed
Free Continental Breakfast
Outdoor Pool
25" Remote TV w/HBO
Jacuzzi Suites
Restaurants and Shops Nearby
Gold Award Winner
EXIT 101 CORDELE, GA
Hampton Inn
Hwy 280 &
I-75 Exit 101,
Cordele, GA
229-273-0737
All Rooms w/Microwave & Refrigerators
25" Remote TV w/HBO
Outdoor Pool & Jacuzzi
FREE Continental Breakfast
All Doubles have Queen Beds
Whirlpool Suites Available
Fitness Center
Non-smoking Rooms
100% Satisfaction Guaranteed

Ashburn
GEORGIA

Ashburn-Turner County Chamber of Commerce
238 East College Ave., Ashburn, Georgia 31714
800-471-9696229-567-9696 **www.turnerchamber.com**

"Flame" the Fire Ant and "The Giant Peanut"

Welcome to the area of Georgia known as "Plantation Trace." Here you will find the vast estates of gentlemen farmers and beautiful downtown avenues lined with Victorian homes and buildings.

Approximately 30,000 vehicles bound for Florida pass through Turner County on a daily basis, many of which stop and photograph the world's largest monument to the peanut (honoring Georgia's top cash crop). The monument is at I-75 exit 82, Ashburn, in the center of the Peanut Belt, and commemorates this crop's processing industry.

Ashburn takes pride in the fact that it has the vast majority of its original homes and buildings still standing pretty much as they were about 100 years ago. Many of these structures are described in detail in the walking-driving tour brochure and map of the historic town, which you can obtain from the Chamber of Commerce.

Notable structures include the completely renovated Turner County Courthouse, which is open for tours Mon. to Fri. 8 a.m.-5 p.m. This landmark historic site was built in 1906-1907 by Dennis and Dennis of Macon, GA, in the Italian style.

Turner County sponsors a number of annual events, pageants and parades. "Flame the Fire Ant" caught my attention! This annual 5-day event is held in late March and celebrates the area's wiregrass heritage. The county promotes the festival with a 24-page newspaper which invites you to "Come Flame a Fire Ant With Us!" filled with expert advice on how to do the thing right. Poor "Flame" is a cartoon fire ant who is roasted in various ways throughout the paper as well as on the Fire Ant window displays all over town.

GEORGIA PARKPASS

If you want to park your vehicle in a state park, you must pay a $2 daily parking fee or you can purchase an annual Georgia ParkPass to display on your vehicle for $25 (seniors, aged 62 and older, pay $12.50). The ParkPass can be purchased at any of the state parks or historic sites. Note: Wednesdays are free for day-use visitors.

A Note on Camping in Georgia's State Parks

Georgia has an impressive 63 state parks and historic sites. While available on a year-round basis, most historic sites and all swimming and golf facilities are not open on Monday (except legal holidays). Forty of the state parks offer camping.

CAMPING
The whole range of camping experiences is offered: tent or trailer camping, RV sites, walk-in camping, pioneer camping and group-camp facilities. The tent/RV/trailer sites have full hookups (water and electricity) as well as cooking grills and picnic tables. They all have dump sites and modern comfort stations, most offer laundry facilities and camp supply stores.

Reservations must be made at least two days prior to arrival but no more than 11 months in advance. Campgrounds are open from 7 a.m. to 10 p.m. and you must register prior to setting up. Late arrivals pay camping fees the following morning. MasterCard and Visa are accepted. Check out time is 1 p.m. You may stay for up to 14 days.

COTTAGES
Almost all of the state parks offer fully equipped cottages with stoves, refrigerators, kitchen and dining utensils, bed linens and blankets and towels. All are heated, almost all the cottages are air-conditioned, most have porches, and woodburning fireplaces or stoves.

A one-night deposit (paid within 7 days) will confirm your reservation, which you can make up to 11 months in advance From June 1 to Labor Day, reservations for less than one week are not allowed unless your reservations are made less than one month in advance and are for at least 2 days. From Labor Day to May 31, a minimum two-day reservation is allowed and 1 night occupancy is allowed with an additional surcharge. Check in time is 4 p.m. - 10 p.m. No registration after 10 pm. Check out is 11 a.m.

LODGES
Five state parks also offer lodges: **Amicalola Falls, George T. Bagby, Little Ocmulgee, Red Top Mountain** and **Unicoi**.

The lodges have between 30 and 100 rooms, and each has its own special features; for example, some have sleeping lofts for children, private porches and suites with separate rooms. All are handicap equipped and offer non-smoking rooms. Maximum occupancy is 4 in double rooms and 6 in loft rooms. A few port-a-cribs are available at each facility. Each room has a television, telephone and individual climate control. Golf, tennis, swimming, hiking and boating facilities as well as restaurant dining is available at some of the parks. Children under 12 stay free. Check in time is 4 p.m. and check out time is 11 a.m.

Interstate I-75-Accessible Georgia State Parks
Reservations: 1-800-864-7275 PARKS

HIGH FALLS PARK. 112 tent/trailer sites, picnic sites, lake, boat rentals, fishing, pool, and hiking. 76 High Falls Park Drive, Jackson, 30233. Just 1.8 miles east of I-75 exit 198. 912-993-3053

FORT MOUNTAIN PARK. 73 tent/trailer sites, 15 cottages, picnic sites, lake, beach, fishing, hiking and mountain biking. 181 Ft. Mountain Pk. Rd., Chatsworth, 30705. About 8 miles east of Chatsworth via GA 52. I-75 exit 296. 706-695-2621

REED BINGHAM PARK. 46 tent/trailer sites, picnic sites, lake, fishing, and hiking. On Route 2, Box 394 B-1, Adel, 31620. 6 mi. W. of Adel on GA 37 via I-75 exit 39. 800-864-7275 or 229-896-3551

RED TOP MOUNTAIN PARK & LODGE. 92 tent/trailer sites, 33 room lodge, 18 cottages, picnic sites, lake, marina fishing, beach, pool, hiking and restaurant. 53 Red Top Mountain Rd. S.E., Cartersville, 30120. 1.5 miles east of I-75 exit 285. 800-864-7275 or 770-975-4226

INDIAN SPRINGS PARK. 90 tent/trailer sites, 10 cottages, picnics, lake, boat rentals, fishing, & beach. 678 Lake Clark Rd., Flovilla, 30216. 5 miles south of Jackson on Hwy. 42. I-75 exit 205. 800-864-7275 or 770-504-2277

GEORGIA VETERANS PARK. 77 tent/trailer sites, 10 cottages, picnic, lake, fishing, pool, beach, and golf. 2459A US Hwy. 280W, Cordele, 31015. 9 mi. W. of Cordele via US 280. Take I-75 exit 101. 800-864-7275 or 229-276-2371

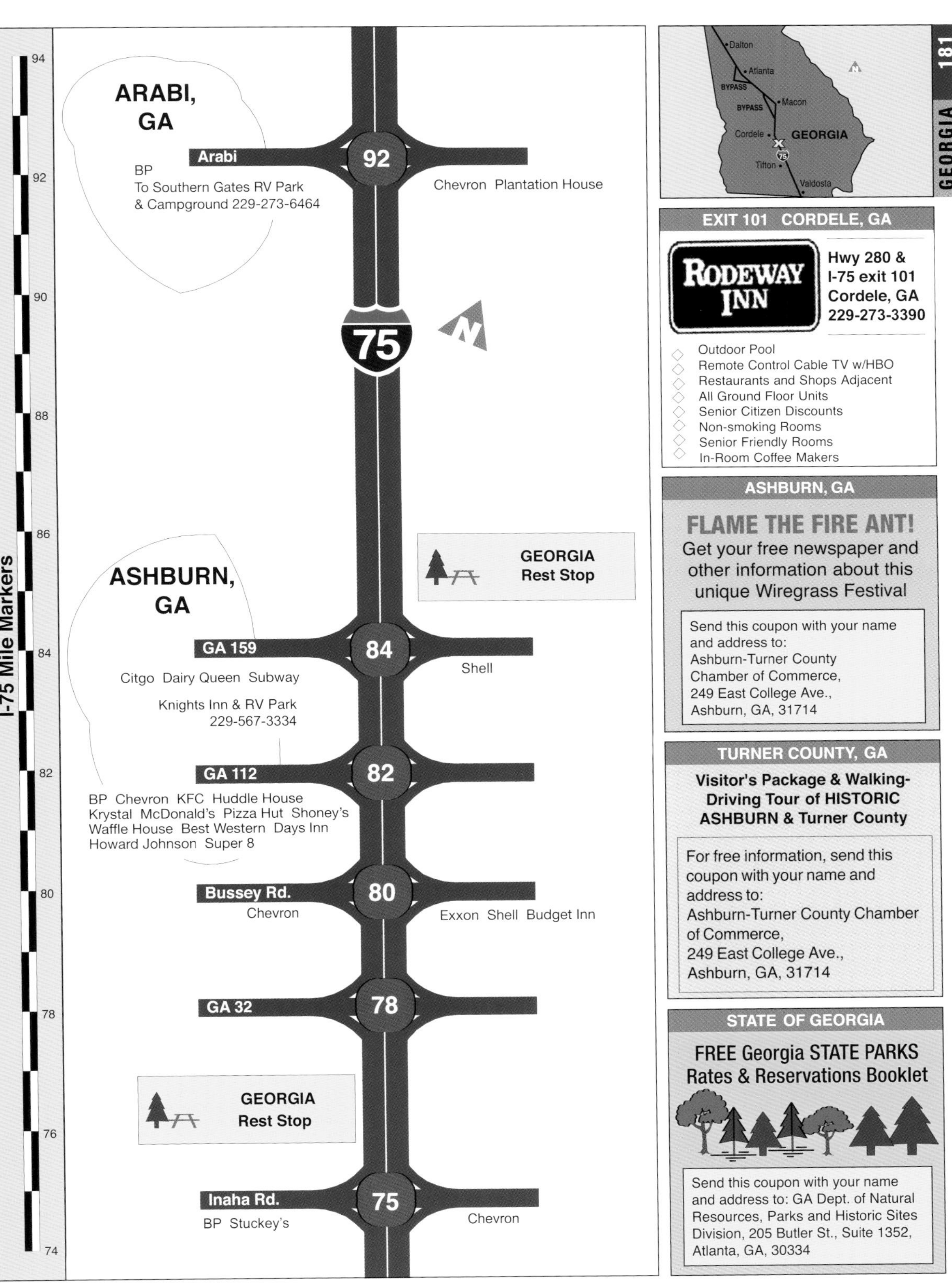
181
GEORGIA
Dalton
Atlanta
BYPASS
BYPASS
Macon
Cordele
GEORGIA
Tifton
Valdosta
I-75 Mile Markers
94
92
90
88
86
84
82
80
78
76
74
ARABI, GA
Arabi
92
BP
To Southern Gates RV Park & Campground 229-273-6464
Chevron Plantation House
75
GEORGIA Rest Stop
ASHBURN, GA
GA 159
84
Citgo Dairy Queen Subway
Knights Inn & RV Park 229-567-3334
Shell
GA 112
82
BP Chevron KFC Huddle House Krystal McDonald's Pizza Hut Shoney's Waffle House Best Western Days Inn Howard Johnson Super 8
Bussey Rd.
80
Chevron
Exxon Shell Budget Inn
GA 32
78
GEORGIA Rest Stop
Inaha Rd.
75
BP Stuckey's
Chevron
EXIT 101 CORDELE, GA
RODEWAY INN
Hwy 280 & I-75 exit 101 Cordele, GA 229-273-3390
Outdoor Pool
Remote Control Cable TV w/HBO
Restaurants and Shops Adjacent
All Ground Floor Units
Senior Citizen Discounts
Non-smoking Rooms
Senior Friendly Rooms
In-Room Coffee Makers
ASHBURN, GA
FLAME THE FIRE ANT!
Get your free newspaper and other information about this unique Wiregrass Festival
Send this coupon with your name and address to: Ashburn-Turner County Chamber of Commerce, 249 East College Ave., Ashburn, GA, 31714
TURNER COUNTY, GA
Visitor's Package & Walking-Driving Tour of HISTORIC ASHBURN & Turner County
For free information, send this coupon with your name and address to: Ashburn-Turner County Chamber of Commerce, 249 East College Ave., Ashburn, GA, 31714
STATE OF GEORGIA
FREE Georgia STATE PARKS Rates & Reservations Booklet
Send this coupon with your name and address to: GA Dept. of Natural Resources, Parks and Historic Sites Division, 205 Butler St., Suite 1352, Atlanta, GA, 30334

Tifton/Tift County, GEORGIA

Tifton-Tift County Tourism Association
115 West 2nd St., Tifton, GA, 31794
229-386-0216 **www.tiftontourism.com**

Home of Georgia Agrirama, Abraham Baldwin Agricultural College, & the "Love Affair" Fine Arts Festival, 1st weekend in May

Tifton was founded in 1872 by H.H. Tift, who built a sawmill in what was then Berrien County. In 1879, Tift bought an engine and built his first tram road. Georgia Southern and Florida railroads arrived in 1888, and homes and businesses followed. Long distance telephone service arrived in 1902; electric lights in March 1903.

In the beginning, Tift named his village "Lena", but a fellow named George Badger, who worked at the sawmill wanted to honor the founder of the village, so he climbed a pine tree and nailed a placard with the bold letters, TIFTON, for "Tift's Town."

On Aug. 15, 1905, Tift County was established. It was named for H.H. Tift, but due to a law that a county should not bear the name of a living man, Nelson Tift of Albany was made honorary beneficiary.

In 1907 Tift County was the county with the most schoolhouses. In 1914, it was the smallest town in the USA with a daily newspaper: *Tifton Gazette Daily*. The last mill whistle blast was June of 1916, marking the end of the lumber era. Tift County was such a rich land that agriculture soon superceded sawmilling as the main "crop." At first cotton was primary, but due to the boll weevil problems, peanuts emerged. When the vegetable industry flourished here, Tifton earned the title "Plant Center of The World." The tobacco industry grew, farming became diversified and the produce and livestock production increased.

The grand opening of the **Tift Theater** in 1937 was greatly anticipated due to its state-of-the-art equipment (said to be the best in South Georgia). The Grand Re-Opening, held in 1993, marked the restoration of the theater to its original design.

GEORGIA AGRIRAMA

Living History Museum has 4 distinct areas: traditional farm community of the 1870s, progressive farmstead of the 1890s, industrial sites complex, and a rural town. 35 structures. 95 acres. Barnyard animals. Costumed interpreters. Special events. Year-round, Mon. to Sat. 9 a.m.-5 p.m. On I-75 exit 63B, Tifton. See photo in "Welcome to Georgia" pages. 912-386-3344

Tifton's Founder, Henry Harding Tift

Henry Harding Tift was born in the town of Mystic, Connecticut on March 16, 1841, the son of Amos Chapman and Phoebe Tift. His father was a merchant who often traded in Southern cities, particularly Key West, and whose two brothers located along the Flint River in Georgia. They were Nelson and Asa F. Tift. These two uncles were to have an influence on Henry Harding and to play a small role in the founding of Tifton.

Henry Harding grew up in the seaport and ship-building town of Mystic, where he developed a natural love for the sea and ships. In 1859 Harding graduated from the East Greenwich Rhode Island Academy and served as an apprentice in the Standard Machine Shop at Mystic.

After completing the course of training in marine engineering, Henry Harding joined the Mallory Steamship Lines as a marine engineer. He continued in the seafaring work until 1870, when his uncles Nelson and A.F. persuaded him to come to Albany to operate a lumber products enterprise which they had organized. Henry Harding accepted and worked for his uncles for the next two years. The move from New England to South Georgia was significant for Tifton.

Two years after arriving in Albany, Captain Tift (the title earned by his seafaring work) bought from his uncles 4,900 acres of virgin timber 40 miles east of Albany. He purchased machinery for a sawmill, mostly from T.H. Willingham, who was to become his father-in-law.

In March 1872, the 31-year-old seafarer-come-lumberman embarked on the trip that was to lead to the founding of Tifton. At Albany, he loaded a 14-by-16 foot shanty on a railroad car and loaded the machinery he had purchased on an ox-drawn wagon.

The next stop was in the heart of the virgin pine forest he had purchased, along the newly opened Brunswick and Western Railroad. Here Capt. Tift unloaded the saw mill machinery and shanty and carved out the area which was to become Tifton.

For 10 years Capt. Tift lived in the shanty near the sawmill. Tift's career was spectacular. He had the trained seaman's eye for good mast material and ship's lumber. He soon made a fortune from the long leaf yellow pine, used primarily for shipsiding in the shipyards of New England.

While Capt. Tift's business enterprises were large, he also was interested in agriculture. He donated two lots of land for the **Cycloneta Experimental Farm** (now SUNSWEET) and in the 1880s established his own model farm on which tobacco, grapes, peaches, pecans, pears, and livestock were grown to illustrate what could be done with South Georgia soil. The first **Tifton Fruit Festival,** The Midsummer Fair, was held in his home and became a major event.

His interest in agriculture led to his most lasting contribution: the establishment in Tifton of the **District A & M School** (now ABAC) in 1907 and the **Coastal Plain Experiment Station** in 1919. He gave his money, land and personal persuasion generously to have the 2 facilities located here.

Education always was a vital concern for Capt. Tift. He gave land for the first school in Tifton; loaned money for its operation, and sold land at a low price for other school facilities. He contributed heavily to **Monroe Female College** at Forsyth where Mrs. Tift had graduated (1878). In 1907, the school's name was changed to **Bessie Tift College** in appreciation of their generosity.

Capt. Tift gave the land for the First United Methodist Church, the First Baptist Church, and the Episcopal Church. When the Methodist's decided to erect a new building, he bought the old frame church and had it moved to the Cotton Mill for religious services there (Bessie Tift Baptist Chapel). He gave a large portion of what is now Fulwood Park to the city for a park and a tract of land to be used as a cemetery-now Oakridge. He set aside a choice tract of land to be sold at a low price to the Tift County Hospital.

On Feb. 4, 1922, at the age of 81, Capt. Tift died peacefully in the large home on Second Street which he had built many years before for his young bride. At his death, he was ranked among the richest men in Georgia and the South.

Text courtesy Tifton-Tift County Tourism Association

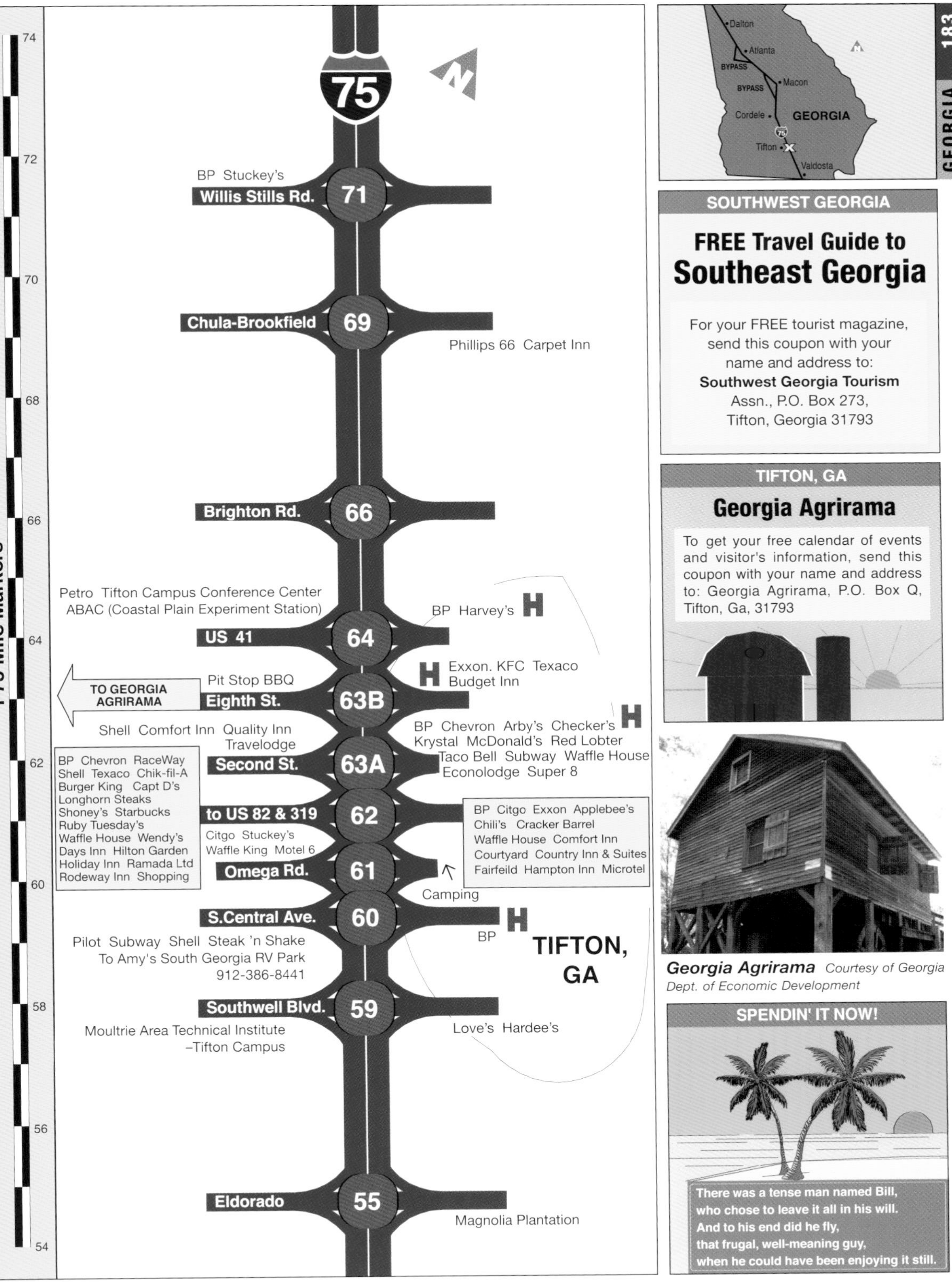

I-75 Mile Markers
74
72
70
68
66
64
62
60
58
56
54
75
N
BP Stuckey's
Willis Stills Rd.
71
Chula-Brookfield
69
Phillips 66 Carpet Inn
Brighton Rd.
66
Petro Tifton Campus Conference Center
ABAC (Coastal Plain Experiment Station)
US 41
64
BP Harvey's
H
TO GEORGIA AGRIRAMA
Pit Stop BBQ
Eighth St.
63B
H
Exxon. KFC Texaco
Budget Inn
Shell Comfort Inn Quality Inn
Travelodge
Second St.
63A
BP Chevron Arby's Checker's
H
Krystal McDonald's Red Lobter
Taco Bell Subway Waffle House
Econolodge Super 8
BP Chevron RaceWay
Shell Texaco Chik-fil-A
Burger King Capt D's
Longhorn Steaks
Shoney's Starbucks
Ruby Tuesday's
Waffle House Wendy's
Days Inn Hilton Garden
Holiday Inn Ramada Ltd
Rodeway Inn Shopping
to US 82 & 319
62
Citgo Stuckey's
Waffle King Motel 6
BP Citgo Exxon Applebee's
Chili's Cracker Barrel
Waffle House Comfort Inn
Courtyard Country Inn & Suites
Fairfeild Hampton Inn Microtel
Omega Rd.
61
Camping
S.Central Ave.
60
H
BP
TIFTON, GA
Pilot Subway Shell Steak 'n Shake
To Amy's South Georgia RV Park
912-386-8441
Southwell Blvd.
59
Love's Hardee's
Moultrie Area Technical Institute
–Tifton Campus
Eldorado
55
Magnolia Plantation
Dalton
Atlanta
BYPASS
BYPASS
Macon
Cordele
GEORGIA
75
Tifton
Valdosta
SOUTHWEST GEORGIA
FREE Travel Guide to
Southeast Georgia
For your FREE tourist magazine, send this coupon with your name and address to:
Southwest Georgia Tourism
Assn., P.O. Box 273,
Tifton, Georgia 31793
TIFTON, GA
Georgia Agrirama
To get your free calendar of events and visitor's information, send this coupon with your name and address to: Georgia Agrirama, P.O. Box Q, Tifton, Ga, 31793
SPENDIN' IT NOW!
There was a tense man named Bill,
who chose to leave it all in his will.
And to his end did he fly,
that frugal, well-meaning guy,
when he could have been enjoying it still.

Georgia Agrirama *Courtesy of Georgia Dept. of Economic Development*

Adel/Cook County, GEORGIA

Adel-Cook County Chamber of Commerce
100 S. Hutchinson Ave., Adel, Georgia 31620
229-896-2281

The South's Premiere Sporting Destination

Georgia's southern tip of the I-75 is a shopper's paradise. A complex of 100 factory outlet stores can be found just off I-75 on exit 5 in Lake Park. Here you will find the famous "King Frog" Outlet Stores, several fast food restaurants, gas stations.

There is also an Official Tourist Center offering discounts on attractions and accommodations and tourism information for areas throughout the southeast (FLA and GA). Open year-round, from Mon. to Sat. 9 a.m. - 9 p.m., and Sun. 10 a.m. -7 p.m. 912-896-4511

The city of Adel is best known for what is outside the city limits! The lake at Reed Bingham State Park is one of Georgia's best boating and water-skiing destinations.

So many people came to see the multitude of Buzzards that roost on the Little River (runs through the State Park), that the informal gathering in January has developed into an annual event, the Buzzard Days Festival. This State Park also offers camping, fishing, swimming, picnic sites and hiking on the Coastal Plains Nature Trail through several different wildlife habitats.

Hidden behind the tall pines and wild wiregrass fields, you will find a 3,000-acre private reserve called Live Oak Plantation which lends its reputation as the South's Premiere Sporting Destination to Adel. This sporting retreat offers southern hospitality to just 15 guests at a time. The Plantation offers a private executive golf course (par 34), and lake-fishing (largemouth bass). More details about Live Oak Plantation are found on this page.

The Adelily Festival is held in Spring in downtown Adel. Call the Chamber for more info: 229-896-2281

Live Oak Plantation

675 Plantation Road, Adel, GA. 31620 1-800-682-HUNT or 1-800-682-4868

HUNTING.
The Live Oak Plantation specialty is quail. The guides are local natives, lifelong hunters and all full-time employees. You'll have access to more than 100 champion-bred pointers, setters and retrievers. A trap Range is available for lessons and practice. Enjoy the complimentary open bar in the lodge following the afternoon hunt.

Proper safety outer wear, including a flame orange hunting jacket, is mandatory. Live Oak Plantation provides hunting caps but do bring your gun and gear. A hunting license not required, as they have a blanket license. The pro shop is well-stocked.

GOLFING.
This is a truly private course, with no crowds, created by a professional designer, with a par 34 that packs enormous challenge into just 3 holes and 3 sets of tees. Did you know that for many years, the legendary old course at St. Andrews played a reversible course (out and then back over the same fairways)? Live Oak Plantation considers its course to be a tribute to the game's Scottish traditions.

Walk or obtain your cart at the on-site pro shop.

RELAXATION.
Home-cooked meals are served three times a day. **Main Lodge** features spacious quarters for nine and handsome antique furnishing in the main lodge, well-stocked complimentary bar, covered decks, screened porch, Game room, and satellite TV/VCR. **Lake Lodge** offers plenty of room for 6 and waterfront relaxation overlooking lake and golf course. The outbuildings are well-suited to business meetings and board retreats.

HONEYBEE FESTIVAL, HAHIRA, GA

In the next county you'll find the town of Hahira, a center for the bee industry.

Hahira holds a **Honey Bee Festival** each October showcasing bee-theme arts and crafts, and bee-keeping demonstrations.

Also a center for the tobacco industry, visitors are welcomed to tour Hahira warehouses and watch the fast-paced tobacco auctioning which takes place from July to October.

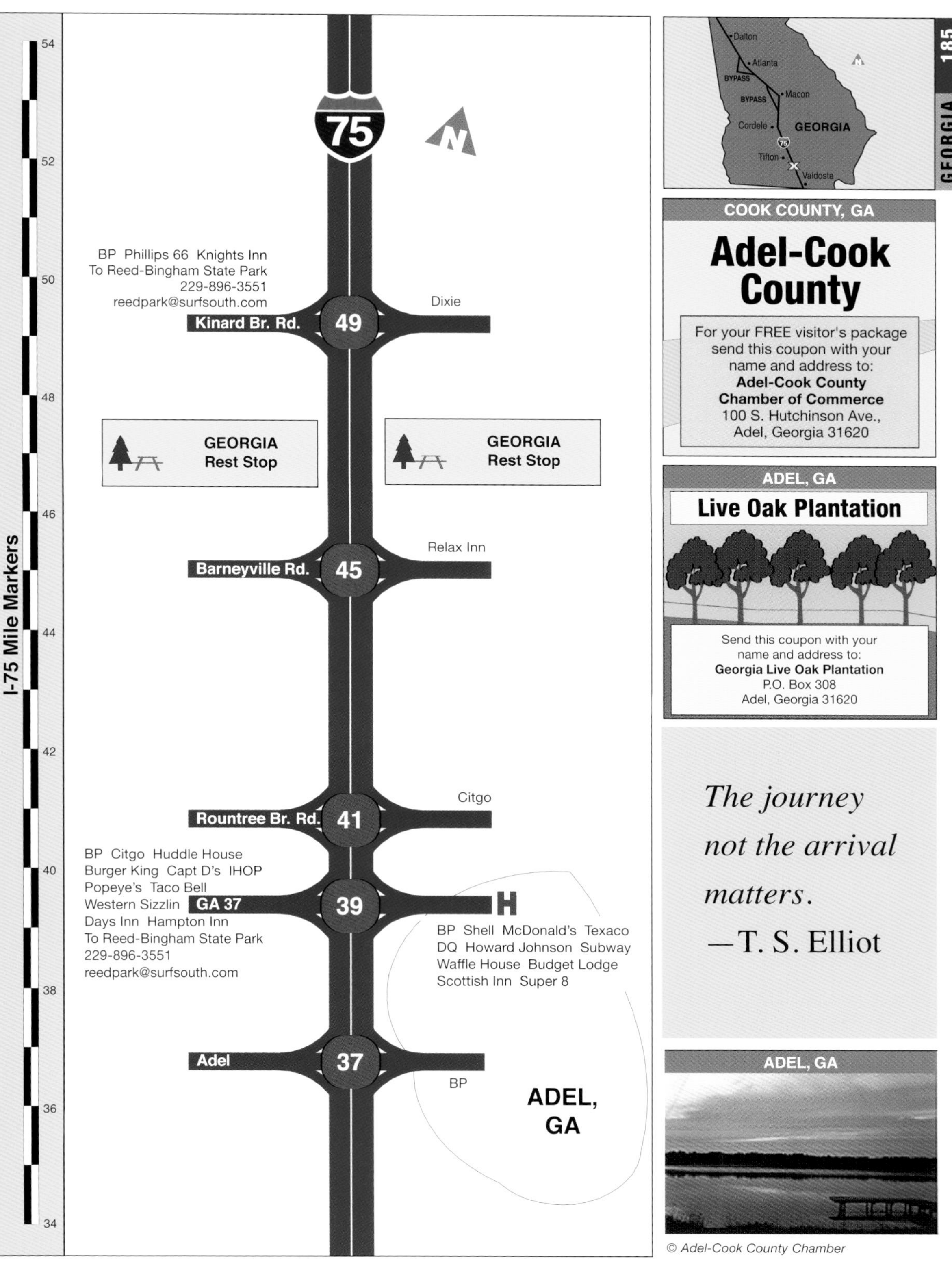

The journey not the arrival matters.
—T. S. Elliot

ADEL, GA

© Adel-Cook County Chamber

Valdosta/Lowndes County
GEORGIA

Valdosta-Lowndes County Conference Center & Tourism Authority
1 Meeting Place, Valdosta, Georgia 31601
1-800-569-TOUR **www.valdostatouris.com**

Valdosta is Georgia's 10th-largest city. Its name means **"Vale of Beauty."** Since its founding in 1860, visitors have looked forward to its mild climate and lush landscapes.

Valdosta is also known as **"the Azalea City."** Flowers abound, as do festivals: the **Ham & Egg Show** in Feb., **Spring Flower show** in Apr., **Day Lily show** in May, **tobacco auctions** in July, **cotton patch festival** in Sept., **Honeybee festival** and antiques show/sale in Oct., **Camellia show** and the **South Georgia Fair** in Nov., and the **Christmas Arts & Crafts Show.**

Located about 4 hours south of Atlanta and 4 hours north of Orlando, Valdosta makes an effort to welcome weary I-75 travelers with four RV parks and 42 hotel/motels, as well as excellent shopping (100 Factory Outlet Stores, the Valdosta Mall and Remerton Mill Village), specialty restaurants and 100 places of worship.

Many stop at Valdosta just to see the **Planetarium** and exhibitions at the **Valdosta State University.** Valdosta's Crescent Complex, one of Georgia's National Treasures, is open to the public.

Historic Valdosta

If you take the driving tour of Historic Valdosta you will see all 3 of the National Register Historic Districts and city's spectacular homes. Perhaps the most beautiful is **Crescent House,** which was built in 1889 by Sen. William S. West. It is known for its mirrored fireplace, ballroom, gold-leaf tiled bathroom, and the circular verandah which is supported by 13 massive columns, one for each of the original American colonies. 904 North Patterson, Valdosta. 229-245-0513

The Lowndes County Historical Society and Museum presents the city's history and its important function as the inland marketing capital for Sea Island cotton. Old Carnegie Library. 305 W. Central Ave., Valdosta. Mon. to Fri. 10 a.m.-5 p.m., Sat. 10 a.m.-2 p.m. 229-247-4780

Old Barber Pitman House
Built in 1915 by the second manufacturer of Coca-Cola products. Open Mon. to Fri. 9 a.m.-5 p.m. for self-guided tours. Guided tours by request at the Chamber of Commerce. 416 N. Ashley St. 229-247-8100

The Legacy of William S. West

William S. West, a native Georgian, was a visionary who worked hard to reach the level of wealth and prominence he eventually obtained. He attended several schools, working and teaching at the same time. Upon his marriage to Ora Lee Cranford, he began plans to build a home. West marked out a crescent shaped line with his walking cane and announced, "This is where I want my front porch to be." And thus began his vision of The Crescent.

In 1898, after 2 years of construction, the 23-room neo-classical mansion was ready for occupancy at an estimated cost of $12,000. The grand ballroom on the third floor was the scene of many elegant parties, boasting guest lists of over 200. One noted dinner guest was Woodrow Wilson, future President of the United States.

By 1914, Col. West was a successful farmer, teacher, lawyer, world traveler, and a business man who had made a fortune. He had served many years in the Georgia legislature, was President of the State Senate and was appointed as a U.S. Senator in 1914 to fill an unexpired term. In December of the same year, West died in his sleep. Mrs. West died in 1933, their son passed in 1937.

By the 1930s, the Wests had suffered financial ruin. This, coupled with the nation-wide depression meant drastic changes for the family. The Crescent was then divided into apartments. By 1950, the building had deteriorated so much that a group of businessmen intended to level it and build a gas station in its place. Instead, 3 dedicated women spearheaded a fundraising drive to preserve the mansion. In just 2 months, the $35,000 needed to buy the mansion was raised and the property was saved.

In 1980, The Crescent was listed in the National Register of Historic Places. Today, it is under the care and ownership of the Valdosta Garden Center, which is made up of 7 garden clubs. Restored and refurbished, the Crescent Complex is open to the public, both for touring as well as for a variety of social functions including weddings and christenings. A library contains 200 books about flower arranging and horticulture. The auditorium is used as a meeting place for business organizations and is the site of flower shows and exhibits. More information on the left of this page.

Text courtesy Valdosta-Lowndes County Convention & Visitors Bureau brochure The Crescent Complex

Mules, Old Cars, Snakes and a Pow Wow

If you are going to Tallahassee or the Florida Panhandle, the folks in Cairo, Georgia's "Hospitality City," would love you to stop by. Count on a good old-fashioned Southern welcome when you get there.

The people in Cairo and Grady County have quite a nice reputation. When the "Great American Race" featuring 100 of the world's most expensive antique cars, made a stopover in Cairo en route to Florida from California, the race entrants were so impressed with the town that they voted Cairo the "Outstanding Great Race City." They had to write in this city's name because Cairo wasn't even among the cities listed on the ballot (like San Diego, Phoenix, or Baton Rouge)!

In the winter, thousands come for the Whigham Rattlesnake Roundup (last Sat. in Jan.). Rattle-snakes are hunted and displayed. Enjoy the arts, crafts, food and entertainment or browse the flea market.

They like mules in Calvary, GA. On the last Sat. of Nov., this community jovially honors mules, who for many years powered their farming equipment and spurred their agricultural prosperity. It's just a fun place to be: a hearty early morning breakfast followed by mule contests, parades, arts, crafts and country entertainment.

May (2nd weekend) features an antique car rally in Cairo, and on the 4th of July, come to Whigham to see the Lower Muscogee Creek Tribe's annual Pow Wow. Native American customs and traditions are presented and the event is open to all. 229-377-3663

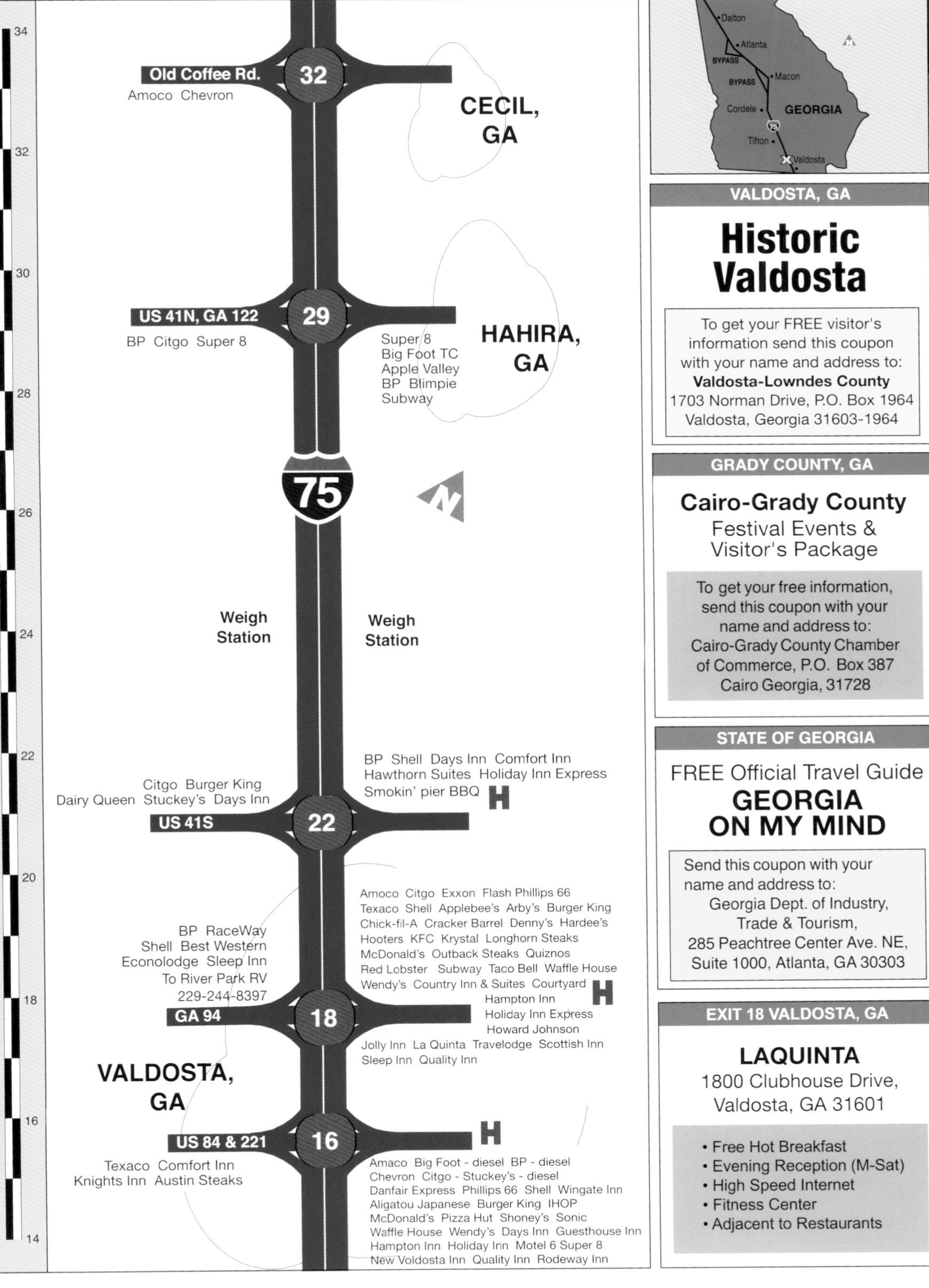

I-75 Mile Markers
34
32
30
28
26
24
22
20
18
16
14
Old Coffee Rd.
32
Amoco Chevron
CECIL, GA
US 41N, GA 122
29
BP Citgo Super 8
Super 8
Big Foot TC
Apple Valley
BP Blimpie
Subway
HAHIRA, GA
75
N
Weigh Station
Weigh Station
Citgo Burger King
Dairy Queen Stuckey's Days Inn
US 41S
22
BP Shell Days Inn Comfort Inn
Hawthorn Suites Holiday Inn Express
Smokin' pier BBQ
H
BP RaceWay
Shell Best Western
Econolodge Sleep Inn
To River Park RV
229-244-8397
GA 94
18
Amoco Citgo Exxon Flash Phillips 66
Texaco Shell Applebee's Arby's Burger King
Chick-fil-A Cracker Barrel Denny's Hardee's
Hooters KFC Krystal Longhorn Steaks
McDonald's Outback Steaks Quiznos
Red Lobster Subway Taco Bell Waffle House
Wendy's Country Inn & Suites Courtyard
Hampton Inn
Holiday Inn Express
Howard Johnson
Jolly Inn La Quinta Travelodge Scottish Inn
Sleep Inn Quality Inn
H
VALDOSTA, GA
US 84 & 221
16
H
Texaco Comfort Inn
Knights Inn Austin Steaks
Amaco Big Foot - diesel BP - diesel
Chevron Citgo - Stuckey's - diesel
Danfair Express Phillips 66 Shell Wingate Inn
Aligatou Japanese Burger King IHOP
McDonald's Pizza Hut Shoney's Sonic
Waffle House Wendy's Days Inn Guesthouse Inn
Hampton Inn Holiday Inn Motel 6 Super 8
New Voldosta Inn Quality Inn Rodeway Inn
Dalton
Atlanta
BYPASS
BYPASS
Macon
Cordele
GEORGIA
75
Tifton
Valdosta

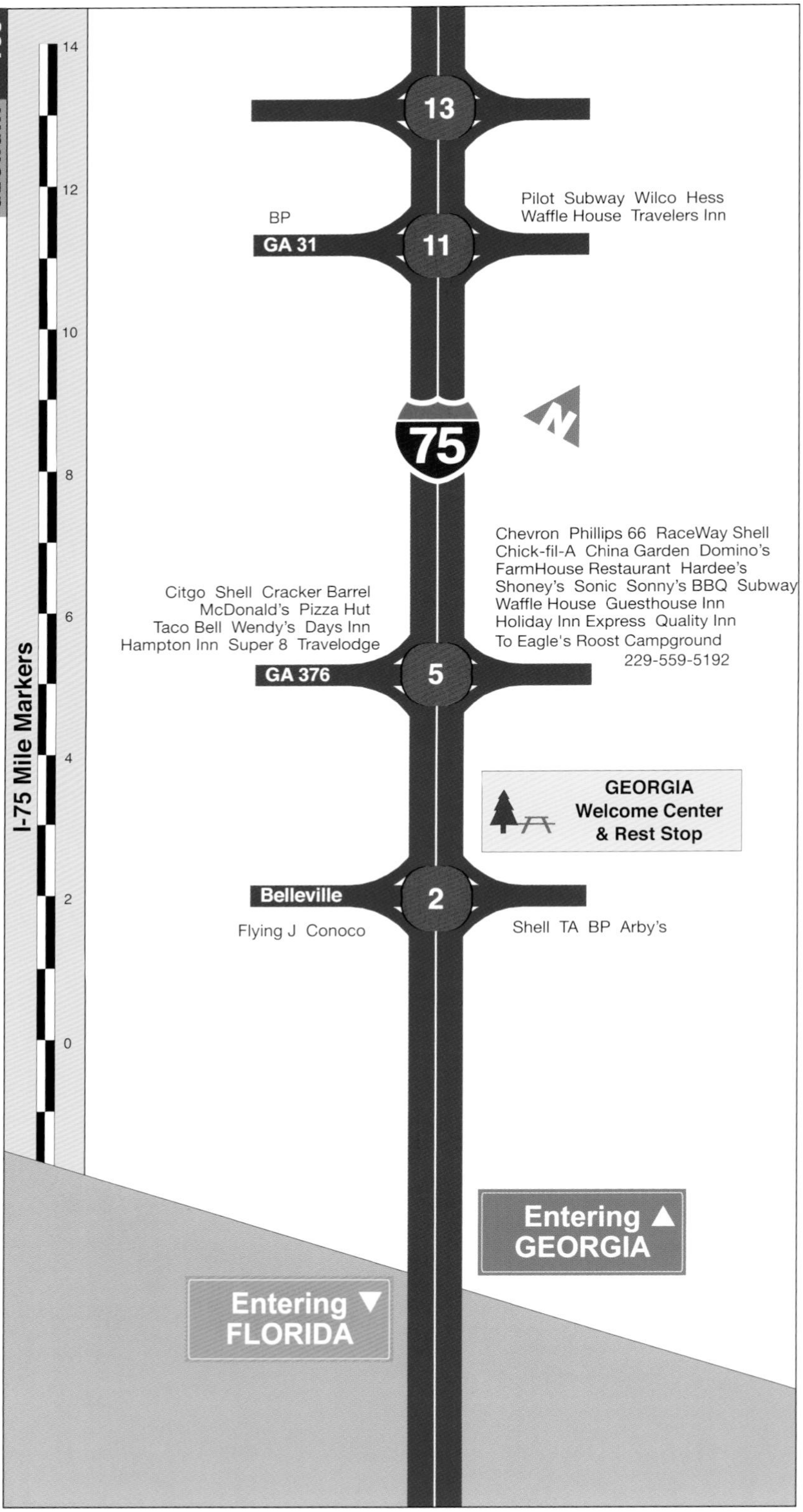

I-75 Mile Markers

14 12 10 8 6 4 2 0

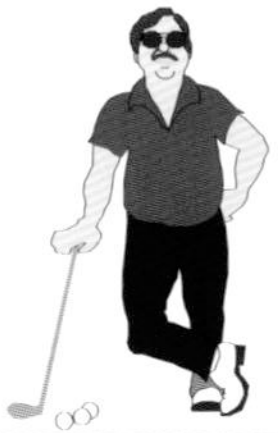

13

BP

GA 31

11

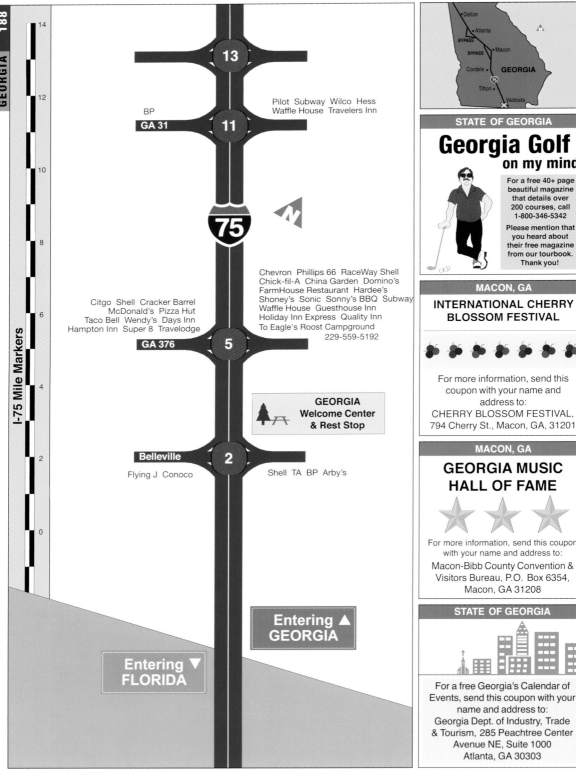

Pilot Subway Wilco Hess
Waffle House Travelers Inn

75

Citgo Shell Cracker Barrel
McDonald's Pizza Hut
Taco Bell Wendy's Days Inn
Hampton Inn Super 8 Travelodge

GA 376

5

Chevron Phillips 66 RaceWay Shell
Chick-fil-A China Garden Domino's
FarmHouse Restaurant Hardee's
Shoney's Sonic Sonny's BBQ Subway
Waffle House Guesthouse Inn
Holiday Inn Express Quality Inn
To Eagle's Roost Campground
229-559-5192

GEORGIA
Welcome Center
& Rest Stop

Belleville

2

Flying J Conoco

Shell TA BP Arby's

Entering GEORGIA

Entering FLORIDA

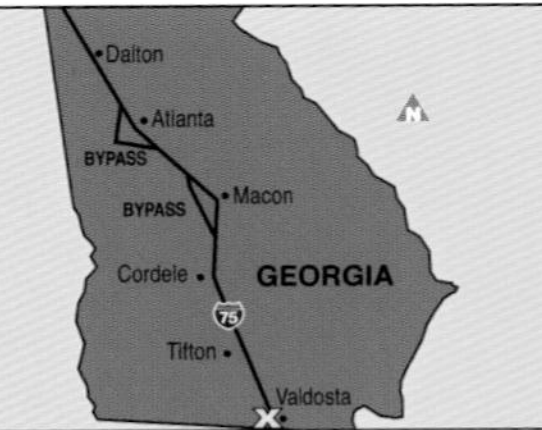

Visit Florida
www.visitflorida.com

2540 W. Executive Center Circle, Suite 200
Tallahassee, FL 32301

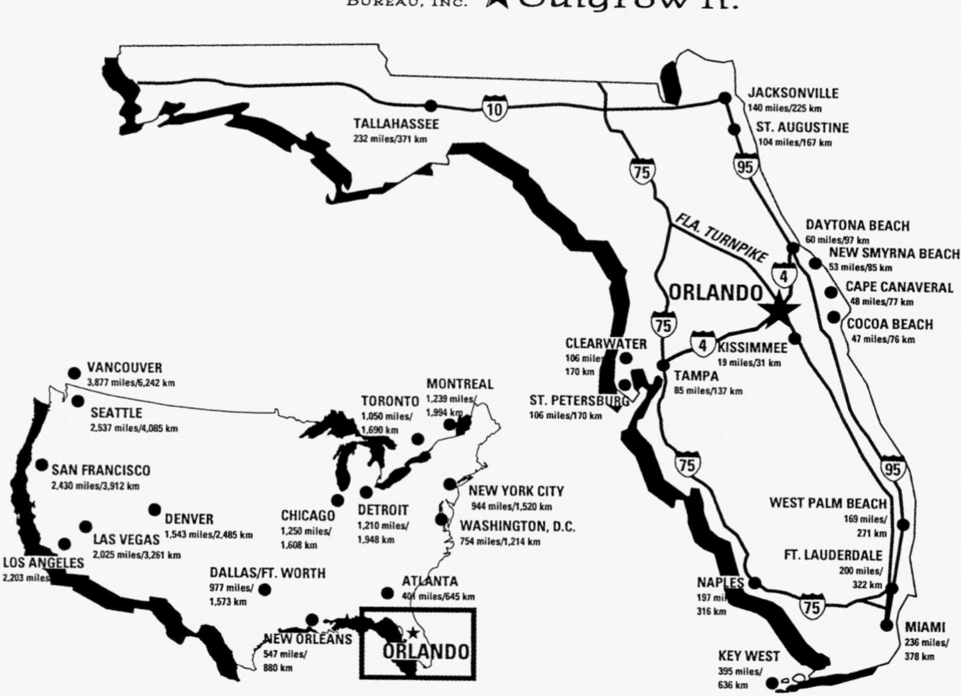

Welcome to Florida

The World's Playground

Florida is the world s playground. There are 7 distinct travel regions in Florida and most every traveler has a favorite. Is yours the temperate Panhandle of Northwest Florida or is it the lush paradise of the Keys in Southeast Florida? Central Florida has 3 distinct divisions: Gulf-side, Ocean-side and the Florida Heartland. The Orlando area in Central Florida is a magnet for fun-lovers the world over, and is the most well-known Florida destination.

Write to the Visit Florida, at the address listed above, and request their Florida Vacation Guide for more information on all of the travel regions.

Orlando: Roads to Excitement

With its unique shape, the peninsula of Florida is easily identifiable. Comprising 58,000 square miles, the Sunshine State is a little larger than England and Greece and can fit into the state of California a little more than 2-1/2 times.

Orlando is located approximately in the center of Florida, midway between Jacksonville and Miami. Its convenient location makes it the ideal vacation spot. Besides being home to more than 80 attractions, more than 92,000 hotel rooms and 3,900 restaurants, its location affords visitors easy access to the Atlantic Coast and the Gulf of Mexico.

Major Florida highways that provide easy connections to Orlando include Interstate 4, which runs from Daytona Beach in the east to St. Petersburg on the west coast; Interstate 10, which enters the state at the southwest tip in Pensacola and extends to Jacksonville in the northeast; Interstate 75, which enters Florida just south of Valdosta, GA. and runs south to Naples and then east to Fort Lauderdale; Interstate 95 which enters Florida just north of Jacksonville and extends south to Miami; and the Florida Turnpike that connects the Interstate 75 south of Ocala, extending southeast through Orlando and on to Miami.

Orlando/Orange County
FLORIDA

Orlando/Orange County Official Visitor Center
8723 International Drive, (southeast corner of International Drive and Austrian Row) 1-800-551-0181 **www.visitorlando.com**

Walt Disney World Resort

Cirque du Soleil's "La Nouba."
Downtown Disney West Side. Acrobatics and state-of-the-art special effects with 70+ artists from around the world. lanoubaorlando.com 407-939-7600

Disney's Animal Kingdom Park
Adventures and encounters with real, exotic animals, and with fictional animals and giant dinosaurs from the prehistoric world. Expedition Everest (high-speed train adventure), "Finding Nemo – The Musical," (30-minute musical show), TriceraTop Spin, Primeval Whirl!, DINOSAUR and Kilimanjaro Safaris. disneyworld.com 407-824-4321

Disney's Blizzard Beach Water Park
One of the world's tallest, fastest free-fall speed slides in a whimsical "winter" setting. The largest of Disney's water parks, 22 water slides and "icy" bobsled runs that stay comfortably warm and thrillingly fast. disneyworld.com 407-939-7812

Disney's Fantasia Gardens Miniature Golf
36-hole golf adventure featuring Fantasia Gardens, an 18-hole mini golf course, and Fantasia Fairways, an 18-hole challenge course designed with strategically placed bunkers and hazards. disneyworld.com 407-560-4870

Disney's Hollywood Studios (formerly Disney-MGM Studios) is a theme park with a complete motion picture and television studio. Feature attractions include Toy Story Mania!; Lights, Motors, Action!; Extreme Stunt Show; Playhouse Disney - Live on Stage!; Rock 'n' Roller Coaster Starring Aerosmith; The Twilight Zone Tower of Terror; and an American Idol attraction (2009). disneyworld.com 407-824-4321

Disney's Typhoon Lagoon Water Park
Twisting tides, roaring rapids and relaxing rivers. 9 water slides – including a water coaster thrill ride, swim with sharks and tropical fish, or conquering waves in the largest wave pool in the U.S.! disneyworld.com 407-939-7812

Disney's Winter Summerland Mini Golf course is an interactive miniature golf experience with two 18-hole wacky, elf-sized golf courses. One carries the zany, snow-covered Florida theme found at Disney's Blizzard Beach Water Park, the other is a more tropical, holiday theme. disneyworld.com 407-560-3000

Our Recommendation For Your Orlando Visit

Disney's Wide World of Sports Complex hosts nearly 200 Amateur Athletic Union events, Atlanta Braves spring training and the Pop Warner Super Bowl each year. Sports lovers can enjoy more than 30 sports. disneyworld.com 407-939-7529

DisneyQuest Indoor Interactive Theme Park is a 5-story, indoor park with cutting-edge technology. Guests river raft on a Virtual Jungle Cruise, ride a roller coaster of their own design on Cyber Space Mountain or become part of a human pinball game in Mighty Ducks Pinball Slam. Some attractions require a separate charge. disneyworld.com 407-828-4600

Epcot takes guests to 11 nations at World Showcase and fast-forwards them to tomorrow in Future World. World Showcase offers a kaleidoscope of nations — The American Adventure, Canada, China, France, Germany, Italy, Japan, Mexico, Morocco, Norway and the United Kingdom. Don't-miss rides include Mission:SPACE, Soarin' (lifts guests 40 feet (12 m) inside a giant projection screen dome), and The Seas with Nemo & Friends (stunning attraction adds the stars of "Finding Nemo" to the live marine life of the huge aquarium in The Living Seas pavilion. disneyworld.com 407-824-4321

Magic Kingdom Park features seven magical lands with attractions, restaurants and shops based on favorite Disney themes of fantasy, yesterday and tomorrow. Popular attractions include Mickey's PhilharMagic, Splash Mountain, Big Thunder Mountain, Buzz Lightyear's Space Ranger Spin, The Many Adventures of Winnie the Pooh, Space Mountain and The Monsters, Inc. Laugh Floor, an interactive adventure inspired by Disney-Pixar's "Monsters, Inc." disneyworld.com 407-824-4321

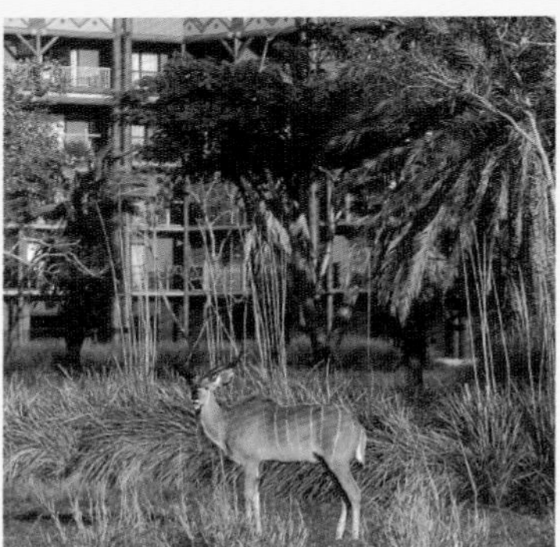

Nickelodeon Family Suites
This must be the most colorful family hotel and resort in Orlando, FL. Play all day — and into the night — at two pool complexes. Dive straight into the excitement of the interactive games. Chat with your favorite Nickelodeon characters over breakfast at the Nicktoons Café, or surround yourself with videogame entertainment in the arcade. Then herd everybody aboard the shuttles for transportation to popular nearby theme parks like Disney and Universal Studios. We loved the various themed hotel rooms, convenient food court, and generous breakfast buffets:

- Located on 24 fabulous acres, in the middle of Orlando, Florida
- One mile from the excitement of Walt Disney World Resort
- Minutes from Universal Orlando, SeaWorld, and tons of other attractions
- Just 20 minutes from Orlando International Airport (MCO)
- 14500 Continental Gateway, Orlando FL 32821 1- (877) NICK-111 www.NickHotel.com

Pirates Dinner Adventure Show
Our favorite Orlando Dinner Show Adventure!! If you are looking for an adventurous time while visiting the International Drive area of Orlando, then book this treat! Pirate's Dinner Adventure is a dinner show attraction that puts you and your family right in the middle of all of the swashbuckling action. Pirate's Dinner Adventure is acclaimed as "the world's most unique interactive dinner show." We loved it.

Guests are entertained with an astonishing display of special effects wizardry, aerial artistry, swashbuckling swordplay, dynamic duels and daring-do; a classic story of good vs. evil that offers the perfect blend of action, adventure, comedy and romance; the opportunity to interact in the adventure; and a sumptuous dining experience. The show is perfect for children and adults alike.

6400 Carrier Dr., Orlando, FL 32819
(407) 248-0590
www.piratesdinneradventure.com

A new breed of resort at Disney's Animal Kingdom Lodge.
Lake Buena Vista, Florida. Photo courtesy The Walt Disney Company.

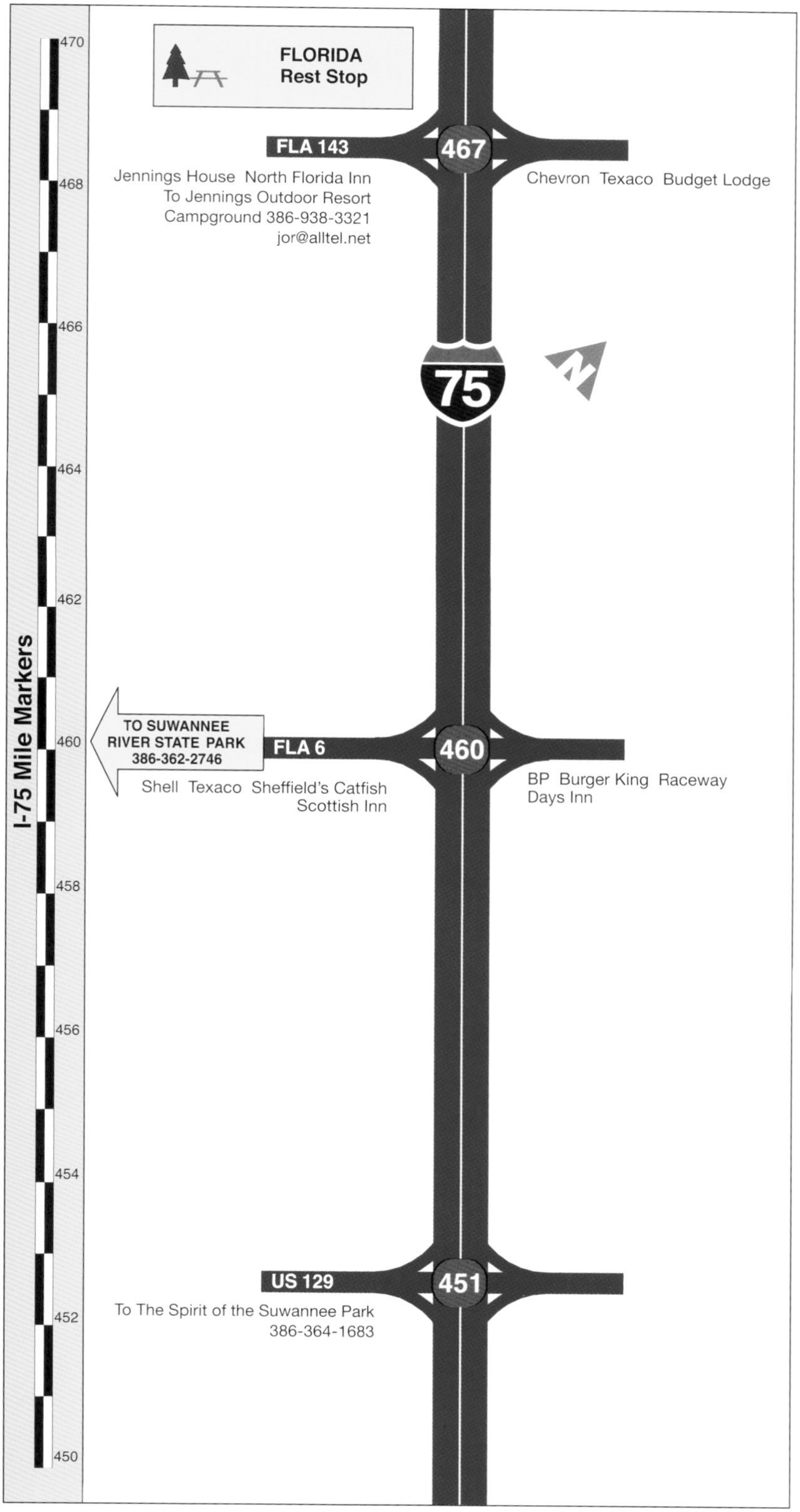

I-75 Mile Markers
470
468
466
464
462
460
458
456
454
452
450
FLORIDA
Rest Stop
FLA 143
467
Jennings House North Florida Inn
To Jennings Outdoor Resort
Campground 386-938-3321
jor@alltel.net
Chevron Texaco Budget Lodge
75
N
TO SUWANNEE
RIVER STATE PARK
386-362-2746
FLA 6
460
Shell Texaco Sheffield's Catfish
Scottish Inn
BP Burger King Raceway
Days Inn
US 129
451
To The Spirit of the Suwannee Park
386-364-1683

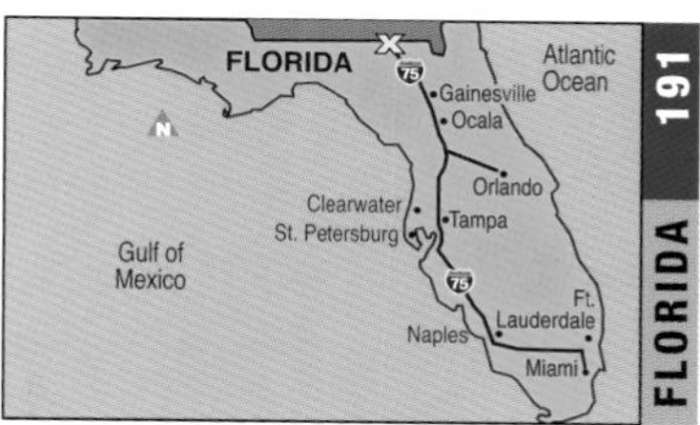

FLORIDA
Atlantic
Ocean
Gainesville
Ocala
Orlando
Clearwater
St. Petersburg
Tampa
Gulf of
Mexico
Naples
Ft.
Lauderdale
Miami
75

STATE OF FLORIDA

Free Florida Accommodations Directory

Official Directory for the Florida Hotel and Motel Association

For a copy of this publication, send this coupon, your name and address to:

Visit Florida
2540 W. Executive Center Circle,
Suite 200, Tallahassee, Florida 32301

STATE OF FLORIDA

Free Florida Official Transportation Map

For a copy of this publication, send this coupon, your name and address to:

Visit Florida

2540 W. Executive Center Circle,
Suite 200, Tallahassee, Florida 32301

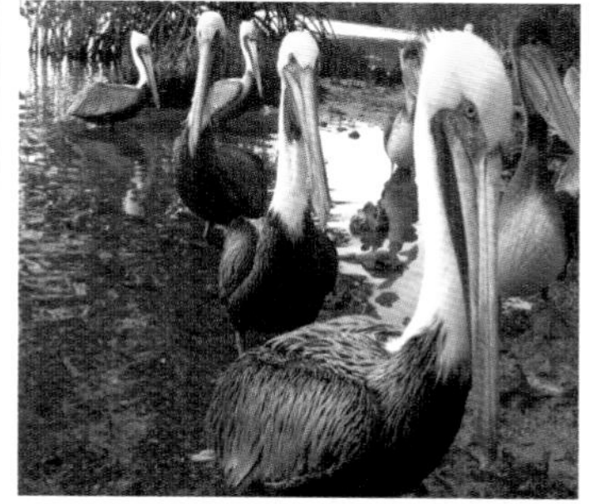

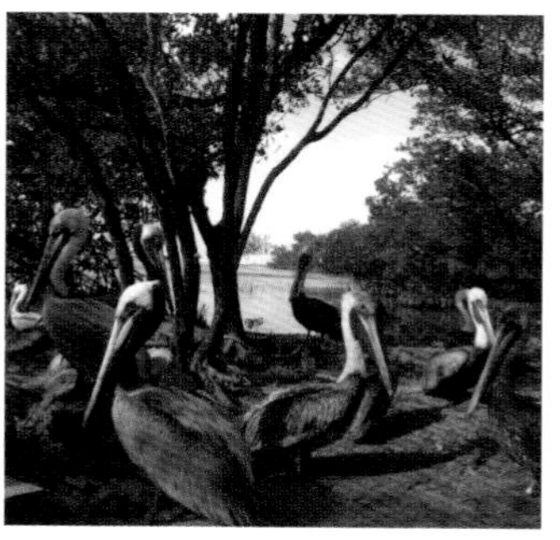

Pelicans *© Emily Marks*

Suwannee County
FLORIDA

Suwannee County Tourist Development Council
601 East Howard Street, P.O. Drawer C, Live Oak, Florida 32060
386-362-3071 **www.suwanneechamber.com/scea/tdc.html**

The **Suwannee River,** forever immortalized by Stephen Foster in 1851, surrounds Suwannee County on three sides and allows the outdoor enthusiast quick access to several fresh-water springs, lakes and rivers.

Certified cave divers know **Suwannee County's** crystal clear underwater caves are some of the longest continuous systems in the world. **Branford** is recognized as the diving capital of the world. Local shops provide equipment, instruction and guided tours.

The rivers are full of gamefish: bass, brim, catfish and sturgeon.

An extensive system of on-and off-road bicycle trails ribbon throughout Suwannee County. The annual Suwannee Bicycle Festival is held each spring in Live Oak. Wildflowers, deer, otters, alligators and beavers are often sighted along the county's extensive nature trails.

THE SPIRIT OF SUWANNEE MUSIC PARK & CAMPGROUND
U.S. 129 N., Rte. 1, Box 98. Live Oak
386-364-1683

SUWANNEE RIVER STATE PARK
Rte. 8, Box 297, Live Oak
386-362-2746

ICHETUCKNEE SPRINGS STATE PARK
Rte. 2, Box 108, Fort White
386-497-4690

Orlando Before Disney

John B. Steinmetz has disappeared into historical obscurity, but little did he know that his idea, an idea that brought national attention to Orlando in 1895, would become the precursor to those of a fellow named Walt Disney.

Steinmetz, a citrus grower, heard opportunity knock in 1895 when his orange groves were devastated by the 1894-95 freeze. The industrious Orlando resident converted his packing house into a skating rink, added picnic facilities and a bath house, and built a toboggan slide that spilled into the springs. His entertainment complex soon made Orlando an important destination.

Seventy years later, **Walt Disney** would soon make Orlando a household word, not only in the nation, but around the world. The announcement that he would build Walt Disney World was made on Nov. 15, 1965, the Cherry Plaza Hotel (now Lee s Lakeside) on Lake Eola, just feet from where Orlando s namesake, **Orlando Reeves,** was struck down

Although its amazing theme parks are what put Orlando on the map, the city existed long before the first roller coaster or castle was ever built. Over the course of more than 150 years, the area has had several names and seen many different industries come and go. What was once a rustic fort in the mid 1800s has emerged as one of the world's most popular vacation destinations.

Welcome to Jernigan?

The City of Orlando came into existence in 1857, but its origins can be traced to the Armed Occupation Act of 1842. Fort Gatlin was established during the Second Seminole War in 1838 and when the war ended in 1842, the government offered land to homesteaders willing to live near the forts. Brothers Aaron and Isaac Jernigan settled near Fort Gatlin in 1843, and in 1850 a post office opened in the settlement then known as Jernigan. The population had soon spread northward, beyond the fort, leaving the exact location of the community in question. But a gift to the county of land for a courthouse near Lake Eola soon settled disputes and led to the creation of a new town called Orlando. While different versions of the origin of the name are recounted, there is no certain story as to how the city of Orlando was named. One story says the name honors soldier Orlando Reeves who died near what is now Lake Eola in downtown Orlando during the Second Seminole War – according to the legend, he warned sleeping soldiers of a coming attack before falling himself. One other popular theory credits early settler Judge Speer as suggesting Orlando, the name of the romantic hero in Shakespeare's play,
As You Like It.

Squeezing the Citrus Market

Orlando's early economy centered around the cattle industry, but the city's greatest growth occurred during several economic booms, the first following the arrival of the South Florida Railroad in 1881 which made it easier to travel to the area. Businesses appeared and hotels opened to accommodate the first wave of tourists. The railroad, renamed the Atlantic Coast Line in 1902, enabled citrus growers to ship fresh fruit to northern markets, making Orlando a major citrus producing center by 1890. With the nation's growing demand for grapefruit, tangerines and oranges, coupled with the extension of the South Florida Railroad into Central Florida in 1880, the citrus industry flourished. On July 21, 1875, by a vote of 22 men from the 85 residents, the city of Orlando was officially incorporated.

In 1894 and 1895, hard freezes hit Central Florida, destroying 95 percent of the citrus trees and severely damaging the citrus industry. It took 15 years for the industry to recover and citrus was a major agricultural industry in Orlando throughout most of the first half of the 20th century. Orlando's second boom paralleled national prosperity and progress. Orlando expanded in the early 20th century as many homes received electrical power. Cars appeared in Orlando in 1903 with a speed limit of 5 mph (8 km/h). The automobile and improved highways brought increased tourism, the growth of business and construction, and the beginnings of suburbanization. The city's population increased from about 9,000 in 1920 to more than 27,000 by 1930.

Flying High

Capitalizing on Orlando's near-perfect, year-round flying weather, aviation brought another economic boom. In 1922, Orlando's first airport opened to haul cargo. Orlando's Municipal Airport, built in 1928, became the Orlando Army Air Base, and quietly contributed to the war efforts both before and during World War II as one of the first places to train bomber pilots. The military built a second airfield near Pine Castle in 1941, which later became McCoy Air Force Base and is now the Orlando International Airport. At the end of the Second World War, Pine Castle Air Base served as the site for top secret X-1 tests and as home to a Strategic Air Command (SAC) unit in the 1950s.
In 1956, a major period of growth resulted when the Glenn L. Martin Company of Baltimore, Md., purchased 10.6 square miles (27.4 square kilometers) of southern Orange County land, and announced plans to build a missile factory. The U.S. Missile Test Center, established at Cape Canaveral in 1955, brought the aerospace industry to Orlando. The Martin Company opened a plant in 1956 and quickly became the area's leading employer. Orlando's population, almost 37,000 in 1940, reached about 52,000 by 1950. Today, the company operates under the name of Lockheed Martin and serves as the backbone of the area's technology industry.

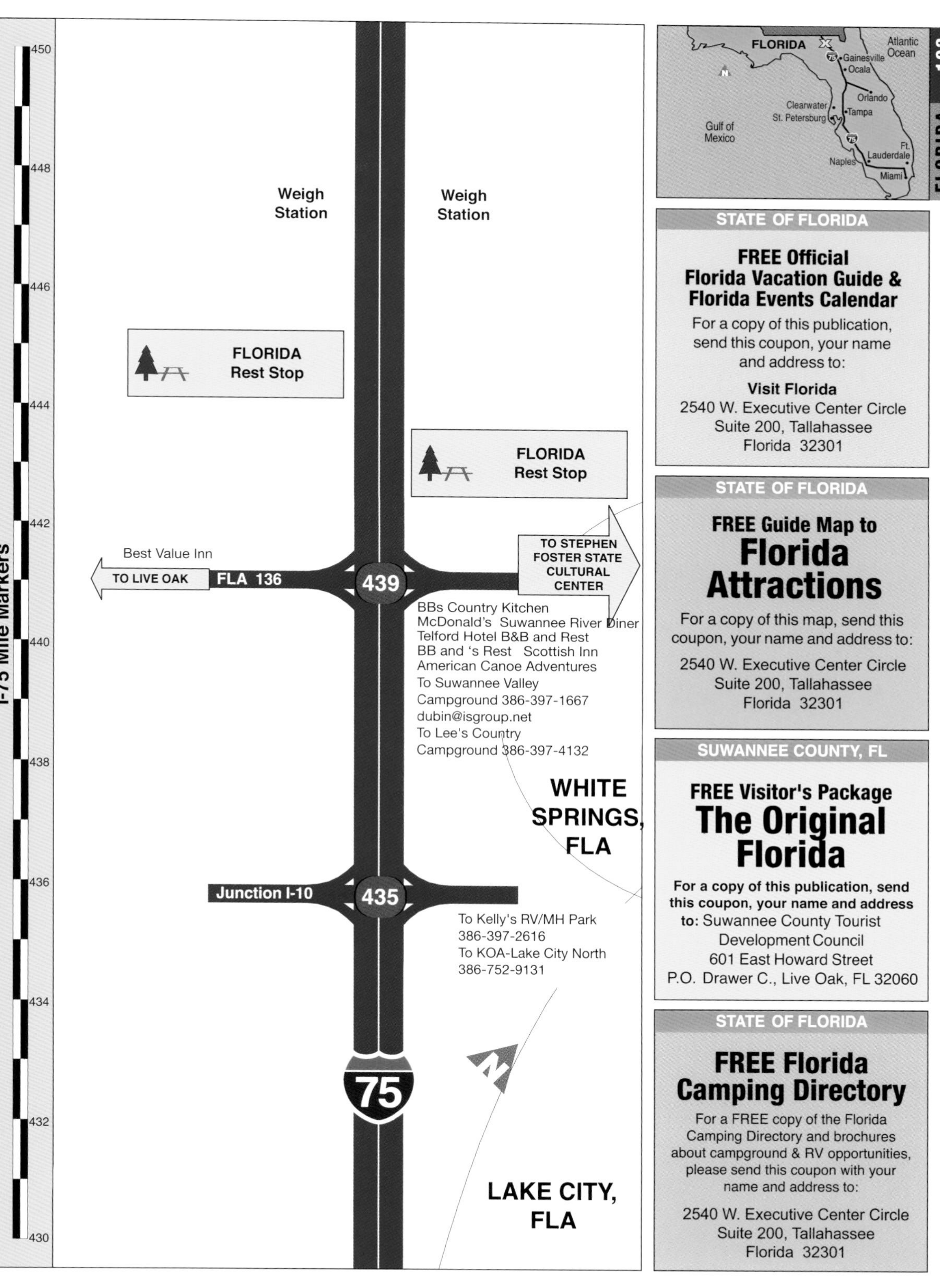

I-75 Mile Markers
450
448
446
444
442
440
438
436
434
432
430
FLORIDA
Atlantic Ocean
Gainesville
Ocala
Orlando
Clearwater
St. Petersburg
Tampa
Gulf of Mexico
Ft. Lauderdale
Naples
Miami
Weigh Station
Weigh Station
FLORIDA Rest Stop
FLORIDA Rest Stop
Best Value Inn
TO LIVE OAK
FLA 136
439
TO STEPHEN FOSTER STATE CULTURAL CENTER
BBs Country Kitchen
McDonald's Suwannee River Diner
Telford Hotel B&B and Rest
BB and 's Rest Scottish Inn
American Canoe Adventures
To Suwannee Valley
Campground 386-397-1667
dubin@isgroup.net
To Lee's Country
Campground 386-397-4132
WHITE SPRINGS, FLA
Junction I-10
435
To Kelly's RV/MH Park
386-397-2616
To KOA-Lake City North
386-752-9131
75
N
LAKE CITY, FLA
STATE OF FLORIDA
FREE Official Florida Vacation Guide & Florida Events Calendar
For a copy of this publication, send this coupon, your name and address to:
Visit Florida
2540 W. Executive Center Circle
Suite 200, Tallahassee
Florida 32301
STATE OF FLORIDA
FREE Guide Map to Florida Attractions
For a copy of this map, send this coupon, your name and address to:
2540 W. Executive Center Circle
Suite 200, Tallahassee
Florida 32301
SUWANNEE COUNTY, FL
FREE Visitor's Package The Original Florida
For a copy of this publication, send this coupon, your name and address to: Suwannee County Tourist Development Council
601 East Howard Street
P.O. Drawer C., Live Oak, FL 32060
STATE OF FLORIDA
FREE Florida Camping Directory
For a FREE copy of the Florida Camping Directory and brochures about campground & RV opportunities, please send this coupon with your name and address to:
2540 W. Executive Center Circle
Suite 200, Tallahassee
Florida 32301

Lake City/Columbia County, FLORIDA

Columbia Tourist Development Office
263 NW Lake City Ave., Lake City, FL 32056
386-758-1312 or 877-746-4778 **www.columbiacountyfla.com**

Historic records reveal that an Indian town once occupied the present-day site of Lake City. In 1817 the leader of this Seminole village was **Chief Alligator** and he gave his name to the settlement. **Chief Alligator** is reported to have been a wise Chief who spoke English and mingled with and even welcomed earlier settlers.

By 1824 several white families were living in Alligator. These settlers kept the town name of Alligator for 2 decades.

A treaty was signed with the Indians in 1824, causing them to relocate to the present-day Ocala area. Once transported, the embittered Seminoles continued to make raids on the white settlements causing the inhabitants to seek refuge in nearby forts; namely, Fort Alligator on Alligator Lake and Fort Lancaster.

The once friendly Chief Alligator achieved notoriety as one of the most cruel and crafty of warriors responsible for the raids and it wasn't long before he and many of the other Florida Seminoles were finally transported to Arkansas.

Columbia County was formed in 1832 and in 1859 the city's name was changed to Lake City. Today, Columbia County with its strategic location is Florida's largest I-75 tourist stopover.

COLUMBIA COUNTY ATTRACTIONS

Olustee Battlefield and Museum
Site of the only major Civil War battle fought in Florida. 386-752-3866

Camp O-Leno State Park
On Sante Fe River at US 41/441. Exits 414. 386-454-1853

Osceola National Forest
Off Hwy. 90, east of Lake City. Day use. 23 miles of trails. I-75 exit 427. 386-752-2577

KOA White Springs/Suwanee Valley Campground
I-75 exit 439. 386-397-1667

Casey Jones Campground
I-75 exit 423. 386-755-0471

Ichetucknee Springs State park
904-497-2511

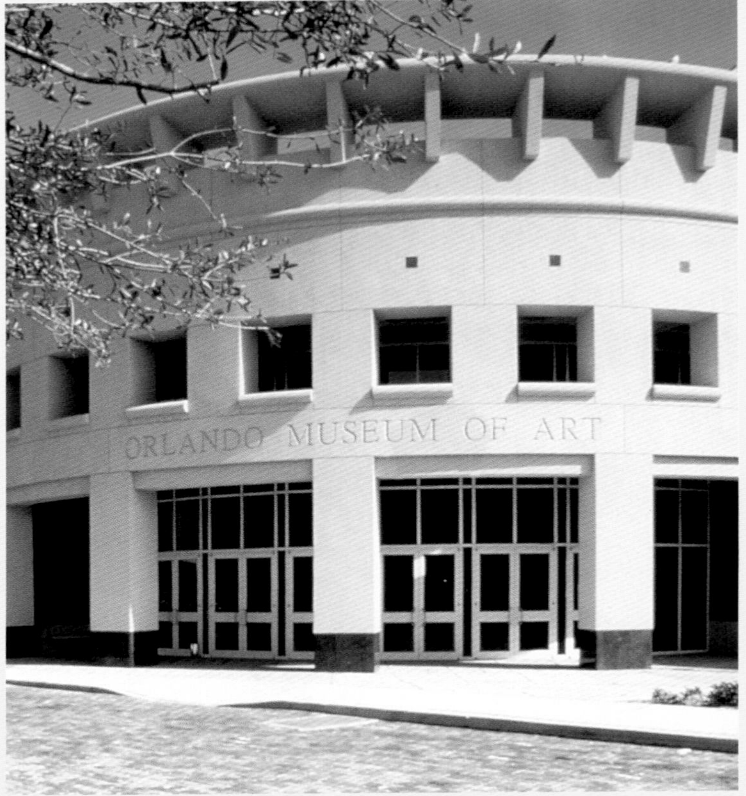

The Orlando Museum of Art *has a large permanent collection of 19th-and 20th-century American art from more than 40 artists. Courtesy Orlando/Orange County CVB, Inc.*

Orlando History

When the second Seminole war ended in 1842, American settlers began following the soldiers into Central Florida.

Originally the town was named **"Jernigan"** after Aaron Jernigan who came from Georgia and settled here in 1843, the town grew slowly around an old Army post, Fort Gatlin, that had been abandoned since 1849.

The town's name was permanently changed to **"Orlando"** in 1857. While different versions of the origin of the name are told, the official account is credited to Orlando Reeves, a U.S. soldier who was killed in 1835 by an Indian's arrow while on sentinel duty at what is now Lake Eola Park in downtown Orlando. By a vote of 22 men from the 85 residents, the two-square-mile city was officially incorporated in 1875.

According to the book Flashback—The Story of Central Florida's Past, the undeveloped expanse of land east of the Orlando International Airport still resembles what the first Orlando settlers saw some 150 years ago.

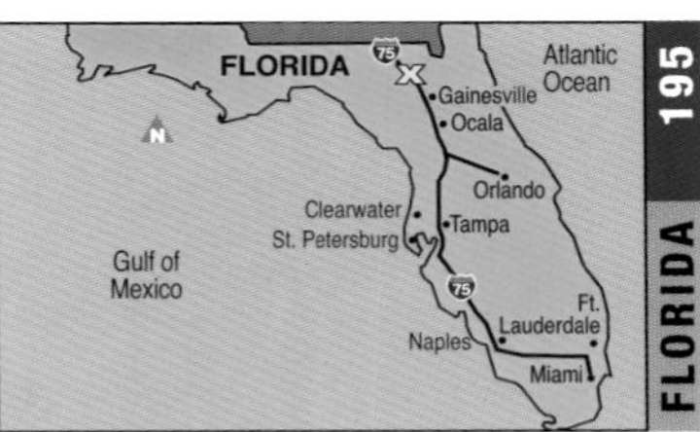

LAKE CITY FLA

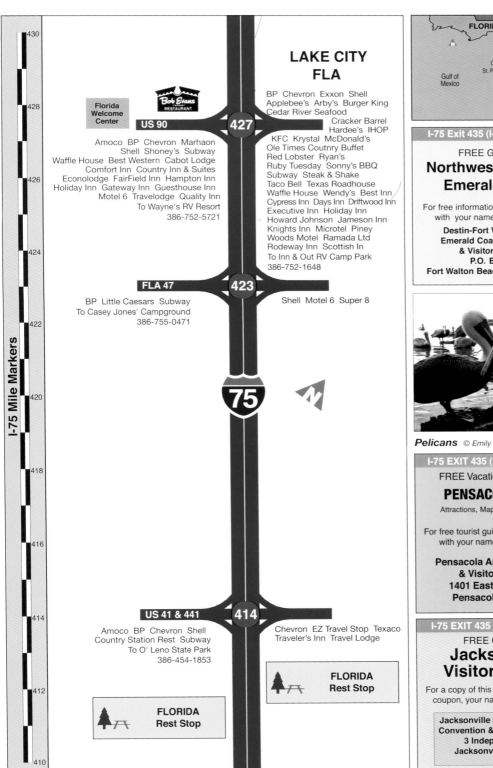

I-75 Mile Markers: 430, 428, 426, 424, 422, 420, 418, 416, 414, 412, 410

Florida Welcome Center

Bob Evans Restaurant

US 90 — Exit 427

West: Amoco BP Chevron Marhaon Shell Shoney's Subway Waffle House Best Western Cabot Lodge Comfort Inn Country Inn & Suites Econolodge FairField Inn Hampton Inn Holiday Inn Gateway Inn Guesthouse Inn Motel 6 Travelodge Quality Inn To Wayne's RV Resort 386-752-5721

East: BP Chevron Exxon Shell Applebee's Arby's Burger King Cedar River Seafood Cracker Barrel Hardee's IHOP KFC Krystal McDonald's Ole Times Coutnry Buffet Red Lobster Ryan's Ruby Tuesday Sonny's BBQ Subway Steak & Shake Taco Bell Texas Roadhouse Waffle House Wendy's Best Inn Cypress Inn Days Inn Driftwood Inn Executive Inn Holiday Inn Howard Johnson Jameson Inn Knights Inn Microtel Piney Woods Motel Ramada Ltd Rodeway Inn Scottish In To Inn & Out RV Camp Park 386-752-1648

FLA 47 — Exit 423

West: BP Little Caesars Subway To Casey Jones' Campground 386-755-0471

East: Shell Motel 6 Super 8

75

US 41 & 441 — Exit 414

West: Amoco BP Chevron Shell Country Station Rest Subway To O' Leno State Park 386-454-1853

East: Chevron EZ Travel Stop Texaco Traveler's Inn Travel Lodge

FLORIDA Rest Stop

FLORIDA Rest Stop

Pelicans *© Emily Marks*

High Springs
FLORIDA

High Springs Chamber of Commerce
25 NE Railroad Ave, High Springs, Florida 32643
386-454-3120 **www.highsprings.com**

High Springs Antiques and the Sante Fe River

Indians, Spaniards and pioneer Americans settled in this area. In 1844 the city of High Springs was established on its present site. High Springs became an important railroad center in 1896 when the Plant System, later absorbed by the Atlantic Coast Line, built engine shops, a round-house, a hospital and offices west of town. Railroad workers came by the hundreds and High Springs expanded. Phosphate mining, timber and agriculture also added to the economy, however, the city's vitality depended on the steam-driven rail system and when diesel power replaced steam in the 1950s, the railyard closed.

The **Santa Fe River**, which runs through the city of High Springs, is fed by springs. This River offers the outdoor enthusiast boating, fishing, canoeing, snorkeling, scuba diving, swimming, camping, hiking and bicycling. North of High Springs is **O'Leno State Park,** known for its deer and accessibility to the Sante Fe River. The Park opens in the morning and boasts a trail that follows alongside the Sante Fe. (Great photo op from the swinging bridge!)

Voted the **"Friendliest Small Town"** and **"Best Antiquing Town"** by Florida Living Magazine, visitors will surely not be disappointed by the many antiques shops, specialty stores and restaurants to be discovered in High Springs.

The **Special Events List** includes Pioneer Days the first full weekend in May, and the High Springs **Antique and Classic Car Show** in Oct.

ATTRACTIONS

Blue Springs State Park P.O. Box 331, Cnty Rd. 340, High Springs, 800-326-3521

The Rustic Inn Bed & Breakfast. 3105 S. Main St., High Springs, 386-454-1223

Ginnie Springs. 7300 NE Ginnie Springs Rd., High Springs, FL 32643 386-454-7188 www.ginniesprings.com

Poe Springs Park. 2880 N.W. 182nd Ave., High Springs, FL 32643 386-454-1992

High Springs Campground. Exit 404. 24004 NW Old Bellamy Rd., High Springs, FL 32643 386-454-1688

Central Florida Side-Trips: Venture for Adventure

Located in the heart of Central Florida, Orlando is the ideal city for a "home base" for visitors who want to take day trips.

CONSIDER:

FANTASY OF FLIGHT
Located on a 300-acre lot in Polk County between Orlando and Tampa, the $30 million aviation-themed museum features 30 antique planes, 2 private grass runways, a gift shop, a pre-1940s-style diner and a flight simulator.

KENNEDY SPACE CENTER SPACEPORT USA
Look into the past and glimpse the future of space travel at the home of the Space Shuttle flights. Just 45 minutes from Orlando, visitors can take a 2-hour, narrated bus tour of the Space Center, view indoor and outdoor exhibits and watch a larger-than-life IMAX movie about the history of space exploration.

BUSCH GARDENS
Located in nearby Tampa, the park is themed in a unique African setting that offers thrilling rides like KUMBA, the largest, fastest steel roller-coaster in the Southeast, as well as variety shows, themed gardens and wild animals.

BEACHES
Basking in the sun, strolling on the warm, sandy beaches, or playing in the surf are pastimes that lure visitors to the East and West Coast beaches located within a 2-hour drive from Orlando.

SILVER SPRINGS
Visitors explore the world's largest natural spring formation aboard famous glass-bottom boats; journey the Florida outback on their Jeep Safari; and meet alligators, giant snapping turtles and a myriad of beautiful waterfowl, wading birds and fish and exotic animals from six countries. Located just north of Orlando, the park is a full day of fun.

CYPRESS GARDENS
Floral canal boat rides, water-ski performances, birds of prey, butterfly conservatory, shows and more than 8,000 varieties of plants and flowers from more than 90 countries make for a memorable day just 40 minutes from Orlando.

Florida is home to many challenging and breathtaking ***golf courses****. Courtesy St. Petersburg/Clearwater Area Convention & Visitors Bureau.*

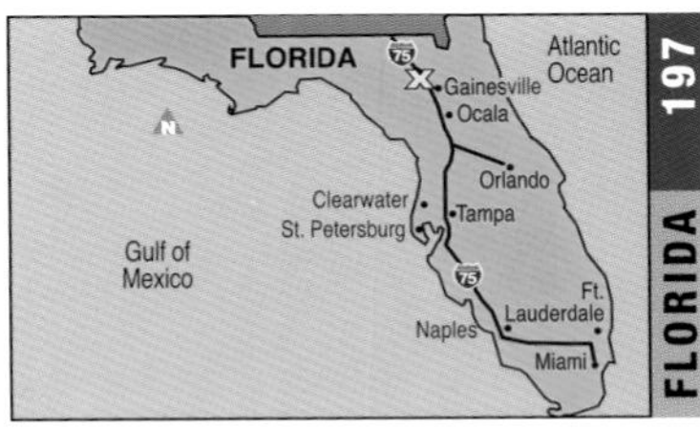

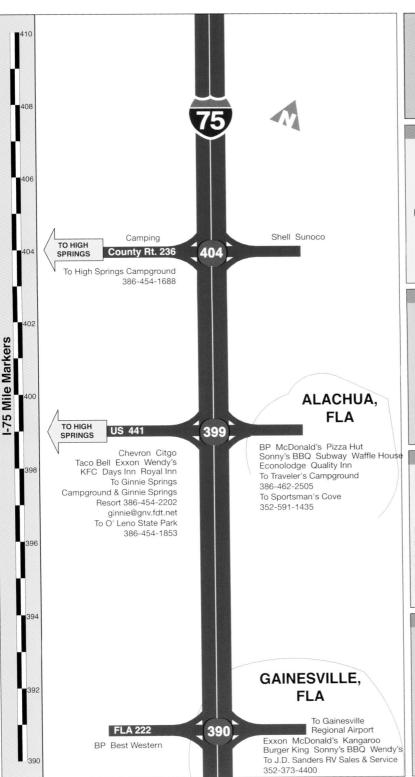

I-75 Mile Markers

410
408
406
404
402
400
398
396
394
392
390

75

Exit 404 — County Rt. 236 — TO HIGH SPRINGS

Camping
To High Springs Campground
386-454-1688

Shell Sunoco

Exit 399 — US 441 — TO HIGH SPRINGS

Chevron Citgo
Taco Bell Exxon Wendy's
KFC Days Inn Royal Inn
To Ginnie Springs
Campground & Ginnie Springs
Resort 386-454-2202
ginnie@gnv.fdt.net
To O' Leno State Park
386-454-1853

ALACHUA, FLA

BP McDonald's Pizza Hut
Sonny's BBQ Subway Waffle House
Econolodge Quality Inn
To Traveler's Campground
386-462-2505
To Sportsman's Cove
352-591-1435

GAINESVILLE, FLA

Exit 390 — FLA 222

BP Best Western

To Gainesville
Regional Airport
Exxon McDonald's Kangaroo
Burger King Sonny's BBQ Wendy's
To J.D. Sanders RV Sales & Service
352-373-4400

Gainesville/Alachua County, FLORIDA

Alachua County Visitors and Conventions Bureau
30 East University Ave., Gainesville, Florida 32601
866-778-5002 **www.visitgainesville.com**

ALACHUA County lies within the quiet beauty of North Central Florida. I-75 Travelers are drawn to the variety of activities: sports, festivals, special events, art culture, shopping and local restaurants.

The population of the county is 247,000 and it is located approximately halfway between Atlanta and Miami. The average temperature is a moderate 71 degrees F with summer highs in the 90s and winter lows in the 40s.

GAINESVILLE is home to the University of Florida and is considered the cultural capital of north central Florida. The Florida Museum of Natural History, the Harn Museum of Art and the Center for the Performing Arts are located on campus. Downtown Gainesville has the Hippodrome Theatre, sidewalk cafes, pubs, night clubs, artists' studios, restaurants and festivals.

Historic Gainesville is centered around the old Clock Tower in Gainesville. The 63-block area around the Clock contains 290 buildings which reflect Florida's architectural style from the 1880s to 1920s. Many are on the National Register of Historical places.

In **CROSS CREEK**, southeast of Micanopy, you can tour the Cracker home of Marjorie Kinnan Rawlings, author of The Yearling and other great novels.

MICANOPY is Florida's second-oldest town and is located 13 miles south of Gainesville on US 441. This charming community seems to be suspended in the 1880s. The antique, art and curio shops are often featured in Hollywood film productions.

HAWTHORNE is renowned for bass fishing. Try out your skill in Lake Orange or Lochloosa. Hawthorne is also the end of the Gainesville-Hawthorne State Trail. This path is popular with hikers, cyclists and horseback riders who are on the lookout for wild stallions, bison, deer, alligators and a great variety of migratory birds.

Gainesville-Hawthorne Rail Trail
This trail, a converted railroad route, begins south of Gainesville and goes eastward to the town of Hawthorne. The Paynes Prairie Preserve, Prairie Creek and Lochloosa Wildlife Management Area are the highlights through the 17 miles of lakes, rivers, springs, freshwater marshes, forests, hammocks and prairies. Region 2 Administration, 4801 S.E. 17th Street, Gainesville, FL 32601 352-955-2135

Alachua County Attractions

Curtis M. Phillips Center for the Performing Arts
This center presents the best in world-class entertainment from Broadway to opera to the superstars of pop, jazz, classical and country music. Opened in 1992, the Center is a state-of-the-art theater with 1800 seats, a large proscenium stage, a versatile orchestra pit and the latest in sound and lighting technology. 315 Hull Rd. and 34th St., Gainesville. 352-392-1900

Devil's Millhopper State Geological Site
Enjoy numerous small waterfalls as you follow 232 steps to the bottom of a 120-foot deep, 500-foot wide sinkhole containing plant species found rarely in Florida. Guided walk 10 a.m. every Saturday. Open 9 a.m. to sunset. Monday & Tuesday. Admission. 4732 Millhopper Rd. (SR 232), Gainesville. 352-955-2008

Florida Museum of Natural History
Explore a full-size limestone cave, a native palace and the Hall of Florida History at the largest natural history museum in the Southeast. The Object Gallery has hundreds of natural specimens for you to examine. The Fossil Study Center exhibits fossil specimens and skeletons and also features computer learning games. Collectors Gift Shop. Visit FMNH's Butterfly Rainforest. Free. Museum Rd. and Newell Dr., University of Florida, Gainesville. 352-846-2000

The Hippodrome State Theatre
Take your seat next to the three quarter round Hippodrome stage and enjoy the very best in contemporary plays. The Second Stage offers exciting cinema series and there is also a local artists' gallery. 25 Southeast 2nd Pl., Gainesville. 352-375-4477

Kanapaha Botanical Gardens
62 acres of woodlands, meadows, vined areas and gardens which feature butterflies, wildflowers, hummingbirds, rocks, carnivorous plants and spring flowers. Here you will find the southeast's largest herb garden, Florida's largest bamboo collection, a palm hammock, water lily pond, fern grotto, and sunken gardens. Gift shop. Plant nursery. Picnic area. Mon., Tues., Fri. open 9 a.m.-5 p.m. Wed., Sat., Sun. open 9 a.m.-Sunset. Closed Thurs. Admission. 4700 S.W. 58th Drive, Gainesville, 32608. 352-374-4981

Marjorie Kinnan Rawlings State Historic Site
Tour the home and farm of Marjorie Kinnan Rawlings just as it was when this noted author of the *The Yearling* lived here. Learn about Florida cracker living in quiet Cross Creek. Guided tours of up to 10 people each, on the hour. Thurs. to Sun. 10 a.m., 11 a.m., and 1 p.m.-4 p.m. Closed Tues. and Wed. Closed Aug. 1 to Sept. 30. Admission. 21 Miles Southeast of Gainesville on Hwy. 325, Cross Creek. 352-466-3672

Morningside Nature Center
Experience the life style of a family farm in North Central Florida in the 1890s. Visit the 278-acre Living History Farm featuring barnyard animals, an 1840 cabin, a turn-of-the-century kitchen, heirloom garden, and barn. Explore the 7-mile long trail and boardwalk through the long leaf pine and cypress forest. Look for the more than 130 bird species, 225 wildflower species, and many mammals and reptiles. Live animal exhibits, educational programs and a wildlife observation blind. 9 a.m.-5 p.m. Free. 3540 East University Ave., Gainesville. 352-334-2170

Samuel P. Harn Museum of Art
One of Southeast University's newest and largest art gallery. The Museum features the best of the traveling exhibits, as well as resident collections of American paintings, African and pre-Columbian collections, and contemporary works. Museum store. Lectures. Tues. to Fri. 11 a.m.-5 p.m., Sat. 10 a.m.-5 p.m., Sun. 1 p.m.-5 p.m. Closed Mon. and state holidays. Free. Hull Rd. and Southwest 34th St., University of Florida, Gainesville. 352-392-9826

Underwater Springs near Gainesville
Photo courtesy of John Jernigan/Alachua County VCB.

GAINESVILLE, FLA

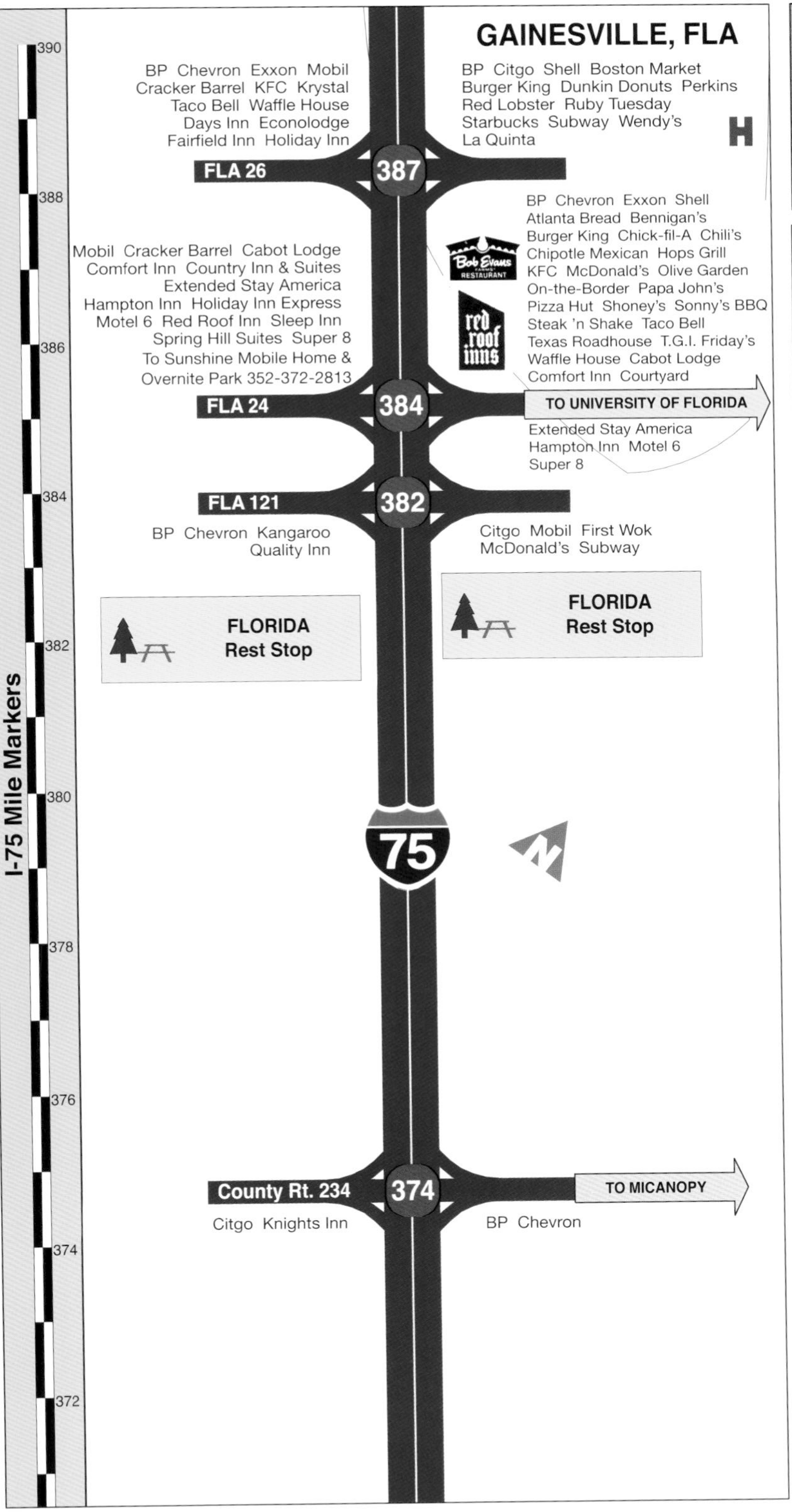

I-75 Mile Markers: 390, 388, 386, 384, 382, 380, 378, 376, 374, 372

FLA 26 — Exit 387

West: BP Chevron Exxon Mobil Cracker Barrel KFC Krystal Taco Bell Waffle House Days Inn Econolodge Fairfield Inn Holiday Inn

East: BP Citgo Shell Boston Market Burger King Dunkin Donuts Perkins Red Lobster Ruby Tuesday Starbucks Subway Wendy's La Quinta

H

FLA 24 — Exit 384

West: Mobil Cracker Barrel Cabot Lodge Comfort Inn Country Inn & Suites Extended Stay America Hampton Inn Holiday Inn Express Motel 6 Red Roof Inn Sleep Inn Spring Hill Suites Super 8 To Sunshine Mobile Home & Overnite Park 352-372-2813

East: BP Chevron Exxon Shell Atlanta Bread Bennigan's Burger King Chick-fil-A Chili's Chipotle Mexican Hops Grill KFC McDonald's Olive Garden On-the-Border Papa John's Pizza Hut Shoney's Sonny's BBQ Steak 'n Shake Taco Bell Texas Roadhouse T.G.I. Friday's Waffle House Cabot Lodge Comfort Inn Courtyard

TO UNIVERSITY OF FLORIDA

Extended Stay America Hampton Inn Motel 6 Super 8

FLA 121 — Exit 382

West: BP Chevron Kangaroo Quality Inn

East: Citgo Mobil First Wok McDonald's Subway

FLORIDA Rest Stop

FLORIDA Rest Stop

75

N

County Rt. 234 — Exit 374

West: Citgo Knights Inn

East: BP Chevron

TO MICANOPY

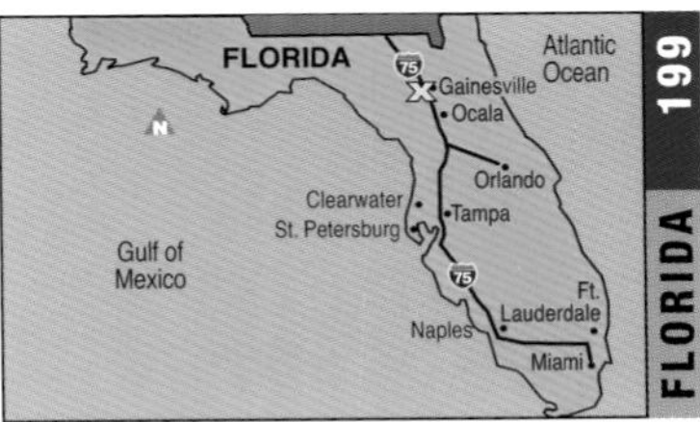

Gainesville at night
Courtesy of visitgainsville.com

Ocala/Marion County
FLORIDA

Ocala-Marion County Chamber of Commerce
110 East Silver Springs Blvd., Ocala, Florida 34470-6613
352-629-8051 **www.ocalacc.com**

The Timucuan Indians were early inhabitants of this region which they called **Ocali.** Hernando de Soto claimed the land for Spain in 1539. Recall that the entire State of Florida was ceded in 1819 to the United States, and by 1844 Marion became a county with Ocala as the county seat. General Francis Marion, the county's namesake, was a leader in the Southern effort during the Revolutionary War. Did you know that Marion is Florida's 5th-largest county and that Ocala is one of the nation's fastest growing areas? (Marion's pop.: 245,000.)

Ocala is about 35 miles south of Gainesville. The Atlantic Ocean is a 70-mile drive east of Ocala through beautiful oak and pine forests in the **Ocala National Forest.** The Gulf of Mexico is 40-mile drive west through Thoroughbred horse farms.

The **Ocala National Forest** occupies a large part of Marion County (covering 366,000 acres) and is a magnet for water sports enthusiasts. The **Ocklawaha River** runs along the western edge of the Forest, as do many smaller streams and lakes, including the **Kerr** and the **George.** The best known feature is **Silver Springs.**

Marion County's temperate climate records an average winter temperature of about 59 degrees F; the May to Sept. average is 92.

Must-sees include the **horse farms** and the **Don Garlits Museum of Drag Racing** near Ocala at exit 341 where you will find the sport's history as well as the memorabilia and car collection of "Big Daddy" Don Garlits, also known as the "King of Speed."

The **Appleton Museum of Art** is a regional landmark which features more than 6,000 works of art from the Classical Greek and Rome periods, the pre-Columbian America period and from 19th-century Europe.

SIDETRIP: DAYTONA BEACH
386-255-0981

The Daytona Beach area is an affordable travel destination. Ormond Beach was once home to the Rockefellers and the Flaglers. The World's Most Famous Beach, Daytona Beach, is the home of NASCAR. Enjoy 23 miles of sand, surf, attractions, culture, shopping, and fine dining. Did you know the beach is a breath-taking 500 feet wide at low tide? And yes, you can drive your vehicle on an 18-mile stretch of hard-packed sand. Feb. to Labor Day.

Attractions

Appleton Art Museum
4333 E. Silver Springs Blvd., Ocala. 352-236-7100

The Ocala Civic Theater
A 400-seat theater with a range of dramatic and musical productions. 4337 E. Silver Springs Blvd., Ocala. 352-236-2274

Florida's Silver Springs or Wild Waters
East of Ocala on State Rte. 40. 350-acre property surrounding the headwaters of the Silver River. Offers glass-bottom boat rides, the world's largest artesian spring, a Jungle Cruise for viewing animals from 6 continents, a Lost River Voyage, a Jeep Safari and a Petting Zoo. Animal shows include: "creature Feature," "Amazing Pets" and "Reptiles of the World." **Wild Waters** is a family water park with water flumes, a huge wave pool, picnic areas and supervised children's areas. 352-236-2121

Moss Bluff North and South Recreation Areas
A 30-acre park with boat ramps above and below the locks, and a handicapped-accessible picnic pavilion and wheelchair fishing. South of County Rte. 314A on County Rte. 464 at the Ocklawaha River.

Collect Antiques?
Try historic McIntosh. I-75 exit 368, east to State Rte. 441, then north on 441.

Carney Island Conservation/ Recreation Area
A 685-acre park with swimming, picnic, playground, and hike/biking trails. Handicapped-accessible. Two miles west of Ocklawah off County Rte. 25 on S.E. 115th Ave. S. 352-671-8560

Rainbow Springs State Campground
109 campsites, swimming area and swimming pool, boat ramp, showers, laundry, tube and canoe rentals and store. On Rainbow River off 180th Ave. between County Rte. 484 and State Rte. 40 near Dunnellon. 352-465-8555

Championship Horses
One of the top four thoroughbred breeding and training areas in the world, Marion County has a passion for Thoroughbreds, Arabians, miniatures, Paso Finos and other breeds of fine horses. There are hundreds of horse farms in Marion County and many invite you to visit. There are also well-attended special events relating to the area's favorite industry. **The HiTS (Horse Show in the Sun)** is an Olympic-caliber hunting and jumping competition held in Feb. The **Hunter/Jumper Competition** is held in May. Ocala Week, in October, highlights the area's famous sale of Thoroughbred horses. The Arabian State Champion Show runs every Nov. 352-629-8051

SIDETRIP: Homosassa & Citrus County

Citrus County is part of "Florida's Nature Coast" on the Gulf of Mexico and is located about 65 miles north of the Tampa/St. Petersburg area. This County is an unspoiled, uncrowded part of paradise within an hour or two of many of the state's main attractions. 800-480-8202

Each minute more than 2 million gallons of glass-clear water pump from underground aquifers to form Citrus County's Crystal River. The **Crystal River** is home to the largest wintering herd of the endangered manatee. Visitors from around the world come here to see these gentle giants.

The **Homosassa River** and **Homosassa Springs State Wildlife Park** is about 7 miles south of the Crystal River. Injured and diseased manatees are treated here. You will also find an underwater observatory into a 55-foot deep spring where visitors can view thousands of fresh-and salt-water fish. 352-628-5343

The **Crystal River State Archaeological Site** preserves a prehistoric Indian settlement. Here you will find mysterious giant mounds made of countless thousands of oyster shells which the tribe had gathered from the local waters. 352-795-3817.

With 13 **golf clubs**, Citrus County ranks high for golf holes per capita. Golfers know that Citrus County is home to the no. 1 course in the Florida: **Black Diamond Ranch Golf and Country Club,** a private course designed in 1988 by Tom Fazio.

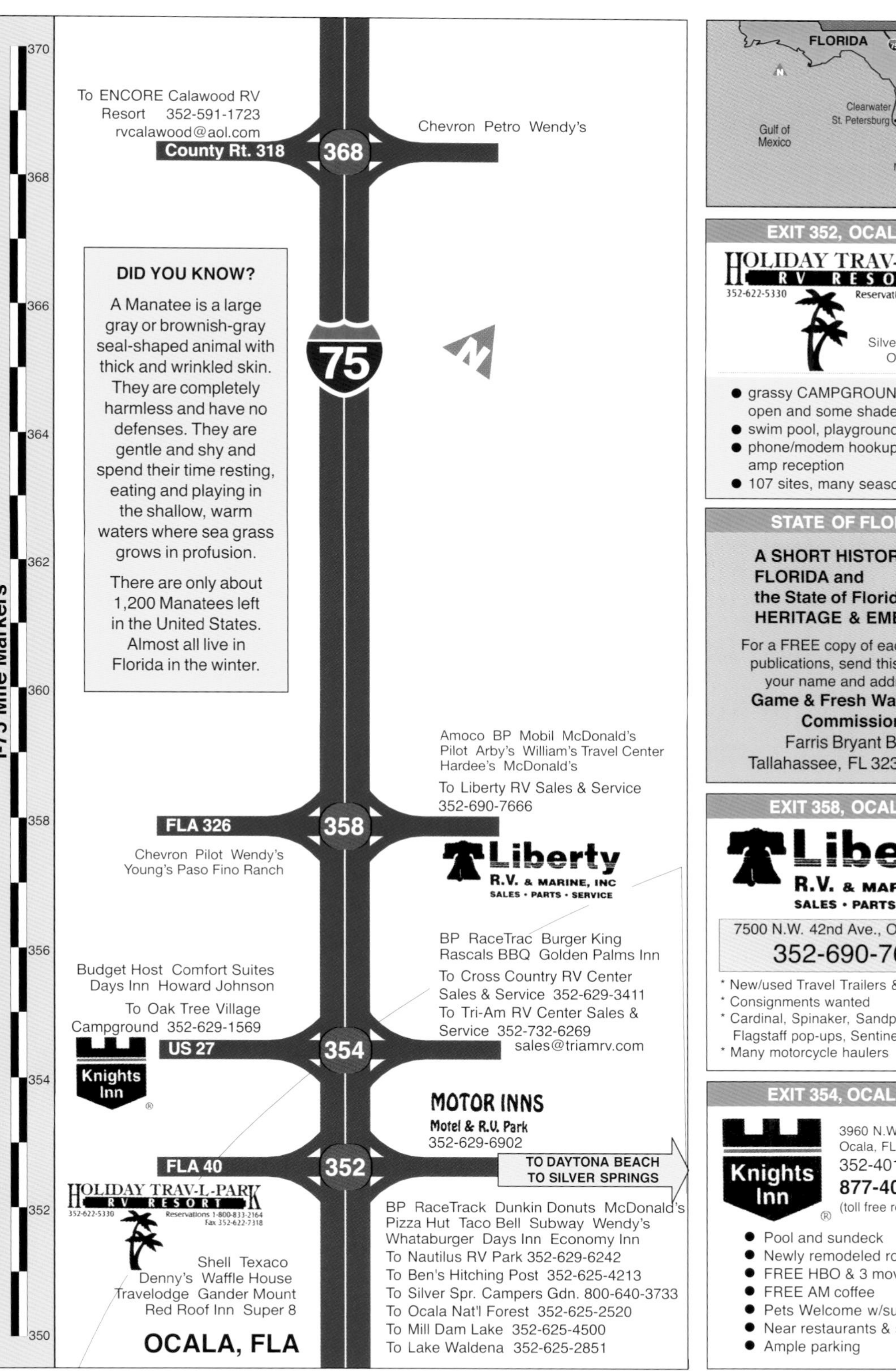

FLORIDA
Gainesville
Ocala
Atlantic Ocean
Orlando
Clearwater
St. Petersburg
Tampa
Gulf of Mexico
Ft. Lauderdale
Naples
Miami

EXIT 352, OCALA, FL

HOLIDAY TRAV-L-PARK RV RESORT

352-622-5330
Reservations 1-800-833-2164
Fax 352-622-7318

4001 W. Silver Springs Blvd.
Ocala, FL 34482

- grassy CAMPGROUND with some open and some shaded sites.
- swim pool, playground equipment
- phone/modem hookup, 30 & 50 amp reception
- 107 sites, many seasonal sites

STATE OF FLORIDA

A SHORT HISTORY OF FLORIDA and the State of Florida's HERITAGE & EMBLEMS

For a FREE copy of each of these publications, send this coupon, your name and address to:

Game & Fresh Water Fish Commission,
Farris Bryant Bldg.
Tallahassee, FL 32399-1600

EXIT 358, OCALA,FL

Liberty R.V. & MARINE, INC
SALES • PARTS • SERVICE

7500 N.W. 42nd Ave., Ocala 34482
352-690-7666

* New/used Travel Trailers & 5th wheels
* Consignments wanted
* Cardinal, Spinaker, Sandpiper, Wildwood, Flagstaff pop-ups, Sentinel park models
* Many motorcycle haulers

EXIT 354, OCALA, FL

Knights Inn

3960 N.W. Blitchton Rd., Ocala, FL 34482
352-401-9800
877-401-9800
(toll free reservations)

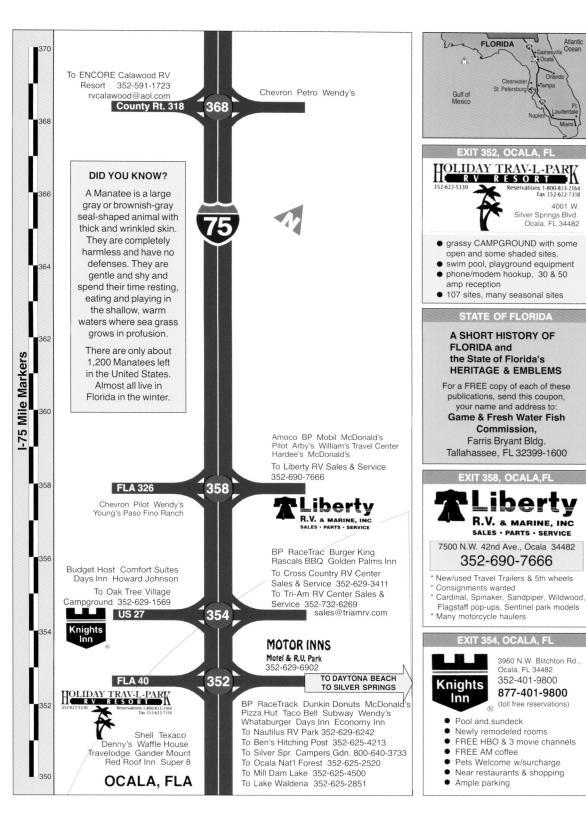

- Pool and sundeck
- Newly remodeled rooms
- FREE HBO & 3 movie channels
- FREE AM coffee
- Pets Welcome w/surcharge
- Near restaurants & shopping
- Ample parking

Orlando/Orange County, FLORIDA

Orlando/Orange County Official Visitor Center
8723 International Drive, (southeast corner of International Drive and Austrian Row).
1-800-551-0181 (U.S. & Canada) or 407-363-5872 **www.visitorlando.com**

Beyond Disney: Many Attractions and Outdoor Activities

Gator Adventure Park. Walk with "trained" alligators. Shows, gator wrestling, hundreds of live gators and a mini golf course. gatoradventurepark.com 407-517-8054

Hawaiian Rumble Adventure Golf. 2 challenging Hawaiian-themed courses featuring a waterfall and a $100,000 musical fountain. hawaiianrumbleorlando.com 407-351-7733

Pirate's Cove Adventure Golf. Two 18-hole courses. Lavish landscaping & delightful pirate themes that are fun for the whole family. piratescove.net 407-352-7378

Ripley's Believe It or Not! Orlando Odditorium, housed in a building that appears to be sinking. Artifacts, collections, weird art/hobbies & interactive exhibits from around the world. ripleysorlando.com 407-351-5803

SkyVenture Orlando, Orlando's high-energy vertical wind tunnel. Indoor sky-diving on a column of air. No parachute, no jumping and no experience necessary. Reservations. skyventureorlando.com 800-759-3861/407-903-1150

The Holy Land Experience re-creates the city of Jerusalem and its religious importance between the years 1450 B.C. and A.D. 66 through costumed characters, enactments and high-tech presentations. The living Biblical museum is home to the Scriptorium, a collection of biblical antiquities dating back to 2200 B.C. theholylandexperience.com 866-872-4659/407-367-2065

Tiki Island Volcano Golf, Two 18-hole courses with four-story volcano with live flame effects, cascading waterfalls and suspended bridges. tikiislandvolcanogolf.com 407-248-8180

Van's Skatepark is Orlando's premier skateboard park designed for beginner to advanced skaters. Multiple ramps, bowls, street courses and an arcade. vans.com 407-351-3881

Wet 'n Wild – Orlando. The Storm washes riders down a towering chute with a splash landing. Disco H2O: groovy 70s musical raft ride . wetnwildorlando.com 800-992-9453/407-351-180

WonderWorks, 100+ interactive exhibits. Virtual reality rock climbing & roller coasters. The Outta Control Magic Comedy Dinner Show is a separate ticket. wonderworksonline.com 407-351-8800

Blue Man Group, wildly successful live entertainment has a permanent home at Universal CityWalk. Music, comedy and multimedia theatrics. universalorlando.com 800-232-7827/407-363-8000

Universal's Islands of Adventure. Technologically advanced thrill rides including The Amazing Adventures of Spider-Man, The High in the Sky Seuss Trolley Train Ride!, the Jurassic Park River Adventure, The Incredible Hulk. In 2010: The Wizardry World of Harry Potter. universalorlando.com 877-688-8011/407-363-8000

Universal Studios Florida. GO into the world of TV and film to "ride the movies." Ride with Shrek and Donkey at Shrek 4-D, battle the supernatural at Revenge of the Mummy – The Ride, and hang out at "Krustyland" with The Simpsons. New high-tech, multi-sensory coaster, Hollywood Rip, Ride, Rockit. universalorlando.com 877-688-8011/407-363-8000

Aquatica – SeaWorld's Waterpark. 2 wave pools, children's areas, 2 lazy rivers, beaches & swimming areas. Plenty of slides, including the Dolphin Plunge amid a lagoon of dolphins. seaworldaquatica.com 407-363-2280

Discovery Cove. Exclusive island oasis. Swim with dolphins, snorkel with tropical fish & rays, hand-feed exotic birds. All-inclusive, reservations-only includes full day of activities, swim/snorkel gear, breakfast & lunch, and 7-consecutive-day pass to either SeaWorld Orlando, Busch Gardens or Aquatica. discoverycove.com 877-434-7268/407-370-1280

SeaWorld Orlando. 200 acres (80 hectares) of sea-themed shows, attractions & rides, including the Manta "flying coaster," Kraken (Orlando's longest, tallest & fastest floorless roller coaster), and Shamu's Happy Harbor (pint-sized rides). Shamu show, "Believe." Polar bears, beluga whales, manatees, sea lions, penguins, dolphins. SeaWorld.com 800-432-1178/407-351-3600

Orlando Brewing. The only organic brewery & taproom in the Southeast, one of 10 in the U.S. Free tours are available & live music. orlandobrewing 407-872-1117

Orlando Science Center. Observatory, giant screen theater & 100s of hands-on exhibits. Coming soon, relocation with distinct children's museum. osc.org 888-672-4386/407-514-2000

Richard Petty Driving Experience puts motor sports fans behind the wheel of a stock car. 1-mile (1.6-km), tri-oval Walt Disney World Speedway and 2.5-mile (4-km) Daytona International Speedway available. At the new Indy Racing Experience Race drive & ride in actual cars used in past Indianapolis 500 events. 1800bepetty.com 800-237-3889/407-939-0130

Wallaby Ranch Hang Gliding Flight Park. Learn to hang glide 2,000 feet (610m) above ground using tandem aerotowing techniques. No experience. wallaby.com 863-424-0070

Biplane Rides Over Kissimmee. Ride in or fly an open cockpit 1943 Boeing Stearman, an authentic World War II trainer. biplaneridesoverkissimmee.com 407-473-9142

Full Speed Race & Golf. Race against other riders in full-motion NASCAR simulators or play a round of golf in an 18-hole, indoor black light miniature golf course. fullspeed.cc 407-397-7455

Gatorland. 1000s of alligators & crocodiles. Petting zoo, bird sanctuary, mini water park, eco-tour & daily alligator wrestlin' shows. gatorland.com 800-393-5297/407-855-5496

Green Meadows Petting Farm. 2-hour guided tour. Pet the animals, take train and hay rides, milk a cow and ride a pony. Picnic areas. greenmeadowsfarm.com 407-846-0770

Old Town Shopping, Dining & Entertainment Attraction. 75 specialty shops, 8 restaurants, 21 rides & Sky Coaster. Free-admission & parking. Experience early 20th century Florida town life. Car shows every Fri/Sat with 100s of classics. old-town.com 800-843-4202/407-396-4888

Warbird Adventures, Inc. Fly in the Premier Fighter-Trainer of WWII — the North American T-6 TEXAN. Thrilling aerobatic adventure or a smooth or straight and level flight? This is a tailored experience. warbirdadventures.com 407-870-7366

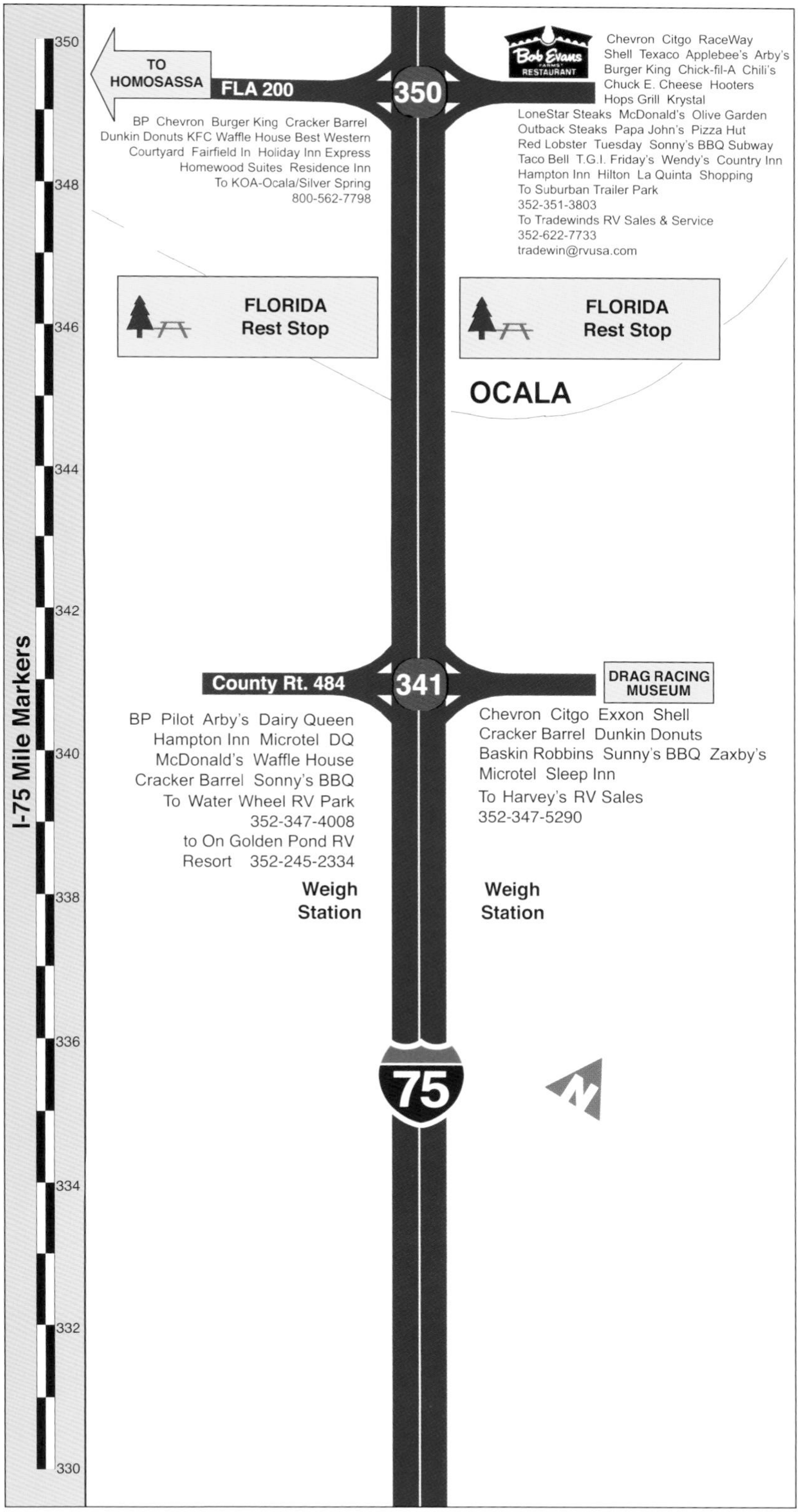

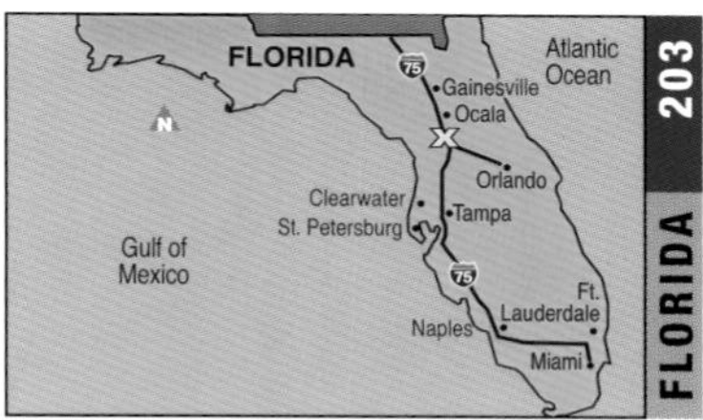

I-75 Mile Markers
350
348
346
344
342
340
338
336
334
332
330
TO HOMOSASSA
FLA 200
350
Bob Evans FARMS RESTAURANT
BP Chevron Burger King Cracker Barrel
Dunkin Donuts KFC Waffle House Best Western
Courtyard Fairfield In Holiday Inn Express
Homewood Suites Residence Inn
To KOA-Ocala/Silver Spring
800-562-7798
Chevron Citgo RaceWay
Shell Texaco Applebee's Arby's
Burger King Chick-fil-A Chili's
Chuck E. Cheese Hooters
Hops Grill Krystal
LoneStar Steaks McDonald's Olive Garden
Outback Steaks Papa John's Pizza Hut
Red Lobster Tuesday Sonny's BBQ Subway
Taco Bell T.G.I. Friday's Wendy's Country Inn
Hampton Inn Hilton La Quinta Shopping
To Suburban Trailer Park
352-351-3803
To Tradewinds RV Sales & Service
352-622-7733
tradewin@rvusa.com
FLORIDA Rest Stop
FLORIDA Rest Stop
OCALA
County Rt. 484
341
DRAG RACING MUSEUM
BP Pilot Arby's Dairy Queen
Hampton Inn Microtel DQ
McDonald's Waffle House
Cracker Barrel Sonny's BBQ
To Water Wheel RV Park
352-347-4008
to On Golden Pond RV
Resort 352-245-2334
Chevron Citgo Exxon Shell
Cracker Barrel Dunkin Donuts
Baskin Robbins Sunny's BBQ Zaxby's
Microtel Sleep Inn
To Harvey's RV Sales
352-347-5290
Weigh Station
Weigh Station
75
N

FLORIDA
Atlantic Ocean
Gainesville
Ocala
Orlando
Tampa
Clearwater
St. Petersburg
Gulf of Mexico
Ft. Lauderdale
Naples
Miami
75

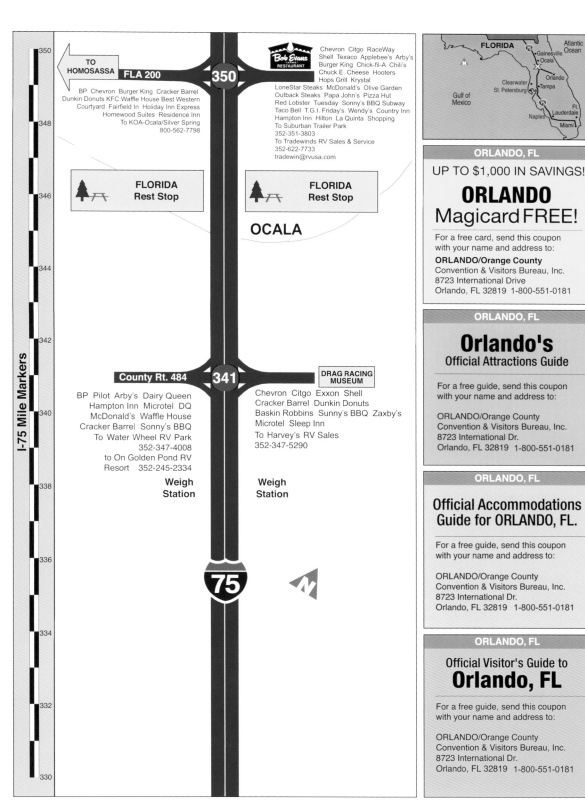

Orlando/Orange County Official Visitor Center
8723 International Drive, (southeast corner of International Drive and Austrian Row).
1-800-551-0181 (U.S. & Canada) or 407-363-5872 **www.visitorlando.com**

Orlando's Special Events & Festivals

Orlando gives visitors the chance to attend unique festivals and special events. Many of these events, such as the Florida Film Festival and Florida Music Festival, consistently receive top awards, such as "Voted Top 25 Best Music Festival in the Southeast" by Weekly Planet and Creative Loafing and "Voted Top Movie Theater" by Florida Trend and Orlando Magazine.

Walt Disney World Marathon and Walt Disney World Half Marathon, early Jan. 20,000 participants. Magic Kingdom, Disney's Animal Kingdom, Disney's Hollywood Studios & Epcot. $115 for half, $125 full. disneyworldsports.com 407-939-7810

MLK Holiday Parade, mid-Jan. Parade down town Orlando, festival and Battle of the Bands at Lake Eola Park. Free. cityoforlando.net 407-246-3661

Kissimmee Bluegrass Festival, late Jan. This four-day event, held at Yeehaw Junction, arts, crafts and carnival fare. originalbluegrass.com/kissimmee 478-949-2036

ArtsFest, early Feb. Ballet, opera, film & art. Central Florida's best. Free. redchairproject.com 407-628-0333

Bud & BBQ, weekends in Feb. SeaWorld and Busch Gardens pair big names in country and classic rock with smokin' barbecue and ice-cold Budweiser. Adult $74.95, Children ages 3-9 $64.95. SeaWorld.com 407-363-2259

Daytona 500, mid-Feb. This legendary event brings together the best stock car drivers in the world to compete for NASCAR's richest and most prestigious race. Single day $105, 2-day packages $150 – $240. daytonainternationalspeedway.com 386-254-2700

Antiques Show & Sale. mid-Feb.: $10. omart.org 407-896-4231, Ext.254

Silver Spurs Rodeo, mid-Feb. Pro circuit, largest rodeo east of the Mississippi. Rated one of the top 50 events by the Pro Rodeo Cowboys Assn. Osceola Heritage Park in Kissimmee. Admission: $15; Children under 10 free. silverspursrodeo.com 407-847-4052

Atlanta Braves Spring Training, Feb/Mar. Disney's Wide World of Sports Complex. disneyworldsports.com 407-939-4263

Bike Week Orlando, late Feb/early Mar. 100,000 Harley-Davidson enthusiasts from across the globe turn out for this annual event, headquartered at the Orlando Historic Factory Dealership where the Harley legend was born. Free. orlandoharley.com 407-423-0346

Valiant Air Command's Tico Warbird Air Show, mid-Mar. Vintage C-47s and sophisticated 440 mph (708 kph) F-86 Saber Jets at one of the biggest air spectacles of the year. Space Coast Regional Airport, south of Titusville. Adults $15, Children ages 4-12 $12. vacwarbirds.org 321-268-1941

Arnold Palmer Invitational Presented by MasterCard at Bay Hill, late Mar. One of the crown jewels of the PGA Tour, attracts one of the strongest international fields of the season. Proceeds benefit the Arnold Palmer Hospital for Children and Winnie Palmer Hospital for Women & Babies. $35-$3,500. arnoldpalmerinvitational.com 407-876-2888

Florida Film Festival, late Mar/early Apr. The best in cutting-edge current cinema; indulgent food and wine; a mix of industry parties and special events; and a star-packed attendee list. More than 25,000 guests $10 (single show) to $800 (multi-show package). enzian.org/FFF 407-629-1088 ext. 225

Ron Jon Surf Shop Easter Surfing Festival, mid- Apr. Cocoa Beach. Championship surfers from ages 12 to 80 from around the world. Surf clinics and demonstrations. Free. eastersurffest.com 321-799-8888

Ginn OPEN, mid-April. The LPGA Tour full-field event is played on Legacy Course, designed by Arnold Palmer, and the Independence Course, designed by Tom Watson. $30-80. ginnopen.com 407-662-1700

Jack Hanna Weekend at SeaWorld Orlando. early May. Hanna introduces unique and exotic animals, shares amazing animal stories and shows hilarious bloopers. Adult $74.95, Children ages 3-9 $64.95. SeaWorld.com 407-363-2259

Florida Music Festival, mid-May. 3-day celebration of up-and-coming musicians, downtown Orlando. More than 250 performers from alternative, pop, cou ntry, urban, hip hop and acoustic formats, along with hundreds of filmmakers and dozens of visual artists. $10 per day, $25 for three days. floridamusicfestival.com

Orlando International Fringe Festival, mid-May. The oldest, non-juried festival in the United States, 12-day celebration of theater, art and music, various venues. True to Fringe roots, all acts remain uncensored. $5-10 per show. orlandofringe.org 407-648-0077

Juneteenth and Jazz Music Festival, mid- June. Oldest nationally celebrated commemoration of the ending of Slavery in the U.S. Free pastinc.org 407-245-7535

Orlando Magical Dining Month, Sept. Indulge the senses at a rare opportunity to indulge in some of the area's fine dining restaurants. Participating restaurants offer 3-course prix fixe dinner menus for $19 or $29. orlandomagicaldining.com 407-363-5872

Rock The Universe at Universal Studios, mid- Sept. Chart-topping Christian music stars from across the nation, 2-day concert. One-night $49.99 plus tax, two-nights $75.99 plus tax. rocktheuniverse.com 407-363-8000

Epcot International Food & Wine Festival, late Sept. World-famous wineries and celebrated chefs, wine and beer seminars, demos and tastings. Included in regular park admission. Adults $75, Children ages 3-9 $63, disneyworld.com 407-824-4321

Global Peace Film Festival. Held in conjunction with the UN's International. CityArts Factory, Orlando Science Center and Rollins College. $8 per film. peacefilmfest.org 407-224-6625

AST Dew Tour, mid-Oct, top professional athletes, skateboarding, BMX & freestyle motocross. Adults $15, Children ages 12 and under $5. astdewtour.com 407-849-2020

Howl-O-Scream, For 16 select nights, Howl-O-Scream transforms Busch Gardens Africa into a nightmare of inescapable fear that will overwhelm the senses with a new spin of horror. buschgardens.com 813-987-5280

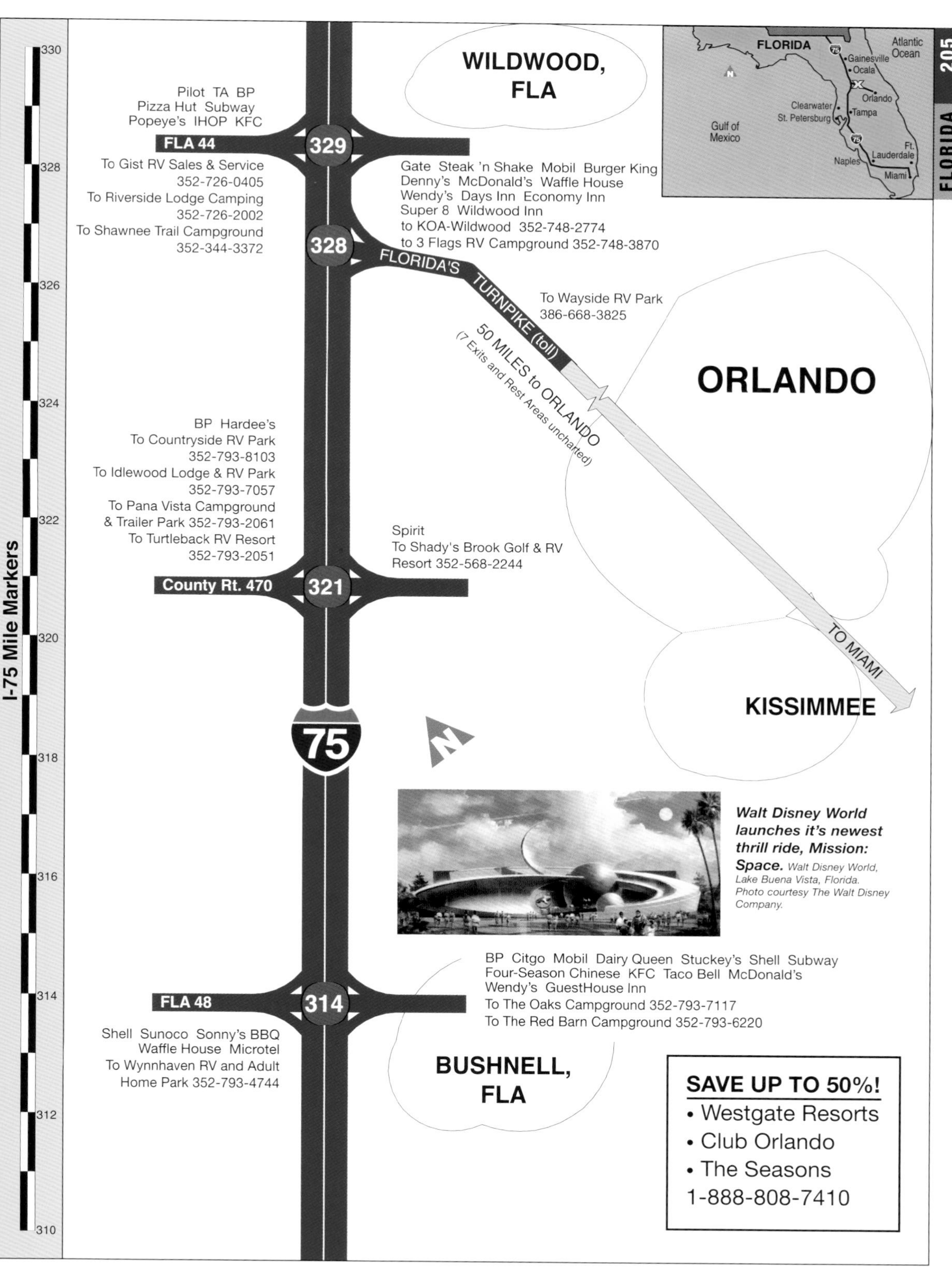

Walt Disney World launches it's newest thrill ride, Mission: Space. *Walt Disney World, Lake Buena Vista, Florida. Photo courtesy The Walt Disney Company.*

Orlando/Orange County
FLORIDA

Orlando/Orange County Official Visitor Center
8723 International Drive, (southeast corner of International Drive and Austrian Row).
1-800-551-0181 (U.S. & Canada) or 407-363-5872 **www.visitorlando.com**

Fast Facts about Orlando

VISITATION
48 million+ visitors each year for business and pleasure, 45.9 million are domestic and 2.8 million are international (approx. 46% from Western Europe, 28% are from Canada).

POPULATION
1.9 million+ residents in Gr. Orlando (Orange, Osceola, Seminole and Lake counties). Median age is a 36 years. The City of Orlando is located in Orange County.

ACCOMMODATIONS
With nearly 450 hotels and 112,000+ guest rooms, Orlando offers luxury resorts and themed hotels, bed and breakfasts, economy hotels/motels and campgrounds. There are 26,000+ vacation home rentals and 16,000+ vacation ownership units.

ATTRACTIONS
100+ attractions keep visitors coming back for more. With theme parks, museums, world-class entertainment and blockbuster rides and attractions, and it would take about 67 eight-hour days to visit all of the entertaining offerings in Orlando.

SHOPPING
Within a 15-mile radius in the heart of Orlando's attractions area, visitors will find 12 amazing shopping malls and factory outlet centers offer the world's most sought-after brands including Burberry, Chanel, Dior, Giorgio Armani, Louis Vitton, Jimmy Choo, among 100 other designer brands.

DINING
5,300+ restaurants, Orlando's dining choices read like a world map — visitors from virtually anywhere in the world can find a taste of home here, with international cuisines ranging from African to Vietnamese.

Wallaby Ranch Hang Gliding Flight Park

Orlando: One Desitnation Turns an Ordinary Vacation into the Holiday of a Lifetime

For families, couples, single travelers and friends, vacation means more than just getting away from home or work. Vacation is a time to recapture the magic and awe of childhood. An Orlando vacation is everything a holiday should be, with a range of accommodations, attractions, dining, shopping and recreation activities to turn an ordinary vacation into an experience of a lifetime.

- Hop aboard a crazy, colorful Dr. Seuss character on the Caro-Seuss-El at Universal's Islands of Adventure.
- Madly spin on the Mad Hatter's Tea Party at Magic Kingdom.
- Visit "Krustyland" with Marge, Homer, Bart and Lisa on The Simpsons Ride at Universal Studios or cheer for Shrek and Fiona on their honeymoon adventure in Shrek 4-D.
- Race against 7 family members and friends on the head-first Taumata Racer at Aquatica-SeaWorld's Waterpark.
- Marvel at eight-ton killer whales performing a graceful water ballet at SeaWorld Orlando's Believe show.
- Strengthen the mother-daughter bond with princess makeovers at Bibbidy, Bobbidy Boutique at Downtown Disney or manicures at a resort spa.
- Watch grandparents and grandchildren connect as they splash around in the hotel swimming pool.

Adrenaline-Pumping Orlando ADVENTURES
Spider-Man and Captain Marvel aren't the only heroes in Orlando. Every day, daring moms and dads, grandmas and grandpas, teens and tots embark on new adventures:

- Live out a fantasy to ride in or drive a stock car at the Richard Petty Driving Experience.
- Ride in the open-air cockpit of a World War II fighter plane at Fantasy of Flight.
- Learn to skydive, or do the next best thing indoors at SkyVenture Orlando.
- Test your skateboarding, rollerblading or BMX skills at Vans Skatepark.
- Get towed into the sky and released by an ultra light plane, hang-gliding back down to Earth at Wallaby Ranch Hang Gliding Flight Park.
- Play in the mud in an ATV or Hummer at Revolution: The Off-Road Experience.
- Soar above the treetops on the Zipline Safari at Forever Florida.

Adventure may mean seeking out Central Florida wildlife — and we mean, WILD life:

- Search for native animals, including intimidating Florida alligators, on a jet-engine powered airboat at Boggy Creek or Black Hammock Airboat Rides.
- Take an eerie nighttime stroll on a wooden walkway at Gatorland's Breeding Marsh, hand feed gators, wrestle a gator, or participate in the park's Trainer for a Day program.
- Get an up-close look as handlers at Reptile World Serpentarium extract venom from some of the world's deadliest snakes, used for medical and herpetological research.

Adrenaline-junkies can brave Orlando's many roller coasters, thrill rides and splash rides:

- The Incredible Hulk Coaster, Dueling Dragons and The Amazing Adventures of Spider-Man at Universal's Islands of Adventure
- Kraken, Orlando's only floorless coaster, and Journey to Atlantis, the water coaster at SeaWorld Orlando
- Rock 'n Roller Coaster Starring Aerosmith, and Tower of Terror (Disney's Hollywood Studios), Expedition Everest (Disney's Animal Kingdom,) the 120-foot (36-m) Summit Plummet (Disney's Blizzard Beach), and Crush 'n' Gusher ("water coaster" at Disney's Typhoon Lagoon)
- Busch Gardens' many coasters, including SheiKra, Florida's tallest coaster.

Orlando adventures may also come in the form of more relaxing activities:

- Horseback riding at Horse World Riving Stables, Westgate River Ranch or Florida Eco-Safaris at Forever Florida.
- Hooking a trophy largemouth bass with fly-fishing lessons by Orvis at The Ritz-Carlton Orlando.
- Embarking on a fresh or saltwater fishing expedition with A Pro Bass Guide Service or Incentive Fishing Charters.
- Renting a pontoon boat from Orlando Pontoons or Water Sports of Kissimmee to go on a self-guided eco-tour.

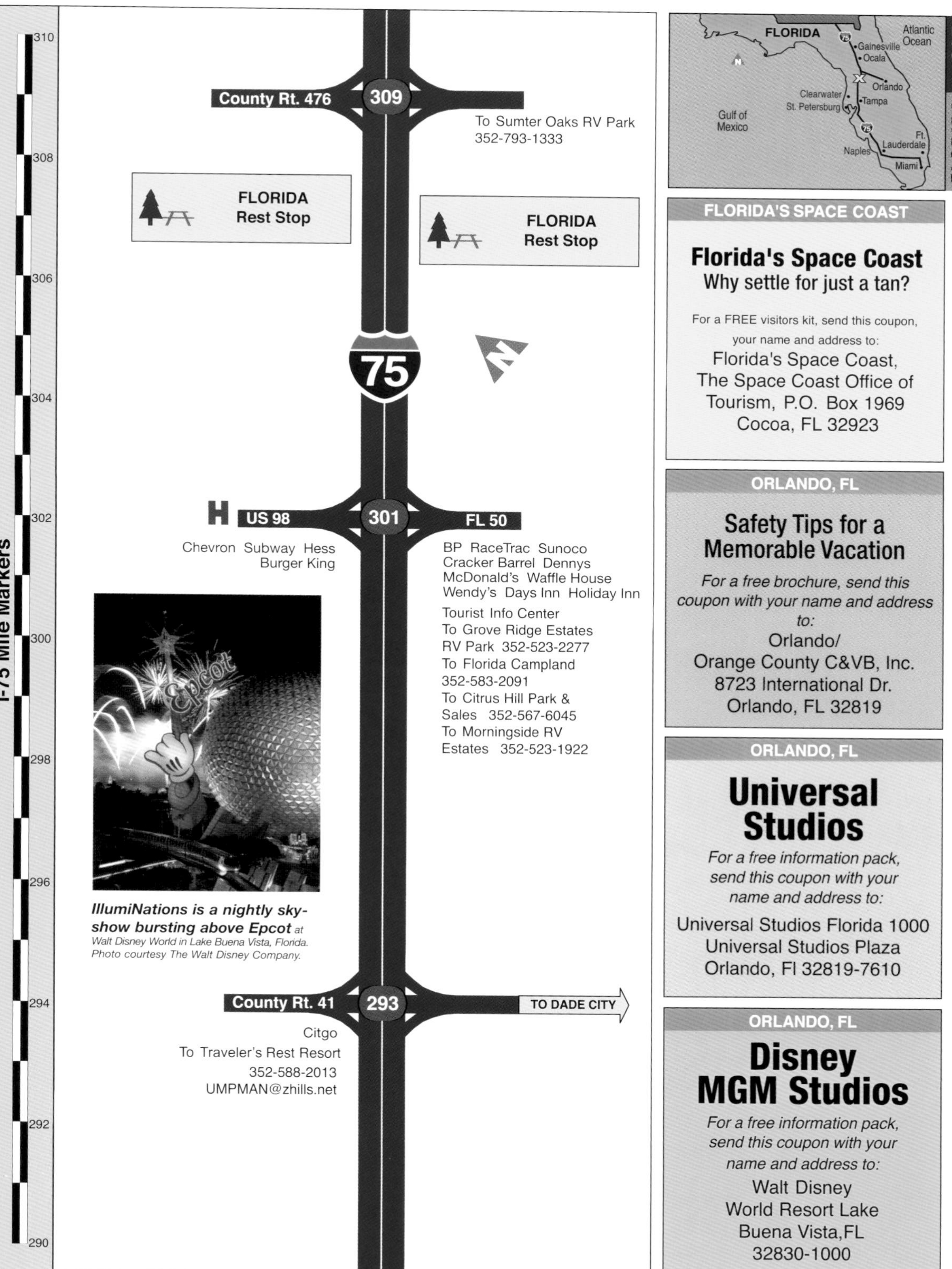
207
FLORIDA
FLORIDA
Atlantic Ocean
Gainesville
Ocala
Orlando
Clearwater
Tampa
St. Petersburg
Gulf of Mexico
Ft. Lauderdale
Naples
Miami
I-75 Mile Markers
310
308
306
304
302
300
298
296
294
292
290
County Rt. 476
309
To Sumter Oaks RV Park
352-793-1333
FLORIDA
Rest Stop
FLORIDA
Rest Stop
75
US 98
301
FL 50
Chevron Subway Hess
Burger King
BP RaceTrac Sunoco
Cracker Barrel Dennys
McDonald's Waffle House
Wendy's Days Inn Holiday Inn
Tourist Info Center
To Grove Ridge Estates
RV Park 352-523-2277
To Florida Campland
352-583-2091
To Citrus Hill Park &
Sales 352-567-6045
To Morningside RV
Estates 352-523-1922
Epcot
IllumiNations is a nightly sky-show bursting above Epcot at Walt Disney World in Lake Buena Vista, Florida. Photo courtesy The Walt Disney Company.
County Rt. 41
293
TO DADE CITY
Citgo
To Traveler's Rest Resort
352-588-2013
UMPMAN@zhills.net
FLORIDA'S SPACE COAST
Florida's Space Coast
Why settle for just a tan?
For a FREE visitors kit, send this coupon, your name and address to:
Florida's Space Coast,
The Space Coast Office of
Tourism, P.O. Box 1969
Cocoa, FL 32923
ORLANDO, FL
Safety Tips for a Memorable Vacation
For a free brochure, send this coupon with your name and address to:
Orlando/
Orange County C&VB, Inc.
8723 International Dr.
Orlando, FL 32819
ORLANDO, FL
Universal Studios
For a free information pack, send this coupon with your name and address to:
Universal Studios Florida 1000
Universal Studios Plaza
Orlando, Fl 32819-7610
ORLANDO, FL
Disney MGM Studios
For a free information pack, send this coupon with your name and address to:
Walt Disney
World Resort Lake
Buena Vista,FL
32830-1000

Tampa
FLORIDA

Tampa Bay Convention and Visitors Bureau
401 East Jackson St., Suite 2100, Tampa, Florida 33602
800-44-TAMPA **www.VisitTampaBay.com**

In Tampa you don't have to look too far for adventure. Packed with excitement, the Bay area offers visitors an explosion of educational, entertaining and cultural attractions.

Explore the wonders of Tampa's scientific playground at MOSI, where you can experience the force of a hurricane; come face-to-face with more than 350 species of animals roaming free on the Serengeti Plain at Busch Gardens; or find what lurks in the depths of the dark icy-cold waters 2,000 feet below the Gulf of Mexico's surface at The Florida Aquarium.

Art enthusiasts will be drawn to the variety of exhibits and cultural events in the Bay area. They can enjoy tours sponsored by the Tampa Museum of Art, or take a self-guided tour and view the many public works of art displayed throughout downtown Tampa.

Take a stroll down Ybor City's Seventh Avenue where the aroma of cigars still linger in the air, and day or night the festive streets of the old "Cigar City" are filled with fun and excitement. Also, visitors can bet they will enjoy the many pari-mutuel sports and attractions Tampa has to offer.

WHAT'S NEW IN THE TAMPA AREA?

Tampa's Historic Streetcar
Almost 110 years ago Tampa's first streetcars whisked the passengers around Ybor City, before they came rolling to a stop in 1946. In the fall of 2000, Tampa will re-experience the nostalgic charm of the electric streetcar with convenient front-door service to major venues.

The International Plaza is the perfect shopping experience. three high end anchors—Neiman Marcus, Nordstrom and lord & Taylor, are complimented by approximately 100 specialty shops, including Tiffany & Co., Charles Jourdan Paris, Nicole Miller, Louis Vuitton, J. Crew, Stuart Weitzman, Jessica McClintock and Christian Dior. The Plaza also includes an outdoor entertainment area called Bay Street Plaza and children's play area for a total of 200 tenants. The $200 million shopping center is located adjacent to Tampa International Airport.

Did you know that Tampa hosted its *third* Super Bowl, **Super Bowl XXXV,** at its state-of-the-art facility, Raymond James Stadium, back in 2001?

Attractions

Adventure Island
Open mid-Feb. to early Oct. and weekends only from mid-Sept. to late Oct. A 25-acre outdoor water theme park. 4500 Bougainvillea Ave. 813-987-5660 888-800-5600 www.adventureisland.com

Photo and text courtesy Tampa/Hillsborough Convention and Visitors Association, Inc.

Busch Gardens
8 themed-sections capture Africa. Rides and entertainment and rides for the whole family. The newest attraction, "Gwazi," is a double wooden roller coaster named after a fabled African lion with a tiger's head. Also popular, "Edge of Africa," pictured above, is a 15-acre animal exhibit which brings visitors face-to-face with lions, giraffes, hyenas and other African animals. 3000 E. Busch Blvd. www.buschgardens.com 888-800-5447 813-987-5000

Canoe Escape
Tours. 9335 E. Fowler Ave. 813-986-2067

Dinosaur World
The world's largest dinosaur attraction, where visitors can mingle with 160 models of prehistoric beasts. Hours are 9 a.m. to dusk. 5145 Harvey Tew Road, Plant City, FL 33565. 813-717-9865 www.dinoworld.net

Florida Aquarium
Learn about the more than 4,300 salt water and fresh water animals and plants. New "Dragons Down Under," "Frights of the Forest" exhibits and also popular, the "Creatures from the Deep" exhibit. Daily. 701 Channelside Dr. 813-273-4000

Henry B. Plant Museum
Tues. to Sat. 10 a.m.-4 p.m., Sun. 12 noon- 4 p.m. 401 W Kennedy Blvd. 813-254-1891

Tampa's Lowry Park Zoo
This open-air natural habitat zoo is ranked in the top 3 for mid-sized zoos. 1,500 animals in lush tropical settings. Free flights aviary. Komodo dragons. Open daily. 1101 W. Sligh Ave., 813-935-8552 www.lowryparkzoo.com

MOSI Science Center/IMAX®
450+ activities. Fri. and Sat. night enjoy the laser show with music. 4801 E. Fowler Ave. 813-987-6100

Seminole Hard Rock Casino
The Seminole Hard Rock Hotel & Casino is located 7 miles east of downtown Tampa on the 37-acre site designated a Federal Indian Reservation. 5223 N. Orient Rd. 813-621-1302 866-762-5463

Salvador Dali Museum
Best collection in the world. 1000 Third St. S., St. Petersburg, 727-823-3767

Tampa Bay Downs
Thorough-breds, Dec. to May. Route 580 and Race Track Rd. 813-855-4401

Tampa Greyhound Track
July to Dec. Off I-275 at Bird St exit. 813-932-4313

Tampa Museum of Art
Classical antiquities gallery re-opened in 1998. Daily. Mon. to Sat. 10 a.m.-5 p.m., Sun. 1 p.m.-5 p.m. 600 N. Ashley Dr. 813-259-1720

Tampa Bay History Center
Tues. to Sat. 10 a.m.-5 p.m., Sun. 1 p.m.-5 p.m. 225 S. Franklin St. 813-228-0097

Ybor City
Tampa's Ybor City is known as the "Nightlife Capital of Florida's West Coast." For more info, see pages 216 and 217. 1818 E. 9th Ave. 813-247-6323

Big Cat Rescue
Non-profit sanctuary for wild and exotic cats is home to the most diverse population of exotic cats in the world. 12802 Easy St., Tampa. 813-920-4130

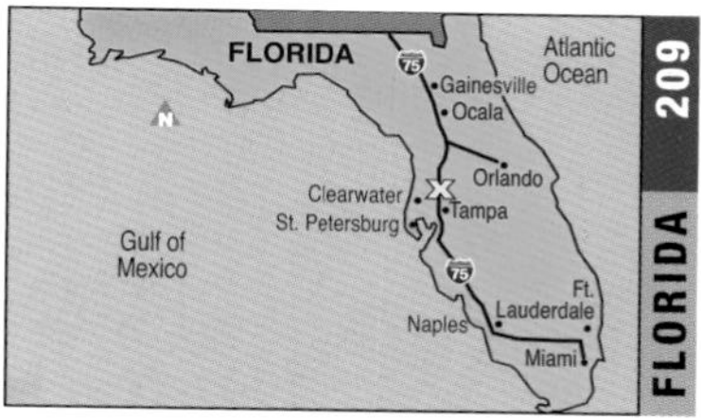

I-75 Mile Markers

290 288 286 284 282 280 278 276 274 272 270

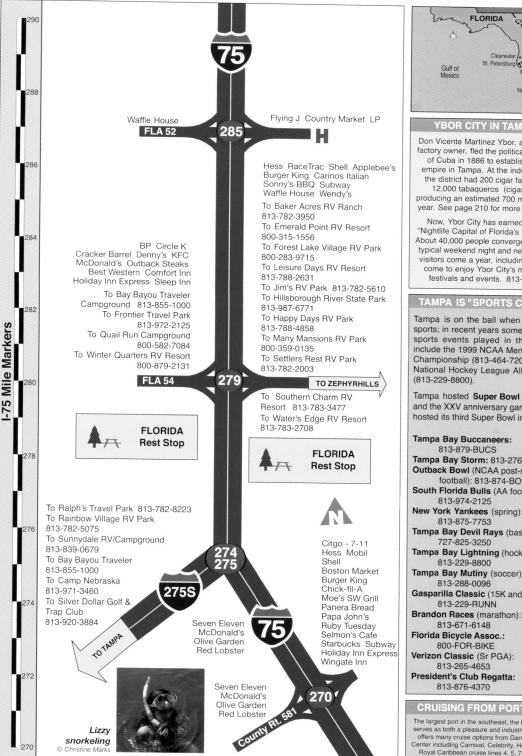

75

Waffle House

FLA 52 — **285** — Flying J Country Market LP H

Hess RaceTrac Shell Applebee's
Burger King Carinos Italian
Sonny's BBQ Subway
Waffle House Wendy's

To Baker Acres RV Ranch 813-782-3950
To Emerald Point RV Resort 800-315-1556
To Forest Lake Village RV Park 800-283-9715
To Leisure Days RV Resort 813-788-2631
To Jim's RV Park 813-782-5610
To Hillsborough River State Park 813-987-6771
To Happy Days RV Park 813-788-4858
To Many Mansions RV Park 800-359-0135
To Settlers Rest RV Park 813-782-2003

BP Circle K
Cracker Barrel Denny's KFC
McDonald's Outback Steaks
Best Western Comfort Inn
Holiday Inn Express Sleep Inn

To Bay Bayou Traveler Campground 813-855-1000
To Frontier Travel Park 813-972-2125
To Quail Run Campground 800-582-7084
To Winter Quarters RV Resort 800-879-2131

FLA 54 — **279** — TO ZEPHYRHILLS

To Southern Charm RV Resort 813-783-3477
To Water's Edge RV Resort 813-783-2708

FLORIDA Rest Stop

FLORIDA Rest Stop

N

To Ralph's Travel Park 813-782-8223
To Rainbow Village RV Park 813-782-5075
To Sunnydale RV/Campground 813-839-0679
To Bay Bayou Traveler 813-855-1000
To Camp Nebraska 813-971-3460
To Silver Dollar Golf & Trap Club 813-920-3884

274 275

Citgo - 7-11
Hess Mobil
Shell
Boston Market
Burger King
Chick-fil-A
Moe's SW Grill
Panera Bread
Papa John's
Ruby Tuesday
Selmon's Cafe
Starbucks Subway
Holiday Inn Express
Wingate Inn

275S

TO TAMPA

Seven Eleven
McDonald's
Olive Garden
Red Lobster

75

Seven Eleven
McDonald's
Olive Garden
Red Lobster

270 County Rt. 581

Lizzy snorkeling
© Christine Marks

YBOR CITY IN TAMPA, FL

Don Vicente Martinez Ybor, a Cuban cigar factory owner, fled the political/labor unrest of Cuba in 1886 to establish his cigar empire in Tampa. At the industry's peak, the district had 200 cigar factories with 12,000 tabaqueros (cigar makers) producing an estimated 700 million cigars a year. See page 210 for more on this story.

Now, Ybor City has earned the name "Nightlife Capital of Florida's West Coast." About 40,000 people converge in Ybor on a typical weekend night and nearly 2 million visitors come a year, including those who come to enjoy Ybor City's many ethnic festivals and events. 813-223-1111

TAMPA IS "SPORTS CENTRAL"

Tampa is on the ball when it comes to sports; in recent years some of the major sports events played in the Bay Area include the 1999 NCAA Men's Basketball Championship (813-464-7200); the 1999 National Hockey League All-Star Game; (813-229-8800).

Tampa hosted **Super Bowl** XVIII in 1984 and the XXV anniversary game in 1991. It hosted its third Super Bowl in 2001.

Tampa Bay Buccaneers: 813-879-BUCS
Tampa Bay Storm: 813-276-7300
Outback Bowl (NCAA post-season football): 813-874-BOWL
South Florida Bulls (AA football): 813-974-2125
New York Yankees (spring): 813-875-7753
Tampa Bay Devil Rays (baseball): 727-825-3250
Tampa Bay Lightning (hockey): 813-229-8800
Tampa Bay Mutiny (soccer): 813-288-0096
Gasparilla Classic (15K and 5K run): 813-229-RUNN
Brandon Races (marathon): 813-671-6148
Florida Bicycle Assoc.: 800-FOR-BIKE
Verizon Classic (Sr PGA): 813-265-4653
President's Club Regatta: 813-876-4370

CRUISING FROM PORT TAMPA

The largest port in the southeast, the **Port of Tampa** serves as both a pleasure and industrial port. Tampa offers many cruise options from Garrison Seaport Center including Carnival, Celebrity, Holland America, Royal Caribbean cruise lines 4, 5, 7- and 14-day itinerairies. Call 813-905-PORT

Tampa Bay Convention and Visitors Bureau
401 East Jackson St., Suite 2100813-223-1111
www.VisitTampaBay.com

Events and Characters Mark Tampa's History

Cigar Rolling at the Tampa Rico Cigar Company. *Photo and text courtesy Tampa/Hillsborough C&V Assoc., Inc.*

Settlement in Tampa began with an Indian fishing village. **De Soto** sailed into the Tampa area in 1539 to search for gold. At the time, he was Governor of Cuba. Native tribes called the village "Tanpa," which meant "sticks of fire." On maps made by the early explorers, the spelling became "Tampa." The area was left untouched for the next 200 years. In 1772, a Dutch cartographer, **Bernard Romans,** named the river, the county and the upper arm of Tampa Bay, in honor of Lord Hillsborough, secretary of state for the Colonies. Fort Brooke attracted traders and enabled the settlement to become a town in 1855.

Don Vicente Martinez Ybor, an influential cigar manufacturer and Cuban exile, moved his cigar business from Key West to a palmetto-covered area east of Tampa in 1885. The following year the first cigar factory opened and more Spanish cigar manufacturers began moving their factories and workers to Tampa. The Spanish, Italian, German and Cuban workers who settled here to work as cigar-makers created the strong, vivacious Latin community known as **Ybor City.** Nearly 12,000 people worked in more than 200 factories making Ybor City the "Cigar Capital of the World." That reputation endured until the emergence of Fidel Castro and the embargo on Cuban tobacco. Now designated one of three landmark districts of Florida, Ybor City is a mixture of historic buildings, galleries, shops and nightclubs.

Henry B. Plant extended the railroad to Tampa in 1883 and started a steamship line from Tampa to Key West to Cuba. In 1891, Plant opened the Tampa Bay Hotel. The hotel cost $3 million to build and furnish. Entertainers, sports figures and dignitaries from around the world visited. The 511-room hotel was the first building in Tampa to be operated by electrical power and served as a winter resort for the wealthy and leisure class of the 19th-century. The building, with its distinctive Moorish architecture, now operates as the University of Tampa.

The six silver onion-shaped minarets that top the building are a Tampa landmark. In 1977, the former hotel was designated a National Historic Landmark by the National Park Service.

With the opening of the **Tampa Bay Hotel,** the city's attention was turned to a sparsely populated area west of the Hillsborough River. Here, in 1886, **O.H. Platt** purchased 20 acres of land and created Tampa's first subdivision, **Hyde Park.** Platt named the area after his hometown Hyde Park, Illinois. During the land boom between 1910 and 1925, this area became home to many prominent citizens. Today, this charming neighborhood reflects the architectural styles of the 19th-century with "bungalow" and "Princess Anne" dwellings. In the heart of this National Register Historic District is **Old Hyde Park Village,** a collection of shops, boutiques and restaurants.

In 1914, due to increasing demands from local residents, a sea wall and brick-paved road was constructed along Hillsborough Bay in the Hyde Park area. Now known as **Bayshore Boulevard,** this picturesque street is lined with some of Tampa's stateliest homes and is a popular site for running, bicycling and skating.

Another Tampa neighborhood that was developed during the Florida land boom was Davis Islands. This area is located just off downtown Tampa near the junction of Hillsborough River and Hillsborough Bay. In 1924, David P. Davis, a real estate entrepreneur, transformed two mosquito-infested islands into a successful, booming residential and commercial development. Today, it is home to an airport, Tampa General Hospital and more than 100 of the original residential, commercial and recreational structures.

Airline history was made in the Tampa Bay area when Tony Jannus piloted the world's first regularly scheduled commercial flight from St. Petersburg to Tampa in 1914. During World Wars I and II, Tampa became a shipbuilding center. World War II also brought the opening of a major military post, MacDill Air Force Base.

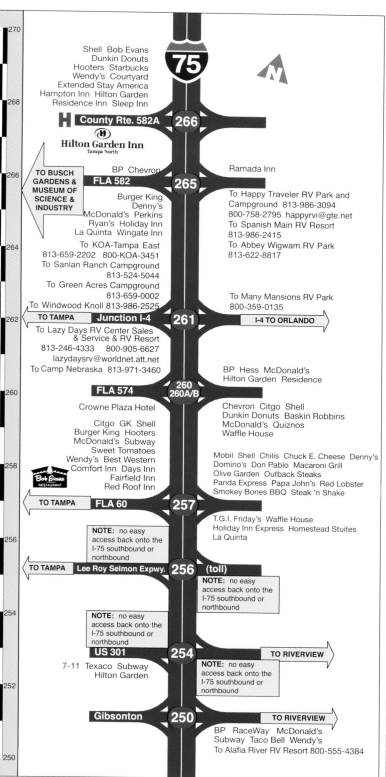

I-75 Mile Markers

270 268 266 264 262 260 258 256 254 252 250

75

N

Shell Bob Evans
Dunkin Donuts
Hooters Starbucks
Wendy's Courtyard
Extended Stay America
Hampton Inn Hilton Garden
Residence Inn Sleep Inn

H **County Rte. 582A** **266**

Hilton Garden Inn
Tampa North

TO BUSCH GARDENS & MUSEUM OF SCIENCE & INDUSTRY

BP Chevron

FLA 582 **265**

Ramada Inn

Burger King
Denny's
McDonald's Perkins
Ryan's Holiday Inn
La Quinta Wingate Inn

To Happy Traveler RV Park and Campground 813-986-3094
800-758-2795 happyrvi@gte.net
To Spanish Main RV Resort
813-986-2415
To Abbey Wigwam RV Park
813-622-8817

To KOA-Tampa East
813-659-2202 800-KOA-3451
To Sanlan Ranch Campground
813-524-5044
To Green Acres Campground
813-659-0002
To Windwood Knoll 813-986-2525

To Many Mansions RV Park
800-359-0135

TO TAMPA **Junction I-4** **261** I-4 TO ORLANDO

To Lazy Days RV Center Sales & Service & RV Resort
813-246-4333 800-905-6627
lazydaysrv@worldnet.att.net
To Camp Nebraska 813-971-3460

BP Hess McDonald's
Hilton Garden Residence

FLA 574 **260 260A/B**

Crowne Plaza Hotel

Chevron Citgo Shell
Dunkin Donuts Baskin Robbins
McDonald's Quiznos
Waffle House

Citgo GK Shell
Burger King Hooters
McDonald's Subway
Sweet Tomatoes
Wendy's Best Western
Comfort Inn Days Inn
Fairfield Inn
Red Roof Inn

Bob Evans RESTAURANT

Mobil Shell Chilis Chuck E. Cheese Denny's
Domino's Don Pablo Macaroni Grill
Olive Garden Outback Steaks
Panda Express Papa John's Red Lobster
Smokey Bones BBQ Steak 'n Shake

TO TAMPA **FLA 60** **257**

T.G.I. Friday's Waffle House
Holiday Inn Express Homestead Stuites
La Quinta

NOTE: no easy access back onto the I-75 southbound or northbound

TO TAMPA **Lee Roy Selmon Expwy.** **256** **(toll)**

NOTE: no easy access back onto the I-75 southbound or northbound

NOTE: no easy access back onto the I-75 southbound or northbound

US 301 **254** TO RIVERVIEW

7-11 Texaco Subway
Hilton Garden

NOTE: no easy access back onto the I-75 southbound or northbound

Gibsonton **250** TO RIVERVIEW

BP RaceWay McDonald's
Subway Taco Bell Wendy's
To Alafia River RV Resort 800-555-4384

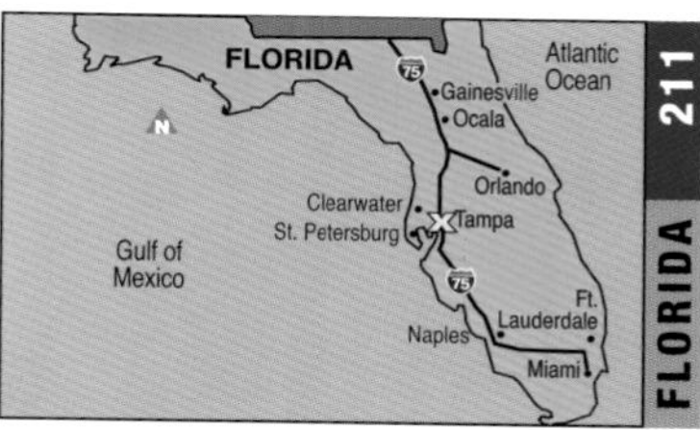

Canoe Escape in Tampa

Just minutes from downtown, **Canoe Escape** enables visitors to surround themselves with the natural beauty of Florida during scenic, serene canoe tours down the Hillsborough River. Canoers view alligators, turtles, ibis, and wood-peckers. The undisturbed tours last from 2 hours to a full day and include paddling instructions as well as the drop-offs and pick-ups. 813-986-2067 or 800-448-2672

Light Tackle Fishing in Tampa

Whether you are a serious sportsfan or relaxed outdoors enthusiast, Bay Area visitors can experience the thrill of light tackle sportfishing. **Light tackle fishing expeditions** offer an angling adventure that brings you and your bait to tarpon, cobia, redfish, trout or snook. A knowledgeable captain will help the odds of getting one of these trophy fish on deck. In-shore fishing also allows passengers the opportunity to see much of the area wildlife such as manatees, dolphins, pelicans, seagulls and stingrays. 813-855-0430 or 800-972-1930

Big Red Balloon of Tampa, FL

Take flight and experience a bird's eye-view of Tampa's skyline, the surrounding gulf and bays and the Sunshine Skyway Bridge. The 4-hour **hot-air balloon flight** provides balloon enthusiasts with a panoramic view to Tampa's nature and wildlife; see wildlife such as deer, alligators and blue herons in their natural habitat. Sunrise flights include a champagne brunch. 813-969-1518 or 800-448-2672

© Emily Marks

St. Petersburg/Clearwater
FLORIDA

St. Petersburg/Clearwater Area Convention & Visitors Bureau
13805- 58th Street North, Suite 2-200, Clearwater, Florida 33760
727-464-7200 877-352-3224 **www.floridabeach.com**

St. Pete Beach. *St. Petersburg/Clearwater has the best beaches in the continental U.S. according to Florida University's Dr. Stephen Leatherman, also known as "Dr. Beach."*
Courtesy St. Petersburg/Clearwater Area CVB.

Special Events

Martin Luther King, Jr. Drum Major for Justice Parade, Battle of the Bands & Drum Line Extravaganza St. Pete. The MLK Festival of Bands features renowned marching bands as they perform their world-famous high-stepping halftime drills in a special salute and tribute to Dr. King. 100,000 average attendance, the largest MLK Commemorative Celebration in the nation. Over 40 marching bands from across the nation. Jan. 727-327-6555

Classic Car Show www.stpetepier.com 727-821-6443

Wine Under the Stars
www.sciencecenterofpinellas.com 727-384-0027

Major League Baseball. Pinellas County is spring training central with Tampa Bay Rays in St. Pete, Philadelphia Phillies in Clearwater and Toronto Blue Jays in Dunedin. Mar. www.tampabay.rays.mlb.com

Bay Area Renaissance Festival. Largo. Discover an enchanted realm of wizards and warriors amongst gourmet treats and unforgettable entertainment. Wander past eight lively stages and street theater featuring jugglers, magicians, fire eaters and specialty acts. Live jousting, human chess matches, 125 shops selling hand crafted wares, minstrels and much more to see. Mar. 800-779-4910 www.renaissancefest.com

Festival of States
St. Pete. 2-week festival of music, the South's largest civic celebration, held since 1921. Bands, 3 parades, concerts, sports. Mar. 727-898-3654 www.festivalofstates.com

Mainsail Arts Festival. St. Pete. One of the "100 Best Fine Art Shows" in the United States. Apr. 727-892-5885 www.mainsailartsfestival.org

Highland Games and Festival
Dunedin. Celebrating Scottish heritage since 1966. U.S./Canadian competitors, dancing, piping, drumming, athletics. Apr. 727-736-5066

Tarpon Springs Arts & Crafts Festival
This show attracts more than 200 artists who compete for excellent prizes! Spring Bayou in Craig Park. Apr. 727-937-6109

American Stage in the Park
St. Pete. Outdoor Shakespeare. 50,000 fans. Wed. to Sun. Apr. 727-823-1600

Fun 'n Sun Festival. Clearwater. 100,000 attend concerts, competitions, food, arts & crafts. Night Parade. Apr. 727-562-4804

St. Anthony's Tampa Bay Triathlon
St. Pete. Florida's largest triathlon. 1,700 athletes compete to qualify for the Ironman Triathlon Championships. Apr. 727-825-1271

Beach Goes Pop. St. Pete Beach. Florida Orchestra and Florida Opera perform sunset concert. Apr. 727-360-6957

Mad Dog Beach Triathalon
May Madeira Beach. 800 competitors. www.madbeachtri.com 727-367-4529

Taste of Pinellas
St. Pete. Fine restaurants set up in Vinoy Park. June. 727-898-7451

Juneteenth. St. Pete. Commemorate the emancipation of slaves at the oldest African-American holiday observance in America. 727-821-3833

Celebrate America! Clearwater. Concerts, crafts, food, fireworks. July. 727-462-6531

Fishathon St. Pete. August. Special event for children under 12. Free awards. 727-892-5874

AVP/Next/Wilson National Beach Finals
Clearwater Beach. Aug.

Don CeSar's Dolphins to Dinosaurs Sand Castle Competition
St. Pete Beach. Sept. 727-360-1881

Florida Birding Festival
Clearwater. One of the biggest urban birding affairs in the U.S. Sept. 877-352-2473

Blues on the Bayou
Tarpon Springs. Some of the country's leading blues acts perform in beautiful Craig Park. Oct. 727-944-3364

Clearwater Jazz Holiday
Top-names. Four-day free extravaganza. Coachman Park on waterfront. Oct. 727-461-5200

Country Jubilee. Largo. Old-time country fair with arts & crafts. Oct. 727-582-2123

John's Pass Seafood Festival
Madeira Beach. 100,000 attend the famous seafood festival. Entertainment, art and crafts. Oct. 727-393-1947

Arts Alive Museum Month
St. Pete. Seven world-class museums offer special events. Salvador Dali Museum, Florida International Museum, Great Explorations, Museum of Fine Arts, Florida Holocaust Museum, Pier Aquarium and St. Pete Museum of History. Nov. 1-800-345-6710 www.stpete.org

Clearwater Cup Regetta. October 100 racing yachts from around the world. 4 race classes. Nov. 727-447-6000

Ribfest
St. Pete. BBQ contest draws chefs from around the globe. Nov. 727-528-3828

St. Petersburg Boat Show
One of the South's largest shows. Nov. 800-940-7642

Arts & Crafts Show. Tarpon Springs. Features 200 artists and crafters from across the US. Nov. 727-937-6109

Arts & Crafts Festival. Indian Rocks Beach. 13,000 attend this semi-annual event in Kolb Park. Nov. 727-596-4331

Suncoast Dixieland Jazz Classic
Nationally prominent bands at Sheraton Sand Key Resort on Clearwater Beach. www.jazzclassic.net 727-595-1611

Snowfest & Holiday Fantasy
St. Pete. Month-long tradition of decorations, choirs, and parade. Dec. 727-821-6443

Lighted Boat Parade
St. Pete. The Pier shows off their Christmas spirit in lighted color. Dec. 727-893-7494

First Night
St. Pete hosts New Year's Eve in a non-alcoholic fashion. 727-823-8906

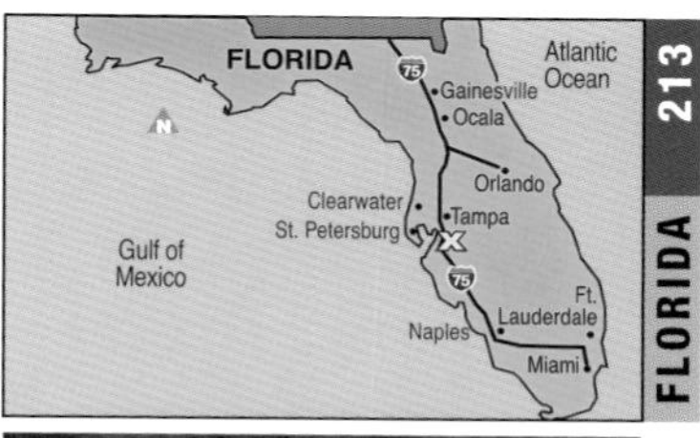

I-75 Mile Markers

250
248
246
244
242
240
238
236
234
232
230

75

Chevron
7-11

TO APOLLO BEACH County Rte. 672 **246**

Applebee's Little Ceaser's.
Mcdonald's Starbucks
Subway Quiznos

TO RUSKIL FLA 674 **240 240AB**

Circle K Hess RaceTrac
KFC McDonald's Subway
To Sun Lake RV Resort
813-645-7860
sunlake@aol.com
To Tampa South RV Resort
813-645-1202
To Hide-A-Way RV Resort
800-607-2532
To River Oaks RV Resort
813-645-2439

Chevron Beef O'Brady's
Bob Evans Denny's
Hungry Howie's King Buffet
Pizza Hut Sonny's BBQ
Taco Bell Wendy's
Comfort Inn

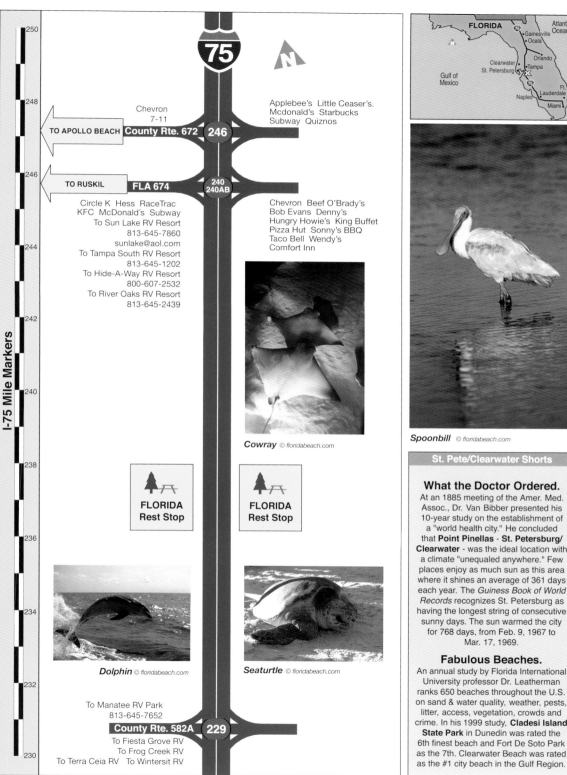

Cowray *© floridabeach.com*

FLORIDA Rest Stop

FLORIDA Rest Stop

Dolphin *© floridabeach.com*

Seaturtle *© floridabeach.com*

To Manatee RV Park
813-645-7652

County Rte. 582A **229**

To Fiesta Grove RV
To Frog Creek RV
To Terra Ceia RV To Wintersit RV

Spoonbill *© floridabeach.com*

St. Pete/Clearwater Shorts

What the Doctor Ordered.

At an 1885 meeting of the Amer. Med. Assoc., Dr. Van Bibber presented his 10-year study on the establishment of a "world health city." He concluded that **Point Pinellas - St. Petersburg/ Clearwater** - was the ideal location with a climate "unequaled anywhere." Few places enjoy as much sun as this area where it shines an average of 361 days each year. The *Guiness Book of World Records* recognizes St. Petersburg as having the longest string of consecutive sunny days. The sun warmed the city for 768 days, from Feb. 9, 1967 to Mar. 17, 1969.

Fabulous Beaches.

An annual study by Florida International University professor Dr. Leatherman ranks 650 beaches throughout the U.S. on sand & water quality, weather, pests, litter, access, vegetation, crowds and crime. In his 1999 study, **Cladesi Island State Park** in Dunedin was rated the 6th finest beach and Fort De Soto Park as the 7th. Clearwater Beach was rated as the #1 city beach in the Gulf Region.

St. Petersburg/Clearwater Area Convention & Visitors Bureau
13805- 58th Street North, Suite 2-200, Clearwater, Florida 233760
727-464-7200 877-352-3224 **www.floridabeach.com**

Sheraton Sand Key Resort

We can't say enough about the beautiful Sheraton Sand Key Resort. For the last few hours of the 2-day drive down to Florida, we start to drive a little faster –we're looking forward to the great beach and pampering we know we can count on at the Sheraton Sand Key Resort! With 10 acres of exclusive beach and comfortable guest rooms and suites, we can confirm that this property will do whatever it takes to help you have the perfect holiday. Whether you're preparing a celebration or just a weekend of soaking up the sun, they can accommodate you. This resort offers 24,000 sq.ft. of extensive conference facilities, a relaxing pool deck, many nearby attractions, and extraordinary cuisine. Come see for yourself why both vacation and meeting planners prefer the Sheraton Sand Key Resort!

- 390 spacious guest rooms and suites
- Award-winning dining
- One of America's most renowned beaches
- Water sport activities and rentals
- Annual events include the 3-day Sun coast Dixieland Jazz Classic in December

1160 Gulf Boulevard
Clearwater Beach, FL 33767-2799
Ph: 727-595-1611 Fax: 727-596-8488
Reservations: 800-456-7263
sheraton@sheratonsandkey.com

Photo © Sheraton Sand Key

Columbia Restaurant on Sand Key in Clearwater Beach—a Florida tradition since 1905.

1241 Gulf Boulevard, Clearwater, FL 33767 (727) 596-8400

After a generous presentation of the most delicious seafood, I managed to find room for a mouthwatering chocolate dessert and a few bites of the girls' fruitier choices as well. You would too. Each flavor lives up to the flair! Waterfront views from the inside dining room or outdoor deck, and the award-winning Spanish/Cuban cuisine, are the specials at the Columbia on Clearwater Beach's Sand Key.

Whether you choose a table looking out onto the radiant blue waters of the Intracoastal Waterway from the Mediterranean dining room, or experience the casual atmosphere from the outdoor deck, you can enjoy the cuisine that has consistently been voted Tampa Bay's Favorite. Here you can satisfy your taste for fresh seafood from the Gulf of Mexico, along with century-old family recipes like Paella "a la Valencia," Snapper "Alicante" Pompano en Papillot and Filet Mignon "Chacho".

Sand Key is located on the West Coast of Florida, directly on the Gulf of Mexico, and is a tropical paradise. The Columbia Restaurant on Sand Key is located just steps from the beach, with two resort hotels nearby. See the article above about the Sheraton Sand Key Resort.

Stop in the on-site gift shop for a selection of unique gifts, fine cigars & accessories. And don't forget to take home "A Taste of Columbia" with their World Famous "1905" Salad ™ Dressing, sangria mix, Cuban and American roast coffee, hot sauce and Columbia seasoning you won't find anywhere else. You will also see a wide variety of unique hand-made and hand painted ceramic pieces imported from Spain.

If you are interested, ask for one of the owners or managers. They are often on site and are proud to tell you the history of this and other restaurants in the family-owned collection of Florida landmarks.

Photos © Columbia Restaurant and www.floridabeach.com

St. Petersburg/Clearwater Area Convention & Visitors Bureau
13805- 58th Street North, Suite 2-200, Clearwater, Florida 233760
727-464-7200 877-352-3224 www.floridabeach.com

Caladesi Island State Park

Is this the best beach in the continental U.S.? See for yourself. All you'll need is your sunscreen and a big beach towel to drape over the rental beach chairs and umbrellas for a real beach experience. Bring a picnic or sample the café's offerings if you prefer. Dr. Beach, also known as Dr. Stephen P. Leatherman (head of the National Healthy Beaches Campaign), consistently ranks the island – just off the coast of Dunedin, north of Clearwater Beach – as one of the nation's top 10 beaches. In 2006 and again in 2007, it reached the No. 2 spot. In 2008, he named it the nation's best beach. But we never saw any of it! We kayaked and were so mesmerized by the natural beauty of the sun-dappled mangroves that we ran out of time and only just made it on the last ferry home.

Caladesi Island is accessible only by boat, a ferry that runs hourly from Honeymoon Island. If you miss the last ferry, you'll be warned by the captain that you'll have to camp out on the island with the rattlesnakes! (Naturally, I didn't want to test him on this!). Caladesi Island is part of the Great Florida Birding Trail and from our kayaks we spotted terns, gulls, osprey and other shorebirds on the outskirts of the island before gliding deeper into the island's interior that was home to many wading birds, including herons and egrets. Adding to the eco-adventure, we watched snakes and tree crabs hidden in the branches, and were startled by splashes made by whatever was watching us.

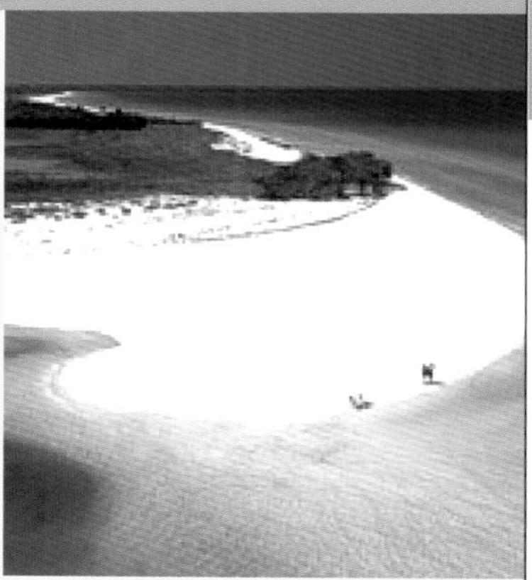

Photos copyright @ 2009 St. Petersburg/Clearwater Area Convention & Visitors Bureau.

Great Explorations! The Children's Museums

Great Explorations, the childrens' museum, is a place where you make discoveries and have a ball! Speaking of balls, here you are invited to launch a tennis ball to the top of the museum, race a car, become a computer animator, make pizza, join a workshop or just people watch in the smartest place in St. Pete! This is a safe place where kids and adults can chill and explore at their own pace. Located next to Sunken Gardens. 1925 4th St. N. St. Petersburg, FL 33704-4307
727-821-8992 727-823-7287
www.greatexplorations.org/

Columbia at The Pier in downtown St. Petersburg

Waterfront views and outstanding Spanish/Cuban cuisine are what you can expect at the Columbia at The Pier in downtown St. Petersburg. A panoramic 360° 4th floor waterfront view of sailboats drifting by and dolphins playing in Tampa Bay enhance their award-winning family recipes for fresh seafood from the Gulf of Mexico and other specialties.

Columbia at the Pier is centrally located in downtown St. Petersburg. Not far from the Pier is an impressive collection of cultural centers that include the St. Petersburg Museum of History, the Museum of Fine Arts, Florida International Museum and the world-renowned Salvador Dali Museum. There are also several waterfront parks to enjoy. For baseball fans, Tropicana Field, home of the Tampa Bay Rays is conveniently located 5 miles from the Pier

Spend a day enjoying nature at the Pier. Take a spin on the Dolphin Queen sightseeing boat tour and you might spot dolphins, manatees and several species of birds. Tours are held 7 days a week. Fishing takes place on the approach to The Pier and around the exterior of the building along the sea walls. Fishing poles can be rented from The Pier Bait House and bait purchased there. Presently, two and four-seater bicycles can be rented at Whimsical Wheels.

Inside the Pier is a collection of sixteen specialty stores. You can also visit the Pier Aquarium on the second floor of the Pier. There, guests explore a variety of marine environments from Tampa Bay to the Caribbean and Pacific coral reefs.

Photos © Columbia Restaurant and www.floridabeach.com

St. Petersburg/Clearwater Area Convention & Visitors Bureau
13805- 58th Street North, Suite 2-200, Clearwater, Florida 233760
727-464-7200 877-352-3224 www.floridabeach.com

Tradewinds Island Grand Resort and Sandpiper Hotel and Suites

5500 Gulf Blvd., St. Pete Beach
(727)367-6461 (727)363-2275
www.sheratonsandkey.com

Swans played in the canal below our balcony while we watched the sunset. How cool is that? These two distinct beach resorts on the island of St. Pete Beach are just steps away from each other on the white sandy beach of Florida's Gulf Coast. This beachfront setting with a hint of the Island tropics offers a colorful mix of relaxation, fun and recreation, along with friendly, four-diamond service and accommodations that encourage you to "just let go".

There was a lot of thought put into the design of this resort. Lakes and canals stocked with big fish meander below picturesque paths and bridges lined with colorful plant life. Two days could never be enough to take it all in. My girls had fun until they hit the pillow. Inbetween switching from the beach to the pools, they stopped for a scream-ride down the towering inflatable beach slide, or to participate in the interactive shows and other planned activities. When we weren't on the beach, I read and snoozed by the pool and visited the tiki bar, knowing the girls were happy and safe on the property together. With convenience stores and a variety of places to get food, drinks and other treats, you'd have little reason to leave this resort complex.
TradeWinds Island Grand is the classic, AAA four-diamond, family-friendly resort, while Sandpiper Hotel and Suites is the more intimate TradeWinds resort with leisurely days of relaxation and tranquility.

Photo left © Christine Marks
Photo above © Tradewinds Island Grand Resort & www.floridabeach.com

Weedon Island Preserve & Sweetwater Kayaks

10000 Gandy Blvd., Saint Petersburg, Florida 33702 (727) 570-4844 www.sweetwaterkayaks.com

Weedon Island Preserve, just north of St. Petersburg, is a 3,700-acre complex of mangrove swamps, mudflats, pine flatwoods and oak hammocks on the western shore of Tampa Bay. If you take the 3000-foot boardwalk (tree top level through a mangrove forest canopy), you'll always remember your roosting pelican's view of a saltwater sea nursery. This is the nursery of the tiny creatures that ultimately will be (or be nutrition for) some of the Gulf of Mexico's biggest fishes.

At this preserve you can explore by kayak the brackish water trail through narrow mangrove tree tunnels formed by over-reaching limbs where leaves drop, decay and feed the smallest creatures that will become food for minnows and crabs. Further into the shallows of Tampa Bay you can expect to see some of the creatures higher on the foodchain -- ospreys, cormorants, egrets, roseate spoonbills, herons, and fishes and rays seemingly too big for this foot-deep water.
Another mission of the preserves is to educate about the healthy relationship between nature and cultures old and modern. At the (air-conditioned!) Cultural and Natural History Center, we took in a short movie and studied the displays to learn the story of the native peoples of the Weedon Island culture who settled the area 1800 years ago and thrived on the fish, shellfish, and lush plantlife.

Weedon Island Preserve features a 4-mile canoe trail, visitor and education center, 9-mile hiking trail and two observation decks, along with a fishing pier and waterfront picnic sites.

Photo © www.floridabeach.com

St. Petersburg/Clearwater Area Convention & Visitors Bureau
13805- 58th Street North, Suite 2-200, Clearwater, Florida 233760
727-464-7200 877-352-3224 **www.floridabeach.com**

Salvador Dali Museum

1000 Third Street South
St. Petersburg, Florida 33701-4901
www.salvadordalimuseum.org

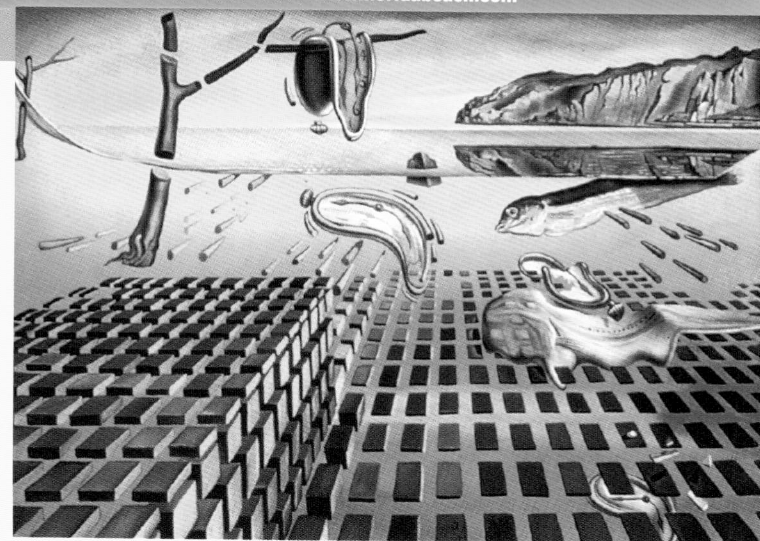

Is it on your "bucket list"? It appears that the Dali Museum is on many people's must-see list. Like most days, the parking lot is quite full before the museum opened. They do it right. It's a big facility and I understand they are building a larger one. We were thrilled that the tour groups were intimate because the lessons added so much to the experience. Over 100 Salvador Dali Museum docents provide regular tours to museum visitors, school groups, and adult groups of all ages. Highly praised by visitors, the docents are scheduled for approximately 6 public tours a day; last year alone they led over 2,300 tours of the museum's galleries.

Dali Museum docents conduct hour-long public tours which are free of charge. While each tour features selections from the permanent collection and highlights from Dali's life, subject matter may touch on Dali's interest in Freud, to mathematics, science, art history or his Spanish and Catalan cultures. Museum docents also lead tours of visiting exhibitions which have ranged from single artist shows of Andy Warhol and James Rosenquist to theme-based shows such as From Pollock to Pop: America's Brush with Dali and Dali & the Spanish Baroque.

The Salvador Dali Museum is the permanent home of the world's most comprehensive collection of the renowned Spanish artist's work. Compiled by A. Reynolds Morse and Eleanor Morse over a 45-year period, it is celebrated for its 95 oil paintings, and features excellent examples from Dali's four major periods - Early (1917-1927), Transitional (1928), Surreal (1929-1939), and Classic (1940-1970s). Pictured here is Nature Morte Vivante (Still Life-Fast Moving) from the permanent collection.

Photos top right, bottom left © www.floridabeach.com

Cha Cha Coconuts at the Pier Restaurant *Best View in Tampa Bay*

800 2ND Ave NE, St Petersburg, FL 33701 727-822-6655

At Cha Cha Coconuts you'll be treated to casual dining with a tropical twist: a savory selection of seafood, sandwiches and other island-style fare. Choose to relax in the dining room or enjoy an outdoor table while sipping on one of our refreshing tropical drinks and sampling from our casual Caribbean menu. You can also relax on the rooftop open-air deck as the breathtaking views of Tampa Bay and warm breeze embrace your senses at the restaurant voted "Best View in Tampa Bay." Favorites include Coconut Shrimp, Fish Tacos and Half-pound Burgers. Live music Friday, Saturday and Sunday. Open daily for lunch and dinner with a Children's menu available. Cha Cha Coconuts at the Pier is centrally located in Downtown St. Petersburg.

Photos © Columbia Restaurant & www.floridabeach.com

Bradenton & Sarasota

Bradenton & Florida's Gulf Island Beaches
P.O. Box 1000, Bradenton, Florida 34206
941-729-9177 or 1-800-4-Manatee www.floridagulfislands.com

Bradenton is in Manatee County, on Florida's central west coast, north of Sarasota and south of Tampa, with the gulf of Mexico to the west and Tampa Bay to the north.

Timucuan and Calusa Indian tribes were the first known inhabitants of Manatee County. It is believed that in 1539 DeSoto led an expedition through the area. Seminole Indians relocated to the area in the last half of the 18th century. Josiah Gates, an early settler, claimed a tract on the Manatee River under the Armed Occupation Act of 1842. This Act was an effort of the U.S. Government to settle Florida and control the Seminoles. Dr. Joseph Addison Braden arrived in the Village of Manatee (now of East Bradenton) in 1843 and built Fort Braden to protect his sugar plantation and mill. Today the main crop is tomatoes. In recognition of Braden, the town was named Bradenton in 1878, although documents sent to Washington misspelt it as "Braidentown." In 1927, it officially became Bradenton.

Manatee County is named for the Manatee, a mammal also called "sea cow." The Manatee River winds for 55 miles from Tampa Bay to the northeast corner of Manatee County.

Lizzy & the manatees

© Christine Marks Mote Marine Laboratory, Sarasota, FL

Eco-Adventures in the Bradenton Area, On Longboat Key & Anna Maria Island

Visit a Remote Tropical Island.
Egmont Key, which lies about 3 miles off the northern tip of Anna Maria Island, is now a virtually abandoned island. This beautiful isle of sand and sea oats separates the open waters of the Gulf of Mexico from Tampa Bay. With a history that dates back to before the Civil War, **Egmont Key** is home to crumbling Fort Dade, a military Fort built in 1900 during the Spanish American War; Florida's sixth-brightest lighthouse; the threatened gopher tortoise and the nesting grounds of many species of sea turtles.

The island can be accessed by private boat or a guided charter trip with the **Miss Cortez Fleet.** A guide from the Miss Cortez offers a walking tour of the island and provides a historical and ecological look at the island. The waters surrounding the islands present some of the most abundant and diverse sea shell collecting on Florida's West Coast. While trekking across this narrow island visitors frequently come across a variety of wildlife, among them the slow-moving **gopher tortoise.** This creature's dull-brown shell is easily spotted along the trails crossing the island.

Egmont Key is truly one of the last island treasures in Florida. Its strategic location at the mouth of Tampa Bay has made for a vibrant history. Because the island is mostly federal property, it remains much as it did before development. For more information about the Cortez Fleet trip to Egmont Key, call 941-794-1223.

Duette Park Expands Park Usage to Include Hiking, Biking and Horseback Riding.
In 1991, the 22,000-acre Duette Park began a wildlife management hunt program. This past year, the park expanded its usage to include hiking and biking and horseback riding trails. Duette Park is a designated watershed conservation area that features some of Florida's most beautiful and diverse ecosystems. Visitors to the park can view palmetto prairie, live oak hammocks, dense pine forests, wildflower meadows and beautiful marsh and wetlands. The park has several distinct species of wildlife including the highly endangered scrub jay and Florida panther. More common sightings in the park include coyote, deer, armadillo, boar, bobcat and birds.

The hunt program, which runs on weekends, Oct. to Nov. and Jan. to March, draws hunters from throughout the state. There are 11 hunts per year, each allowing 150 hunters. There are two archery hunts, one muzzleload hunt, and three general gun hunts for deer and hog only. 941-742-5923

Manatee Airboat Tours Teach Conservation and Preservation.
Visitors wishing to learn more about the marine ecology of the barrier islands will enjoy the "Turbulance," the Bradenton area's only airboat tour. The tour which lasts about 1 hour departs from the Perico Bay Marina, just west of Anna Maria Island on Manatee Ave. The airboat, which holds up to 6 people, glides through the inland bays and narrow mangrove hammocks. Sites along the coastline include a look at many species of native birds including a trip to the nesting grounds of some species such as the roseate spoonbill, reddish egret, ibis, sandhill crane and the native wood stork. In the water, visitors may get a glimpse of a porpoise family at play, sea turtles and tropical fish. For further information on Manatee Airboat Tours call 941-730-1011.

Canoe Adventures Abound in the Bradenton Area.
Climb into a canoe for an exciting eco-adventure on the beautiful Upper Manatee River. Head up the Manatee River and enjoy the wide variety of subtropical vegetation and an area rich in wildlife. Spot herons, egrets, hawks, ospreys, otters, bobcats and turtles.

Once the main route to the Florida interior for the area's first settlers, the Manatee River has hidden white sandy beaches, fresh clear waters and a large stock of striped bass, bream, speck and the area's largest freshwater catfish. Head further north and spend your day canoeing on the Little Manatee River, one of Florida's last remaining unspoiled water-ways. Designated by the Florida legislature as an Outstanding Florida Waterway, the river is enjoyed by every level of canoe enthusiast. Call 941-747-3909 or 941-634-2228 for more information.

We highly recommend Bungalow Beach Resort, Anna Maria, FL. www.bungalowbeach.com

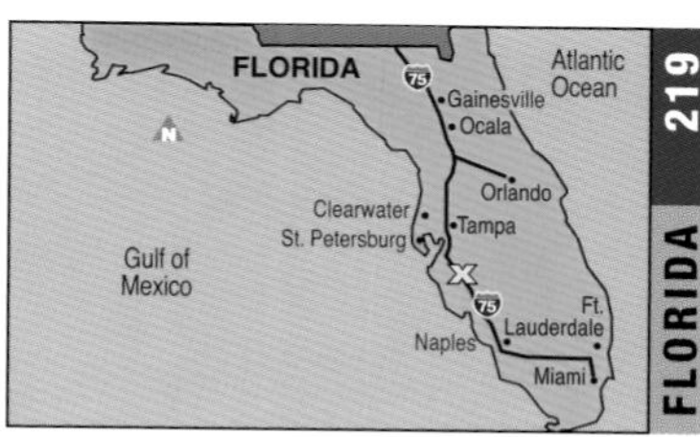

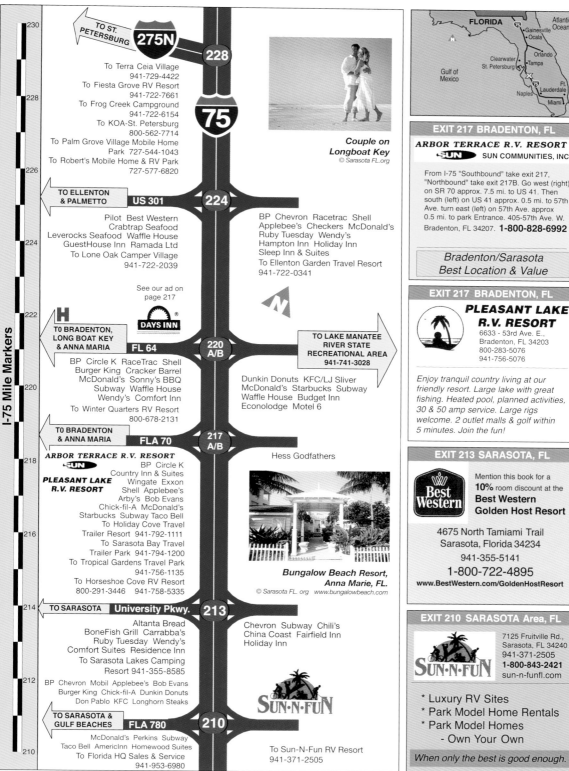

I-75 Mile Markers

230 228 226 224 222 220 218 216 214 212 210

TO ST. PETERSBURG 275N

228

To Terra Ceia Village 941-729-4422
To Fiesta Grove RV Resort 941-722-7661
To Frog Creek Campground 941-722-6154
To KOA-St. Petersburg 800-562-7714
To Palm Grove Village Mobile Home Park 727-544-1043
To Robert's Mobile Home & RV Park 727-577-6820

75

Couple on Longboat Key
© Sarasota FL.org

TO ELLENTON & PALMETTO US 301

224

Pilot Best Western
Crabtrap Seafood
Leverocks Seafood Waffle House
GuestHouse Inn Ramada Ltd
To Lone Oak Camper Village 941-722-2039

BP Chevron Racetrac Shell
Applebee's Checkers McDonald's
Ruby Tuesday Wendy's
Hampton Inn Holiday Inn
Sleep Inn & Suites
To Ellenton Garden Travel Resort 941-722-0341

See our ad on page 217

DAYS INN

N

H

TO BRADENTON, LONG BOAT KEY & ANNA MARIA FL 64

220 A/B

TO LAKE MANATEE RIVER STATE RECREATIONAL AREA 941-741-3028

BP Circle K RaceTrac Shell
Burger King Cracker Barrel
McDonald's Sonny's BBQ
Subway Waffle House
Wendy's Comfort Inn
To Winter Quarters RV Resort 800-678-2131

Dunkin Donuts KFC/LJ Sliver
McDonald's Starbucks Subway
Waffle House Budget Inn
Econolodge Motel 6

TO BRADENTON & ANNA MARIA FLA 70

217 A/B

ARBOR TERRACE R.V. RESORT
SUN
PLEASANT LAKE R.V. RESORT

BP Circle K
Country Inn & Suites
Wingate Exxon
Shell Applebee's
Arby's Bob Evans
Chick-fil-A McDonald's
Starbucks Subway Taco Bell
To Holiday Cove Travel Trailer Resort 941-792-1111
To Sarasota Bay Travel Trailer Park 941-794-1200
To Tropical Gardens Travel Park 941-756-1135
To Horseshoe Cove RV Resort 800-291-3446 941-758-5335

Hess Godfathers

Bungalow Beach Resort, Anna Marie, FL.
© Sarasota FL. org www.bungalowbeach.com

TO SARASOTA University Pkwy.

213

Altanta Bread
BoneFish Grill Carrabba's
Ruby Tuesday Wendy's
Comfort Suites Residence Inn
To Sarasota Lakes Camping Resort 941-355-8585

BP Chevron Mobil Applebee's Bob Evans
Burger King Chick-fil-A Dunkin Donuts
Don Pablo KFC Longhorn Steaks

Chevron Subway Chili's
China Coast Fairfield Inn
Holiday Inn

SUN-N-FUN

TO SARASOTA & GULF BEACHES FLA 780

210

McDonald's Perkins Subway
Taco Bell AmericInn Homewood Suites
To Florida HQ Sales & Service 941-953-6980

To Sun-N-Fun RV Resort 941-371-2505

Sarasota
FLORIDA

Sarasota Convention & Visitors Bureau
701 N. Tamiami Trail, Sarasota, Florida 34236
941-957-1877 or 1-800-800-3906 **www.SarasotaFL.org**

Siesta Key: The Finest, Whitest Sand in the World

It all started as a friendly competition over "bragging rights" about what beach has the finest, whitest sand in the world. More than 11 years ago tourism professionals in the Sarasota and Bradenton area persuaded scientists from the Woods Hole Oceanographic Institution in Woods Hole, Massachusetts, to judge the "Great International White Sand Beach Challenge," with more than 30 entries from beaches around the state and around the world. The competition was held in Manatee County in 1987, and on that day Siesta Key was named the winner of the worldwide title, which remains in effect today.

According to a report from the Geology Department of Harvard University: "The sand from Siesta Key is 99% PURE QUARTZ grains—the grains being somewhat angular in shape. The soft, floury texture of the sand is due to its very fine grain size. It contains no fragments of coral and no shell. The fineness of the sand which gives it its powdery softness, is emphasized by the fact that the quartz is very hard, graded at 7 in the hardness scale of 10—the diamond being rated 10 in that scale."

Strollers, joggers, bathers and sun-worshippers flock to the island to enjoy the pristine sands of the wide, 2-3/4 mile-long **Crescent Beach,** including **Siesta Key Public Beach** at the north end. Seashell searchers find their rewards farther south at **Turtle Beach,** where shell treasures abound.

Within easy walking distance from the sand, visitors will find a quaint and charming village with art galleries, boutiques, delightful restaurants, entertainment and every service and amenity.

Two bridges connect Siesta Key to Sarasota County, **"Florida's Cultural Coast."** Denizens of the theater can choose from the **Florida Studio Theatre, The Asolo Theatre** in the **FSU Center for the Performing Arts, Theatre Works, Players of Sarasota** and the **Golden Apple Dinner Theatre.** There is also a new theater company called the **Banyan Theater Company**. The **Sarasota Opera** offer world-class performances. The **John and Mable Ringling Museum of Art** boasts a magnificent location on the water, a first-class collection of Baroque art, a whimsical **Circus Museum** and the breathtaking Ringling mansion, **Ca'd'Zan.** A dazzling display of orchids, bromeliads and other exotic flora blooms at the **Marie Selby Botanical Gardens** of Sarasota Bay, while **Mote Aquarium** brims with sharks, sea turtles, manatees and other local aquatic life. Ecology and nature enthusiasts can take in the unfettered wildlife at **Myakka River** and **Oscar Scherer State Parks.** For history lovers, **Historic Spanish Point** is a must-see.

Elizabeth at The John and Mable Ringling Museum of Art. *Here, we sketched feverishly in the courtyard beneath the sun and the towering Statue of David. We then spent several hours marveling at the Baroque and modern art treasures. Finally we collapsed in the grass and soaked in the spicy fragrances of the Museum's rose test garden.*

Venice Beach

Scoring the perfect shell is one thing, but finding the perfect fossilized sharks' tooth is quite another!

Venice Beach calls itself the "Sharks Tooth Capital of the World" and the visitors bureau suggested that the fossilized teeth were plentiful. We were skeptical but decided to go and see if we could find one. Not one of us was disappointed! There they were, black and shiny, literally peppering the beach. Some of the sharks teeth rested on the sand, but we found our luck vastly improved with an "archeological dig." Just a few inches below the surface, the teeth were nicer for collecting, often unbroken and somewhat larger.

Venice Beach, just a short walk from the public parking area, is clean, uncrowded and wheelchair accessible.

Siesta Key Beach

Siesta Key Beach

I am going to retire here.

I had read about the baby powder sand, and heard of its legendary sunsets so I expected a fairly nice beach. I did not expect to see my girls plop down and plunge their hands wrist deep into the softness just for the sheer pleasure of it! Two steps onto the sand and my daughters were shoveling it into their plastic pails to "bring some home for Gramma!" This beach is truly surprising.

And again, we weren't prepared for the sunset. Sunsets are often beautiful, but here, at Siesta Key Beach, the atmosphere, the latitude, or some magical element, sets the colors aglow in such mesmerizing patterns, the folks on the beach rarely fold up their chairs till the sun has disappeared completely and the resulting applause of the crowd has ceased.

Sarasota Convention & Visitors Bureau
701 N. Tamiami Td., Sarastora, Florida 34236
800-800-3906 941-957-1877 **www.sarasotafl.org**

Mote Marine Laboratory

1600 Ken Thompson Pkwy., Sarasota, FL 34236. (941) 388-4441 - (800) 691-MOTE www.Mote.org

Take out your red pen and circle this attraction. If you've used any of our past editions, you'll know how I had to bribe my daughters in order to leave this wonderful place. We have visited Mote twice before, and could have easily spent another great day here, but as travel authors we have to cover ground every day. If you have any interest in nature, especially in the marine world –this world renowned research and education center must make it on to your "to do" list! From its humble beginnings in a tiny shed in a small Florida town, Mote Marine Laboratory continues to expand its 10.5-acre campus in Sarasota, Fla., with field stations and public exhibits in Key West and field stations in Summerland Key and Charlotte Harbor. Florida's extensive coastline is the perfect marine and estuarine environment for the Mote scientists to build this research environment.

Originally focused on sharks, Mote research now has seven major areas of concentration, however as the Mote scientists have partnered with others within the complex, this integrated effort across a number of fields has established Mote as a global leader in many areas of marine science. Mote Marine Laboratory is one of the world's few remaining private marine research laboratories and, as a nonprofit organization, is funded through federal, state and local grants and through the vast generosity of individual donors and foundations.

Show and Tell. Mote conducts extensive public outreach and operates a public aquarium that serves nearly 400,000 visitors a year. Here is one of the few organizations in the world that combines marine research with public outreach through a full-fledged aquarium. It is simply incredible the caliber of volunteer guides this aquarium attracts. Every visit, we were offered the breadth and depth of education we sought from the very educated, very experienced guides. Emily was interested in lobster migration and although that was not the specialty of the retired marine biologist (Ph.D. on the tag) we were chatting with about flounders, he knew another volunteer scientist at a different tank area would have more to offer on this, and happily found her for us – you just can't put a value on that dedication. How exciting to be in the thick of all that! The lessons we learned have stayed with us and hopefully inspired at least one of my daughters to consider furthering her education in this area.

Historic Spanish Point

337 North Tamiami Trail (PO Box 846), Osprey, FL 34229 941-966-5214 www.historicspanishpoint.org/

Historic Spanish Point museum is open to the public seven days a week and serves over 28,000 visitors annually who take in the major archaeological exhibition "A Window to the Past," and the renovated Osprey School, a 1927 Spanish Colonial Revival style building that is now a Visitors Center with an orientation theater, lecture hall, meeting room, administrative offices, museum store, and an exhibit gallery for temporary exhibitions.

- Historic Spanish Point is a significant horticulture site with a Wetland Garden
- "A Window to the Past" is the only place in the country to go inside a prehistoric shell midden where you are surrounded on three sides by evidence of the past.
- 140 year old pioneer heritage preserved and interpreted at Historic Spanish Point
- Enjoy the 3 gardens– the Sunken Garden, Duchene Lawn, and Jungle Walk, the classical styled Pergola overlooking Little Sarasota Bay which is the site of wedding ceremonies and Living History Performances.

Jungle Walk at historic Spanish Point
© Sarasota Convention and Visitors Bureau

Longboat Key Club and Resort

301 Gulf of Mexico Drive, Longboat Key, FL 34228 941.383.1512 www.longboatkeyclub.com

Like stumbling on a chest of gold and diamonds, this is treasure in paradise. As my daughter Lizzy said, it was "luxury-everything." The unofficial motto seemed to be "just ask, we'll take care of it." The suites were more like apartments, and so well appointed we were delighted. It was towards the end of a two-week fact-finding trip that we stayed at the Longboat Key Club, and that was perfect timing for the pampering. Oh, the pampering! We used the kitchen to prepare our own dinner for our candle-lit balcony farewell meal. Dozens of stories high, the view of the sunset on the water over the sparkling lights of the grounds was serene. I said good night to the girls ....their suite was so far away, I couldn't hear them at all while I soaked in the king-size Jacuzzi tub. If you sleep in late like I did, just blame it on that heavenly bed.

- AAA Four Diamond
- Private white-sand beach
- 218 newly renovated rooms with private balconies
- Island House Spa
- Championship golf (45 holes)
- 6 restaurants
- Tennis Academy
- Kids Club

Photo © Longboat Key Club & Resort

Sarasota
FLORIDA

Sarasota Convention & Visitors Bureau
701 N. Tamiami Td., Sarastora, Florida 34236
800-800-3906 941-957-1877 **www.sarasotafl.org**

WIZ The Science Museum

**1001 Boulevard of the Arts,
The Blivas Science & Technology Center, Sarasota, FL 34236
941.309.GWIZ (4949) www.gwiz.org**

I underestimated the time we would need to see this playground of science! I've always been interested in science and technology and this place fascinated at every turn, but the girls wore me out. I didn't want to rush them so I was thankful there were many welcoming places to sit and wait for them to finish an exhibit before moving on to the next. Soon after it opened to the public as the Gulf Coast World of Science (GCWS) in 1990, it

was granted membership in the Association of Science & Technology Centers (ASTC). Then, just 10 months later GCWS expanded to 6,000 feet. In May 1993, with its new permanent home, and working with Hands-On, a nationally recognized museum planning company, a fresh image was created for the evolving science center which became the Gulfcoast Wonder & Imagination Zone, "G.WIZ" in 2000. The $3.5 million 33,000 sq. ft. facility located downtown on Sarasota's bay front is the perfect contrasting backdrop for this a world-class science and technology center.

Photo © Sarasotafl.org

Capri Inn at the Beach

**6782 SaraSea Circle,
Sarasota, FL 34242 941-684-3244
www.capriinternational.com**

If you want to test-drive retirement, an ideal choice for Sarasota & Siesta Key Beach hotel and vacation rentals is the Capri Inn at the Beach. The Capri Inn offers a variety of lodging directly on beautiful Siesta Key Beach which has the highest rated sugar white sand beaches in the world! We chose the brand new condominium-style accommodations featuring full kitchens and hotel amenities so we could grocery shop in Siesta Key Village.

The Capri Inn offers rentals available daily (which is hard to find in this area), weekly and monthly rates. With 200 steps to the Gulf of Mexico, The Capri Inn at the Beach is the perfect spot for sunning, shelling, or taking a siesta, but Capri Inn is also known for its resort amenities: a heated swimming pool, spacious courtyard with barbeque grills. While I barbecued, the girls chased the little lizards around the courtyard and chatted with the host (from Italy) and with other guests (from Germany, England, and New York). You can rent beach chairs and cabanas. All of these extras are easily accessible from any of the well-furnished yet casual one bedroom suites or efficiencies.

You'll have easy access to the Sarasota area attractions, including Mote Marine Laboratory, St. Armand's Circle, Siesta Village, John & Mable Ringling Museum of Art, Marie Selby Botanical Gardens, Sarasota Jungle Gardens, Aslo Theatre, Van Wezel Performing Arts Hall and Ed Smith Stadium (Cincinnati Reds Spring Training Home) and are not at all far from the Sarasota Memorial Hospital and Sarasota Bradenton International Airport.

Sarasota Bay Explorers

Sea Life Encounter Cruise

**At Mote Aquarium,
1600 Ken Thompson Pkwy., City Island,
Sarasota, FL 941.388.4200**

We paired this excursion with a visit to Mote Marine Laboratory and made a day of it. I wished I had a video camera trained on the marine biologist for this 1 hour, 45 minute cruise through Sarasota and Roberts Bays. What a first hand eco-education! I've been on these cruises before and was happy that the groups were small and that our guide was audible. It's almost a given that you will see the resident population of bottlenose dolphins while learning about the ecology, history, and folklore of the area. Florida manatees are also possible sightings at the right time of the year! Our guide lead us on a short nature walk on an uninhabited island where we were afforded the unique opportunity to view pelicans, herons, ibis and egrets in their nesting habitat. The guides collected a sample of marine life with a trawl net. We saw and the girls handled some of the curious residents of Sarasota Bay: puffer fish, sea horses (they were bright yellow!), stone crabs, and cow fish.

The 40-foot pontoon boats, the Explorer I and IV, are Coast Guard-inspected covered vessels equipped with on-board restrooms, comfortable seating, cold drinks and snacks. This trip is pleasure for all ages. Reservations are recommended. Check-in is 30 minutes prior to departure.

Photos © Sarasotafl.org

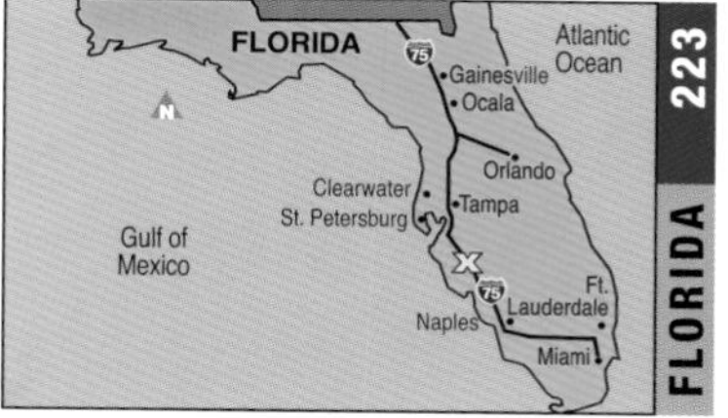

I-75 Mile Markers

210

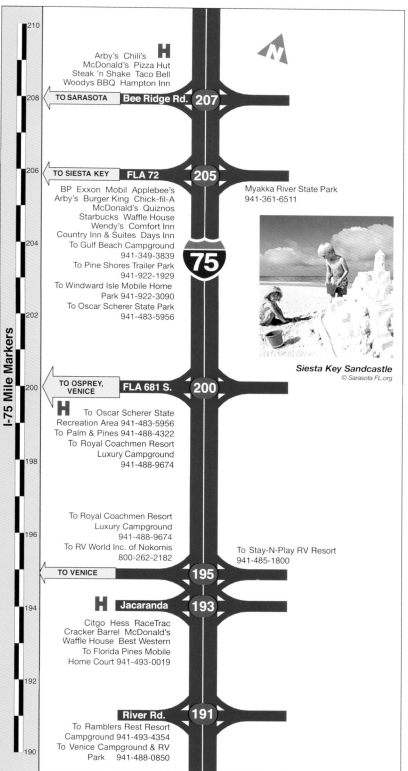

Arby's Chili's
McDonald's Pizza Hut
Steak 'n Shake Taco Bell
Woodys BBQ Hampton Inn

208

TO SARASOTA — Bee Ridge Rd. — 207

206

TO SIESTA KEY — FLA 72 — 205

BP Exxon Mobil Applebee's
Arby's Burger King Chick-fil-A
McDonald's Quiznos
Starbucks Waffle House
Wendy's Comfort Inn
Country Inn & Suites Days Inn
To Gulf Beach Campground
941-349-3839
To Pine Shores Trailer Park
941-922-1929
To Windward Isle Mobile Home
Park 941-922-3090
To Oscar Scherer State Park
941-483-5956

Myakka River State Park
941-361-6511

204

75

202

Siesta Key Sandcastle
© Sarasota FL.org

200

TO OSPREY, VENICE — FLA 681 S. — 200

To Oscar Scherer State
Recreation Area 941-483-5956
To Palm & Pines 941-488-4322
To Royal Coachmen Resort
Luxury Campground
941-488-9674

198

To Royal Coachmen Resort
Luxury Campground
941-488-9674
To RV World Inc. of Nokomis
800-262-2182

196

To Stay-N-Play RV Resort
941-485-1800

TO VENICE — 195

194

Jacaranda — 193

Citgo Hess RaceTrac
Cracker Barrel McDonald's
Waffle House Best Western
To Florida Pines Mobile
Home Court 941-493-0019

192

River Rd. — 191

To Ramblers Rest Resort
Campground 941-493-4354
To Venice Campground & RV
Park 941-488-0850

190

Venice Beach
© www.SarasotaFL.org

Venice Beach Sharks Tooth Festival
© www.SarasotaFL.org

Sarasota
FLORIDA

Sarasota Convention & Visitors Bureau
701 N. Tamiami Trail, Sarasota, Florida 34236
941-957-1877 or 1-800-800-3906 **www.SarasotaFL.org**

Sarasota County Sinks Its Teeth Into Eco-Tourism

Visitors looking for a taste of the "Real Florida" that predates condos, concrete and chic can find the unspoiled, environmental delights of Sarasota County. Already known for its white sand beaches, spectacular scenery and cultural opportunities, appreciative travelers are discovering the Sarasota area's abundant uncivilized resources. Some of the best-known include **Mote Marine Laboratory, Marie Selby Botanical Gardens, Pelican Man's Bird Sanctuary,** and **Sarasota Jungle Gardens.**

South of Sarasota is **Venice Beach,** the "Sharks Tooth Capital of the World." On the this uncrowded, sandy shore of the Gulf of Mexico, the gentle surf deposits millions of prehistoric sharks' teeth and other interesting marine fossils. All species of shark repeatedly shed their teeth and grow new ones, so there is a never-ending supply of teeth to be found. They vary in color from black to brown to gray, depending on the minerals in the soil surrounding them. They can be as small as one-eighth of an inch or as big as your hand! Every April, the Venice Area celebrates with "Sharks Tooth and Seafood Festival."

Twelve miles south of Venice, in the town of **Warm Mineral Springs,** a 2 1/2-acre lake is the focal point of a resort and spa. Some 9-million gallons of water flow naturally into the lake everyday, and maintain a constant temperature of a soothing 87 degrees. Bathers of all ages find immersion in the warm, mineral-laden water soothing and rejuvenating.

Over 1,000 acres of flora and fauna flourish in their natural habitat at the **Oscar Scherer State Park,** north of Venice on Route 41 in Osprey. The park is noted for its population of Florida scrubjays, one of Florida's endangered bird species. During the winter months, nature lovers can spot bald eagles, bobcats, river otters and alligators around the park. The scrubby flatwoods, is home to the rapidly disappearing gopher tortoise, gopher frog and indigo snake. Oscar Scherer offers visitors abundant outdoor activities, including camping, hiking through the pine flatwoods' nature trails, swimming in the freshwater lake, fishing and canoeing in South Creek.

East of U.S. 41 on State Road 72 in Sarasota is an eco-tourist's "must-stop:" **Myakka River State Park.** Named for the Myakka River which flows through the park for 12 miles, this is one of Florida's largest and most diverse natural areas, covering almost 45-square-miles of preserved oak and palm hammocks, grassy marshes, open expanses of dry prairie, pine flatwoods and small wetlands. Deer, raccoon and many species of birds are easily viewed along the park drive and on a wooden bird-walk. Birdwatching, backpacking, guided walks, horseback riding, bicycling and rustic camping are all popular activities. Hikers can roam the 7,500-acre park and look for cottontail rabbits, deer, bobcat, red-shouldered hawks and other native wildlife. A guided air boat tour is available on Upper Myakka Lake, and canoeing opportunities are excellent. Anglers cast their lines for bass, bream, and catfish in the freshwater lake.

Canoeing at Myakka State Park.
Courtesy Sarasota CVB

Attractions

Asolo Repertory Theatre
Professional and young Companies perform classic to modern. Up to 4 plays per weekend. 5555 N. Tamiami Trail, Sarasota, FL 34243. 941-351-8000 or 1-800-361-8388 www.asolo.org

Sarasota Orchestra
709 N. Tamiami Trail, Sarasota, FL 34236. 941-953-4252

Flying Fish Fleet
Deep Sea Fishing. Grouper, snapper, kingfish. 941-366-3373 www.flyingfishfleet.com

Gulf Coast Wonder and Imagination Zone (G. Wiz)
Adults $7, children two or over $5, seniors $6. 1001 Boulevard of the Arts, Sarasota, FL 34236. 941-309-4949 www.gwiz.org

Historic Spanish Point
Mon. to Sat. 9 a.m.-5 p.m., Sun. 12 noon-5 p.m. 337 N. Tamiami Trail, Osprey, FL 34229. 941-966-5214 www.historicspanishpoint.org

Kayak Rentals & Sailing Charter
Sales and lessons. 941-922-9671 Sail the "Enterprise" 41-foot sailboat. 941-951-1833

Pelican Man's Bird Sanctuary
Rehabilitation center for 39 species of Florida birds on Longboat Key. 10 a.m.-5 p.m. Adults $6, children 4-17 $2. 1708 Ken Thompson Pkwy. 941-388-4444

St. Armands Circle on St. Armands Key
Island shopping center with gourmet restaurants. 210, west on St. Rte. 780, 941-388-1554 www.starmandscircleassoc.com

Sarasota Jungle Gardens
Exit 213. Just off US 41, 2 miles south of the Sarasota Airport. 3701 Bay Shore Rd. 877-861-6547 www.sarasotajunglegardens.com

Sarasota Ballet
5555 N. Tamiami Trail, Sarasota, FL 34243. 941-359-0099 www.sarasotaballet.org

Sharks Tooth Festival in August. The Greater Venice Area. 800-940-7427 www.sharktoothfest.com

Sarasota Classic Car Museum
5500 N. Tamiami Trail, Sarasota, FL. Rolls Royce, Pierce Arrow, Auburn, Delorean, Bricklin. 100 antique games. Exit 40 west to U.S. 41. 941-355-6228 www.sarasotacarmuseum.org

Sarasota Opera House
61 N. Pineapple Ave., Sarasota, FL 34236-5716. 941-366-8450 www.sarasotaopera.org

Selby Gallery & Ringling School of Art & Design. Free. Local talent and known works of art. 2700 N. Tamiami Trail, Sarasota, FL 34234. 941-359-7563

Van Wezel Performing Arts Hall
941-953-3366 www.vanwezel.org

Warm Mineral Springs Resort & Spa
12200 San Servando Ave., Warm Mineral Springs, FL 34287. 941-426-1692

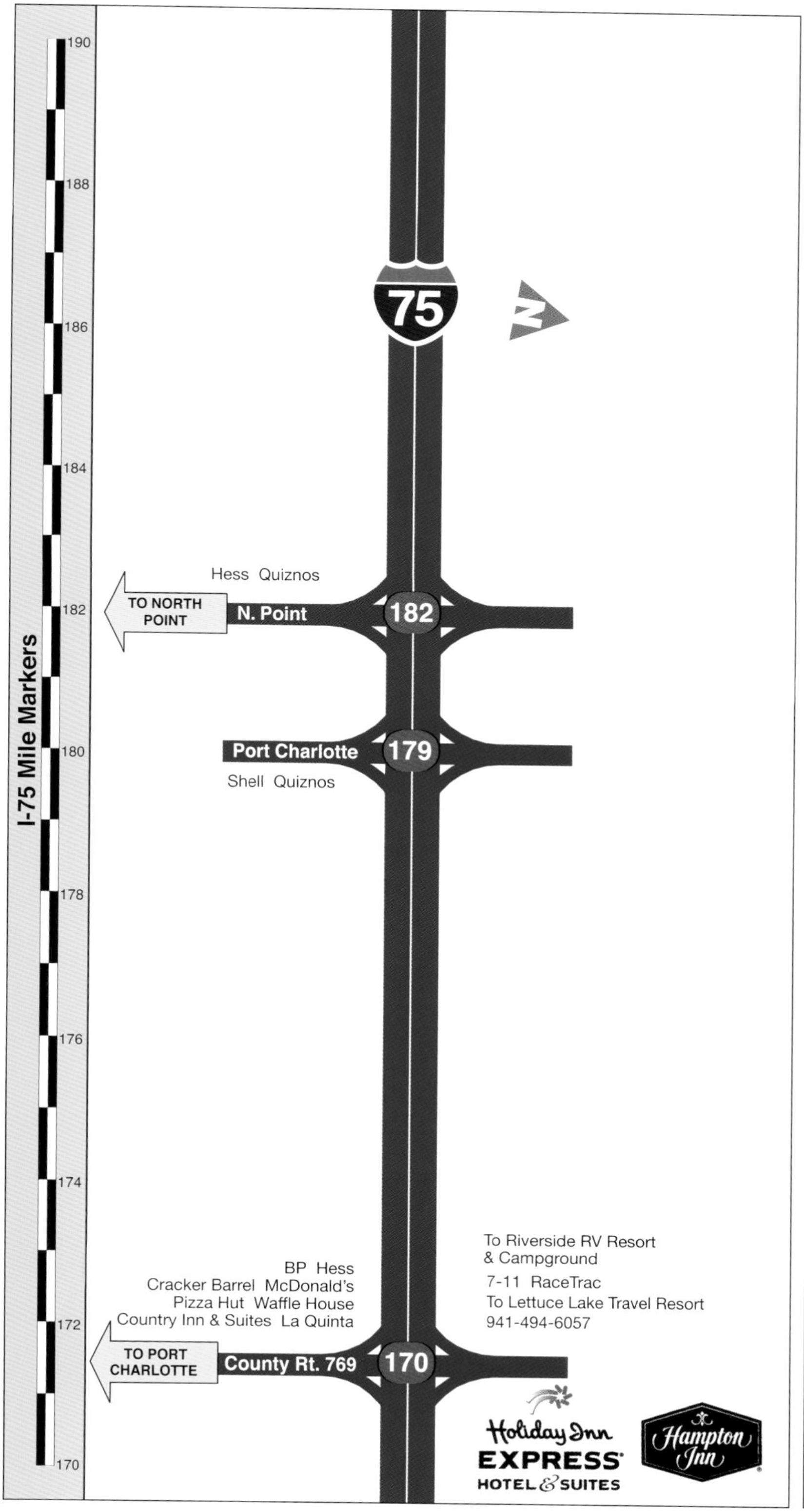

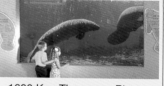

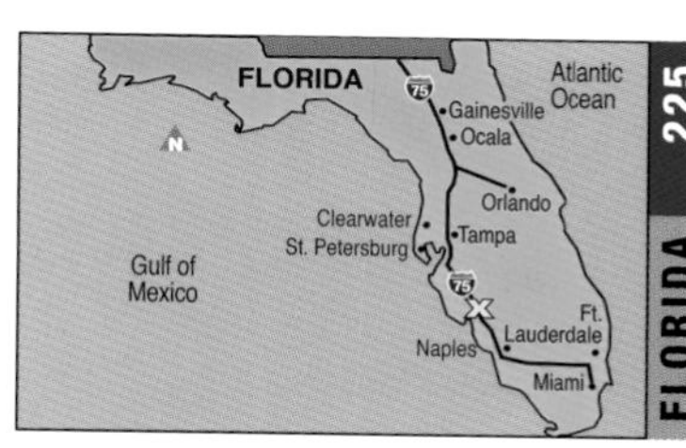

I-75 Mile Markers
190
188
186
184
182
180
178
176
174
172
170
75
N
Hess Quiznos
TO NORTH POINT
N. Point
182
Port Charlotte
179
Shell Quiznos
BP Hess
Cracker Barrel McDonald's
Pizza Hut Waffle House
Country Inn & Suites La Quinta
To Riverside RV Resort & Campground
7-11 RaceTrac
To Lettuce Lake Travel Resort
941-494-6057
TO PORT CHARLOTTE
County Rt. 769
170
Holiday Inn EXPRESS HOTEL & SUITES
Hampton Inn

FLORIDA
Atlantic Ocean
Gainesville
Ocala
Orlando
Clearwater
St. Petersburg
Tampa
Gulf of Mexico
Ft. Lauderdale
Naples
Miami
75

Punta Gorda
FLORIDA

Charlotte County Visitor's Bureau
18501 Murdock Circle, Suite 502, Port Charlotte, Florida 33952
941-743-1900 **www.pureflorida.com**

Punt Gorda & Charlotte County

Charlotte County is on the Gulf Coast of southwest Florida, 50 miles south of Sarasota on U.S. Highway 41 (the historic "Tamiami Trail"). Charlotte County is 125 miles from Orlando and 162 miles from Miami. The population of the county is approximately 154,000. The seasonal population, including part-time inhabitants who may live for several months of the year in Charlotte County or the city of Punta Gorda, but who have usual residence elsewhere, is estimated at a 30% increase from January to April.

At five feet to 25 feet above sea level, Charlotte County enjoys a sub-tropic climate. The average annual rainfall is 49 inches, with approximately 2/3 occurring July through September. The average annual temperature is 75 degrees. The average low month, January, is 63 degrees. The average high month, August, is 82.8 degrees.

The communities of Charlotte County surround Florida's second-largest estuary system, Charlotte Harbor, providing unspoiled beauty to its full-time residents and vacationers.

Money magazine: "Best Places to Live in the South" Golf Digest: "Best in America, ranked 3rd in US for place to live and golf." National Wildlife Federation: "One of most popular sport-fishing locales in Florida." US News 2008: "City of Punta Gorda is the Best Healthy Place to Retire" Sail Magazine: "One of the top ten sailing destinations."

This county provides the sports enthusiast a veritable paradise. Fishing, baseball, golfing, hunting, boating and eco-touring opportunities are everywhere.

CHARLOTTE HARBOR
& THE Gulf Islands
Florida's Best-Kept Secret

Use I-75 exits 179 to 158 to access Charlotte County.

Annual Events

Golfing in Charlotte County.
Courtesy of the Charlotte County Visitor's Bureau

Sullivan St. Craft Fair, Punta Gorda. January.

Annual Lemon Bay Festival, Englewood. February

Peace River National Arts Festival, Laisley Park. February

Placinda Rotary Seafood Festival, Fishery Restaurant. March

Florida International Air Show, Punta Gorda. March

Redfish Cup, Tourney & Fesitval. Laishley Park Marina. May

Annual Florida Frontier Days, Bayshore Live Oak. May

Annual National Hibiscus Fest, Punta Gorda. June

Annual Englewood Jaycees Pioneer Days. July

Charlotte Harbor Nature Festival. November

Annual Christmas Light Canal Tours. December

Annual Peace River Lighted Boat Parade, Punta Gorda. December

Punta Gorda

The city of Punta Gorda is a charming waterfront community which traces its history to DeSoto's landing on **Live Oak Point** on the Peace River in 1539. Ponce de Leon visited Charlotte Harbor in 1513 & 1521. "Punta Gorda" means "Broad Point" in the language of the Conquistadors.

Early attempts by Spanish explorers to colonize the outer islands were stopped by Calusa aboriginal peoples, but the area was slowly settled by the English. In 1885, Col. Isaac Trabue from Kentucky bought the land from British investors and renamed the settlement **Trabue,** a name never truly accepted by the town and finally rejected in favor of the Spanish one when the **Punta Gorda** was incorporated in 1887.

Port Charlotte

This is a growing community was developed in the late 1950s. The population is approximately 46,000, and the community has all the necessary amenities and services, including golf courses, yacht clubs, tennis clubs, parks, boating facilities, pools and beach swimming.

Englewood

Englewood is directly on the Gulf of Mexico and is part of both Charlotte and Sarasota counties. This area was founded by two brothers who farmed vast lemon groves. The greatest attractions are the long stretches of white sandy beach and the fresh water fishing in the miles of canals.

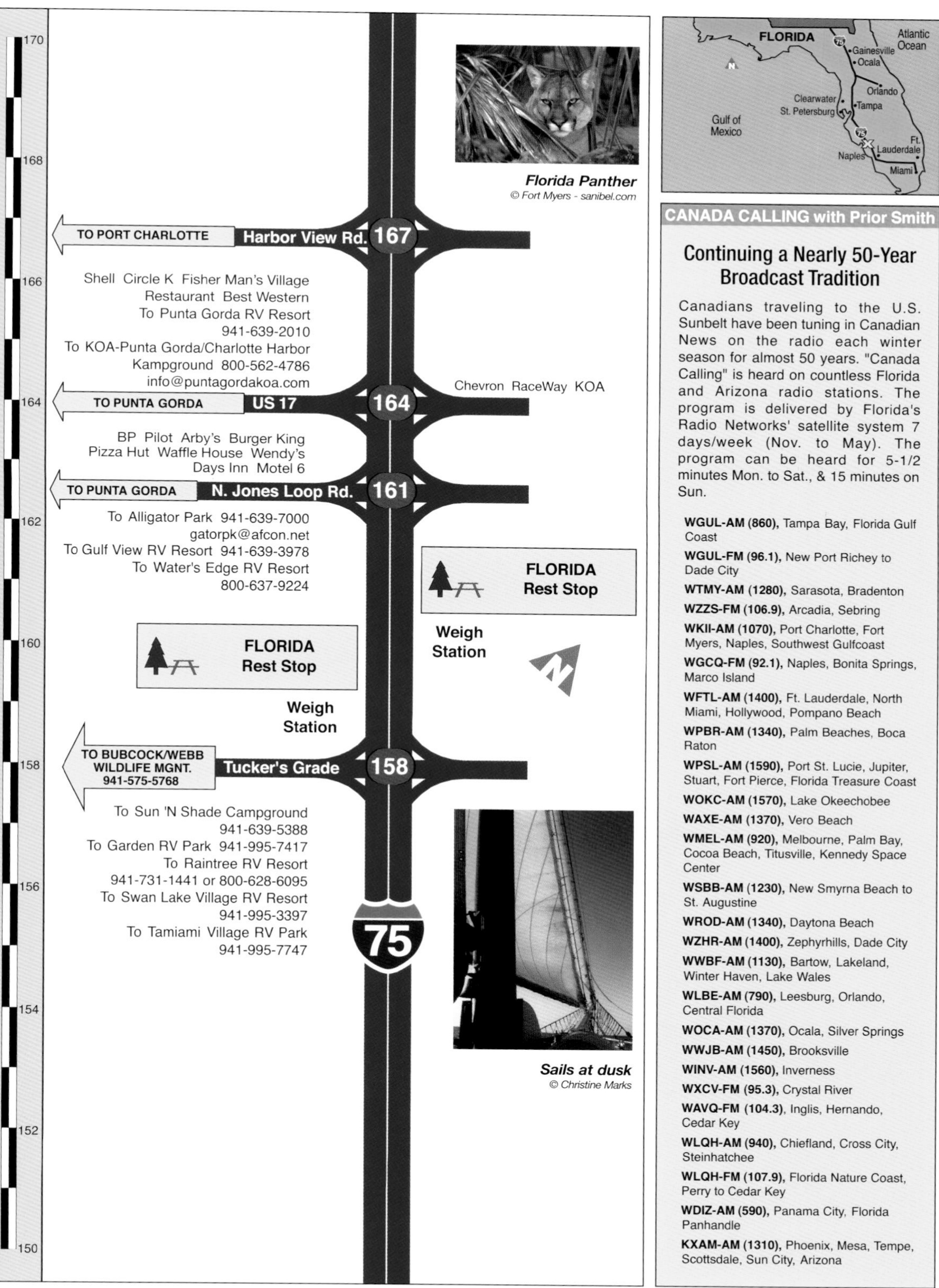

Florida Panther
© Fort Myers - sanibel.com

Sails at dusk
© Christine Marks

CANADA CALLING with Prior Smith

Continuing a Nearly 50-Year Broadcast Tradition

Canadians traveling to the U.S. Sunbelt have been tuning in Canadian News on the radio each winter season for almost 50 years. "Canada Calling" is heard on countless Florida and Arizona radio stations. The program is delivered by Florida's Radio Networks' satellite system 7 days/week (Nov. to May). The program can be heard for 5-1/2 minutes Mon. to Sat., & 15 minutes on Sun.

WGUL-AM (860), Tampa Bay, Florida Gulf Coast

WGUL-FM (96.1), New Port Richey to Dade City

WTMY-AM (1280), Sarasota, Bradenton

WZZS-FM (106.9), Arcadia, Sebring

WKII-AM (1070), Port Charlotte, Fort Myers, Naples, Southwest Gulfcoast

WGCQ-FM (92.1), Naples, Bonita Springs, Marco Island

WFTL-AM (1400), Ft. Lauderdale, North Miami, Hollywood, Pompano Beach

WPBR-AM (1340), Palm Beaches, Boca Raton

WPSL-AM (1590), Port St. Lucie, Jupiter, Stuart, Fort Pierce, Florida Treasure Coast

WOKC-AM (1570), Lake Okeechobee

WAXE-AM (1370), Vero Beach

WMEL-AM (920), Melbourne, Palm Bay, Cocoa Beach, Titusville, Kennedy Space Center

WSBB-AM (1230), New Smyrna Beach to St. Augustine

WROD-AM (1340), Daytona Beach

WZHR-AM (1400), Zephyrhills, Dade City

WWBF-AM (1130), Bartow, Lakeland, Winter Haven, Lake Wales

WLBE-AM (790), Leesburg, Orlando, Central Florida

WOCA-AM (1370), Ocala, Silver Springs

WWJB-AM (1450), Brooksville

WINV-AM (1560), Inverness

WXCV-FM (95.3), Crystal River

WAVQ-FM (104.3), Inglis, Hernando, Cedar Key

WLQH-AM (940), Chiefland, Cross City, Steinhatchee

WLQH-FM (107.9), Florida Nature Coast, Perry to Cedar Key

WDIZ-AM (590), Panama City, Florida Panhandle

KXAM-AM (1310), Phoenix, Mesa, Tempe, Scottsdale, Sun City, Arizona

Fort Myers and Fort Myers Beach

Lee Island Coast Visitors and Convention Bureau
12800 University Dr., Suite 550, Fort Myers, Florida 33907
239-338-3500 or 1-800-237-6444 www.fortmyerssanibel.com

History Touches Lee Island Coast

Named in honor of General Robert E. Lee, even though he never visited the area, Lee County was founded in 1887 with almost 1,500 residents. Today, Lee County's population exceeds 370,000, attracting perhaps twice as many seasonal residents and more than 1.9 million vacationers each year.

Numerous historic homes and sites have been preserved as reminders of the area's past. Inventor **Thomas Edison,** automobile magnate **Henry Ford** and tire manufacturer **Harvey Firestone** called Lee County home, at least in winter. (See page 59 for the primary residences of Ford and Edison). The **Thomas Edison winter home** in Fort Myers is the best beloved by visitors and local residents. The inventor of the lightbulb, phonograph and holder of more than 1,000 patents during his lifetime, made his winter home in Lee County for 46 winters. He came south to the sleepy, sub-tropical cattle town when he was 37 years old, on the advice of his physician.

Open daily (except Thanks-giving and Christmas) tours run 9 a.m.-5:30 p.m. Mon. to Sat., and from noon-5:30 p.m. on Sun. 2350 McGregor Blvd.

Treat yourself to an efficiency unit overlooking the pool at the Outrigger Beach Resort. We did and we had the most relaxing stay! The convenience of the sparkling kitchenette allowed more time for romping around the resort, touring the town and especially enjoying the fabulous white sand at Fort Myers Beach! The band that played from the Tiki bar was a luxury while we splashed in the pool. We took so many pictures of this lush tropical resort (the plants were identified), and that is surely an indication of how much we enjoyed it!
Outrigger, 6200 Estero Blvd., Fort Myers Beach, FL 33931 800-655-8997

Great Calusa Blueway

New paddling trail to entertain nature enthusiasts along The Beaches of Fort Myers & Sanibelin southwest Florida.

LEE COUNTY, FL.—Recognized as among the best U.S. kayaking destinations by both and *Canoe & Kayak* magazines, The Beaches of Fort Myers & Sanibel has opened the first 40 miles of a new paddling trail. This initial phase will treat paddlers to extraordinary up-close-and-personal encounters with diverse wildlife and history from the Imperial River in Bonita Springs north to Punta Rassa in Fort Myers.

The Great Calusa Blueway will begin in ***Bonita Springs,*** *the southernmost point of the Lee Island Coast. Photos courtesy Lee Island Coast Visitors and Convention Bureau.*

After over a year in the planning stages, "The Great Calusa Blueway" will begin in Bonita Springs, the southernmost point of the Lee County area, where paddlers will enjoy exploration of the calm waters of the Imperial River and back bays. Birdwatchers will be delighted to share Lovers Key State Recreation Area and the back bays of Black Island with roseate spoonbills and many other wading birds. The area is home to one of the world's largest populations of Atlantic bottlenose dolphins, and paddlers will observe these incredible creatures in the Estero Bay Aquatic Preserve, designated as Florida's first Aquatic Preserve in 1966.

The fascinating history of the Calusa Indian tribe awaits paddlers at the Mound Key State Archaeological Site. Listed on the National Register of Historic Places, it is believed that the 125-acre subtropical jungle island was constructed from oyster shells and other natural discards by the Calusa Indians who inhabited the island from about 100—1750 A.D. The site includes a 32-foot ceremonial shell mound, engineered canal systems, and now dry inland lakes.

To the north, adventurous paddlers will find remnants of a religious sect established in 1894 at the Koreshan State Historic Site. Paddlers can camp, picnic, and fish, while learning about this unique utopia, inspired by an "illumination" that promoted a communal lifestyle.

The Beaches of Fort Myers & Sanibel Paddling Trail

The blueway continues west through the back bays of Fort Myers Beach, offering paddlers stopping points with a wide variety of overnight accommodations and dining options.

The first phase of the paddling trail ends at Bunche Beach, near the Sanibel Causeway. The second phase will take canoes and kayaks through the scenic bays of Sanibel, Captiva, and Pine islands, ending at Cayo Costa, in the northern part of the Lee Island Coast.

To enhance the paddling experience, The Great Calusa Blueway will utilize the latest technology, Global Positioning System (GPS). Key points will be marked along the trail to aid in navigation.

"Along The Great Calusa Blueway, paddlers will definitely enjoy the true serenity that our waters provide," said Nancy MacPhee, recreation supervisor for Lee County Parks and Recreation. "Besides signage marking the trail, the project will include a designated map, two helpful tools for paddlers to explore the area without a guide."

Considered one of the fastest growing water sports, kayaking is a popular activity for Lee Island Coast visitors. For observing a variety of wildlife, gliding through scenic mangroves, or mastering paddle techniques, the area offers some of the best year-round kayak water in the eastern U.S. Several outfitters provide expert guidance for novice, intermediate, and experienced paddlers. From outings lasting for a few hours to weeks-long adventures, the educational and entertaining Great Calusa Blueway promises to provide memorable experiences. Royal Palm Tours of Fort Myers is organizing a 7 day/6 night paddling package or customized trips. For details, call (800)296-0249.

Funded by the area's tourist development tax, the canoe and kayak trail is a project of Lee County Parks and Recreation and the Lee County Visitor and Convention Bureau.

EDITOR'S NOTE: The Beaches of Fort Myers & Sanibel (formerly the Lee Island Coast) include: Sanibel & Captiva islands, Fort Myers Beach, Fort Myers, Bonita Springs & Estero, Cape Coral, Pine Island, Boca Grande & Outer islands, North Fort Myers, Lehigh Acres. For information go to www.FortMyers-Sanibel.com.

Outrigger Beach Resort

6200 Estero Boulevard, Fort Myers Beach, FL 33931 239-463-3131 800-655-8997 www.outriggerfmb.com

When someone says "relax and breathe and imagine your happy place" – my girls and I will come up with the same perfect vision. It's the Outrigger Beach Resort, on Fort Myers Beach. Long a family tradition, this is the place we've most often recommended to Florida bound travelers because it's everything a Florida resort should be and still affordable. Recommended to us by the Lee Island Coast Visitors and Convention Bureau as a beautiful and exciting place for a woman to bring her kids, that's exactly what we found. With a variety of accommodation styles to chose from, we've enjoyed both the smaller pool-side, "bachelor" efficiencies and the larger, gulf-view apartment-style suites.

Twice we planned our trip so we could see the international sand-carving competition. It is heart breaking that those magnificent sand creations are so temporary!

Fort Myers Beach is on a strip of land and The Outrigger Beach Resort is on the main road, so you are just a few minutes from the festive tourist areas. Souvenir shops, artwork, beach clothing and jewelry shops are calling! The local traffic rules favor pedestrians, so park your car. Many people rent a moped or bikes to get around.

This resort is the perfect base camp. From the Outrigger it is no trouble at all to hop in the car and get to the shopping, restaurants and attractions on the "mainland" of the Fort Myers. When we're not out exploring, we're very happy at home on the resort. The wide, sandy beach is the obvious attraction – you never know what will wash ashore– we'd run out with our flashlights in the morning and collect buckets of good shells. Other times we found more rare treasures like sand dollars and horse shoe crab shells. The shark's head still puzzles us!

The rooms are cheery and so are the staff. They seem to have caught the infectious charm of the on-site PR lady, Jeanne Bigos. They will take care of you and mean it when they say "No trouble at all!" Here's just a little example. Ask for a wake-up call! Go on, I'm not kidding – what a riot! I have no idea who is singing, but it's the old Beatles tune "Get up, get out of bed…drag a comb across your head…and have a great day at the Outrigger!" Children's crafts and other planned activities, the fabulous pool and sports courts are an added bonus. The

beach-themed masterpieces my girls made at craft-time 4 years ago are still on display in our living room as a constant happy reminder of all the fun we had at the Outrigger.

Good live music draws many of the other tourists out of the pool to relax or dance by the Tiki bar. We enjoyed the on-site restaurant and other restaurants that were within walking distance but also made good use of the local grocery store and the kitchenette in our unit. With a convenience store right across the street, a dash out for a late night ice cream was not a problem either.

What else can you do while staying at the Outrigger? Rent a Jet Ski, Snuggle in a cushioned Beach Cabana, Heard of Mountain Biking – Try Beach Biking, Book a Deep Sea Fishing Adventure, Canoe or Kayak the Great Calusa Blueway, Reserve a Sunset Cruise, Practice your Putting, Check your email, Shuffleboard...

Photos © fortmyerssanibel.com

Tropic Star of Pine Island–Cruises

Pineland Marina, 13921 Waterfront Dr., Pineland, FL 33945 239-283-0015 www.tropicstarcruises.com

Open Year-Round, 8:30 a.m. - 5 p.m. daily. Tour Duration: up to 8 hours
Ask the locals. They will tell you that the Tropic Star is the go-to resource for a wide variety of water based cruises and adventures ranging from a few peaceful hours on a private beach for shelling and swimming to overnight camping and cottage excursions.

The distractingly handsome Captain Tapager pointed out the wildlife we encountered and gave us the history of the Pine Island Sound area as he ferried us aboard the 59 passenger TROPIC STAR (resembles the "African Queen") to Cabbage Key. We were looking forward to a good lunch at the famous Cabbage Key Inn. This is the bar and restaurant made famous by the Jimmy Buffet song "Cheeseburger in Paradise". For good luck, we added our dollar bill to the thousands of others taped to the walls and ceiling. The money goes to local conservation efforts. After lunch we grabbed our towels and headed for the legendary private beach. As promised, the shelling was simply excellent, especially as we wandered further along the unspoiled coast.

Courtesy: Lee Island Coast Visitors and Convention Bureau

Fort Myers and Fort Myers Beach

Lee Island Coast Visitors and Convention Bureau
12800 University Dr., Suite 550, Fort Myers, Florida 33907
239-338-3500 or 1-800-237-6444 **www.fortmyerssanibel.com**

Gaea Guides, Fort Myers

Gaea Guides, Fort Myers
239-694-5513 866-256-6388
www.gaeaguides.com

Benefit from a Florida Master Naturalist guide, trained by the University of Florida, if you want to explore the hundreds of miles of back bays, aquatic preserves, wildlife refuges, creeks, bayous, rivers and mangrove forests of Southwest Florida's newest attraction: the Great Calusa Blueway. Ours was a casual paddle, and we were encouraged to stop and use all of our senses, we listened to the nearby dolphins breathe, smelled the mangrove islands, and watched the pelicans dive. The other birds which were identified for us, and because of all this we thoroughly enjoyed an unforgettable eco-education. The tours are flexible, tailored to your interest, and can be arranged at a time to suit your needs: choose from Estuary Tours, Full Moon Kayak Tours, Archeological Tours, Sunset Kayak Tours, Manatee Tours (seasonal), Bird Rookery Tours, Great Calusa Blue-way, Hickey Creek Paddle, Kayak Clinic, River Tours, and Bat Tours.

J.N. "Ding" Darling National Wildlife Refuge

J.N. "Ding" Darling National Wildlife Refuge www.fws.gov/dingdarling
The J. N. "Ding" Darling National Wildlife Refuge is located on the subtropical barrier island of Sanibel in the Gulf of Mexico. The refuge is part of the largest undeveloped mangrove ecosystem in the United States. It is world famous for its spectacular migratory bird populations. There are many ways to experience the Refuge, including hiking and kayaking.

Bird-watching for Roseate Spoonbill at J.N. "Ding" Darling National Wildlife Refuge. *Courtesy Lee Island Coast Visitors and Convention Bureau*

Of Note: the narrated sealife cruise offered by the Tarpon Bay Explorers, was exceptional.
www.tarponbayexplorers.com
239.472.8900

Babcock Ranch with Babcock Wilderness Adventures

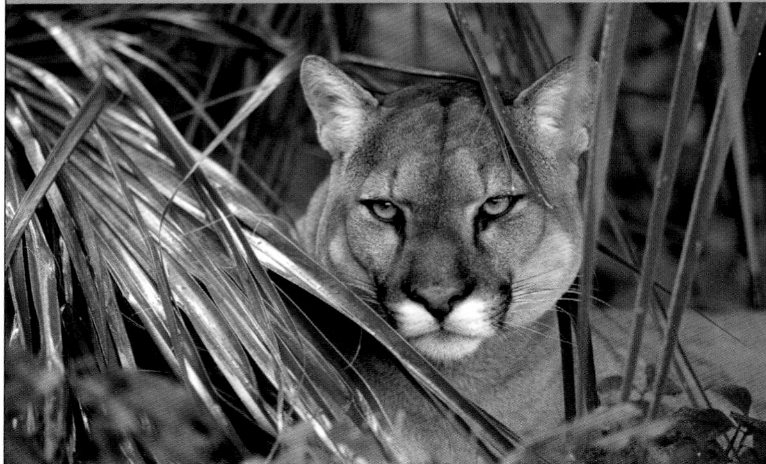

8000 State Road 31, Punta Gorda, Florida 33982 1-800-500-5583
www.babcockwilderness.com

Babcock Ranch offers something for everyone. From swamp buggy tours with Babcock Wilderness Adventures to overnight accommodations at the Cypress Lodge, you'll find yourself face to face with wildlife in an Old Florida setting. We enjoyed the swamp buggy tour and encourage you to follow the guide on the boardwalk side trip through the cypress swamp – where we were lucky to catch a glimpse of the rare Florida cougars protected by the Ranch.

Photos © fortmyerssanibel.com

Edison & Ford Winter Estates

2350 McGregor Blvd – Fort Myers, FL 33901 239-334-7419 www.efwefla.org

Call ahead for tour times at the Edison/ Henry Ford Winter Estates. No visit to Fort Myers is complete without this experience. Here your guide will interpret for you the home, botanical gardens, and laboratory of Thomas Edison as well as the home of Henry Ford. The collection, preservation, and exhibition of artifacts relating to the lives and work of these two great men places special emphasis on their experiences in the City of Fort My-ers. Growing up in Windsor, Ontario, just across the river from Detroit, made this attraction somewhat like a pilgrimage for me! If you are a history buff, or are fasci-nated by science and technology, there is a quite alot to take in, so you might want to plan for a extended visit.

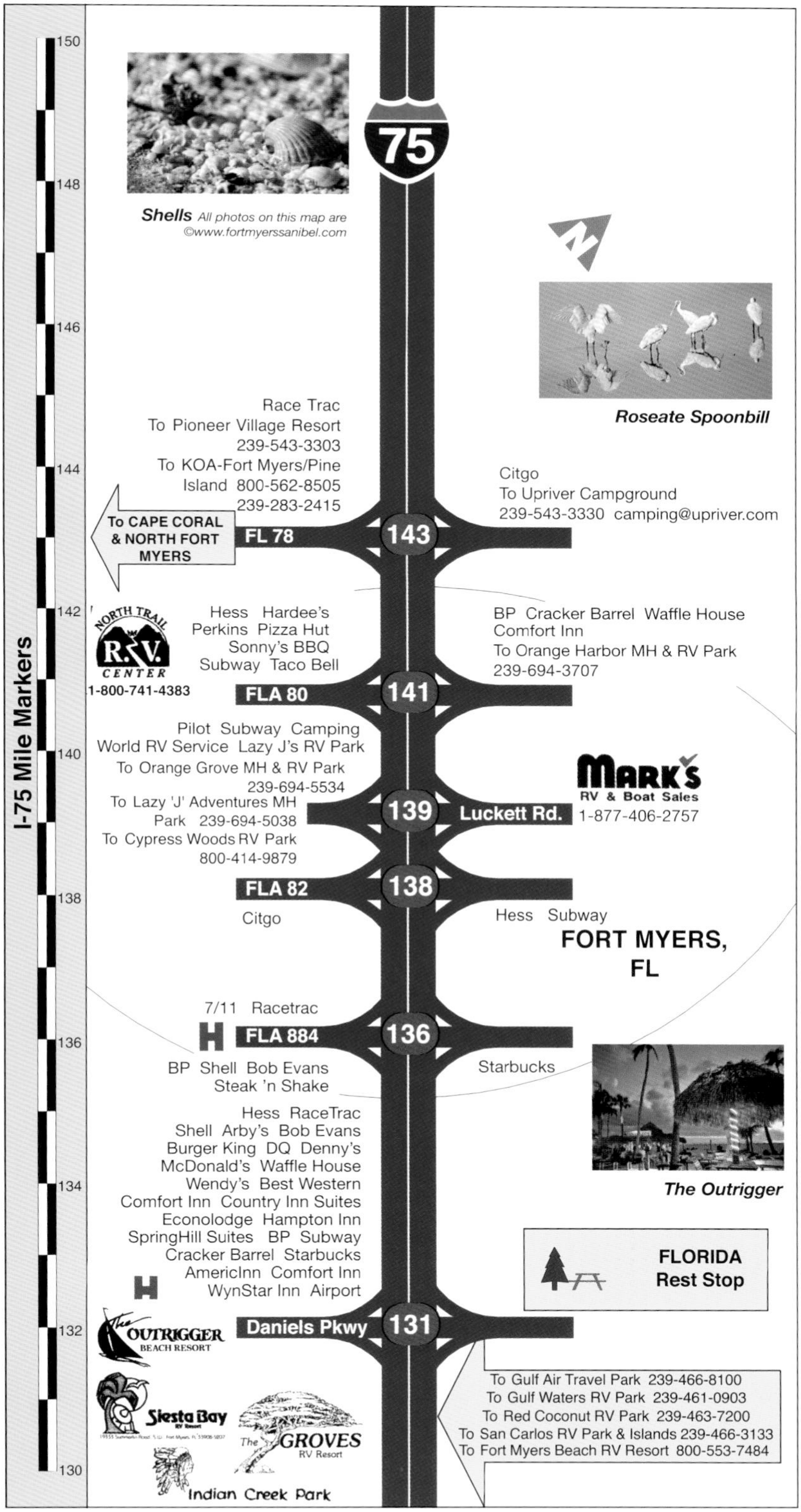

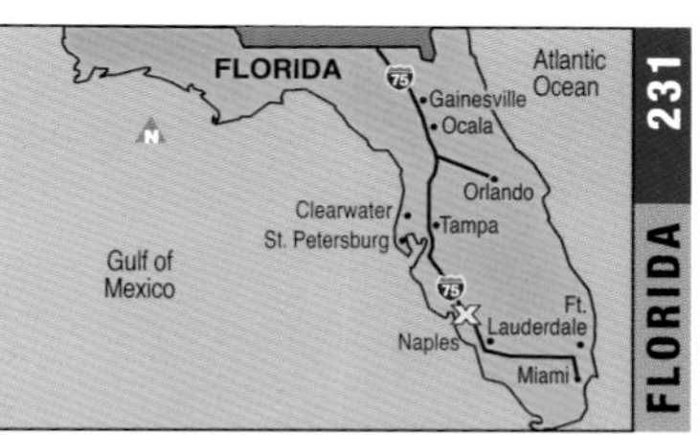

I-75 Mile Markers

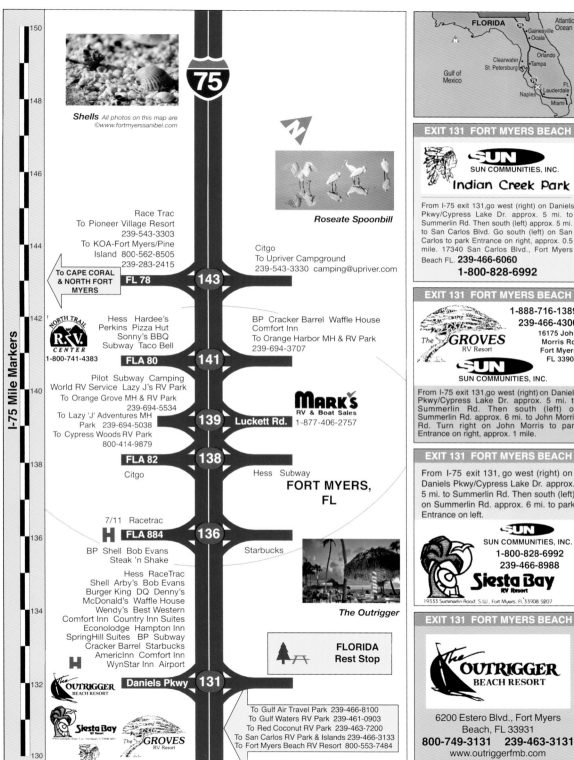

Shells *All photos on this map are ©www.fortmyerssanibel.com*

Roseate Spoonbill

Exit 143 — FL 78 — To CAPE CORAL & NORTH FORT MYERS

West: Race Trac; To Pioneer Village Resort 239-543-3303; To KOA-Fort Myers/Pine Island 800-562-8505 239-283-2415

East: Citgo; To Upriver Campground 239-543-3330 camping@upriver.com

Exit 141 — FLA 80

West: Hess Hardee's Perkins Pizza Hut Sonny's BBQ Subway Taco Bell

NORTH TRAIL R.V. CENTER 1-800-741-4383

East: BP Cracker Barrel Waffle House Comfort Inn; To Orange Harbor MH & RV Park 239-694-3707

Exit 139 — Luckett Rd.

West: Pilot Subway Camping World RV Service Lazy J's RV Park; To Orange Grove MH & RV Park 239-694-5534; To Lazy 'J' Adventures MH Park 239-694-5038; To Cypress Woods RV Park 800-414-9879

East: MARK'S RV & Boat Sales 1-877-406-2757

Exit 138 — FLA 82

West: Citgo

East: Hess Subway

FORT MYERS, FL

Exit 136 — FLA 884

West: 7/11 Racetrac; BP Shell Bob Evans Steak 'n Shake

East: Starbucks

The Outrigger

FLORIDA Rest Stop

Exit 131 — Daniels Pkwy

West: Hess RaceTrac Shell Arby's Bob Evans Burger King DQ Denny's McDonald's Waffle House Wendy's Best Western Comfort Inn Country Inn Suites Econolodge Hampton Inn SpringHill Suites BP Subway Cracker Barrel Starbucks AmericInn Comfort Inn WynStar Inn Airport

OUTRIGGER BEACH RESORT; Siesta Bay RV Resort; The GROVES RV Resort; Indian Creek Park

East: To Gulf Air Travel Park 239-466-8100; To Gulf Waters RV Park 239-461-0903; To Red Coconut RV Park 239-463-7200; To San Carlos RV Park & Islands 239-466-3133; To Fort Myers Beach RV Resort 800-553-7484

Lee Island Coast
FLORIDA

Lee Island Coast Visitors and Convention Bureau
12800 University Drive, Suite 550, Fort Myers, Florida 33907
239-338-3500 or 1-800-237-6444 **www.fortmyerssanibel.com**

DID YOU KNOW?

Captiva Island, on Florida's Lee Island Coast, has been ranked as one of the country's most romantic beaches for two consecutive years by Stephen Leatherman, Ph.D., recognized as the nation's foremost beach authority. *Conde' Nast Traveler* named Sanibel Island as the best place to view a sunset in 1994. Lee County beaches are some of the best in the nation for shelling, with more varieties found here than anywhere else in the U.S.

(Above) Simple pleasures, Fort Meyers Beach. *Each sunrise brought treasures anew from the Gulf. We delighted in the myriad of tiny live shells the first morning, sand dollars the next, and star fish on our last day at the* ***Outrigger beach Resort.***

(Left) Pausing to read the trail guidebook at Calusa Nature Center.
Text courtesy Lee Island Coast CVB

The Calusa Nature Center and Planetarium in Fort Myers!

Tour Lee Island Coast if you want to experience the natural side of Florida. Numerous opportunities abound for ECO-touring including the **Calusa Nature Center & Planetarium.** Truly breathtaking, we spent 4 rolls of film on the winding trail which lead us through the 105-acre Calusa Nature preserve, and at each marker educated ourselves with our borrowed guide book. With a museum, Audubon aviary, and planetarium, this is the idyllic place to learn.

3450 Ortiz Ave., Fort Myers FL 33905
239-275-3435 www.calusanature.com

Other extraordinary parks and attractions of Lee Island Coast include the J.N. "Ding" Darling National Wildlife Refuge and the the Babcock Wilderness Adventure.

Lee Island Coast: Treasures for Shell Seekers

Southwest Florida's **Lee Island Coast** boasts more than 100 coastal islands hugging 50 miles of sandy, white beaches which shelter some of the best shelling in the United States. Tourists and residents alike search the shoreline for Neptune's treasures. Some even don miner's hats so they can arise before sunrise and find the best specimens. Or, visit the **Bailey-Matthews Shell Museum** on Sanibel Island, it has extensive shell exhibits and experts on hand to tell you about them.

The barrier and coastal islands, which make up the Lee Island Coast, cling lightly to the Southwest Florida coastline, yielding some 400 species of seashells. You'll find the common scallop and clam as well as exotic shells such as tulips, olives, and fragile paper fig shells. Maybe you'll capture the rarest of them all, the brown speckled junonia.

Many seashell creatures are hidden just beneath the surface of the sand where the surf breaks. Many shells never make it over this point and can be collected by wading or snorkeling along the surf line and sifting through the numerous shells deposited by the waves. Another tip: monitor the feeding of shorebirds such as terns to locate the Gulf's treasures. "Typical winter cold fronts produce great shelling on the southwest side of the barrier islands," said Mike Fuery, a fishing and shelling charter captain on Captiva Island. Changing tides, strong currents and weather conditions create ever-changing formations. "A brand new island has formed off North Captiva providing exciting and challenging adventures. Miniature sand dollars, as well as olives, nauticas and small whelks are bountiful."

Lee County has taken measures to protect this natural attraction. Shell activists want to preserve this natural resource which lures visitors to this area as well as protect live shells from being overharvested and becoming endangered. The city of Sanibel Island banned all live shelling as of Jan. 1, 1995.

Lee County's Board of Commissioners endorsed a law which bans the collection of live seashells from the waters off Lee County. The collection of dead shells, ones where the animals or mollusks are already dead or gone from the shell, is unlimited and encouraged.

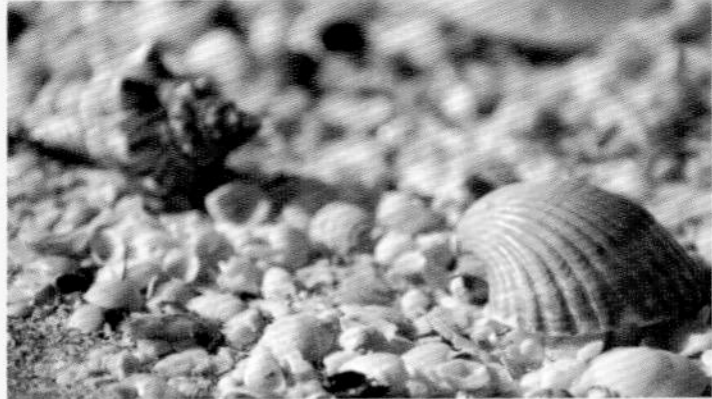

Shells *© www.fortmyerssanibel.com*

FLORIDA
Atlantic Ocean
Gainesville
Ocala
Orlando
Clearwater
Tampa
St. Petersburg
Gulf of Mexico
Ft. Lauderdale
Naples
Miami
N
75

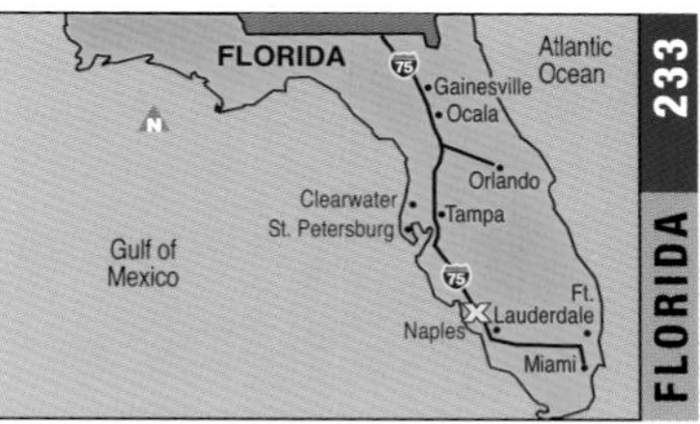

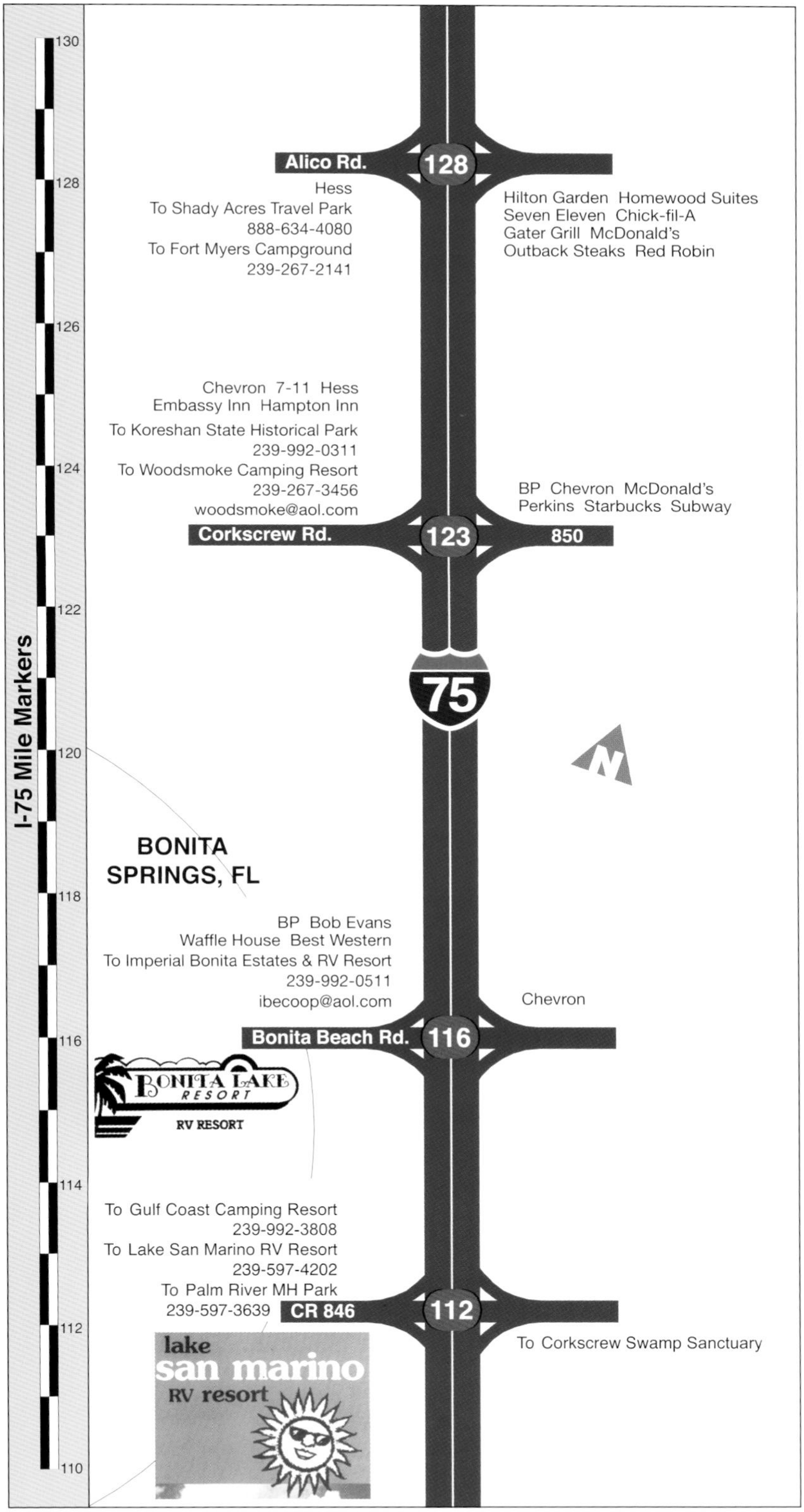

I-75 Mile Markers
130
128
126
124
122
120
118
116
114
112
110
Alico Rd.
128
Hess
To Shady Acres Travel Park
888-634-4080
To Fort Myers Campground
239-267-2141
Hilton Garden Homewood Suites
Seven Eleven Chick-fil-A
Gater Grill McDonald's
Outback Steaks Red Robin
Chevron 7-11 Hess
Embassy Inn Hampton Inn
To Koreshan State Historical Park
239-992-0311
To Woodsmoke Camping Resort
239-267-3456
woodsmoke@aol.com
BP Chevron McDonald's
Perkins Starbucks Subway
Corkscrew Rd.
123
850
75
N
BONITA SPRINGS, FL
BP Bob Evans
Waffle House Best Western
To Imperial Bonita Estates & RV Resort
239-992-0511
ibecoop@aol.com
Chevron
Bonita Beach Rd.
116
BONITA LAKE RESORT
RV RESORT
To Gulf Coast Camping Resort
239-992-3808
To Lake San Marino RV Resort
239-597-4202
To Palm River MH Park
239-597-3639
CR 846
112
To Corkscrew Swamp Sanctuary
lake san marino RV resort

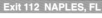

Naples/Collier County, FLORIDA

Naples Area Chamber of Commerce
2390 Tamiami Trail N., Naples Florida 34103
239-262-6141 **www.napleschamber.org**

Collier County is named for Tennessean businessman Barron F. Collier. Prior to Collier's arrival, in 1887, the Naples Improvement Company, headed by publisher Walter N. Haldeman and his associates, had begun their push to bring more tourists and developers to the area.

The Naples Hotel and the original pier was built in 1890, and soon after waterfront lots for $10 apiece were being sold to new residents.

Barron Collier purchased just about the whole of Marco Island in 1922, then he began the completion of the Tamiami Trail *(p.s., Tamiami = tampa + miami).* Working with the State of Florida, the Trail was completed in 1928.

By 1922, Collier had purchased some 900,000 acres of land in the county but Marco Island did not experience major development until 1964.

Excavations on Marco Island in the 1970's unearthed a civilization that dated to 3500 B.C. These ancestors of the Calusa Indians left artifacts and the enormous shell mounds. Many purposes for these mounds have been postulated: lookouts, protection from the high waves, ceremonial, garbage heaps...

Why not explore this fascinating area and come up with your own theory or two?

Naples is an exclusive destination and the shops and restaurants are exquisite. Craig and I enjoyed two fantastic dinners in downtown Naples under the stars and are looking forward to returning

Photo courtesy Lee Island Coast Convention and Visitors Bureau.

Naples & Marco Island Attractions

FORT MYERS BASEBALL CLUB
The Miracles (the Twins' farm club) from April to August. 239-768-4210

COLLIER COUNTY MUSEUM
Local history, artifacts, Florida garden and park adjacent. 239-774-8476

NAPLES DEPOT. Restored building now home to the United Arts Council of Collier County, and the unique Whistle Stop Shop. 239-262-1776

PALM COTTAGE
The famous "tabby mortar" home was built in 1895 just steps from the Naples Pier. Tours Nov. to Apr. 2 p.m.-4 p.m. 239-261-8164

PHILHARMONIC CENTER FOR THE ARTS/MIAMI CITY BALLET
239-597-1900

TEDDY BEAR MUSEUM OF NAPLES
3,000 bears in a forested "den." Storytellings and other exhibits. 239-598-2711

BAREFOOT BEACH PRESERVE
342 acres on lush barrier island. 8 a.m.-sundown. 239-353-0404

BRIGGS NATURE CENTER. Gateway to 10,000 Islands eco-system. Boardwalk, exhibits, butterfly garden, canoe/guided boat tours. Year-round, Mon. to Fri. 9 a.m.-4 p.m. Shell Island Rd., off SR 951. 239-775-8569

CLAM PASS COUNTRY PARK
Boardwalk through mangrove leads to the beach. Walk or take the tram. 8 a.m. -sundown. Free. 239-353-0404

CONSERVANCY NATURE CENTER
Self-guided nature trails, aquarium and natural science museum. Special touch tank. Nature store, rehab clinic for animals and birds, tours. 239-262-0304.

CORKSCREW SWAMP SANCTUARY
Run by the National Audubon Society, this virgin 500-year old cypress tree forest, is home to many species of birds and wildlife. Guided tours available or self-guided with illustrated tourbook. 8 a.m.-5 p.m., daily. 239-657-3771

DELNOR-WIGGINS PASS STATE RECREATION AREA
Beach with picnic, fishing, and wheelchair access on narrow barrier island. 8 a.m.-sundown. 239-597-6196.

MARCO ISLAND The largest of Florida's Ten Thousand Islands. www.marco-island-florida.com

NAPLES MUNICIPAL BEACH and **FISHING PIER**
The 1,000-foot pier is a historical landmark. Open 24 hours. Concessions, restrooms, bait house, cleaning tables, chickee shelter. 239-434-4696

And Highly Recommended...

BIG CYPRESS NATIONAL PRESERVE
On U.S. 41 between Naples and Miami. Primitive camping, picnic tables, hiking trails on 716,000 acres of "Everglades-like" terrain. 239-263-3532

EVERGLADES NATIONAL PARK
On U.S. 41. Third-largest national park. Group boat tours from the Shark Valley Visitor Center from 8:30 a.m. to 6 p.m. 305-221-8776

CARIBBEAN GARDENS Nationally accredited zoo in 52 acres of jungle. We loved the Primate Expedition Cruise! 1590 Goodlette Rd., Naples. 239-262-5409

CHOKOLOSKEE ISLAND
Use U.S. 41, go east to SR 29, south on SR 29 through Everglades City and over causeway. Smallwood's Store and Old Trading Post is a museum preserving the days of outlaw gunfights, "gator hunting and smuggling. Open daily from late Nov. to May. Chokoloskee is the gateway to the 10,000 Islands and one of Florida's last frontiers. 239-695-2989

COLLIER-SEMINOLE STATE PARK
On U.S. 41. Nation's only walking dredge (the construction equipment used on Tamiami Trail). Hiking trails through cypress swamps, salt marshes and tropical hardwood hammock. Abundant wildlife. 13.6-mile canoe trip for experienced paddlers. Nature cruises. 239-394-3397

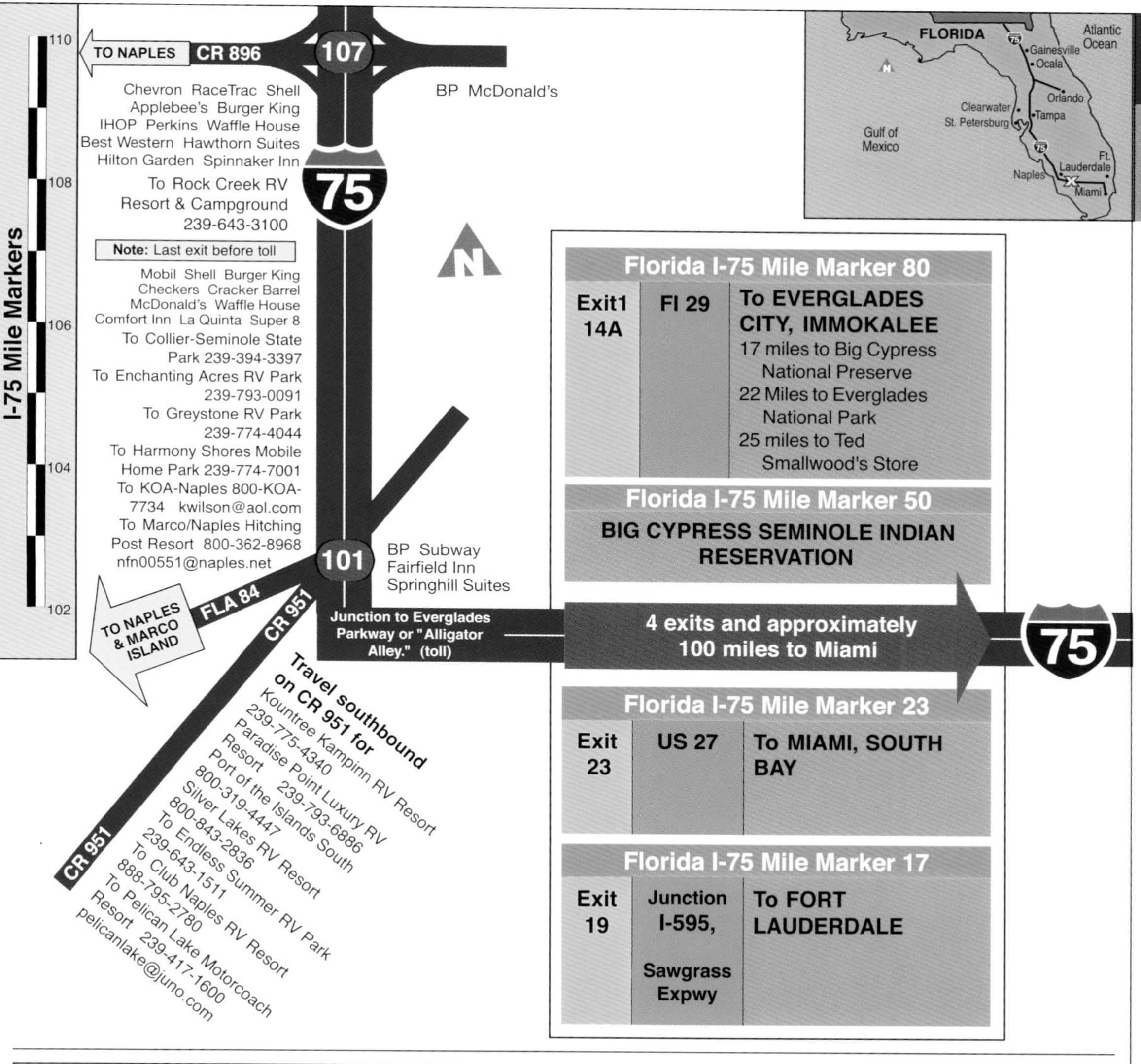

Florida I-75 Mile Marker 80		
Exit1 14A	Fl 29	To EVERGLADES CITY, IMMOKALEE 17 miles to Big Cypress National Preserve 22 Miles to Everglades National Park 25 miles to Ted Smallwood's Store

Florida I-75 Mile Marker 50
BIG CYPRESS SEMINOLE INDIAN RESERVATION

Florida I-75 Mile Marker 23		
Exit 23	US 27	To MIAMI, SOUTH BAY

Florida I-75 Mile Marker 17		
Exit 19	Junction I-595, Sawgrass Expwy	To FORT LAUDERDALE

Q. Which Florida destination can boast all of the following:

First to dredge the Everglades. Elected Florida governor in 1904, Napoleon Bonaparte Broward was responsible for dredging the Everglades. Very much a man of his time, Broward knew little about the Everglades ecology. Like most, he thought the seemingly useless swamp should be drained and turned into farmland. However, the canals that now crisscross south Florida made it possible for millions of people to live here and provides South Florida's drinking water.

Florida's First Boat Parade. A spectacular nighttime parade that has become a holiday tradition. Decorated yachts float up the Intracoastal waterway. Celebrated for almost 40 years, the annual Parade is held early to mid-Dec.

Florida's First Water Taxis. 300 miles of navigable waterways lend this city the nickname of "Venice of America." An all-day pass is $5. You can catch a water taxi to take you shopping, to restaurants, to the theater or sightseeing.

First spring break mecca. In the early 1930s, swim teams from northern schools traded the arctic winds for balmy breezes and practiced here in the winter months. Each year the crowds grew until the 1960 classic movie *Where the Boys Are* triggered spring break mania. In 1985, this destination's peak year, 350,000 students visited these sunny shores. Today just 10,000 students spend spring break in Fort Lauderdale. **Fort Lauderdale** is no longer "where the boys are," but where well-heeled Europeans, sophisticated Northerners and laid-back Mid-Westerners come to relax.

Florida's First Blue Wave Beaches: Certified by the Clean Beaches Council of Washington, D.C. as user friendly and safe.

Fort Lauderdale
FLORIDA

Greater Fort Lauderdale Convention and Visitors Bureau
100 East Broward Blvd, Suite 200, Fort Lauderdale, Florida 33301
954-765-4466, Ext. 223 or 1-800-22-SUNNY **www.sunny.org**

The Promenade. *Photo/text courtesy the Greater Fort Lauderdale CVB*

Life Is More Than a Beach In Greater Fort Lauderdale

Money Magazine voted **Fort Lauderdale** the best place to live in America in 1996, which did not surprise the 1.7 million inhabitants of the city and its neighboring municipalities who comprise Greater Fort Lauderdale/Broward County or the 8.1 million non-residents who came from all over North and South America, Europe and Asia last year for fun or business. The fact is, all of Greater Fort Lauderdale is a terrific place to visit because it is a great place to live.

So what do the residents and loyal visitors of Florida s fastest growing, most diverse and dynamic vacation and business travel destination know that the rest of the world should find out? For starters there are 23 miles of wide sandy beaches stretching enticingly along calm, azure Atlantic waters from Palm Beach in the north to Miami in the south. More than 300 miles of navigable inland waterways wind through palatial estates, citrus groves and the unique and exotic Everglades, beckoning boats of all sizes and shapes.

It is the Intracoastal Waterway and the waterfront homes that dot it, that have earned Greater Fort Lauderdale its reputation as the **"Venice of America"** and, with more than 44,000 registered boats, the label "yachting capital of the world." Then there are the cultural attractions, museums, sports, sailing, Scuba, dining, shopping, entertainment, natural wonders, festivals and celebrations, friendly folk, cruise ships, water taxis, horse-drawn carriages, butterflies, and alligators ...

Greater Fort Laud-erdale/Broward County covers an area of 1,197 square-miles, two-thirds of which lie in the Ever-glades or "river of grass." It's no wonder that sun-seekers from all over the world come here to live, play, relax, and sometimes, even work. Broward County is one of the fastest growing residential areas in the country. Part of the reason is accessibility. Greater Fort Lauderdale is easy to reach by air, train or interstate highway.

The newly expanded **Fort Lauderdale/ Hollywood International Airport** is one of the most efficient in the world, served by more than 30 carriers from most air-departure points across the U.S. and Canada. With three airports to select from in South Florida, the Fort Lauderdale/ Hollywood International facility is fast becoming the number one choice with visitors who want to avoid overcrowding, long lines, confusion and miles of corridors. The airport's location makes it easy to land, collect luggage, rent a car and be at the beach, board a cruise ship or make a meeting at the Convention Center in minutes.

These are some of other reasons why Greater Fort Lauderdale is rapidly becoming South Florida's #1 place to be:

• **Accommodations for Every Taste.** With some 33,000 hotel rooms in the area, finding the right one is never a problem. Broward County's accommodations range from small inexpensive, family-run hostelries to deluxe resorts, operated by such international award-winning lodging companies as Hyatt, Hilton, Marriott, Westin, Sheraton, Doubletree and others. For those with a taste for more intimate surroundings, there are the *Superior Small Lodging* properties that feature charm, location and the personality and character of South Florida's early days. The area also boasts two spa resorts as well as hotels and resorts with golf and other activities.

• **World Class Dining with Down-Home Hospitality.** From the haute to the hot dog, Greater Fort Lauderdale s 3,000 restaurants guarantee satisfaction for everyone, and especially those with a taste for the finest, a palate for adventure or a craving for casual fare. An international array of ethnic specialty restaurants includes Caribbean, Chinese, Cuban, French, German, Indian, Italian, Jamaican, Mexican, Soul, South African, Spanish, Swiss, Thai, Vietnamese, American (nouvelle and traditional) and classic South Florida.

Eight of the top South Florida restaurants cited by Gourmet Magazine in Oct. 1998 are located in Greater Fort Lauderdale. Elegant continental restaurants offer a panoramic view of the Intracoastal Waterway or a penthouse view of the city. Arrive by **Water Taxi** at some, dine waterside and beachfront at others, and watch those calories at a whole new generation of dining spots that serve up delicious, fresh and healthy fare.

• **To Shop, To Shop.** The most popular pastime for vacationers is said to be shopping. From diamonds and precious antiques to discounted designer wear, Greater Fort Lauderdale has many opportunities. Modern malls, such as the famed *Galleria,* with Neiman-Marcus, Saks, Cartier, and Ann Taylor purvey the upscale in this 1.4 million-square-foot complex a short walk from the beach. *Sawgrass Mills,* Florida's largest value and entertainment mall, offers over 300 brand-name and designer outlets, specialty shops and restaurants. **Festival Market Place** in Pompano offers bargains in air-conditioned comfort.

Landscaped, gas-lighted and chic ***Las Olas Boulevard*** is lined with one-of-a-kind boutiques, galleries and restaurants. Antique lovers head for *Antique Row* in nearby Dania Beach, with 150 shops in a one-block area just south of the airport. For treasure and trivia hunters, 75 acres of garage sales, farmers market, international bazaar and county fair comprise the south's largest flea market: the *Fort Lauderdale Swap Shop. Outdoor World Bass Pro Shops* mega sporting goods store will delight sportsmen and women.

Fort Lauderdale
FLORIDA

Greater Fort Lauderdale Convention and Visitors Bureau
100 East Broward Blvd, Suite 200, Fort Lauderdale, Florida 33301
954-765-4466, Ext. 223 or 1-800-22-SUNNY **www.sunny.org**

Water Taxi. *Photos/text courtesy the Greater Fort Lauderdale CVB*

• **The World's #1 Five-Star Cruise Port.** More than 2-million people cruise out of modern *Port Everglades* each year, making it the world's second largest cruise port. More than 50 depart from the port, destined for the Caribbean and points south. Port Everglades is port of call for Celebrity, Costa, Crystal, Holland America, Princess, Mediterranean Shipping Cruises, Royal Olympic, Royal Caribbean, Seabourn and Silversea.

• **Off the Beach Attractions and Activities.** With the opening of *Broward Center for the Performing Arts,* Greater Fort Lauderdale has become the center for theater, music and dance in South Florida. The biggest Broadway musicals including "Miss Saigon," "Phantom of the Opera," "Les Miserables," "Rent," "Sunset Boulevard" and "Beauty and the Beast" play the 2,700 seat *Au-Rene Theater,* which has also presented Tony Bennett and Liza Minnelli.

Other performing arts venues such as *Bailey Hall,* offer music concerts, theater productions and dance performances; the *Sunrise Musical Theater,* presents everything from the Moscow Ballet to pop, rock and country artists; and the *Vinnette Carroll Theatre,* offers multicultural productions.

For a look at **"Old Florida,"** historic sites abound: *Bonnet House* (named for the lilies which are native to the nearby Everglades) is the Fort Lauderdale oceanfront estate of the late painter Frederic Bartlett; *Stranahan House* is the oldest home in Broward County and *Flamingo Gardens and Wray Botanical Collection,* one the area's first citrus groves, is now a botanical garden.

The *Fort Lauderdale Museum of Art* is home to one of the world's premier collections of early 20th-century art. The museum is also home of the most comprehensive collection of work by American Impressionist William Glackens. *The Museum of Discovery and Science,* and *Blockbuster 3D IMAX Theater,* the most visited museum in Florida, explores science, space and the environment.

Festivals here are frequent and have broad appeal. The *Air and Sea Show* kicks off the summer season in May and the spectacular *Cingular Wireless Winterfest Boat Parade Presented by Nokia* caps the month-long December *Winterfest* celebration. The *Pompano Beach Seafood Festival* and *Fishing Rodeo* in April, celebrate the bounty of the sea. Art and food festivals, jazz festivals and boat shows make for many other special happenings.

Butterfly World, is one of Broward County's most popular attractions. Set in Tradewinds Park, a specially designed screened enclosure lets thousands of butterflies free in their native habitats. A hummingbird exhibit and a hatchery complete this unique "world."

Racing fans can choose thoroughbred racing at ***Gulfstream Park*** in Hallandale (host of the prestigious Breeders Cup and the annual Florida Derby festival), trotters at *Pompano Park Harness Track,* greyhound racing in Hollywood and *Jai Alai* in Dania Beach.

Golfers will recognize the names of famous courses, among the more than 56 public and private clubs in Broward County. **The PGA *Eagle Trace*** is perhaps the best known, but others are wonderfully challenging and accessible. Greater Fort Lauderdale is also home to pro golf tournaments including the Honda Golf Classic at TPC in Heron Bay and the LPGA Tournament of Champions at Weston Hills Country Club. Tennis, too, is world-class here with 550 tennis courts. When the time comes to let the pros handle the action, Greater Fort Lauderdale comes alive as "sports central" for the Southeast. This is one of only 4 areas in the nation to serve as home to Dolphins pro football, Florida Marlins pro baseball, Heat pro basketball and Florida Panthers pro hockey franchises. Broward County is also home to baseball spring training of the Baltimore Orioles, Dolphin football training at Nova Southeastern University and more. The ***International Swimming Hall of Fame*** enables spectators to watch Olympic hopefuls.

The Office Depot Center in Sunrise and serves as home to the Florida Panthers pro hockey team as well as major concerts.

Special-interest visitors can attend schools for sailing or motor-boating, learn board-sailing, ride an airboat or swampbuggy in the Everglades and seep-sea fish for big sails and marlin. **Scuba divers** will find clear water and coral formations as elaborate and spectacular as those in the fabled Florida Keys with one big advantage: the reefs are a lot less crowded and more accessible. At the *International Game Fish Association World Fishing Center* at the Sportsmen's Park in Dania Beach you can visit the galleries and conservation center and even virtual fish.

For the last few years, Broward County has made a concerted effort to create an ideal environment for diverse artificial reef building process that is essentially "reforesting" the sea and introducing divers to dozens of new and interesting sights. More than two dozen sanitized freighters and other vessels have been sunk off the coast, primarily around Fort Lauderdale and Pompano Beach. In September, divers both novice and experienced can enjoy ***Oceanfest,*** a dive trade show on the beach that actually offers diving.

The ***Jungle Queen*** offers guided day tours and dinner cruises through the canals and waterways, complete with music and colorful commentary. The *Fort Lauderdale Water Taxi* provides a delightful and more scenic mode of transportation to and from many hotels, attractions, restaurants and shops. The water taxi captains are friendly and knowledgeable about local lore, hotspots and current who's who.

Miami
FLORIDA

Greater Miami Visitors and Convention Bureau
701 Brickell Ave., Suite 2700, Miami, Florida 33131
305-539-3000 or 800-933-8448 **www.miamiandbeaches.com**

Miami Beach. *Photo/ text courtesy Greater Miami C&VB*

Greater Miami

Probably no other single community, at least in recent years, has set as many trends nor trampled as many traditions as Greater Miami and the Beaches.

Today's Greater Miami is a dynamic international crossroad of commerce, culture, sports, tourism entertainment and transportation. The cosmopolitan city boasts some of the world's most beautiful beaches, right next to one of the world's most vibrant urban centers. For those torn between "getting away from it all" and "being part of it all," Greater Miami is a great compromise.

Greater Miami will exhaust the visitor long before the visitor can exhaust Greater Miami. But it's worth the effort, especially for people who appreciate diversity.

Greater Miami is conch fritters, black beans and rice, cowbells and castanets, salsa and compas, jig and rumba. It's a blend of 21st-century and Old World architecture, fast sports and leisurely sunbaths, big-city culture and small-town neighborhoods.

Visitors can battle a marlin with rod and reel, explore the historic and "happening" **Art Deco District**, spot alligators in the Everglades, enjoy the ballet, opera or symphony, windsurf over the ocean, sip Cuban coffee, skip a cigarette boat across the bay, savor a plate of stone crabs, dive a coral reef, touch parrots and porpoises, dance and feast through a street festival, or contemplate nature on a serene sandbar. The spectator sports inventory includes NFL, NBA, major league baseball, professional hockey and arena football action, the Orange Bowl Classic, Jai Alai, horse and dog racing, world-class boating, one of the nation's top college football teams, Grand Prix auto racing and the two sports seemingly invented for South Florida: golf and tennis. For participants, the outdoor sports season never really ends.

• **Rejuvenating the Senses.** Miami is one of the few urban centers in the world capable of completely rejuvenating the human senses. Gardenias, bougainvillea and hibiscus are exotic plants in some cities, but not in Miami. Here, they are indigenous and thrive even in downtown areas where their scents are as common as that of ocean spray.

• The **Miami skyline** represents a radical departure from the symmetrical lines prevalent in most of urban America The cutouts, tiered and scalloped facades, nautical themes, spiral staircases and the unconventional use of color suggests Miami is already in the 21st-century. Across sparkling Biscayne Bay, Miami Beach is a living mural, an alliance of pastel buildings opposite the white Pompano sand and aquamarine sea.

• **The Crossroad of America.** Logistics are especially kind to Greater Miami. The community is located at the crossroad of the Americas, making it a most convenient transit point. Visits to Greater Miami can be easily combined with trips to just about anywhere. You can hop a jet to London, sail to the Caribbean or around the world, or rent a car for a relatively short trip to the Florida Keys, the Gulf of Mexico or Walt Disney World.

As a product of the 20th-century, Greater Miami is tailored for the automobile. The area's comprehensive network of roads makes every part of Dade County accessible within a reasonable time. Moreover, car rental rates in Greater Miami are among the country's lowest.

Trips across the causeways that span Biscayne Bay are short and scenic, connecting mainland Miami to the seaside attractions. Bal Harbour, Surfside, Sunny Isles, Key Biscayne and Miami Beach are minutes from the heart of the city.

The perimeters of Greater Miami are reachable via the Florida Turnpike, I-95, U.S. 1 and many east-west expressways. Yet no matter where you are in Greater Miami, wildlife is never far. Within minutes of the skyscrapers is the only living coral reef in North America, a diver's paradise extending south along the Florida Keys. Several miles west of the city is the Everglades, the only subtropical zone in N. America.

• ***Everglades National Park*** comprises thousands of acres of rare and unspoiled wilderness, a sprawling sanctuary for vanishing species of birds and other rare creatures such as the Florida panther and alligator. *Biscayne National Park* offers glass-bottom boat rides through mangroves, islands and out to tropical coral reefs rising 25 feet.

• Nature also abounds closer to the city, in the guise of subtropical "jungles" that provide counterpoint to the glass-and-steel downtown. These are some of Greater Miami's most enduring and endearing attractions: ***Parrot Jungle*** *and Gardens,* a haven for exotic flowering trees sheltering some of the world's loveliest birds; and ***Monkey Jungle,*** where visitors are caged to safely observe the antics of free-roaming primates. The 83-acre *Fairchild Tropical Garden* is the largest tropical botanical garden in the continental U.S., and features a rare plant house, sunken gardens and newly landscaped tracts.

• **The New Miami Beach.** Sitting at an alfresco cafe on Miami Beach in the early evening is a windfall for the human spirit. When the moon rises over the ocean and a cruise ship crawls across the horizon, it is difficult to imagine a finer place to be. These days, along Ocean Drive's impressive row of Art Deco hotels and restaurants, a new generation is rediscovering Miami Beach. The renaissance of South Beach resounds from the festive crowds in the

Greater Miami Visitors and Convention Bureau
701 Brickell Ave., Suite 2700, Miami, Florida 33131
305-539-3000 or 800-933-8448 **www.miamiandbeaches.com**

Coconut Grove. *Photo/text courtesy the Greater Miami C&VB*

Deco clubs to the new red sidewalks and palm trees along spruced-up Ocean Drive.

Miami nightlife is full of fresh energy with live music, from progressive to hot rock and cool blues and jazz. Intimate theaters, where patrons sit just a few feet from the actors, are springing up throughout the Art Deco district. Restaurants, galleries and boutiques dot the pastel-hued streets. European cafe society finds one of the best American expressions in Ocean Drive's inviting sidewalk tables facing the sea.

The Deco District is also making a case for itself as the heart of Greater Miami's cultural renaissance. **The *Lincoln Road Mall*,** once known as the "Fifth Avenue of the South" is regaining its sizzle as a hub of the arts. The street now houses the *South Florida Arts Center,* the *Colony Theatre,* and the headquarters of the New World Symphony and Miami City Ballet. New tenants include trendy restaurants, art galleries and boutiques.

The "beautiful people" have discovered the District too. The Deco architecture, ocean vistas and soft, tropical light serve as a backdrop for glamorous models posing for catalogs, advertisements, television commercials and films. There are about 15 modeling agencies operating in South Beach and at least five have set up shop on Ocean Drive.

In upper Miami Beach, the old favorites remain: the Mediterranean-style neighborhoods, the horse-drawn carriages, famous convention hotels such as the Fontaine-bleau Hilton, fashionable boutiques and, incredibly wide beaches.

The remarkable weather of Miami Beach features about 13 inches less rainfall each year on the beach than inland. The temperatures rarely hit the 90-degree mark here, even on summer afternoons.

• **Oceanfront Enclaves.** North of Miami Beach but occupying the same island are several enclaves with their own identities.

• **Surfside** has the feel of Hometown, USA. Uncrowded, yet full of activity, it first garnered attention as the setting for the classic Warner Brothers TV show of the '60s, "Surfside 6."

Surfside shares the Broad Causeway with *Bal Harbor,* a village which may have invented the term "casually elegant." Well before the mega-mall, the Bal Harbor Shops had firmly established a niche as the Miami-area choice of discriminating shoppers from around the world. Cascading waterfalls and abundant foliage bring the tropics indoors to share space with Gucci, Cartier, Neiman Marcus, Tiffany and Company, and others.

In *Sunny Isles,* the emphasis is on the outdoors. The area has inviting stretches of sand perfect for basking or sports. Families appreciate the beach proximity offered by Sunny Isles' hotels and restaurants, as well as the community's affordable ease.

• **Tropical Bohemia.** Coconut Grove is a bohemian state of mind played out in curbside cafes, pubs, arcades, art galleries, specialty shops and red brick sidewalks. A visit to this eclectic, energetic, triangular-shaped limestone bluff is almost mandatory. The Grove is a microcosm of Greater Miami and a parade for nonconformity: Socialites in evening gowns and white gloves are as commonplace as rollerbladers in polka-dot bikinis.

Energy levels run high along the sidewalks that stretch south from Grand Avenue along Main Highway, opposite a towering forest of bayfront, wind-swept Australian pines. Pictures of the short side streets that cut away from the two-lane main drag can easily be mistaken for postcards from the Left Bank. And they're lined with flaming-red bottlebrush trees that sweeten the air.

Nearby, the $38-million Cocowalk center fills the Grove with excitement. Designed to complement and blend with the Grove's distinctive architecture and ambiance, the center draws crowds to its shops, nightclubs, restaurants and comedy club.

Dining in the Grove can be very casual at a bayfront pub, or extremely elegant. Some of Greater Miami's finest hotels, restaurants, designer shops, and museums are found here. Don't miss ***Vizcaya Museum & Gardens***. Cloistered in a densely wooded area along Biscayne Bay, just north of the Grove, this 70-room Italian Renaissance-style villa and its surrounding 10-acre gardens are open to the public 7 days a week.

• **Bayside**. The flamingo-colored, shoebox-shaped pavilions that comprise Bayside Marketplace have helped Miami establish a new sense of city style. Upscale shops, boutiques, retail booths, gourmet restaurants and fast-food outlets give Bayside a festive atmosphere enhanced by gondola rides, Biscayne Bay cruises, strolling musicians and sidewalk entertainers.

Bayside's dining options include seafood and trendy fare served outdoor overlooking the water, as well as more upscale dining where a sweeping panorama of water and skyline are served with the cuisine.

Bayside's newest attraction, the *Hard Rock Cafe Miami,* delivers up an internationally recognized combination of American cuisine and rock memorabilia.

Bayside's colossal fast-food section is a gastronomic playground where the fast-food outlets deliver options from souvlaki to pasta to plantain chips.

A breezy bazaar between the pavilions is lined with booths and carts displaying jewelry, leather goods, hats, T-shirts, novelties and other wares.

Miami
FLORIDA

Greater Miami Visitors and Convention Bureau
701 Brickell Ave., Suite 2700, Miami, Florida 33131
305-539-3000 or 800-933-8448 **www.miamiandbeaches.com**

Adjacent to Baywalk is a scenic promenade that traces the shoreline of Biscayne Bay 1/3 of a mile, leading pedestrians to the *Miami Convention Center* and other downtown attractions. Near Bayside is 28-acre *Bayfront Park,* wit the recent additions of the *Claude and Mildred Pepper Fountain,* the waterfront amphitheater, and a 100-foot laser light tower that sheds a whole new light on downtown Miami.

• **The Neighborhoods.** Greater Miami's urban and suburban neighborhoods preserve the community's unique blend of cultures. *Coral Gables, Opa-Locka, Little Havana* and *Little Haiti* are particularly intriguing.

Planned during Miami's 1920s boom era, ***Coral Gables*** features residential and commercial districts famous for their Mediterranean-style piazzas, fountains, and entrances. Along *Coral Way,* giant ficus trees form a natural canopy over the residential street. Also worth exploring are the individual villages of the Gables, with their distinctive Spanish-Mediterranean, Colonial, Dutch South African, Chinese and French Provincial architectural designs.

The main streets in ***Opa-Locka,*** named for characters in the Arabian Nights, are laid out in the shape of a crescent moon. In downtown Opa-Locka, buildings sport a Moorish motif, and the keyhole arches of the train station entrance way are framed in handpainted tiles, crowned by domes and a crenelated parapet.

Little Havana is the hub of Greater Miami's vibrant Cuban community. Here, the chimneys and porch piers of single-family bungalows are made of native coral limestone, and the Cuban restaurants on S.W. 8th Street (Calle Ocho) serve the finest picadillo and arroz con pollo in the free world.

A sensory paradise, *Little Havana* exudes life from every corner: the enticing aroma of Cuban coffee, an explosion of color in hand-painted murals, staccato Spanish spoken on the streets, and the contagious energy of mambo and merengue rhythms.

Caribbean influence also pervades **Little Haiti**. Creole lilts through the air, against the beat of compas, soca and protest songs.

Finally, there is ***Key Biscayne.*** This tropical island is just a scenic bridge away from downtown Miami.

Along the ***Rickenbacker Causeway*** leading to the key, the multi-colored sails of windsurfers and Hobie Crafts criss-cross the bay, while jet skis hum in a cove on the opposite side of the bridge. Ahead is the geodesic dome of the *Miami Seaquarium* (Florida's first oceanarium) and to the left stretches a dramatic view of the downtown skyline.

Although hotels, restaurants and a small business district cater to visitors' needs, much of the island is preserved as parkland. In these refuges, towering pines, sabal palms, massive banyans, undisturbed mangroves and beaches offer a respite from the urban pace.

The surprising, the exotic, the unexpected, all help to make Greater Miami the "sophisticated tropics."

The Miami Seaquarium *provides a fascinating look into the underwater world. Lolita the Killer Whale, acrobatic dolphins and lovable manatees are just a few of the hundreds of sea creatures here.*

White Tiger at the Miami Metrozoo. *The 290-acre habitat provides the excitement of the world's jungles with more than 900 animals of 240 species. Wildlife shows, special exhibits and an elevated, air-conditioned monorail are all a part of the Miami Metrozoo experience. Photos/text courtesy Greater Miami Convention and Visitors Bureau.*

Greater Miami Visitors and Convention Bureau
701 Brickell Ave., Suite 2700, Miami FL 33131
305-539-3000 or 800-933-8448 **www.miamiandbeaches.com**

Newport Beachside Hotel & Resort

16701 Collins Avenue,
Miami Beach, Florida 33160
305-949-1300 1-866-323-7931
www.newportbeachsideresort.com

Sunny Isles Beach, Florida's # 1 Destination as Reported By TripAdvisor Travel Cast Top 10 Destinations In The US for 2008.

You are promised world-class service and outstanding value at a beautiful ocean-front setting, just minutes from Miami and Fort Lauderdale in Sunny Isles Beach, FL, at the Newport Beachside Hotel & Resort. "The place" from the beginning, The Newport Beachside Hotel & Resort once attracted a steady crowd of more than 600 VIPS nightly, including famous entertainers such as Sammie Davis Jr., Tina Turner, The Platters and Jimi Hendrix. We were all ready impressed, but we are looking forward to our next visit to the resort because with the latest wave of interior and exterior renovations, more modern services are being offered to guests.

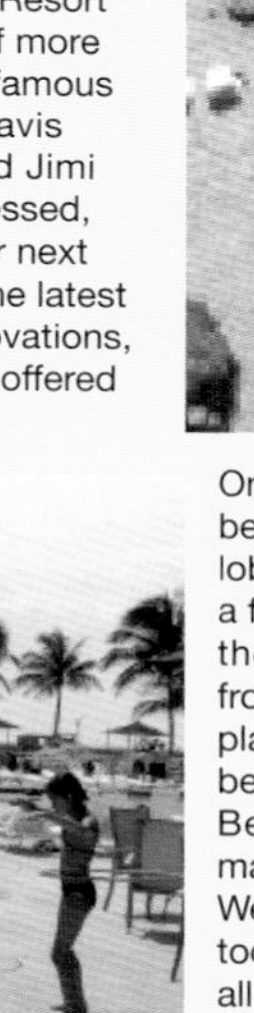

Once through the valet parking, expect to be surprised by the trademark gorgeous lobby! Our suite was well designed with a family in mind. Dozens of floors above the white sand, the view of the ocean from our balcony was breath-taking. With planned activities, a huge pool and wide beach, this is a popular resort for families. Between the beach and the pool, we managed to find time to tour Sunny Isles. We were at the end of our trip, and that's too bad. We could have filled our car up all over again with deals from the Outlet centers and malls!

Photos © website for Newport Beachside Hotel & Resort

Miami Area Cultural Venues

Lowe Art Museum
University of Miami, 1301 Stanford Dr. Coral Gables, FL 33124, 305/284-3535

Jewish Museum of Florida
301 Washington Ave. Miami Beach, FL 33139, Miami Beach - Art Deco District/ South Beach 305/672-5044

The Miami Beach Cinematheque
512 Espanola Way, Miami Beach, FL 33139, Miami Beach - Art Deco District/ South Beach 305/673-4567

Museum of Contemporary Art
770 NE 125th St. Miami, FL 33161, North Miami Area, 305/893-6211

Miami Beach Botanical Garden
2000 Convention Center Dr., Miami Beach 33139, Miami Beach - Art Deco District/ South Beach, 305/532-4855

World Erotic Art Museum (WEAM),
1205 Washington Ave., Miami Beach, FL 33133, Miami Beach - Art Deco District/ South Beach, 305/532-9336

Miami Art Museum
101 W. Flagler St., Miami, FL 33130, Downtown Miami Area, 305/375-3000

Miami Children's Museum
980 Macarthur Causeway, Miami, Florida 33132 305/373.KIDS (5437)

Miami
FLORIDA

Greater Miami Visitors and Convention Bureau
701 Brickell Ave., Suite 2700, Miami FL 33131
305-539-3000 or 800-933-8448 **www.miamiandbeaches.com**

Circa 39 Hotel

3900 Collins Avenue,
Miami Beach, FL 33140
Main Hotel Telephone: 305.538.4900
Reservations: 877.8.CIRCA39

If you are ever offered a magic lamp, rub it and say "Take me to the Circa 39 Hotel." You'll know what a riot this place is as soon as you step into the lobby! We've absolutely enjoyed many of the hotels and resorts we've explored. Sometimes you just want your digs to be predictable when you travel, but sometimes you can appreciate something different. Surprise, surprise! Circa 39 is truly in a class of its own. The artsy, fun loving lobby is full of comfortable chaise lounges, couches and ottomans in bold colors and patterns. Large, overstuffed pillows seem to say "stay awhile." My girls and I were mesmerized by the hotel's signature custom centerpiece frame with nine panels of neon color, which changed to the beat of the hotel music. Funky accessories and fixtures like an Art Deco fireplace add pizzazz. The simple use of a purple light in the elevator added to our list of surprises. Between the two main buildings is a shaded courtyard where guests were relaxing in private cabanas. And if that's not enough, wait till you see your room! The whole package is inviting, just try not to extend your stay.

Circa 39 is located in a serene neighborhood that is only a short walk from Miami's glistening, sandy beaches and just a few minutes away from South Beach's energetic scene. The history of the property is dramatic, reaching back to –you guessed it ---1939. The owner and staff will be proud to fill you in, so don't hesitate to approach them.

After a breakfast to brag about, we took our books to the teak chaise lounges off the sun deck and pool area where, later in the afternoon, cocktails and light fare would be offered. Included in the hotel fee is a beach service if you want to take chairs and towels to the nearby beach. We had a lot of exploring to do in the Miami area and this hotel was the perfect springboard. At the end of the day, you can count on the cozy bar and pool areas for a quiet drink or lively conversation.

Photos © websitefor CIRCA 39 Hotel

South Beach's Art Deco District

Known as a super chic destination of celebrities, the Art Deco District of South Beach has attracted eccentric residents who have restored and protected more than 800 architectural treasures from the 1930s and 40s. Considered "south" of downtown, this glamorous visitor destination has a mix of luxury resorts, chic hotels, inexpensive hostels and moderately-priced national chain hotels. While Ocean Drive is known worldwide for its see-and-be-seen cafes, bikini-clad in-line skaters and beaches packed with beautiful young sunseekers, nearby Lincoln Road has emerged a hot spot of exclusive nightclubs and high end retail.

Photo © Lizzy Marks

Miami
FLORIDA

Greater Miami Visitors and Convention Bureau
701 Brickell Ave., Suite 2700, Miami FL 33131
305-539-3000 or 800-933-8448 **www.miamiandbeaches.com**

Island Queen Cruises

www.islandqueencruises.com
(305) 379-5119, 401 Biscayne Blvd, Miami, Fl 33132

Head down to the pier a little early for some unique shopping opportunities while you wait to board one of the Island Queen cruises out onto Miami's Biscayne Bay area. They tell you to relax and enjoy the narrated tour, and encouraged you to enjoy a beverage, but the bartender wasn't that busy. People just didn't have any free hands -- the cameras were clicking like crazy! From the fantastic Miami skyline to the mind-boggling properties on Millionaire's Row, there was so much to see! My girls both remarked that we've all seen these sights so many times in movies and on TV, it felt like we'd been there before. Check the website for special trips and vessels.

View of Millionaire's Row cruise from the Island Queen *Photo © Emily Marks (all rights reserved)*

Miami Area Cultural Venues

One of the top 10 zoos in the U.S., the cageless Miami MetroZoo is 5x larger than the average U.S. zoo. Of the 740 acres on the property, 300 are used for the care of 1,300 animals from over 400 species, including 48 endangered species. Don't miss the largest Asian aviary in the U.S. (over 70 species of birds). Dr. Wilde's World is an the indoor gallery of discovery with opportunities for close encounters. TheZoo features an elevated monorail, safari cycle rentals, paddle boat rides, a unique wildlife carousel, guided tram tours, behind-the-scenes zookeeper tours, animal feeding encounters, exotic animal presentations, and much more.

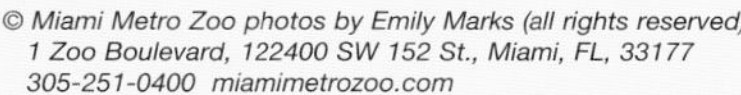

© Miami Metro Zoo photos by Emily Marks (all rights reserved)
1 Zoo Boulevard, 122400 SW 152 St., Miami, FL, 33177
305-251-0400 miamimetrozoo.com

Florida Keys & Key West FLORIDA

Florida Key & Key West Visitors Information
1201 White Street, Suite 102, Key West Florida 33040
1-800-FLA-KEYS **www.fla-keys.com**

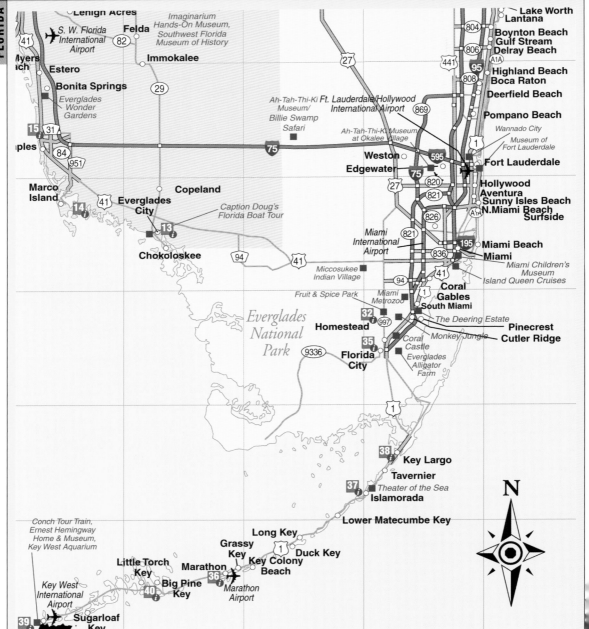

Lehigh Acres
S. W. Florida International Airport
Felda
Imaginarium Hands-On Museum, Southwest Florida Museum of History
Immokalee
Myers
Beach
Estero
Bonita Springs
Everglades Wonder Gardens
Naples
Marco Island
Everglades City
Copeland
Caption Doug's Florida Boat Tour
Chokoloskee
Ah-Tah-Thi-Ki Museum/ Billie Swamp Safari
Ft. Lauderdale/Hollywood International Airport
Ah-Tah-Thi-Ki Museum at Okalee Village
Weston
Edgewater
Lake Worth
Lantana
Boynton Beach
Gulf Stream
Delray Beach
Highland Beach
Boca Raton
Deerfield Beach
Pompano Beach
Wannado City
Museum of Fort Lauderdale
Fort Lauderdale
Hollywood
Aventura
Sunny Isles Beach
N.Miami Beach
Surfside
Miami International Airport
Miami Beach
Miami
Miami Children's Museum
Island Queen Cruises
Miccosukee Indian Village
Fruit & Spice Park
Miami Metrozoo
Coral Gables
South Miami
The Deering Estate
Pinecrest
Cutler Ridge
Monkey Jungle
Coral Castle
Everglades Alligator Farm
Homestead
Florida City
Everglades National Park
Key Largo
Tavernier
Theater of the Sea
Islamorada
Lower Matecumbe Key
Long Key
Duck Key
Grassy Key
Key Colony Beach
Marathon
Marathon Airport
Little Torch Key
Big Pine Key
Conch Tour Train, Ernest Hemingway Home & Museum, Key West Aquarium
Key West International Airport
Sugarloaf Key

Ocean Pointe Suites at Key Largo

Near Mile Marker 92.5
500 Burton Drive, Tavernier, Florida 33070 305-853-3000
800-882-9464 (USA & Canada)
www.opsuites.com

Photo courtesy of Ocean Pointe Suites at Key Largo (From their website)

A luxurious hotel, located just inside the gateway to the fabulous Florida Keys, offers the perfect tropical vacation setting. What I especially appreciated about our apartment-styled accommodations, like all the others here, was the fully equipped kitchen, private balcony and whirlpool tub in the master bathroom. Naturally, the girls loved the huge heated pool. We took many photos of the breathtaking views of the ocean from our balcony. The bar, near the private beach area, has a grill going almost all the time and it is stocked with pop and snacks you can pick up on the way to the beach. We sunbathed for a bit and chatted with other guests, then walked about the marina and out on the pier to watch the snorkelers. There is about 60 acres of tropical elegance at the Ocean Pointe resort, as well as wilder areas to explore beyond the beach. We chose the untamed areas and hiked along the shore into the brush trails for photo opportunities of the birds and flowers. If you have the time, consider joining other guests of the resort who may be taking out a kayak to explore the coastline. If you are looking for something a little more exciting, the friendly people at the Ocean Pointe Suites will arrange para sailing and jet skiing excursions for you in the area. Staffed by locals, make the most of your stay by asking about the local attractions and restaurants. We were grateful to learn about the Wild Bird Rehabilitation Center and the Rain Barrel artists' alcove further ahead down the Keys.

Want to call home and rub it in? Wireless internet is available in public areas and is free of charge.

Take the Florida Turnpike south. Continue south on Turnpike until it becomes US1. Follow US1 until you see signs for Burton Drive/Harry Harris Park, turn left. The Ocean Pointe Suites entrance will be on your right side approximately ¼ mile from US1.

• Fine restaurants and shopping are just minutes away, along with boating, fishing, snorkeling, diving, Everglades eco-tours, glass bottom boat reef trips, parasailing, waverunners and swimming with the dolphins. Everything you could want for the perfect Keys vacation!

Florida Keys Wild Bird Rehabilitation Center

Near mile marker 93
93600 Overseas Highway Tavernier, Florida 33070 305-852-4486
www.fkwbc.org

Florida Keys Wild Bird Center *courtesy Christine Marks, all rights reserved.*

After touring the injured birds rehabilitation areas, we were lucky enough to win a few moments with the center's very busy founder (Laura Quinn). It was like an episode from a public television show: heart-wrenching one moment, inspiring the next! Laura never set out to dedicate all of her retirement years to helping wild birds fight for their lives, but life is like that sometimes. She told a fascinating story of the (often struggling) history of the center while I watched my girls take photos of the beautiful pelicans and other wild birds sunbathing and preening near the Bay. I said we'd surely come back to witness the celebrated daily feeding of the wild birds later in the day, and regret missing it. I was just so tired from the solo 3-day drive down to the Keys that I fell asleep at the hotel. What a shame we didn't make it back, I heard many of the locals say this is truly a spectacular sight. The Florida Keys Wild Bird Sanctuary receives little government funding, relying mostly on donations from people near and far to meet its operating expenses. Thankfully, it's not just money that is donated. Every time a hurricane washes over the Keys, the center is destroyed. Just try not to be moved as she tells you how the volunteers come in with their own hammers and wood to rebuild the center for her again and again. This reputation, and her success story is known around the world. Make sure you stop in – and don't miss feeding time!

Florida Keys & Key West FLORIDA

Florida Key & Key West Visitors Information
1201 White Street, Suite 102, Key West Florida 33040
1-800-FLA-KEYS **www.fla-keys.com**

Rain Barrel Artists Village

Near mile marker 86
www.keysdirectory.com/rainbarrel

Another local favorite, the Rain Barrel Artists Village in Islamorada was the dream of owner Carol Cutshall, who came to the Keys from Pennsylvania 35 years ago for a 2-week vacation and never went home. That happens a lot in the Keys. Thanks to her you can spend hours in this artists' colony in the Upper Keys, located at mile marker 86 bayside. The quaint, open-air village showcases the galleries of the 10 resident artists — as well as thousands of works by 500+ diverse artists from all around the world. We were amazed by the blown glass fish ornaments and lamps, and bought hand-painted keepsakes. 9 a.m. to 5 p.m. seven days per week. For more information, call 305- 852-3084.

Photo © Rain Barrel website

Robbie's Marina

Near Mile Marker 77
(305) 664-9814 www.Robbies.com

We took some good advice and headed down to Robbie's to feed the tarpon from the docks. As you walk down the pier with your smelly bucket of fish,you can almost hear the theme music from "Jaws." The mob of huge, sleek tarpon have their eyes on you as they wrestle for the front row below the dock. It's just one photo opportunity after the other. Feeding the huge tarpon is one of the more popular activities at Robbies, but this is also the favorite hub for most of marine activities in the area including fishing, snorkeling and scuba excursions. Rent a kayak, hire a Backcountry or Patch Reef Fishing Guide, or chart your own course with a Rent-A-Boat. Hungry Tarpon Restaurant offers Keys-style meals and you'll understand why the parking lot in front of the restaurant is full of local tags --- the food is great! If you've caught fish, they'll cook them up any way you like. You can also rent a house boat from Robbie's for the ultimate Keys experience!

Photos © Christine Marks

Theatre of the Sea

Near Mile Marker 84
84721 Overseas Hwy.
Islamorada, FL, (305) 664-2431
www.theaterofthesea.com

The second oldest marine mammal museum in the world, Theater of the Sea is an educational and entertaining marine animal park where the bottlenose dolphin performances are up close and personal. The marine animals live in natural salt-water lagoons which you tour in glass bottomed boat. The nature walk was educational and refreshing.

Turtle Hospital

Near mile marker 48 2396 Overseas Hwy, Marathon, FL 33050, (305) 743-2552 www.turtlehospital.org

State certified, the non-profit Turtle Hospital raises 95% of its revenue from visitors programs. You'll be motivated to help after learning about the plight of the world's population of sea turtles in the theater room and touring the operating/emergency rooms of the hospital. Every patient has a story and most turn out to be successes! Like a doctor on call, you'll hear a detailed history of the illness, the strategies, the prognosis of each of the convalescing turtles and, if you want, get an emailed update from the hospital as the healthier turtles are returned to the wild.

Photo © Turtle Hospital website

Florida Keys & Key West FLORIDA

Florida Key & Key West Visitors Information
1201 White Street, Suite 102, Key West Florida 33040
1-800-FLA-KEYS **www.fla-keys.com**

Islander Resort

Near Mile Marker 82, Oceanfront, Islamorada, FL 33036 305-664-2031 800-753-6002 islanderfloridakeys.com

Best Kept Secret in the Florida Keys

Just an hour from the mainland, the Islander Resort encourages you to leave your cares behind and escape to the beauty of the fabulous Florida Keys. We lavished in an Oceanside villa with a screened in lanais and views of the Atlantic Ocean. This place gets it right -- the suite gives you what you are looking for in a tropical hotel with its vintage island décor and 20 acres of beautifully landscaped grounds, but then also gives you a modern way to say "wish you were here" with high-speed internet in every suite. The free breakfast buffet was generous and appealing and you'll probably not need lunch. If you don't want to cook dinner in your fully stocked kitchen, you can enjoy delicious food from the resort's full-service restaurant, Bluewater Tiki Bar. The resort's coral sand beach and perfect, blue water is made for water sports. The pool area is unparalleled with its choice of fresh-water or salt-water pools and hot tub areas. I wasn't the only one snoozing on the lounge chair! It must have been the intoxicating scent of the ocean and flowers, or the sounds of the piped in music and laughter of the guests that left me so relaxed, because both nights we stayed out until it was too dark to read. To my girls, that's the perfect holiday.

Located in Islamorada, known as the "Sportfishing Capital of the World," this oceanfront resort is the perfect home base for your "American Caribbean" adventures.

Photos © Islander Resort website

The Florida Keys History of Diving Museum

Near Mile Marker 83 Bayside, Islamorada, Florida 305-664-9737 www.DivingMuseum.org

The Florida Keys History of Diving Museum is a not-for-profit educational institution focused on the story of Man's Quest to Explore Under the Sea. The Museum is dedicated to collecting, preserving, displaying and interpreting artifacts, antiques, books, documents, photographs and oral history relative to the History of Diving. The Museum's artifacts have been provided through the generous support of its founders, Drs. Joe and Sally Bauer, who hold the world's largest collection of historic diving equipment and research documents. As a diver, I was practically giddy to have discovered this Museum but my girls were just as fascinated by the highly entertaining and interactive exhibits!

World Wide Sportsman

Near Mile Marker 81
81576 Overseas Hwy.
(305) 664-9271 1-800-BASS-PRO
www.basspro.com

Drawing tourists from as far away as Europe, this sports outlet is every sportsman's vision. There is a replica of Ernest Hemingway's boat on display that you may board and an aquarium wall providing an opportunity for an eyeball-to-eyeball meeting with tarpon, cobia, and bonefish.

Photo courtesy Florida Keys History of Diving Museum

Florida Keys & Key West FLORIDA

Florida Key & Key West Visitors Information
1201 White Street, Suite 102, Key West Florida 33040
1-800-FLA-KEYS **www.fla-keys.com**

Attractions We Recommend In Key West

Mallory Square,
1 Whitehead St., Key West, FL
33040 www.mallorysquare.com

The famous Mallory Square is a Key West must see! Here at the center of Key West's historic waterfront, Mallory Square stages the famous Key West sunset celebration. Historic Mallory Square and the city of Key West both had their beginning along this deep harbor waterfront — the wrecking schooners, the frigates and warships of the US Navy, the Cuban cigar makers' tobacco warehouses, and government offices connected to make Key West a foothold out on the frontier of a young America. That history has been well preserved. Today, you will find exciting carnival atmosphere complete with buskers and artisans who can hold the attention of the huge crowds only until the sun starts to dip into the horizon when all eyes face outward and the applause begins.

Jim Croce's Pirate Soul Museum
524 Front Street, Key West, FL
33040 305-292-1113
www.piratesoul.com

Port Royal, Jamaica, in late 1690's is the setting for the ultimate pirate museum. Wander through the winding alleys of the museum – where you'll be invited into the various "buildings" to discover the collections of authentic pirate artifacts and replicas. The modern interactive technology and audio-animatronics will drop you into the Golden Age of Piracy where you'll peer into the lives of the era's most infamous pirates. This attraction was a highlight for all of us, and felt more like a theme park than a museum.

Shipwreck Historeum Museum of Key West
1 Whitehead Street, Mallory Square,
Key West, FL 33040 305-292-8990.
www.shipwreckhistoreum.com

In 1851, Key West was the richest city in the United States. Why? Step back in time to the treacherous world of shipwrecking and see for yourself. The live actors will make this era come alive for you and the artifacts, laser technology and a 60' lookout tower will add to your unique experience at the Shipwreck Historeum.

Mel Fisher's Maritime Museum
200 Greene Street, Key West, FL
33040 1-800-434-1399
www.melfisher.com

The Learning Channel declared Mel Fisher's Maritime Museum to be the most amazing treasure in the world. There's more than $20 million in treasure and historical objects housed here and we took our time to see every exhibit including the gold and silver bars, silver coins, gold chalice (known as the "poison cup"); and a six-inch gold cross that was set with some of the finest emeralds in the world. We also were awestruck by the swords, guns, pottery, and personal effects from the sunken fleets. The museum chronicles the fate of four ships, the Nuestra Señora de Atocha and the Santa Margarita, both of which sank in a hurricane in 1622; The St. John's Wreck, a vessel of exploration that carried conquistadors to the Caribbean in roughly 1560; and the Henrietta Marie, an English merchant slaver that sank off the Florida Keys in 1700.

View of Key West from the 60ft. tower at the Shipwreck Historeum, *courtesy Christine Marks*

Key West Aquarium
Mallory Square - 1 Whitehead St.,
Key West, Florida, 33040
305-296-2051
www.keywestaquarium.com

Key West's first attraction. The aquarium, built in 1934, features the turtles, sharks, game and tropical fish that are native to the waters of Key West. We stayed a little longer to play in the touch tank. The interpreters are knowledgeable, make sure you follow them to the outdoor exhibits. You don't want to miss their lectures by the shark tank (feedings) or above the lagoon full of large tropicals.

Touch tank at Key West Aquarium
courtesy Christine Marks

Florida Key & Key West Visitors Information
1201 White Street, Suite 102, Key West Florida 33040
1-800-FLA-KEYS **www.fla-keys.com**

Key West Butterfly Conservatory

1316 Duval St., Key West, FL 33040 (305) 293-9258 www.keywestbutterfly.com

Prepare to be intoxicated! You will spend more time than you expect when you visit this tropical paradise. Flowering plants, cascading waterfalls and trees set the stage for an ever-changing masterpiece painted by nature that could be called "flowers of the sky." Bring your camera, there are 50 to 60 different species of butterflies as well as a variety of colorful birds to capture. Just as interesting, I would have loved to have photographed the pure delight and wonder of the other visitors, young and old, who visited this controlled, glass-enclosed habitat. The giftshop offers many butterfly and nature inspired souvenirs created by local artists.

Photos © Christine Marks

Old Town Trollery Tours

6631 Maloney Ave, Key West, FL 33040, (305) 296-6688 www.trolleytours.com

A piece of advice? There is no better way to explore the 100 points of interest in Key West than with Old Town Trolley Tours. Take it all in while your expert tour guide gives you a lively history from days of Indians, pirates, wreckers and the Civil War. Some of the stories you'll hear include the lucrative ship wrecking industry, the success and disaster of Henry Flagler's railroad and the fierce Calusa Indians. Your guide has been extensively trained and is proud to share the history, lore and legends of Key West. Count on them to show you where the best shops and restaurants are as well. What we really appreciated was the on and off privileges. For one price, do the whole loop but take all the time you want at each stop — you can just reboard when you are ready!

Florida Keys & Key West FLORIDA

Florida Key & Key West Visitors Information
1201 White Street, Suite 102, Key West Florida 33040
1-800-FLA-KEYS **www.fla-keys.com**

Liberty Clipper

Key West, PO Box 1662,
Key West, FL 33041 (305) 292-0332
www.Libertyfleet.com

Get ready to be pressed in for service. And get happy about it. How often do you get the chance to help hoist the sales on a 125 ft schooner? This is genuine Tall Ship sailing with an experienced crew and you are not going to forget it. Completed in 1983 the steel vessel is a replica of a 19th-century clipper ship.

Although the afternoon cruise is popular, we opted for a sunset sail and it was incredible. After your hard work with the ropes: its eat, drink and be merry while the dazzling sights and sounds of Key West pass you by. We chatted with the other guests and crew while we sampled the appetizers but passed on the wine, beer and champagne. And once the sun starts to set, that's when you'll be really glad you remembered your camera. Something about feeling like you are on the tip of the world makes this simple spectacle all the more brilliant.

Photos © Christine Marks

Sweets of Paradise

291 Front Street #5,
Key West, FL 33040 (305) 296-1611
http://sweetsofparadise.com

wicked evil grin We fully intended to share, but the bags of homemade fudge and cookies we tried to bring back home for everyone never got past the state line. Yes, I did feel a little remorse when we had to tell Gramma what happened to her tasty souvenirs but as I write this I know she'd simply given us an impossible task. I bet you couldn't help yourselves either – we're talking about a trip to heaven with every bite, ok?! Sweets of Paradise is owned by Walt and Leslie Kramer and they are famous for their baked fresh daily cookies and classic chocolate fudge but we encourage you to try their tropical fudge and key lime goodies too. Psst! You don't have to go to the ends of the earth to get your share of heaven! You can simply order on-line!!

Photos © Sweets of Paradise website

Lazy Dog Island Outfitters & Outdoor Adventure Company

5114 Overseas Highway, #7,
Key West, FL 33040
305-293-9550 1-866-293-9550
www.kayakthekeys.com

The natural beauty of Key West's backcountry is best explored by kayak. The shallow, calm, blue-green waters and the mangroves and wildlife of the Key's inhabitants will give you a different adventure each time. Three guides took us out that afternoon and pointed out tropical fish, crabs, sea stars, jellyfish, sea cucumbers, sponges and various aquatic birds, and even invited the braver paddlers to handle some of these creatures! Choose from 2 and 4 hour guided tours or rent your kayak for the day and explore the local waters on your own. Paddle away under the sun, there will be a friendly bunch with a barbecue and cold beer waiting for you at pub/restaurant when you get back! And yes, there is a "lazy dog" who loves to accompany the guides on the kayak tours.

The Island City House Hotel

Photo of pool area
Courtesy Island City House Hotel

In Key West we found our family's most beloved hotel:

THE ISLAND CITY HOUSE HOTEL
411 William Street, Key West, FLA
800-634-8230
www.Islandcityhouse.com

We'd driven practically three days to get here — the rave reviews were compelling — but we had absolutely no idea how extraordinary our stay would be!! Our first glimpse of those charismatic wrap-around porches on all three levels and lush landscaping made us smile, but the property's most charming aspects are just beyond the gate. If a picture is worth a thousand words, I'd like to write you a book with my selection of photos but I think you just need to click on the website to see all the other reasons why we just love this Hotel.

All twenty-four fully stocked suites have private baths, air conditioning, kitchens, ceiling fans, hardwood floors, televisions, and direct dial telephones. The fun is selecting from the property's 3 distinct lodging choices.

THE ARCH HOUSE
The Arch House is a traditional Key West Bed and Breakfast with six suites, all furnished in a casual Caribbean Style. The two suites on the first floor have two separate bedrooms each with one queen-sized bed, a living/dining room with a kitchen, bathroom, and a small porch. The studio-suites on the second floor of the Arch House have one queen-sized bed in an alcove, a sitting area with a kitchenette, and either a street-side balcony with a porch swing or a garden view balcony with a hammock. Built as a carriage house to the Main house in 1880, it remains the only standing carriage house on the island.

THE ISLAND CITY HOUSE, the main building, has ten one-bedroom parlor suites, and two two-bedroom parlor suites. The parlor suites are furnished in an island Victorian style with lace curtains and many antique pieces and other luxuries like granite countertops and basins. The two bedroom suites have a king bed in one room and a queen bed in the other room, a living/dining room with a full kitchen, one bathroom and a large porch. The one-bedroom suites have one queen-size bed and a separate sitting area with a kitchen. Many of these suites also have a sleeper sofa (for children or a third adult) or a wide porch overlooking the gardens. Originally built as a private home for a wealthy Charleston merchant family in 1880, this grand three-story Victorian mansion was then converted into the Island City House Hotel by its owners, in anticipation of the railroad's arrival in 1912.

THE CIGAR HOUSE is a poolside building and home to the six largest one-bedroom suites nestled quietly in the rear garden and shaded by tall palms. All of these suites are decorated in a tropical plantation style with rattan furniture, Bahama ceilings, French doors and hardwood flooring. The first and second floor suites have a king-size bed in the bedroom, a separate living room with a full kitchen, and a hammock on the poolside porch or balcony. The two suites tucked away on the third floor have a queen-size bed in the bedroom, a separate living room with a full kitchen, and an open balcony overlooking the pool. This red cypress wood house was built to replicate the Alfonso Cigar Factory that once occupied this site approximately one hundred years earlier. We could have taken the bicycles, but the Mallory Square attractions, shopping and restaurants were only a few minutes walk from the Island City House. We loved the elegance of our suite at the Island City House and can't get over all the rest that property offers: genuinely friendly hosts, a feast of a breakfast, the famous resident cats, the stunning pool and large sun deck, the Widow's walk (bathing suit optional!), lush tropical gardens, and coin-op guest laundry facilities. The grounds are so stunning that magazine photo shoots keep selling out the place so make sure you call well in advance for reservations.

So hop on the website!
www.Islandcityhouse.com and see for yourself why many of the Hotel's international and local guests are regular visitors.

3 Photos of property courtesy Christine Marks

Composite Trip Diary

Based on our last two trips to Florida, fall of 2001 and 2003.
Diarists: Elizabeth "Lizzy" Marks, Emily Marks and Christine Marks

November 1, leaving Hamilton, Ontario
Emily. The car is so loaded we had to sit on the trunk to close it. We have to drive 1633 miles to get to Fort Myers Beach; that means 816.5 miles each day since we want the drive to take two days. Mom says that is about 13 to 15 hours of driving each day!

Lizzy. Windsor-Detroit. Wow! Look at the Detroit skyline! It took over 20 minutes to get over the border. This is going to be a long drive but I know it's going to be worth it when we get to Florida.

November 2, Richmond, Kentucky
Emily. We drove and drove and drove the whole day and stopped a little past Lexington. We followed along in the book and cheered every time we crossed the border to another state. So far we've been in Michigan, Ohio and Kentucky. The people drive really fast in Michigan. Ohio looked a lot like Ontario. You should see how pretty Cincinnati looks all lit up! I'm going to bed.

Lizzy. I've been in the back seat all day. When mom goes to the bathroom I'm going to jump up and down on the hotel bed.

Christine. The girls were great! Excellent navigators and no fighting; I think the book gives them something to do. I wanted to get a little further tonight but when we saw the sign advertising such an excellent rate (less than $40) for the Quality Quarters Inn at Exit 87, Richmond, KY, I decided we would do without the comforts of a room at a hotel chain and that this would be a good enough place to put our head down for a few hours. What a surprise! The room was huge, the beds were very comfortable and the property extremely clean. I was so impressed that we waited to meet the owner, Mr. Patel, in the morning. On our way back home, I've made a note to stay here again.

November 3, Fort Myers Beach, Florida
Emily. Made it to Fort Myers Beach. What a great suite we have at the Outrigger Beach Resort! Just like a little house with a kitchenette, two TVs, and a big balcony that looks out onto the beach. They even had a bouquet of flowers waiting for us. We didn't stay in the room for long though! Even though it was getting dark we put our bathing suits on and ran out to the Gulf of Mexico to watch the sunset. It's a family tradition.

Christine. They always take such good care of us at the Outrigger. When friends ask why we always start our Florida trip here I tell them that here is where our family reconnects. This is where we forget about work and school, bills and homework, bullies and bosses, and just focus on enjoying each other's company. Yes, that can be found elsewhere in Florida but the Outrigger has become a tradition. Say the name and we all light up. The resort encourages family interaction with planned events, craft hours, and nature education; but on the larger scale the Lee Island Coast area truly allows our family to grow stronger through our experiences. This area celebrates nature like no other part of Florida. You just don't see masses of bill boards and other neon reminders to 'buy this' or 'visit that.' The attraction is the place itself: go explore this river, here's a map of the bay, come see the alligators in the swamp, take a look at the sunset from this beach—wonderful experiences for families and couples to share.

Lizzy. The air smells so good around here! Like a jungle—tropical. I love the sunset, you can see so many colours! It makes me feel like painting. I'm going to wake mom up early tomorrow.

November 4, Fort Myers Beach and Sanibel Island, Florida
Christine. Woke up with a start to someone tickling my eyelashes. I usually have to drag Lizzy out of bed by her toenails to get her to school and here she is jumping all over my bed while it's still dark. Every bone in my body hurts but we've got to go "shelling" with all the others who know that this it the time to find the prettiest specimens. As of March 2002 all live shelling has been banned along the Lee Island Coast, thank goodness. After breakfast, we've planned to visit Sanibel Island where the shells are also bountiful and varied. Then before supper back to the Outrigger Resort to try and chat with the wonderful sand castle artists who are busily creating early stages of their masterpieces. Each November the Resort is the host of an invitational sand castle competition that attracts some of the world's more creative artists and thousands of spectators.

Emily. I found lots of seashells on Bowman's Beach on Sanibel Island. We had so much fun in the water, the waves were bigger than on Fort Myers Beach. I saw a lady get squirted by a tiny octopus that was hiding in a beautiful shell! That was funny! Later we went back to Fort Myers Beach andcollected more shells and some white sand dollars. The waves made a little pool of water with a little island in it. We made "rivers" and locks from one side to another. It was warm and sunny all day long and I love it here.

Lizzy. I fell on a cactus in the parking lot for the beach on Sanibel. Cactus grows like weeds here! I collected a water bottle full of sand for my homework. The sand on Sanibel is a little whiter than Fort Myers Beach, feels softer and it has bigger pieces of broken shell in it. The shells are mostly the large flat white ones called Sunray Venus and the big brown ones called Atlantic Giant Cockles (Nancy Hamilton from the Visitors and Convention Bureau gave me a Nature Guide with pictures of all the shells and wildlife we can find on Lee Island Coast). This morning back at the Outrigger we found lots of Pear whelks with their shiny insides, Junonias with their bold patterns, Calico scallops that have the same shape as the Shell gas station signs, and Sharks eyes that look just like what they are called.

November 5, Naples, Florida
Christine. Met Ron Friedman, the Marketing Director for "Caribbean Gardens: The Zoo in Naples" who told me that the zoo was founded as a botanical garden in 1919 and that Caribbean Gardens was recently accredited by the prestigious American Zoo and Aquarium Association. I was impressed with the natural settings and the emphasis on teaching conservation to the visitors.

*Lizzy.*We spent some time at a beautiful zoo in Naples. We walked through a tropical jungle and rode on a boat to see the animal habitats. The small lake had islands that were the home to many different kinds of primates. I liked looking at the gibbons, lories, and other animals this way; I always felt sad at the other zoos that kept the animals behind bars.

Emily. I hope the picture turns out! I was petting an alligator! We watched a man lower some meat on a long rope towards a pond and huge alligators jumped almost out of the water to snap at it. Later we went to the beach at Fort Myers and saw dolphins jumping out of the waves.

November 5, Lover's Key, Florida
Christine. Lee Rose at the Lee Island Coast Visitors and Convention Bureau arranged for us to meet Connie Langmann, a most interesting woman, who owns and is the chief naturalist guide of Gaea Guides. She will be offering our introduction to the much celebrated and newest Lee Island Coast attraction: The Great Calusa Blueway. Paddlers from around the world are anxious to explore these many remarkable rivers, bays, backwaters and shorelines of Southwest Florida. Pleasure tours of an hour or two to more extensive 7-day/6-night trip packages are now available. The world class trail meanders through two distinct regions of the Gulf of Mexico, Estero Bay and Pine Island Sound. Natural and historic highlights are identified by trail markers and a detailed map of suggested routes for canoes and kayaks that shows random Global Positioning System (GPS) coordinates along the trail is also available. The GPS markers are listed on www.GreatCalusaBlueway.com and the map is free if you send a self addressed return envelope to: Lee County Natural Resources, (Boaters Guide), P.O. Box 398, Fort Myers, FL 33902.

Lizzy. Connie took us out for two hours of paddling on Tarpon Bay! She showed us islands where the pelicans live (it was kind of smelly!), mangrove islands covered in crabs, and took us out into the bay where we saw so many dolphins. We just floated along and got so close to the dolphins one time that we could hear them breathing, it was wonderful.

Emily. Now I know the difference between a cormorant and an anhinga, how to tell a young pelican from and older one, how mangroves spread, how the snowy egrets and great egrets almost became extinct (their feathers were used to make hats!) and the marine law about abandoned vessels. The kayaking was fun, but I'm tired! I want to do this again, but next time I'll bring splash pants and a rain coat!

Christine. Connie was patient and, being first time paddlers, let us explore at our own speed. She is a great teacher and always had answers to our many questions. We learned more from her than from all our naturalist books on the area. She offers several other tours that we want to take advantage of on our next visit: Full Moon tours, Bat tours, Sunset tours and a few more.

Emily. We went for supper at a nice place along the beachfront, the Junkanoo, and while we were eating our seafood ceasar salads mom spotted dolphins out near the surf's edge. She gave us the nod and Lizzy and I ran out of the restaurant to the water and then ran alongside the dolphins as they played with each other down by the shore! We were so close we could see their eyes! I think they were looking at us too! It's wonderful here!

November 6, Fort Myers Beach, the Peace River near Arcadia, Florida
Lizzy. Somebody is getting married at the beach tonight at the Outrigger. They have made a pretty aisle of palm trees leading up to the waves and it aims right where the sun sets. I want to get married here too.

Christine. I'm already sore from yesterday's paddling but the girls want to canoe down the Peace River. We've never canoed before, as a three-some that is, but the "Peace River", how bad can that be—count me in. The brochure says this is a hot spot for fossils, especially mastodon and shark (different Eras) and they encourage paddlers to take breaks and use the archaeological tools provided to see what they can find along the river.

Emily. The "Peace River," suuuuure, it's full of alligators! The lady that owns the Peace River Outfitters told us that we probably wouldn't see any but when we went to wait at the dock while her helpers loaded our canoe onto the trailer, we saw a great big one the size of a canoe resting on the other side of the shore. "Oh, that's just our pet, he stays right over there, don't worry at all. Besides, if you see any alligators, they'll be more afraid of you anyway." They drove us quite away down the stream, plopped the canoe onto the shore and laughed when we paddled in a nice circle right back to our launch site. Mom was laughing, so I did too. Most of the time we zig-zagged down the river but we got used to the paddling and the current carried us along anyway. It stayed sunny but was lightly raining off and on and that made it like a scene out of a fantasy movie. Green misty light on the thick vegetation that was draping down from the trees and covering the shore plus the sound of all the many kinds of birds was magical. We saw osprey, green herons, great blue herons, great egrets, snowy egrets, ibises, and cormorants and many others that I didn't know the names of. Everything was wonderful until Lizzy had to go to the bathroom.

Christine. On occasion, I noticed a few dark green "logs" following along behind us but didn't want the girls to worry so I neglected to point that out to them and spoil the "magic" as Emily called it.

Lizzy. I told mom I couldn't hold it anymore, I had to go!

Christine. That was exciting. My heart was beating so fast as we paddled up onto a sandy bank with a bit of hill (alligator protection). I urged the girls to scurry up onto the overhang where we could rest. I was so afraid that the girls would see the alligators and they did, but we all made it safely back into our canoe only to notice that another hundred feet downstream harboured a fenced-in paddock area with a portable toilet! We all had a good laugh. It's my favourite "Florida" story. I would recommend the canoe trip to anyone.

November 7, Sanibel Island
Emily. We met Chip, one of the owners of Tarpon Bay Outfitters, and he talked to us about wildlife conservation. Then we went on a pontoon boat out into J.N. "Ding" Darling National Wildlife Refuge and saw manatee and some dolphin jumping out of the water.

Christine. My friend, Cheryl Edgecombe, told me about what a wonderful place this is for birders. Ding Darling Refuge is a 6000-acre tract on the northeast side of Sanibel Island that is known world-wide for its abundance and variety of wildlife, especially birds.

Lizzy. I have no idea how our guide could tell what it was, it looked like a tiny pink speck out in the distance to me, but what we saw was a cotton-candy coloured roseate spoonbill! I thought the oyster island was interesting too. It was great to see all those birds soaring over our heads. Maybe I want to be a marine biologist.

November 8, Florida Everglades
Christine. We're being chauffeured to the next adventure from Naples. I'm looking forward to visiting the fabled Florida Everglades National Park.

Emily. We went to the Everglades sanctuary. We went on an airboat tour and sat in the front and I was glad that mom made us bring raincoats! We got so wet. We flew so fast through the swamp that the air from the fan at the back of the boat could have blown a kite to the moon! We saw a softshell turtle and some smaller alligators. The water was not very deep and you could see to the bottom. Every once in a while the pilot would stop and point out plants and animals to us. After the airboat ride we went to a small zoo and watched a man jump in the alligator pit full of gators with their mouths wide open. The biggest was 14 feet long! He demonstrated how quickly an alligator can snap its jaw shut with his baseball cap. Apparently he loses 5 or 6 caps a week when the alligator wins. I didn't get a chance to count his fingers.

Lizzy. There were gigantic snakes in the Everglade Zoo that looked like they could wrap themselves around our car and crush it into a garbage can. I learned why alligators have bumps all down their backs! It helps warm them, the bumps or studs radiate the heat from the sun. I definitely don't want to be an alligator wrestler when I grow up.

November 9, North Fort Myers and then Venice Beach on our way to Siesta Key, near Sarasota, FL
Christine. Lee Rose (Lee Island Visitors and Convention Bureau) and Jeannie Bigos (Marketing Director for the Outrigger Beach Resort) are treating us to an end-of-stay breakfast. They have treated us so well and I feel like I have friends here, we'll be back soon.

Emily. On our way to Sarasota we stopped at the Babcock Wilderness Adventures. It's a 90,000 acre cattle farm and nature preserve. We explored the Cypress Swamp and piney wood flat lands by swamp buggy. Our guides, Marilyn and Max, were great! They explained the importance of fire to the flat land eco-system, pointed out the wild turkeys and showed where the wild boars made paths through the slash pines and saw palmettos. Then we went into a swamp full of alligators. I didn't know that swamps aren't the same as marshes.

Composite Trip Diary

Based on our last two trips to Florida, fall of 2001 and 2003.
Diarists: Elizabeth Lizzy Marks-Cyr (age 8), Emily Marks-Cyr (age 11), Christine Marks: Thirty-something

d you know that swamps have water that is moving and marshes e stagnant. More mosquitoes live in marshes than swamps because ey need still water to lay eggs. She taught me that the heat in an ligator's nest will determine the sex of the baby alligators. Did you now that if the temperature in the nest is over 90 degrees then)% of the babies will be male and if the nest temperature is less an 85 degrees, then 90% of the babies will be females. I think at's amazing.

izzy. I took a lot of photos at Babcock. We got out of the swamp uggy to take a boardwalk path and see what we could see in the ypress swamp. It was so beautiful with the great big triangular ypress treetrunks draping into the water. I saw snakes in the trees nd alligators all over the place. Sometimes it was so quiet all you ould hear was the water moving under the boardwalk. At the end f the boardwalk we saw the florida Cougar. He was beautiful! When e got home I collected some Fort Myers Beach sand for my omework, it's very light beige and has small bits and pieces of shell.

hristine. It was finally explained to me what the term "Cracker" eans. I knew it meant someone who didn't migrate to Florida from lichigan or Minesota and the term could also be used to describe particular style of home. Courtesy of our Babcock guide, I now now it has to do with the first settlers to Florida and the way they sed to crack their whips to drive the cattle. Babcock is home to ne of the remaining herds of "cracker" cattle whose ancestors can e directly traced to the ones Ponce de Leon introduced to the area 1521. Another point of interest: the movie "Just Cause" with ean Connery was filmed here.

izzy. It's a good thing that we stopped at Venice Beach on our way o Sarasota. I am always the luckiest. Same as last time, I found he most fossilized shark's teeth! I met some nice adults from New 'ork and they showed me how to scoop up wet sand from just nder where the waves crash and dump it on the beach. I think I ave about 12 shiny, black shark's teeth and two of them are big nd perfect! I also collected another bottle of sand for my project. t's so dark, like pepper.

Emily. I love Venice beach! The sand is so dark and it's great fun to earch for the shark's teeth. Gotta love my tan! I can't wait to see Kelly Yatcko again at the Sarasota Visitors and Convention Bureau. She's so nice, she feels like family. We're meeting the new marketing director as well, Jenny Martin.

Christine. Wow! Sarasota again. Just like the Lee Island Coast area, get excited every time we return to Sarasota, but for different reasons. Just as Lee Island means "celebrate nature" to me; Sarasota means "celebrate humanity." It truly is the cultural centre for Florida. On any given night there's opera, plays, dinner theatre, dance performances, musical concerts, art shows and more. Of course Sarasota is known for its contribution to conservation and there are many opportunities to explore nature here as well. We are staying for a few days at a pretty little place, the Capri Beach Motel at Siesta Key. It's just a minute's walk to the beach and is a member of the Sara Sea association of hotels who share the property (the pools, the lush gardens, the entertainment and the private beach). The rates are excellent.

Lizzy. This is my favourite beach! Siesta Key is my favourite place ever! The sand is as white as snow and feels as soft as baby powder. I've filled two bottles, one for my teacher and one for my Grandma. You can see right down to your toes when you go out into the water. We have a private beach with the motel and there are a few people with kids here for me to play with.

Emily. First thing you have to do when you go to Siesta Key is jump in the water, get your whole body wet and run up onto the beach and roll around in the white sand. You can make yourself look just like a statue with all the sand caked onto your body and stuck in your hair! I really like the courtyard of the hotel we are staying at, it is full of colourful flowers and tropical trees I've never seen before. I try to catch the little lizards that scurry out from everywhere and sometimes I'm lucky. This hotel is just like a small apartment. Our neighbours are from England and Germany. The owner, Vera Giancristoforo, is Italian. Everyone is friendly here and likes my questions.

Christine. Do you know of Easter Island? That island with all those great statues with their eyes glued upon the sea? That's what sunset at Siesta Key reminds me of. A daughter on each arm, we too stood still among the colourfully-clad beachgoers,767oohing and aahhing, delightedly watching the sun set into the waves. Siesta Key sunsets are masterpieces. You watch an artist wildly painting his canvas with bold strokes the shades of fire, right before your eyes. The collective clapping of the spectators sent shivers up and down my spine and is unforgettable.

November 10, Sarasota, FL
Christine. Took the girls back to Mote Aquarium even though I know I will have to put up with the fuss when it's time to go. It's not just the informative exhibits that sets this attraction apart from other aquariums we have visited, it's the volunteers. We are not passive tourists. My girls both love marine biology and have endless questions. This is one place that never tires of providing them with answers. Just inside the door we were met by a quiet man, I noticed Ph.D. and retired marine biologist on his volunteer identification badge. I sat back and watched Emily duel with him with delight. First topic of debate: the voltage produced by a fish called a Stargazer. Second issue: lobster migration; then onto jellyfish locomotion, seahorse propagation, what is it about flounders shifting their eyes to one side of their head, clown fish and anemones poison—*laughing*. I waited for this patient man to ask me the question that I knew was coming: 'How old is she?" When I answered 11 he asked me to introduce my girls to his wife, another volunteer at the Aquarium who studies marine biology. This place is a treat.

Lizzy. I didn't want to play the computer game that teaches you about the food chain because I don't know how to play video games but when the volunteer came to show me how to beat my mom and sister, I wanted to play again. This is something new at Mote and it's fun when you get the hang of it. You sit in a theatre with a big screen and you have a smaller video in front of each player where you touch the screen and act out the parts of all the sea creatures. You compete with all the other visitors who are playing, and it is so much fun. I won! We also saw the two manatees again, Hugh and Buffet, and listened to their voices through the underwater microphone. We actually got to touch conchs, starfish and urchins in one touch tank and played with the stingrays in the other touch tank. The stingrays feel like slippery pieces of jello.

Emily. There's a university in Florida where you can get a degree in Marine Biology. I think I want to go there. We just visited Mote Aquarium and I learned tons of things I didn't know. It's my third time there and this was the best. Ocean life is so much more interesting than land ecosystems to me. Mom had to pull me by my hair to get me to leave (heehee, actually she bribed me with $5 US). The Pelican Man's Bird Sanctuary is just across the parking lot and that is another favourite place of mine. Injured birds from all around the world are nursed back to health but will stay with the Pelican man if they are too hurt to survive in the wild. If you go, find the crow and talk to her. She says "No Fair!" It's really funny. You can also see hawks, kestrels, eagles, owls, herons, ibises and many other birds here.

Christine. Back to the beach for the sunset, don't ever want to miss it. This time as we watched the colours unfurl, it reminded me of the magic trick where the magician pulls endless streams of brilliantly-coloured handkerchiefs from seemingly nowhere.

November 11, Sarasota and Spanish Point, FL
Lizzy. G-Whiz is my dream come true! It is a science museum where you can learn all about how things work by playing with the exhibits. I learned about sound and light and magnets. There were games you could play to see how fast you can run, how strong your hands are and how high you can jump. I learned about spinning objects create energy and how our eyes create after-images. I even saw how movies are made one snapshot at a time. I got to make a movie of my mom and I shaking hands (too bad we couldn't save it!). We stayed in the butterfly room for quite a while and held a corn snake and a huge frog. I was the only one that would touch the giant hissing cockroach from South America! Mom had to pay me 5 bucks to leave. HA HA!

Emily. Have you ever been on a real archeological dig? That's what they let the kids do at Spanish Point! We found lots of interesting artefacts that were buried in a midden (Native American "landfill") but the archaeologist wouldn't let us keep them because "if everyone kept what they found, the next people wouldn't get to see anything." Then we watched a movie about the history of the area and learned about Native culture. There was so much more to do here, but mom is getting tired so we had to leave.

Christine. Not going to miss that sunset!

November 12, Long Boat Key
Christine. I'm not complaining but I've got sand everywhere and I needed to be pampered. So we went for a couple of nights at The Resort at Longboat Key Club. This place is heaven. I have never stayed at a better location: it makes me blush to say it but the suite was decorated much nicer than most houses I've been in, including my own home! The girls had their own comfortable room and full bath, the kitchen was state-of-the art and beautifully stocked with extras, and the crowning glory in my room was the Jacuzzi. We ate our own homecooked supper on the wraparound balcony (the 9th floor) by candlelight. The grounds were lovely and so were the private beach, tennis courts, and on-site golf course. I noticed that the unofficial motto seemed to be "just ask." Just before I slid into that daydream of a bed, I called everyone I knew to gloat! I am such a meanie.

Lizzy. Too bad mom needs a rest, I wanted to go to the John & Mable Ringling Museum again. I remember how wonderful it felt to sit in the courtyard and sketch the sculptures. Oh well, we need to do our homework since there's only a few more days left of this trip.

November 13, Orlando, FL
Christine. Laurie Smithberger and Angie Ranck of the Orlando/ Orange County Convention and Visitors Burea have arranged for us to stay at the Holiday Inn Family Suites Resort and I am so thrilled with this location. The creators of this original concept have designed several different suites, each with their own theme. We stayed in the Jungle theme Kidsuite, a room full of energy and surprises like the see-through remote control and telephone, the surround sound stereo and Ninendo games in the kids bedroom that could be played from each bunk bed, the jungle animals and plants painted all over the walls and curtains, and more. Our room had a full kitchen and private rooms. The other suites special treats are given away by their names: Sweetheart Suite, Residential Suite, Cinema Suite, Classic 2 Bedroom Suite. The resort complex centred around a courtyard that contained a huge splashpad full of water games and rides, two pools (one for tots), a pond with swans, a couple of Jacuzzis, mini-puts, table tennis, a couple of jungle gyms, shuffle board, lounge chairs and patio tables...and more. A huge buffet breakfast is available in the huge cafeteria or you are welcome to visit the fast food restaurants or general store. The lobby is a turn-of-the-century train depot and serves as the hub of activities for the hotel. Fine details of this property are too numerous to write. I suggest the website www.hifamilysuites.com or 1-877-387-KIDS

Lizzy. Wow! I can't thank mom enough for letting us go to the Holiday Inn Family Suites. Our hotel is amazing!!! We played in the pool and at the splash pad all afternoon! But later, after supper, mom wanted to go see Orlando. I don't think mom likes driving in Orlando. Maybe I shouldn't talk about this but it was kind of funny. It was raining and dark when we left the Holiday Inn and mom was trying to read the map to get us to the Pirate's Dinner Adventure. I guess the roads change names and direction too many times for her. We stopped at a gas station and I could still hear her saying bad words from inside the car. We watched her rip up the map and stomp all over it in a puddle and we very quiet when she came back into the car. I suggested she go ask the gas station guy how to get there and then we all started laughing.

Emily. We made it to the Pirate's Adventure and it was so much fun. If your parents ask what is the one thing you want to do in Orlando besides Disney, pick this one. While you are waiting in the big lobby for the show to start, they feed you snacks and offer to take your picture as a pirate. Mom got her fortune read and we bought some great souvenirs in the shop (a Florida sunken treasure map and a sabre). The show starts out in the lobby where they introduce you to the story and then you are seated into different coloured section inside the theatre. Each section has it's own pirate who you cheer for; ours wore an orange sash. Every time your pirate does something heroic, you swing your imaginary mug of beer and sing. If another pirate does something great you Boo! It felt like you were a part of the story. I really liked it when I was chosen to go back stage, get into a costume, and join the pirates on the ship in the centre of the stage! I won't ever forget that!

Lizzy. It was fun to watch Emily have to swear allegiance to "The Black Pirate" and promise to always eat my vegetables.

Christine. There is so much to do in Orlando. It's a pity I'm not feeling that well, I know the girls really want to go to Seaworld and all the other attractions. We were supposed to be here for 4 or 5 days, but I think I'm only good for one more—we'll go see Disney tomorrow and go home. We can always come back.

November 14, Orlando
Lizzy. This was my first time to go to Disney. I was so happy and excited because all my life I've been watching Disney movies and hearing my friends talk about their Disney trips. We were given "go to the front of the line" passes because Mom is an author but there weren't that many people there because it was rainy. My favourite rides were Space Mountain (Emily turned green!) Haunted House, Splash Mountain, Big Thunder Mountain Railroad, Peter Pan's flight and Swiss Family Robinson's treehouse. I loved seeing the Disney characters and getting to take my picture with them. I was surprised when I was looking around for Mickey Mouse and he popped up right behind me. We saw a beautiful parade, too. Cinderella's Castle was smaller than it looks but still beautiful. I can't wait to tell all my friends about this day.

Christine. Road trip tomorrow. We'll be back next year!

Composite Trip Diary

Diary excerpts from more recent travels...
Diarists: Elizabeth Lizzy Marks-Cyr (age 13), Emily Marks-Cyr (age 16), Christine Marks: Forty-something

St Petersburg / Clearwater
Sheraton Sand Key Resort
Emily: Ugh. Long, long drive but I'm excited. We're here. This hotel was truly a treat. We stayed in a very comfortable suite, and because I guess they were happy to see us, it was complete with loads of snacks and presents like huge yellow beach towels. Our room has a view of the most beautiful beach and I couldn't wait to get out there. It looks like there's a lot to do here, but the beach itself has got to be the highlight of the resort. Like a postcard, it is white and wide, and immaculately free of debris and litter.

Christine: The older I get, the longer the drive down here. Like most, I try to time the drive so we can get a bit of beach time when we get there. I know the twists and turns of the highway so well, some of the views are as familiar as the streets of my home town. Some things have changed a lot though. I still have a mid size car and my two teenagers don't fit into it that well any more. It's a long hot drive, so I should have known to pack some Febreeze. Everyone must have seen or smelled the "cloud" that came into the lobby with us. Never mind. It's a classy location and we were well received . I was surprised by an exquisite suite full of presents from the St. Pete's/ Clearwater area CVB. After a quick shower, we grabbed our new beach towels and toys and went for a splash. On the way out I saw more of the resort and although we have a lot of places to see, I want to make sure we get to try the restaurants and pools here.

Lizzy: I'm glad we came here first. It's soooo Florida. Flowers and palm trees all over the place, and what a beach!

Caledesi Island State Park
Lizzy: We were ferried to Caledesi State Island along with 30 or so other people, they went to a special beach and we went alone on a kayaking trip through mangroves! We each had our own kayak and we paddled along in a single file: Emmy first, then me, then mom. There were so many things here you could never see anywhere else! Our kayaking trip took so much time we never got to see the world famous beach everyone was so excited about.

Emily: The three of us ended up taking a private kayaking excursion through the mangrove tunnels on an uninhabited island. Unfortunately, mother and I were pushed by the current when we tried to change positions and we got stuck in the tangled mangrove branches, and Elizabeth was stuck paddling by herself for a short time. The trees were nearly covered in iguanas, tree crabs and spiders and the sea was a nursery for fish and birds.

Christine: I'm looking at the girls' entries and wondering why they forgot to mention that we had to have the Coast Guard come find us. I'm not saying this was a disaster, it turned out ok, but there were some tense moments today. The warden of the State Park was at a conference, and so was the deputy. We were outfitted by a helper who forgot to give us a map. That was the lesson here and what I hope the readers will take from this entry. It was an extraordinary experience that I would still recommend...as long as you have a guide and a map. The numbered markers are obvious enough as you paddle through the dark tunnels into the mangrove thatches but once you emerge from the island out into open water there's no indication of whether you need to paddle to the left or to the right to get back to the docks. We were all tired by that time, and I paddled out a little from the harbor to look for markers and came back quickly to the girls as a flash thunder storm began to drench and toss us about in the harbor. I was still stressed from "losing" Elizabeth out there for a few minutes about an hour earlier (I think it was a sibling rivalry thing, she wanted to get out to the front and get a big lead) and on top of all that there was the ferry captain's remark: "there's only one ferry back. It leaves at 4 and it you're not on it you sleep out here with the rattle snakes." I didn't have much coverage with my cell phone ... after getting voicemail at the State Park, the outfitters hut, and the CVB, I called the Coast Guard. Luckily the storm passed quickly, the Coast Guard found us, and the ferry waited. I happily endured the glares of the other ferry boat guests who were clueless to our ordeal and only knew that we were the reason why they were getting back late. I actually kissed the pavement of the parking lot, I was that scared today. Lesson learned.

Columbia Restaurant on Sand Key
Lizzy: The Columbia has the most amazing tall chocolate cake I have ever tasted, and the seafood plate I had was also delicious. Everyone was full and happy and I would definitely ask if we could go back there if I had the chance.

Emily: The Columbia celebrates Latin culture with their fine array of Cuban and Spanish-inspired dishes. The gift shop had all kinds of stuff you can bring home for souvenirs!

Tradewinds island Grand Resort
Lizzy: This hotel was amazing! There were streams running between and around all of the buildings, with swans and paddle boats. It seemed like everywhere you turned, there was a game, something to play on or an interesting show. There was a pirate and bird show that was fun but the best thing was the massive inflated slide on the beach. It was like being at an amusement park.

Christine: This is the perfect place to take a family. They've thought of everything. I packed a few books and water bottles and wandered between the pool and the beach while the girls explored the resort. There's a lot for kids of all ages to do here while the parents get some R&R. With convenience stores and fast food court areas, and all the planned activities and play areas, I felt completely at ease with giving the girls some freedom now that they are a little older.

Snorkeling at Egmont Key
Emily: Although not personally my best experience snorkeling, I still had fun. A boat takes you out to an array of reefs and ruins, where you are free to snorkel around and see both the ruins and the underwater creatures. Unfortunately, there were jellyfish in the water, and I was too spooked to do much sightseeing. My sister, however, dove right in and enjoyed herself enormously watching the fish.

Weedon Island Preserve
Emily: A serious trip into history, this preserve and museum is dedicated to the lives of the Native Americans who once lived there. This was the natural home of the aboriginals, until European settlers shot and diseased them out of existence. The boardwalk tours were well laid out over the marshes and hammocks, and the information at each station was insightful. We could have taken out kayaks but after yesterday's experience, we let that one go.

Great Explorations Museum
Lizzy: It was so interesting! There were so many things to learn by doing. With everything scientific and fun packed into one massive room and second floor balcony, this was heaven for me. I like science more than my mom and sister, so I took my time wandering from exhibit to exhibit on my own while they took breaks and watched.

Dali Museum
Lizzy: The Dali Museum holds many of the abstract paintings of Salvador Dali. Everyone knows the painting of the melting clock. They hold tours that bring you through the whole museum and tell you about the history of the pieces of art and about Dali's life. It was very interesting to me since I love to add wild colour to the abstract paintings I do (mom let me draw all over my bedroom walls!), and I would recommend it to all ages because of the uniqueness and beauty of his art.

Emily: I've always been interested in Salvador Dali's take on abstract and surrealist art, and being able to see it up close and personal was a tour de force. Especially because of the gigantic pieces that dominated some walls, I was completely amazed by his skill. Anyone who appreciates art, or even surrealism should see this.

Christine: What a story! Dali was one of history's more colorful commentators. This was a little mature-themed, but the girls were not bothered. I've always wanted to see this gallery and will mark it as a highlight of the trip.

Miami
Afterglo
Lizzy: The Afterglo was advertised as a top 10 restaurant in the world and now I know why. Everything was organic and bursting with flavor. The décor of the whole place was calming and lovely to the last detail. There were many different styles of food on the menu all made with healthy organic, hand picked ingredients. I thought I would try a bison rib eye steak and, never having had bison before, was a bit unwilling to eat it, but the moment I took a bite I couldn't stop until my plate was clean.

Circa 39 Hotel
Lizzy: Down in the lobby there was a wall covered in lighted squares that changed color to the beat of the music. The whole place was very unique and "happy." We were close to everywhere we wanted to go and I would love to get to stay there again the next time we go to Miami.

Emily: A minute or two's walk away from the beach is Circa 39. Breathtakingly designed, from top to bottom, this was a really neat place. Our entire suite was in white, with a few colourful accents. It's the kind of place that just makes you smile. Great pool and deck and the restaurant was super. We took a lot of pictures of the art deco area (the strip that's in all the movies) and were treated to a cruise around Millionaire's Row.

Seaworld
Emily: I made the mistake of sitting too close to the front row in the walrus exhibit. Guess who got sprayed all over? I've been to a lot of marine parks and this one is a must see for people of all ages.

The Florida Keys
Rain Barrel
Emily: This charming village hosts painters and potters and other artists from around the world. My favourite was a man who blew glass into the shapes of undersea creatures, most notably octopi. They were fragile, but very beautiful. The village had a very wholesome feel, as nature and building often intertwined in imaginative ways. Plus, an overhead canopy of leaves dappled the light in such a way so you'd think the buildings were just part of a forest.

Turtle Hospital
Lizzy: It was really interesting to see all the types of turtles that they had there. Each one had been saved from an injury caused by people: some ate plastic bags, others were cut by propellers. Before visiting each of the patients, the tour guide showed us a movie about turtles in general, took us to the operating room, and then told us the story of each survivor, from emergency.... to recovery ....and release.

Wild Bird Rehabilitation Center
Emily: Created by a kind-hearted woman who's been living in the Keys since the new bridges were built, the Wild Bird Rehabilitation Center is a huge humanitarian gesture. It's amazing that sick birds seem to know to come here, although most of the "patients" were brought here by compassionate volunteers.

Lizzy: If you're going to visit, check ahead to see when it is feeding time. Pelicans and other birds from the surrounding area swoop in for their snacks. We were so tired that day and mom had to leave before the feeding, but she says it's on our "bucket list."

Robbie's Marina
Lizzy: Get ready to be amazed. This marina is host to the largest and friendliest group of tarpon you're likely to ever see. I reached into my bucket of fish and fed them one by one.

Emily: Tarpon are huge fish that normally you'd shy away from. But, at Robbie's Marina, you're welcomed to share their company, and tease them with buckets of smaller fish to lure them out from under the docks.

Mel Fisher Diving Museum
Emily: This museum is dedicated to the discovery of several crashed merchant and slaving vessels from past centuries. Inside, you'll find informative tours on diving in general, and separate floors devoted to individual shipwrecks.

Lizzy: The best part was definitely looking at the cases and cases of treasure hauled up from the ocean floor, especially with the thorough explanations next to each one. I touched a real bar of gold!!

The Islander Resort
Emily: We stayed in perfect luxury here. Right on the beach, this resort has so much to offer. Our suite, complete with screened in porch, had a kitchenette and internet access. Outside out on a huge deck were heated pools, saltwater and freshwater options. The beach was close by but the pools were so fabulous we stayed by the deck till it was dark.

Lizzy: Look at Emily's entry. All she missed was the fabulous huge breakfast buffet. What more could you want?

Theater of the Sea
Lizzy: Great for families with smaller children.

History of Diving Museum
Emily: Very informative. I'd recommend it to anyone with an interest in diving, as it completely details the history of diving from the beginning to today. Mom is a scuba diver and Lizzy and I hope to get our licenses soon too.

Ocean Pointe Suites
Emily: The suite were more like real apartments — huge, very clean, had everything you'd have at home but with a gorgeous view of the ocean.

Lizzy: The sunset was breathtaking out on our balcony, and you could see down onto a trail that followed a stream through a sedge forest. WE suntanned by the little beach area and looked at the boats in the marina. The rooms made you feel very at home, with beautiful Florida decor.

Composite Trip Diary

Based on our last two trips to Florida, fall of 2001 and 2003.
Diarists: Elizabeth Lizzy Marks-Cyr (age 8), Emily Marks-Cyr (age 11), Christine Marks: Forty-something

Sunset Cruise on the Liberty Clipper boat in Key West
Lizzy: It was a beautiful sail. The crewmates (aka customers) were invited to take part in the raising of the sails. The best part was the sunset, we were out on the water and so had an unparalleled view. I took a lot of photos that I am happy about.

Emily: We even got snacks—fruit, cheese and crackers, as much as you wanted! The crew was really friendly and helpful, and seemed to like answering all of my sister's questions about living on a sailboat. I would definitely go on this cruise against, and recommend it to anyone.

Island City House
Emily: I'm only sixteen, but if I had to give up travelling right now, I would be content with having at least seen this place. Where to even begin? Our room was so clean and beautiful, with the most charming design scheme we've ever seen. The property itself was a tropical jungle, complete with paths and cats meandering everywhere. Breakfast was down in the paths below the buildings, and better than any I've ever had at a restaurant.

Christine: You may have noticed. My entries are scarce. This is just like what I've been telling the girls every day: "I drive. I pay. Nothing else." Do you know how many miles I've driven? I don't want to even say it. But I have to say something about this hotel. The Island City House is now our family's favorite. Go back in time when you stay at this century old completely restored gem, but take all of today's upgrades with you! I loved the whitewashed, wrap-around porches on all three levels, the marble pedestal sinks, gleaming hardwood, and granite countertops. Get the hosts to show you around. There are surprises everywhere: each building has a history you want to hear. On a relatively small piece of property, the three main buildings are closely set around the pool and courtyard, but we still needed an hour to get acquainted with the premises. And I stopped the girls just in time — the widow's walk is clothing optional! It's easy to see why so many of the guests are regulars and why this location features in magazine shoots and tv spots.

Butterfly Museum
Lizzy: They had every kind of butterfly imaginable, all in beautiful colours. I found it very relaxing. I was standing on the bridge just watching them and kind of in a dream, and a few of them actually landed on my shoulder! I think the pictures will be very good.

Sweets of Paradise
Emily: Amazing, just amazing. I have never had fudge so good in my life. It practically melted right in my mouth as soon as it hit my lips.

Pirate Soul Museum
Lizzy: Jack Sparrow was always one of my favourite movie characters. Here was a museum devoted to pirates! This was very interesting to me, because I had always wondered about how true pirates lived in the same times as the Pirates of the Caribbean movies were set. They even had information I'd never thought to wonder about, presented through clever portholes full of interesting views and interactive displays. What a fun and interesting place, I think it was my favorite museum.

Shipwreck Museum
Emily: This was just packed full of artifacts. Actors play out the story for you as they point out interesting treasures from the past. Key West has always been a shipwrecking town, and this museum is devoted to the lives of wreckers in the area. You learn about the wharves built to hold all the stuff, and the estates that were built on these riches. To top it all off, you got to climb a tower for a bird's eye view of the whole town of Key West.

Key West Aquarium
Lizzy: The aquarium was awesome. They had a touch tank where you could actually reach in and grab sea creatures. They also had tours that guided you around so you wouldn't miss any of the exciting features of the aquarium, and then they lead you outside for a shark feeding!

Lazy Dog Kayaking
Emily: I love kayaking, its seems to be something I was born to do, and this kayak trip was one of my favourites, all-time. For sure. We all set out in a little flotilla following a few helpful guides and of course, their dog. The guides had marine biology backgrounds and while they taught us what they knew about the area and its inhabitants, they would gently lift sea creatures right off the sea floor from time to time and pass them around, so that everyone could get right up close and have a personal experience. We spent a lot of the day kayaking between islets and in currents and all of it was fun. It was a great experience and the perfect thing to do last before heading back home. I'm looking forward to posting my photos. It's been a great trip.

Lizzy: I loved getting to touch the horseshoe crabs. There were many things to see because the water is so shallow. We saw schools of colorful fish, an octopus, and many sponges and birds. I think this is one of those things that you can go back to again and again because each time would be different. I'm pretty good with the kayak now and love to glide across the water. I'm so happy right now, I don't want to go home.

Christine: There. I am so proud of myself. I always wanted to show the girls the Florida Keys, and give them a taste of the Caribbean without having to leave the safety of the U.S. I loved the unique and natural beauty of the Keys area when my grandparents brought me and now I'm sure to have passed this love to my girls, its time to head home.

Christine Marks © Stephen D'Agostino

Reader Comments

Diary excerpts from more recent travels...
Diarists: Elizabeth Lizzy Marks-Cyr (age 13), Emily Marks-Cyr (age 16), Christine Marks: Thirty-something

I've taken excerpts from a few emails I've received from Ontario travelers. We're always happy to hear from travelers everywhere! Please send your travel stories, and comments and suggestions for the next edition of this travel guide to: cem@estatemultipliers.com

"My husband and I just returned from a trip to Orlando and used your reference guide. I just had to e-mail and state what a fabulous book it was. Forget the trip tick from the local automobile club, we just used yours. It was so much easier to use not to mention extremely interesting with all the different tidbits from all the various states listed along the way plus of course the rest stops, gas stops and restaurants. Kudos to Christine Marks. Thank you again for making our road trip a very, very easy and enjoyable one."
Sincerely, Alan & Lindsay McK., Hamilton, Ont.

"I would love to have an (updated) copy of your book and so would my sister in law. Both families travel to Florida each winter and books like yours are so very helpful." Jean R, Wasaga Beach, Ont.

"...just wanted to say that I love your book – very helpful. I'm driving to Florida for the first time this winter and I definitely plan to use your book." Thanks! Anita V., Ont.

"I wanted to write to you and thank you for writing a good book. This book came in handy when we were driving to Florida. It was nice to have a book/map that was easy to read and understand. Keep up the good work." Kim & Don DeL., Ont.

"We have your I-75 travel book and we just love it when we drive to Florida. It is the best reference book on the market!! Thanks and keep the good work up." Rudi & Donna P., Bracebridge, Ont.

"Your book is very informative. I will be making my first trip to Florida this winter via I75. Thank-you," Young Lee, Toronto, Ont.

"We just returned from Florida using I75 for the first time. We found your book very useful." Colin D., Ont.

"My wife and I are planning quick trip to Florida shortly so we stopped in at the St. Thomas CAA to pick up Dave Hunter's book "Along I-75" when we spied your book. My wife is never one to turn down the opportunity to acquire coupons and low and behold your book offer just such things..." Jim R., Springfield, Ont.

"I purchased the above book in January 2005 to assist our drive to Florida at the end of January. We found it a great help in finding accommodations, meals, gas, etc.....Thanks" Ellie R. L., Ont.

"Hi! I just wanted to let you know we enjoyed the book. If you are reporting on Sarasota (My husband had proposed marriage to me at an evening picnic on Siesta Key where we enjoyed a lovely sunset)....then you might want to go to Turtle Beach where the whole neighbourhood gets together to enjoy it....it's kind of neat to see that kind of community! I wish you had more on seafood restaurants....for some of us, Florida isn't the same without eating a load of seafood!" Karen & Rob A., Ont.
....Karen, check out the Columbia family of restaurants in Florida, thanks, CEM

"We recently returned to Toronto from Florida and we used the subject travel guide by Christine Marks. We found the guide extremely helpful and enjoyable. I think it's the first travel guide that I really used and found to be worth the price." Jack N., Ont.

"Hi Christine, My wife and I have used your book for many trips to Florida. Is there a later version and if so were can we purchase it? Thanks in advance," Bill H. Ont.